CASH FLOW AND SECURITY ANALYSIS

CASH FLOW AND SECURITY ANALYSIS

SECOND EDITION

Kenneth S. Hackel
President, Systematic Financial Management, LP

Joshua Livnat
Leonard N. Stern School of Business, New York University

IRWIN
Professional Publishing

Chicago • Bogatá • Boston • Buenos Aires • Caracas
London • Madrid • Mexico City • Sydney • Toronto

This book is dedicated to our families

Irwin Professional Book Team
Executive editor: Ralph Rieves
Marketing manager: Kelly Sheridan
Production supervisor: Pat Frederickson
Assistant manager, desktop services: Jon Christopher
Project editor: Denise Santor-Mitzit
Designer: Matthew Baldwin
Compositor: Douglas & Gayle Limited
Typeface: 11/13 Palatino
Printer: Quebecor/Kingsport
▀▼▟ Times Mirror
M Higher Education Group

Hackel, Kenneth S.
    Cash flow and security analysis / Kenneth S. Hackel—2nd ed.
        p.   cm.
    Includes bibliographical references and index.
    ISBN 0-7863-0407-3
    1. Investment analysis.   2. Cash Flow.   I. Livant, Joshua.
    II. Title.
    HG4529.H33   1996   95-38516
    658.15′244—dc20   CIPO

Printed in the United States of America

1 2 3 4 5 6 7 8 9 0 QK 2 1 0 9 8 7 6 5

Preface

Investment professionals can be broadly characterized as those who follow a top-down process, which identifies first the economic sectors and industries in which the portfolio should be invested, and a bottom-up approach which selects individual stocks into a portfolio based on desirable characteristics. At present, pension-fund consultants classify money managers (and investors) as growth investors, market timers, sector rotators, and value investors. The latter category includes a wide variety of investment criteria such as low price/earnings multiples, asset values, or private market values. However, given the severe measurement problems in accounting, more and more professional investors are beginning to focus on an entity's cash flows.

The new edition this book describes in further detail the investment approach based on free cash flows. Instead of focusing on earnings of a firm that can be manipulated by the selection of accounting methods, we focus on the maximum amount of cash that can be distributed to shareholders without sacrificing future growth. The investment approach is a *bottoms-up* process, which identifies firms that are consistent generators of free cash flows, that have low financial leverage, and that have low free cash flow multiples. This investment approach does not attempt to identify firms with superior growth prospects, which may or may not be realized. Instead, it focuses on solid firms that are temporarily mis-priced by the market. We provide evidence about the superiority of this investment approach.

The current world of money management and equity investment is changing at a pace not seen before. More sophisticated pension sponsors, new legal requirements, and the growth of quantitative techniques in risk measurement are forcing security analysts and investment advisors to improve their analysis and investment process. Central to this improvement is a better understanding of cash flow analysis, the focal point of this book. Furthermore, with the growing integration of U.S. and foreign capital markets and the increasing difficulties of comparing reported earnings of U.S. and foreign firms, cash flow analysis will become essential for successful international portfolio selection. In this book, we show how international investments can yield superior returns when using our free cash flow approach.

Acknowledgments

We would like to thank many individuals and corporations who helped in the preparation of the second edition of this book, or who showed a strong commitment to investments based on cash flows. Foremost among them, we should thank Sumner Levine, who accompanied the process from its inception and contributed many valuable suggestions to our work.

We received great encouragement from our parents, Bernice and David Hackel (OB"M) , and Rachel and Meyer (OB"M) Livnat, to seek knowledge and better understanding of the world around us. We were lucky to have the support of our wives, Gail and Shoshana, and our children, Emily, Eli and Betsy, and Orit, Ofer and Shira, who never treated the book as a competitor for our time. We greatly benefitted from our teachers, Professors Ronen, Schiff and Sorter at New York University, and from many colleagues at the Leonard N. Stern School of Business at New York University, who have commented on earlier drafts, and used the first edition in their classes.

We obtained considerable of help from employees at Systematic Financial Management, L.P., Yvonne McNair at New York University, David Hill from Factset, and Ralph Rieves and the dedicated staff of Richard D. Irwin. We also wish to thank Advest, Inc., A.G. Edwards & Sons, Inc., Frank Russell Co., Interstate/Johnson Lane, PaineWebber, Inc., Prudential Securities, Inc., Raymond James & Associates, Inc., Smith Barney, and Wheat, First Securities, which exhibited their strong commitment to investments based on free cash flows. Special thanks are due to many consultants in Fund Evaluation Group, GS2 Securities, Inc., Montford Associates, Performance Analytics, and other firms who took the time to understand and learn what cash flow analysis is all about.

Contents

Chapter One

Introduction

Everything flows and nothing stays

Heraclitis

People work, save, invest, and start businesses primarily to obtain cash. Their success in those endeavors is usually measured by the cash return on these activities, expressed as a percent increase of cash, but discounted at an appropriate rate of interest. An important dimension of the cash return is how reliably an individual can continue to expect that return. Investors and creditors are therefore primarily interested in future cash flows and, in particular, in the amounts, timing, and uncertainty of cash flows. This book introduces the reader to the world of investments that use these three dimensions of cash flows.

PURPOSE OF THE BOOK

This book was written with the underlying assumption that cash flow analysis is the most important tool at the investor's (or creditor's) disposal. Although investors, academicians, and businessmen have developed a widespread arsenal of valuation techniques and procedures throughout the years, cash flow analysis must eventually enter the picture. This is true whether the analyst evaluates a bond, a share of stock, or a nonpublic business. Even though appraisals may be an important determinant of the selling price for asset-based sales, cash flow analysis is also important because cash is what eventually pays for the cost of the asset.

Unfortunately, the current corporate reporting system in the United States does not reflect properly how business decisions are made. For example, hiring decisions, purchasing decisions, financing decisions—in essence, all important corporate decisions—must be made only after considering the entity's ability to maximize its free cash flow and recover the cash invested in the firm. However, accounting descriptions of these important decisions deviate from their cash effects, sometimes to a considerable degree.

The purpose of this book is to advocate a fundamental approach to investment in equity securities based on the analysis of free cash flows. *Free cash flow* can be loosely applied as the cash a firm collects from its customers minus any expenditures required to sustain the current growth rate of the firm. Although this definition of free cash flow has been used before, its application has varied considerably across users of financial statements. In this book, we describe in detail a novel procedure for estimating free cash flow, which we consider the most comprehensive estimation method. We further show that this definition of free cash flow can be used to select firms for a portfolio that earns superior returns.

We describe in this chapter the components we will be highlighting throughout this text. We believe they will be attractive—and crucial—to money managers, security analysts, investors, creditors, financial statement users and preparers, and students of business.

THE MARKET SETTING

The United States capital market is characterized by three major markets in which equity securities trade; the New York Stock Exchange (NYSE), the American Stock Exchange (ASE), and the over the counter (OTC) market. Currently, about 2,300 securities are traded on the NYSE, about 750 on the ASE, and an additional 5,500 securities are traded over the counter. Thus, an investor can include more than 8,000 securities in a portfolio. The major question facing an investor is how to select a subset of these securities for investment, because direct investment in all of these securities is prohibitively costly and inefficient. One can invest in an index fund, which is a fund that holds a portfolio of securities similar to a widely accepted index such as the S&P (Standard & Poor's) 500. However, an index fund investment will not yield any superior returns (above the index). Thus, an investor who wishes to outperform a market index has to invest in a subset of the available securities. He or she must decide how to focus on a subset of securities for investment.[1]

The first step in the investment process is to screen potential investment candidates and select a subset of firms for a more detailed investigation. Many screening criteria are available. One that has attracted wide attention (but that we show, in Chapter 8, to be an undesirable criterion in recent periods) is the price to earnings ratio (P/E). After sorting firms according to their P/E ratios, one can focus on the subset with the lowest P/E ratios for further analysis. Also, if the investor wants to ensure enough liquidity in the portfolio, he or she might impose another criterion—for example, a minimum of $100 million market value (or a minimum trading volume) for firms available for investment. Other screening criteria are also available, such as the exclusion of certain industries (e.g., financial services) or the exclusion of foreign firms.

Regardless of the specific screening criteria, however, after screening all available securities, the investor obtains a list of firms that constitutes possible candidates for investment. He or she must then obtain more information on these firms to determine which ones to include in the final portfolio. The information the investor needs will depend on other important factors. For example, some investors are interested in the market position of the firm—does it have any monopolistic advantages (such as patent or special licenses)? Some investors are concerned about the firm's management team, its labor relationships, and so forth. This information should be collected after the initial screening, but before the final investment decision is made.

---

[1] Some funds or portfolio managers have a very clearly defined but narrow investment focus. For example, some portfolios are concentrated in a specific industry. Others hold only small stocks or are designed to maximize dividend yield (i.e., tilt funds). However, such investments may expose the investor to a greater than market risk.

Finally, the investor should identify his or her investment goals and their implications for selling decisions. The investor should determine *a priori* when a security is overpriced and should be sold. For example, one may decide that a security should be sold if the ratio of its price to free cash flow exceeds the median ratio of firms included in the S&P 500. Or one may decide to sell the securities of a firm engaged in taking over another firm, where the new entity is too leveraged or if the basic nature of the business changed considerably or if a significant legal challenge has been brought against the acquiring firm. One's selling criteria are an integral part of the investment strategy and should be decided upon when the investment is made. Figure 1–1 describes the three steps of the investment process.

SOFT AND HARD INFORMATION

Information about firms can be classified into two major types; quantitative, or hard, information and qualitative, or soft, information. In making investment decisions, investors use both types of information. For initial screening of firms, investors usually use quantitative information, which is readily available in a computer-readable format such as the Standard & Poor's Compustat database, now available on a CD-ROM. Hard information is reasonably homogeneous across firms, and it can be used through a computer program or a computer screening routine. However, an in-depth analysis of a firm will usually include some qualitative information. For example, the management strength or the quality of a firm's products are two attributes based on soft information.

In Chapter 2, we present a checklist of attributes an investor may want to consider before making an investment decision. From our long experience in security analysis, we have compiled a list of attributes most investors assess either formally or informally. Some investors go through such a list explicitly for every firm they analyze, while others consider the information implicitly or intuitively. We believe that an organized checklist is a powerful tool for systematic investment decisions. Therefore, we begin this book by providing such a list.

FIGURE 1–1
The Investment Process

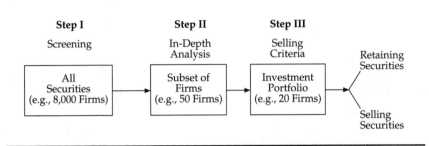

The list of attributes in the next chapter includes items that relate to the macroeconomy in which the firm operates, the industries in which the firm does business, and some firm-specific attributes. For this checklist of items, we describe their possible effects on future operating cash flows, on free cash flows, and on the expected operating performance of the firm. We also provide the reader with a possible list of data sources (i.e., where one can find information about these attributes). Figure 1–2 illustrates the checklist of items and its potential use in the investment process.

We believe that the list of attributes we provide in the next chapter will enable the investor to construct a formal process of investment decision making *after* a subset of firms is identified, and to set up some screening variables. For example, in Chapter 2 we describe the diversification strategy a firm may follow. Typically, a firm may diversify into related areas of its business or into unrelated areas. When an investor sets up a screen for investment, the screen may include a desirable diversification strategy, such as a measure for unrelated diversification. Thus, some of the attributes on our list can be used for screening as well as for further in-depth analysis.

THE STATEMENT OF CASH FLOWS

The astute reader may wonder why we need to calculate or estimate free cash flows if a statement of cash flows is now routinely provided by firms on an annual and even a quarterly basis. To

FIGURE 1–2
Variables Used in Making Investment Decisions

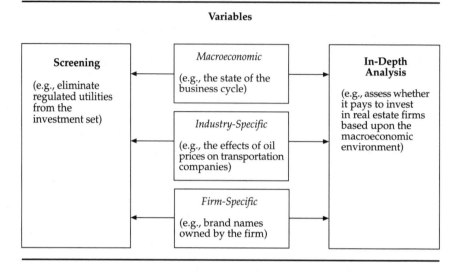

understand the limitations of the statement of cash flows for investment analysis, we devote Chapters 3 and 4 to a detailed discussion of this statement.

Chapters 3 and 4 explain the objectives of the statement of cash flows and describe the major components of this statement. Generally, the statement of cash flows is intended to provide investors with information about cash flows from operating, investing, and financing events. The chapters explain why these events are of paramount importance to investors and creditors of the firm. Chapter 3 illustrates in detail the construction of a statement of cash flows for one particular firm. Figure 1–3 illustrates how the underlying economic environment of a firm affects its decisions and how these decisions are captured by the statement of cash flows.

In Chapters 3 and 4, we take a critical view of the way most firms report operating cash flows—the indirect method. This method provides substantially less information about components of cash flows from operations than the direct method and is used by most firms. We show how the components of cash flows from operating activities can be estimated, and in Chapter 5 we extend the estimation to free cash flows.

FIGURE 1–3
Economic Decisions of a Firm

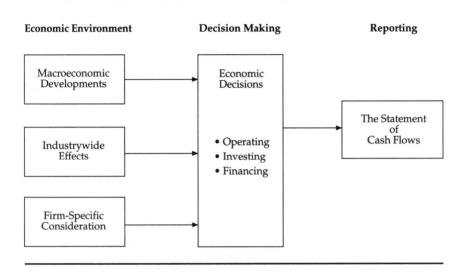

Just as we do throughout the book, Chapter 4 provides a very rich set of illustrations and examples of disclosures from real-world financial statements of firms. We illustrate the different components of cash flows that firms choose to report in the statement of cash flows. Our illustrations begin with examples that are very common and proceed to describe some uncharacteristic disclosures by firms. In the latter cases, we evaluate the disclosure practices and speculate on the motives for such disclosures.

Chapter 4 also contains a detailed analysis of factors that an investor should consider when evaluating a firm. We describe the process that a careful investor may want to follow in analyzing the major components of cash flows. For example, we show the importance of the components of cash flows from operations, the stability of net operating cash flows, and the relationships among the components of investing cash flows. We believe that such an analysis is important for most investors, even if they do not use free cash flow as the primary component in their investment decision.

EARNINGS, CASH FROM OPERATIONS, AND FREE CASH FLOWS

Chapter 5 is the focal chapter in this book. In it, we provide detailed procedures to estimate free cash flows. We examine the limitations of earnings and net operating cash flows for investment analysis and provide the reasons for estimation of free cash flows. We show the superiority of free cash flows for investment purposes in Chapters 8–10 of this book.

Earnings of firms are highly publicized in the investment community, and sudden changes in earnings attract wide attention of analysts, investors, creditors, and the financial press. Prior academic studies showed that earnings changes are positively associated with security returns, that is, earnings increases are likely to be associated with price increases and earnings decreases with price declines. Nevertheless, earnings is a number that is subject to managerial discretion and, in particular, the accounting methods used to construct earnings. We feel that investors would probably be better off using a number that is less subject to managerial discretion.

Net operating cash flow has been suggested as an alternative to earnings. In Chapter 5, we discuss the importance and limitations of operating cash flows for investment purposes. In particular, net operating cash flows as reported currently by firms may contain nonrecurring elements, such as the proceeds from a lawsuit against a competitor for infringement of a patent. Also, net operating cash flows do not include any investments that the firm has to make in order to sustain its current level of growth. Thus, while the ability of the business entity to generate positive operating cash flow is important, it is not the end of the investment process.

Free cash flow is subject to less managerial discretion; it is unaffected by the choice of accounting methods and by managerial discretion with respect to real cash expenditures. Free cash flow is estimated as net cash collected from customers minus all expenditures necessary to sustain the current rate of growth. Figure 1–4 shows the financial statements used to derive the free cash flows, net operating cash flows, and earnings of a firm.

In Chapter 5, we show two approaches to estimating free cash flow using real-world examples. We describe a process that can be used by investors and creditors and develop detailed

FIGURE 1–4
*Sources for Earnings, Net Cash from Operations,
and Free Cash Flows*

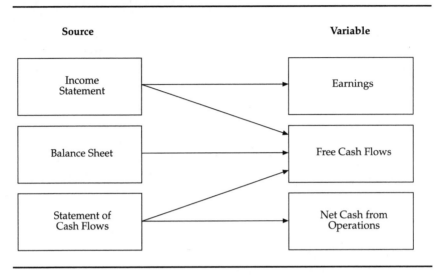

procedures that can be used to construct a screen based on free cash flows. This screen is used in Chapter 8–10 to devise an investment strategy.

EQUITY VALUATION BASED ON FREE CASH FLOW

Chapter 6 deals with the important issue of security valuation. Simple models of security valuation are based on discounting future dividends to determine the firm's current value. Such models require assumptions relating to expected future dividends and the required rate of return used to discount these future dividends. However, some firms do not pay cash dividends, while others (such as utilities) sometimes borrow to pay dividends. Those firms that do pay cash dividends attempt to set dividends low enough so that they can be sustained in good as well as bad economic periods. Thus, dividends per se may be a poor indicator of expected future cash flows to an investor in the firm.

In Chapter 6, we develop a model of security valuation based on free cash flows. This model is appealing because it does not require a firm to distribute the free cash flows, but only to generate them. It recognizes that undistributed free cash flows can be invested or used to retire debt, thereby increasing the value of the firm's equity. The developed model is conservative; it assumes that free cash flows are expected to remain at their most recent levels, and it assumes that firms would not need additional future borrowing to sustain the current rate of growth. Thus, the model identifies a subset of firms for investment—firms that have shown a consistent ability to generate free cash flows and that have low financial leverage. This model provides the theoretical basis for the investment strategy we advocate in Chapters 8–10.

TOTAL DEBT OF A FIRM, INCLUDING OFF-BALANCE-SHEET LIABILITIES

The decade of the 1980s will be remembered because of the large wave of acquisition activity that was financed mostly by debt, including management-led and leveraged buyouts (LBO). The underlying economic rationale had been that acquired firms were believed capable of generating strong and consistent cash flows that would be used to pay off the assumed debt. As a result of the LBO boom, however, many firms found themselves with excess amounts of debt when they entered the 1990 recession. In contrast, the decade of the 1990s found firms with substantially lower financial and operating leverage than before, which helped their international competitiveness and made them more attractive to investors. Still, it is important to identify firms that have excessive amounts of total debt.

We feel excess debt can be very dangerous to the viability of a firm and should be examined as closely by investors as it is by major creditors. Furthermore, we believe that investors and creditors should carefully scrutinize the financial statements to determine whether the firm has any obligations that have not been recorded on the balance sheet. The purpose of Chapter 7 is to discuss the relationship between free cash flows and debt, where debt consists not only of liabilities on the balance sheet but also of off-balance-sheet liabilities.

Unlike the prior literature on the relationship between debt and earnings or cash flows, we develop a measurement of financial leverage that is based on the relationship between debt and free cash flows. Free cash flows represent an amount that a firm generates from its operations that it does not have to reinvest in the business in order to sustain current growth. Thus, free cash flows can be either distributed entirely to shareholders without affecting future cash flows or used to pay down debt not due, again without affecting future cash flows. Therefore, we measure the debt capacity of a firm by the ratio of total debt (including off-balance-sheet liabilities) to free cash flows. The larger this ratio, the longer it will take the firm to pay off its debt.

Chapter 7 covers several areas that include potential off-balance-sheet liabilities such as operating leases, pensions, and other postretirement benefits. It shows how investors and creditors should adjust total debt to include these obligations that are not recorded on the balance sheet. The importance of these adjustments and consideration of the debt capacity is shown and discussed in Chapter 8, where we show that firms with low financial leverage perform better, in the long run, than those firms with greater financial leverage.

PORTFOLIO SELECTION AND PERFORMANCE

Chapter 8 provides comparisons of the stock market performance of three portfolios—one based on P/E ratios, one based on net operating cash flows, and one based on free cash flows. It shows that portfolios based on free cash flows perform better than those based on P/E ratios or net operating cash flows.

To form portfolios, one can use several screening criteria that identify subsets of firms for investment purposes. One such screening variable is the P/E ratio, which is widely quoted in the financial press. It is typically believed that one should hold long securities with low P/E ratios and sell short securities with high

P/E ratios. Our results show that securities with low P/E ratios did *not* outperform the market in recent years. Thus, one cannot rely on P/E ratios for identifying investment candidates.

We follow a similar investment strategy that is based on the ratio of market value to net cash flow from operating activities. This ratio is similar to the P/E ratio in that it measures (roughly) the number of years it will take an investor to recapture the initial investment in the firm by the cash generated from operations. As with the portfolios based on P/E ratios, we find that net operating cash flows cannot be used to identify a subset of firms that earn abnormal returns in the testing period.

However, we find that a portfolio that is based on the ratio of market value to free cash flows has earned abnormal returns consistently over the testing period. This portfolio is selected based on several criteria; firms in this portfolio must have a low ratio of market value to average free cash flow over the past four years. These firms must also have a low ratio of debt to average free cash flow. They also have to show positive growth in their net operating cash flows over the most recent four- and eight-year periods. We find that very few firms fulfill all these requirements. Those that do are firms with very stable patterns of free cash flows that are underpriced by the market, possibly because of lower accounting earnings, although free cash flows remain strong. The returns on holding this portfolio exceed the returns on holding the S&P 500 or securities with similar size. Figure 1–5 portrays examples of screening criteria that are used in Chapter 8 to form portfolios for investment.

In Chapter 8, we provide results of back-testing the investment strategy based on free cash flow, as well as results of live portfolios for a long period. We explain in the chapter that both types of evidence are needed to support the superiority of the investment strategy. The back-tests are artificial in terms of timing of investment or liquidation of a security. However, they ensure that no other considerations beyond the specified investment strategy are used for investment. Live portfolio results are deemed to be superior because they adjust for transaction costs and information bias and demonstrate that a strategy can be applied successfully. However, results of a live portfolio cannot guarantee that other considerations were not responsible for investment or liquidation decisions.

FIGURE 1–5
Screening Criteria Used in the Book

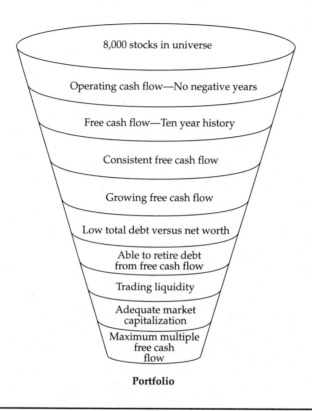

8,000 stocks in universe

Operating cash flow—No negative years

Free cash flow—Ten year history

Consistent free cash flow

Growing free cash flow

Low total debt versus net worth

Able to retire debt from free cash flow

Trading liquidity

Adequate market capitalization

Maximum multiple free cash flow

Portfolio

We feel the two approaches (live and back-tests) are important complements to each other and we report the results for both.

OTHER APPLICATIONS OF PORTFOLIOS BASED ON FREE CASH FLOW

The portfolio approach we advocate—investment in firms with consistent free cash flows, with low financial leverage, and with low free cash flow multiples—seems to be ideally suited to other areas of investment as well. We explore two of these in Chapters 9 and 10.

One of the most attractive areas for investment is small-capitalization stocks. Such stocks were shown to outperform the general market and their larger capitalization counterparts during much of the last 20 years. However, small firms carry additional dimensions of risk, which are not typical for large firms. Small firms are usually less diversified than large firms and are more dependent on a single product for their survival. Thus, their operating risk is usually greater than that of larger firms, which are usually not exposed to economic hardships with all their products at the same time. Also, small firms have a limited debt capacity; debt and equity holders are unlikely to aid the smaller firm during bad economic times for fear of bankruptcy. Indeed, the rate of bankruptcy is greater for smaller firms than for large firms, as we show in Chapter 9.

We recommend investment in small- and mid-capitalization firms that fit our criteria: consistent ability to generate free cash flows, low financial leverage, and low free cash flow multiples. Such firms are usually more diversified, or at least have more stable operations than most small firms. Such firms also have lower financial risk because of their lower levels of debt and a greater potential for price appreciation due to their low free cash flow multiples. Indeed, as we show in Chapter 9, such portfolios are able to earn returns that are superior to the market as a whole and to portfolios of firms with similar size, similar systematic risk (beta), and similar book/market ratios. The chapter also provides evidence on superior returns earned on a live portfolio of small- and mid-capitalization stocks managed according to this strategy.

Another natural area of a free cash flow based strategy is investments in foreign firms. Such firms usually prepare financial statements according to their local accounting principles, which may be very different from U.S. accepted accounting principles. In order to perform an initial screening of a large population of foreign firms, one has to devise a measure that would abstract from the different accounting methods followed in different countries. In Chapter 10, we suggest free cash flow as the common benchmark that can be used for such analysis. We show how one can estimate free cash flows from foreign financial statements, although they are prepared according to different accounting methods. The chapter shows that a portfolio based on our free cash flow strategy earns returns that are higher than the universe of all foreign firms included in the database, as well as portfolios of firms with similar size and book/market ratios.

SUMMARY

The purpose of this book is to educate the reader in what we believe is an important investment concept—free cash flow. We believe that one can use this concept to screen many candidates for investment and select a subset of firms for an in-depth analysis. The estimation of free cash flow enables investors to use a sophisticated level of fundamental analysis in a computer screen that identifies a subset of firms for in-depth fundamental analysis. We believe the methods advocated in this book will help investors make better and more informed investment decisions.

Chapter Two

The Firm's Economic Environment

INTRODUCTION

Before one begins any analysis of a firm, whether it is a cash flow analysis, ratio analysis, credit analysis, investment analysis, or any general financial statement analysis, it is very important to become familiar with the firm's economic environment. Familiarity with the economic environment is achieved on three levels: macroeconomic developments, industrywide events, and firm-specific attributes. (See Figure 2–1.)

MACROECONOMIC ENVIRONMENT

Generally, one wants to become familiar with the macroeconomy in which the firm operates, how the firm is affected by various stages of the business cycle, the firm's own product life cycle, and the general forecasts of future economic developments. These macroeconomic developments will affect the firm's cash flows and, therefore, the firm's market value.

Example

Firms that sell consumer goods may be directly affected by the general condition of the economy and the particular stage of the business cycle. Firms that sell consumer electronics normally see their sales decline when the economy contracts and increase rapidly when the economy expands. In order to induce consumers to purchase goods, such firms reduce prices at an economic downturn, leading to lower operating cash flows for the firms. Many marketers of electronic goods offered deep

FIGURE 2-1
Financial Analysis of a Firm

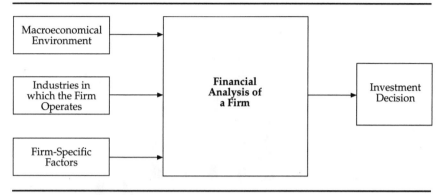

discounts on their merchandise during November and December of 1990, in anticipation of bad holiday sales due to the economic recession.

Figure 2–2 shows the sensitivity of Sony's profits and cash flows to the world recession in the early 1990s. Sony's profits continued to grow through 1992, but its free cash flows did not grow after 1988 and began declining after 1990, reflecting severe competitive pressures for consumer electronics and the rise of the Yen during that period.

Example

A notable casualty of the 1980s was the banking industry, whose cash and deposits include amounts required to be maintained at the Federal Reserve, while loans, which make up the major share of its assets, are not "liquid" in the sense they are usually rolled over rather than paid. When rising interest rates caused wide negative spreads, cash flows of banks evaporated. When interest rates fell, cash flows soared.

As can be seen in Figure 2–3, United Jersey Bank's profits and cash flows were sensitive to the spread between the prime rate and the yield on short-term Treasury bills. They generally rose when the spread increased and fell when the spread decreased.

INDUSTRYWIDE EFFECTS

The second level of analysis is the industry (or industries) in which a firm operates. Recognizing the particular forces that affect the entity or industry is vitally important. The analysis of cash flows

FIGURE 2–2
Sony Corporation

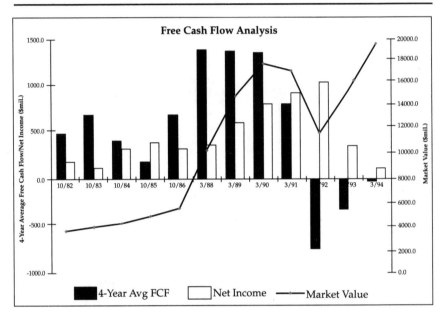

can differ from one entity to another and from one industry to another, depending on the particular industries in which the firm operates. The analyst wishes to identify expected growth rates for the industry, expected operating capacity, expectations for technological advances, and the like. The analyst should also examine interrelationships among several industries in those cases where a firm operates in more than one industry, or is dependent on another industry or on some other economic factor. For example, firms and industries may be sensitive to the exchange rate of the dollar against other currencies, or dependent on a single supplier or a major customer. The industrywide events are likely to affect the firm's own cash flows in a significant manner.

Example

Tobacco firms generally enjoy a loyal brand clientele, although its potential market decreases with the decrease in the number of smokers in the population. Nevertheless, tobacco firms' cash flows are stable and predictable and are affected mostly by industry-specific

FIGURE 2–3
United Jersey Bank Corporation: Free Cash Flow Analysis

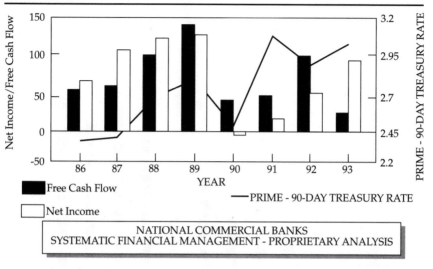

events such as governmental regulations (and taxes), the ability to increase selling prices, or the price of raw tobacco, as opposed to economywide events. Such firms may be severely affected by an unfavorable decision in a legal case of product liability against them. Stock prices of tobacco firms are greatly affected by major court cases in these areas, and would see their operating and free cash flows soften if they were to lose such a case.

Figure 2–4 illustrates the free cash flows and profits of Philip Morris and Co., the largest tobacco firm in the United States. Its free cash flows increased nicely over the period shown, although its profits declined in 1993. Its market value declined when the firm announced plans to lower prices, resulting in an industry price war. Furthermore, the proposed tax on cigarettes to finance the national health care bill caused declines in prices of tobacco-related-stocks.

Example

Banks and other financial intermediaries that do not maintain a good maturity balance (of assets and liabilities) have shown a high propensity for failure, as those institutions that borrowed "short-term" and lent "long-term" found out.

FIGURE 2–4
Philip Morris and Co.

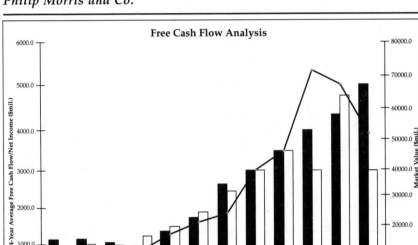

For manufacturing concerns, liquidity may appear to be in balance. However, if assets are more liquid than liabilities, there could be a surplus of short-term cash that can be used to repay interest-bearing debt; if the reverse is true, there could be a cash flow deficiency.

In the growing service sector, where the typical investment in fixed assets is low compared to liabilities, there is a greater need to estimate the *timing* of cash inflows.

It is the chief responsibility of the cash flow analyst to be cognizant of permissible industry/accounting methods, how they differ from other industries, and new accounting proposals and tax legislation that affect cash flows. For analysts who take pride in their earnings forecasts, assessing operating and free cash flows is invaluable in determining the quality of those earnings and to aid in setting an appropriate price/earnings multiple. Earnings quality is partially determined by the ease with which reported income is converted into cash.

Firm-Specific Factors

Finally, the analyst should focus on firm-specific characteristics: any unique resources (or problems) that cannot be identified for other firms in the same industry. Firms that have a monopoly in producing one product (e.g., a utility company or certain computer operating system), or firms that rely on a single supplier of raw materials are examples. Positive factors will increase cash flows for the particular firm and will result in higher stock prices, whereas firms with negative factors may have more volatile cash flows.

Example

When Microsoft announced its Windows 95 operating system, stock in the company jumped as it is expected most personal computers will upgrade to the system. Dataquest, a research firm, estimated that Windows 95 would sell 30 million copies in the first four months alone.

Example

Drexel Burnham and Lambert, a small security firm became a large operation due to its development and large market share of the high-yield bond market ("junk" bonds, as they were known). With the deterioration in this market (and the allegations of illegal trading), the firm lost its unique competitive advantage and was forced into bankruptcy.

In this chapter, we develop a checklist of items that should be considered in an analysis of the economic environment of a firm, and provide examples of data sources that are available for this analysis.

THE MOTIVES FOR UNDERSTANDING THE ECONOMIC ENVIRONMENT

There are three main reasons why an analyst who is studying cash flows would like to understand the economic environment of a firm. Figure 2–5 illustrates these reasons, which are explained below in more detail.

1. Evaluation of past performance. In many cases, an analyst wishes to evaluate a firm's historic operating cash flows, as reflected in its published financial reports. He or she should

FIGURE 2–5
Applications of Financial Statement Analysis

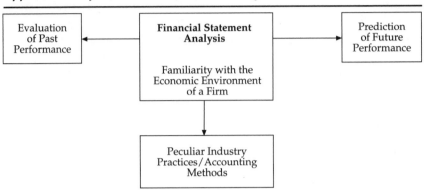

have a good idea of the economic environment that prevailed during the period covered by the financial statements, to better understand the reasons for success or failure of the firm.

Example

Suppose that the analysis concerns a firm in the oil business during the years 1973–1974. The analyst who is familiar with the firm and its economic environment will expect to see a major increase in revenues and in free and operating cash flows between 1974 and prior years due to the oil embargo, which was imposed by oil producers in 1973. Evaluation of past performance that ignores the effects of the oil embargo may erroneously conclude that management was able to increase sales and cash flows substantially due to greater market penetration or similar reasons. Conversely, the decline in oil prices during the latter part of the 1980s and 1993 caused declines in free cash flows for most energy-related firms.

Example

A tender offer for Revco Corporation, a large drug store chain, was made at the height of its operating cycle, a time when retail sales were higher than normal. Subsequent to the tender offer, retail sales fell and cash flow was insufficient to repay the new debt, thereby forcing the firm into bankruptcy. The cash flow analyst should be familiar with the economic conditions, including cash flows during prior recessions, so that he or she can evaluate retail sales and cash flows in future periods even if those turn out to be extreme cases.

2. Prediction of future performance.   Often, the analyst examines published financial reports in order to make predictions about the future performance of the firm. This is often called feedback. In making these predictions, the analyst should have a good understanding of possible economic scenarios a firm may face. The analyst should take into consideration any expectations of changes from the historical growth rates for the particular industry, as well as other microeconomic and macroeconomic factors.

Example

Throughout the mid 1980s, computer manufacturers of mainframes or personal computers enjoyed a very high growth rate of revenues and cash flows. However, market expectations in the mid-1980s for future growth rates declined considerably, and competitive pressures along with advances in technology severely reduced selling prices. Therefore, an analyst who based predictions of future sales solely on historical results, would have grossly overstated future growth rates in earnings and cash flows, given the changed outlook for such firms.

Example

Many entities that went private via leveraged buyout (LBO) ran into difficulties when the economy slowed during the early 1990s. The retailing industry is a notable example. Large companies enjoyed good growth during the 1982–1990 economic expansion. But many companies either fell into bankruptcy or were faced with prospects of bankruptcy when demand fell, and when very large debt payments associated with the LBO eroded cash flows.

Figure 2-6 illustrates the free cash flows and profits of the retailer R. H. Macy, which was taken private in a management buyout that saddled the firm with large amounts of debt. As can be seen in the figure, cash flows and profits declined substantially, forcing the firm into bankruptcy proceedings.

3. Identification of particular business practices and accounting rules.   Certain industries follow business practices and accounting rules that are different from those of most firms. When an analyst examines firms from these industries, it is important to understand the context of business transactions, as well as their accounting descriptions.

FIGURE 2–6
R. H. Macy

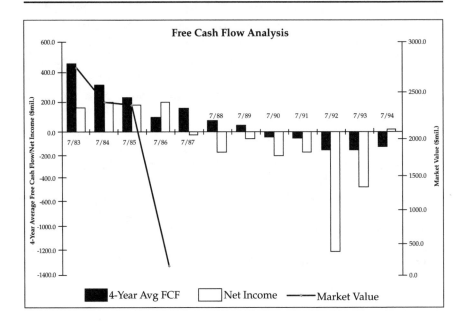

Example

Firms in the broadcasting industry may invest resources in creating a program or a movie that is expected to generate future cash flows from future broadcasting or screening. In such cases, the original expenditures on the program or movie are capitalized and amortized over the expected life of the program. The analyst should be aware of that practice when analyzing financial statements of a firm in the broadcasting industry, and should be able to assess whether the amortization period that the firm chooses is adequate or too liberal, as well as its effects on estimating cash flows.

Example

Headquartered in Des Moines, Iowa, Meredith Corp. is a Fortune 500 diversified media company involved in magazine and book publishing, television broadcasting, and residential real estate marketing and franchising.

In its 1993 financial statements, Meredith states:

e. Unearned Subscription Revenue and Deferred Subscription Acquisition Cost. Gross unearned subscription revenue and gross deferred subscription acquisition costs are recorded and recognized pro rata as delivery of magazines is made, beginning with the month of initial delivery. In prior periods, unearned subscription revenues were reported net of deferred subscription acquisition costs on the Company's Consolidated Balance Sheets and Consolidated Statements of Cash Flows. In fiscal 1993, the presentation was changed to show each in its gross amount and also to show the long-term and current portions of both unearned subscription revenues and deferred subscription acquisition costs. (The long-term and current portions are determined based on the delivery month of the subscription.) Prior periods have been reclassified to make the presentation of the consolidated financial statements more meaningful. In addition, current and noncurrent portions of deferred income taxes were reclassified in prior years to reflect this change in presentation. The reclassifications have no effect on the Consolidated Statements of Earnings.

f. Deferred Film Rental Costs. Deferred film rental costs reflect the value of all programming available for showing and are stated at cost less amortization. Film rental costs are charged to operations on an accelerated amortization basis over the contract period. The cost of broadcast film rental estimated to be charged to operations during the next fiscal year has been classified as a current asset.

Note that Meredith needs to show not only its policy regarding the recognition of revenues and income from its magazine subscriptions, but also its accounting policy regarding the costs of film rentals. Both of these items should be understood by the cash flow analyst prior to any serious analysis of the financial statements.

THE FIRM'S BUSINESS SEGMENTS

In *Statement of Financial Accounting Standards (SFAS) No. 14* (1976), the Financial Accounting Standards Board (FASB) required firms to disclose information about their business segments. A business segment is any group of similar businesses that contributes at least 10 percent to revenues, operating profits, or identifiable assets of a firm (para. 15). The FASB required the disclosure of revenues, operating profits, and identifiable assets by segments. Many firms also disclose capital expenditures and depreciation by segments. The FASB required firms to disclose geographical distribution of sales for firms that operate in more than just one part of the world, and the disclosure of sales to major customers who purchase at least 10 percent of total revenues.

Example

General Electric (GE) reported operations in 10 different segments during 1993. Although GE is well-known for its electric appliances and light bulbs, it is less famous for its power generating equipment or financial services. A firm may actually derive most of its revenues (or cash flows) from lines of business that are less known. In the case of GE, electric appliances constitute less than 10 percent of consolidated revenues.

Figure 2–7 portrays the distribution of revenues across GE's segments.

Example

Singer Co. is probably familiar to most people for its sewing machines. In fact, Singer sold the division that produced sewing machines in 1986. In 1987, it operated in four segments, and was greatly dependent on the U.S. government for defense-related projects.

Example

Black & Decker manufactures, markets, and services power tools, household products, and other labor-saving devices. Products include drills, saws, toaster ovens, coffee makers, electric mowers, and so on. However, in its 1988 financial statements, Black & Decker did not disclose segment data, claiming that it operated in just a single line of business:

> The Corporation operates in one business segment—the manufacturing, marketing and servicing of a wide range of power tools, household products and other labor-saving devices generally used in and around the home and by professional users [1988 annual report, p.32].

FIGURE 2–7
General Electric's Business Segments—1993

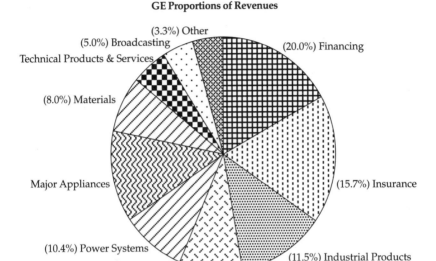

GE Proportions of Revenues

(3.3%) Other
(5.0%) Broadcasting
Technical Products & Services
(8.0%) Materials
Major Appliances
(10.4%) Power Systems
(10.5%) Aircraft Engine
(20.0%) Financing
(15.7%) Insurance
(11.5%) Industrial Products

In 1993, Black & Decker reported operations in the following segments: (*a*) consumer and home improvement products, (*b*) commercial and industrial products, and (*c*) information systems and services. Although the firm provided some breakdown of its revenues, it still lumped together in one segment power tools and hand-held mixers, toasters, and the like. Thus, the breakdown to consumer and commercial products often masks a large variety of products within a single segment.

Example

In its 1992 annual report, Ford Motor Co. reports information in two business segments—automotive products and financial services. Within each segment, Ford reports the results of its operations in the following geographical areas:

(in millions)	1992	1991	1990
Geographic Area—Automotive			
Sales to unaffiliated customers:			
United States	$ 51,918	$ 40,627	$ 48,761
Europe	22,777	22,228	23,736
All other	9,712	9,196	9,347
Total	$ 84,407	$ 72,051	$ 81,844
Operating(loss)/income:			
United States	$ (582)	$ (3,238)	$ (230)
Europe	(1,283)	(711)	460
All other	90	180	86
Total	$ (1,775)	$ (3,769)	$ 316
Geographic Area—Financial Services			
Revenues			
United States	$ 12,514	$ 13,182	$ 13,010
Europe	2,051	1,847	1,662
All other	1,160	1,206	1,134
Total	$ 15,725	$ 16,235	$ 15,806
Income before income taxes and cumulative effects of changes in accounting principles:			
United States	$ 1,452	$ 1,163	$ 955
Europe	266	184	195
All other	107	118	70
Total	$ 1,825	$ 1,465	$ 1,220

As can be seen from the footnote, although Ford's European operations were profitable in 1990, they actually dragged down profits considerably in 1992, reflecting the weak economic conditions in Europe during 1992.

Example

General Mills is a leading producer of consumer foods and an operator of chain restaurants. The company also makes and sells food products in Canada, Europe, Japan, Korea, and Latin America. Products are distributed to retail food chains, co-ops and wholesalers.

General Mills includes the following data in a footnote to its 1993 financial statements:

Note Seventeen: Segment Information

(in millions)	Consumer Foods	Restaurants	Unallocated Corporate Items (a)	Consolidated Total
Sales:				
1993	$5,397.2	$2,737.4		$8,134.6
1992	5,233.8	2,544.0		7,777.8
1991	4,939.7	2,213.5		7,153.2
Operating profits:				
1993	772.6	181.4	$ (110.0)	844.0
1992	744.3	190.8	(90.6)	844.5
1991	689.5	172.2	(96.1)	765.6
Identifiable assets:				
1993	2,576.4	1,605.0	469.4	4,650.8
1992	2,481.2	1,419.3	404.5	4,305.0
1991	2,189.2	1,256.4	456.2	3,901.8
Capital expenditures:				
1993	321.6	301.2	1.0	623.8
1992	397.1	297.0	1.2	695.3
1991	277.6	273.0	4.0	554.6
Depreciation expense:				
1993	154.2	115.2	1.4	270.8
1992	140.3	99.4	2.3	242.0
1991	131.7	79.7	2.0	213.4

In addition to a footnote about segments in the annual report, segment information is also available in the first section of Form 10-K, which must be filed with the Securities and Exchange Commission (SEC) once a year. The first section of this report contains general information about the various businesses of the firm, its major products and additional information that is relevant for other subsections of this chapter. One can use the description of products and lines of business to identify the industries in which the firm operates.

The Bureau of the Census has used a widely accepted system to classify firms into industries, which is known as the Standard Industrial Classification (SIC) system. Under this system, each broad industry is assigned a two-digit SIC code, such as 20 for the food and kindred products group. Within this broad industry, businesses are assigned to more specified industries with three- and four-digit SIC codes, such as 202 for dairy products, and 2024 for ice cream and frozen desserts. The Bureau of the Census has classified each business establishment of each surveyed firm into one of 214 four-digit SIC industries. When a firm has establishments in just one four-digit SIC industry, it is classified as a single-industry company. When it has establishments in more than one four-digit SIC industry, it is classified as a multi-industry company. The cash flow analyst may compare firms from the same four-digit SIC industry, and may attempt to forecast future cash flows within a particular industry.

According to the 1987 census, most employees (a ratio of about 3:1) in the manufacturing sector were employed by multiestablishment businesses (i.e., firms that have more than one business location), and in many cases by firms operating in more than one line of business. Such firms also accounted for the majority of wages and sales in the overall economy. Indeed, most large publicly traded firms operate in more than one industry.

A very useful source of information about the SIC industries in which a firm operates can be found in Standard & Poor's *Registrar of Corporations.* In addition to data about the firm's address, telephone number, directors, and so on, this source lists the four-digit codes of the SIC industries in which a firm operates.

Example

Although Black & Decker indicated that it operated in a single line of business it its 1988 annual report, Standard & Poor's showed operations in eight different four-digit SIC industries for Black & Decker in 1989.

It is very important to understand the various businesses the firm operates before analyzing its financial statements. Traditionally, a firm is assigned to an industry according to its segment with the largest revenues. This may be misleading for a firm that operates in more than one major line of business because the firm's highest cash flow generator may not be the same segment that contributes the largest amount of revenues. A convenient way of assessing the extent of operations in more than one industry is to construct a table that shows the percentage of total revenues, profits, or assets that each of the segments is responsible for.

This gives an immediate indication about the diversity of operations across business segments.

It should be noted that current disclosure of segment data is insufficient to estimate the major components of cash flows from operating, financing, or investing activities. Most firms disclose data about sales, operating profits, and identifiable assets in each of their segments, but there is usually no disclosure of each segment's balance sheet, income statement, or cash flow statements. Thus, an analyst cannot estimate components of cash flows for each of a firm's segments unless the segment discloses a complete set of financial statements because it is required to do so by regulators, or because of other reasons, such as a part of a due diligence review that precedes a takeover process. However, in most cases the analyst is limited to segment information about revenues, operating profits, identifiable assets, depreciation, and capital expenditures. These data are available in footnotes to the financial statements and can be accessed from computer data bases and analyzed easily.

Example

National Service Industries is a diversified firm that has four major segments. Factset, an information service firm, provides the analysis of National Service Industries shown in Table 2–1.

TABLE 2–1
National Service Industries Inc.

	8/94	8/93	8/92	8/91	8/90	8/89	8/88
Lighting Equipment (3646, 3645)							
Net sales	763.6	691.9	683.5	657.4	717.2	658.7	602.8
COGS and SGA	698.0	636.5	629.9	607.9	638.0	590.7	540.9
Depreciation and amortization	15.5	16.8	18.3	17.7	15.3	12.8	11.3
Operating profits	50.1	38.6	35.4	31.8	63.9	55.2	50.6
Operating cash flow	65.6	55.4	53.6	49.5	79.2	68.0	61.9
Capital expenditures	13.2	10.2	10.0	18.9	30.0	20.3	14.0
Identifiable assets	323.3	298.6	280.2	278.4	295.1	263.5	241.7
Percent change analysis:							
Net sales	10.4	1.2	4.0	-8.3	8.9	9.3	
Operating profits	29.7	9.2	11.2	-50.2	15.6	9.1	

TABLE 2–1 *(continued)*
National Service Industries Inc.

	8/94	8/93	8/92	8/91	8/90	8/89	8/88
Profitability analysis:							
Asset turnover	2.46	2.39	2.45	2.29	2.57	2.61	NA
× Operating margin	6.6	5.6	5.2	4.8	8.9	8.4	8.4
= Operating ROA	16.1	13.3	12.7	11.1	22.9	21.9	NA
Operating cash ROA	21.1	19.2	19.2	17.3	28.4	26.9	NA
Textile Rental (7213, 7218)							
Net sales	544.5	546.9	444.1	437.5	397.0	355.8	321.0
COGS and SGA	464.0	466.7	377.2	376.2	335.7	301.8	272.4
Depreciation and amortization	31.7	31.1	24.1	21.9	17.8	15.5	12.9
Operating profits	48.8	49.1	42.8	39.5	43.6	38.5	35.8
Operating cash flow	80.5	80.2	66.9	61.4	61.3	54.1	48.7
Capital expenditures	21.0	55.0	28.2	53.3	23.1	22.6	17.5
Identifiable assets	433.0	433.4	343.3	330.9	251.6	213.8	189.3
Percent change analysis:							
Net sales	-0.5	23.1	1.5	10.2	11.6	10.8	
Operating profits	-0.5	14.8	8.4	-9.4	13.1	7.7	
Profitability analysis:							
Asset turnover	1.26	1.41	1.32	1.50	1.71	1.77	NA
× Operating margin	9.0	9.0	9.6	9.0	11.0	10.8	11.1
= Operating ROA	11.3	12.6	12.7	13.6	18.7	19.1	NA
Operating cash ROA	18.6	20.7	19.9	21.1	26.4	26.8	NA
Chemical (2841, 2842)							
Net sales	332.3	318.1	253.9	239.6	232.9	218.1	200.0
COGS and SGA	290.5	278.3	216.1	203.3	198.1	185.6	166.8
Depreciation and amortization	6.4	6.5	4.3	3.0	2.4	2.1	2.0
Operating profits	35.4	33.3	33.6	33.4	32.4	30.4	31.2
Operating cash flow	41.8	39.8	37.8	36.4	34.8	32.5	33.2
Capital expenditures	5.3	12.7	4.6	11.5	12.1	6.6	3.5
Identifiable assets	169.0	173.2	112.7	110.3	90.4	81.6	72.0
Percent change analysis:							
Net sales	4.5	25.3	6.0	2.9	6.8	9.0	
Operating profits	6.3	-0.8	0.6	3.0	6.6	-2.5	

TABLE 2–1 *(continued)*
National Service Industries Inc.

	8/94	8/93	8/92	8/91	8/90	8/89	8/88
Profitability analysis:							
Asset turnover	1.94	2.23	2.28	2.39	2.71	2.84	NA
× Operating margin	10.6	10.5	13.2	13.9	13.9	13.9	15.6
= Operating ROA	20.7	23.3	30.1	33.2	37.7	39.6	NA
Operating cash ROA	24.4	27.8	33.9	36.2	40.5	42.3	NA
Other (1742, 2677)							
Net sales	241.5	247.9	252.2	267.1	300.7	306.9	290.4
COGS and SGA	226.9	231.2	232.4	251.1	276.8	275.9	269.1
Depreciation and amortization	5.8	6.4	6.2	6.7	6.5	5.5	4.6
Operating profits	8.8	10.3	13.6	9.3	17.4	25.5	16.6
Operating cash flow	14.6	16.6	19.8	16.0	23.9	31.1	21.3
Capital expenditures	2.7	4.0	5.1	6.0	9.8	12.1	8.9
Identifiable assets	75.6	104.9	101.6	120.8	131.6	124.4	123.8
Insulation service	NA	NA	127.0	116.0	117.0	127.0	118.0
Marketing services	NA	NA	37.0	41.0	42.0	41.0	48.0
Envelopes	NA	NA	88.0	92.0	93.0	89.0	77.0
Percent change analysis:							
Net sales	-2.6	-1.7	-5.6	-11.2	-2.0	5.7	
Operating profits	-14.1	-24.3	45.6	-46.5	-31.6	53.3	
Profitability analysis:							
Asset turnover	2.68	2.40	2.27	2.12	2.35	2.47	NA
× Operating margin	3.7	4.1	5.4	3.5	5.8	8.3	5.7
= Operating ROA	9.8	10.0	12.2	7.4	13.6	20.6	NA
Operating cash ROA	16.2	16.1	17.8	12.7	18.7	25.0	NA
Company Totals							
Net sales	1881.9	1804.8	1633.8	1601.7	1647.8	1539.5	1414.2
COGS and SGA	1679.4	1612.7	1455.6	1438.4	1448.5	1353.9	1249.2
Depreciation and amortization	59.3	60.8	52.9	49.3	42.0	36.0	30.8
Operating profits	143.1	131.3	125.3	114.0	157.3	149.7	134.2
Operating cash flow	202.4	192.1	178.2	163.3	199.3	185.6	165.0
Capital expenditures	42.2	82.0	47.8	89.6	75.0	61.6	44.0
Identifiable assets	1000.9	1010.0	837.8	840.4	768.6	683.3	626.8

TABLE 2–1 *(concluded)*
National Service Industries Inc.

	8/94	8/93	8/92	8/91	8/90	8/89	8/88
Percent change analysis:							
Net sales	4.3	10.5	2.0	-2.8	7.0	8.9	
Operating profits	9.0	4.8	9.9	-27.6	5.1	11.5	
Profitability Analysis:							
Asset turnover	1.87	1.95	1.95	1.99	2.27	2.35	NA
× Operating margin	7.6	7.3	7.7	7.1	9.5	9.7	9.5
= Operating ROA	14.2	14.2	14.9	14.2	21.7	22.8	NA
Operating cash ROA	20.1	20.8	21.2	20.3	27.5	28.3	NA
Percent of Company Totals							
Sales:							
Lighting equipment	40.6	38.3	41.8	41.0	43.5	42.8	42.6
Textile rental	28.9	30.3	27.2	27.3	24.1	23.1	22.7
Chemical	17.7	17.6	15.5	15.0	14.1	14.2	14.1
Other	12.8	13.7	15.4	16.7	18.2	19.9	20.5
Operating Profits:							
Lighting equipment	35.0	29.4	28.2	27.9	40.6	36.9	37.7
Textile rental	34.1	37.4	34.2	34.6	27.7	25.7	26.7
Chemical	24.7	25.4	26.8	29.3	20.6	20.3	23.2
Other	6.2	7.8	10.8	8.2	11.1	17.1	12.4
Capital Expenditures:							
Lighting equipment	31.3	12.4	20.8	21.1	40.0	33.0	31.8
Textile rental	49.8	67.1	58.9	59.5	30.8	36.7	39.9
Chemical	12.6	15.5	9.6	12.8	16.1	10.7	8.0
Other	6.4	4.9	10.6	6.7	13.1	19.6	20.3
Identifiable Assets:							
Lighting equipment	32.3	29.6	33.4	33.1	38.4	38.6	38.6
Textile rental	43.3	42.9	41.0	39.4	32.7	31.3	30.2
Chemical	16.9	17.1	13.5	13.1	11.8	11.9	11.5
Other	7.6	10.4	12.1	14.4	17.1	18.2	19.8

Note that in the above example, National Service Industries, a firm with total sales of about $1.88 billion in 1994 has four major segments; lighting equipment, textile rental, other, and chemical segments. At the bottom of Factset's analysis, one can find the contribution of each segment to sales, operating profits, capital expenditures, and identifiable assets. In addition, for each of the segments, Factset estimates operating cash flows by adding back depreciation to operating profits of the segment. As we shall see in the next chapter, this is just a rough approximation of operating cash flows. For each segment, Factset reports the percentage change in sales and operating profits, and two profitability measures. The first profitability measure is based on multiplying asset turnover (sales divided by average identifiable assets in the most recent two years) by the operating margin (operating profit divided by sales times 100). The second is identical to the first, except that operating cash flow replaces operating profit in the margin ratio.

It should be noted that the segment analysis reported by Factset is not at all exhaustive; other analysts can add their own unique ratios or other types of analysis. However, with the limited data available on segments, there is not much broader analysis that can be applied. Note that the cash flow analyst can have a reasonable idea about which segments generate operating (free) cash flows and which ones actually use cash flows generated by the other segments.

Sometimes a firm will report that it operates in a single line of business. In this case, the cash flow analyst will have little information about revenues, profits or cash flows for various parts of the business, such as for different brands or important products.

Example

H. J. Heinz Co. has the following comment in its 1992 Management Discussion and Analysis section of the annual report:

> The company is engaged principally in one line of business—processed food products—which represents over 90% of consolidated sales.

However, Heinz reports data about operations in various geographical regions.

In some cases, the assignment of firms into a particular four-digit SIC industry yields an industry that has very dissimilar firms.

Example

SIC Industry code 1400 includes DeBeers Mines, which has interests primarily in diamond mining and distribution. SIC code 1400 also includes Vulcan Materials, which sells construction materials and chemicals.

Evaluation of Diversification

An analysis of the business segments should include an assessment of the firm's diversification. There are two major types of corporate diversification—related and unrelated. In related diversification, the firm diversifies into areas of business that use similar input factors, similar manufacturing techniques, or similar distribution channels. Unrelated diversification is characterized by operations that have no commonalties. The advantage of related diversification is the synergies that are created from using similar inputs for the various products. The disadvantage of related diversification is that most businesses tend to move together. Downturns in the economy affect all segments simultaneously, and so one or more segments would not offset the poor operating cash flows of the down-cycle segments. The main advantage of unrelated diversification is the stability of operations and cash flows; not all segments are equally affected by the business cycle at the same time. The disadvantage of unrelated diversification is that economies of scale or economies of scope are likely to be suboptimal because the firm may be unable to fully utilize its assets within the firm. Management of firms that diversified into unrelated areas of business may also be unable to apply the same priorities that made the core business successful, and troubles in one division can actually drag cash flows of the entire firm down.

Example

Nashua Corporation began as a marketer of copiers and office supplies, and later expanded into manufacturing of discs for the computer industry. When the disc drives business collapsed in 1991, so too did Nashua's earnings and market value, as can be seen in Figure 2–8.

The analyst should assess whether the firm followed a strategy to diversify into related or unrelated areas of business. The analyst should also examine segmental exposure to the business cycle, and what one should expect to find in the amount, growth, and stability of cash flows for each line of business.

Example

In the example of National Service Industries used previously, the firm operated in the following segments: lighting equipment, textile

FIGURE 2–8
Nashua Corp.

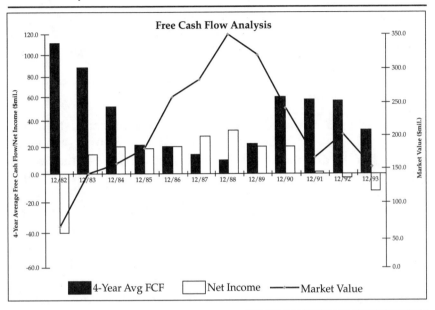

rental, other, and chemical. The primary SIC codes for the segments were 3646, 7213, 1742, and 2841, respectively. It can be seen that there is very little similarity in operations of the four segments. They operate in four different SIC industries, even at the two-digit SIC level. Thus, the firm may be perceived to have diversified into unrelated areas of business.

In terms of the sensitivity of the firm to the business cycle, it should be noted that the four segments are probably not affected by the business cycle at the same time. Lighting equipment and the insulation service (the major component of the other segment) are probably affected by the housing market, which tends to lead the business cycle. Textile rental and chemical either lag behind the business cycle or coincide with the business cycle. Thus, the firm seems to be less sensitive to the business cycle than firms that operate in a single sector of the economy, and can be considered a defensive stock.

Example

In a previous example, we showed that General Mills operates in consumer foods and in restaurants. One can immediately think about related areas of business in the two segments, including products, research and development, marketing, sharing of technology, managerial expertise, ability to test products, and the like. Thus, the firm may be perceived as one that chose to diversify into related areas of business. It should be noted that General Mills will be affected by the business cycle in a similar manner across both of its segments, with the restaurants segment affected by the business cycle to a greater degree. However, the food business is usually considered very stable in terms of operating cash flows.

Another area of investigation is the geographical distribution of revenues. When a firm has a seasonal product, it may be worthwhile to diversify into the other part of the hemisphere to take advantage of smoothing sales and increasing cash flows. Quaker Oats is attempting to do this with its popular Gatorade sports drink. It is also important to assess the risks of such seasonal operations, as well as the risks of operating in specific countries. These risks can be driven by economic factors, such as interest rate changes, and by political risks, such as instability in oil producing regions.

The cash flow analyst should also examine the firm's disclosure of cash flows by segment, or at least the disaggregation of cash flows from industrial and financial activities.

Example

Ashland Oil Inc. reports segment cash flows from operations in its 1992 financial statements. These are as follows:

(in millions)	1992	1991
Cash Flows from Operations:		
Ashland Petroleum	$102	$183
SuperAmerica Group	49	56
Valvoline	48	41
Chemical	102	97
Construction	76	78
Engineering	–	–
Exploration	64	102
Coal investments	7	9
Corporate	(175)	(109)
Change in operating assets and liabilities	125	16
	$398	$473

The cash flow analyst can assess the contribution of each segment to total cash flows from operating activities. Figure 2-9 shows the contribution of each of the segments in a graph.

Example

In its 1991 annual report, Sun Co. shows statements of cash flow for its businesses. In these statements, Sun reports data on its refining and marketing segment, international exploration and production segment, its Canadian operations, its coal division, and its corporate group. The statements show abbreviated operating cash flows and investing cash flows, but not financing cash flows, which are probably more difficult to desegregate by segments.

Finally, the capital expenditures made in each of the segments may indicate where the firm feels the best potential lies, and what areas it decides to shrink. The firm also signals which businesses are more capital-intensive than others, and which businesses are subject to frequent replacement of capital assets due to rapid technological advances. The analyst could compare the expectations of the firm, as evidenced by the relative investments in each of the segments, with market expectations about each of these industries.

Example

Some firms provide a lot of information on their segments in the management discussion and analysis (MD&A) section of the annual report. According to SEC rules, management is required to provide additional analysis and explanation of its operating results and liquidity in the MD&A section. In its 1991 annual report, Monsanto provides a detailed discussion of each of its segments, and includes in the discussion an analysis of the factors that contributed to (reduced) operating income. Such factors include the effects of selling prices, sales volume and mix, raw materials and other manufacturing costs, restructuring and divestitures, and so on. It also provides an outlook for each of the segments.

RELIANCE ON MAJOR CUSTOMERS

The reliance on one or a few major customers exposes the firm to greater business risk. If a major customer goes out of business, or if it is adversely affected by any external events, the firm's sales and

FIGURE 2–9
Ashland Oil—1992 Cash Flows by Segments

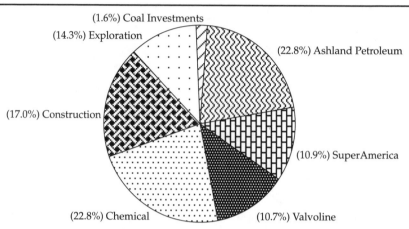

consequently its cash flows may be badly hurt. Data about major customers are sometimes found in the footnote on segment reports or in the business description section of Form 10-K. The analyst should consider the extent of the additional risk that is imposed on the firm due to its reliance on one or a few major customers.

Example

Harsco manufactures military vehicles and defense systems, scaffolding and concrete forming equipment, plastic piping, propane tanks, seamless steel cylinders, and it provides materials handling and engineering services to steel producers.

In its 1992 annual report, Harsco reports the following information about its sales to the U.S. government:

(in millions)	1992	1991	1990
Net sales to unaffiliated customers:			
United States	$1,468.1	$1,799.1	$1,619.2
International	156.8	144.0	140 3
Total	$1,624.9	$l,943.1	$1,759.5
Export sales and major customer information			
Export sales from the United States	$ 585.4	$ 533.5	$ 277.5
Sales to U.S. government agencies, principally by Defense Group	$ 563.6	$ 860.1	$ 627.1

As can be seen, Harsco is very dependent on the U.S. defense budget. With the cuts in the defense budget, Harsco's sales were reduced since 1991. However, Harsco managed to contain its costs, and its free cash flows actually increased in recent years. See Figure 2–10.

Example

Oil refiners are very dependent on oil prices, not only for cash flows and profits, but also for their capital spending. In December 1993, Maxus Energy was quoted by *The Wall Street Journal* as saying that every $1 decline in the price of a barrel of crude oil reduces the company's cash flows by 4 percent, or $8 million, a year. Since oil firms rely on internally generated cash flow for their spending, such declines have immediate effects on oil exploration activities.

RELIANCE ON MAJOR SUPPLIERS

Most firms rely on outside sources for their input factors such as raw materials, components used in production, labor force, and the like. An ideal situation for the manufacturing entity is when there are many suppliers of these input factors and they therefore compete intensely for customers. In such cases, the firm is virtually guaranteed a steady source of supply at competitive prices. However, when a firm relies on one supplier, or just a few suppliers of important input factors, the firm is exposed to greater risk because of possible disruption of supply. The supplier may go out of business, may decide to halt the supply of a certain component, or may decide (or be forced) to raise prices. In all these cases, production is likely to be interrupted and the dependent firm is likely to be adversely affected. The analyst can find information about major suppliers in the business description section of Form 10-K, or in a recent prospectus.

Example

Airlines are dependent on the price of oil for their profitability. When the supply of fuel is hampered or when there are perceptions that future supply may be falling, profitability of the airline is negatively affected because oil prices will reflect the expected shortages. Although the airline may not be dependent on any individual supplier of fuel,

FIGURE 2–10
Harsco. Co.

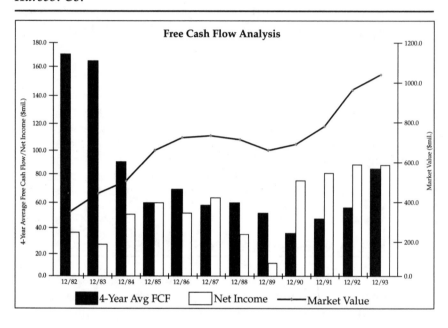

it is greatly dependent on world supply of oil. The analyst should have some expectations about future prices of fuel in analyzing the future prospects of an airline.

Example

Southwest Airlines provides air transportation services on routes between 29 cities in the Southwest and Midwest regions of the United States. Southwest Airlines showed in its 1985 annual report that fuel costs comprised over 27 percent of operating costs, and in some years as much as 40 percent of operating costs.

Year Ended December 31, 1985

	Consolidated	Southwest	Muse Air	1984
Fuel cost per gallon	80.49¢	80.52¢	79.80¢	80.53¢
Fuel's % of operating costs	27%	27%	29%	31%

Southwest Airlines explicitly recognizes it in its discussion of operations in its 1989 report:

> We experienced significant operating cost increases throughout 1989, however, which served to dampen an otherwise very successful year. Fuel costs, in particular, escalated in the fourth quarter to a system average of 66 cents per gallon and then skyrocketed in January 1990 to 79 cents per gallon. As an energy-dependent Company, we are continually exploring ways to manage this risk more effectively, in addition to continually adding more fuel-efficient aircraft to the fleet (the 737-300 and -500). Even so, we are consistently among the lowest in the industry in terms of the average cost of fuel per gallon. Aircraft maintenance was the other cost category where larger increases were experienced in 1989 and are expected in 1990 due, in part, to the increase in the fleet of 737-300s, which is more expensive to maintain than their 737-200 predecessor. Thus, the increased maintenance cost offsets, to an extent, the fuel savings obtained from these aircraft.

A different perspective about the number of available suppliers has gained momentum in recent years. According to this view, it is preferred to rely on a small number of suppliers who would work closely with the firm in designing the parts they supply, and in ensuring a proper quality and the availability of units when those are required by the firm. In fact, such reliance helped the Japanese automobile manufacturers attain leaner production lines and higher quality than their U.S. counterparts. Even within the United States, Chrysler and Ford rely more on suppliers of parts than GM, which still manufactures most of its parts internally.

COMPETITION IN THE INDUSTRY

Economic theory suggests that the more competitive an industry, the lower the profit and cash flow margins to any firm that operates in that industry. Thus, it is important to assess the degree of competition in each of the industries where the firm sells its products. The analyst should assume that if the industry is very competitive, the firm is unlikely to obtain any abnormal cash flows. However, if the industry is not competitive, it can indicate that the major firms in the industry may earn abnormal cash flows and be characterized by a better ability to generate free cash flows.

Example

During 1994, an agreement between the world's primary major aluminum producers was successful in lifting the price of the metal and in boosting cash flows of aluminum companies. This resulted in rising market values of aluminum companies.

One can assess the competition in an industry by examining concentration ratios in the industry. For example, one can examine the percentage of industry sales made by the four (or eight) largest firms in the industry. The larger this ratio, the more concentrated the industry—and the less competitive it is likely to be. The Bureau of the Census publishes concentration ratios for four-digit SIC industries. Alternatively, the analyst can construct this ratio from published sources, such as Standard & Poor's Compustat database.

Example

Checking the Standard & Poor's Compustat database showed that two industries, pharmaceutical and computer makers, have largely different four-firm concentration ratios. In the pharmaceutical industry, denoted by SIC code 2834, the largest four firms sell about 36 percent of total sales of firms included in the Compustat database. However, computer manufacturers, excluding IBM, denoted by Compustat industry 3571, had a four-firm concentration ratio of 61 percent. (Tables 2–2 and 2–3 provide a partial list of firms in these two industries and their sales during 1993). This clearly shows that the pharmaceutical industry is less concentrated than the computer industry, corresponding with our intuition. Had IBM been included in the calculations of the computer industry, the results would have been even more accentuated.

Additional discussion of the competition in the firm's industries may also be available in the business discussion of Form 10-K or in a recent prospectus.

Example

The broadcasting industry is dominated by three major networks that control most of the noncable programming through affiliates. However, in 1994, some of the affiliates of CBS have decided to switch to the fourth largest network, Fox, creating more competitive tension in the industry. Still, in most areas, the three largest networks dominate by far their local competitors and are able to attract the best local stations.

TABLE 2–2
Pharmaceutical Firms—SIC Industry 2834

Ticker	Name	1993 Sales ($millions)
JNJ	JOHNSON & JOHNSON	$14,138.0
BMY	BRISTOL MYERS SQUIBB	11,413.0
MRK	MERCK & CO	10,498.2
SBE	SMITHKLINE BEECHAM PLC -AD	9,246.0
ABT	ABBOTT LABORATORIES	8,407.8
AHP	AMERICAN HOME PRODUCTS CORP	8,304.8
GLX	GLAXO HOLDINGS PLC -ADR	7,987.0
PFE	PFIZER INC	7,477.7
ZEN	ZENECA GROUP PLC -SPON ADR	6,626.6
LLY	LILLY (ELI) & CO	6,452.4
WLA	WARNER-LAMBERT CO	5,793.7
SGP	SCHERING-PLOUGH	4,341.3
RPR	RHONE-POULENC RORER	4,019.4
UPJ	UPJOHN CO	3,653.4
WEL	WELLCOME PLC -ADS	3,034.1
MKC	MARION MERRELL DOW INC	2,818.0
SYN	SYNTEX CORP	2,123.0
NVO	NOVO-NORDISK A/S -ADR	1,863.7
AGN	ALLERGAN INC	858.9
CAR	CARTER-WALLACE INC	656.2
IVX	IVAX CORP	645.3
GNE	GENENTECH INC -RED	608.2
PRGO	PERRIGO COMPANY	570.8
TEVIY	TEVA PHARM INDS -ADR	502.0
SPI	SPI PHARMACEUTICALS INC	404.0
SHR	SCHERER (R.P.)/DE	398.0
BMD	A.L. LABORATORIES INC -CL	338.2
MDV	MEDEVA PLC -SPON ADR	296.1
FRX	FOREST LABORATORIES -CL A	285.4
GENZ	GENZYME CORP	270.4
AZA	ALZA CORP	219.8
MYL	MYLAN LABORATORIES	212.0
NBTY	NATURE'S BOUNTY INC	138.4
ELN	ELAN CORP PLC -ADR	135.8
NATR	NATURES SUNSHINE PRODS INC	127.2
BCL	BIOCRAFT LABORATORIES INC	124.9
CHTT	CHATTEM INC	105.4

TABLE 2–3
Computer Firms (without IBM)—SIC Industry 3571

Ticker	Name	1993 Sales ($millions)
AAPL	APPLE COMPUTER INC	$7,977.0
CPQ	COMPAQ COMPUTER CORP	7,191.0
SUNW	SUN MICROSYSTEMS INC	4,308.6
DELL	DELL COMPUTER CORP	2,873.2
TDM	TANDEM COMPUTERS INC	2,031.0
GATE	GATEWAY 2000 INC	1,731.7
AMH	AMDAHL CORP	1,680.5
ASTA	AST RESEARCH INC	1,412.2
SGI	SILICON GRAPHICS INC	1,091.2
INGR	INTERGRAPH CORP	1,050.3
CYR	CRAY RESEARCH	894.9
CEN	CERIDIAN CORP	886.1
CBU	COMMODORE INTL LTD	590.8
SRA	STRATUS COMPUTER INC	513.7
SQNT	SEQUENT COMPUTER SYSTEMS IN	353.8
PYRD	PYRAMID TECHNOLOGY	233.7
CCUR	CONCURRENT COMPUTER CP	220.5
ZEOS	ZEOS INTL LTD	216.2
DPT	DATAPOINT CORP	205.8
CNX	CONVEX COMPUTER CORP	193.1
AALR	ADVANCED LOGIC RESEARCH INC	169.3
8580B	NORSK DATA A S -ADR	168.2
3NGCP	NORTHGATE COMPUTER CORP	124.4

Example

CPI Corp. operates permanent studios in Sears stores and a chain of one-hour photofinishing stores. In both of these segments, the competition is very intense, although CPI enjoys a 26 percent market share of the preschool portrait market, and about 12 percent of the one-hour photofinishing market. The competition in the portrait business is intense, but it comes mostly from four firms that operate studios in other main chain stores such as Kmart and Wal-Mart. However, the competition in the one-hour photofinishing business comes mainly from mom-and-pop small stores.

RELATED FIRMS

One of the most noticeable differences between Japanese and American corporations is the extent of intercorporate investments. In Japan, many corporations are interlocked with other corporations through intercorporate investments. Many directors serve on the board of more than one firm, and operations of firms are much more coordinated than would be the case without these special relationships. For example, one of the reasons it is easier to adopt a just-in-time inventory system in Japan than in the United States is intercorporate investments where a firm may have a significant equity holding in a supplier. In the United States, it is less frequent to see such strong relations among firms. However, when such relations do exist, it is useful to assess the potential benefits (or costs) that may be obtained by both firms. In particular, such firms can obtain economies of scale, economies of scope, ability to obtain financing at a cheaper rate, and the like.

Example

Many firms find it beneficial to have a separate entity that operates as a finance subsidiary. The finance subsidiary usually purchases the receivables of the parent company and collects those receivables on its own. It also issues its own debt, which is secured by the accounts receivable it purchased. The finance subsidiary can branch to its own operations, which do not involve the parent's receivables. For example, it can factor the receivables of other firms or engage in leasing transactions with other firms. Most of the automobile manufactures have their own finance subsidiaries, such as GMAC with GM. Clearly, it is worthwhile to know about the relationship between GMAC and GM when analyzing the cash flows of GMAC or GM.

Example

Westinghouse Electric Corp. took a $1.68 billion pre-tax charge in the third quarter of 1991 due to loan problems at its Westinghouse Financial Services Division. The finance subsidiary of Westinghouse made bad real estate loans and was forced to take a pre-tax charge against income of $975 million in the prior year, in addition to the $1.68 billion charge in 1991. The firm had to restructure its operations, reducing its workforce by about 4,000 jobs. Due to these problems, Westinghouse had difficulties in placement of its commercial paper, and its credit ratings were reduced.

Example

When problems surfaced at its Kidder Peabody financial services unit in 1994, General Electric replaced top management of the unit with managers from other parts of GE and infused more cash into the unit to make it a more attractive operation for future sale.

Example

In September 1992, Digital Equipment announced that it was selling its 7.8 percent stake in Olivetti & Co., the Italian firm that transformed itself from a typewriter company into a computer and information services firm. Digital's decision was motivated by its own restructuring and by problems at Olivetti, which was unable to reduce its costs and become the lowest-cost manufacturer in its industry. Digital actually made the effects of its announcement worse for Olivetti, when it disclosed that it was going to sell its position in the open market, instead of finding a strategic buyer for its position. The stock price of Olivetti reacted unfavorably to both of these news.

Example

When the Japanese economy and stock market dropped at the beginning of the 1990s, some Japanese corporations began selling their stock holdings of some banks in an attempt to maintain liquidity. For example, Yoko Shibata reports in the April 1992 issue of *Global Finance* that Kyokuyo, a marine products company, decided to sell stocks it owned in six banks, realizing both cash and profits from this sale. Thus, the typical relations between members of a conglomerate can be subject to strains when economic conditions are bad, if members of the conglomerate are not fully owned by one parent company.

To find out about related firms, one has to observe whether certain related transactions are reported in the financial statements. Further information can be obtained from the Form 10-K, which lists the firm's subsidiaries, and from the proxy statement, which lists major investors (owning more than 5 percent of outstanding stock) in the firm.

EXPERIENCE IN THE INDUSTRY

Experience in a particular business may aid managers in adapting to changes in business conditions, to changes in the political environment, and to changes in the microstructure of the firm. Experienced managers are more likely to be aware of changes that affect the business, and they are more likely to react faster to these changes. Furthermore, experience in an industry may enhance long-term planning and formulation of strategy and, in particular, the ability to forecast and attain future cash flow levels. Most business failures occur at the first three years of a business's life. Presumably, an older and more experienced business management team, one that has shown it can adapt to changes, is less prone to the mistakes that are typical of new and inexperienced businesses. Good managers will adjust discretionary spending to maintain a certain level of free cash flows during business contractions and be more adept at managing the balance sheet. The analyst should attempt to assess whether the firm's management has enough experience in the business, whether it was able to survive a recession before, and whether or how it still incurs development-stage expenses. All these factors may either increase the business risk or increase the economic benefits to a firm. For these reasons, it is important to study the volatility of cash flows over several business cycles.

Example

Dynatech Corp. designs, manufactures, and sells a diverse line of electronic and mechanical instruments and systems used in measurement, analysis, and control in the communications and scientific markets and by some government agencies. Dynatech started as an R&D contract firm and 31 years later developed into a diversified high-technology firm. In its discussion of operations for 1989, Dynatech writes:

> Given the speed at which technology changes and the susceptibility of single-product companies to broad market swings, this recipe has spurred Dynatech's development from an R&D contract firm to a diversified, high-technology company which designs, manufactures, and markets more than 1,000 products through 40 well-focused operating subsidiaries to customers around the globe.

In the high-technology world, firms often turn to acquire other firms' patents or development efforts, because internal research and development efforts are often unsuccessful. Thus, the ability of Dynatech to develop over such a long period bodes well for its management.

Example

The management of Chrysler Corporation was quick to recognize the market demand for mini-vans in the early 1990s, bringing the company back from possible financial crisis while generating very substantial cash flow for the company.

Example

Norfolk Southern is a railroad firm with lines primarily in the Southeast and Midwest. In addition, it owns the North American Van Lines trucking company. The firm has been in operation for a long time and gained substantial experience in weathering economic contractions. Its earnings and cash flows during the most recent economic downturn show its ability to react well to adverse economic conditions. (See Figure 2–11.)

AGE OF THE BUSINESS

Related to experience in a business is the age of the business. However, age may also affect the financial statements of a firm because of the historical-cost assumption embedded in Generally Accepted Accounting Principles. Under this assumption, the firm uses historical acquisition cost of assets as the carrying value on the balance sheet, without any adjustments to market values. Thus, older firms may have greater discrepancies between market value of assets and their book values. Obviously, the most likely assets to be affected by this bias are property, plant, and equipment (PPE), with a particular emphasis on properties and plant. Other assets include noncurrent investments that are carried at the lower of cost or market value.

A direct way of finding the age of a business is through the date of incorporation, which is available for example in Moody's guides. Alternatively, the analyst can consult the differences between book and current-cost values of assets for 1979–1983, when such data were required to be disclosed. The analyst can also examine Form 10-K, which provides information

FIGURE 2–11
Norfolk Southern Co.

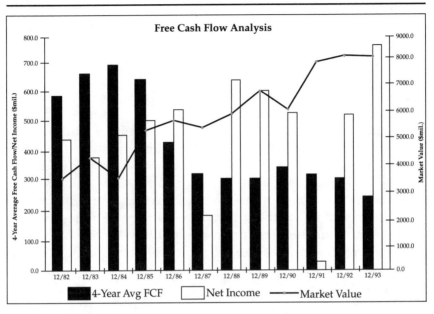

about additions and acquisitions of property, plant and equipment. If the firm provided these data for a long-enough period, the analyst can construct an estimate of current values of PPE. Notice that in many foreign countries, firms often revalue their PPE on the balance sheet to reflect current market prices.

Example

An interesting example involves the air rights above the Sea Land Inc. terminal in Hong Kong. These rights are not included in the balance sheet, but are discussed in management's letter as follows.

> We put up the air rights over our terminal plus $15 million cash, as our 50 percent share of this investment. Our partner is putting up the balance of $145 million to earn his 50 percent interest.
> Hong Kong is the busiest container port in all Asia. The six-story, high-rise warehouse, with 2.2 million square feet of floor space, promises to be the largest building in all of Asia. It will increase our present capacity in Hong Kong fourfold . . . and offer significant opportunities for us to provide a unique service to our customers while generating substantial incremental revenues.

BRAND-NAME RECOGNITION

Some firms are fortunate in having a very high level of brand-name recognition that can lead to high and constant operating cash flows. For example, Coca-Cola is world famous for its Coke brand and enjoys a strong market share because of it. Xerox is famous as the manufacturer of the first copier and still obtains benefits from this position in its industry. Such brand-name recognition can be very important to the continuing success of a business, and, in particular, the growth and stability of future cash flows. In analyzing the financial statements of a firm, the analyst should attempt to assess whether the firm has a brand or brands of products that are recognized within that industry, or whether the firm occupies a market niche. Alternatively, the analyst should determine whether other firms within the industry have leading brand names. This analysis should indicate whether the firm may reap future benefits from its leading position in the industry, or whether the firm will need to invest additional resources in order to gain market share.

Example

Hillenbrand Industries writes in its first quarterly report for 1991:

> Our objective is to be the recognized leader in each of our markets. We will never be satisfied with second place. Leadership companies generate higher cash flows that can be used to strengthen leadership positions and invest in related niche markets.

Indeed, Hillenbrand has a major market share of the hospital beds industry (estimated as 60 percent) through its Hill-Rom subsidiary and was the subject of an investigation by the Federal Trade Commission in 1993. The FTC cleared Hill-Rom from any violation of antitrust rules in 1995.

Example

The Quaker Oats Company reports in its 1993 financial statements that 77 percent of worldwide sales come from brands that hold the number one or number two position in their respective categories. Among them are Quaker Oatmeal, Gatorade, Aunt Jamima's products, and Felix cat food. The firm attributes its high profitability and stable cash flows to these brand-name products.

Example

The advertising industry is one in which the largest firms have grown through consolidation, penetrated the market that is held by other firms, and have acquired brand-name recognition through aggressive worldwide diversification.

MANAGEMENT TEAM

A good management team is a most valuable asset to a firm because its decisions and actions can lead the firm to higher cash flows. Good managers steer the firm in the right direction, develop it properly, and increase the value of shareholders' investments in the firm. In contrast, bad managers waste cash through bad or unnecessary investments, thereby reducing cash flows that otherwise could have been transferred back to shareholders or channeled into higher-yielding investments.

Publicly held companies are characterized by a separation between owners and managers. The owners or their representatives (the board of directors) monitor the actions and decisions of management, but management is responsible for the daily operations of the firm. In the evaluation of a firm, the analyst must assess the quality of management and the quality of directors in a firm, including the degree of the directors' independence from management. Limited information about managers and directors is available in the proxy statement of a firm. This information should be studied to determine whether managers and directors have experience in the industry or in the business, and whether managers have the required skills for their position. Also, the analyst should assess the degree of nepotism in the firm or whether the board is composed of cronies of a major stockholder, or whether the board is simply an antitakeover tool. Are managers and directors related? Is it possible that members of a particular family accept the public's money, but manage it poorly and cover up their mismanagement through improprieties?

Example

Tyco Toys designs, develops, manufactures, and distributes a variety of toy products. Tyco products are sold through over 2,500 large retail chains, wholesalers, and independent retailers.

During 1990, Tyco Toys had on its board of directors the chairman of the firm and one of his sons. In addition, the outside attorney for Tyco Toys was on the board of directors, and in the 1990 proxy statement, another son was nominated for the board of directors. After some pressure from stockholders, the chairman of the board and his sons agreed to remove themselves from the board of directors.

Example

Carlo De Benedetti, the Italian executive, acquired a strong reputation as an excellent manager who can take over troubled firms and turn them around in a short time. When rumors spread through the Italian stock exchange that he had been interested in a publicly traded Italian firm, its stock price shot up close to 40 percent. This was in anticipation of a good manager coming aboard that firm.

Example

On January 25, 1993, American Express's board decided to retain James Robinson III as chairman in spite of opposition by three board members. On February 1, 1993, just days afterwards, James Robinson III announced his resignation. Figures 2–12 and 2–13 show the price and volume reactions to these two announcements.

FIGURE 2–12
Price of American Express Stock

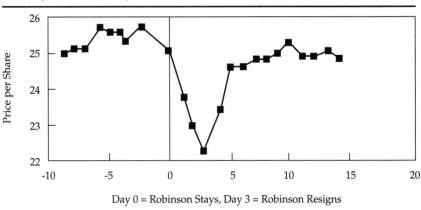

Day 0 = Robinson Stays, Day 3 = Robinson Resigns

FIGURE 2–13
Volume of American Express Stock

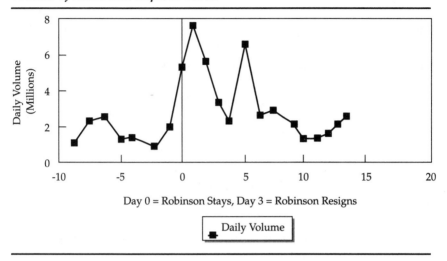

Day 0 = Robinson Stays, Day 3 = Robinson Resigns

Daily Volume

As can be seen in these graphs, market prices dropped significantly after the first announcement and increased to their prior levels immediately after the resignation announcement. The volume followed a similar pattern, with unusual volumes on both days, showing that investors cared and evaluated the firm in part based on its management.

Example

When Barry Diller agreed to buy into QVC Network and become its chairman in 1992, stock prices of QVC rose sharply. Diller, who had been very successful at running Fox, was considered to add an important managerial dimension to QVC. At a subsequent period, CBS has considered merging with QVC in order to attract Diller to run the entire combined firm.

LABOR RELATIONS

When the contracts in the automobile industry are up for renewal, the financial press is usually full of rumors, speculations, and reports of recent developments in the contract negotiations. Indeed, the extent of unionization of employees in a firm has a material effect on its future production, wage demands, flexibility, and on cash flows. During an economic upswing, a firm with a strong union is likely to be less flexible in adopting to changes in the environment. It is more likely to have greater disruptions in production due to strikes, labor insistence on enforcing work rules, and so on. The analyst should therefore attempt to assess the degree of unionization (including make-up and changes in union officials) and the type of labor relations of the firm (i.e., a history of wage increases and all other factors that may be important in analyzing both the cost of operations, through wages, and revenues, through potential work stoppage). Information about these items can be obtained from the business discussion in the beginning of Form 10-K, or through an examination of newspaper clippings about the firm. For example, one may consult *The Wall Street Journal Index,* trade publications, local newspapers where the firm is headquartered, or the *Index of Business Periodicals* for recent information about the firm. From these sources, one can determine the length of former union contracts, the terms and length of the current contract, and the firm's historical relationship to the union. One can also assess labor relations by direct discussions with union and management personnel.

The analyst should also investigate the extent of the employees' ownership of a firm. When employees own a substantial portion of the firm, they have a greater incentive to make the firm more prosperous. Recently, because of favorable tax treatments, many firms have experienced large investments by their employees through an Employee Stock Ownership Plan (ESOP). An ESOP aligns the interests of investors and employees to a greater extent and improves the productivity of such firms. Information about ESOPs can be obtained in footnotes to the financial statements, in proxy statements, or from the ESOP Council in Washington.

Example

General Motors Corp. has to negotiate its labor contracts with the Automobile Workers Union, which is very powerful in the industry. Furthermore, GM manufactures a large proportion of the components that go into its automobiles instead of purchasing them from suppliers that are not subject to union contracts. Consequently, GM is less flexible than its competitors in its contract renegotiations. The firm reported that in 1992–3, it had to pay idle workers about $1 billion, although it had jobs available for these workers in other plants. According to union rules, GM was unable to relocate workers from one plant to another if the plants were more than a certain distance apart. This resulted in idle laborers who were getting full wages.

Example

Big B, Inc., operates a chain of retail drug stores and stores that sell and rent medical equipment for home use.

In its 1990 letter to shareholders the chairman and the president of the firm writes:

> The past year has been a most difficult one, resulting in the first annual net loss in the twenty-three year history of Big B. Despite the loss of $1,465,000, fiscal 1991 had more positives than negatives. The biggest positive is the way all of Big B's employees pulled together to correct gross margin and expense problems which became evident during the year, and in recognition of this tremendous effort we gratefully dedicate this annual report to them. The fruits of their efforts are evident in our fourth quarter earnings of $2,455,000, the highest fourth quarter net income from operations in the history of the Company.

Example

McKesson's largest shareholder is its ESOP, which holds more than 17 percent of the firm's common stock in trust for its participating employees. Alan Sleenfreund, the chairman and CEO, explained the decision to form an ESOP by saying:

> We established our ESOP because we really believe in sharing with our employees value that they help create. We are in a business that is driven by customer service and the need to constantly improve productivity. That makes it critical that employees recognize and understand that they benefit financially when McKesson achieves improved financial performance. [*McKesson Today*, December 1990, p. 1].

Example

In its 1991 review, Potlatch enclosed a schedule of labor contract expiration dates for 1992. In this schedule, it provided also the location of the plant, the union involved, and the number of employees represented by this union. This is very useful information to the cash flow analyst who wishes to assess future cash flow effects of labor contracts on the firm.

Example

One of the fundamental factors in Japanese large corporations had been lifetime employment. This factor helped Japanese firms to reduce labor mobility and turnover rates, and it made investment in human capital more attractive. However, when market conditions deteriorated in the late 1980s and the beginning of the 1990s, Japanese firms found themselves with an implicit employment contract that was hard to maintain. These firms reacted by shifting employees to projects that would not have been adopted otherwise, leading to reduction in future cash flows. Other firms saw their cash flows and profits deteriorating when they could not pass on their high-cost structure to their consumers. In contrast, U.S. firms have gone through major waves of restructuring their manufacturing and overhead processes in the same period, and many experts consider the U.S. sector to be very competitive in the mid-1990s.

SERVICE TO CUSTOMERS

In their book *In Search of Excellence* (1983), Peters and Waterman document the importance of service to customers for the excellent firm. According to their research, the group of excellent firms became excellent partly through meticulous service to customers, sometimes when it is seemingly uneconomic to do so. For example, Frito-Lay services over 99 percent of the vending machines in which it sells products on a daily basis, even though some machines are not out of their products on a daily basis. Frito-Lay believes that in the long run, such a strategy pays off because of consumer loyalty and the good relationships with owners of the vending machines. Thus, the analyst should attempt to assess whether the firm is noted for good service to its customers. This can be gleaned from trade magazines, consumer publications, and the number of service centers the firm has. Better service to the customer may have a negative effect on immediate cash flows, since larger amounts of cash are expended on providing quality service to customers. However, future cash flows are likely to grow due to customers' loyalty and increases in market share.

Example

Toys R Us, the world's largest toy retailer, will return a customer's money—not credit—for any reason, within 90 days with a receipt. This is probably a more lenient return policy than that of their competitors, indicating the firm wants to maintain better service to the customer.

Example

IBM always prided itself on providing customers with excellent service. Indeed, customers who are happy with a firm's service level are likely to continue their service contracts with the firm. In 1993, IBM's revenues from services and maintenance reached $9.7 and $7.3 billion, respectively, out of total revenues of $62.7 billion. Indeed, while revenues from hardware and software sales declined in 1993, revenues from services actually increased from 1992 to 1993.

Example

At the 1994 annual meeting of shareholders, Sun Company's chairman promised shareholders a concentrated effort on making customers "enthusiastic" and not just "satisfied." Sun, which markets gasoline under the Sunoco brand, attempts to achieve this high level of customer enthusiasm in order to ensure customers' loyalty in this very competitive market.

PRODUCT QUALITY

It is well-known that Japanese firms place a great deal of emphasis on product quality and quality control. The literature is abundant with examples of Japanese firms that invest great resources to reduce slightly the rate of defective units in their production process. Superficially, it seems that these Japanese firms are not getting a proper rate of return on their investment in product quality; the amount of resources needed to reduce the number of defective units beyond a certain threshold cannot be justified by the direct savings on the repairs of these units. Nevertheless, the Japanese firms make huge investments in quality control because they expect greater consumer confidence and loyalty to their products, which are later manifested by the consistent growth of operating cash flows. Inevitably, higher quality may lead to a larger market share and greater operating cash flows, even in periods of declining markets.

The analyst should therefore assess the quality of the firm's products or services as an integral part of the analysis, especially since, as stated earlier, higher quality can result in greater product visibility (e.g., Coke) and can by itself greater market share and cash flows. Information about product quality can be obtained from consumers' rankings, industry publications, description of businesses in Form 10-K, discussions with company employees, industry experts, and from assessing the extent of returns and expenses for repairs in the financial statements.

Example

One of the important lessons American firms learned from their Japanese counterparts is the cultivation of close relationships with suppliers. Japanese firms work very closely with a small number of suppliers who promise to increase the quality of their products and who promise to deliver their products on time. This enables the purchasing firms to reduce their inventories due to their receipt of deliveries close to production time (just-in-time inventories), and it also enables them to reduce expenses on quality control inspections and on the need to rework defective units. As a result, pressures are mounting on firms that supply parts or raw materials to American firms to increase quality substantially. A related article appeared in *The Wall Street Journal* (August 16, 1991, p. B-1).

OWNERSHIP STRUCTURE

Academic studies, as well as anecdotal evidence, suggest that the ownership structure of a firm is important to its profitability and risk[1]. It has been shown that firms that are controlled by owners are more profitable and have a greater tendency to diversify into related areas of business than firms that are controlled by managers. Empirically, such studies define a management-controlled firm as one that has a diffuse ownership structure, with no single shareholder holding more than 5 percent of the outstanding stock. An owner-controlled firm is one in which a single investor or entity holds at least 20 percent of the outstanding stock. As mentioned before, it is hypothesized (and verified empirically) that, *on average,* owner-controlled firms are more profitable and less diversified into unrelated areas of business than management-controlled firms. The explanation for these findings is that managers in

---

[1]A recent survey of academic studies in this area can be found in Hunt (*Journal of Accounting Literature*, 1986).

management-controlled firms tend to divert corporate resources for their own personal gains because they are less likely to be closely supervised than they would be in owner-controlled firms. Similarly, it is hypothesized, because they wish to diversify the large human-capital investments in their own firms, managers in management-controlled firms invest in unrelated areas of business. This results in a more diversified firm, although the extent of diversification may be suboptimal from the shareholders' point of view.

The analyst should determine whether the firm under analysis is manager controlled or owner controlled. Even if it is an owner-controlled firm, the analyst should attempt to assess whether management seems to be diverting assets to its own personal use at the expense of stockholders or is using assets sub-optimally. Data about ownership structure, as well as about compensation and borrowing by officers, are available in the proxy statement of a firm, where shareholders with more than 5 percent of the outstanding stock are listed. One can examine who are the major shareholders, whether they are represented on the board of directors, on the various subcommittees that run the firm, and so on.

Example

Brown Forman is a very well managed consumer goods company. It is an excellent generator of operating and free cash flows and is certainly an owner-controlled firm as can be seen from the data in its proxy statement which appears on page 55.

Example

In their book, *Barbarians at the Gate,* (1990), Burrough and Helyar describe the extravagant lifestyle that professional managers enjoyed in RJR-Nabisco prior to its going private. At that time, RJR was not controlled by any individual stockholder, and management had to account only to the board of directors, some of whom enjoyed many personal benefits from the firm at the discretion of management.

With the new pressure by shareholders and regulators, the Securities and Exchange Commission (SEC) has expanded its disclosure requirements in the proxy statement. Corporations now must discuss all forms of management compensation, including stock options and other benefits. They also have to compare the performance of the firm's stock prices to its industry peers and another wide index. See Figure 2–14.

Brown/Forman Proxy

SECURITY OWNERSHIP OF CERTAIN
BENEFICIAL OWNERS AND MANAGEMENT

Voting Security Ownership of Certain Beneficial Owners. At April 30,1989, the following persons were known to the management of the Corporation to be the beneficial owners of more than five percent of Class A Common Stock of the Corporation, the only class of voting securities of the Corporation:

Name and Address of Beneficial Owner	Amount and Nature of Beneficial Ownership			Percent of Class
	Sole Voting and Investment Power	Shared Voting and Investment Power[1]	Total	
W. L. Lyons Brown, Jr. 850 Dixie Highway Louisville, Kentucky	441,420	4,354,170	4,795,590	45.4
Owsley Brown Frazier 850 Dixie Highway Louisville, Kentucky	262,896	3,712,260	3,975,156	37.6
Dace Brown Farrer Hillcrest Farm Prospect, Kentucky		2,996,187	2,996,187	28.3
Owsley Brown II 850 Dixie Highway Louisville, Kentucky	290,389	1,618,662	1,909,051	18.1
Ina Brown 5900 Burlington Avenue Louisville, Kentucky	326,383	1,116,127	1,442,510	13.6
Robinson S. Brown, Jr. 5208 Avish Lane Harrods Creek, Kentucky	95,939	906,906	1,002,845	9.5
Harry S. Frazier 4810 Cherry Valley Road Prospect, Kentucky	194,448	705,438	899,886	8.5
Laura Lee Brown Deters 7001 U.S. Highway 42 Louisville, Kentucky	262,730	477,867	740,597	7.0

(1) Shared voting and investment powers are held by the above named beneficial owners as members of advisory committees of certain trusts and estates of which First Kentucky Trust Company of Louisville, Kentucky, is trustee or executor, and in addition, W. L. Lyons Brown, Jr., Owsley Brown II and Ina Brown are three of the eight trustees of the W. L. Lyons Brown Foundation which owns 11,451 shares of Class A Common Stock and 126,625 shares of Class B Common Stock. **As a result of the shared voting and investment powers described above, several persons are shown as the beneficial owners of the same securities.** Counting such shares only once, the aggregate number of shares of Class A Common Stock beneficially owned by the above named persons is 7,406,825 shares, or 70% of the outstanding shares of such stock.

Source: Brown/Forman, Proxy Statement, 1989.

FIGURE 2–14
Exerpt from the General Mills' 1993 Proxy Statement

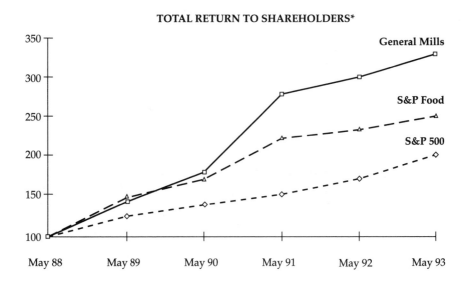

TOTAL RETURN TO SHAREHOLDERS*

	1988	1989	1990	1991	1992	1993
General Mills	100	144	183	274	302	319
S&P Food	100	151	176	225	236	247
S&P 500	100	127	148	165	181	202

*Total return assumes reinvestment of dividends and assumes $100 invested on May 31, 1988, in General Mills Common Stock, S&P 500 index, and S&P Food Group index.

Summary Compensation Table

| Name and Principal Position | Year | Annual Compensation | | | Long-Term Compensation | | | All Other Compensation ($) (3) |
| | | Salary ($) | Bonus ($) | Other Annual Compensation ($) | Awards | | Payouts | |
					Restricted Stock Awards ($) (1)	Options (#)	LTIP Payouts ($) (2)	
H. B. Atwater, Chairman of the board and chief executive officer	1993	$607,689	$777,800	—	$194,488	$137,798	0	$88,533
	1992	620,591(4)	786,900	—	196,656	146,280	0	46,895
	1991	607,882	823,500	—	205,856	175,662	290,636	48,759
J. R. Lee, vice chairman	1993	388,523	437,600	—	109,400	63,868	0	46,597
	1992	396,771(4)	442,700	—	110,635	65,372	0	42,616
	1991	357,229	372,400	—	93,084	94,400	540,338	21,066
S. W. Sanger, vice chairman	1993	297,500	329,800	$27,328(5)	82,446	56,246	0	25,431
	1992	238,496(4)	242,700	—	60,646	53,918	0	18,968
	1991	185,677	181,400	—	45,319	39,780	0	16,799
C. L. Whitehill, senior vice president and general counsel	1993	238,095	266,340	—	0	37,424	0	24,756
	1992	243,150(4)	269,445	—	0	41,238	0	17,480
	1991	238,171	281,980	—	0	50,258	0	20,074
M. H. Willes, vice chairman	1993	433,353	532,400	—	133,050	79,972	0	50,864
	1992	442,553(4)	538,700	—	134,614	92,834	116,000	53,483
	1991	433,490	563,800	—	140,965	114,092	0	50,257

(1) This amount reflects the value of restricted stock awarded under the EIP. Recipients must deposit with the Company one personally owned share of Common Stock for each share of restricted stock awarded. The restricted shares vest 50% at three years and 50% at six years, provided the participant's shares remain on deposit until the end of the corresponding restricted period. Regular dividends are paid on the restricted shares. Restricted stock under the EIP vests in the event of a Change of Control as defined in the 1993 Plan on page A-7. At May 30, 1993, the number and value of the aggregate restricted stockholdings for the named officers was:

H. B. Atwater, Jr.	21,836 shares	$1,432,988
J. R. Lee	9,424	618,450
S. W. Sanger	3,714	243,731
C. L. Whitehill	0	0
M. H. Willes	12,632	828,975

(2) The amounts reflected in this column are cash withdrawals from performance unit accounts, described in footnote (1) on page 28 to the table entitled "Option Grants in Last Fiscal Year." These withdrawals caused cancelation of the number of corresponding stock options with a value equal to the amount of the withdrawal.

(3) These amounts are the Company's contributions or allocations to defined contribution (savings) plans (tax-qualified and supplemental) on behalf of the named officers.

(4) 53-week fiscal year.

(5) The amount represents the "above-market" portion of the earnings on deferred compensation credited and paid to Mr. Sanger for fiscal 1993 which were based on the performance of the Big G cereal division. Under the Company's Deferred Compensation Plan, election of such a crediting rate is available only to eligible key managers with respect to the business operation for which they are responsible. Mr. Sanger is no longer eligible to elect this crediting rate.

Option Grants in Last Fiscal Year

	Individual Grants (1)				Potential Realizable Value at Assumed Annual Rates of Stock Price Appreciation for Option Term ($) (2)		
Name	Options Granted (#)	% of Total Options Granted to Employees in Fiscal Year	Exercise Price ($/share)	Expiration Date	0% ($) (3)	5% ($)	10% ($)
Atwater	80,000(4)	2.36	63.8125	05/01/01	0	2,760,620	6,772,771
	46,300(5)	1.37	70.5000	10/21/02	0	2,073,600	5,267,016
	11,498(6)	0.34	68.4375	05/01/01	0	397,463	962,095
Lee	40,000(4)	1.18	63.8125	07/22/02	0	1,621,514	4,118,701
	17,400(5)	0.51	70.5000	10/21/02	0	779,280	1,979,397
	6,468(6)	0.19	68.4375	01/14/03	0	281,202	714,264
Sanger	36,000(4)	1.06	63.8125	07/22/02	0	1,459,362	3,706,831
	16,700(5)	0.49	70.5000	10/21/02	0	747,929	1,899,766
	3,546(6)	0.10	68.4375	01/14/03	0	154,166	391,586
Whitehill	20,000(4)	0.59	63.8125	05/01/01	0	690,155	1,693,193
	14,000(5)	0.41	70.5000	10/21/02	0	627,007	1,592,618
	3,424(6)	0.10	68.4375	05/01/01	0	118,361	286,503
Willes	50,000(4)	1.48	63.8125	07/22/02	0	2,026,892	5,148,376
	22,100(5)	0.65	70.5000	10/21/02	0	989,775	2,514,061
	7,872(6)	0.23	68.4375	01/14/03	0	342,243	869,308
All stockholders	NA	NA	NA	NA	0	6,792,422,918(7)	17,254,647,682(7)
All optionees	3,384,144	100%	66.64(8)	(8)	0	143,250,816	363,897,004
As a % of all stockholders gain	NA	NA	NA	NA	NA	2.1%	2.1%

(1) All options are granted at the fair market value of the Common Stock on the grant date and generally expire 10 years and one month from the grant date. All options vest in the event of a Change of Control as defined in the 1993 Plan on page A-7. Options include the right to pay the exercise price in cash or in previously acquired Common Stock (which must be owned for six months or not used in the previous six months for an option exercise) and the right to have shares withheld by the Company to pay withholding tax obligations due in conjunction with the exercise. Performance units also were granted as an exercise alternative with certain options under the 1988 Plan. The exercise of the option or a withdrawal of the corresponding performance units (in cash only) cancels the other on a one-for-one basis. Performance units awarded in fiscal 1993 will be valued at the end of fiscal 1995 by a formula determined in June 1992 by the Committee. Each performance unit could have a maximum value of $15 based on growth in earnings per share over the three-year period and return on average stockholders' equity for fiscal 1995. These performance units will have no value if the Company's compound growth rate in earnings per share for the three-year period is less than 4% and the after-tax return on average stockholders' equity for fiscal 1995 is less than 14%. In June 1995 the value (if any) of the performance units will be credited to a participant's account and thereafter credited quarterly with an amount equal to interest at a rate determined by the Committee. As a result of the strong performance of the Company over the last five years (see chart on page 25) the market value of the Company's Common Stock has exceeded the value of performance units granted to date under the 1988 Plan and therefore it is not expected that units will be exercised by the participants, since a cash withdrawal of a performance unit cancels the corresponding option on a one-for-one basis.

(2) These assumed values result from certain prescribed rates of stock price appreciation. The actual value of these option grants is dependent on future performance of the Common Stock and overall stock market conditions. There is no assurance that the values reflected in this table will be achieved. The Company did not use an alternative formula for a grant date valuation, as it is not aware of any formula which will determine with reasonable accuracy a present value based on future unknown or volatile factors.

(3) No gain to the optionees is possible without stock price appreciation, which will benefit all stockholders commensurately. Zero percent stock price appreciation will result in zero dollars for the optionee.

(4) This regular stock option grant under the 1988 Plan becomes exercisable four years from the grant date.

(5) This option, granted under the 1990 Salary Replacement Stock Option Plan, benefits the Company by reducing the cash compensation paid to executives, with corresponding reductions in cash bonuses, lower pension accruals and similar effects on other benefits which are tied to base salary. It further increases the percentage of key employee compensation and benefits tied to stock ownership, in keeping with the Company's philosophy to more closely align stockholder and employee interests. This option becomes exercisable over a four-year period beginning on the grant date.

(6) To encourage retention of the Common Stock, this deposit stock option grant (which becomes exercisable three years from the grant date) requires the deposit of one share of owned Common Stock for every two option shares granted. The maximum number of shares permitted for deposit is based on the number of shares with a fair market value at the date of grant equivalent to 50% of the executives's prior year cash incentive payment.

(7) "All Stockholders" value is calculated from $66.64, the weighted average exercise price for all options awarded in fiscal 1993, based on the outstanding shares of Common Stock on May 30, 1993.

(8) Options expire on various dates through the year 2003. Exercise price shown is a weighted average of all options awarded in fiscal 1993.

BACKLOG

In some industries, information about backlog is extremely important for forecasting future developments of the market. Firms that are involved in construction or in manufacturing that takes a long time are required to provide information on their backlog. The cash flow analyst can use this information for predictions of future cash flows.

Example

On April 25, 1994, Cray Research Inc. announced its sales and earnings report for the first quarter of 1994. In its release, Cray indicated that net earnings reached $21,953,000, or $.84 per share, on revenue of $248,866,000 for the first quarter ended March 31, 1994, compared to net earnings of $15,024,000, or $.58 per share, on revenue of $202,597,000 for the 1993 first quarter. Thus, both revenues and earnings exceeded random-walk expectations, and were very consistent with analysts' predictions at that point. However, in the same release, Cray disclosed that the net contract value of orders signed during the quarter was $59 million compared to $124 million in the 1993 first quarter, and that backlog at quarter's end totaled $271 million compared to $381 million at March 31, 1993. The stock market reacted negatively to the news, resulting in sharply lower price and higher-than-usual trading volume.

As Figures 2–15 and 2–16 show, the price of Cray Research declined sharply immediately after the announcement of the decline in backlog, although both earnings and sales were above their expected level. A similar picture emerges for the volume of trading that was unusually high around the press release date.

FIGURE 2–15
Price of Cray Research (around 4/25/94)

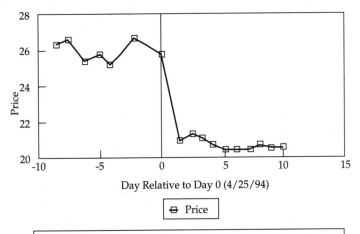

Day Relative to Day 0 (4/25/94)

⊟ Price

On 4/25/94 Cray Research Announced Increase in First Quarter
Sales and Earnings but a Decline in Backlog

FIGURE 2–16
Volume of Cray Research (around 4/25/94)

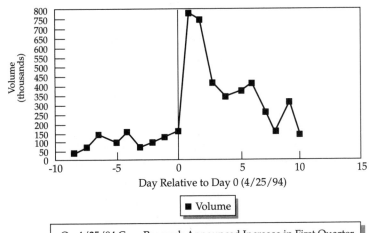

Day Relative to Day 0 (4/25/94)

■ Volume

On 4/25/94 Cray Research Announced Increase in First Quarter
Sales and Earnings but a Decline in Backlog

Chapter Three

The Statement of Cash Flows

T his chapter introduces the reader to the statement of cash flows. Understanding the role of this statement is crucial for a general analysis of cash flows and, in particular, for an analysis that is based on free cash flows. In the chapter, we will see how the statement of cash flows is constructed and discuss the important components of the statement. We will also introduce the motivation for the statement of cash flows, historical developments in the disclosure of fund flows, and a detailed example for the construction of the statement.

The purpose of the statement of cash flows is to disclose information about economic events that affect cash during the accounting period. Three general types of economic events or activities are described in the statement: operating cash flows, financing cash flows, and investing cash flows. Operating cash flows are ongoing operations of a business entity that affect cash, such as collections from customers, payments to suppliers and employees, and the like.[1] Financing cash flows are events that affect the financial structure of a firm, such as borrowing of cash, repurchase of common stock, and dividend payments. Investing cash flows are those events that affect the long-term assets of a firm, such as purchases of property, plant, and equipment (PPE), sale of investments in subsidiaries, and so forth.

The statement of cash flows provides information about these events if they affect cash during the accounting period. Presumably, those events that affect cash during a period are very impor-

---

[1]We provide exact definitions for these three categories of cash flows in the next chapter.

tant to investors, suppliers, creditors, and employees. Information about operating cash flows indicates the business's ability to generate cash from its continuing operations. Information about investing cash flows indicates how the business used (received) cash for capital items or liquidated capital to survive downturns. Information about financing cash flows illustrates how the business financed its expansion and partially rewarded shareholders. If a financing event, for example, does not involve cash (such as the conversion of preferred stock to common stock), the information is disclosed in a separate portion, normally called "Supplemental information" at the bottom of the cash flow statement, or in the footnotes of the statement of cash flows. To understand the current disclosure requirements of cash flows, it is useful to review the historical developments of the statement.

HISTORICAL BACKGROUND

The use of cash flow analysis as an investment yardstick is not new. William Morse Cole's 1908 accounting treatise includes flow of funds statements.[2] Corporate treasurers have long used cash flow as the basis to invest in capital projects, that is, the net present value of cash returned on a project must be greater than the initial outlay of cash.

Only about half century after Morse's accounting text, in 1963, did the precursor of the Financial Accounting Standards Board (FASB), the Accounting Principles Board (APB), in *Opinion No. 3*, "The Statement of Source and Application of Funds," recommend presentation of a statement in the annual report that would provide information about sources and uses of funds.

In 1969, the Securities and Exchange Commission (SEC) mandated a funds statement in annual filings. In 1971, the APB released *Opinion No. 19*, "Reporting Changes in Financial Position," which for the first time required a flow of funds statement for each period in which an income statement was presented. In this opinion, the APB did not specify the definition of funds that firms should use,

---

[2]William Morse Cole, *Accounts: Their Construction and Interpretation for Businessmen and Students of Affairs* (Boston: Houghton Mifflin, 1908).

and the majority of firms used net working capital as their definition of funds. Further, the APB required firms to disclose information about sources and uses of funds, but allowed firms to define sources and uses of funds (and present these events in the financial statements) as their managers saw fit.

On December 15, 1980, the FASB issued a *Discussion Memorandum*, "Reporting Fund Flows, Liquidity, and Financial Flexibility," which explains the reasons for the FASB's interest in a fund flow statement:

1. *Income and Funds Are Different.* A business often experiences significant differences between income and fund flows. Those differences vary from business to business, and from time to time. They are particularly important when large price changes take place. Investors, creditors, and others are likely to need information about fund flows for assessments of future cash flows. Managers are familiar with the importance of information about fund flows for the evaluation of investment opportunities and for other kinds of budgeting.

2. *Information about Liquidity and Financial Flexibility Is Needed for Making Assessments of Future Cash Flows.* Information about liquidity and financial flexibility is useful for assessments of the timing and uncertainty of future cash flows. Financial flexibility is a measure of the adaptability of a business. The need for adaptability may be offensive or defensive. A business may need financial flexibility to take advantage of an unexpected new investment opportunity or to survive a crisis resulting from a change in operating conditions. Financial flexibility comes from quick access to cash. A financially flexible business has large inflows of cash from operations, large borrowing capacity, or assets that can be realized quickly in significant amounts. Information about liquidity may help the assessment of financial flexibility. It is a measure of the nearness to cash of assets and liabilities—the time interval that will lapse before assets become cash and before liabilities have to be paid.

3. *There Appears to Be a Problem with Current Practice.* People have criticized current practice for reporting fund flows as confusing because it compresses too much information

into one statement and does not focus on any specific definition of funds. The concepts of liquidity and financial flexibility have not yet been developed in the authoritative literature.

4. *It Is Needed as Part of a Conceptual Framework for Financial Accounting and Reporting.*

In November 1981, the FASB issued an Exposure Draft of a proposed concepts *Statement*, "Reporting Income, Cash Flows, and Financial Position of Business Enterprises." This Exposure Draft discussed the role of a funds statement and guidelines for reporting components of fund flows, concluding that reporting funds flows should focus on cash rather than on net working capital.

During its deliberations on the 1981 Exposure Draft, the FASB decided that detailed cash flow reporting should be addressed only on the standards level, but deferred consideration of the standards project until the results of a voluntary initiative by the Financial Executives Institute (FEI) were assessed. In late 1981, the FEI encouraged its members to change the definition of funds in the funds flow statement to cash and short-term investments. It also encouraged enterprises to experiment with alternative formats, such as grouping items by operating, investing, and financing activities. That experimentation with cash flow reporting in statements of changes in financial position was consistent with *APB Opinion No. 19*, which allowed flexibility in the focus and form of the statement.

In December 1983, the Board issued another Exposure Draft of a concepts *Statement*, "Recognition and Measurement in Financial Statements of Business Enterprises," which also discussed the role of the cash flow statement. In December 1984, the FASB issued *Statement of Financial Concepts No. 5*, "Recognition and Measurement in Financial Statements of Business Enterprises," which includes general guidance on a statement of cash flows and concludes that, in concept, a cash flow statement should be part of a full set of financial statements.

In April 1985, the FASB added to its agenda a cash flow reporting project of limited scope (*a*) to establish the objectives of a statement of cash flows, (*b*) to define the major components of cash flows to be presented in the statement, and (c) to decide whether to require a statement of cash flows as part of a full set of financial statements for all enterprises.

In May 1985, the FASB staff organized a Task Force on Cash Flow Reporting, and in June 1985, the FASB staff met with the task force to discuss appropriate objectives for a statement of cash flows. In November 1985, the staff met again with the task force to discuss the identification and definition of major elements of cash flows, the classification of certain transactions, the reporting of noncash transactions, and the methods for presenting cash flow from operating activities.

In March 1986, an Advisory Group on cash flow reporting by financial institutions was organized. In April 1986, the FASB met with the advisory group to discuss whether a statement of cash flows should be included in a complete set of financial statements of a financial institution, as well as other cash flow reporting issues related to financial institutions.

In July 1986, the FASB issued an Exposure Draft, "Statement of Cash Flows." It proposed standards for cash flow reporting that require a statement of cash flows as part of a full set of financial statements of all business enterprises in place of a statement of changes in financial position.

In November 1987, the FASB issued *Statement of Financial Accounting Standards No. 95*, "Statement of Cash Flows" which established standards for cash flow reporting and required a statement of cash flows as part of a full set of financial statements. *SFAS No. 95* superseded *APB Opinion No. 19*, "Reporting Changes in Financial Position." It requires companies to present a statement of cash flows that classifies cash receipts and cash payments according to whether they result from operating, investing, or financing activities and provides a definition of each category. With the introduction of *SFAS No. 95*, the FASB has made an undeniable move toward emphasizing the important role of cash flow analysis for investors and creditors. From then on, investors and creditors experienced a continued shift toward emphasizing the use of cash flow in security analysis and lending decisions.

In February, 1989, the FASB issued *SFAS No. 102*, "Statement of Cash Flows—Exemption of Certain Enterprises and Classification of Cash Flows from Certain Securities Acquired for Resale."

SFAS No. 102 exempted from the statement of cash flows defined benefit plans covered under *SFAS No. 35*, "Accounting and Reporting by Defined Benefit Plans," and certain other employee benefit plans and highly liquid investment companies that meet specified conditions. *SFAS No. 102* also required that certain cash receipts and cash payments resulting from acquisitions and sales of securities and other assets that are acquired specifically for resale and are carried at market value or at the lower-of-cost-or-market (LCM) value be classified as operating cash flows in a statement of cash flows.

In December 1989, the FASB issued *SFAS No. 104*, "Statement of Cash Flows—Net Reporting of Certain Cash Receipts and Cash Payments and Classification of Cash Flows from Hedging Transactions." *SFAS No. 104* amended *SFAS No. 95* to permit banks, savings institutions, and credit unions to report in a statement of cash flows certain net cash receipts and cash payments for (*a*) deposits placed with other financial institutions and withdrawals of deposits, (*b*) time deposits accepted and repayments of deposits, and (*c*) loans made to customers, and principal collections of loans. *SFAS No. 104* also permitted cash flows resulting from futures contracts, option contracts, or swap contracts that are accounted for as hedges of identifiable transactions or events to be classified in the same category as the cash flows from the items being hedged, provided that this accounting policy is disclosed.

We now provide a detailed example to illustrate the construction of a statement of cash flows.

EXAMPLE

To construct the statement of cash flows we use information from the balance sheet at the beginning and at the end of the accounting period, information about some economic events from the income statement, and minor additional information about events that are not incorporated in the income statement. To illustrate the construction of the statement, we use information that is adopted from the 1993 financial statements of Quaker Oats Co. The data were modified for ease of exposition, and minor additional assumptions were made when data were unavailable in the financial statements. The financial statements of Quaker Oats Co. are available at the end of this section. We also provide additional real-life examples of the statement of cash flows at the end of this chapter.

Quaker Oats Co.
Consolidated Balance Sheet
For Years Ended December 31, 1992 and 1993
(in millions)

	1993	1992	Difference
Cash	$61.00	$95.20	($34.20)
Accounts receivable	$478.90	$575.30	($96.40)
Inventories	$354.00	$435.30	($81.30)
Current assets—other	$173.70	$150.40	$23.30
Investments	$88.80	$83.00	$5.80
PPE	$2,059.20	$2,066.10	($6.90)
Accumulated depreciation	($831.00)	($792.80)	($38.20)
Intangibles	$431.30	$427.40	$3.90
Total assets	**$2,815.90**	**$3,039.90**	
Short-term debt	$128.00	$61.00	($67.00)
Current long-term debt	$48.90	$57.90	$9.00
Accounts payable	$391.60	$420.20	$28.60
Accrued payroll	$161.30	$147.00	($14.30)
Accrued advertising	$130.60	$120.20	($10.40)
Taxes payable	$33.70	$82.60	$48.90
Accrued liabilities	$211.00	$198.60	($12.40)
Long-term debt	$632.60	$688.70	$56.10
Other liabilities	$426.20	$171.70	($254.50)
Deferred taxes	$89.50	$242.00	$152.50
Preferred stock	$100.00	$100.00	$0.00
Deferred compensation	($85.90)	($90.50)	($4.60)
Preferred treasury	($2.70)	($1.60)	$1.10
Common stock	$420.00	$420.00	$0.00
Paid-in capital	$0.00	$2.90	$2.90
Retained earnings	$1,190.10	$1,162.30	($27.80)
Cumulative translation	($65.40)	($24.50)	$40.90
Deferred compensation	($154.00)	($160.40)	($6.40)
Treasury stock	($839.60)	($558.20)	$281.40
Total liabilities and equity	**$2,815.90**	**$3,039.90**	

Example   77

It should be noted that the differences in the account balances between 1992 and 1993 sum up to zero. This is expected because we begin 1993 with a balanced balance sheet (assets equal to liabilities plus equities), and end it with a balanced balance sheet. Thus, the sum of the changes should be equal between the debit and credit sides.

Quaker Oats Co.
Income Statement
For the Year Ended December 31, 1993
(in millions)

	1993
Sales	$5,730.6
Cost of goods sold	-2,858.4
Selling general adm.	-2,279.4
Interest expense	-55.1
Other expenses	-70.1
Tax	-180.8
Accounting change	-115.5
Net income	$ 171.3

We begin the construction of the statement of cash flows with the construction of operating cash flows, using information from the balance sheet and income statement. We proceed to explain changes in balance sheet accounts by using the events described in the income statement. Those changes we cannot explain by events in the income statement will have to be explained by using additional information.

Operating Cash Flows

1. Collections from customers.

	(in millions)
Sales	$5,730.60
Minus change in accounts receivable	(96.40)
Collections from customers	**$5,827.00**

The collections from customers are estimated by assuming that all sales are on credit. Since annual sales are at $5,730.6 million, we expect that accounts receivable would have increased by that amount. In fact, accounts receivable decreased by $96.4 million, implying that not only were the current sales collected, but also some of the beginning accounts receivable, or a total $5,827 million had been collected from customers.

2. Payments to suppliers and employees

	(in millions)
Cost of goods sold	$(2,858.40)
Selling, general, and administrative expenses	(2,279.40)
Subtract change in inventories	81.30
Subtract change in other current assets	(23.30)
Add change in accounts payable	(28.60)
Add change in accrued payroll	14.30
Add change in accrued advertising	10.40
Add change in accrued liabilities	12.40
Add depreciation	131.00
Add deferred compensation	11.00
Payments to suppliers and employees	**$(4,929.30)**

To estimate payments to suppliers and employees, we aggregate cost of goods sold (under which there may also be a labor component) and selling, general, and administrative expenses, which are assumed for a moment to represent cash payments to our suppliers for purchases of merchandise and to our employees for their services during the period. We also assume that all other overhead expenses incurred during the period were in cash. We add to this amount the decrease in inventory because some of the goods sold during 1993 were actually paid for in 1992 when they were manufactured. We subtract the increase in other current assets (such as prepaid expenses, which are assumed to be made in cash during 1993). Now we subtract the decrease in accounts payable during 1993, because suppliers were paid not only for current purchases, but also for purchases made in 1992. However, we add the increases in the three accounts accrued payroll, accrued advertising, and accrued liabilities, because these increases

Example 79

represent credit that was received from our suppliers and employees for expenses which have not yet been paid during 1993, but would be paid in 1994. We further add the annual depreciation expense because it is included in the above expenses (cost of goods sold and SG&A), but it represents a mere accounting entry which does not require a cash outflow. We do not add the amortization of goodwill because it is included among other expenses on the income statement, and not among cost of goods sold or the selling, general, and administrative expenses, as can be verified in Note 16. We also add back $11 million of deferred compensation (see Note 8), which is included as an expense in cost of goods sold and selling, general, and administrative expenses, because it is not a cash expense. The offset to this expense is the reduction of the deferred compensation accounts included in the stockholders equity section of the balance sheet.[3] Thus, total payments to suppliers and employees amount to $4,929.3 million.

3. Payment for taxes

	(in millions)
Tax expense	$(180.80)
Subtract change in taxes payable	(48.90)
Subtract change in deferred taxes	(152.50)
Add tax effect of accounting change	90.00
Tax payments	**$(292.20)**

To estimate tax payments during the period, we initially assume that all the tax expense on the income statement was deferred to future periods. This should have increased the deferred tax liability on the balance sheet by $180.8 million. Instead, we observe that the deferred tax liability decreased by $152.5 million. Thus,

---

[3]This transaction is related to the employee stock ownership program (ESOP), which is founded by the ESOP's borrowing (guaranteed by Quaker). The borrowing is included on the balance sheet of Quaker, and the cash proceeds were used to repurchase common and preferred stock. As payments are made on these borrowings, both the long-term debt (for the principal) and cash are reduced. At the same time, the deferred compensation account is reduced, reflecting the allocation of common and preferred stock to individual ESOP participants and the same amount is included in cost of goods sold and selling, general, and administrative expenses to reflect current compensation (but noncash) expense.

the sum of these two amounts, $333.3 million, became current taxes, and we thus expect the taxes payable account to increase by $333.3 million. However, the taxes payable account actually decreased by $48.9 million, so current tax payments would have been $382.2 million. The only adjustment we have to make is for the tax benefit of the accounting method switch to *SFAS No. 106*, which was not included in the tax expense of $180.8 million. This tax benefit was $90 million, and we thus have to reduce the estimated tax payments by $90 million (see Note 17), to obtain $292.2 million. As we shall point out later, under *SFAS No. 95*, the actual cash tax payment has to be disclosed. In its 1993 annual report (Note 17), Quaker Oats reports a tax payment of $213.3 million. Our estimates of the cash flows can be very different from those of the firm, because the firm has detailed records of cash and other balance sheet accounts as well as superior information about events that cause changes in these accounts, such as foreign tax credits. We only have aggregated account information, and even then we do not have sufficient information about events that caused changes in the accounts. Calls to the company's chief financial officer can clarify this issue. For international conglomerate like Quaker Oats, tax accounts can be quite complex.

4. Interest payments

Interest expense (net of interest income)	$(55.10)

To estimate the interest payments during the period, we begin by the interest expense during the year, which we assume is all cash. We then modify it if there are interest payable or receivable accounts on the balance sheet. In this case, there are no interest receivable or payable accounts, so we assume that the interest payment is identical to the interest expense. As is the case for tax payments, the actual payment of interest is disclosed under *SFAS No. 95*. In its 1993 annual report (Note 15), Quaker reports interest payments of $74.3 million. Note that our estimate of $55.1 million is net of interest income of $10.5 million, which indicates that after adjusting for interest received in cash, our estimate is not that different from actual cash payments for interest. Again, absent the detailed records of the firm itself, our estimates may

Example 81

contain errors that can be clarified by a call to a company's CFO. We are now ready to calculate cash from operating activities.

5. Total operating cash flows

Collections from customers	$5,827.00
Payments to suppliers and employees, etc.	($4,929.30)
Tax payments	($292.20)
Interest payments	($55.10)
Net operating cash flow	$ 550.40

At this point, we can summarize the steps we took so far in a partial spreadsheet (see Table 3–1).

Investing Cash Flows

To estimate investing cash flows, we use the changes in the balance sheet accounts that are not classified as current assets. We begin with the property, plant, and equipment (PPE) accounts, which include the original cost of PPE, and the accumulated depreciation of PPE. The two additional accounts we investigate are other receivables and investments and intangible assets, net of amortization. Here, we require additional information about the transactions that affected those accounts, part of which is available in the notes.

Note 4 in the 1993 annual report provides additional information about PPE and accumulated depreciation. In particular, it shows additions to PPE during 1993 of $187.3 million, retirements and sales of $113 million, and other changes, which are mostly decreases due to translation of foreign financial statements to the U.S. dollar when the dollar depreciated against foreign currencies. The accumulated depreciation account increased in 1993 by the depreciation expense of $131 million, accumulated depreciation on assets retired or sold of $55.3 million, and the translation of accumulated depreciation of foreign PPE in the amount of $37.5 million.

We assume that all PPE was acquired for cash, and thus show cash outflows of $187.3 million. We also calculate the net book value of PPE retired or sold as ($113 − $55.3), or $57.7 million. From Note 16 we find that the loss on divestitures, restructuring charges, and asset write-offs (plus other miscellaneous expenses) was $28.7 million in 1993. Thus, Quaker Oats realized the difference, $29

TABLE 3-1
Quaker Oats—1993

	1993	1992	Difference	Collections	Payments to Suppliers	Taxes	Interest
Cash	61.0	95.2	-34.2				
Accounts receivable	478.9	575.3	-96.4	96.4			
Inventories	354.0	435.3	-81.3		81.3		
Current assets	173.7	150.4	23.3		-23.3		
Investments	88.8	83.0	5.8				
PPE	2,059.2	2,066.1	-6.9				
Accumulated depreciation	-831.0	-792.8	-38.2		131		
Intangibles	431.3	427.4	3.9				
Total assets	2,815.9	3,039.9					
Short-term debt	128.0	61.0	-67.0				
Current long-term debt	48.9	57.9	9.0				
Accounts payable	391.6	420.2	28.6		-28.6		
Accrued payroll	161.3	147.0	-14.3		14.3		
Accrued advertising	130.6	120.2	-10.4		10.4		
Taxes payable	33.7	82.6	48.9			-48.9	
Accrued liabilities	211.0	198.6	-12.4		12.4		
Long-term debt	632.6	688.7	56.1				
Other liabilities	426.2	171.7	-254.5				
Deferred taxes	89.5	242.0	152.5			-152.5	
Preferred stock	100.0	100.0	0.0				
Deferred compensation	-85.9	-90.5	-4.6		4.6		
Preferred treasury	-2.7	-1.6	1.1				

TABLE 3–1 (concluded)

	1993	1992	Difference	Collections	Payments to Suppliers	Taxes	Interest
Common stock	420.0	420.0	0.0				
Paid-in capital	0.0	2.9	2.9				
Retained earnings	1,190.1	1,162.3	-27.8				
Cumulative translation	-65.4	-24.5	40.9				
Deferred compensation	-154.0	-160.4	-6.4		6.4		
Treasury stock	-839.6	-558.2	281.4				
Total liabilities & equity	2,815.9	3,039.9					
Total difference			-0.0				
Quaker Oats Co. *Income Statement*	1993						
Sales	5,730.6			5,730.6			
Cost of goods sold	-2,858.4				-2,858.4		
Selling general administration	-2,279.4				-2,279.4		
Interest expense	-55.1						-55.1
Other expenses	-70.1						
Tax	-180.8					-180.8	
Accounting change	-115.5					90	
Net income	171.3						
Collections				5,827			
Payments					-4,929.3		
Tax payment						-292.2	
Interest payment							-55.1

($55.7 − $28.7) million, in a cash inflow. We shall deal with the effects of currency translations shortly.

Since investments in other firms increased by $5.8 million, we assume that Quaker spent this amount in cash outflows to acquire these investments. In addition, we find out in Note 16 that amortization of intangibles was $26.3 million. Thus, we expect that intangibles (net of amortization) should decline by $26.3 million. However, net intangibles actually increased by $3.9 million during 1993, prompting us to assume that cash outlays for investments in other firms had been associated with goodwill of $30.2 ($26.3 + $3.9) million. Thus, total cash outflows for investments amounted to $36 ($30.2 + $5.8) million.

Let us summarize the above computations in the following table (in millions of dollars):

		Cash
Additions to PPE		$(187.30)
Retirement of PPE:		
Original cost of PPE sold	$113.00	
Accumulated depreciation	(55.30)	
Loss on sale	(28.70)	29.00
Investments and acquisitions:		
Increase in investments	(5.80)	
Increase in intangibles	(3.90)	
Amortization of intangible	(26.30)	(36.00)
Total investing cash flows		**$(194.30)**

Note that at this point all the changes in asset accounts on the balance sheet have been incorporated in our analysis, except for cash. Let us see the effects of these events on the accounts in a partial spreadsheet (see Table 3–2).

Financing Cash Flows

To estimate the effects of events that affect financing cash flows, we focus now on the changes in the liability and equity accounts that were not explained earlier. Once more, we need additional information about events that affect these accounts. We are

TABLE 3-2
Quaker Oats—1993

	1993	1992	Difference	Collections	Payments to Suppliers	Taxes	Interest	PPE Additions	PPE Sales	Investment
Cash	61.0	95.2	-34.2							
Accounts receivable	478.9	575.3	-96.4	96.4						
Inventories	354.0	435.3	-81.3		81.3					
Current assets	173.7	150.4	23.3		-23.3					
Investments	88.8	83.0	5.8							-5.8
PPE	2,059.2	2,066.1	-6.9					-187.3	113	
Accumulated depreciation	-831.0	-792.8	-38.2		131				-55.3	
Intangibles	431.3	427.4	3.9							-3.9
Total assets	2,815.9	3,039.9								
Short-term debt	128.0	61.0	-67.0							
Current long-term debt	48.9	57.9	9.0							
Accounts payable	391.6	420.2	28.6		-28.6					
Accrued payroll	161.3	147.0	-14.3		14.3					
Accrued advertising	130.6	120.2	-10.4		10.4					
Taxes payable	33.7	82.6	48.9			-48.9				
Accrued liabilities	211.0	198.6	-12.4		12.4					
Long-term debt	632.6	688.7	56.1							
Other liabilities	426.2	171.7	-254.5							
Deferred taxes	89.5	242.0	152.5			-152.5				
Preferred stock	100.0	100.0	0.0							
Deferred compensation	-85.9	-90.5	-4.6		4.6					
Preferred treasury	-2.7	-1.6	1.1							
Common stock	420.0	420.0	0.0							
Paid-in capital	0.0	2.9	2.9							

TABLE 3–2 (*concluded*)

	1993	1992	Difference	Collections	Payments To Suppliers	Taxes	Interest	PPE Additions	PPE Sales	Investment
Retained earnings	1,190.1	1,162.3	-27.8							
Cumulative translations	-65.4	-24.5	40.9							
Deferred compensation	-154.0	-160.4	-6.4		6.4					
Treasury stock	-839.6	-558.2	281.4							
Total liabilities & equity	2,815.9	3,039.9								
Total difference			-0.0							
Quaker Oats Co.										
Income Statement	1993									
Sales	5,730.6			5,730.6						
Cost of goods sold	-2,858.4				-2,858.4					
Selling general administration	-2,279.4				-2,279.4					
Intrest expenses	-55.1						-55.1			
Other expenses	-70.1								-28.7	-26.3
Tax	-180.8					-180.8				
Accounting change	-115.5					90				
Net income	171.3									
Collections				5,827						
Payments					-4,929.3					
Tax payment						-292.2				
Interest payment							-55.1			
Operating cash flow										
Foreign currency tr										
PPE additions								-187.3		
PPE retirements									29	
Investment										-36

Example   87

going to infer these events from the footnotes and from the statement of stockholders equity.

Let us begin with the change in the long-term debt account. This account shows a reduction of $56.1 million during 1993, which for a moment we assume became current. Thus, the current portion of long-term debt should have increased by that amount. Instead, we find that the current portion of long-term debt actually decreased by $9.0 million, which means that Quaker retired long-term debt of $65.1 ($56.1 + $9) million during 1993. However, short-term debt increased by $67 million, so the net effect on borrowing is $1.9 ($67 − $65.1) million of cash inflow from creditors in 1993.

Quaker Oats adopted *SFAS No. 106* in 1993, increasing its other liabilities by $205.5 million, as indicated in Note 12. However, other liabilities actually increased by $254.5 million in 1993, indicating an increase of $49 million, which we assume to be a cash inflow to the firm.[4]

The preferred stock in the treasury account increased by $1.1 million, and the common stock in treasury increased by $281.4 million during 1993. Thus, net repurchases of stock amounted to $282.5 ($281.4 + $1.1) million. However, we find that paid-in capital decreased by $2.9 million, probably due to issuance of common stock from stock held in treasury. Thus, the net cash outflow for repurchases of stocks should be increased by this amount to obtain a total of $285.4 ($282.5 + $2.9) million. To figure out the amount of cash dividends, we see that retained earnings increased during the period by $27.8 million. We expect an increase of $171.3 million, which is net income in 1993. The difference, $143.5 million, represents cash outflow for dividend payments.

Finally, let us examine the foreign currency cumulative translation adjustment. This account indicates an additional loss of $40.9 million. Part of this loss can be explained by the losses on translation of PPE, as seen in Note 4, of $82.1 million minus accumulated

---

[4]Actually, the increase in other liabilities may be the results of operations, in which case the change should reduce payments to suppliers and employees. Alternatively, it may be additional obligations assumed when purchasing a subsidiary or a new business. Then, the net investment is classified as cash outflow for investing activities. Absent any other details in the financial statements, we assume it to be a financing cash inflow.

depreciation of $37.5 million. In addition, Note 16 reports foreign exchange losses of $15.1 million included in other expenses on the income statement. Thus, the cash effect of foreign currency can be estimated as $40.9 million minus ($81.2 − $37.5) million plus $15.1 million, or a net negative cash flow effect of $12.3 million.

Let us summarize these events in a table:

	Cash (in millions)	
Reduction in long-term debt	$(56.10)	
Reduction in the current portion of long-term debt	(9.00)	
Increase in short-term debt	67.00	
Net borrowing:		$ 1.90
Increase in liabilities due to postretirement benefits	(205.50)	
Increase in the other liabilities account	254.50	
Net financing from other liabilities:		49.00
Increase in treasury preferred stock	(1.10)	
Increase in treasury common stock	(281.40)	
Decrease in paid-in-capital	(2.90)	
Net stock repurchases:		(285.40)
Net income	(171.30)	
Increase in retained earnings	27.80	
Dividend payments:		(143.50)
Increased losses in the cumulative translation adjustment	(40.90)	
Additional translation loss on PPE	81.20	
Additional loss on accumulated depreciation	(37.50)	
Foreign exchange losses in other expenses	(15.10)	
Net effect of foreign currency translation		(12.30)
Net financing cash flow		**($390.30)**

Note that at this point all the changes in balance sheet accounts have been explained by events that affected cash flows during the period. The only account we have not yet explained is the cash account itself, which decreased by $34.2 million in 1993. If our analysis is mathematically correct, the change in the cash account should be equal to the net effect of the cash flows from operating, investing and financing events. Specifically:

Net operating cash flow	$550.40
Net investing cash flow	(194.30)
Net financing cash flow	(390.30)
Net change in cash	**$(34.20)**

This analysis can be captured in the following spreadsheet (see Table 3–3).

TABLE 3-3
Quaker Oats—1993

	1993	1992	Difference	Collections	Payments To Suppliers	Taxes	Interest	PPE Additions	PPE Sales	Investments	Foreign Exchange	Post Retirement	Debt	Treasury Stock	Dividend	Cash Change
Cash	61.0	95.2	-34.2													-34.2
Accounts receivable	478.9	575.3	-96.4	96.4												0.0
Inventories	354.0	435.3	-81.3		81.3											0.0
Current assets	173.7	150.4	23.3		-23.3											0.0
Investments	88.8	83.0	5.8							-5.8						0.0
PPE	2,059.2	2,066.1	-6.9					-187.3	113		81.2					0.0
Accumulated depreciation	-831.0	-792.8	-38.2		131				-55.3		-37.5					0.0
Intangibles	431.3	427.4	3.9							-3.9						0.0
Total Assets	2,815.9	3,039.9														0.0
Short-term debt	128.0	61.0	-67.0										67			0.0
Current long-term debt	48.9	57.9	9.0										-9			0.0
Accounts payable	391.6	420.2	28.6		-28.6											0.0
Accrued payroll	161.3	147.0	-14.3		14.3											0.0
Accrued advertising	130.6	120.2	-10.4		10.4											0.0
Taxes payable	33.7	82.6	48.9			-48.9										0.0
Accrued liabilities	211.0	198.6	-12.4		12.4											0.0
Long-term debt	632.6	688.7	56.1										-56.1			0.0
Other liabilities	426.2	171.7	-254.5									254.5				0.0
Deferred taxes	89.5	242.0	152.5			-152.5										0.0
Preferred stock	100.0	100.0	0.0													0.0
Deferred compensation	-85.9	-90.5	-4.6		4.6											0.0

TABLE 3–3 *(concluded)*

	1993	1992	Difference	Collections	Payments To Supplies	Taxes	Interest	PPE Additions	PPE Sales	Investments	Foreign Exchange	Post Retirement	Debt	Treasury Stock	Dividend	Cash Change
Preferred treasury	-2.7	-1.6	1.1											-1.1		0.0
Common stock	420.0	420.0	0.0													0.0
Paid-in capital	0.0	2.9	2.9											-2.9		0.0
Retained earnings	1,190.1	1,162.3	-27.8												-143.5	-171.3
Cumulative translation	-65.4	-24.5	40.9								-40.9					0.0
Deferred compensation	-154.0	-160.4	-6.4		6.4											0.0
Treasury stock	-839.6	-558.2	281.4											-281.4		0.0
Total liabilities & equity	2,815.9	3,039.9														
Total difference			-0.0													0.0
Quaker Oats Co. Income statement	*1993*															
Sales	5,730.6			5,730.6												
Cost of goods sold	-2,858.4				-2,858.4											0.0
Selling general administration	-2,279.4				-2,279.4											0.0
Intrest expense	-55.1						-55.1									0.0
Other expenses	-70.1								-28.7	-26.3	-15.1					0.0
Tax	-180.8					-180.8										0.0
Accounting change	-115.5					90						-205.5				0.0

TABLE 3–3 (concluded)

	Post Dividend Change	1993	1992 Treasury	Difference ence	Cash Collections tions	Differ- Supplies	Collec- Taxes	Payments To Interest	Additions	Sales	Invest- ments	PPE Exchange	PPE Retirement	Invest- Debt	Foreign Stock
Net Income			171.3												-171.3
Collections					5,827										5,827.0
Payments						-4,929.3									-4,929.3
Tax payment							-292.2								-292.2
Interest payment								-55.1							-55.1
Operating cash flow															0.0
Foreign currency tr											-12.3				-12.3
PPE additions									-187.3						-187.3
PPE retirements										29					29.0
Investments											-36				-36.0
Other liabilities												49			49.0
Debt issuance													1.9		1.9
Repurchase of stock														-285.4	-285.4
Dividends														-143.5	-143.5
															-34.2

We can see that the change in the cash account is exactly identical to the aggregate of the events that affect cash during the period. We are now ready to present the statement of cash flows for 1993:

Quaker Oats Co.
Statement of Cash Flows
For the Year Ended December 31, 1993

	(in millions)
Collections from customers	$5,827.00
Payments to suppliers and employees, etc.	(4,929.30)
Tax payments	(292.20)
Interest payments	(55.10)
Net operating cash flow	**$ 550.40**
Additions to PPE	(187.30)
Proceeds from sale of PPE	29.00
Investments and acquisitions	(36.00)
Net investing cash flows	**$ (194.30)**
Net borrowing	1.90
Net financing from other liabilities	49.00
Net stock repurchases	(285.40)
Dividend payments	(143.50)
Net financing cash flow	**$ (378.00)**
Net effect of currency translation	**$ (12.30)**
Net cash decrease	**$ (34.20)**

We can also reconcile the net cash flow generated from operating events to net income in 1993 using the following schedule in million:

Net income		**$171.30**
Adjustments to income:		
Depreciation	$131.00	
Amortization	26.30	
Deferred compensation	11.00	
Decrease in deferred taxes	(152.50)	
Net effect of accounting change	115.50	
Tax effect of accounting change	90.00	
Net loss on sale of PPE	28.70	
Net loss on foreign translation	15.10	
Net adjustments		**265.10**

Example   93

	(concluded)	
Changes in assets/liabilities:		
Accounts receivable	96.40	
Inventories	81.30	
Other current assets	(23.30)	
Accounts payable	(28.60)	
Accrued payroll	14.30	
Accrued advertising	10.40	
Taxes payable	(48.90)	
Accrued liabilities	12.40	
Net change in assets/liabilities		**114.00**
Net operating cash flow		**$550.40**

The reconciliation of net income to net operating cash flow is based on adjusting net income for revenue and expense events that did not affect cash, and to revenue and expense events that cannot be considered operating cash flows. In the above schedule, we add back depreciation, amortization, and deferred compensation, which are noncash charges to income. In addition, the change in accounting method for other postretirement benefits has been a charge of $205.5 ($115.5 + $90) million against income, although it had no effect on current cash payments to retirees. However, the deferred taxes decreased during the period, indicating that tax payments exceeded the tax expense in net income. Finally, the losses on sale of PPE and foreign translation are not operating cash flows and have to be adjusted.

The other set of adjustments to income are caused by balance sheet changes that indicate that portions of the revenues and expenses were not in cash. For example, the increase in other current assets indicates that, in addition to those expenses included in 1993 income, there was another cash outlay of $23.3 million that increased other current assets. Since most of these changes were explained earlier, we will not go through every one of them again.

The above schedule is intended to explain why net income and net operating cash flows differ. It is required whenever the statement of cash flows is prepared using the "direct" method. We now explain the differences between the "direct" and "indirect" method of reporting cash flows from operations. (See the sections from the Quaker Oats Annual Report on page 113–134.)

THE DIRECT AND INDIRECT METHODS FOR OPERATING CASH FLOWS

The FASB has provided firms with the option of reporting cash flows from operations using the direct or the indirect method. Under the direct method, the main categories of operating cash flows are reported on the statement in a way that is very similar to what we did in the previous example. However, the FASB has also allowed firms to report the operating cash flows by using the indirect method. The basis for this method is the accounting identity:

Net Income = Revenues − Expenses

We can examine individual revenues and expenses and exclude those that are noncash revenues or expenses, as well as those that are not due to operating events. For example, a firm may record income from unconsolidated subsidiaries that are carried on the balance sheet using the equity method. This income is included in net income, but is a noncash event if cash dividends are not paid by the subsidiary. Similarly, suppose the firm sold some old PPE at a gain. This gain is included in net income, but it reflects an investing cash flow and not an operating cash flow. Examples of noncash expenses include depreciation and deferred taxes. Thus, we can rewrite the accounting identity as:

Net Income = (CR + NCR) − (CE + NCE)

where CR is defined as cash revenues from operating activities, NCR is revenues that are noncash revenues or that are nonoperating cash flows. Similarly, CE is defined as cash expenses from operating activities, and NCE as noncash expenses or nonoperating cash flows that are included among the expenses. Simple algebra yields:

(CR − CE) = Net Income + NCE − NCR

By definition, (CR − CE) is identical to the cash from operating activities. It can be derived by adjusting net income for revenue and expense events that are either noncash, or that are nonoperating cash flows. In particular, we *add* noncash (or nonoperating) expenses because they were subtracted from income to derive net income, and *subtract* noncash (or nonoperating) revenues because they were added to income in deriving net income. In effect, we have done exactly that at the bottom of the statement of cash flows in the schedule that reconciles net income with net operating cash flows in the example of Quaker Oats.

The FASB has encouraged firms to use the direct approach in reporting operating cash flows. However, it required firms that use the direct method for reporting operating cash flows to add a schedule that reconciles net income to net operating cash flow. Thus, when a firm adopts the direct method for reporting cash flows from operating activities it has to supply *all* the information that is required from a firm that uses the indirect method, but, *in addition*, it has to supply information about the major components of operating cash flows. Obviously, reasonable managers will opt to minimize their exposure to costly *additional* disclosure and will mostly use the indirect method for reporting cash flows from operations. Indeed, most firms today (about 97–99 percent according to recent surveys) use the indirect method of reporting cash from operations.

We show below how we can estimate the components of operating cash flows even when a firm reports net operating cash flow using the popular indirect method.

QUAKER OATS STATEMENT OF CASH FLOWS—DISCUSSION

At this point, let us examine the statement of cash flows reported by Quaker Oats for 1993 (see pages 113–134). As can be seen, Quaker uses the indirect method to report its net operating cash flow. This can be seen by the fact that we begin with net income of $171.3 million and make adjustments to derive net cash provided by operating activities. Furthermore, had Quaker used the direct method, we would have seen such items as cash collected from customers, payments to suppliers and employees, and so forth. The absence of the components of operating cash flows and the existence of adjustments to net income indicate that the firm uses the indirect method to report operating cash flows.

It is instructive to compare the adjustments to net income in the statement of cash flows with those we made earlier in the reconciliation of net operating cash flow to net income. Quaker added back $115.5 million for the net effect of the accounting change, just as we did. This is an expense on the income statement that has no immediate cash flow consequences. Similarly, Quaker adds back the depreciation and amortization expenses of $156.9 million because they represent just accounting entries and not cash outflows. Note that we had a total depreciation and amortization of $157.3 million, since we used information from the footnotes to statements. Quaker has the detailed records of these accounts and can be more accurate in its adjustments. Quaker reports a decrease in deferred taxes and other items of $46.4 million, whereas we reported a decrease of deferred taxes of $152.5 million, which after netting out the tax effect of the accounting change in the amount of $90 million and the deferred compensation of $11 million is equal to a net reduction of $51.5, close but not equal to the $46.4 million adjustment reported by Quaker. Again, it should be emphasized that the firm's numbers are more accurate because it has the detailed records, which are unavailable to us. Finally, Quaker adjusts net income for restructuring charges and loss on disposition of PPE by adding back $44.3 million. In our reconciliation, we adjusted for the loss on PPE and translation of foreign transactions in the amount of $43.8 million, which is very similar to what Quaker reported in its statement of cash flows.

Moving to the adjustments for balance sheet changes, we find that Quaker reports changes in balance sheet accounts that are different from the changes reported in the balance sheet. For example, we had seen a decrease of accounts receivable of $96.4 million on the balance sheet, and adjusted the net income accordingly, whereas Quaker reports a decrease of only $59.1 million. Similarly, we show a decrease in inventories of $81.3 million, whereas Quaker adjusts for decreases of inventories of only $41.9 million. There may be several reasons for these differences. The firm may segregate the effect of foreign currency translation on the statement of cash flows but not on the balance sheet. The firm may also exclude accounts receivable that are due to investing activities (such as those from sale of PPE). Thus, the changes in balances from the balance sheet may not agree with the adjustments to net income on the statement of cash flows. However, we can see that in the case of Quaker the net operating cash flow which we estimated ($550.4 million) is very similar to that reported by the firm ($558.2 million).

Turning to investing cash flows, we find that Quaker Oats reports cash outflows for additions to PPE of $172.3 million, whereas we included $187.3 million from Note 4. The difference probably stems from two effects: some of the additions to PPE can be caused by acquisitions which are reported separately in the statement of cash flows of Quaker Oats, and the additions to PPE may not be entirely financed by cash outflow. Thus, we can also expect changes in the other investing activities that are probably aggregated differently in the statement of cash flows of Quaker Oats. Note, however, that the net cash flow spent on investing activities is very similar in the statement and in our calculations ($196.7 and $194.3 million, respectively).

Examination of the financing activities shows that the total of financing activities and the effects of foreign currency translations are very similar between Quaker's statement of cash flows and our calculations. However, individual amounts differ. For example, dividends are different between our computations and the statement due to cash dividends on preferred stock. Quaker shows a net cash inflow of $8.5 million from debt issuance, whereas we showed a net effect of $1.9 million. The possible explanation here is that some of our difference can be caused by foreign currency translation of foreign liabilities. Quaker also shows net cash outflow for repurchase of stock of $300.9 million, whereas we show only $285.4 million. Finally, we included an increase in other liabilities of $49 million as another cash flow from financing, whereas this amount is missing completely from Quaker's statement of cash flows. This difference can be explained, again, by the effects of translating foreign liabilities. We have no way of finding this effect without additional information, which Quaker Oats alone possesses.

To sum up, we find that our estimates provide reasonably close approximations to both net operating and investing cash flows. Our estimates for net financing activities and foreign currency translation effects are less accurate because we do not possess enough detail about foreign liabilities of Quaker Oats. The individual components of investing and financing activities are mostly reasonable approximations to those reported by Quaker Oats, although some of the smaller items may be very different, because we do not have the detailed records and worksheets that Quaker has. However, our estimates are reasonably close to those reported by Quaker Oats as a whole, and we can use them when a detailed statement of cash flows is not provided (before 1987, or for foreign firms in countries that do not require a statement of cash flows).

ESTIMATING COMPONENTS OF OPERATING CASH FLOWS

To estimate the components of cash flows from operating activities, we use the information in the income statement and the schedule that reconciles net income to cash flows from operating activities. Let us illustrate this technique for the 1989 annual report of Sara Lee Corp. These statements provide the following information (in millions of dollars):

	Year Ended 7/1/89
Net sales	$11,717.67
Cost of sales	(8,040.44)
Selling, general, and administrative	(2,936.14)
Interest expense	(153.78)
Interest income	20.58
Unusual items, net	31.59
Income taxes	(228.98)
Net Income	$ 410.50
Net income	410.50
Adjustments for noncash items:	
Depreciation and amortization	279.95
Unusual items, net	(31.59)
Increase in deferred taxes	42.51
Other noncash credits, net	(102.13)
Changes in current assets and liabilities,	
net of businesses acquired and sold	(105.83)
Net cash from operating activities	$ 493.41

	Year Ended 7/1/89
Components of the changes in current assets and liabilities:	
Increase in trade accounts receivable	(14.68)
Increase in inventories	(181.36)
Increase in other current assets	(37.78)
Increase in accounts payable	209.13
Decrease in accrued liabilities	(49.32)
Decrease in accrued income taxes	(31.82)
Change in current assets and liabilities	$ (105.83)

From these data, we can estimate the individual components of operating cash flows by using the information on operating events from the income statement, and information about changes in account balances from the schedule that reconciles net income to net operating cash flows.

Sara Lee Corp.: Consolidated Statements of Income

CONSOLIDATED STATEMENTS OF INCOME

| | | Years ended | |
(in thousands except per share data)	July 1, 1989	July 2, 1988	June 27, 1987
Net Sales	$11,717,678	$10,423,816	$9,154,588
Cost of sales	8,040,447	7,096,756	6,309,565
Selling, general and administrative expenses	2,936,149	2,717,504	2,328,704
Interest expense	153,781	119,925	105,632
Interest income	(20,588)	(23,705)	(37,159)
Unusual items, net	(31,592)	–	–
	11,078,197	9,910,480	8,706,742
Income before income taxes	639,481	513,336	447,846
Income taxes	228,989	188,261	180,787
Net Income	410,492	325,075	267,059
Preferred dividend requirements	(14,358)	(9,394)	(4,125)
Earnings available for common stockholders	$ 396,134	$ 315,681	$ 262,934
Net Income per Common Share	$ 3.50	$ 2.83	$ 2.35
Average shares outstanding	113,395	111,670	111,687

1. Cash collections from customers:

	Year Ended 7/1/89
Net sales	$ 11,717.67
Increase in trade accounts receivable	(14.68)
Cash collections from customers	**$ 11,702.99**

2. Cash payments to suppliers and employees:

Cost of sales	$ (8,040.44)
Selling, general, and administrative	(2,936.14)
Depreciation and amortization	279.95
Other noncash credits, net	(102.13)
Increase in inventories	(181.36)
Increase in other current assets	(37.78)
Increase in accounts payable	209.13
Decrease in accrued liabilities	(49.32)
Cash payments to suppliers and employees	**$(10,858.09)**

Sara Lee Corp.: Consolidated Balance Sheets

CONSOLIDATED BALANCE SHEETS

(dollars in thousands except share data)	July 1, 1989	July 2, 1988	June 27, 1987
Cash and equivalents	$ 117,498	$ 178,552	$ 302,862
Trade accounts receivable, less allowances of $63,862 in 1989, $54,850 in 1988 and $47,084 in 1987	813,672	717,532	609,998
Inventories			
Finished goods	830,340	674,186	640,723
Work in process	171,560	109,213	86,382
Materials and supplies	450,064	344,054	284,614
	1,451,964	1,127,453	1,011,719
Other current assets	116,587	65,335	35,827
Total current assets	2,499,721	2,088,872	1,960,406
Investments in associated companies	188,989	88,763	116,320
Trademarks and other assets	265,867	258,053	230,133
Property, at cost			
Land	68,988	64,203	51,023
Buildings and improvements	965,215	822,594	720,741
Machinery and equipment	1,607,377	1,345,120	1,356,151
Construction in progress	221,840	210,043	100,354
Assets under capital leases	23,823	42,599	38,700
	2,887,243	2,484,559	2,266,969
Accumulated depreciation	1,114,227	1,067,855	1,026,399
Property, net	1,773,016	1,416,704	1,240,570
Intangible assets	1,795,139	1,159,678	644,246
	$6,522,732	$5,012,070	$4,191,675

3. Cash payment for taxes:

Income taxes	$(228.98)
Increase in deferred taxes	42.51
Decrease in accrued income taxes	(31.82)
Cash payment for taxes	**$(218.29)**

Sara Lee Corp.: Consolidated Balance Sheets (continued)

CONSOLIDATED BALANCE SHEETS

	July 1, 1989	July 2, 1988	June 27, 1987
Notes payable	$ 279,026	$ 94,599	$ 219,354
Accounts payable	966,508	769,733	510,580
Accrued liabilities	988,084	905,180	766,322
Accrued income taxes	10,143	11,813	20,892
Current maturities of long-term debt	31,665	24,836	78,114
Total current liabilities	2,275,426	1,806,161	1,595,262
Long-term debt	1,488,230	893,434	632,624
Deferred income taxes	346,470	298,952	280,527
Other liabilities	315,243	213,426	192,307
Preferred stock (authorized 13,500,000 shares; no par value)			
Convertible adjustable: Issued and outstanding—607,000 in			
1989 and 1,500,000 in 1988 and 1987; redeemable at			
$50 per share	30,350	75,000	75,000
Auction: 1,500 shares issued and outstanding in 1989 and			
1988; redeemable at $100,000 per share	150,000	150,000	—
Convertible ESOP: 4,827,586 shares issued in 1989	350,000	—	—
Unearned deferred compensation	(347,903)	—	—
Common stockholders' equity			
Common stock: (authorized 300,000,000 shares; $1.33 1/3 par value)			
113,667,303 shares issued in 1989 and			
119,596,068 in 1988 and 1987	151,556	159,461	159,461
Capital surplus	18,779	24,212	3,667
Retained earnings	1,750,961	1,597,259	1,408,504
Foreign currency translation adjustments	(6,380)	15,337	20,048
Treasury stock, at cost: None in 1989, 9,037,505 shares			
in 1988 and 8,872,115 shares in 1987	—	(221,172)	(175,725)
Total common stockholders' equity	1,914,916	1,575,097	1,415,955
	$6,522,732	$5,012,070	$4,191,675

4. Cash payment for interest:

Interest expense	$(153.78)
Interest income	20.58
Cash payment for interest	**$(133.20)**

Sara Lee Corp.: Consolidated Statements of Common Stockholders' Equity

CONSOLIDATED STATEMENTS OF COMMON STOCKHOLDERS' EQUITY

(dollars in thousands except per share data)	Total	Common Stock	Capital Surplus	Retained Earnings	Foreign Currency Translation Adjustments	Treasury Stock
Balances at June 28, 1986	$1,154,678	$ 79,730	$ 6,965	$1,320,475	$(42,350)	$(210,142)
Net income	267,059	—	—	267,059	—	—
Cash dividends						
Common ($.95 per share)	(102,148)	—	—	(102,148)	—	—
Convertible adjustable preferred ($2.75 per share)	(4,125)	—	—	(4,125)	—	—
Stock issuances						
Two-for-one stock split	—	79,731	(28,426)	(51,305)	—	—
Public offering	21,893	—	10,919	—	—	10,974
Business acquisitions	39,538	—	18,698	—	—	20,840
Stock option and purchase plans	27,633	—	375	—	—	27,258
Company acquired under pooling-of-interests	41,073	—	(16,167)	(21,452)	—	78,692
Treasury stock purchases	(100,003)	—	—	—	—	(100,003)
Translation adjustments	62,398	—	—	—	62,398	—
Other	7,959	—	11,303	—	—	(3,344)
Balances at June 27, 1987	1,415,955	159,461	3,667	1,408,504	20,048	(175,725)
Net income	325,075	—	—	325,075	—	—
Cash dividends						
Common ($1.15 per share)	(126,926)	—	—	(126,926)	—	—
Convertible adjustable preferred ($3.03 per share)	(4,547)	—	—	(4,547)	—	—
Auction preferred ($3,231.13 per share)	(4,847)	—	—	(4,847)	—	—
Stock issuances						
Business acquisitions	18,000	—	8,990	—	—	9,010
Stock option and purchase plans	34,028	—	(5,203)	—	—	39,231
Treasury stock purchases	(91,653)	—	—	—	—	(91,653)
Translation adjustments	(4,711)	—	—	—	(4,711)	—
Other	14,723	—	16,758	—	—	(2,035)
Balances at July 2, 1988	1,575,097	159,461	24,212	1,597,259	15,337	(221,172)
Net income	410,492	—	—	410,492	—	—
Cash dividends						
Common ($1.38 per share)	(155,304)	—	—	(155,304)	—	—
Convertible adjustable preferred ($3.70 per share)	(3,714)	—	—	(3,714)	—	—
Auction preferred ($7,096.00 per share)	(10,644)	—	—	(10,644)	—	—
Stock issuances						
Business acquisitions	80,140	—	34,430	—	—	45,710
Stock option and purchase plans	33,066	716	11,956	—	—	20,394
Conversion of convertible adjustable preferred stock	44,650	—	16,299	—	—	28,351
Treasury stock purchases	(37,388)	—	—	—	—	(37,388)
Retirement of treasury stock	—	(8,606)	(72,067)	(87,128)	—	167,801
Translation adjustments	(21,717)	—	—	—	(21,717)	—
Other	238	(15)	3,949	—	—	(3,696)
Balances at July 1, 1989	$1,914,916	$151,556	$ 18,779	$1,750,961	$ (6,380)	$ —

5. Other cash flows:

Unusual items, net	$ 31.59
Unusual items, net (adjusted to show it is a nonoperating-cash item)	(31.59)
Other cash flows	**$ 0.00**
Total operating cash flow	**$493.41**

Sara Lee Corp.: Consolidated Statements of Cash Flows

CONSOLIDATED STATEMENTS OF CASH FLOWS

(dollars in thousands)	Years ended		
	July 1, 1989	July 2, 1988	June 27, 1987
Cash Flows from Operating Activities			
Net income	$ 410,492	$325,075	$267,059
Adjustments for non-cash items included in net income:			
Depreciation and amortization of intangibles	279,945	250,920	201,607
Unusual items, net	(31,592)	—	—
Increase (decrease) in deferred income taxes	42,509	15,102	(10,629)
Other non-cash credits, net	(102,134)	(10,897)	(28,945)
Changes in current assets and liabilities, net of			
businesses acquired and sold	(105,827)	152,080	227,536
Net cash flows from operating activities	493,393	732,280	656,628
Cash Flows from Investing Activities			
Purchases of property and equipment	(541,483)	(448,974)	(286,547)
Acquisitions of businesses	(910,147)	(881,442)	(236,293)
Investments in associated companies	(176,107)	(6,019)	(86,216)
Dispositions of businesses	484,668	227,243	70,870
Sales of property	21,377	157,235	32,237
Other	1,095	10,665	2,211
Net cash flows used in investing activities	(1,120,597)	(941,292)	(503,738)
Cash Flows from Financing Activities			
Issuance of convertible ESOP stock in 1989 and			
auction preferred stock in 1988	350,000	150,000	—
Issuances of common stock	33,066	34,028	49,526
Purchases of common stock	(37,388)	(91,653)	(100,003)
Borrowings of long-term debt	257,273	393,092	10,916
Repayments of long-term debt	(44,813)	(125,860)	(41,516)
Short-term borrowings (repayments), net	184,427	(124,755)	123,743
Payments of dividends	(169,662)	(136,320)	(106,273)
Net cash flows from financing activities	572,903	98,532	(63,607)
Effect of changes in foreign exchange rates on cash	(6,753)	(13,830)	57,420
Increase (decrease) in cash and equivalents	(61,054)	(124,310)	146,703
Cash and equivalents at beginning of year	178,552	302,862	156,159
Cash and equivalents at end of year	$ 117,498	$178,552	$302,862
Components of the Changes in Current Assets and Liabilities			
(Increase) decrease in trade accounts receivable	$ (14,682)	$ 49,199	$104,865
(Increase) in inventories	(181,359)	(38,207)	(31,556)
(Increase) decrease in other current assets	(37,777)	(25,127)	2,961
Increase in accounts payable	209,126	109,482	67,570
(Decrease) increase in accrued liabilities	(49,318)	91,996	111,063
(Decrease) in accrued income taxes	(31,817)	(35,263)	(27,367)
Changes in current assets and liabilities	$(105,827)	$152,080	$227,536
Supplemental Disclosures of Cash Flow Information			
Cash paid during the year for:			
Interest	$ 129,877	$110,474	$ 94,286
Income taxes	233,343	215,661	222,048

In the above estimation, we have used all the information on the income statement and the information in the reconciliation schedule. Thus, the net operating cash flow is identical to that reported

by the firm. Still, there are two important differences that should
be highlighted; the estimates for tax and interest payments are
not identical to those reported by the firm. Under *SFAS No. 95*,
firms must disclose payments for taxes and interest, *even* if they
use the indirect method to report cash flows from operating activities. Accordingly, Sara Lee Corp. reports the following data:

	Year Ended 7/1/89
Tax payments as reported	$(233.34)
Estimated payments for taxes	(218.29)
Error in estimation	(15.05)
Interest payments as reported	(129.88)
Estimated payments for interest	(133.20)
Error in estimation	3.32
Total (underestimation) error	**$ (11.73)**

In the above estimation, we can use the actual numbers reported
by the firm, and since the underestimation error is small, we can
assign it to "other" cash flows from operating activities. Thus,
our estimates will be:

Cash collections from customers	$11,702.99
Cash payments to suppliers and employees	(10,858.09)
Tax payments as reported	(233.34)
Interest payments as reported	(129.88)
Other operating cash flows	(11.73)
Net operating cash flow	$ 493.41

Let us perform the same procedure for Lotus Development Corp.,
which reports operating cash flows using the direct method. Initially,
we will use the same procedures as those above to estimate the
components of cash flows from operating activities and then compare
the results to the actual components reported by the firm.

Lotus Development Corporation

The company's financial statements provide the following information (in thousands of dollars):

	Year Ended 12/31/89
Net sales	$556,033.00
Cost of sales	(104,949.00)
R&D	(94,343.00)
Sales and marketing	(221,745.00)
General and administrative	(61,078.00)
Interest income, net	5,644.00
Other income, net	5,389.00
Provision for income taxes	(16,990.00)
Net income	$ 67,961.00
Net income	$ 67,961.00
Depreciation and amortization	33,827.00
Increase in accounts receivable	(10,028.00)
Increase in inventory	(6,095.00)
Increase in accounts payable and accrued expenses	16,569.00
Net change in other working capital items	23,201.00
Net cash provided by operations	$125,435.00

Lotus Development Corporation: Consolidated Statements of Operations

LOTUS DEVELOPMENT CORPORATION
CONSOLIDATED STATEMENTS OF OPERATIONS
Years ended December 31,

(In thousands, except per share data)	1989	1988	1987
Net sales	$556,033	$468,547	$395,595
Cost of sales	104,949	90,825	68,676
Gross margin	451,084	377,722	326,919
Operating expenses:			
Research and development (Note B)	94,343	83,837	58,420
Sales and marketing	221,745	170,750	126,848
General and administrative	61,078	54,124	46,546
Total operating expenses	377,166	308,711	231,814
Operating income	73,918	69,011	95,105
Interest income, net (Note J)	5,644	9,568	3,960
Other income, net (Note K)	5,389	1,295	3,853
Income before provision for income taxes	84,951	79,874	102,918
Provision for income taxes (Note H)	16,990	20,949	30,875
Net income	$ 67,961	$ 58,925	$ 72,043
Net income per share	$1.61	$1.29	$1.58
Weighted average common and common equivalent shares outstanding	42,301	45,551	45,720

Lotus Development Corporation: Consolidated Balance Sheets

LOTUS DEVELOPMENT CORPORATION
CONSOLIDATED BALANCE SHEETS

(In thousands)	December 31, 1989	December 31, 1988
Assets		
Current assets:		
Cash and short-term investments	$274,977	$192,433
Accounts receivable, less allowances for doubtful accounts of $4,200 and $3,936	97,712	92,035
Inventory (Note C)	23,171	18,088
Other current assets	13,937	7,430
Total current assets	409,797	309,986
Property and equipment, net of accumulated depreciation and amortization of $75,418 and $55,482 (Note D)	129,702	86,953
Software and other intangibles, net of accumulated amortization of $36,972 and $35,802 (Note B)	27,100	16,026
Investments and other assets (Note E)	37,678	9,157
Total assets	$604,277	$422,122

It should be noted that the reconciliation schedule here reports different increases in accounts receivable and inventories than those calculated by subtracting the balances on the balance sheet. For example, the increase in accounts receivable on the balance sheet amounts to $5.677 million, whereas the increase reported in the reconciliation schedule is of $10.028 million. The difference between these two figures stems from accounts receivable that are not due to trade receivables. For example, if some of these receivables are caused by sale of fixed assets, these receivables should *not* be considered for the change in operating cash flows, since these receivables are related to disinvesting cash flows. Similarly, the increase in inventories according to the balance sheet is of $5.083 million, whereas the reconciliation schedule reports an increase of $6.095 million. Obviously, the firm has examined the change in inventories carefully and excluded those items that do not represent operating cash flows. Normally, it is a good procedure to compare the changes in the reconciliation schedule with those reported on the balance sheet to identify any material differences and their possible sources. In many cases, these differences arise because of acquisitions or divestitures, where the balance sheet differences are likely to include the effects of the acquisition, but the reconciliation schedule in the cash flow statement does not. These differences are likely to be included as part of the acquisition costs in the investing activities section of the statement of cash flows.

Lotus Development Corporation: Consolidated Balance Sheets (continued)

	December 31,	
(In thousands)	1989	1988
Liabilities and Stockholders' Equity		
Current liabilities:		
Notes payable to banks (Note I)	$ 2,975	$ 9,441
Accrued employee compensation	17,688	11,771
Accounts payable and accrued expenses	63,125	45,491
Deferred revenue (Note B)	15,798	16,592
Income taxes payable (Note H)	10,253	1,231
Total current liabilities	109,839	84,526
Deferred income taxes (Note H)	13,693	10,400
Long-term debt (Note I)	202,440	95,000
Commitments and contingencies (Notes E and F)		
Stockholders' equity (Note G):		
Preferred stock, $1.00 par value, 5,000,000 shares authorized, none issued	–	–
Common stock, $.01 par value, 100,000,000 shares authorized; 57,940,650 and 55,561,312 issued; and 41,607,816 and 41,666,344 outstanding	579	556
Additional paid-in capital	139,762	109,429
Retained earnings	334,246	266,285
Treasury stock, 16,332,834 and 13,894,968 shares at an average cost of $11.94 and $10.37 per share	(194,937)	(144,030)
Translation adjustment	(1,345)	3
Deferred employee compensation	–	(47)
Total stockholders' equity	278,305	232,196
Total liabilities and stockholders' equity	$604,277	$422,122

To estimate operating cash flows using the information above:

1. Cash collections from customers:

	Year Ended 12/31/89
Net sales	$556,033.00
Increase in accounts receivable	(10,028.00)
Decrease in deferred revenue	794.00
Cash collections from customers	**$546,799.00**

Lotus Development Corporation: Consolidated Statements of Cash Flows

LOTUS DEVELOPMENT CORPORATION
CONSOLIDATED STATEMENTS OF CASH FLOWS
Years ended December 31,

(In thousands)	1989	1988	1987
Cash flows from operations:			
Cash received from customers	$545,997	$425,601	$394,300
Cash paid to suppliers and employees	(429,245)	(359,693)	(270,600)
Interest received	18,153	11,980	7,560
Interest paid	(14,884)	(3,614)	(3,258)
Income taxes recovered (paid)	9,270	(12,438)	(20,371)
Other, net	(3,856)	258	1,127
Net cash provided by operations	125,435	62,094	108,758
Cash flows from investments:			
Payments for purchase of property and equipment	(68,906)	(55,161)	(25,258)
Payments for investments	(24,513)	(1,004)	(4,800)
Payments for software and other intangibles	(23,197)	–	(17,624)
Net cash used for investments	(116,616)	(56,165)	(47,682)
Cash flows from financing activities:			
Proceeds from issuance of long-term debt	107,440	65,000	–
Purchase of common stock for treasury	(43,552)	(56,205)	(1,279)
Issuance of common stock	15,916	10,649	8,042
Net short-term borrowings under credit facilities	(6,079)	2,151	3,913
Net cash provided by financing activities	73,725	21,595	10,676
Net increase in cash and short-term investments	82,544	27,524	71,752
Cash and short-term investments at beginning of year	192,433	164,909	93,157
Cash and short-term investments at end of year	$274,977	$192,433	$164,909

(In thousands)	1989	1988	1987
Reconciliation of net income to net cash provided by operations:			
Net income	$67,961	$58,925	$72,043
Depreciation and amortization	33,827	37,253	27,984
(Increase) in accounts receivable	(10,028)	(49,359)	(5,652)
(Increase) in inventory	(6,095)	(9,163)	(1,633)
Increase (decrease) in accounts payable and accrued expenses	16,569	13,837	(3,116)
Net change in other working capital items	23,201	10,601	19,132
Net cash provided by operations	$125,435	$62,094	$108,758

Lotus Development Corporation: Consolidated Statements of Stockholders' Equity

LOTUS DEVELOPMENT CORPORATION
CONSOLIDATED STATEMENTS OF STOCKHOLDERS' EQUITY

Years ended December 31, 1987, 1988 and 1989. (Note G) (In thousands)	Common Stock	Additional Paid-In Capital	Retained Earnings	Translation Adjustment	Treasury Stock	Deferred Employee Compensation	Total
Balance, December 31, 1986	$526	$66,624	$135,317	($776)	($83,135)	($3,963)	$114,593
Acquisition of 174,375 shares of common stock	–	(184)	–	–	(4,608)	184	(4,608)
Exercise of 461,695 incentive stock options	5	2,886	–	–	–	–	2,891
Exercise of 1,406,119 non-qualified stock options	14	7,566	–	–	–	–	7,580
Income tax benefit related to exercise of stock options	–	5,483	–	–	–	–	5,483
Issuance of 63,002 shares of common stock under employee stock purchase plan	1	899	–	–	–	–	900
Amortization of deferred employee compensation	–	–	–	–	–	2,145	2,145
Currency translation effect	–	–	–	1,019	–	–	1,019
Net income	–	–	72,043	–	–	–	72,043
Balance, December 31, 1987	546	83,274	207,360	243	(87,743)	(1,634)	202,046
Acquisition of 3,282,087 shares of common stock	–	–	–	–	(56,287)	–	(56,287)
Exercise of 377,060 incentive stock options	4	2,904	–	–	–	–	2,908
Exercise of 490,839 non-qualified stock options	5	4,833	–	–	–	–	4,838
Income tax benefit related to exercise of stock options	–	15,434	–	–	–	–	15,434
Issuance of 136,858 shares of common stock under employee stock purchase plan	1	2,984	–	–	–	–	2,985
Amortization of deferred employee compensation	–	–	–	–	–	1,587	1,587
Currency translation effect	–	–	–	(240)	–	–	(240)
Net income	–	–	58,925	–	–	–	58,925
Balance, December 31, 1988	556	109,429	266,285	3	(144,030)	(47)	232,196
Acquisition of 2,437,866 shares of common stock	–	–	–	–	(50,907)	–	(50,907)
Exercise of 407,864 incentive stock options	4	3,471	–	–	–	–	3,475
Exercise of 1,750,513 non-qualified stock options	17	16,354	–	–	–	–	16,371
Income tax benefit related to exercise of stock options	–	7,083	–	–	–	–	7,083
Issuance of 220,961 shares of common stock under employee stock purchase plan	2	3,425	–	–	–	–	3,427
Amortization of deferred employee compensation	–	–	–	–	–	47	47
Currency translation effect	–	–	–	(1,348)	–	–	(1,348)
Net income	–	–	67,961	–	–	–	67,961
Balance, December 31, 1989	$579	$139,762	$334,246	($1,345)	($194,937)	$–	$278,305

2. Cash payments to suppliers and employees:

Cost of sales	$(104,949.00)
R&D	(94,343.00)
Sales and marketing	(221,745.00)
General and administrative	(61,078.00)
Depreciation and amortization	33,827.00
Increase in inventory	(6,095.00)
Increase in accounts payable and accrued expenses	16,569.00
Net change in other working capital items (without taxes and deferred revenue)	13,385.00
Cash payments to suppliers and employees	**$(424,429.00)**

3. Cash receipts from taxes:

Provision for income taxes	$(16,990.00)
Increase in deferred taxes	3,293.00
Increase in accrued income taxes	$ 9,022.00
Income tax paid	**$ (4,675.00)**

4. Cash payment and receipt of interest:

Interest expense	$(15,494.00)
Capitalized interest	(1,808.00)
Cash payment for interest	**$(17,302.00)**
Interest income	$ 19,330.00
Cash receipt from interest	**$ 19,330.00**

5. Other cash flows:

Other income, net	$ 5,389.00
Cash receipt from other income	**$ 5,389.00**
Total operating cash flow	**$125,112.00**
Total operating cash flow	$ 125,112
As reported	(125,435)
Difference	$ (323)
Difference explained by:	
Increase in deferred taxes	3,293
Interest capitalized (twice)	(3,616)
Total	$ (323)

(Both items were not included specifically in the company's reconciliation schedule.)

Comparison of Estimated to Reported Components

	As Reported	Estimated	% Error
Cash received from customers	$545,997	$546,799	(1)
Cash paid to suppliers and employees	(429,245)	(424,429)	1
Interest received	18,153	19,330	(6)
Interest paid	(14,884)	(17,302)	(16)
Income tax recovered	9,270	(4,675)	150
Other, net	(3,856)	5,389	(240)
Total	$125,435	$125,112	1

As can be seen from the previous table, estimating net cash flows from operations can be calculated fairly accurately. Furthermore, given the information available in the reconciliation schedule, estimates of the cash received from customers and cash paid to suppliers and employees are reasonably close to the amounts that the firm would have reported had it used the direct method. Significant differences may occur for interest received or paid, because for most firms only the income statement interest expense/income are available, but not changes in balance sheet amounts. Obviously, these amounts are available to the firm, which uses them to report the actual cash received or paid for interest. It should be noted that the FASB required firms to disclose the amount of cash paid for interest if they used the indirect method for deriving cash from operating activities.

Another item with large differences between reported and estimated amounts for Lotus is the taxes paid. Normally, large differences occur when not all tax-related balance sheet accounts are separately disclosed on the balance sheet. For example, some prepaid taxes or deferred taxes that represent an asset may be included with prepaid and other assets on the balance sheet. Some deferred tax liabilities may be included with other liabilities. Thus, in these cases, it is impossible to estimate the taxes paid during a period in a reasonable manner. Again, it should be emphasized that the actual cash paid for taxes should be separately disclosed in the statement of cash flows (or in footnotes) for firms that use the indirect method to derive cash from operating activities.

Finally, by definition, very little information will be available to estimate the "other operating cash flows." More than anything else, it would probably be a "plug" figure and is likely to contain an estimation error. However, one should not be too concerned about these errors since most of these "other" operating cash flows would not recur and would therefore not have any important consequences for future cash flows.

SUMMARY

In this chapter, we have described the basics of the statement of cash flows using the information from the 1993 financial statement of Quaker Oats. We showed how one can reconstruct the statement from information that is available in the income statement, balance sheets, and some footnote information. This procedure is useful, not only to gain a better understanding of the statement of cash flows, but also because some foreign countries do not require a statement of cash flows, and it therefore has to be compiled by the analyst from available financial statement data. We also explained the differences between the derivation of net operating cash flow using the direct or indirect method. We showed how we can estimate the components of operating cash flows even if the firm uses the indirect method. This will become useful in later chapters when we show the estimation of free cash flow.

In the next chapter, we will provide exact definitions of cash flows from financing, investing, and operating activities. We will also provide many examples of such activities as reported in publicly available statements and discuss how these cash flows should be interpreted. Immediately following, however, are examples of entire statements of cash flows from published financial statements of domestic and foreign corporations.

The Quaker Oats Company

Dollars in Millions (Except Per Share Data)

Year Ended June 30	1993	1992	1991
Net Sales	**$5,730.6**	**$5,576.4**	**$5,491.2**
Cost of goods sold	2,858.4	2,817.7	2,839.7
Gross profit	2,872.2	2,758.7	2,651.5
Selling, general and administrative expenses	2,279.4	2,213.0	2,121.2
Interest expense—net of $10.5, $9.6 and $9.0 interest income, respectively	55.1	67.4	86.2
Other expense—net	70.1	56.8	32.6
Income from Continuing Operations Before Income Taxes and Cumulative Effect of Accounting Changes	**467.6**	**421.5**	**411.5**
Provision for income taxes	180.8	173.9	175.7
Income from Continuing Operations Before Cumulative Effect of Accounting Changes	**286.8**	**247.6**	**235.8**
(Loss) from discontinued operations—net of tax	—	—	(30.0)
Income Before Cumulative Effect of Accounting Changes	**286.8**	**247.6**	**205.8**
Cumulative effect of accounting changes—net of tax	(115.5)	—	—
Net Income	**171.3**	**247.6**	**205.8**
Preferred dividends—net of tax	4.2	4.2	4.3
Net Income Available for Common	**$ 167.1**	**$ 243.4**	**$ 201.5**
Per Common Share:			
Income from Continuing Operations Before Cumulative Effect of Accounting Changes	**$ 3.93**	**$ 3.25**	**$ 3.05**
(Loss) from discontinued operations	—	—	(0.40)
Income Before Cumulative Effect of Accounting Changes	**3.93**	**3.25**	**2.65**
Cumulative effect of accounting changes	(1.59)	—	—
Net Income	**$ 2.34**	**$ 3.25**	**$ 2.65**
Dividends declared	**$ 1.92**	**$ 1.72**	**$ 1.56**
Average Number of Common Shares Outstanding (in thousands)	71,974	74,881	75,904

See accompanying notes to the consolidated financial statements

The Quaker Oats Company (continued)

Consolidated Statements of Cash Flows

Dollars in Millions

Year Ended June 30	1993	1992	1991
Cash Flows from Operating Activities:			
Net income	$171.3	$247.6	$205.8
Adjustments to reconcile net income to net cash provided by operating activities:			
Cumulative effect of accounting changes	115.5	155.9	—
Depreciation and amortization	156.9		177.7
Deferred income taxes and other items	(46.4)	(1.0)	14.0
Restructuring charges and gains on divestitures—net	20.5	23.1	10.0
Loss on disposition of property and equipment	23.8	84.7	17.9
Decrease (Increase) in trade accounts receivable	59.1	(14.3)	(116.6)
Decrease (Increase) in inventories	41.9	(10.1)	30.7
(Increase) Decrease in other current assets	(25.8)	24.0	5.1
(Decrease) Increase in trade accounts payable	(7.6)	132.5	19.2
(Decrease) Increase in other current liabilities	(6.4)	11.6	56.6
Change in deferred compensation	11.0	(43.1)	(0.2)
Other items	44.4	(29.6)	27.4
Change in payable to Fisher-Price	—		29.6
Change in net current assets of discontinued operations	—		66.0
Net Cash Provided by Operating Activities	558.2	581.3	543.2
Cash Flows from Investing Activities:			
Additions to property, plant and equipment	(172.3)	(176.4)	(240.6)
Change in other receivables and investments	(25.6)	(20.0)	(10.7)
Purchases and sales of property and businesses, net	1.2	16.5	
Discontinued operations	—		(19.8)
Net Cash Used in Investing Activities	(196.7)	(179.9)	(271.1)
Cash Flows from Financing Activities:			
Cash dividends	(140.3)	(132.8)	(123.0)
Change in short-term debt	67.0	(19.6)	(265.6)
Proceeds from long-term debt	0.5	1.1	1.8
Reduction of long-term debt	(59.0)	(46.2)	(39.7)
Proceeds from short-term debt to be refinanced	—	50.0	
Proceeds from issuance of debt for Fisher-Price spin-off	—		141.1
Issuance of common treasury stock	23.3	20.3	25.6
Repurchases of common stock	(323.1)	(235.1)	
Repurchases of preferred stock	(1.1)	(0.9)	(0.7)
Net Cash Used in Financing Activities	(432.7)	(363.2)	(260.5)
Effect of Exchange Rate Changes on Cash and Cash Equivalents	37.0	(17.6)	(6.0)
Net (Decrease) Increase in Cash and Cash Equivalents	(34.2)	20.6	5.6
Cash and Cash Equivalents—Beginning of Year	95.2	74.6	69.0
Cash and Cash Equivalents—End of Year	$ 61.0	$ 95.2	$ 74.6

See accompanying notes to the consolidated financial statements.

The Quaker Oats Company (continued)

Consolidated Balance Sheets	June 30	1993	1992	1991
	Assets			
	Current Assets:			
	Cash and cash equivalents	**$ 61.0**	$ 95.2	$ 74.6
	Trade accounts receivable—net of allowances	**478.9**	575.3	655.6
	Inventories:			
	Finished goods	**241.5**	302.8	309.1
	Grains and raw materials	**73.1**	93.7	86.7
	Packaging materials and supplies	**39.4**	38.8	26.5
	Total inventories	**354.0**	435.3	422.3
	Other current assets	**173.7**	150.4	150.0
	Total Current Assets	**1,067.6**	1,256.2	1,302.5
	Other Receivables and Investments	**88.8**	83.0	79.1
	Property, plant and equipment	**2,059.2**	2,066.1	1,914.6
	Less accumulated depreciation	**831.0**	792.8	681.9
	Property—Net	**1,228.2**	1,273.3	1,232.7
	Intangible Assets—Net of Amortization	**431.3**	427.4	446.2
	Total Assets	**$2,815.9**	$3,039.9	$3,060.5

See accompanying notes to the consolidated financial statements.

115

The Quaker Oats Company (continued)

June 30	1993	1992	1991
			Dollars in Millions
Liabilities and Shareholders' Equity			
Current Liabilities:			
Short-term debt	$ 128.0	$ 61.0	$ 80.6
Current portion of long-term debt	48.9	57.9	32.9
Trade accounts payable	391.6	420.2	395.3
Accrued payroll, pension and bonus	161.3	147.0	116.3
Accrued advertising and merchandising	130.6	120.2	105.7
Income taxes payable	33.7	82.6	58.5
Payable to Fisher-Price	—	—	29.6
Other accrued liabilities	211.0	198.6	165.8
Total Current Liabilities	1,105.1	1,087.5	984.7
Long-term Debt	632.6	688.7	701.2
Other Liabilities	426.2	171.7	231.9
Deferred Income Taxes	89.5	242.0	236.9
Preferred Stock, no par value, authorized 1,750,000 shares; issued 1,282,051 of $5.46 cumulative convertible shares (liquidating preference $78 per share)	100.0	100.0	100.0
Deferred Compensation	(85.9)	(90.5)	(94.5)
Treasury Preferred Stock, at cost, 34,447 shares; 21,315 shares; and 10,089 shares, respectively	(2.7)	(1.6)	(0.7)
Common Shareholders' Equity:			
Common stock, $5 par value, authorized 200,000,000 shares; issued 83,989,396 shares	420.0	420.0	420.0
Additional paid-in capital	—	2.9	7.2
Reinvested earnings	1,190.1	1,162.3	1,047.5
Cumulative translation adjustment	(65.4)	(24.5)	(52.9)
Deferred compensation	(154.0)	(160.4)	(168.0)
Treasury common stock, at cost, 14,533,157 shares; 10,586,091 shares; and 7,660,675 shares, respectively	(839.6)	(558.2)	(352.8)
Total Common Shareholders' Equity	551.1	842.1	901.0
Total Liabilities and Shareholders' Equity	$2,815.9	$3,039.9	$3,060.5

The Quaker Oats Company *(continued)*

Consolidated Statements of Common Shareholders' Equity

	Common Stock Issued	
	Shares	Amount
Balance as of June 30, 1990	83,989,396	$420.0
Net income		
Cash dividends declared on common stock		
Cash dividends declared on preferred stock		
Distribution of equity to shareholders from spin-off of Fisher-Price		
Common stock issued for stock purchase and incentive plans		
Current year foreign currency adjustments (net of allocated income tax provisions of $(3.0))		
Deferred compensation		
Other		
Balance as of June 30, 1991	83,989,396	$420.0
Net income		
Cash dividends declared on common stock		
Cash dividends declared on preferred stock		
Common stock issued for stock purchase and incentive plans		
Repurchases of common stock		
Current year foreign currency adjustments (net of allocated income tax benefits of $8.3)		
Deferred compensation		
Other		
Balance as of June 30, 1992	83,989,396	$420.0
Net income		
Cash dividends declared on common stock		
Cash dividends declared on preferred stock		
Common stock issued for stock purchase and incentive plans		
Repurchases of common stock		
Current year foreign currency adjustments (net of allocated income tax provisions of $(12.6))		
Deferred compensation		
Other		
Balance as of June 30, 1993	83,989,396	$420.0

See accompanying notes to the consolidated financial statements.

The Quaker Oats Company (continued)

Dollars in Millions

Common Shares Outstanding	Additional Paid-in Capital	Reinvested Earnings	Cumulative Translation Adjustment	Deferred Compensation	Common Stock in Treasury		Total
					Shares	Amount	
75,586,525	$12.9	$1,164.7	$(29.3)	$(164.1)	8,402,871	$(386.7)	$1,017.5
		205.8					205.8
		(118.7)					(118.7)
		(4.3)					(4.3)
		(200.0)					(200.0)
742,196	(8.3)				(742,196)	33.9	25.6
			(23.6)				(23.6)
				(3.9)			(3.9)
	2.6						2.6
76,328,721	$ 7.2	$ 1,047.5	$ (52.9)	$ (168.0)	7,660,675	$ (352.8)	$ 901.0
		247.6					247.6
		(128.6)					(128.6)
		(4.2)					(4.2)
619,084	(9.4)				(619,084)	29.7	20.3
(3,544,500)					3,544,500	(235.1)	(235.1)
			28.4				28.4
				7.6			7.6
	5.1						5.1
73,403,305	$ 2.9	$ 1,162.3	$ (24.5)	$ (160.4)	10,586,091	$ (558.2)	$ 842.1
		171.3					171.3
		(136.1)					(136.1)
		(4.2)					(4.2)
805,434	(8.4)	(3.2)			(805,434)	41.7	30.1
(4,752,500)					4,752,500	(323.1)	(323.1)
			(40.9)				(40.9)
				6.4			6.4
	5.5						5.5
69,456,239	$ —	$1,190.1	$ (65.4)	$ (154.0)	14,533,157	$(839.6)	$ 551.1

The Quaker Oats Company (continued)

Geographic Segment Information

Year Ended June 30	5-Year Compound Growth Rate	Net Sales		
		1993	1992	1991
United States	3.3%	$ 3,705.7	$ 3,599.8	$ 3,623.3
Canada	4.7%	224.6	242.5	236.9
U.S. and Canadian Grocery Products	3.4%	3,930.3	3,842.3	3,860.2
Europe	6.7%	1,335.8	1,354.5	1,326.4
Latin America and Pacific	16.3%	464.5	379.6	304.6
International Grocery Products	8.7%	1,800.3	1,734.1	1,631.0
Net Sales and Operating Income from Continuing Operations(a)	4.9%	$ 5,730.6	$ 5,576.4	$ 5,491.2
Less: General corporate expenses				
Interest expense—net				
Foreign exchange loss (gain)—net				
Income from continuing operations before income taxes and cumulative effect of accounting changes				
Provision for income taxes				
Income from continuing operations before cumulative effect of accounting changes				
Income from continuing operations per common share before cumulative effect of accounting changes				

(a) See Management's Discussion and Analysis for discussion of fiscal 1991 through 1993 restructuring charges and gains on divestitures.
(b) Fiscal 1989 results include a pretax restructuring charge of $124.3 million or $1.00 per share for plant consolidations and overhead reductions and a pretax charge of $25.6 million or $.20 per share for a change to the LIFO method of accounting for the majority of U.S. Grocery Products inventories.

Segments of the Business

The principal product lines of U.S. and Canadian Grocery Products and International Grocery Products are described in the Operations Review beginning on pages 21 and 28, respectively.

The Quaker Oats Company (continued)

Dollars in Millions (Except Per Share Data)

	Net Sales			5-Year Compound Growth Rate	Operating Income(a)					
	1990	1989	1988		1993	1992	1991	1990	1989(b)	1988
	$3,377.7	$3,413.9	$3,143.3	6.1%	$428.2	$414.8	$408.5	$354.7	$241.2	$318.9
	232.3	216.0	178.6	5.5%	18.8	20.2	20.5	17.8	15.1	14.4
	3,610.0	3,629.9	3,321.9	6.0%	447.0(c)	435.0	429.0	372.5	256.3	333.3
	1,084.6	968.6	967.5	1.3%	52.2	41.2	68.3	88.6	52.6	49.0
	336.0	280.9	218.6	20.8%	76.0	64.0	35.7	83.1	40.7	29.5
	1,420.6	1,249.5	1,186.1	10.3%	128.2	105.2	104.0	171.7	93.3	78.5
	$5,030.6	$4,879.4	$4,508.0	6.9%	575.2	540.2	533.0	544.2	349.6	411.8
				(0.9%)	37.4	38.2	40.4	34.3	39.3	39.1
				6.1%	55.1	67.4	86.2	101.8	56.4	41.0
				—	15.1	13.1	(5.1)	25.7	14.8	17.1
				8.2%	467.6	421.5	411.5	382.4	239.1	314.6
				8.9%	180.8	173.9	175.7	153.5	90.2	118.1
				7.9%	$286.8	$247.6	$235.8	$228.9	$148.9	$196.5
				9.8%	$ 3.93	$ 3.25	$ 3.05	$ 2.93	$ 1.88	$ 2.46

(c)Fiscal 1993 results include a pretax restructuring charge of $14.5 million, or $.12 per share, due to the adoption of FASB Statement #106
(d)Exclude results of businesses reported as continuing operations

The Quaker Oats Company (continued)

Dollars in Millions

Geographic Segment Information

Year Ended June 30	1993	1992	1991	1990	1989
Identifiable Assets					
United States	$ 1,772.3	$ 1,892.2	$ 2,114.8	$ 2,035.1	$ 1,969.6
Canada	105.0	105.7	113.9	115.1	85.6
U.S. and Canadian Grocery Products	1,877.3	1,997.9	2,228.7	2,150.2	2,055.2
Europe	562.9	687.5	533.5	517.7	378.3
Latin America and Pacific	182.4	154.4	122.5	120.2	103.4
International Grocery Products	745.3	841.9	656.0	637.9	481.7
Total Continuing Businesses	2,622.6	2,839.8	2,884.7	2,788.1	2,536.9
Corporate(a)	193.3	200.1	175.8	589.3	589.0
Total Consolidated	$ 2,815.9	$ 3,039.9	$ 3,060.5	$ 3,377.4	$ 3,125.9
Capital Expenditures					
U.S. and Canadian Grocery Products	$ 107.2	$ 110.7	$ 167.0	$ 210.3	$ 174.5
International Grocery Products	65.1	65.7	73.6	59.7	40.6
Total Continuing Businesses	172.3	176.4	240.6	270.0	215.1
Corporate	—	—	—	5.6	8.1
Total Consolidated	$ 172.3	$ 176.4	$ 240.6	$ 275.6	$ 223.2
Depreciation and Amortization					
U.S. and Canadian Grocery Products	$ 117.6	$ 116.6	$ 112.9	$ 97.9	$ 89.2
International Grocery Products	38.2	38.2	36.4	29.8	26.1
Total Continuing Businesses	155.8	154.8	149.3	127.7	115.3
Corporate	1.1	1.1	1.0	0.8	—
Total Consolidated	$ 156.9	$ 155.9	$ 150.3	$ 128.5	$ 115.3

(a) Corporate identifiable assets include the net assets of businesses reported as discontinued operations, corporate cash and cash equivalents, certain other current assets and miscellaneous investments and investments.

121

Notes to the Consolidated Financial Statements

Note 1
Summary of Significant Accounting Policies

Consolidation. The consolidated financial statements include The Quaker Oats Company and all of its subsidiaries ("the Company"). All significant intercompany transactions have been eliminated. Businesses acquired are included in the results of operations since their acquisition date. Fisher-Price, a toy and juvenile products business spun off to shareholders on June 28, 1991, is reflected in the accompanying fiscal 1991 consolidated financial statements as a discontinued operation (see Note 2). Certain prior year amounts have been reclassified to conform to the current presentation.

Foreign Currency Translation. Assets and liabilities of the Company's foreign affiliates, other than those located in highly inflationary countries, are translated at current exchange rates, while income and expenses are translated at average rates for the period. For entities in highly inflationary countries, a combination of current and historical rates is used to determine foreign currency gains and losses resulting from financial statement translation. Translation gains and losses are reported as a component of shareholders' equity, except for those associated with highly inflationary countries, which are reported directly in the consolidated statements of income.

Futures, Swaps, Options and Forward Contracts. The Company enters into a variety of futures, swaps, options and forward contracts in its management of foreign currency and commodity price exposures. Realized and unrealized gains and losses on foreign currency options and forward contracts are recognized currently in other income and expense. Realized and unrealized gains and losses on foreign currency options that hedge exchange rate exposure on future raw material purchases are deferred and recorded in inventory in the period in which purchases occur. Realized and unrealized gains and losses on foreign currency options, currency swaps and forward contracts that are effective as net investment hedges are recognized in a component of shareholders' equity. Realized and unrealized gains and losses on commodity futures contracts and options are deferred and recorded in inventory in the period in which purchases occur.

Cash and Cash Equivalents. Cash equivalents are composed of all highly liquid investments with an original maturity of three months or less. As a result of the Company's cash management system, checks issued but not presented to the banks for payment may create negative book cash balances. Such negative balances are included in trade accounts payable and amounted to $45.9 million, $37.6 million and $61.7 million as of June 30, 1993, 1992 and 1991, respectively.

Inventories. Inventories are valued at the lower of cost or market, using various cost methods, and include the cost of raw materials, labor and overhead. The percentage of year-end inventories valued using each of the methods was as follows:

June 30	1993	1992	1991
Last-in, first-out (LIFO)	53%	57%	61%
Average quarterly cost	35%	31%	27%
First-in, first-out (FIFO)	12%	12%	12%

If the LIFO method of valuing these inventories was not used, total inventories would have been $17.2 million, $13.9 million and $18.9 million higher than reported at June 30, 1993, 1992 and 1991, respectively.

Property and Depreciation. Property, plant and equipment are carried at cost and depreciated on a straight-line basis over their estimated useful lives. Useful lives range from 5 to 50 years for buildings and improvements and from 3 to 20 years for machinery and equipment.

Intangibles. Intangible assets consist principally of excess purchase price over net tangible assets of businesses acquired (goodwill). Goodwill is amortized on a straight-line basis over periods not exceeding 40 years. Gross goodwill as of June 30, 1993, 1992 and 1991 was $528.0 million, $522.0 million and $520.0 million, respectively. Accumulated goodwill amortization as of June 30, 1993, 1992 and 1991 was $113.3 million, $103.2 million and $86.5 million, respectively.

Software Costs. The Company defers significant software development project costs. Software costs of $5.0 million, $13.2 million, and $12.2 million were deferred during fiscal 1993, 1992 and 1991, respectively, pending the projects' completion. Amounts deferred are amortized over a three-year period beginning with a project's completion. As of June 30, 1993, $34.6 million of completed project costs were subject to amortization. Total amortization expense was $7.7 million, $2.6 million and $0.4 million in fiscal 1993, 1992 and 1991, respectively.

The Quaker Oats Company (continued)

Income Taxes. Deferred income taxes are provided when tax laws and financial accounting standards differ with respect to the amount of income for a year and the bases of assets and liabilities. Effective July 1, 1992, the Company adopted FASB Statement #109, "Accounting for Income Taxes," which requires an asset and liability approach to financial accounting and reporting for income taxes. The Company adopted the statement through a cumulative adjustment in the first quarter of fiscal 1993. See Note 17 for further discussion. Federal income taxes have been provided on $127.7 million of the $298.5 million of unremitted earnings from foreign subsidiaries. Taxes are not provided on earnings expected to be indefinitely reinvested.

Postretirement Benefits. The Company provides certain health and life insurance benefits for eligible retirees. Effective July 1, 1992, the Company adopted FASB Statement #106, "Employers' Accounting for Postretirement Benefits Other Than Pensions," whereby the cost of postretirement benefits is accrued during the years that employees render service. The Company has elected to immediately recognize the prior periods' obligation in a cumulative adjustment in the first quarter of fiscal 1993. See Note 12 for further discussion.

Note 2
Acquisitions and Discontinued Operations

In May 1993, the Company purchased the *Chico-San* rice cakes business. Pro forma operating results are not presented as they are not material. Subsequent to year-end, the Company purchased the *Near East* flavored rice business. The results of the *Near East* business will be included in the Company's consolidated results beginning in fiscal 1994.

In April 1990, the Company's Board of Directors approved in principle the distribution of Fisher-Price to the Company's shareholders. Accordingly, Fisher-Price has been reflected as a discontinued operation in the consolidated financial statements for fiscal 1991. The tax-free distribution was completed on June 28, 1991, and Fisher-Price, Inc., an independent free-standing company, was created. The distribution reduced reinvested earnings by $200.0 million and required a final cash settlement. The $29.6 million payable to Fisher-Price as of June 30, 1991, represented an estimate of the final cash settlement pursuant to the Distribution Agreement and approximated the final settlement. Each holder of Quaker common stock on July 8, 1991, received one share of Fisher-Price, Inc. common stock for every five shares of Quaker common stock held as of such date. Fisher-Price, Inc. common stock is publicly traded.

In fiscal 1991, the Company recorded a $50.0 million pretax charge ($30.0 million after-tax), or 40 cents per share, to discontinued operations. The charge related primarily to receivables credit risk exposure, product recall reserves and severance costs. Fisher-Price sales and operating loss for fiscal 1991 were $601.0 million and $35.0 million, respectively.

Note 3
Trade Accounts Receivable Allowances

Dollars in Millions

	1993	1992	1991
Balance at beginning of year	$16.6	$18.7	$16.5
Provision for doubtful accounts	5.7	7.2	5.8
Provision for discounts and allowances	13.8	13.5	15.8
Write-offs of doubtful accounts—net of recoveries	(4.4)	(5.4)	(4.6)
Discounts and allowances taken	(16.7)	(17.4)	(14.8)
Balance at end of year	$15.0	$16.6	$18.7

Note 4
Property, Plant and Equipment

Dollars in Millions

1993	Balance at Beginning of Year	Additions	Retirements and Sales	Other Changes	Balance at End of Year
Gross property:					
Land	$ 29.8	$ 0.1	$ (0.1)	$ (1.1)	$ 28.7
Buildings and improvements	448.4	21.1	(17.3)	(10.7)	441.5
Machinery and equipment	1,587.9	166.1	(95.6)	(69.4)	1,589.0
Total	$2,066.1	$187.3	$(113.0)	$(81.2)	$2,059.2
Accumulated depreciation:					
Buildings and improvements	$ 118.4	$ 12.6	$ (7.0)	$ (3.7)	$ 120.3
Machinery and equipment	674.4	118.4	(48.3)	(33.8)	710.7
Total	$ 792.8	$131.0	$ (55.3)	$(37.5)	$ 831.0

The Quaker Oats Company (continued)

Dollars in Millions

1992	Balance at Beginning of Year	Additions	Retirements and Sales	Other Changes	Balance at End of Year
Gross property:					
Land	$ 31.0	$ —	$ (2.2)	$ 1.0	$ 29.8
Buildings and improvements	427.2	20.7	(10.0)	10.5	448.4
Machinery and equipment	1,456.4	155.7	(69.8)	45.6	1,587.9
Total	$1,914.6	$176.4	$ (82.0)	$ 57.1	$2,066.1
Accumulated depreciation:					
Buildings and improvements	$ 104.1	$ 13.2	$ (2.2)	$ 3.3	$ 118.4
Machinery and equipment	577.8	119.3	(40.2)	17.5	674.4
Total	$ 681.9	$132.5	$ (42.4)	$ 20.8	$ 792.8
1991					
Gross property:					
Land	$ 31.0	$ 0.8	$ (0.2)	$ (0.6)	$ 31.0
Buildings and improvements	395.2	41.5	(4.4)	(5.1)	427.2
Machinery and equipment	1,319.4	198.3	(38.1)	(23.2)	1,456.4
Total	$1,745.6	$240.6	$ (42.7)	$ (28.9)	$1,914.6
Accumulated depreciation:					
Buildings and improvements	$ 94.1	$ 13.6	$ (1.8)	$ (1.8)	$ 104.1
Machinery and equipment	497.4	115.0	(23.0)	(11.6)	577.8
Total	$ 591.5	$128.6	$ (24.8)	$ (13.4)	$ 681.9

Included in the "Other Changes" column for fiscal 1993, 1992 and 1991 were net (decreases) increases of $(45.8) million, $31.9 million and $(18.1) million, respectively, reflecting the effect of translating non-U.S. property at current exchange rates as required by FASB Statement #52.

Note 5
Short-term Debt and Lines of Credit

Dollars in Millions

	1993	1992	1991
Notes payable—			
Non-U.S. subsidiaries	$ 35.6	$111.0	$ 67.6
Commercial paper—U.S.			
Dealer-placed on the open market	142.4	—	13.0
Short-term debt to be refinanced	(50.0)	(50.0)	—
Total short-term debt	$ 128.0	$ 61.0	$ 80.6
Weighted average interest rates on debt outstanding at end of year:			
Notes payable—non-U.S.(a)	9.0%	10.8%	12.1%
Commercial paper—U.S.	3.2%	—	5.9%
Weighted average interest rates on debt outstanding during the year:			
Notes payable—non-U.S. (computed on month-end balances)(a)	10.6%	11.5%	14.8%
Commercial paper—U.S. (computed on daily balances)	3.3%	4.0%	7.2%
Average amount of debt outstanding during the year	$121.3	$105.5	$263.5
Maximum month-end balance during the year	$178.0	$170.2	$391.4

(a) Annual interest rates in highly inflationary countries have been adjusted for currency devaluation to express interest rates in U.S. dollar terms.

The consolidated balance sheets as of June 30, 1993 and 1992, include the reclassification of $50.0 million of short-term debt to long-term debt, reflecting the Company's intent and ability to refinance this debt on a long-term basis. See Note 6 for discussion of long-term debt.

The Company has a Revolving Credit Agreement with various banks, which supports its commercial paper borrowings and is also available for direct borrowings. The Agreement, which expires no sooner than June 30, 1998, requires a commitment fee of three-sixteenths percent per annum, payable on any available and unused portion. There were no borrowings under the Agreement during fiscal 1993, 1992 or 1991. In August 1993, the Company supplemented the existing $250.0 million Agreement with an additional $100.0 million short-term credit facility. The terms of the additional facility are essentially the same as the Agreement.

The Quaker Oats Company (continued)

The Company has an Adjusted Principal Revolving Credit Agreement. Each quarter, the Company may borrow a predetermined amount up to $31.0 million. The amount borrowed may be repaid based upon an index of foreign currency rates. The Agreement is in effect through fiscal 1996 and bears interest at market rates in effect at the time of each borrowing. There were no borrowings under the Agreement during fiscal 1993.

The Company's non-U.S. subsidiaries have additional unused committed lines of credit of $32.3 million as of June 30, 1993.

Under the most restrictive terms in effect as of June 30, 1993, the Company must not exceed certain debt ratios as defined in various loan agreements.

Note 6
Long-term Debt

Dollars in Millions	1993	1992	1991
7.83% Senior ESOP Notes due through 2002	$ 85.9	$ 90.5	$ 94.5
8.07% Senior ESOP Notes due through 2002	140.3	145.0	148.2
8.75% ESOP installment loan due through 1996	7.9	10.2	12.2
7.4%-7.9% Series A Medium-term Notes due through 2000	86.8	101.7	119.6
5.415% and 6.63% deutsche mark swaps due 1993 and 1998, respectively	16.3	30.4	25.6
8.15%-9.34% Series B Medium-term Notes due through 2020	248.0	250.0	250.0
Industrial Revenue Bonds:			
6.0%-11.5% due through 2010, tax-exempt	35.6	35.6	39.0
4.5%-8.375% due through 2003, taxable	0.9	6.7	7.1
Sinking Fund Debentures:			
7.7% due through 2001	—	14.0	16.1
8.0% due through 1999	—	—	8.4
Non-interest bearing installment note due 2014	4.0	3.5	3.1
Short-term debt to be refinanced	50.0	50.0	—
Other	5.8	9.0	10.3
	$ 681.5	$ 746.6	$ 734.1
Less: Current portion	48.9	57.9	32.9
Long-term Debt	$ 632.6	$ 688.7	$ 701.2

All amounts are presented in tabled units.

Aggregate required payments of maturities of long-term debt for the next five fiscal years are as follows:

Dollars in Millions	1994	1995	1996	1997	1998
Required payments	$ 48.9	$ 45.3	$ 37.2	$ 54.0	$ 67.4

In September 1992, the Company redeemed the 7.7 percent sinking fund debentures, and in April 1992, the Company redeemed the 8.0 percent sinking fund debentures, which were an obligation of Stokely-Van Camp Inc., a wholly owned subsidiary of the Company.

In January 1990, the Company filed a shelf registration with the Securities and Exchange Commission covering $600.0 million worth of debt securities. No securities have been issued under the registration statement as of June 30, 1993. Subsequent to year-end, the Company filed a prospectus supplement for the intended issuance of $200.0 million of medium-term notes under the shelf registration. The proceeds of the medium-term notes may be used to refinance debt, repurchase outstanding common stock and for other general corporate purposes.

In fiscal 1989, The Quaker Employee Stock Ownership Plan (ESOP) issued $250.0 million of Senior ESOP Notes. The proceeds from these notes were used to purchase the Company's common and preferred stock. Both issues of Senior ESOP Notes are unconditionally guaranteed by the Company.

The non-interest bearing installment note for $55.5 million has an unamortized discount of $51.5 million, $52.0 million and $52.4 million as of June 30, 1993, 1992 and 1991, respectively, based on an imputed interest rate of 13 percent.

Note 7
Capital Stock

During the first six months of fiscal 1993, 1.75 million shares of the Company's outstanding common stock were repurchased for $107.0 million, completing a two million share repurchase program announced in April 1992. In January 1993, the Company announced a program to repurchase three million shares of its outstanding common stock and completed this program by June 30, 1993, for $216.1 million. Subsequent to year-end, the Company announced its intent to repurchase, from time to time, up to five million shares of its outstanding common stock through open market purchases and privately negotiated transactions.

The Company is authorized to issue one million shares of redeemable preference stock, none of which had been issued as of June 30, 1993. The Company is also authorized to issue 10 million shares of preferred stock in series, with terms fixed by resolution of the Board of Directors. One million shares of Series A Junior Participating Preferred Stock have been reserved for issuance in connection with the Shareholder Rights Plan (see Note 10). In fiscal 1989, 1,750,000 shares of Series B ESOP Convertible Preferred Stock were designated in connection with the Company's ESOP plan. As of June 30, 1993, 1,282,051 shares of the ESOP preferred stock had been issued and are each convertible into 1.0788 shares of the Company's common stock. The ESOP preferred stock will be issued only for the ESOP and will not trade on the open market.

The Dividend Reinvestment and Stock Purchase Plan exists for eligible employees and shareholders. The Plan allows for the use of open market, unissued or treasury shares. The shares used in fiscal 1993, 1992 and 1991 were open market shares.

Note 8
Deferred Compensation

The ESOP was established to issue debt and to use the proceeds of such debt to acquire shares of the Company's stock for future allocation to ESOP participants. The ESOP borrowings are included as long-term debt on the Company's consolidated balance sheets. See Note 6 for a further description of the ESOP notes.

Deferred compensation of $239.9 million as of June 30, 1993, primarily represents the Company's payment of future compensation expense related to the ESOP. As the Company makes annual contributions to the ESOP, these contributions, along with the dividends accumulated on the common and preferred stock held by the ESOP, are used to repay the outstanding loans. As the loans are repaid, common and preferred stock are allocated to ESOP participants, and deferred compensation is reduced by the amount of the principal payment on the loans.

The following table presents the ESOP loan repayments:

Dollars in Millions	1993	1992	1991
Principal payments	$ 11.6	$ 9.3	$ 7.4
Interest payments	19.4	20.2	20.9
Total ESOP payments	$ 31.0	$ 29.5	$ 28.3

As of June 30, 1993, 1,517,705 shares of common stock and 335,337 shares of preferred stock were held in the accounts of ESOP participants.

Note 9
Employee Stock Option and Award Plans

In fiscal 1990, the Company's shareholders approved the adoption of The Quaker Long-Term Incentive Plan of 1990 ("the Plan"). The purpose of the Plan is to promote the interests of the Company and its shareholders by providing the officers and other key employees with additional incentive and the opportunity through stock ownership to increase their proprietary interest in the Company and their personal interest in its continued success. The Plan provides for benefits to be awarded in a variety of ways, with stock options being used most frequently. Nine million shares of common stock have been authorized for grant under the Plan. Previously, stock options were issued under the 1984 Long-Term Incentive Plan, which expired by its terms on December 31, 1990. Officers and other key employees may be granted options for the purchase of common stock at a price not less than the fair market value at date of grant. Portions of the option awards have been granted at exercise prices that are higher than the fair market value at the date of grant. Options are generally exercisable after one or more years and expire no later than 10 years from date of grant. As of June 30, 1993, 665 persons held such options. Changes in stock options outstanding are summarized as follows:

	Shares	Option Price (Per Share)
Balance as of June 30, 1990	3,455,237	$ 7.08-57.00
Granted	781,100	49.50
Exercised	(600,065)	7.08-57.00
Expired or terminated	(210,554)	28.69-57.00
Balance as of June 30, 1991	3,425,718	$ 8.30-57.00
Adjustment due to Fisher-Price spin-off	293,241	—
Granted	1,492,792	70.69-88.36
Exercised	(564,540)	7.64-52.50
Expired or terminated	(89,683)	7.64-88.36
Balance as of June 30, 1992	4,557,528	$ 9.83-88.36
Granted	1,602,646	63.56-79.45
Exercised	(780,724)	9.83-70.69
Expired or terminated	(83,303)	9.83-88.36
Balance as of June 30, 1993	5,296,147	$ 14.03-88.36

The Quaker Oats Company (continued)

As of June 30, 1993, options for 2,770,578 shares were exercisable and the average per share option price of unexercised options expiring during the period January 1994 to September 2002 was $61.43.

In July 1991, the number and exercise price of all options outstanding at the time of the Fisher-Price spin-off (see Note 2) were adjusted to compensate for decreases in the economic value of the options as a result of the distribution to shareholders. This adjustment increased the number of options outstanding by 293,241 and decreased the exercise price of the options outstanding by approximately 8 percent.

Under the Plan, restricted stock awards grant shares of the Company's common stock to key officers and employees. These shares are subject to a restriction period from the date of grant, during which they may not be sold, assigned, pledged or otherwise encumbered. The number of shares of the Company's common stock awarded were 70,800, 24,000 and 172,700 in fiscal 1993, 1992 and 1991, respectively. Restrictions on these awards lapse after a period of time designated by the Compensation Committee of the Board of Directors.

Note 10
Shareholder Rights Plan

The Company's Shareholder Rights Plan, adopted July 9, 1986 and amended July 12, 1989, is designed to deter coercive or unfair takeover tactics and to prevent a person or group from gaining control of the Company without offering a fair price to all shareholders.

Under the terms of the Plan, all common shareholders of record on July 30, 1986, received for each share owned one "Right" entitling them to purchase from the Company one one-hundredth of a share of Series A Junior Participating Preferred Stock at an exercise price of $300.

The Rights become exercisable (1) 10 days after a public announcement that a person or group has acquired shares representing 20 percent or more of the voting power of the Company's capital stock, (2) 10 business days following commencement of a tender offer for more than 20 percent of such voting power, or (3) 10 business days after a holder of at least 15 percent of such voting power is determined to be an adverse person by the Board of Directors. The time periods can be extended by the Company.

Unless the Board of Directors has made a determination that any person is an adverse person, the Company can redeem the Rights for $.05 per Right at any time prior to their becoming exercisable. The Rights will expire on July 30, 1996, unless redeemed earlier by the Company.

If after the Rights become exercisable the Company is involved in a merger or other business combination at any time when there is a holder of 20 percent or more of the Company's stock, the Rights will then entitle a holder, upon exercise of the Rights, to receive shares of common stock of the acquiring company with a market value equal to twice the exercise price of each Right. Alternatively, if a 20 percent holder acquires the Company by means of a reverse merger in which the Company and its stock survive, or if any person acquires 20 percent or more of the Company's voting power or acquires 15 percent of the Company's voting power and is determined by the Board of Directors to be an adverse person, each Right not owned by such 20 percent shareholder or adverse person would, upon exercise of the Right, entitle the holder to common stock of the Company (or in certain circumstances other consideration) having a market value equal to twice the exercise price of the Right. The Rights described in this paragraph shall not apply to an acquisition, merger or consolidation which is determined by a majority of the Company's independent directors, after consulting one or more investment banking firms, to be fair and otherwise in the best interest of the Company and its shareholders.

Note 11
Pension Plans and Other Postemployment Benefits

The Company has various pension plans covering substantially all of its domestic and certain foreign employees. Plan benefits are based on compensation paid to employees and their years of service. Company policy is to make contributions to its U.S. plans within the maximum amount deductible for Federal income tax purposes. Plan assets consist primarily of equity securities and government, corporate and other fixed-income obligations.

The Quaker Oats Company (continued)

The components of net pension cost for defined plans are detailed below:

Dollars in Millions	1993	1992	1991
Service cost (benefits earned during the year)	$41.5	$35.6	$28.5
Interest cost on projected benefit obligation	51.9	46.6	39.7
Actual return on plan assets	(64.8)	(65.3)	(70.5)
Net amortization and deferral	(8.5)	(5.8)	9.8
Subtotal	20.1	11.1	7.5
Multi-employer plans	0.2	0.4	0.7
Foreign plans	—	—	3.2
Net pension cost	$20.3	$11.5	$11.4

Reconciliations of the funded status of the Company's defined benefit plans to the prepaid (accrued) pension costs included in the consolidated balance sheets were as follows:

Dollars in Millions	Overfunded 1993	1992	1991	Underfunded 1993	1992	1991
Vested benefits	$549.3	$438.6	$363.6	$66.0	$71.0	$43.6
Non-vested benefits	10.1	8.5	8.1	4.7	1.2	0.2
Accumulated benefit obligation	559.4	447.1	371.7	70.7	72.2	43.8
Effect of projected future salary increases	80.8	64.5	54.2	12.3	11.1	5.4
Projected benefit obligation	640.2	511.6	425.9	83.0	83.3	49.2
Plan assets at market value	750.5	669.2	588.2	23.3	31.9	28.0
Projected benefit obligation less (greater) than plan assets	110.3	157.6	162.3	(59.7)	(51.4)	(21.2)
Unrecognized net (gain)	(46.2)	(90.5)	(81.3)	(4.4)	(11.3)	(14.1)
Unrecognized prior service cost	11.2	10.8	10.4	6.4	10.3	5.6
Unrecognized net (asset) liability at transition	(66.4)	(59.8)	(83.8)	4.0	4.7	5.6
Prepaid (accrued) pension costs	$ 8.9	$ 18.1	$ 7.6	$(53.7)	$(47.7)	$(24.1)

Assumptions:
Weighted average discount rate: 8%
Rate of future compensation increases: 5%
Long-term rate of return on plan assets: 8.5%

Beginning in fiscal 1992, disclosures required by FASB Statement #87 are presented for foreign pension plans and include unfunded termination indemnity reserves of $14.1 million and $17.8 million as of June 30, 1993 and 1992, respectively.

In November 1992, the FASB issued Statement #112, "Employers' Accounting for Postemployment Benefits." The Company has not yet adopted this statement, which must be implemented no later than fiscal 1995. The Company is currently determining the impact, if any, this statement will have on its financial position.

Note 12
Postretirement Benefits

The Company has various postretirement health care plans covering substantially all domestic employees and certain foreign employees. The plans provide for the payment of certain health care and life insurance benefits for retired employees who meet service-related eligibility requirements. The Company funds only the plans' annual cash requirements.

Effective July 1, 1992, the Company adopted FASB Statement #106, "Employers' Accounting for Postretirement Benefits Other Than Pensions." This statement requires that the expected cost of these benefits be charged to expense during the years that the employees render service. This is a significant change from the Company's previous policy of recognizing these costs on a cash basis. The statement was adopted through a cumulative pretax charge of $205.5 million, or $125.4 million after-tax, which represents the accumulated postretirement benefit obligation for years prior to fiscal 1993. The incremental effect on fiscal 1993 results of adopting FASB Statement #106 was a pretax charge of $14.8 million. Cash expenditures are not affected by this accounting change.

The components of postretirement benefit costs for fiscal 1993 were as follows:

Dollars in Millions	1993
Service cost (benefits earned during the year)	$ 6.2
Interest cost on projected benefit obligation	18.3
Total postretirement benefit costs	$24.5

The Quaker Oats Company (continued)

The Company's unfunded accumulated postretirement benefit obligation as of June 30, 1993, included in the consolidated balance sheet, was as follows:

Dollars in Millions

	1993
Current retirees	$122.5
Current active employees—fully eligible	12.0
Current active employees—not fully eligible	100.0
Subtotal	234.5
Unrecognized net loss	(11.1)
Accrued postretirement benefit costs	$223.4

Assumptions:		
Weighted average discount rate: 8%		
Health care trend rates (varies by plan):	1994	2004 and Beyond
Pre-age 65:	11-15%	4-6%
Age 65 and over:	11-15%	5-6%

If the health care trend rates were increased one percentage point, the current-year postretirement benefit costs would have been $4.1 million higher and the accumulated benefit obligation as of June 30, 1993, would have been $31.7 million higher.

Postretirement benefit costs incurred and expensed in fiscal 1992 and 1991 amounted to $9.2 million and $7.4 million, respectively.

Note 13
Lease and Other Commitments

Certain equipment and operating properties are rented under non-cancelable operating leases that expire at various dates through 2002. Total rental expense under operating leases was $34.3 million, $41.0 million and $44.5 million in fiscal 1993, 1992 and 1991, respectively. Contingent rentals and subleases are not significant. Capital leases, which are included in fixed assets, and minimum lease payments under such leases are not significant.

The following is a schedule of future minimum annual rentals on non-cancelable operating leases, primarily for sales offices, warehouses and corporate headquarters, in effect as of June 30, 1993:

Dollars in Millions

	1994	1995	1996	1997	1998	Later	Total
Total payments	$26.2	$21.6	$19.6	$19.4	$18.7	$40.6	$148.1

The Company enters into executory contracts to promote various products. As of June 30, 1993, future commitments under these contracts amounted to $88.0 million.

Note 14
Supplementary Expense Data

Dollars in Millions

	1993	1992	1991
Advertising, media and production	$ 282.0	$ 288.8	$ 277.5
Merchandising	1,193.0	1,160.8	1,129.9
Total advertising and merchandising	$1,475.0	$1,449.6	$1,407.4
Maintenance and repairs	$ 105.6	$ 96.2	$ 96.1
Depreciation expense	$ 129.9	$ 129.7	$ 125.2
Research and development	$ 52.4	$ 52.1	$ 44.3

Note 15
Interest Expense

Dollars in Millions

	1993	1992	1991
Interest expense	$66.1	$78.5	$103.8
Interest expense capitalized—net	(0.5)	(1.5)	(1.9)
Subtotal	65.6	77.0	101.9
Interest income	(10.5)	(9.6)	(9.0)
Net interest allocated to discontinued operations	—	—	(6.7)
Interest expense—net	$55.1	$67.4	$ 86.2

Interest paid in fiscal 1993, 1992 and 1991 was $74.3 million, $74.7 million and $101.7 million, respectively. Fiscal 1991 interest paid includes amounts related to Fisher-Price.

Note 16
Other Expense

Dollars in Millions

	1993	1992	1991
Foreign exchange loss (gain)—net	$15.1	$13.1	$ (5.1)
Amortization of intangibles	26.3	23.6	22.4
Gains on divestitures, restructuring charges and asset write-offs—net	28.2	7.1	8.8
Miscellaneous	0.5	13.0	6.5
Other expense—net	$70.1	$56.8	$32.6

The Quaker Oats Company (continued)

Note 17
Income Taxes

Effective July 1, 1992, the Company adopted FASB Statement #109, "Accounting for Income Taxes," which requires an asset and liability approach to financial accounting and reporting for income taxes. The cumulative effect of adopting FASB Statement #109 was to increase income by $9.9 million.

Provisions for income taxes applicable to continuing operations were as follows:

Dollars in Millions	1993	1992	1991
Currently payable—			
Federal	$129.2	$109.9	$103.0
Non-U.S.	25.0	23.8	36.6
State	29.7	24.1	21.8
Total currently payable	183.9	157.8	161.4
Deferred—net			
Federal	(6.7)	8.2	6.7
Non-U.S.	2.7	5.6	4.1
State	0.9	2.3	3.5
Total deferred—net	(3.1)	16.1	14.3
Provision for income taxes	$180.8	$173.9	$175.7

The components of the deferred income tax provision were as follows:

Dollars in Millions	1993	1992	1991
Accelerated tax depreciation	$15.0	$ 9.3	$ 8.4
Postretirement benefits	(5.8)	—	—
Accrued expenses	(8.6)	—	—
Receipt of tax benefits	(0.9)	(1.9)	(1.3)
Other—net	(2.8)	8.7	7.2
(Benefit) Provision for deferred income taxes	$ (3.1)	$16.1	$14.3

The sources of pretax income from continuing operations were as follows:

Dollars in Millions	1993	1992	1991
U.S. sources	$389.3	$346.2	$328.7
Non-U.S. sources	78.3	75.3	82.8
Income from continuing operations before income taxes and cumulative effect of accounting changes	$467.6	$421.5	$411.5

A reconciliation of the statutory Federal income tax rate to the effective income tax rate was as follows:

Dollars in Millions	1993 Amount	1993 % of Pretax Income	1992 Amount	1992 % of Pretax Income	1991 Amount	1991 % of Pretax Income
Tax provision based on the Federal statutory rate	$159.0	34.0%	$143.3	34.0%	$139.9	34.0%
State and local income taxes—net of Federal income tax benefit	19.7	4.2	17.8	4.2	16.7	4.1
Repatriation of foreign earnings	(2.4)	(0.5)	(2.9)	(0.7)	4.3	1.0
Non-U.S. tax rate differential	1.7	0.4	6.7	1.6	8.2	2.0
Miscellaneous items—net	2.8	0.6	9.0	2.2	6.6	1.6
Provision for income taxes	$180.8	38.7%	$173.9	41.3%	$175.7	42.7%

The consolidated balance sheet as of June 30, 1993, included the following deferred tax assets and deferred tax liabilities:

Dollars in Millions	1993 Deferred Tax Assets	1993 Deferred Tax Liabilities
Depreciation and amortization	$ —	$196.5
Postretirement benefits	85.9	—
Other benefit plans	42.0	13.5
Accrued expenses	59.1	4.1
Loss carryforwards	20.8	—
Other	21.8	34.6
Subtotal	229.6	248.7
Valuation allowance	(18.1)	—
Total	$211.5	$248.7

The Quaker Oats Company (continued)

As of June 30, 1993, the Company had $58.5 million of operating and capital loss carryforwards available to reduce future taxable income of certain international subsidiaries. These loss carryforwards must be utilized within the carryforward periods of these international jurisdictions. The majority of loss carryforwards have no expiration restrictions. Those with restrictions expire primarily in five years. A valuation allowance has been provided for a portion of the deferred tax assets related to these loss carryforwards.

Total income tax provisions (benefits) were allocated as follows:

Dollars in Millions	1993
Continuing operations	$ 180.8
Cumulative effect of accounting changes	$ (90.0)
Items charged directly to common shareholders' equity	$ 2.6

Income taxes paid in fiscal 1993, 1992 and 1991 were $213.3 million, $182.1 million and $88.7 million, respectively. Fiscal 1991 income taxes paid include amounts related to Fisher-Price.

Note 18
Financial Instruments

Foreign Currency Forward Contracts. As of June 30, 1993, the Company had forward contracts for the purchase and sale of European, Canadian and other currencies, with purchases totaling $2.3 million and sales totaling $237.4 million. These contracts hedge balance sheet and operating income currency exposures. While the contracts generally mature in less than 12 months, total sales include obligations to sell $8.2 million in British pounds in fiscal 1998.

Deutsche Mark Swap. In fiscal 1988, the Company swapped $25.0 million for deutsche marks in two separate transactions. In August 1992, the Company repaid 18.5 million deutsche marks for $12.6 million. The Company is required to exchange 27.9 million deutsche marks for $15.0 million in August 1997 and to make semi-annual interest payments of 0.9 million deutsche marks through August 1997.

The estimated fair values of the Company's financial instruments as of June 30, 1993, were as follows:

Dollars in Millions	1993
Cash and cash equivalents	$ 61.0
Short-term debt	$(176.9)
Long-term debt	$(730.7)
Foreign currency contracts	$ 5.9
Commodity futures contracts	$ (1.0)

The following methods and assumptions were used to estimate the fair value of each class of financial instruments:

Cash and Cash Equivalents. The carrying amounts approximate fair value because of the short-term maturity of the instruments.

Short-term Debt. The carrying amounts approximate fair value because of the short-term maturity of the instruments.

Long-term Debt. Fair-value estimates were based on market prices for the same or similar issues or on the current rates offered to the Company for similar debt of the same maturities.

Foreign Currency Contracts. Fair-value estimates were based on quotes from financial institutions.

Commodity Futures Contracts. Fair-value estimates were based on quotes from brokers.

The Quaker Oats Company (continued)

Note 19
Litigation

On December 18, 1990, Judge Prentice H. Marshall of the United States District Court for the Northern District of Illinois issued a memorandum opinion stating that the Court would enter judgment against the Company in favor of Sands, Taylor & Wood Co. The Court found that the use of the words "thirst aid" in advertising *Gatorade* thirst quencher infringed the Plaintiff's rights in the trademark THIRST-AID. On July 9, 1991, Judge Marshall entered a judgment of $42.6 million, composed of $31.4 million in principal, plus prejudgment interest of $10.6 million and fees, expenses and costs of $0.6 million. The order enjoined use of the phrase "THIRST-AID" in connection with the advertising or sale of *Gatorade* thirst quencher in the United States. The Company and its subsidiary, Stokely-Van Camp, Inc., ceased use of the words "thirst aid" in December 1990. The Company subsequently appealed the judgment. On September 2, 1992, the Court of Appeals for the Seventh Circuit vacated the District Court's judgment. The appellate court affirmed the finding of infringement, but found that the monetary award was an inequitable "windfall" to the Plaintiff. The case was remanded to the District Court for further proceedings. The Company filed a request for rehearing that was denied. The Company also filed a Petition for Certiorari with the U.S. Supreme Court that was denied. On June 7, 1993, Judge Marshall issued a judgment on remand of $26.5 million, composed of $20.7 million in principal, prejudgment interest of $5.4 million and fees, expenses and costs of $0.4 million. The Company has filed a Notice of Appeal with respect to this judgment. Management, with advice from outside legal counsel, has determined that the amount of liability that might ultimately exist in this case will not be material.

The Company is not a party to any pending legal proceedings that it believes will have a material adverse effect on its financial position or results of operations.

Note 20
Quarterly Financial Data (Unaudited)

Dollars in Millions (Except Per Share Data)

1993	First Quarter(a)(b)	Second Quarter(a)(c)	Third Quarter(a)(d)	Fourth Quarter
Net sales	$1,494.2	$1,332.7	$1,358.1	$1,545.6
Cost of goods sold	740.5	677.5	667.7	772.7
Gross profit	$ 753.7	$ 655.2	$ 690.4	$ 772.9
Income before cumulative effect of accounting changes	$ 60.2	$ 56.2	$ 77.0	$ 93.4
Net income	$ (55.3)	$ 56.2	$ 77.0	$ 93.4
Per common share:				
Income before cumulative effect of accounting changes	$ 0.81	$ 0.77	$ 1.05	$ 1.30
Net income	$ (0.78)	$ 0.77	$ 1.05	$ 1.30
Cash dividends declared	$ 0.48	$ 0.48	$ 0.48	$ 0.48
Market price range:				
High	$ 65	$ 71	$ 70	$ 77
Low	$ 56¼	$ 60¼	$ 62¾	$ 60¾

(a)Quarterly information for the first three quarters of fiscal 1993 have been restated for the adoption, retroactive to July 1, 1992, of FASB Statements #106 and #109. Income before cumulative effect of accounting changes for the first and second quarters has been reduced by $2.3 million or $.03 per share and for the third quarter by $2.2 million or $.03 per share for the fiscal 1993 after-tax incremental charge for FASB Statement #106. Net income in the first quarter was reduced by $115.5 million or $1.59 per share for the after-tax cumulative effect of adopting both FASB Statements #106 and #109.

(b)Includes a $55.6 million pretax charge ($26.9 million after-tax or $.37 per share) for the consolidation of production facilities at pet foods plant.

(c)Includes a $17.4 million pretax gain ($10.5 million after-tax or $.14 per share) for the sale of two Italian businesses and a $9.7 million pretax charge ($5.9 million after-tax or $.08 per share) for European cost reduction programs.

(d)Includes a $16.4 million pretax gain ($8.8 million after-tax or $.11 per share) for the sale of a business in the United Kingdom.

Note 20
(Continued)

Dollars in Millions (Except Per Share Data)

1992	First Quarter (a)	Second Quarter (a)	Third Quarter (b)	Fourth Quarter (a)(c)
Net sales	$ 1,355.8	$ 1,342.8	$ 1,335.2	$ 1,542.6
Cost of goods sold	694.0	691.5	674.6	757.6
Gross profit	$ 661.8	$ 651.3	$ 660.6	$ 785.0
Net income	$ 42.4	$ 44.7	$ 56.6	$ 103.9
Per common share:				
Net income	$ 0.54	$ 0.58	$ 0.75	$ 1.38
Cash dividends declared	$ 0.43	$ 0.43	$ 0.43	$ 0.43
Market price range:				
High	$ 66 ½	$ 75 ¼	$ 74 ⅛	$ 57 ⅞
Low	$ 55 ⅛	$ 55 ⅞	$ 54 ½	$ 50 ¼

(a) Includes an $8.5 million pretax charge ($5.3 million after-tax or $.07 per share) during the first quarter and an additional $3.8 million pretax charge ($2.4 million after-tax or $.03 per share) during the second quarter for a recall of certain Van Camp's and Wolf Brand products. Fourth-quarter results include a $7.5 million pretax ($4.7 million after-tax or $.06 per share) downward adjustment to the reserves.
(b) Includes an $11.0 million pretax gain ($6.8 million after-tax or $.09 per share) for the sale of the Ghirardelli chocolate business, largely offset by $10.0 million in pretax restructuring charges ($6.2 million after-tax or $.08 per share).
(c) Includes a $5.5 million credit ($3.4 million after-tax or $.05 per share) for LIFO and other favorable inventory variances that were not projected in the prior fiscal 1992 quarters.

Report of Independent Public Accountants

To the Shareholders of The Quaker Oats Company:

We have audited the accompanying consolidated balance sheets of The Quaker Oats Company (a New Jersey corporation) and subsidiaries as of June 30, 1993, 1992 and 1991, and the related consolidated statements of income, common shareholders' equity and cash flows for the years then ended. These financial statements are the responsibility of the Company's management. Our responsibility is to express an opinion on these financial statements based on our audits.

We conducted our audits in accordance with generally accepted auditing standards. Those standards require that we plan and perform the audit to obtain reasonable assurance about whether the financial statements are free of material misstatement. An audit includes examining, on a test basis, evidence supporting the amounts and disclosures in the financial statements. An audit also includes assessing the accounting principles used and significant estimates made by management, as well as evaluating the overall financial statement presentation. We believe that our audits provide a reasonable basis for our opinion.

In our opinion, the financial statements referred to above present fairly, in all material respects, the financial position of The Quaker Oats Company and subsidiaries as of June 30, 1993, 1992 and 1991, and the results of their operations and their cash flows for the years then ended in conformity with generally accepted accounting principles.

As indicated in Note 12 and Note 17, the Company changed their accounting for postretirement benefits other than pensions and income taxes.

Arthur Andersen & Co.

Chicago, Illinois
August 3, 1993

Report of Management

Management is responsible for the preparation and integrity of the Company's financial statements. The financial statements have been prepared in accordance with generally accepted accounting principles and necessarily include some amounts that are based on management's estimates and judgment.

To fulfill its responsibility, management maintains a strong system of internal accounting controls, supported by formal policies and procedures that are communicated throughout the Company. Management also maintains a staff of internal auditors who evaluate the adequacy of and investigate the adherence to these controls, policies and procedures.

Our independent public accountants, Arthur Andersen & Co., have audited the financial statements and have rendered an opinion as to the statements' fairness in all material respects. During the audit, they obtain an understanding of the Company's internal control systems and perform tests and other procedures to the extent required by generally accepted auditing standards.

The Board of Directors pursues its oversight role with respect to the Company's financial statements through the Audit Committee, which is composed solely of non-management directors. The Committee meets periodically with the independent public accountants, internal auditors and management to assure that all are properly discharging their responsibilities. The Committee approves the scope of the annual audit and reviews the recommendations the independent public accountants have for improving internal accounting controls. The Board of Directors, on recommendation of the Audit Committee, engages the independent public accountants, subject to shareholder approval.

Both Arthur Andersen & Co. and the internal auditors have unrestricted access to the Audit Committee.

Additional 10-K Information

Description of Property

As of June 30, 1993, the Company operated 56 manufacturing plants in 16 states and 12 foreign countries and owned or leased distribution centers, warehouses and sales offices in 21 states and 17 foreign countries. The number of locations utilized by each segment of the business was as follows:

Geographic Segment	Owned Mfg. Locations U.S.	Foreign	Owned and Leased Distribution Centers U.S.	Foreign	Leased Sales Offices U.S.	Foreign
U.S. and Canadian Grocery Products	29	3	20	1	40	5
International Grocery Products	—	24	—	24	—	25
Total	29	27	20	25	40	30

The Company owns a research and development laboratory in Barrington, Illinois, and a pet food nutrition facility in Lake County, Illinois. The corporate offices are maintained in leased space in downtown Chicago, Illinois. Management believes manufacturing, warehouse and office space owned and leased are suitable and adequate for the business and productive capacity is appropriately utilized.

The Quaker Oats Company (concluded)

Additional 10-K Information

Trademarks

The Company and its subsidiaries own a number of trademarks and is not aware of any circumstances that could affect its continued use of these trademarks. Among the most important of the domestic grocery product trademarks owned by the Company are *Quaker*, *Cap'n Crunch*, *Quaker 100% Natural*, *Quaker Oat Squares* and *Life* for breakfast cereals; *Gatorade* for thirst-quenching beverages; *Quaker*, *Chico-San* and *Quaker Chewy* for rice and grain-based snacks; *Van Camp's* for canned bean products; *Ken-L Ration*, *Kibbles'n Bits'n Bits'n Bits*, *Gravy Train*, *Cycle* and *Gaines* for dog foods; *Puss'n Boots* and *Pounce* for cat foods; *Rice-A-Roni* for value-added rice; *Noodle Roni* for value-added pasta; *Golden Grain* and *Mission* for pasta; *Quaker* and *Aunt Jemima* for mixes, syrups and corn goods; *Aunt Jemima* and *Celeste* for frozen foods; *Wolf* for chili, hot dog sauce, tamales and beef stew; *Ardmore Farms* for citrus and fruit juices; *Continental* and *Continental WB* for coffee; *Mrs. Richardson's* for ice cream toppings; and *Pritikin* for numerous food products and services. Many of the grocery product trademarks owned by the Company in the United States are registered in foreign countries in which the Company does substantial business. Internationally, the key trademarks owned include *Cruesli* and *Sugar Puffs* for breakfast cereals; *Cuore* for edible oils; *Felix* and *Miauu* for cat foods; *Fido* and *Bonzo* for dog foods; *Coquerro* for fish; *Toddy* and *ToddYnho* for chocolate beverages; and *Carlos V* and *Larin* for chocolate candy.

U.S. and Canadian Grocery Products Description

The Company is a major participant in the competitive packaged food industry in the United States and is the leading manufacturer of hot cereals, pancake mixes, grain-based snacks, cornmeal, hominy grits, value-added rice products and canned pork and beans. In addition, the Company is the second-largest manufacturer of dog food, syrups and value-added pasta products and is among the five largest manufacturers of ready-to-eat cereals and dry pasta products. The Company also purchased by consumers through a wide range of food distributors. The Company maintains full-time sales forces and has distribution centers throughout the country, each of which carries an inventory of most of the Company's grocery products.

In addition, the Company markets a line of over 400 items for the food service market, including *Quaker* hot and ready-to-eat cereals; *Wolf* Brand chili; *Aunt Jemima* frozen breakfast products and mixes; *Continental* coffee; *Ardmore Farms* single-serve frozen fruit juices; *Gatorade* thirst quencher; a specialty line of custom-blended dry baking mixes; ready-to-bake biscuits; *Burry* cookies and crackers; and *Mrs. Richardson's* syrups, ice cream toppings and condiments.

International Grocery Products Description

The Company is broadly diversified, both geographically and by product line, and participates in the human foods and pet foods markets. The Company manufactures and markets its products in Argentina, Brazil, Canada, Colombia, France, Germany, Italy, Mexico, the Netherlands, the United Kingdom and Venezuela. The Company also markets products in many countries throughout the world and is the leading hot cereals producer in many countries and has other leading market positions for products in a number of countries, including the following: the leading producer of edible seed oils in Italy; the leading producer of chocolate candy and chocolate beverages in Brazil; the leading canned fish processor in Brazil; the leading honey company in Mexico; the leading canned fish processor in Brazil; the leading honey company in the Netherlands and the second-largest pet food company in continental Europe.

Raw Materials

The raw materials used in manufacturing include oats, wheat, soy products, corn, rice, sweeteners, orange juice concentrate, almonds, coffee beans, raisins, beef, chicken, corn oil, cocoa beans, shortening, meat by-products, dry beans and fish, as well as a variety of packaging materials. While most of these products are purchased on the open market, the Company purchases commodity futures contracts, when considered appropriate, in order to assure supply at predictable prices. This practice has tended to limit the impact of volatile commodity costs. Energy availability is important in maintaining production, and costs have been stable. Supplies of all raw materials have been adequate and continuous.

Champion International Corporation Statements of Cash Flows

In Thousands of Dollars Years Ended December 31	1993	1992	1991
Cash flows from operating activities			
Net income (loss)	$(156,243)	$ (440,394)	$ 40,343
Adjustments to reconcile net income (loss) to			
net cash provided by operating activities			
Extraordinary item	14,266	—	—
Cumulative effect of accounting changes	7,523	454,314	—
Depreciation expense	360,240	338,004	282,310
Cost of timber harvested	83,194	72,496	59,261
Gain on sale of assets	(9,973)	(103,778)	(92,705)
Deferrals of pre-operating and start-up costs	(18,819)	(16,999)	(42,340)
(Increase) decrease in receivables	(28,235)	(11,274)	18,514
(Increase) in inventories	(13,529)	(4,830)	(1,194)
(Increase) decrease in prepaid expenses	(2,789)	5,091	5,502
(Decrease) in accounts payable			
and accrued liabilities	(61,296)	(10,263)	(887)
(Decrease) increase in income taxes payable	(3,032)	(1,517)	1,895
Increase (decrease) in other liabilities	21,164	(2,027)	(2,252)
(Decrease) increase in deferred income taxes	(26,843)	(11,904)	17,197
All other — net	35,167	(9,144)	84,068
Net cash provided by operating activities	200,795	257,775	369,712
Cash flows from investing activities			
Expenditures for property, plant and			
equipment	(475,633)	(622,976)	(603,668)
Timber and timberlands expenditures	(130,147)	(95,313)	(57,801)
Purchase of investments	(123,978)	(203,424)	(59,627)
Proceeds from redemption of investments	230,561	145,461	43,457
Proceeds from sales of property, plant and			
equipment and timber and timberlands	304,773	174,417	130,328
All other — net	(17,448)	(9,096)	49,578
Net cash used in investing activities	(211,872)	(610,931)	(497,733)
Cash flows from financing activities			
Proceeds from issuance of long-term debt	1,382,715	770,052	1,247,611
Payments of current installments of			
long-term debt and long-term debt	(1,307,909)	(439,646)	(991,320)
Cash dividends paid	(46,334)	(46,326)	(67,273)
All other — net	1,580	(6,942)	(7,281)
Net cash provided by financing activities	30,052	277,138	181,737
Increase (decrease) in cash and cash			
equivalents	18,975	(76,018)	53,716
Cash and cash equivalents			
Beginning of period	36,678	112,696	58,980
End of period	$ 55,653	$ 36,678	$ 112,696
Supplemental cash flow disclosures			
Cash paid during the year for			
Interest (net of capitalized amounts)	$ 225,764	$ 201,925	$ 196,463
Income taxes (net of refunds) (Note 11)	11,867	15,181	(6,075)

The accompanying notes are an integral part of this statement.

American Stores Company Statements of Cash Flows

(In thousands of dollars)	1993	1992[1]	1991[1]
Cash flows from operating activities:			
Net earnings	$247,090	$207,466	$199,282
Adjustments to reconcile net earnings			
to net cash provided by operating activities:			
Cumulative effect of a change in accounting principle			67,890
Depreciation and amortization	384,307	370,439	386,916
Net loss (gain) on asset sales	16,060	34,227	(100,519)
Deferred income taxes	(53,722)	(38,766)	21,105
Self-insurance reserves and other [2]	(45,610)	(37,114)	(11,021)
(Increase) decrease in current assets: [2]			
Receivables	3,063	(21,792)	(49,966)
Inventories	36,889	(3,864)	7,436
Prepaid expenses	(14,308)	24,372	(10,394)
Increase (decrease) in current liabilities: [2]			
Accounts payable	189	(3,869)	6,119
Other current liabilities	28,774	(67,466)	62,723
Accrued payroll and benefits	1,507	(6,231)	(4,283)
Income taxes payable	86,207	13,380	(105,446)
Total adjustments	443,356	263,316	270,560
Net cash provided by operating activities	690,446	470,782	469,842
Cash flows from investing activities:			
Expended for property, plant and equipment	(593,785)	(386,106)	(354,940)
Proceeds from disposition of divisions		429,952	286,287
Proceeds from sale of assets	38,007	48,271	11,458
Net cash (used in) provided by investing activities	(555,778)	92,117	(57,195)
Cash flows from financing activities:			
Proceeds from long-term borrowing	100,000	401,602	239,528
Reduction of long-term debt	(170,467)	(935,128)	(606,773)
Principal payments for obligations under capital leases [2]	(9,850)	(16,735)	(16,719)
Proceeds from exercise of stock options	7,532	14,553	7,235
Other changes in equity	554	6,572	1,674
Cash dividends	(56,905)	(51,007)	(43,592)
Net cash used in financing activities	(129,136)	(580,143)	(418,647)
Net increase (decrease) in cash and cash equivalents	5,532	(17,244)	(6,000)
Cash and cash equivalents:			
Beginning of year	54,048	71,292	77,292
End of year	$ 59,580	$ 54,048	$ 71,292

[1] Restated to reflect adoption of Statement of Financial Accounting Standards No. 109, "Accounting for Income Taxes," as if effective at the beginning of fiscal 1989.
[2] Amounts reflected are net of effects of the disposition of divisions.

See notes to consolidated financial statements

Borden Company Consolidated Statements of Cash Flows

Consolidated Statements of Cash Flows

(In millions)		Year Ended December 31.	1993	1992	1991
Cash Flows From Operating Activities	Net (loss) income		$(630.7)	$ (364.4)	$ 294.9
	Adjustments to reconcile net income to net cash from operating activities:				
	Depreciation and amortization.............		224.0	227.6	216.9
	Loss on disposal of discontinued operations.............................		637.4		
	Change in accounting estimates...........		94.1		
	Restructuring..............................		52.5	316.5	(65.0)
	Non-pension postemployment benefit obligation		36.1	317.7	
	Net changes in assets and liabilities:				
	Trade receivables		47.8	(30.3)	19.9
	Inventories.............................		21.2	1.0	7.6
	Trade payables.........................		(0.5)	(4.4)	(15.1)
	Current and deferred taxes..............		(242.4)	(175.3)	63.4
	Other assets...........................		(34.2)	(9.6)	(99.0)
	Other, net.............................		(132.9)	14.1	(74.8)
	Discontinued operations		79.9		
			152.3	292.9	348.8
Cash Flows From Investing Activities	Capital expenditures.........................		(177.0)	(286.2)	(376.0)
	Divestiture of businesses		53.4	123.0	94.1
	Purchase of businesses		(9.5)	(20.1)	(29.5)
			(133.1)	(183.3)	(311.4)
Cash Flows From Financing Activities	(Decrease) increase in short-term debt		(536.2)	255.5	(310.4)
	Reduction in long-term debt		(128.7)	(266.1)	(244.2)
	Minority interest............................				500.0
	Long-term debt financing		274.6	45.2	223.1
	Sale of receivables..........................		400.0		
	Dividends paid		(126.7)	(170.4)	(165.0)
	Issuance of stock under stock options and benefits and awards plans		12.1	3.9	7.2
	Acquisition of treasury stock				(1.6)
			(104.9)	(131.9)	9.1
	(Decrease) increase in cash and equivalents...		(85.7)	(22.3)	46.5
	Cash and equivalents at beginning of year		186.0	208.3	161.8
	Cash and equivalents at end of year		$ 100.3	$ 186.0	$ 208.3
Supplemental Disclosures of Cash Flow Information	Interest paid.................................		$ 133.3	$ 130.4	$ 177.5
	Taxes paid		20.5	67.1	102.6

See Notes to Consolidated Financial Statements

Bally Manufacturing Corporation Statement of Cash Flows

BALLY MANUFACTURING CORPORATION
CONSOLIDATED STATEMENT OF CASH FLOWS

	Years ended December 31		
	1993	1992	1991
			(In thousands)
OPERATING:			
Loss from continuing operations	$ (16,026)	$ (9,028)	$(67,688)
Adjustments to reconcile to cash provided —			
Depreciation and amortization	113,824	108,942	109,029
Deferred income taxes	(24,244)	9,117	(32,171)
Provision for doubtful receivables	74,740	117,344	125,477
Interest accretion on discount notes	7,194		
Gain on repurchase of debt for sinking fund requirements	(596)	(4,512)	(14,694)
Change in operating assets and liabilities	(55,722)	(142,049)	(31,780)
Other, net	(1,704)	(2,024)	816
Cash provided by continuing operating activities	97,466	77,790	88,989
INVESTING:			
Acquisitions of businesses, net of cash acquired	29,838	(746)	(642)
Purchases of property and equipment	(97,277)	(40,152)	(39,057)
Other	(24,636)	(3,387)	4,076
Cash used in investing activities	(92,075)	(44,285)	(35,623)
FINANCING:			
Debt transactions —			
Proceeds from issuance of long-term debt	920,181		1,361
Net payments under revolving credit agreements	(108,000)	(73,153)	(140,437)
Payments on other long-term debt	(616,180)	(24,596)	(50,271)
Debt issuance costs	(35,533)	(1,138)	(8,685)
Cash provided by (used in) debt transactions	160,468	(98,887)	(198,032)
Equity transactions —			
Proceeds from exercise of stock options	590	699	
Cash provided by (used in) financing activities	161,058	(98,188)	(198,032)
DISCONTINUED OPERATIONS:			
Proceeds from disposal		58,743	94,910
Dividends received from discontinued operations and other, net		2,913	23,111
Cash provided by discontinued operations	—	61,656	118,021
Increase (decrease) in cash and equivalents	166,449	(3,027)	(26,645)
Cash and equivalents, beginning of year	36,609	39,636	66,281
Cash and equivalents, end of year	$ 203,058	$ 36,609	$ 39,636

Bally Manufacturing Corporation Statement of Cash Flows

BALLY MANUFACTURING CORPORATION
CONSOLIDATED STATEMENT OF CASH FLOWS — (continued)

	Years ended December 31		
	1993	1992	1991
		(In thousands)	
SUPPLEMENTAL CASH FLOWS INFORMATION:			
Changes in operating assets and liabilities, net of effects from acquisitions and dispositions, were as follows —			
Increase in receivables	**$ (79,313)**	$ (80,342)	$ (36,050)
(Increase) decrease in other current assets and other assets	**9,295**	(3,598)	11,876
Increase (decrease) in accounts payable and accrued liabilities	**10,012**	(22,238)	22,529
Increase (decrease) in income taxes payable	**12,261**	(11,414)	(5,519)
Increase (decrease) in deferred revenues	**8,229**	(21,356)	(18,588)
Decrease in other long-term liabilities	**(16,206)**	(3,101)	(6,028)
	$ (55,722)	$(142,049)	$ (31,780)
Cash was invested and common stock was issued in acquisitions of businesses as follows —			
Fair value of assets acquired (including goodwill of $19,888, $7,307 and $442)	**$(475,833)**	$ (14,304)	$ (442)
Liabilities assumed (including long-term debt of $259,950 and $1,254)	**390,305**	7,978	
Minority interests in business acquired	**43,280**		
Issuance of common stock		4,614	
Cash and equivalents acquired	**72,402**		
Increase (decrease) in earn-out liabilities	**(316)**	966	(200)
	$ 29,838	$ (746)	$ (642)
Cash payments for interest and income taxes for continuing operations were as follows —			
Interest paid	**$ 106,800**	$ 119,983	$ 135,547
Interest capitalized	**(1,026)**	(432)	(1,150)
Income taxes paid (refunded)	**7,866**	(3,667)	(2,705)
Investing and financing activities exclude the following non-cash activities —			
Acquisition of Bally's Grand, Inc. common stock in exchange for Bally Gaming International, Inc. common stock	**$ 18,838**	$	$
Accrued purchases of property and equipment	**8,558**		
Issuance of common stock in satisfaction of preferred stock dividends, interest and other obligations	**4,190**	34,710	
Securities exchanged for debt		5,491	46,418
Exchange of exclusive gaming machines license for liability reduction		3,500	
Common stock issued upon conversion of preferred stock . .			680
Stock option and benefit plan transactions	**500**	98	3,878

Autodesk, Inc., Statement of Cash Flows

(In thousands)	Fiscal year ended January 31,		
	1994	1993	1992
Operating activities			
Net income	$ 62,166	$ 43,873	$ 57,794
Adjustments to reconcile net income to net cash provided by operating activities:			
Depreciation and amortization	20,568	16,386	14,783
Changes in operating assets and liabilities, net of business combinations:			
Accounts receivable	(8,283)	(11,518)	(10,172)
Inventories	8,049	(5,644)	(612)
Deferred income taxes	(9,133)	(2,944)	(529)
Prepaid expenses and other current assets	923	1,910	(1,617)
Accounts payable and accrued liabilities	5,031	20,095	6,803
Accrued income taxes	9,532	6,450	6,408
Net cash provided by operating activities	88,853	68,608	72,858
Investing activities			
Purchases of marketable securities	(438,405)	(231,480)	(138,597)
Sales of marketable securities	426,168	230,581	117,860
Purchases of computer equipment, furniture and leasehold improvements	(21,503)	(11,008)	(9,863)
Business combinations, net of cash acquired	(6,536)	(15,037)	
Capitalization of software costs and purchases of software technologies	(2,479)	(2,782)	(13,517)
Other	1,474	(4,970)	(4,006)
Net cash used in investing activities	(41,281)	(34,696)	(48,123)
Financing activities			
Proceeds from issuance of common shares	47,899	20,819	14,109
Repurchase of common shares	(71,586)	(43,145)	(6,638)
Dividends paid	(11,388)	(11,538)	(11,345)
Net cash used in financing activities	(35,075)	(33,864)	(3,874)
Net increase in cash and cash equivalents	12,497	48	20,861
Cash and cash equivalents at beginning of year	73,107	73,059	52,198
Cash and cash equivalents at end of year	$ 85,604	$ 73,107	$ 73,059

See accompanying notes.

Asarco Incorporated Statement of Cash Flows

FOR THE YEARS ENDED DECEMBER 31,	1993	1992	1991
OPERATING ACTIVITIES			
(in thousands)			
Net earnings (loss)	S 15,619	$ (83,091)	$ 45,957
Adjustments to reconcile net earnings (loss) to net cash provided from operating activities:			
Depreciation and depletion	80,641	86,642	74,869
Provision (benefit) for deferred income taxes	(19,639)	(60,200) ·	2,387
Treasury stock used for employee benefits	4,743	4,140	3,318
Undistributed equity earnings	(26,114)	(1,772)	(11,788)
Net gain on sale of investments and property	(18,823)	(2,600)	(10,125)
Cumulative effect of change in accounting principle by SPCC	(86,295)	–	–
Provision for plant closures and disposals	13,156	31,900	–
Increase (decrease) in reserves for closed plant and environmental matters	(38,012)	36,781	(24,944)
Provision for postretirement benefit obligation at adoption	–	81,764	–
Cash provided from (used for) operating assets and liabilities, net of acquisitions:			
Accounts receivable	21,765	(5,255)	53,759
Inventories	37,462	(19,200)	(10,174)
Accounts payable and accrued liabilities	42,231	13,553	(7,762)
Other operating liabilities and reserves	12,149	6,960	(52,171)
Other operating assets	(709)	15,620	3,888
Foreign currency transaction losses	687	447	262
Net cash provided from operating activities	38,861	105,689	67,476
INVESTING ACTIVITIES			
Capital expenditures	(112,315)	(134,574)	(282,917)
Business acquisitions, net of cash acquired	–	–	(17,392)
Proceeds from sale of securities and property	176,024	72,389	116,384
Purchase of investments, principally marketable securities	(139,592)	(73,374)	(77,998)
Net cash used for investing activities	(75,883)	(135,559)	(261,923)
FINANCING ACTIVITIES			
Debt incurred	387,788	84,781	267,654
Debt retired	(349,371)	(20,195)	(9,466)
Retirement of common stock purchase warrants, net	–	–	766
Net treasury stock transactions	321	1,209	(955)
Dividends paid	(20,792)	(33,043)	(65,796)
Net cash provided from financing activities	17,946	32,752	192,203
Effect of exchange rate changes on cash	(1,672)	(4,844)	2,861
Increase (decrease) in cash and cash equivalents	(20,748)	(1,962)	617
Cash and cash equivalents at beginning of year	33,248	35,210	34,593
Cash and cash equivalents at end of year	S 12,500	$ 33,248	$ 35,210

( ) See notes to financial statements
   Descriptions of material noncash transactions and supplemental disclosures are included in Notes 3, 6, 8 and 9.

Baltimore Gas and Electric Company Statements of Cash Flows

CONSOLIDATED STATEMENTS OF CASH FLOWS

Year Ended December 31,	1993	1992	1991
		(In thousands)	
Cash Flows From Operating Activities			
Net income	$ 309,866	$ 264,347	$ 253,426
Adjustments to reconcile to net cash provided by operating activities			
Cumulative effect of change in the method of accounting for income taxes	–	–	(19,745)
Depreciation and amortization	314,027	273,549	244,017
Deferred income taxes	53,057	26,914	30,725
Investment tax credit adjustments	(8,444)	(8,854)	(6,225)
Deferred fuel costs	51,445	105,430	102,754
Write-down of financial investments and real estate projects	–	–	23,563
Allowance for equity funds used during construction	(14,492)	(13,892)	(23,596)
Equity in earnings of affiliates and joint ventures (net)	(4,655)	(11,525)	8,707
Changes in current assets	(37,252)	(26,206)	(6,563)
Changes in current liabilities, other than short-term borrowings	71,153	(9,614)	(6,027)
Other	(31,919)	(31,005)	(5,373)
Net cash provided by operating activities	702,786	569,144	595,663
Cash Flows From Financing Activities			
Proceeds from issuance of			
Short-term borrowings (net)	(11,900)	(139,600)	(15,530)
Long-term debt	1,206,350	603,400	1,015,950
Preference stock	128,776	–	34,801
Common stock	57,379	355,759	32,263
Reacquisition of long-term debt .	(1,012,514)	(687,052)	(959,379)
Redemption of preference stock	(144,310)	(2,924)	(22,800)
Common stock dividends paid	(211,137)	(189,180)	(176,007)
Preferred and preference stock dividends paid	(42,425)	(42,300)	(42,743)
Other	(7,094)	(399)	(442)
Net cash used in financing activities	(36,875)	(102,296)	(133,887)
Cash Flows From Investing Activities			
Utility construction expenditures	(477,878)	(389,416)	(456,244)
Allowance for equity funds used during construction	14,492	13,892	23,596
Nuclear fuel expenditures	(47,329)	(39,486)	(1,854)
Deferred nuclear expenditures	(13,791)	(15,809)	(22,681)
Deferred energy conservation expenditures	(32,909)	(19,918)	(3,489)
Nuclear decommissioning trust fund	(9,699)	(8,900)	(8,900)
Financial investments	6,523	52,616	67,282
Real estate projects	(30,330)	(23,385)	(45,322)
Power generation systems	(26,841)	(31,483)	(33,204)
Other	8,965	4,746	(3,422)
Net cash used in investing activities	(608,797)	(457,143)	(484,238)
Net Increase (Decrease) in Cash and Cash Equivalents	57,114	9,705	(22,462)
Cash and Cash Equivalents at Beginning of Year	27,122	17,417	39,879
Cash and Cash Equivalents at End of Year	$ 84,236	$ 27,122	$ 17,417
Other Cash Flow Information			
Cash paid during the year for:			
Interest (net of amounts capitalized)	$ 183,266	$ 183,209	$ 189,271
Income taxes	$ 126,034	$ 87,693	$ 16,078

See Notes to Consolidated Financial Statements.

Certain prior-year amounts have been restated to conform to the current year's presentation.

Bethlehem Steel Corporation Statements of Cash Flows

Consolidated Statements of Cash Flows

	Year Ended December 31		
(Dollars in millions)	1993	1992	1991
Operating Activities:			
Net loss	$(266.3)	$(550.3)	$(812.7)
Adjustments for items not affecting cash from operating activities:			
Estimated restructuring losses (Note D)	350.0	—	635.0
Cumulative effect of changes in accounting (Note B)	—	340.0	—
Depreciation	277.5	261.7	241.4
Deferred income taxes	(87.0)	(45.0)	—
Other–net	19.6	26.5	11.4
Working capital*:			
Receivables	(99.9)	5.2	33.2
Inventories	—	172.8	(41.6)
Accounts payable	—	(59.2)	18.4
Employment costs and other	(5.6)	(17.6)	13.0
Other–net	14.9	1.0	20.6
Cash Provided from Operating Activities	203.2	135.1	118.7
Investing Activities:			
Capital expenditures	(327.1)	(328.7)	(563.9)
Cash proceeds from sales of businesses and assets	15.2	124.9	83.7
Other–net	5.6	7.2	0.4
Cash Used for Investing Activities	(306.3)	(196.6)	(479.8)
Financing Activities:			
Pension financing (funding) (Note I):			
Pension expense	183.6	188.7	184.6
Pension funding	(261.1)	(40.2)	(130.7)
Revolving and other credit borrowings (payments)–net	(80.0)	(74.0)	144.0
Long-term debt borrowings (Note F)	171.2	104.0	125.8
Long-term debt and capital lease payments (Notes F and G)	(73.8)	(105.3)	(68.6)
Restructured facilities payments	(28.4)	(36.1)	(30.8)
Cash dividends paid (Note M)	(36.1)	(22.5)	(52.9)
Preferred Stock issued (Note M)	248.4	—	—
Common Stock issued (Note M)	—	171.3	—
Cash Provided from Financing Activities	123.8	185.9	171.4
Net Increase (Decrease) in Cash and Cash Equivalents	20.7	124.4	(189.7)
Cash and Cash Equivalents–Beginning of Period	208.2	83.8	273.5
–End of Period	$ 228.9	$ 208.2	$ 83.8
Supplemental Cash Payment Information:			
Interest, net of amount capitalized	$ 55.7	$ 57.1	$ 44.4
Income taxes (Note E)	$ 3.7	$ 1.3	$ 1.9

*Excludes Financing Activities and Investing Activities.

The accompanying Notes are an integral part of the Consolidated Financial Statements.

Blockbuster Entertainment Corporation Statements of Cash Flows

	1993	1992	1991
CASH FLOWS FROM OPERATING ACTIVITIES:			
Net income	$ 243,646	$ 148,269	$ 89,112
Adjustments to reconcile net income to cash flows from operating activities:			
Depreciation and amortization	396,122	306,829	223,672
Amortization of film costs	87,281	—	—
Additions to film costs and program rights	(110,422)	—	—
Interest on subordinated convertible debt	6,362	8,945	8,267
Gain from equity investment	(2,979)	—	—
Changes in operating assets and liabilities, net of effects from purchase transactions:			
Increase in accounts and notes receivable	(29,444)	(9,347)	(14,203)
(Increase) decrease in merchandise inventories	(83,333)	1,379	(38,606)
(Increase) decrease in other current assets	(974)	(5,254)	386
Increase (decrease) in accounts payable and accrued liabilities	(62,529)	(37,159)	24,831
Increase in income taxes payable and related items	83,655	20,391	39,786
Other	(5,101)	16,732	17,106
	522,284	450,785	350,351
CASH FLOWS FROM INVESTING ACTIVITIES:			
Purchases of videocassette rental inventory	(451,116)	(296,139)	(221,996)
Disposals of videocassette rental inventory	40,595	37,618	22,648
Purchases of property and equipment	(164,541)	(98,393)	(78,698)
Net cash used in business combinations and investments	(673,241)	(252,888)	(8,244)
Other	(2,216)	(22,893)	(15,603)
	(1,250,519)	(632,695)	(301,893)
CASH FLOWS FROM FINANCING ACTIVITIES:			
Proceeds from the issuance of common stock, net	595,698	80,769	11,516
Proceeds from long-term debt	2,373,786	328,583	87,717
Repayments of long-term debt	(2,152,239)	(222,523)	(144,410)
Cash dividends paid	(18,275)	(7,154)	—
Other	(18,839)	(6,071)	(3,375)
	780,131	173,604	(48,552)
INCREASE (DECREASE) IN CASH AND CASH EQUIVALENTS	51,896	(8,306)	(94)
CASH AND CASH EQUIVALENTS AT BEGINNING OF YEAR	43,358	51,664	51,758
CASH AND CASH EQUiVALENTS AT END OF YEAR	$ 95,254	$ 43,358	$ 51,664

Chapter Four

Cash Flows from Investing, Financing, and Operating Activities

In the previous chapter, we described the preparation of the statement of cash flows, but did not define exactly the major components of the statement, that is, cash flows from investing, financing, and operating activities. In this chapter, we provide detailed explanations of the components of cash flows, as well as real-life examples from published financial statements. We show common examples of these components, but also some unusual examples that we encountered when scouring financial statements. Finally, we discuss how the cash flow analyst should interpret the cash flows from investing, financing and operating activities.

CASH FLOWS FROM INVESTING ACTIVITIES

In its *Statement of Financial Accounting Standards (SFAS) No. 95*, the FASB defines cash flows from investing activities as follows:

> Investing activities include making and collecting loans and acquiring and disposing of debt or equity instruments and property, plant, and equipment and other productive assets, that is, assets held for or used in the production of goods or services by the enterprise (other than materials that are part of the enterprise's inventory) (*SFAS No. 95*, para. 15).

Thus, the definition of investing cash flows includes cash outflows used as investments in financial or fixed assets, as well as cash receipts from disposition of such investments. Furthermore, investing cash flows are for investments in financial instruments as well as investments in real assets (PPE). The FASB further describes cash inflows and outflows from investing activities as:

Inflows

    a. Receipts from collections or sales of loans made by the enterprise and of other entity's debt instruments (other than cash equivalents) that were purchased by the enterprise.

    b. Receipts from sales of equity instruments of other enterprises and from returns of investment in those instruments.

    c. Receipts from sales of property, plant, and equipment and other productive assets. (*SFAS No. 95,* para. 16).

Outflows

    a. Disbursements for loans made by the enterprise and payments to acquire debt instruments of other entities (other than cash equivalents).

    b. Payments to acquire equity instruments of other enterprises.

    c. Payments at the time of purchase or soon before or after purchase to acquire property, plant, and equipment and other productive assets. (*SFAS, No. 95,* para. 17)

It is more natural to discuss first the cash outflows for investing activities. The statement requires the classification of investments in PPE and other productive assets as investing activities. It further restricts the inclusion of these investments on the statement of cash flows to those amounts that were paid at the time of purchase or soon before or after the time of purchase. Thus, an advance payment for PPE, or a down payment, will be included. However, a loan by the seller of the PPE will not be included as a cash flow from investing activity because the buyer had not paid for it in cash.

The FASB includes in investing cash flows those investments in equity instruments of *other* enterprises (repurchases of the firm's own securities are classified as financing cash flows), or investments in debt instruments of other enterprises, or loans made to other enterprises. The FASB notes that investments in debt instruments of other entities should be "other than cash equivalents." This is an important distinction since the statement of cash flows can be prepared using "cash and cash equivalents." Cash equivalents are short-term, highly liquid investments that are both:

a. Readily convertible to known amounts of cash.

b. So near their maturity that they present insignificant risk of changes in value because of changes in interest rates. (*SFAS, No. 95*, para. 8).

The FASB states that generally only investments with original maturities of three months or less qualify under the definition of a cash equivalent. Thus, when a treasurer purchases a Treasury note that has 60 days to maturity by using cash, an increase of cash and cash equivalents is recorded for the period.[1] However, if the treasurer purchased a 120-day Treasury note, an investing cash flow is recorded on the statement of cash flows. Clearly, these rules leave management some room for manipulation close to the end of the accounting period. It should be noted that the FASB ruled that if a seven-year note, for example, is *purchased* less than 90 days before maturity, it can be classified as a cash equivalent. However, if it had been purchased more that 90 days before maturity, it does *not* get reclassified as a cash equivalent when the balance sheet date falls within 90 days of its maturity.

Example

Morrison Knudsen Corp. operates in two main segments—engineering, construction, and environmental clean-up efforts, and manufacturing of locomotives and railway cars. In its 1993 annual report, Morrison Knudsen states that "cash equivalents consist of investments in highly liquid securities having an original maturity of three months or less."

Example

In its 1993 annual report, Boeing Co. defines cash and short-term investments as follows: "Cash and cash equivalents consist of highly liquid instruments such as certificates of deposit, time deposits, treasury notes, and other money market instruments which generally have maturities of less than three months. Short-term investments are carried at cost, which approximates market value."

---

[1]The decrease in cash is exactly offset by the increase in cash equivalents, the Treasury note, since the maturity of the note is less than 90 days.

It seems reasonable that cash and cash equivalents will include only those items that could be readily converted to cash and also used by the business entity immediately. In some cases, a portion of the available dash is restricted by compensating balance agreements or by other agreements. It seems that restricted cash should not be included in "cash and cash equivalents" for purposes of the statement of cash flows. However, in some cases firms deviate from this line of reasoning.

Example

Foundation Health Co. administers the delivery of managed health care services through its HMO and government contracting subsidiaries. A footnote to the financial statements of Foundation Health Co., provided as part of its prospectus, stated: "Cash equivalents include investments with maturities of three months or less. Included in cash and cash equivalents at June 30, 1989 was $4,000,000 on deposit at The Bank of New York as a compensating balance in connection with the Company's term loan agreement. During the nine month period ended March 31, 1990, the compensating balance restriction on these funds was removed." It should be noted that cash and cash equivalents on June 30, 1989, were shown on the balance sheet at about $34 million. Thus the $4 million of compensating balances were a significant portion of that amount.

These examples show that we should examine what the firm classifies as cash and cash equivalents. Also, the firm may affect its investing activities by purchases of short-term investments with maturities of less than 90 days. Such investments may be shown as cash equivalents and may be omitted from investing activities.

It should be noted that cash flows from investing activities include both cash outflows and cash inflows. The inflows occur when a firm disposes of its investments in financial instruments or fixed assets.[2] The cash proceeds from such sales are included among the cash flows from investing activities, and represent disinvesting activities by the firm. Can a firm net cash inflows against cash outflows? For example, can a firm net the proceeds from sales of PPE against additions to PPE? Usually, accountants are against offsetting any type of inflows

---

[2]Capital payments on debt instruments in which the firm invested are also considered cash inflows from investing activities; these are, in effect, disinvesting activities. However, interest payments on such debt are classified as operating cash inflows.

with outflows, assets against liabilities, or revenues against expenses. However, if the amount of the proceeds is immaterial, the firm may report the net purchases of PPE.

Let us now examine several examples of investing activities:

Example

Eaton Corp. reports the following investing cash flows in its 1993 financial statements (in millions):

Investing activities:	1993	1992	1991
Expenditures for property, plant, and equipment	$(227)	$(186)	$(194)
Acquisitions of businesses	(14)	(22)	(17)
Purchases of short-term investments	(108)	(86)	(39)
Maturities and sales of short-term investments	22	—	138
Other—net	8	36	5
Net cash used in investing activities	$(319)	$(258)	$(107)

Note that the single most significant item is expenditures for PPE, as it is for most manufacturing firms. The firm had also made some acquisitions, which required cash outflows. The third item represents new short-term investments the firm made ($108 million during 1993), but the firm sold some other short-term investments (about $22 million in 1993). Other—net may include items such as proceeds from sale of PPE, proceeds from sale of long-term investments, and the like.

Example

Federal Express reports in its 1993 statement of cash flows the following investing cash flows (in millions):

Investing activities:	1993	1992	1991
Purchases of property and equipment, including deposits on aircraft of $177,564, $212,291, and $92,587	$(1,023,723)	$(915,878)	$1,027,736)
Proceeds from disposition of property and equipment:			
Sale-leaseback transactions	216,444	400,433	275,347
Other	5,984	12,851	5,699
Purchase of businesses, net of cash acquired	—	—	(24,322)
Other, net	1,992	621	—
Net cash used in investing activities	$ (799,303)	$(501,973)	$ (771,012)

The capital expenditures of Federal Express in 1993 ($1.023 billion), include $177 million that represent deposits on aircraft. The aircraft would be delivered to Federal Express in the future, but since cash was used to acquire the aircraft in 1993, these amounts are shown as investing cash outflows. Note also that in 1993 Federal Express showed cash inflows from sale-leaseback transactions of $216 million. The firm sold some of its fixed assets to a financial intermediary but agreed to lease this equipment back from the new owner. Federal Express received cash from the sale, which it includes as a disinvesting activity in its investing cash flows. In future years, the cash outflows (payments on the lease) will be shown as operating cash outflows.

Example

Fleming Companies Inc. reports in its 1993 financial statements the following cash flows from investing activities:

Cash flows from investing activities:	1993	1992	1991
Collections on notes receivable	$ 82,497	$ 88,851	$ 95,045
Notes receivable funded	(130,846)	(168,814)	(193,643)
Notes receivable sold	67,554	44,970	81,986
Purchase of property and equipment	(55,554)	(66,376)	(67,295)
Proceeds from sale of property and equipment	2,955	3,603	4,748
Investments in customers	(37,196)	(17,315)	(21,108)
Business acquired	(51,110)	(8,233)	—
Proceeds from sale of investment	7,077	9,763	7,156
Other investing activities	197	(353)	(8,428)
Net cash used in investing activities	$(144,426)	$(113,904)	$(101,539)

Fleming shows cash inflows from investing activities that are mainly due to collections on notes receivable. These collections represent the principal of the notes, since the interest receipts are reported as operating cash inflows. Note that Fleming shows a cash outflow of $37 million for investments in customers. These cash outflows are not intended as marketing expenses (like purchases of goods and supplies, which are included in operating cash flows), but long-term relationships with major customers who would continue to buy products from Fleming.

Example

Sunshine Mining is a holding company whose subsidiaries produce silver, gold, crude oil, and natural gas. Sunshine's principal subsidiaries are Sunshine Precious Metals Inc. and Sunshine Oil & Gas Inc. Sunshine Mining discloses the following cash flows from investing activities in its 1989 financial statements:

Additions to property, plant, and equipment	$(17,308)
Proceeds from the disposal of property, plant, and equipment	3,460
Purchases of futures, forward, and option contracts	(19,221)
Sales of futures, forward, and option contracts	19,534
Investment in PT corporation	3,290
Other, principally investments	(8,188)

There are two interesting items on this section of the statement of cash flows. First, the purchases and sales of futures, forward, and option contracts are investments in financial instruments by Sunshine Mining, which are covered by FASB Statement No. 104. The firm states in its annual report that it "periodically enters into forward and option contracts to hedge its exposure to price fluctuations on oil and precious metals transactions." The firm mostly hedges its silver operations and its future oil production, although it is active in the forward market as an investor, too. Note that these hedge transactions represent investments in financial instruments, and although they may actually hedge current or future inventories, they are accounted as investing activities. Note further that these contracts cover about 18 percent of current assets, or 5 percent of total assets, of Sunshine Mining as of the balance sheet date.

The second interesting item is the investment in PT Corporation, which is shown as a cash inflow from investing activities of about $3.3 million. Thus, it may represent the cash proceeds from sale of this investment, or an increase in the value of this investment. To clarify which one of these explanations is correct, we need to consult the footnotes to the annual report. The annual report shows that PT had unrealized losses on its own investments, which were large enough to wipe out stockholders equity. Thus, the investment in PT on the books of Sunshine Mining was put at a value of zero on 12/31/89. However, PT had transferred dividends and other cash distributions to Sunshine of about $4.9 million and income that was included from PT for the year on Sunshine's books amounted to $1.7 million, or net proceeds of about $3.2 million. It seems odd, though, that not all the $4.9 million were shown as cash flows from investing activities, that is, Sunshine had not subtracted the $1.7 million of income from net income when it derived cash flows from operations. Thus, cash flows from operating activities are overstated by $1.7 million (Sunshine reported net operating cash flow of about $0.2 million for 1989).

Example

When a firm acquires or disposes of entire businesses, one has to be careful in interpreting the relevant items on the statement of cash flows because the amounts shown on the statement represent only the portion of the transaction that involved cash payments or receipts. The entire transaction may have involved a much larger amount.

Halliburton is one of the world's largest diversified oil field service engineering and construction companies. It also provides insurance services.

Halliburton reports in its 1989 financial statements:

Payments for the acquisitions of businesses, net of cash acquired $(42.4)
Receipts from dispositions of businesses, net of cash disposed   88.2

The supplemental schedule provides the following additional information:

Liabilities assumed in acquisitions of businesses $51.2
Liabilities disposed of in dispositions of businesses   663.9

During 1989, Halliburton effected two acquisitions and two dispositions. For stockholder reporting purposes, Halliburton recorded a $3.6 million pre-tax gain. The cash effect was dramatically different due to cash received as payment on the transactions. However, the balance sheet effect was not as large as the amount shown in the table. For instance, the $72 million cash receipt for The Life Insurance Company of the Southwest excludes the $40 million in cash the company had on its balance sheet. To summarize:

Halliburton—Cash Effect due to Business Transactions—1989 (in millions)

Name of Company	Type of Transaction	Cash Effect*	Income Effect
Sierra Geophysics	Acquisition	$0	—
C. F. Braun	Acquisition	$(39.0)	—
Life Insurance Co. of the Southwest	Disposal	$ 72.0	$ 5.5
Zapata Gulf Marine	Disposal	$ 31.5	$(1.9)
Total		$ 64.5	$ 3.6

*Cash effect is cash outlay or receipt of cash only.

Thus, it seems that the acquisitions of business were for $42.4 million cash plus assumed obligations of the acquired firms of $51.2 million or a total consideration of $93.6 million. Similarly, the cash proceeds from the dispositions of businesses amounted to $88.2 million, plus liabilities that were assumed by the buyers of $663.9 million, or a total consideration of $752.1 million. In Notes 8 and 13 to the financial statements, the firm discloses that cash used for one acquisition from internal sources was approximately $39 million, and the total goodwill in the acquisitions amounted to approximately $33.5 million. Thus, the net assets of the two acquired firms were approximately $60.1 million (93.6 − 33.5). The firm also reports total cash receipts for the two firms disposed during 1989 of approximately $103.5 million (31.5 + 72). Thus, cash on hand in the two disposed subsidiaries was about $15.3 million (103.5 − 88.2).

Example

Among the wave of mergers and buyouts in the defense-related industries after the downfall of the Soviet Union, Martin Marrietta acquired GE Aerospace. In its 1993 report, Martin Marrietta shows an investing cash outflow for the acquisition of GE Aerospace of $883 million. However, at the bottom of the statement of cash flows, it reports that noncash consideration in the acquisition included assumption of certain payment obligations of $750 million and the issuance of preferred stock for $1 billion. Thus, the acquisition price was greater than that reported in investing cash flows, since the latter include only the cash part of the acquisition.

Example

The Travelers Corporation, an insurance firm, shows in 1989 the following items on its statement of cash flows:

Investment repayments:	
Fixed maturities	$2,022
Mortgage loans	1,309
Carrying value of investments sold:	
Fixed maturities	5,153
Equity securities	732
Mortgage loans	—
Investment real estate	328

(continued)

Investments in:

Fixed maturities	(9,153)
Equity securities	(1,013)
Mortgage loans	(1,308)
Investment real estate	(109)
Policy loans, net	(110)
Short-term securities purchased, net	(340)
Other investments	(179)
Securities transactions in course of settlement	(360)
Proceeds from disposition of subsidiaries and operations	124
Other	(75)

As an insurance firm the Travelers makes investments in financial assets, out of which it pays its claims. The financial assets include securities with fixed maturities, mortgage loans, equity securities, and investments in real estate. The items on the portion of the cash flow statement that relate to investing activities usually describe these financial investments or collections of principal on these investments. However, one of the items in the above list is securities transactions in course of settlement, which represents additional investments in securities where cash was used to purchase certain financial instruments but where the financial instruments were not yet the property of the firm on the balance sheet date. It also represents financial instruments that were lent to other business entities and were not available for use by the Travelers as of the balance sheet date. Thus, it properly represents a cash flow from investing activity and not cash flows from operating activity.

In some cases, investing activities represent payments for investments in intangible assets of firms.

Examples

Handleman Co. reports in its 1993 financial statements a cash outflow of $2.4 million for the purchases of video licenses.

Measurex Co. manufactures and services computer integrated manufacturing systems that control continuous batch manufacturing processes serving such industries as paper, plastics, and metals. Measurex Corp. shows as part of its investing activities capitalized software of about 3 million for 1989. The firm had cash expenditures of about $3 million on developing software after the technical feasibility of the software products had been established (costs prior to this point cannot be capitalized). These expenditures are capitalized as an asset and are subsequently amortized over three years.

Bic Corp., North America's leading ball-point pen producer (which also produces disposable butane lighters, disposable pencils, disposable razors, sailboards, and car racks), shows in its 1989 statement of cash flows a cash purchase of trademarks and patents for about $440,000. These are intangible assets, although they will probably help the firm generate greater cash flows in the future.

CASH FLOWS FROM FINANCING ACTIVITIES

The FASB defines financing activities broadly, as follows:

> Financing activities include obtaining resources from owners and providing them with a return on, and a return of, their investment; borrowing money and repaying amounts borrowed, or otherwise settling the obligation; and obtaining and paying for other resources obtained from creditors on long-term credit. (*FASB Statement No. 95*, para. 18)

It further clarifies the nature of cash inflows or cash outflows from financing activities in the following manner:

> Cash inflows from financing activities are:
>   *a.* Proceeds from issuing equity instruments.
>   *b.* Proceeds from issuing bonds, mortgages, notes, and from other short- or long-term borrowing.
>
> Cash outflows for financing activities are:
>   *a.* Payments of dividends or other distributions to owners, including outlays to reacquire the enterprise's equity instruments.
>   *b.* Repayments of amounts borrowed.
>   *c.* Other principal payments to creditors who have extended long-term credit. (*FASB Statement No. 95*, paras. 19–20)

The logic underlying the definition of financing activities seems very clear; all the events that represent increases of internal or external capital are financing cash flows, whereas events that represent decreases of internal or external capital are disfinancing cash flows. Loosely speaking, internal capital is capital invested by shareholders in the firm, whereas external capital represents lending to the firm by creditors.

One important asymmetry in the treatment of internal and external capital under SFAS No. 95 should be highlighted at this point; dividends paid to shareholders are classified as financing cash outflows because they represent disfinancing events. However, payments of interest on a loan do not represent cash outflows from financing activities; instead, as we shall see in the next subsection, they represent an operating cash outflow. This is an asymmetric treatment because both represent a return on capital to providers, and there should not be any distinction between a return to creditors and return to shareholders. The inclusion of interest payments among operating cash flows will bias the concept of cash flows generated from ongoing operations and the concept of free cash flows, as it is generally defined.

Let us provide now examples of financing cash flows from financial statements of firms:

Example

Briggs and Stratton Corp. produces gasoline engines for outdoor power products such as lawn mowers. In its 1994 annual report, the firm includes the following financing cash flows:

Net borrowings on loans and notes payable	$ 5,396,000
Cash dividends paid	(26,034,000)
Purchase of common stock for treasury	(791,000)
Proceeds from exercise of stock options	266,000
Net cash used in financing activities	$(21,163,000)

The financing cash flows reported above are straightforward—net borrowing of $5.4 million, proceeds from the exercise of stock options $266,000, cash outflows for dividends $26 million, and cash used to repurchase common stock of the firm $791,000. The net result is a financing cash outflow of $21.2 million, which the firm was able to cover from the cash it generated by operations. Many firms acquire some amounts of stock for treasury, usually to reissue those shares to employees who exercise stock options. However, from time to time, a firm may decide to acquire a significant proportion of its own common stock because it believes the price to be considerably undervalued, or to distribute free cash flows back to shareholders.

Example

Delta Airlines reports the following financing activities in its 1993 financial reports:

Issuance of Series C convertible preferred stock, net	$1,126,000
Issuance of long-term obligations	1,426,587
Issuance of common stock	1,392
Net short-term borrowing	(800,692)
Repurchase of common stock	(38)
Payments on long-term debt and capital lease obligations	(518,678)
Cash dividends	(138,499)
Proceeds from sale and leaseback transactions	683,816
Net cash provided by financing activities	$1,779,888

Delta Airlines financed about $1.78 billion in 1993, although it generated about $677 million from operations, because it budgeted about $1.33 billion for new equipment. Most of the financing came from three sources—issuance of debt ($1.4 billion), issuance of preferred stock ($1.1 billion), and sale and leaseback transactions. The latter represent the sale of equipment by Delta to a third party, with an obligation to lease the equipment back from the buyer. The economic substance of sale and leaseback transactions is very similar to a mortgage on property, except that the title to the equipment is transferred to the buyer who can use the depreciation expense for tax purposes. Thus, treating the proceeds of sale and leaseback transactions as financing cash flows seems to be justified.

To pare intevert expense Delta decided to pay down some of its debt—about $800 million of short-term borrowing and $519 million of long-term debt and capital lease obligations. To explain the capital lease obligations, recall that under *SFAS No. 13* assets under capital leases are included on the balance sheet as both assets and liabilities. The asset/liability is the present value of future payments on the lease. Future payments under the lease agreement consist of interest payments on the loan, which is implicit in the lease, and also of a reduction in the principal obligation (or loan), which is implicit in the lease. The interest payment is included under operating cash flows, whereas the reduction of the principal is included among the financing cash flows, as a disfinancing event. Finally, the firm paid out dividends of about $138 million.

Example

Standard Motor Products Inc. is a manufacturer of replacement parts for the electrical, fuel, brake, and temperature control systems of motor vehicles. Parts are used by cars, trucks, marine, and industrial engines. The company includes the following items in its 1989 statement of cash flows among the financing activities:

Net borrowings under line-of-credit agreements	$ 13,600
Proceeds from issuance of long-term debt	49,229
Principal payments of long-term debt	(4,436)
Reduction of loan to ESOP	1,676
Proceeds from exercise of employee stock options	567
Tax benefits applicable to ESOP	82
Loan to ESOP	(16,779)
Dividends paid	(4,191)

Among the items that should be noted are those related to the employee stock ownership plan (ESOP). Under the plan, employees are induced to purchase stock in the firm because there are tax benefits to all parties. The firm may lend money to the plan, so that the plan can purchase additional shares. Standard Motor Products lent about $16.8 million to the plan in 1989; which is shown as a financing cash outflow, not as an investing cash outflow. The reason is that funds lent to the ESOP are used to purchase shares in the firm. Thus, the economic substance of the transaction is very similar to the repurchase of common stock, which is shown as a disfinancing cash flow.

Example

Amax Inc. explores for, mines, refines, and sells aluminum, coal, gold, and molybdenum. The company also explores for and produces oil and natural gas, tungsten, magnesium, specialty metals, and zinc. Amax includes the following items as financing cash flows on its 1989 statement of cash flows:

Repayments of long-term debt	$(124,900)
Share repurchase payment	(60,600)
Repayments of sales of future production	(52,100)
Dividends paid on common and preferred stock	(51,900)
Decrease in unearned revenue	(25,900)
Decrease in capital lease obligation	(4,800)
Issuance of common shares	48,400
Issuance of long-term debt	44,000
Increase in short-term borrowings	1,000

Among the uncommon items are the repayments of sales of future production and the decrease in unearned revenue. The firm shows a balance sheet liability entitled proceeds from sales of future production, which represents a loan to the firm that is guaranteed by future sale of coal. During 1989, the loan was reduced by approximately $52.1 million and is shown as a disfinancing event on the statement of cash flows. Similarly, unearned revenue represents loan facilities that will be satisfied by future delivery of gold and silver. Upon such delivery, the firm records sales, cost of goods sold, and a reduction of the liability unearned revenue. During 1989, the firm paid about $26 million of loan facilities, mostly by the delivery of gold.

Example

In its 1993 statement of cash flows, the Dial Corp. reports a cash outflow for extraordinary charge for early retirement of debt in the amount of $21.9 million. This amount represents a cash outflow made when the firm paid down its debt, which was carried on the books at present-value using the effective interest rate when the debt was issued. Subsequently, interest rates declined, so the firm decided to refinance its high interest rate debt with lower interest rate debt. However, to induce holders of old debt to give up their high interest rate receipts, the firm had to make an extra payment of $21.9 million to recall the debt. This payment is an accounting loss, since the carrying value of the debt is lower than the cash outflow to pay down the debt. However, the firm would benefit over time from lower interest payments on its new debt. Because of this anomaly (accounting loss but economic gain), the accounting profession classifies this loss as an extraordinary loss. In the statement of cash flows, the Dial Corp. classified this cash flow for retirement of old debt as a financing cash outflow.

In the same section of financing activities, Dial reports cash payments on interest rate swaps of $32.9 million in 1993. Interest rate swaps are intended either to transform a fixed-rate debt into a variable (adjusted) interest rate debt, or to transform a variable interest rate to a fixed interest rate. In both cases, when a firm makes payments on such agreement, it offsets interest payments that it makes on its own debt. Since interest payments are reported as operating cash flows, it seems logical to expect the payments (receipts) on interest rate swaps that offset regular interest payments to be reported on the operating cash flows of the firm, not on its financing cash flows. If the interest rate swaps were taken as an investment and not as a hedge, then they should be reported among investing cash flows, not among the financing cash flows.

Example

Bethlehem Steel Corp. is the second largest domestic steel producer, although it has fabricating and other operations as well. Its products are used largely in heavy construction and capital goods markets. Bethlehem includes two interesting items among its financing activities for 1988:

	($millions)
Pension financing (funding)	$(514.3)
Discontinued assets and facilities payments	(63.2)

The first item represents payments to the pension fund to reduce the firm's outstanding pension liability. Can this be shown as a financing cash flow? Normally, payments made to the pension fund are included as an operating cash flow, like all other payments made to employees. In this case, a substantial portion of the firm's obligation for postretirement benefits is to former employees in its discontinued facilities. The firm may have decided to show the funding of this obligation as a repayment of a loan, since the obligation was accrued on the balance sheet before as part of the expected future costs of the discontinued operations.

The second item seems to represent payments that are made on discontinued assets, probably to cover retirement benefits to employees in discontinued facilities. The firm uses proceeds from sales of assets to reduce these payments. It probably shows the proceeds from the sale of assets as an investing cash flow.

Example

Ethyl Corp. is a producer of specialty industrial and petroleum chemicals that also has interests in insurance. It is the largest domestic supplier of lead antiknock additives. The 1989 statement of cash flows for Ethyl Corp. includes a financing cash inflow of $100 million, which is represented as a dividend received from Tredegar Industries. Normally, the receipt of dividends is included as an operating cash inflow, not as a financing cash flow. However, in the case of Ethyl, the firm combined some of its aluminum, plastics, and energy businesses into Tredegar. The shares of the new firm were distributed to shareholders of Ethyl, except for $100 million, which was transferred as a dividend from Tredegar to Ethyl. Ethyl used this dividend, together with other cash, to pay off about $152.5 million of maturing notes. Thus, Ethyl classified this special dividend as a financing activity because it deemed this special dividend to be related to the retirement of debt. This interpretation seems to be at odds with *SFAS No. 95*, which would probably require the dividend to be shown as a cash inflow from operating activities or as a disinvesting activity.

Example

MNC Financial Co., a holding company, owns Maryland National Bank (the largest bank in that state), American Security Bank in Washington D.C., Virginia Federal S&L, and MBNA America, which conducts extensive credit card operations. The company is also engaged in providing services for smaller corporations, real estate lending, and retail banking.

MNC Financial reports the following financing activities for the three months ending on 3/31/1990:

Net decrease in noninterest bearing demand deposits, interest bearing transactions, and savings accounts $	(74,369)
Net decrease in short-term borrowings	(1,180,536)
Net increase in certificates of deposit	1,234,702
Proceeds from issuance of long-term borrowings	2,705
Maturities of long-term borrowings	(12,087)
Proceeds from the issuance of common stock	3,042
Dividends paid	(26,479)
Decrease in other financing activities	(275)

The first item represents a decline in deposits, which are, in effect, loans made to MNC Financial. Note that MNC had an inflow of cash through issuance of certificates of deposit, which helped the firm bridge the decline in short-term borrowing.

Example

McGraw-Hill includes in its 1993 statement of cash flows a financing cash inflow of $337.5 million for the acquisition of Macmillan/McGraw-Hill. It also includes a cash outflow of $323.9 million for acquisition of businesses and equity interests among its investing cash flow. This treatment assumes that the issued debt is totally separate from the payment for the acquisition. Otherwise, the firm should have reported the information in the supplemental schedule.

Example

First Missisipi Corp. reports in its 1993 statement of cash flows a cash outflow for financing activities of $13.4 million for the purchase of gold to repay a loan repaid with gold, not cash. Typically, cash outflows for purchases of any asset should be reported as an investing cash flow. However, since in this case the loan is denominated in gold, the purchase of gold is to discharge the loan and is therefore not different from a cash outflow to pay down debt. Thus, it is properly classified as a financing activity.

Example

In its 1993 statement of cash flows, Enserch Corp. reports a cash inflow of $23 million from the settlement of foreign currency swap. This settlement should probably be reported as either an operating or investing cash flow rather than a financing cash flow. It may be reported as a financing cash flow only if it hedges a specific foreign-currency-denominated debt.

Example

In its 1993 statement of cash flows, ConAgra Inc. includes a cash inflow of $15 million from the sale of accounts receivable. Typically, the proceeds from a sale of accounts receivable are included in operating cash flows because this sale amounts to a collection of accounts receivable, except that the collection is not from customers but from the buyer of the receivables. However, if the firm sold the receivables with recourse, then the sale can be construed just as a way of borrowing against the accounts receivables. In such cases, it may be justified to include the proceeds from the sale as a financing cash inflow. But note that some companies include the proceeds from sale of receivables as an operating cash inflow.

CASH FLOWS FROM OPERATING ACTIVITIES

The FASB defined cash flows from operating activities as "all transactions and other events that are not defined as investing or financing activities." It broadly explained that "operating activities generally involve producing and delivering goods and providing services. Cash flows from operating activities are generally the cash effects of transactions and other events that enter into the determination of net income." (*FASB Statement No. 95*, para. 21) The FASB provided a list of specific cash flows from operations:

   a. Cash receipts from sales of goods or services, including receipts from collection or sale of accounts and both short- and long-term notes receivable from customers arising from those sales.
   b. Cash receipts from returns on loans, other debt instruments of other entities, and equity securities-interest and dividends.
   c. All other cash receipts that do not stem from transactions defined as investing or financing activities, such as amounts

received to settle lawsuits; proceeds of insurance settlements except for those that are directly related to investing or financing activities such as from destruction of a building; and refunds from suppliers. (*FASB Statement No. 95*, para. 22)

It further described cash outflows for operating activities as:

a. Cash payments to acquire materials for manufacture or goods for resale, including principal payments on accounts and both short- and long-term notes payable to suppliers for those materials or goods.

b. Cash payments to other suppliers and employees for other goods or services.

c. Cash payments to governments for taxes, duties, fines, and other fees or penalties.

d. Cash payments to lenders and other creditors for interest.

e. All other cash payments that do not stem from transactions defined as investing or financing activities, such as payments to settle lawsuits, cash contributions to charities, and cash refunds to customers. (*FASB Statement No. 95*, para. 23)

Clearly, the FASB treated cash flows from operations as the "residual" cash flow; it comprises all events that are not classified as either investing or financing activities. For many firms, the net cash flow from operating activities is likely to contain special items that are not easily assignable to investing or financing cash flows, and that may not recur in the future, such as the settlement of a law suit. Thus, the analyst should, ideally, separate those nonrecurring and special items from other operating cash flows. However, this is not easily done in practice because most firms follow the indirect approach to disclosing the cash flows from operating activities.

Indeed, the FASB states:

In reporting cash flows from operating activities, enterprises are encouraged to report major classes of gross cash payments and their arithmetic sum—the net cash flow from operating activities (the direct method). Enterprises that do so should, at minimum, separately report the following classes of operating cash receipts and payments:

a. Cash collected from customers, including lessees, licensees, and the like.

b. Interest and dividends received.

c. Other operating cash receipts, if any.

 d. Cash paid to employees and other suppliers of goods or
 services, including suppliers of insurance, advertising, and
 the like.
 e. Interest paid.
 f. Income taxes paid.
 g. Other operating cash payments, if any.

Enterprises are encouraged to provide further breakdowns of operating cash receipts and payments that they consider meaningful and
feasible. For example, a retailer or manufacturer might decide to
further divide cash paid to employees and suppliers (category d above)
into payments for costs of inventory and payments for selling, general,
and administrative expenses. (FASB Statement No. 95, para. 27)

Let us examine several disclosures of operating cash flows using
the direct method:

Example

Longs Drug Stores Inc. reports the following information about its
operating activities in its 1993 statement of cash flows:

Receipts from customers	$ 2,490,558
Payments for merchandise	(1,840,876)
Payments for operating, administrative, and occupancy expenses	(503,891)
Income tax payments	(31,628)
Net cash provided by operating activities	$ 114,163

This is a simple example of an application of the direct method
to calculate the net operating cash flow. It lists the main categories
that the FASB encouraged firms to use, excluding interest pay-
ments/receipts, which are excluded probably because they do not
exist or are immaterial. It is instructive at this point to show the
reconciliation of net income with net operating cash flow, which is
required from any firm that uses the direct method. It is also the
information that would have been required if the firm would have
used the indirect approach.

Net income	$ 57,782
Adjustments to reconcile net income to cash provided by operating activities:	
Depreciation and amortization	33,241
Deferred income taxes	2,857
Restricted stock awards	1,350

Common stock contribution to benefit plans	5,530
Tax benefits credited to stockholders' equity	(324)
Cumulative effect of accounting change	3,031
Changes in assets and liabilities net of effects from acquisition of Bill's Drugs, Inc.:	
Pharmacy and other receivables	(8,868)
Merchandise inventories	4,586
Other current assets	(433)
Current liabilities	20,411
Net cash provided by operating activities	$114,163

As can be seen, the direct method provides more information about the relevant components of operating activities without going through the cumbersome adjustments of net income to net operating cash flows.

Example

Commerce Clearing House Inc. (CCH) publishes current information, primarily in the fields of tax and business law. Detailed information about operating cash flows can be found in Commerce Clearing House's 1989 financial statements:

Receipts from customers	$ 674,356
Interest income	12,821
Miscellaneous	2,861
Payments to suppliers	(308,039)
Payments to employees	(266,482)
Payments for pensions and profit sharing plans	(12,610)
Income taxes paid	(36,795)
Interest paid on long-term obligations	(3,217)

In this statement of cash flows, there is substantially more disclosure; payments to suppliers and employees are separated into two items, and payments for fringe benefits such as pensions and profit sharing plans are segregated from direct payments to employees. Note also that CCH is a net creditor, as is evidenced by interest income (interest received in cash) exceeding interest payments.

Example

Manitowoc Company Inc. designs, manufactures, and markets commercial ice cubes machines, shipbuilding equipment, cranes, and excavators. The firm reports the following cash flows from operating activities in its 1989 financial statements:

Cash received from customers	$ 186,283,043
Cash paid to suppliers and employees	(189,686,352)
Interest and dividends received	4,120,622
Income taxes paid	(1,527,514)
Restructuring costs paid	(4,679,097)
Miscellaneous cash receipts	211,343
Net cash used in operating activities	$ (5,277,955)

As can be seen in the above disclosure, Manitowoc had more cash payments than cash receipts in its operations. Normally, this is not a favorable signal, because a business entity is expected to generate cash inflows from its operations. However, Manitowoc, which had substantial liquid assets, had a positive operating cash flow when interest and dividend income are taken into account. We should also note that restructuring costs amounted to about $4.7 million, most of the $5.3 million of net cash outflows on operating activities. The firm hopes restructuring costs are nonrecurring, or else management changes may be indicated. Thus, an analyst who wishes to predict future cash flows should not concentrate on net cash flows from operating activities, but on those cash flows that are expected to recur in the future.

Example

Lubrizol Corp. engages primarily in the development, manufacturing, and marketing of automotive chemical additives, fuel additives, lubricants, and specialty oils. Lubrizol reports the following cash flows from operating activities in its 1988 financial statements:

Received from customers	$1,109,333
Paid to suppliers and employees	(957,945)
Received from patent litigation settlement	80,000
Income taxes paid	(44,566)
Received from the sale of investments	16,529
Interest and dividends received	11,640
Interest paid	(5,447)
Other, net	2,238
Cash provided from operating activities	$ 211,782

Note that net operating cash flow is positive (inflow) and amounts to about $212 million. However, a careful examination of the individual items reveals that almost one-half of the net operating cash inflow comes from a patent litigation settlement ($80 million), a cash inflow that is usually nonrecurring. Furthermore, the firm reports about $17 million received from sales of investments. This item is classified as an operating cash flow, although proceeds from disposal of investments should be classified, typically, as a cash inflow from investing activity.

Example

Comdisco Inc. is the largest independent lessor and marketer of computer and high-technology equipment. It leases, places, and remarkets IBM computer equipment, as well as other high-tech equipment. It also operates data centers and telecommunication sites, as an alternative data processing and telecommunication centers of customers in cases of power outages or other disasters (such as the 1988 earthquake in San Francisco).

In its 1994 financial statements, Comdisco reported the following items for operating cash flows (in millions of dollars):

Operating lease and other leasing receipts	$1,122
Direct financing and sales-type leasing receipts	907
Leasing costs, primarily rentals paid	(49)
Sales	283
Sales costs	(147)
Disaster recovery receipts	240
Disaster recovery costs	(200)
Other revenue	48
Selling, general and administrative expenses	(193)
IBM litigation settlement	(70)
Interest	(268)
Income taxes	(34)
Net cash provided by operating activities	$1,639

The firm reports the cash receipts (and cash outlays) from three major sources—leasing of equipment (both operating leases and capital leases), sales of equipment, and the disaster recovery services. It also provides information about cash inflows from other revenues and cash outflows for selling, general, and administrative expenses. In addition, it discloses information about payments for interest and taxes, which is required even if the firm had been using the indirect method of calculating net operating cash flows. Note also the payment to IBM in settlement of litigation, which is classified as an operating cash outflow because it cannot be classified as either financing or investing cash flow.

It is interesting to also examine the reconciliation of net income to net cash provided by operating activities:

Net earnings	$ 53
Adjustments to reconcile net earnings to net operating cash flow:	
Leasing costs, primarily depreciation and amortization	955
Leasing revenue, primarily principal portion of direct financing and sales-type lease rentals	491
Cost of sales	78
Income taxes	2
Interest	(5)
Depreciation and amortization of buildings, furniture and other	37
Bad debt expense	10
Contribution charge	10
Other, net	8
Net cash provided by operating activities	$1,639

The two most prominent adjustments regard leasing costs, which are shown on the statement of cash flows above as a $49 million cash outflow and are also shown in the income statement as $1,004 million of expense. The difference between these two amounts, $955 million, is shown as a source of cash in the adjustments to net income. In reality, this is not a source of cash but an elimination of an accounting expense that is much higher than cash outflow during the period. The second largest adjustment is for revenues from leasing, which the income statement shows as $1,538, but which the statement of cash flows shows were actually $2,029 ($1,122 + $907). Thus, we need an adjustment to net income to reflect another cash inflow of $491 million. This is an actual cash inflow that is not yet recorded in the income statement as revenue and has to be adjusted in calculating net cash provided by operations from net income.

Example

The Continental Corp., an insurance company, provides operating cash flow information in its quarterly financial supplement. This report includes cash inflows from premiums collected and investment income received. It also includes such cash disbursements as losses and loss expenses paid, insurance operating expenses paid, interest on corporate debt, and other expenses. Thus, an investor is provided with quarterly operating cash flows prepared according to the direct method.

Example

Ethyl Corp. provided in its 1993 annual report an analysis of its operations by stating that it used the revenues it received on the following items: materials and services (63.8 percent), payrolls and employee benefits (16.8 percent), current taxes (4.8 percent), regular dividends (3.6 percent), interest expense (2.3 percent), and for use in the business including expansion and modernization (8.7 percent). Although not prepared with a cash flow orientation, this schedule provides information on the major components of Ethyl's operations.

The FASB allowed firms to disclose information about operating cash flows using the indirect method. In particular, it stated:

Enterprises that choose not to provide information about major classes of operating cash receipts and payments by the direct method as encouraged in paragraph 27 shall determine and report the same amount for net cash flow from operating activities indirectly by adjusting net income to reconcile it to net cash flow from operating activities (the indirect or reconciliation method). That requires adjusting net income to remove (a) the effects of all deferrals of past operating cash receipts and payments, such as changes during the period in inventory, deferred income, and the like, and all accruals of expected future operating cash receipts and payments, such as depreciation, amortization of goodwill, and gains and losses on sales of property, plant, and equipment and discontinued operations (which relate to investing activities), and gains or losses on extinguishment of debt (which is a financing activity) (*FASB Statement No. 95*, para. 28).

Let us examine several examples of disclosure according to the indirect method.

Example

Eli Lilly and Co. reports the following derivation of net cash flows from operating activities in its 1993 financial statements:

Net income	$ 480.2
Adjustments to reconcile net income to cash flows from operating activities:	
Depreciation and amortization	398.3
Change in deferred taxes	(231.6)
Restructuring and special charges—net of payments	1,041.3
Cumulative effect of changes in accounting principles	10.9
Other noncash (income)—net	(53.1)
	1,646.0
	(continued)

Changes in operating assets and liabilities:

Receivables—decrease	(32.1)
Inventories—increase	(192.3)
Other assets—increase	(104.5)
Accounts payable and other liabilities—increase	199.8
	(129.1)
Net cash flows from operating activities	$1,516.9

Eli Lilly uses the indirect method, as can be seen from the reconciliation of net income to net operating cash flows, without the disclosure of components of operating cash flows such as collections from customers, payments to suppliers, employees, and the like. To derive net operating cash flow from net income, the firm makes two general types of adjustments; (a) items that are included in income but either do not involve cash or are not considered operating activities, and (b) items that involve cash but are not included in income. Eli Lilly includes depreciation and amortization among the first type because it is included in income, but does not represent a cash outflow. Similarly, the change in deferred taxes was included as a reduced tax expense (or an increase of income) of $231.6 million and is therefore subtracted when calculating cash from operations because it has no cash flow implications in 1993. However, the most significant adjustment is the $1,041.3 million for restructuring expenses, net of cash payments. Here, the restructuring charge was deducted from income, but most of it did not involve cash outflows. Thus, just like depreciation, it has to be added back to income in computing net cash from operating activities.

Among other type of adjustments, Eli Lilly reduces net income for the increases in current assets—inventories and other assets. The acquisition of these assets necessitated the outflow of cash, but since they are still outstanding on the balance sheet date, they are not yet included in income in 1993. These assets would be included in cost of goods sold or other expenses in 1994, when the inventories are sold, or when the other current assets are utilized. Similarly, the increase in accounts receivable indicates that sales revenues included in income for 1993 were not fully collected in 1993 and are therefore reduced by the amount not yet collected, $32.1 million. Finally, net income includes expenses of $199.8 million, which were not yet paid in 1993, but represent increases in accounts payable and other liabilities which would be paid in 1994 or afterwards.

Example

In its 1993 statement of cash flows, First Interstate Bankcorp reports net income of $736.7 million and net operating cash flows of $976.0 million. Among the items that reconcile the two is a depreciation and amortization expense of $124.4 million and a provision for credit losses of $112.6 million. The second item represents bank loans that are not expected to be collected and are written off. This is done by an accounting entry similar to depreciation and does not represent a cash outflow. Thus, it is added back to income in calculating net cash flow from operating activities.

Example

Meredith Corp. is a Fortune 500 diversified media firm engaged in magazine and book publishing, television broadcasting, and residential real estate marketing. It reports 1993 cash from operating activities as follows:

Cash flows from operating activities:	
Earnings from continuing operations	$18,626
Adjustments to reconcile net earnings to net cash provided by operating activities:	
Depreciation and amortization	32,393
Amortization of film contract rights	26,908
Deferred income taxes	4,936
Decrease in receivables	565
(Increase) in inventories	(6,234)
Decrease in supplies and prepayments	1,855
(Decrease) in accounts payable and accruals	(112)
Decrease in deferred subscription costs	4,432
Reductions in unearned subscription revenues	(3,514)
Reductions in other deferred items	(9,469)
Net cash provided by operating activities	$79,972

As can be seen, Meredith amortizes its film contract rights. This amortization does not involve cash and is similar to the depreciation of tangible assets. Thus, Meredith adds this charge back, since it was subtracted in deriving net income. Note that the reduction in unearned subscription revenue is subtracted from net income in computing net cash flow from operations. The reduction in unearned revenues occurs because these revenues were earned during the current period and therefore were included in net income. However, the cash for these subscriptions had been received in the prior year, and thus we have a revenue event that is not a cash event in 1993. Therefore, it is subtracted from net income in computing net cash from operating activities.

Example

A. T. Cross manufactures and markets high-quality writing instruments such as ball point and fountain pens and mechanical pencils. It also markets luggage, leather goods, and various gift items. The company reports the following items on its 1989 statement of cash flows:

Net income	$36,001,500
Adjustments to reconcile net income to net cash provided by operating activities:	
Depreciation	5,185,348
Amortization	2,986,762
Provision for losses on accounts receivable	702,552
Deferred income taxes	(1,456,126)
Provision for warranty costs	1,760,927
Changes in operating assets and liabilities, net of effects from acquisitions - Note G:	
Accounts receivable	(3,585,809)
Inventories	(8,924,315)
Other assets—net	(2,434,214)
Accounts payable	(3,881,963)
Other liabilities—net	5,069,781
Warranty costs paid	(1,560,927)
Foreign currency transaction (gain) loss	30,670,817
Net cash provided by operating activities	30,534,333

A. T. Cross adds back to net income the provision for losses on accounts receivable since the provision is a noncash expense that was subtracted in deriving net income. Note that A. T. Cross also adds back the provision for warranty costs for exactly the same reason. However, unlike the provision for losses on accounts receivable, it subtracts actual payments made under its warranty. This is unnecessary with accounts receivable that are written off, because no cash is involved when accounts receivables are written off; it is just an accounting entry.

Example

Harsco Corp. manufactures military vehicles and defense systems, scaffoldings and concrete-forming equipment, plastic piping, propane tanks, and various steel products. Harsco reports the following items in its 1989 disclosure of operating cash flows:

Net income	$ 11,362
Adjustments to reconcile net income to net cash provided by operating activities:	
Depreciation	56,229
Other, net	3,324
Changes in assets and liabilities, net of the effect of businesses acquired:	
Notes and accounts receivable	8,457
Inventories	(59,719)
Other current assets	(16,313)
Accounts payable	4,158
Accrued long-term contract costs	56,689
Other current liabilities	5,164
Advance deposits on long-term contracts	63,296
Other noncurrent assets and liabilities	(3,100)
Net cash provided by operating activities	$129,547

Note that Harsco subtracts about $60 million from net income because of the increase in inventory. However, it then adds back to net income about $57 million for the *decrease* in accrued long-term costs and about $63 million for advance deposits on long-term contracts. The first of these latter two items represents costs that are recognized for the production of inventory (i.e., work performed on the manufacturing of long-term contracts), although they have not been paid during the accounting period. The second of the two items represents payments that were made by customers for the long-term contracts. These payments qualify as cash inflows from customers and should be added to operating cash flows, as Harsco did.

Example

Sonat Inc. is a diversified firm that operates in the oil and gas fields. It is active in the transmission and sale of natural gas, contract drilling, and exploration and production of oil and gas. Sonat reports the following items on its 1989 operating cash flows:

Cash flows from operating activities:	
Net income (loss)	$108,978
Adjustments to reconcile net income to	
net cash proved by operating activities:	
Depreciation, depletion, amortization and	
valuation adjustments	163,120
Deferred income taxes and investment tax credits	37,523
Equity in (earnings) of joint ventures, less distributions	(9,021)
(Gain) on sale of assets	(11,004)
Reserves for regulatory matters	(334,074)
Natural gas purchase contract settlement costs	210,986
Other	17,791
Change in working capital	60,566
Net cash provided by operating activities	$244,865

Two items stand out in this schedule: the reserves for regulatory matters and natural gas purchase contract settlement costs. The first is subtracted from income because in 1989 the regulating body approved prior rate increases for one of the firm's subsidiaries. Thus, additional revenue was recognized in 1989, although the cash inflows representing these revenues were actually received by the firm much earlier. Instead of recognizing these revenues immediately, the firm created reserves for fear that future refunds to customers would be needed if the regulating body did not approve the rate increases. When the rate increases were approved, revenues and income increased, but cash flows in 1989 were unaffected. Thus, the firm had to subtract this item from income in deriving cash from operating activities. The second item, natural gas purchase contract settlement costs, reflects reserves for future potential losses on existing contracts to purchase natural gas. This was needed since the company agreed to purchase natural gas at significantly higher prices. Since no cash is involved yet, it represents a noncash accounting entry similar to depreciation expense or reserves for future repairs under warranty, and it is added back to income to derive cash from operating activities. These two items together account for about one-half of the cash from operations. Still, as we emphasized, these items do *not* represent cash flows.

Example

Sunshine Mining Company, which is engaged in the production of gold, silver, crude oil, and natural gas, reports the following items on its 1989 statement of cash flows (in thousands):

	1989
Cash Provided (Used) by Operations	
Net loss	$(38,345)
Adjustments to reconcile net loss to net cash provided (used) by operations:	
Depreciation, depletion, amortization and impairment provisions	37,134
Amortization of discount on silver indexed bonds	1,916
Gain on the sale of fixed assets	(828)
Common stock issuances for:	
Interest on silver indexed bonds	—
Services provided and other	791
Net (increase) decrease in:	
Accounts receivable	(1,800)
Inventories	2,374
Other current assets	1,341
Other assets and deferred charges	(657)
Net increase (decrease) in:	
Accounts payable—trade	578
Oil and gas proceeds payable	1,947
Accrued expenses	(3,435)
Other liabilities and deferred credits	(784)
Other, net	(10)
Net cash provided (used) by operations	$ 222

As can be seen, Sunshine added the common stock that was issued for services provided of $791,000 to net income in computing cash from operations. To understand this item, it can be assumed that some other entity provided services to Sunshine, for which the entity was compensated with common stock. The services were recorded as operating expenses and were subtracted in deriving net income. However, these services did not necessitate an outflow of cash; therefore, they are added back to net income in deriving cash from operations. This item does *not* appear in the section of financing cash flows, because no cash was received for the issued shares. However, if the amount was material, it should have been disclosed in the schedule of noncash financing events.

Example

Ethyl Corp. computes net cash flow from operating activities using the indirect method. In 1992, it subtracted from net income $30 million for the after-tax gain on sale of 20 percent interest in First Colony

Corporation. Ethyl included this gain in its 1992 income, which does not represent an operating cash flow but an investing cash flow. Thus, it had to subtract this gain from net income in deriving net cash from operating activities. Indeed, the 1992 investing cash flows include proceeds from the sale of 20 percent interest in First Colony Corporation of $256.3 million. However, in 1993, Ethyl subtracted $60.6 million from net income in deriving net operating cash flow for income tax payment on 1992 gain on sale of 20 percent of First Colony Corporation. This is appropriate since the actual cash outflow for the gain on the sale occurred in 1993, although the tax expense on the gain was included in 1992 income. Thus, to derive net cash flows from operating activities in 1993 from net income, we have to add a cash outflow of $60.6 million for taxes, which is not included in 1993 income. Note that this transaction reflects the use of the problems in relying on information for a single year; 1992 investing cash flow and 1993 operating cash flows are affected significantly by the sale of the 20 percent interest in First Colony Corporation. Thus, our reliance on four-year averages of operating and free cash flows discussed in Chapter 5, seems to be preferable to an analysis based on any single year.

Example

In its 1993 statement of cash flow, Con Agra, Inc., uses the indirect method to calculate net cash from operating activities. One of its most significant adjustments is $210.9 million provision for nonpension postretirement benefits, which is added to 1993 net income of $270.3. This provision relates to the recent accounting rule for postretirement benefits other than pensions, which are required to be accrued throughout the employees' service, although they are to be paid only after retirement. This represents an accounting expense that is included in income, but that would not involve cash outflows until after the employees retire. Thus, it is added back to income in deriving net cash from operating activities. The firm adopted this standard for the first time in 1993, as required by the FASB, and this is the reason for the magnitude of the adjustment. Most firms include a similar adjustment in their 1993 statements, except it is called an adjustment for the cumulative effect of an accounting change.

Outside the United States, countries differ in their requirements for a statement of cash flows in general, and the way to derive net operating cash flow in particular. New Zealand requires firms to use the direct method for reporting operating cash flows. Japan does not require a statement of cash flows, but only a statement of sources and uses of funds, which can be shown on a working capital basis instead of using cash. The British way of reporting the statement of cash flows is to begin with net cash flow from operating activities, which does not include interest received or paid or tax payments. Interest and dividends are subtracted from operating cash flows on the body of the statement, as is the payment of taxes. The remainder of the statement is very similar to a U.S. statement. At the end of this chapter, we present the cash flow statement of Hongkong Telecom, which is prepared using the British method.

INTERPRETATION OF OPERATING CASH FLOWS

Net cash flow from operating activities indicates the amount of cash that the firm was able to generate from (or needed to spend on) its ongoing business activities. Ideally, a firm should be able to generate cash from its business activities in every period. However, in reality, many financially healthy firms generate cash from their business activities in most periods, but spend more cash on their business activities than they receive from customers in some periods. Also, a firm may be in the development stage of its business. It may invest in developing its products or in setting production facilities and distribution channels (investment activities), while larger cash receipts from customers are expected to occur only in the future. Another example is a seasonal business that invests in setting up inventories during one or two quarters, while most sales are made during other quarters (such as during the holiday season). Operating cash flows are likely to be negative during the quarters when inventories are built, but positive in quarters when inventories are sold.

For some periods, and for some firms, a negative net cash flow from operations is acceptable, such as a manufacturer who works on long-term contracts (e.g., Boeing) and must re-tool and build inventories during the initial stages of production. However, in the majority of cases, a positive net cash flow from business activities is expected. A business that spends more cash on its ongoing activities than it generates has to finance these activities somehow. It can just use up its cash reserves, it can borrow additional cash, it can raise additional equity, or it can liquidate investments or fixed assets. But none of these options can be sustained for prolonged periods. For example, it is unlikely that creditors will keep lending to a business that continuously does not generate an acceptable level of cash from its operations. Similarly, liquidation of necessary assets may reduce the chances of generating cash flows from operations in the future. Thus, continuous negative cash flows from operating activities (which are unrelated to a seasonal business or the operating cycle of the business) should be examined carefully by the cash flow analyst.

In addition to net cash flows from operating activities, one should examine the components of cash flows. Actual cash inflows begin with the collection of cash from accounts receivable. The ease with which the entity collects its accounts receivable is an important determinant of its financial flexibility. Improvements in the collection period begin at the credit approval. For small, unknown, or startup entities, a greater degree of due diligence by the credit analyst is needed to enhance operating cash flows.

Reductions in accounts receivable, next to planned reductions in inventory, are the most sought after way to increase operating cash flow. Faster collection periods, made possible by vastly improved credit analysis computer software that enables the credit analyst to review prospective and existing accounts, has upgraded and abated operating cash flow. Additionally, the conservative use of customer credits and discounts along with great strides on accounts receivable software packages have helped improve the flow of collections.

Because of the growth and ease in software programs, credit department analysts today have at their fingertips, among other treasury department schedules, an aging schedule of the entity's accounts receivable. Although some analysts like to look at the average collection period,[3] the formula does not provide them with the more important collection and credit information such as (1) which clients pay their bills on time and might be accorded credits

---

[3]The average collection period is defined as 360/average accounts receivable turnover. In turn, the accounts receivable turnover is defined as net sales/average accounts receivable.

and (2) which clients have run into such severe payment problems that further delivery of goods is unjustified—and whose accounts should probably be classified as bad debt.

Example

According to an article in Corporate Cashflow (May 1994), United States Gypsum Co. (USG) was able to provide a price discount to a cash-rich customer who was willing to pay 30 days ahead of schedule. The customer received a better return on its cash than was available elsewhere, and USG managed to provide a price discount that was lower than their cost of financing.

Computer software has made the job of the credit manager much easier. With the push of a button, most credit managers can check the payment history of their clients over many years, thereby making the credit approval process much quicker, simpler, and more accurate. Credit managers still use time-honored techniques to reduce their bad debt expense and aid the accounts receivable process (i.e., minimize the nominal amount of receivables outstanding). Credit service agency reports, such as Dun & Bradstreet (D&B) credit reports, are still widely used, although many credit managers feel the data in such reports are to a great extent outdated. D&B reports can be helpful if they show lawsuits against the company, show the company's financial statement, or show the employment and educational backgrounds of key employees.

Trade references, which also help the credit analyst gather information about potential clients, come in a variety of sources. The new-account customer application designates areas for both trade and bank referrals. Sales professionals, who visit the prospective new account's offices and facilities are likely to spot the products of companies who can be called for references, even though these firms might not be listed on the credit application. The credit application itself usually provides useful information to the credit analyst.

Good credit analysis is vitally important to helping the enterprise's cash flow, as errors by credit department analysts can be very costly to the entity. Trade shows and reference checks of the client's competitors are also very useful. So are telephone leads resulting from the questioning of competitors. Analyzing financial statements for trends in operating free cash flow, free cash flow, and leverage are essential to the credit analyst, since cash flow trends is a leading indicator of financial failure. Newspapers and magazines are also likely to bring a flow of financial information to the credit department, especially for the larger customer. Some credit managers take a very careful approach to rumored takeover candidates, since credit downgrades often result after a takeover.

A pattern of declining receipts from customers may indicate a maturing product, softening of demand, lenient credit policy toward customers, and the like. The cash flow analyst may be interested in ascertaining the reasons for this development—and may do so—by examining other firms in the industry and management discussion of activities (and liquidity) in the reports, or by directly inquiring of the firm's management.

Example

In some cases, a manufacturer uses its ability to finance the customer's receivables as a strategic weapon. Boeing Co. reports in 1992 customer financing of slightly above $2 billion out of total assets of about $18 billion. In the same period, McDonnell Douglas suffered in its competition with Boeing because it could not offer its customers attractive financing agreements.

A simple ratio that can illustrate the credit-granting policy of the firm, or its ability to collect its accounts receivable, is the ratio of collections to sales. Collections from customers can be estimated as shown in the previous section by sales minus the change in accounts receivable. One can divide collections during a period by sales in the same period. When operations are relatively stable, this ratio is likely to hover around 1; that is, most sales are collected within the year of sales. However, if the ratio shows a declining trend, the quality of a firm's receivables should be questioned by the cash flow analyst.

Similarly, if one observes a significant increase in cash payments to employees and suppliers that is beyond the proportionate increase in cash receipts from customers, the cash flow analyst should examine whether the firm experienced unfavorable business conditions. For example, the firm may have problems marketing its products and therefore is caught with unwanted buildup of inventories. It may spend more cash on selling, general, and

FIGURE 4–1
Norfolk Southern: Collections and Payments Ratio

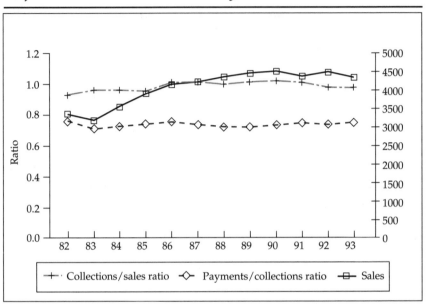

administrative expenses than is warranted by the level of activities. Again, sometimes a firm may incur greater administrative costs in one period because it may make substantial changes in its operations (such as computerizing its operations). However, one should not observe continuous increases in cash payments to suppliers and employees beyond those called for by increases in demand.

In Figure 4–1, we see that sales of Norfolk Southern, a transportation firm, increased slightly over the period 1982–1993. The ratio of collections to sales is very stable around 1, and the ratio of payments to suppliers and employees to collections is again very stable throughout that period around 0.8. This is to be expected given the relatively stable business of railroads.

Figure 4–2 shows Macy's sales during the period 1983–1994. The graph shows that Macy's sales increased smoothly until 1990, when they began to fall slowly. The ratio of collections to sales was very stable around 1 during that period, as would be expected for a retailer with a lot of cash or credit card sales. However, its

FIGURE 4–2
Macy (H.R.): Collections and Payments Ratio

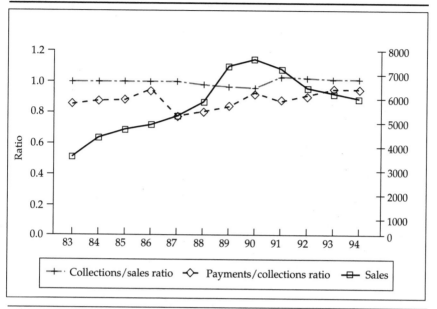

margins, as measured by the ratio of payments to suppliers and employees to cash collections, decreased since 1989, reflecting Macy's financial difficulties.

While "involuntary" increases in the current asset accounts do occur, with advances in computer software programs for inventory control and accounts receivable/payable, such involuntary buildups are less frequent than they were prior to the 1980s and are now more easily controlled. Such software improvements are part of the explanation for the longevity of the business expansion that began in 1982. Even the recession that started at the end of the 1980s did not find most businesses with excess inventories.

Example

In its discussion of cash flows during 1990, Ashland Oil Inc. comments on an increase in its cost of crude oil: "However, as long as product prices move reasonably in tandem with crude oil prices, there is little impact on working capital from higher crude oil costs because the payment terms on our crude oil purchases are longer than the terms for our receivables."

This indicates the importance of examining the relationships between costs of the product and the ability of the firm to roll these costs over to the customer. Furthermore, it indicates the importance of assessing the credit terms of the firm from its suppliers and the credit terms it grants to its own customers.

In order to determine the quality of inventories, one has to measure the inventory turnover for the different products the entity sells, because almost all firms have products that are hot sellers and products that sell poorly. Unfortunately, this is impossible to do with published information. If the inventory turnover for an individual firm is showing a slowing trend, the analyst should question management about which product lines are contributing to the inventory buildup.

If the entity's products are not what its customers are demanding, operating and free cash flow will be affected and perhaps signal that management should be taking the appropriate measures to correct the problems. The solution may not lie with the product itself but how it is being promoted (analyze advertising expenditures compared to the industry), or its cost of manufacture, which may be too high relative to the industry.

When management decides to reduce prices of slow-moving inventory, operating cash flows increase as the goods are sold, although profit margins and earnings decrease compared to what they would have otherwise been. Nevertheless, this strategy is probably superior to a strategy that lets the inventory remain on the shelves.

Inventory bulges can be expensive and there is no guarantee inventory can be sold at a profit. Cash tied up in inventory could otherwise be used to reduce interest-bearing debt or earn a money market rate of return.

Example

In its 1990 first quarter report to shareholders, Federal-Mogul writes:

> The [warehouse] facility has also implemented a new computer system that provides better order and inventory management, and freight consolidation. It tracks a product from the time an order is placed with a supplier, to the moment it is shipped, then received by a customer.

This new system allows us to forecast and manage inventory more accurately, and at the same time serve our customers better and save the company money.

However, such improvements in warehousing and shipping can backfire if they are not implemented properly. For example, Stride Rite Co. installed a new warehouse and distribution center, which was supposed to ship products to customers within three hours from the receipt of an order. This type of service was meant to induce retailers to prefer Stride Rite shoes. In 1993, Stride Rite's distribution center had many problems and contributed significantly to reduced sales in 1993 and 1994.

Not surprisingly, many advances in the production process are directly related to minimizing inventory, such as just in time (JIT) inventory control techniques, process mapping, reducing cycle time, and total quality management. Advances such as cell manufacturing, in which the production process divides the workforce into groups, or cells, has improved both the quality of the product and the level of inventories. In cell manufacturing, raw material is ordered and inspected by the same group that is also responsible for its portion of the production process. Levels of work-in-process inventory are controlled by the continuous passage of goods from one cell to the next, and by the elimination of space for storing work-in-process inventory within a cell.

Example

Martin Marietta Corp. practices total quality management (TQM), a team approach to the productive process. The company defines TQM as follows:

1. TQM recognizes workers as experts and gives them the freedom and decision-making authority they need if they are to develop new and better ways of performing their jobs.
2. TQM advocates the goal of zero defects for every employee throughout the company.
3. TQM provides quantification, measurement, and feedback about quality to employees.
4. TQM is teamwork: workers and managers working as a team. It has been proven time and again that if management shares the decision-making process authority with workers, the very

things managers are supposed to manage—cost, quality, and production schedules—begin to improve automatically.

Example

One of the areas in which retailers were able to increase their efficient use of inventories is by moving to vendor-directed inventory management. In such a system, the vendor actually manages the inventory of items that the retailer sells. In one such example, Richard Gamble reports (*Corporate Cashflow,* September 1994) that Johnson Wax was able to increase the in-stock rate from 80 percent to 90 percent in Kmart stores, while simultaneously reducing inventory from 16 weeks of normal sales to 2–4 weeks of sales. This represents cash savings for both companies. In other cases, retailers or manufacturers strongly suggest to a supplier to move its operations closer to them so that inventory can be delivered at the desired time to the buyer.

Another area that received a lot of attention recently is the cycle time in a manufacturing process. Cycle time is defined as the length of time from the receipt of a customer's order until it is shipped to the customer. Firms have a clear incentive to reduce cycle time because short delivery periods constitute a strategic advantage. Furthermore, the experience of many manufacturers shows that short cycle times lead to smaller inventories, reduced inventory costs, and fewer defects.

Cycle time can be reduced by emphasis on quality improvement. Firms find that improvements in quality can be caused by simplifying the design and then the production process for any specific product. It is found that setup costs and switching costs can be substantially reduced by simpler designs of the product or by greater investment in the production process. These investments may cause lower utilization rates of the firm's capacity, but greater quality, reduced cycle time, and greater customer satisfaction and reliability. In the long run, reductions in cycle time and increases in quality pay off handsomely.

The cash flow analyst should investigate whether the firm seems to improve the quality of its products and reduce its cycle time. Such information can be found in the management discussion and analysis portion of financial statements, or in press releases or conversations with the firm. The analyst may also inquire if management intends to apply for the Baldrige National Quality Award or has been nominated for or has received other quality awards. Additionally, the analyst can examine the turnover ratios of the firm; these should increase if the firm is able to conduct its operations with smaller inventories, fewer assets, or with more efficient credit policy.

Example

FAB Industries is a firm in the textile milling business. It operates over 200 machines to produce several types of materials. The introduction of cheap textile imports from the Far East in the 1980s and the 1990s forced many U.S. textile producers and processors either to produce efficiently or to go out of business. However, the recent emphasis on inventory reduction by U.S. retailers is helping the surviving domestic textile producers and processors. The retailers now insist that orders should be supplied within two weeks or less, causing domestic suppliers to obtain the business simply because foreign competitors cannot ship the goods within such a short period. This is evident in the cash flows and market value of such domestic producers as FAB Industries (see Figure 4–3).

Payments for taxes is another area that the cash flow analyst should investigate in detail. In some cases, a firm may defer its tax payments to the future. The analyst should examine the tax expense and its relationship to actual cash payments for taxes. When the two differ significantly, the analyst should investigate the reasons for these differences. Are they expected to reverse in the near future? When? What are the causes for these differences? Do they result from tax loss carryforwards? If yes, what is the amount that is still available to be utilized in the future for both tax and financial reporting purposes? The answers to these questions should affect the projections for future cash payments to the tax authorities and financial reporting. Of course, loss carryforwards can be a very valuable asset if the company is expected to utilize the credits in future periods.

Example

Inter-Regional Financial Group (IFG, a broker-dealer) has been able to take advantage of tax loss carryforwards. As shown in its 1990 annual report, IFG was able to generate $4.8 million in operating cash flow from utilizing tax loss carryforwards.

FIGURE 4–3
FAB Industries: Free Cash Flow Analysis

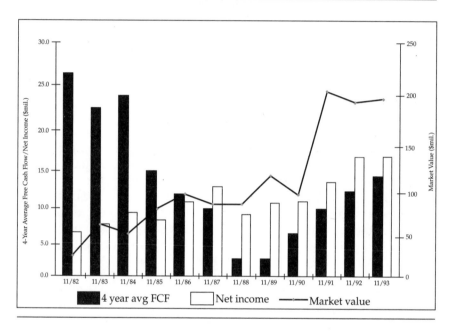

Example

In a meeting with analysts, Marathon Oil Co. discussed its tax outlook in detail. Among the comments made at the meeting:

We believe that the U.K tax regime is politically stable. Our confidence in the U.K. tax regime is evidenced by our aggressive capital investment program. Future changes in the tax regime are generally expected to be neutral or beneficial and not detrimental.

In Tunisia, the tax system is based on variable royalty and tax rates. The system is similar in philosophy with the PRT in that the investor is allowed to recover his investment plus a return before being burdened with tax and royalty. We expect to pay tax and royalty in 1991 for the Ezzaouia Concession on the Zarzis Permit.

Unlike the U.K., where exploration and production incentives enacted by the government have resulted in a substantial increase in exploration and production activity in the U.K., the United States has enacted tax law changes that act as disincentives to production and exploration activity in the States. As a result, exploration and production in the States has steadily declined throughout the '80s and early '90s.

Such information is important to the cash flow analyst because it helps not only in prediction of future tax payments but also in the feasibility of future capital expenditures. Lower taxes lead to greater free cash flows. In Chapter 7, we devote more analysis to the effects of accounting for income taxes and show disclosure examples.

Other operating cash flows should probably receive close scrutiny by the cash flow analyst who is interested in forecasting future cash flows. The analyst should investigate whether these cash flows are expected to persist in the future. For example, cash payments or receipts from settlement of legal cases may not persist in the future. Thus, the analyst may choose to exclude these from predictions of future cash flows from operating activities.

Finally, operating cash flows include payments for interest. As discussed previously, the cash flow analyst may be interested in examining the cash flows generated from operations before interest payments are subtracted. The analyst can then make the necessary adjustments to different levels of debt if the firm is considering floating new debt or if it is reasonable to assume that it will float new debt in the future. Focusing on the current level of interest payments or interest received may also be misleading in comparisons of firms from the same industry. Presumably, net operating cash flows may differ across firms just because of different levels of financial leverage in firms' capital structure. Thus, it seems more reasonable to exclude interest from operating cash flows in the initial stages of the analysis and include it again when focusing on the free cash flows.

The analyst should also examine the growth rate and stability of the enterprise's operating cash flows. For companies like Food Lion and Wal-Mart, which have a high rate of growth due to rapid store expansion, one should also see a rapid rate of growth in operating cash flow, but not necessarily free cash flow, as we shall see in the next chapter.

INTERPRETING CASH FLOWS FROM FINANCING ACTIVITIES

Cash flows from financing activities should first be segregated to cash inflows and cash outflows from financing activities. The net cash flows from financing activities will be determined by the net cash generated from operating activities minus net cash used for investing activities minus the increase in the cash balance. Thus, once the cash flow analyst examines the cash generated from operations and cash investments, net cash financing is of little relevance. However, the composition of net cash from financing activities is of great relevance.

The most significant source of financing for most firms is borrowing. The academic literature is unclear about the implications of debt financing. Debt financing is generally considered favorable because interest on debt is tax deductible. However, a firm that is overly leveraged increases the risk of bankruptcy and thus, the expected costs of bankruptcy to shareholders. Most firms have some optimal level of debt; increases beyond this level are undesirable for the firm, whereas increases up to that point are favorable. Other fortunate firms are such strong cash flow producers that all growth opportunities are easily financed through internal operations. The cash flow analyst may wish to consider whether the firm's increase in debt financing is favorable or not, depending on the analyst's assessments of the optimal level of debt for the firm and the relation of debt to both the magnitude of cash flows. One way of assessing the optimal level of debt is to assess the pro forma ability of the firm to meet scheduled debt payment from free cash flows (we provide a more detailed discussion of this point in Chapter 7).

Another implication of debt financing is that current owners/shareholders of the firm indicate they wish to retain full ownership in the firm, possibly because they perceive a high probability that the value of the firm will grow. Thus, increases in debt financing, or at least increases in debt financing that are not accompanied by increases in equity financing, may be perceived as favorable signals about the future prospects of a firm. However, increases in debt financing may cause conflicts of interest between stockholders and bondholders, which, in turn, may lead management to invest in suboptimal projects. These conflicts may lead to undesirable consequences or to wasted resources that are dedicated to reducing this conflict. Thus, issuance of debt may sometimes be viewed negatively by the cash flow analyst.

Example

In the fourth quarter of calendar 1994, Quaker Oats Co. decided to acquire Snapple for $1.7 billion in cash, which Quaker Oats borrowed. The acquisition was supposed to utilize synergies between Snapple and Gatorade, two soft drinks for the athletic and health-conscious segment of market. On the day of the announcement, the price of Quaker Oats declined by about 10 percent. The share price declined for several reasons. First, Snapple was known to be a huge cash user. Second, many investors viewed the acquisition as an attempt by Quaker Oats' management to prevent a takeover of Quaker Oats, which was rumored to be an acquisition target during the second half of 1994. Substantially increasing the firm's financial leverage greatly reduced the likelihood of an unfriendly takeover of Quaker Oats, which led investors who favored a takeover to sell their stock. During the ensuing quarters, Quaker Oats reported dissappointing financial results and declining cash flows.

Another aspect of debt financing is the composition of debt; is it short-term or long-term debt? What are the interest rates on the debt? And what does the principal payment schedule look like? Traditionally, it is recommended that short-term debt be used to finance short-term assets, whereas long-term debt should be used to finance long-term projects. The logic behind this recommendation can be seen by a firm that invests in a long-term project expected to yield 12 percent annually and finances it with a short-term loan carrying an interest rate of 10 percent. Suppose that after three years short-term interest rates increase to 14 percent, and the firm still needs to finance its project. The project will be cash flow negative, although it could have been cash flow positive had the firm financed the project initially with long-term debt, even if that debt had carried interest of 10.5 percent. This problem occurred in banks that borrowed funds at the short-term rate and lent these funds at the long-term rate. Such banks had financial difficulties and had to be bailed out by the government. Thus, the analyst should assess the composition of debt and relate it to investments by the firm. In particular, the analyst should examine whether old debt is being refinanced or retired or whether net new debt is being issued, what it is used for, and whether the firm's poor creditworthiness precludes borrowing long-term funds at reasonable interest rates. The analyst should also examine whether the debt is denominated in foreign currency, whether it carries fixed or variable interest rate, and whether the firm has undertaken any interest rate swaps or purchased any derivatives in an attempt to hedge its debt exposure. Such information is available in the footnotes for long-term debt.

Example

Tecumseh Products Co. had on December 31, 1993, total assets of $1.133 billion and $445.9 million in total liabilities, of which $11.2 million represented long-term debt. Note 8 to its 1993 financial statements reads as follows:

> Short-term debt consists of borrowings by foreign subsidiaries at varying interest rates under revolving credit agreements and overdraft arrangements with banks used in the normal course of business. The U.S. dollar equivalent of this debt was $10.5 and $19.8 million at December 31, 1993 and 1992, respectively.
>
> Long-term debt consists of the following;
>
> 1. Unsecured borrowings, primarily with banks, by foreign subsidiaries with interest rates ranging from 7.9 percent to 10.3 percent. The U.S. dollar equivalent of these borrowings was $9.2 and $12.4 million at December 31, 1993 and 1992, respectively.
> 2. A $5.5 million ($4.8 million in 1992) bank repurchase agreement bearing interest at 1/2 percent above the London Inter-Bank Offered Rate (LIBOR) due in 1995.
>
> Scheduled maturities of long-term debt outstanding at December 31, 1993 are as follows: 1994—$3.5 million; 1995—$9.4 million; 1996—$1.2 million; 1997—$0.5 million; 1998 and beyond—$0.1 million. Interest paid was $3.6 million in 1993, $5.2 million in 1992, and $6.0 million in 1991. The carrying value of short- and long-term debt at December 31, 1993 and 1992, approximates fair market value.

Note that although the total debt of Tecumseh is not substantial compared to its assets or even to total liabilities, the firm provides detailed footnote information on the composition of its short- and long-term debt. We learn the amounts outstanding, the average interest rates, whether the debt is denominated in domestic or foreign currency, whether the debt has a fixed interest rate or is linked to some index (such as LIBOR), and the maturities of debt in the following five years. This information is important for the cash flow analyst in deriving a forecast of future cash flows. Additional information about balances of short-term borrowing during the year may be obtained from Form 10-K.

Example

General Signal Corp. issued a press release on June 1, 1992, informing the public about the issuance of $100 million of convertible subordinated notes that carried an interest rate of 5.75 percent. These notes were intended to replace short-term borrowing of $25 million with an interest rate of 8.94 percent, $21 million of 8.675 percent debentures, and $53 million for other short-term borrowing at 4.36 percent. Thus, the main purpose of these notes was to replace costly borrowing with cheaper and longer-term borrowing.

Turning to equity financing, the cash flow analyst should examine whether the issued equity causes the debt-to-equity ratio to move away from or toward the optimal level. Also, the analyst should examine the type of securities issued, whether they are common stock, preferred stock, other securities or financial instruments, and their potential conversion to common stock. A common view is that current owners of a firm will invite others to invest in their firm only if they expect future prospects to be worse, or if they view their stock to be overvalued, in effect, inviting others to share their burden. Thus, a negative reaction is expected to stock issuance.

A symmetric argument can be made for repurchases of a firm's common stock. It can be argued that the firm decides to invest its excess cash flows in an identical risk-return trade-off: its own securities. Moreover, management possesses inside information that future prospects are favorable, and the stock market does not share these expectations. Thus, management decides to repurchase stock at low prices. Indeed, academic evidence points out a positive market reaction when the firm announces a significant (greater than 5 percent) stock repurchase program.

Finally, the payment of a cash dividend is considered an important signaling mechanism by most—management will signal its expectations about the future by increases or decreases of cash dividends. When cash dividends are increased, management signals that it expects future cash flows to be favorable, so that a higher level of dividends can be sustained. When a firm reduces its cash dividend, the market can interpret it as a negative signal about future cash flows, which are expected to decrease or remain low and will be insufficient to sustain the current level of cash dividends.

It may be useful to examine the stability of operating cash flows, which generally relates to the level of cash dividends. Firms that consistently generate strong operating cash flow, such as Philip Morris (the tobacco and food company) and regulated companies like public utilities, usually have a higher payout ratio than firms with large swings in operating cash flows. Cyclical companies usually pay lower cash dividends, since they can maintain a lower level of cash dividend payments from their operations. For example, the cash flow statements at the end of this chapter include both Boeing Co., with large swings in its cash from operations and Pfizer Inc., which has consistent operating cash flows. Pfizer pays out about 40–50 percent of its operating cash flows in dividends to shareholders, whereas Boeing has a rate of 10–20 percent. Thus, stability of operating cash flows is an important factor for the cash flow and credit analyst.

INTERPRETING CASH FLOWS ON INVESTING ACTIVITIES

As we saw earlier, most firms disclose in this section cash outlays on capital expenditures, acquisitions, investments in financial instruments, investments in unconsolidated subsidiaries, and purchases of additional shares from minority shareholders. Clearly, each of these investing activities has an opposite counterpart of a disinvesting activity, for instance, the sale of investments.

The cash flow analyst should investigate the capital expenditures of a firm and the retirement of PPE during the accounting period. Capital expenditures should be sufficient at least to sustain the current levels of operations. They can be compared to past capital expenditures, levels of investments by competitors, improvements in technology, current levels of PPE, and the firm's unit growth rates. A significant increase in the sale of PPE may indicate that the firm is suffering from cash shortage and decides to generate cash by selling fixed assets. This strategy means that the firm is reducing the scale of operations or that it is gradually liquidating. However, the firm may be just selling underutilized capital or making a strategic shift in its business. Thus, the cash flow analyst wishes to examine these events carefully because of the implications for future cash flows.

The firm has two major options in its future expansion—to expand internally through further investments in capital expenditures or to invest in the existing operations of other firms through acquisitions. Most studies to date show that, on the average, it is detrimental for a firm to expand through acquisition of other firms; most such acquisitions do not work as originally intended.[4] Thus, the cash flow analyst may want to assess the chances of success for the firm's acquisitions and the related costs of these acquisitions in terms of additional debt that is assumed or issued. The analyst should also assess the potential synergies that can be created through acquisition. These may have favorable effects on future cash flows by eliminating redundant operations.

Finally, the cash flow analyst should examine additional investments in unconsolidated subsidiaries (which are subsidiaries in which the firm has less than 50 percent of the stock), investments in joint ventures, and investments in other financial instruments. The analyst should carefully assess potential future cash flow consequences of such investments. Usually, investments in other entities, where the investing firm does not control the investee, are considered less desirable than investments in entities where a

---

[4]For example, Eastman Kodak was forced to sell Sterling Drug after admitting that large diversification attempt failed. Also, Deluxe, the largest U.S. check-printing firm, reported weak 1994 results as attempts to diversify out of its primary business has not succeeded.

firm has full control. Similarly, the analyst should examine the reasons for investments in financial instruments; are these made merely to park cash that will be needed in the near future for investments, or are they made because the firm has no superior investment opportunities?

Sometimes the distinction between investing or operating cash flows is not clear-cut. For example, a cash payment may pertain to an item that could be considered either as inventory or as a productive asset. If so, the appropriate classification shall depend on the activity that is likely to be the predominant source of cash flows for the item. For example, the acquisition and sale of equipment to be used by the enterprise or rented to others is generally considered an investing activity. However, equipment sometimes is acquired or produced to be used by the enterprise or rented to others for a short period of time and then sold. In those circumstances, the acquisition or production and subsequent sale of those assets can be considered an operating activity.

Needless to say, this ambiguity in reporting requirements leads to different interpretations in practice by many firms. Some leasing companies include the collections of principal on their capital leases as cash flows from operating activities on the grounds that the equipment leased is in fact inventory. Other leasing entities include such payments in investing activities on the grounds that the leases represent investments in the traditional sense. Thus, the cash flow analyst needs to carefully examine the accounting treatment of capital leases and their classification as investing or operating cash flows.

Similarly, the analyst should examine the implications of disinvesting events as carefully as investing events. Also, the cash flow analyst should note that the current requirements of *SFAS No. 95* are that *only* the cash portion of these events is disclosed in the statement of cash flows. It is reasonable in most cases to focus not only on the cash portion of the transaction but also on the noncash portion because of its future consequences. For example, the sale of a division for cash, notes receivable, and stocks will likely yield future cash inflows. These should be incorporated by the cash flow analyst, as well as the current inflow of cash from the sale of the division, which is reported in the statement of cash flows. Such information is usually disclosed as supplemental information to the statement. This leads us naturally to a discussion of the supplemental information to the statement of cash flows.

SUPPLEMENTAL INFORMATION

SFAS No. 95 requires firms to disclose additional information about their important economic events during the period beyond the direct cash flow implications of these events. For example, when a firm engages in a transaction that is, in effect, a financing or an investing event, but where the entire consideration is not in cash, the firm should report the transaction in a separate schedule, usually at the bottom of the statement of cash flows. Supplemental disclosure is necessary because financing and investing events are significant economic events, they affect the long-run viability of the firm, and they should be disclosed to investors and creditors regardless of whether they involve cash alone or combine cash and other consideration.

The FASB also requires firms that report net operating cash flows using the indirect approach to report the tax payments and the interest payments during the period. Let us examine several disclosures of these items.

Example

In its 1993 statement of cash flows, Gillette Co. reports the following supplemental information:

Supplemental disclosure of cash paid for (in millions):	
Interest	$ 72.5
Income taxes	180.9
Noncash investing and financing activities:	
Acquisition of businesses:	
Fair value of assets acquired	705.8
Cash paid	481.1
Liabilities assumed	$224.7

Note that the first part of the supplemental schedule is very standard. Firms report the cash payment for interest and income taxes either in the body of the cash flow statement or in footnotes to the statements. Most often, tax payments can be found in the income taxes footnote, and interest payments in the long-term borrowing footnote.

Among its investing activities, Gillette reports a cash outflow of $452.9 million for acquisition of business less cash acquired. Thus, although the fair value of the acquired business had been $705.8 million, it was shown among the investing cash outflows only at $452.9 million, the cash portion paid for it. The amount that was not paid in cash, but was assumed in additional liabilities, is not shown as a financing activity because it did not involve cash. Thus, the firm properly reports information about this noncash portion in the supplemental disclosure section.

Example

In its 1989 annual report, Ingersoll Rand reports the following items:

Noncash activity:	
Notes receivable from asset disposals	$ 2,325
Cash paid during the year for:	
Interest, net of amount capitalized	37,150
Income taxes	102,944

Ingersoll Rand reports proceeds from the sale of property, plant, and equipment of $8,194 in its cash flows from investing activities. However, part of the consideration received for these asset disposals was in the form of a note, so the firm reported an additional noncash consideration for disposal of assets in the amount of $2,325.

Example

Hercules Inc. reports the following items at the bottom of its 1993 statement of cash flows:

Supplemental Disclosure of Cash Flow Information	
Cash paid during the year for:	
Interest (net of amount capitalized)	$ 38,529
Income taxes, net	132,827
Noncash investing and financing activities:	
Conversion of notes and debentures	18,524
Contribution of net assets to joint ventures	—
Incentive plan stock issuance	61,600
Accounts payable for common stock acquisitions	22,046
Premium for early retirement of debt	4,144

As before, Hercules reports its payments for interest and taxes. It also reports additional items about events that did not affect cash, the first of which is the conversion of notes and debentures into other items that did not involve cash. The next item, although not applicable in

1993 (but a $52.2 million item in 1992), represents an investment in a joint venture that is effected through the transfer of noncash items into a joint venture with another entity. Since it is done without using any cash, the firm reports it in the supplemental schedule as an investment event that did not require cash. The following item is stock issuance to employees as incentive for their efforts. Since the employees did not pay cash for these stocks, this amount cannot be included among the financing activities of the cash flow statement. Similarly, the firm reacquired its own shares and included $320.5 million as a financing cash outflow in 1993. However, it reacquired additional shares (probably very close to year-end) for which it agreed to pay approximately $22 million in 1994. This amount will be included as a financing cash outflow in 1994, but is reported in the supplemental schedule in 1993 because it is material noncash financing event. Finally, the firm refinanced some of its long-term debt in 1993, incurring a charge of $4.1 million for early retirement of debt. Since this amount is refinance without a cash outflow, the firm reports it in the supplemental schedule.

FINANCIAL SUBSIDIARIES

The free cash flow analyst must take particular account of the cash flow implications of a firm's financial subsidiaries. Finance subsidiaries are large cash borrowers when the parent entity is in the growth stage and large cash providers when the parent is in the mature stage of growth or during economic downturns. Bad debts of finance subsidiaries can prove to be a terrible burden for the parent if the parent is holding the paper instead of selling it without recourse.

Example

Inter-Regional Financial Corp. (IFG), the parent company of two regional brokerage firms, saw its stock price tumble from $27.125 a share to $12.5 the year its leasing division ran into trouble. Ironically, when the brokerage business picked up, IFG was able to take full advantage of the tax losses created by its leasing division.

For entities with finance divisions, it is necessary to analyze the leasing component separately from the operating company. The leasing entity represents a separate and distinct asset with separate and distinct operating and free cash flow characteristics. Leasing affiliates are dependent on the financial health of the parent for its own success, including the parent's ability to meet its fixed income obligations. It is appropriate, when analyzing the operating cash flows of an entity like Unisys Corp. with a finance and insurance subsidiary, to adjust for the cash transfers in and of the financial subsidiaries.

Example

Trinity Industries, Inc., is a large manufacturer of heavy metal products such as railcars, marine products, and containers; it also has a leasing subsidiary.

In its statement of cash flows, Trinity separates its depreciation expense and capital spending for its leasing operation. It is imperative to review and analyze the statement of cash flows for Trinity's leasing operation for which it files separate 10-Ks and 10-Qs. The investment activities sections for Trinity and its leasing division are closely intertwined. For example, Trinity has entered into an agreement (the "Fixed Charges Coverage Agreement") with the leasing subsidiary whereby Trinity is obligated to make such payments to the subsidiary as may be required to maintain "the Registrant's" net earnings available for fixed charges (as defined) at an amount equal to but not less than one and one-half times the fixed charges (as defined) of the subsidiary. The fixed charge coverage agreement will terminate in accordance with its terms at such time as all amounts payable by the subsidiary under the 10 5/8 percent Equipment Trust Certificates due January 31, 1995, have been paid in full, and the subsidiary shall have delivered a certificate of its certified public accountants demonstrating that net earnings available for fixed charges, without considering any payments by Trinity, have not been less than one and one-half times the fixed charges in each of the five most recently completed fiscal years provided that the subsidiary and Trinity may agree in connection with "Future Financing Agreements" to maintain the fixed charges coverage agreement in force and in effect during the term of such "Future Financing Agreements."

OTHER EXAMPLES AND DISCLOSURE REQUIREMENTS

The statement of cash flows for Sunshine Mining Company, a natural resource holding company, principally in silver and gold, is quite interesting on several counts. To begin, Sunshine pays interest on its "Silver Indexed Bonds" and contributions to

Trinity Industries: Consolidated Statement of Cash Flows

CONSOLIDATED STATEMENT OF CASH FLOWS

(in millions)

	Year Ended March 31		
	1990	1989	1988
Cash flows from operating activities:			
Net income	$38.2	$30.3	$13.0
Adjustments to reconcile net income to net cash provided by operating activities:			
Depreciation:			
Excluding Leasing Subsidiaries	21.6	17.8	15.3
Leasing Subsidiaries	12.4	13.1	13.9
Deferred provision for income taxes	15.0	14.9	6.7
(Gain) loss on sale of property, plant and equipment	(1.9)	0.4	(0.9)
Accretion of discount on long-term debt	6.2	6.1	6.2
Payment of prepayment premium	–	–	(2.2)
Other	1.4	(0.6)	–
Change in assets and liabilities:			
Increase in receivables	(17.1)	(30.1)	(16.8)
(Increase) decrease in inventories	37.4	(68.5)	(36.7)
(Increase) decrease in other assets	(1.9)	0.6	0.2
Increase (decrease) in accounts payable and accrued expenses	(7.6)	10.8	(3.4)
Increase (decrease) in other liabilities	(9.7)	16.7	8.6
Total adjustments	55.8	(18.8)	(9.1)
Net cash provided by operating activities	94.0	11.5	3.9
Cash flows from investing activities:			
Proceeds from sale of property, plant and equipment	4.8	9.0	14.9
Capital expenditures:			
Excluding Leasing Subsidiaries	(28.1)	(21.9)	(10.3)
Leasing Subsidiaries	(10.0)	(18.0)	(41.9)
Payment for purchase of acquisitions, net of cash acquired	(16.8)	(36.0)	(5.5)
Net cash required by investing activities	(50.1)	(66.9)	(42.8)
Cash flows from financing activities:			
Issuance of common stock	2.0	1.8	1.7
Net borrowings under short-term debt	(2.5)	17.0	15.0
Proceeds from issuance of long-term debt	0.2	62.7	95.6
Payments to retire long-term debt	(30.8)	(18.4)	(78.9)
Dividends paid	(11.8)	(8.9)	(8.6)
Net cash (required) provided by financing activities	(42.9)	54.2	24.8
Net increase (decrease) in cash and cash equivalents	1.0	(1.2)	(14.1)
Cash and cash equivalents at beginning of period	6.4	7.6	21.7
Cash and cash equivalents at end of period	$ 7.4	$ 6.4	$ 7.6

Excluding Leasing Subsidiaries, interest paid in fiscal 1990, 1989, and 1988 was $11.4, $7.6, and $5.1, respectively. Leasing Subsidiaries' interest paid in fiscal 1990, 1989, and 1988 was $25.6, $22.0, and $20.8, respectively.

employee retirement plans with stock in the company, an operating expense. Sunshine is also an active participant in the futures markets, taking both hedging and speculative positions. Option premiums and gains or losses related to these contracts are included in revenues (Operating Activities). Proceeds on its

Trinity Industries Leasing Company Statement of Cash Flows (in millions)

	Year Ended March 31		
	1990	1989	1988
Cash flows from operating activities:			
Net income	$ 10.6	$ 10.6	$ 9.4
Adjustments to reconcile net income			
to net cash provided by operating activities:			
Depreciation	13.7	13.3	12.7
Deferred provision for federal income tax	3.0	5.5	5.5
(Gain) loss on retirement of equipment	(0.4)	0.4	—
Payment of prepayment premium	—	—	(2.2)
Other	0.1	0.2	0.2
Changes in assets and liabilities:			
(Increase) decrease in other assets	1.3	(0.5)	2.3
Decrease in accounts payable and			
accrued liabilities	(0.6)	(0.1)	(3.1)
Increase in other liabilities	1.0	2.3	1.6
Total adjustments	18.1	21.1	17.0
Net cash provided by operating activities	28.7	31.7	26.4
Cash flows from investing activities:			
Proceeds from retirement of equipment	3.3	8.7	12.5
Capital expenditures	(10.0)	(18.0)	(41.9)
Net cash required by investing activities	(6.7)	(9.3)	(29.4)
Cash flows from financing activities:			
Increase in notes receivable from Trinity	(8.5)	(74.0)	(33.4)
Proceeds from issuance of long-term debt	—	61.6	95.6
Payments to retire long-term debt	(13.0)	(9.6)	(68.5)
Decrease in long-term obligation under capital lease	(0.5)	(0.4)	(0.5)
Transfer from Trinity of deferred tax liability	—	—	3.8
Net cash required by financing activities	(22.0)	(22.4)	(3.0)

hedged positions are shown under Investing Activities. Gains on unhedged positions are included as part of other—net under Operating Activities.

FASB Statement No. 104 permitted hedged transactions to be classified in the same category as the cash flows being hedged, provided that the accounting policy is disclosed, as is the case with Sunshine in its notes to Form 10-K. However, it is impossible, based solely on a review of Sunshine's Investment Activity section in its statement of cash flows, to determine the profitability of the forward contracts, since the Investment Activities include only closed-out positions. Profitability is listed in the footnote to Form 10-K. Except for 1987, speculative trading has been unrewarding.

Under Sunshine's Operating Activities, an extraordinary gain on settlement of pension obligations is debited since the cash was actually received a year earlier, in 1986, but a book gain was not recorded until a year later. The company deferred recognition of the gain until it could determine whether any significant future benefits were due its employees other than what was known and accounted for. This information is found in Sunshine's Form 10-K for 1989.

The Charles Schwab Corporation, a large brokerage firm, splits its operating activities into two major areas. It differentiates between operating cash flows and operating cash flows that result from changes in customer-related balances. This simplifies the analytical process since a brokerage firm can easily create operating cash flows through the short-term investments account. Furthermore, transactions taken specifically for customers can obscure the firm's own transactions.

Ethyl Corporation breaks down its cash flows from various activities in its major operating segments, chemicals, and insurance. Entities can be as creative in their reporting as they would like. The type of reporting in which the statement of cash flows is broken down by the various operating groups is extremely helpful to the cash flow analyst.

Sunshine Mining: Notes to Consolidated Financial Statements Showing Unhedged Position

---

SUNSHINE MINING COMPANY
NOTES TO CONSOLIDATED FINANCIAL STATEMENTS

The Company periodically enters into forward and option contracts to hedge its exposure to price fluctuations on oil and precious metals transactions. At December 31, 1989, the Company had entered into contracts designated as hedges which included forward sales contracts covering 750,000 ounces of silver at prices ranging from $5.50 to $6.45 per ounce. The Company also had forward sales contracts covering 100,000 barrels of oil at prices ranging from $20.50 to $1.41 per barrel, and sold call option contracts covering 550,000 barrels of oil at prices ranging from $19.40 to $21.00 per barrel. Option premiums, and gains and losses related to changes in values of these contracts, which are deferred and included in revenues when the related products are sold, increased revenues by approximately $2.0 million in 1989 and $563,000 in 1988.

Sunshine Mining Company: Consolidated Statements of Cash Flows

SUNSHINE MINING COMPANY

CONSOLIDATED STATEMENTS OF CASH FLOWS
For the Years Ended December 31, 1989, 1988 and 1987
(In Thousands)

	1989	1988	1987
Cash provided (used) by operations:			
Net loss	$(38,345)	$(54,017)	$(51,771)
Adjustments to reconcile net loss to net cash provided (used) by operations:			
Depreciation, depletion, amortization and impairment provisions	37,134	38,166	46,446
Amortization of discount on Silver Indexed Bonds	1,916	1,617	1,365
Extraordinary loss on extinguishment of debt	—	—	3,393
Extraordinary gain on settlement of pension obligations	—	—	(4,007)
Gain on the sale of fixed assets	(828)	—	—
Common stock issuances for:			
Interest on Silver Indexed Bonds	—	6,183	6,180
Services provided and other	791	616	2,089
Net (increase) decrease in:			
Accounts receivable	(1,800)	9,494	3,430
Inventories	2,374	(2,445)	1,290
Other current assets	1,341	(5,301)	(814)
Other assets and deferred charges	(657)	(556)	(3,864)
Net increase (decrease) in:			
Accounts payable — trade	578	(15,686)	2,373
Oil and gas proceeds payable	1,947	(793)	(1,462)
Accrued expenses	(3,435)	2,755	(4,865)
Other liabilities and deferred credits	(784)	(425)	(5,945)
Other, net	(10)	(2,098)	(5,646)
Net cash provided (used) by operations	222	(22,490)	(11,808)
Cash provided (used) by investing activities:			
Additions to property, plant and equipment	(17,308)	(17,170)	(8,894)
Proceeds from the disposal of property, plant and equipment	3,460	5,430	8,912
Purchases of futures, forward and option contracts	(19,221)	(8,786)	(12,851)
Sales of futures, forward and option contracts	19,534	9,656	18,834
Investment in PT Corporation	3,290	(3,400)	—
Other, principally investments	(8,188)	527	(2,758)
Net cash provided (used) by investing activities	(18,433)	(13,743)	3,243
Cash provided (used) by financing activities:			
Issuance of long-term debt	—	153,583	122,549
Principal repayments and retirements of long-term debt	(4,598)	(86,295)	(183,625)
Issuance of common stock	—	355	89,921
Exercise of warrants and stock options	—	339	2,959
Net cash provided (used) by financing activities	(4,598)	67,982	31,804
Increase (decrease) in cash and cash investments	(22,809)	31,749	23,239
Cash and cash investments, January 1	82,839	51,090	27,851
Cash and cash investments, December 31	$ 60,030	$ 82,839	$ 51,090
Supplemental cash flow information — interest paid in cash	$ 21,814	$ 13,798	$ 13,318

Charles Schwab Corporation: Consolidated Statement of Cash Flows

THE CHARLES SCHWAB CORPORATION
Consolidated Statement of Cash Flows
(IN THOUSANDS)

	Year Ended December 31, 1989	Year Ended December 31, 1988	Nine Months Ended December 31, 1987	Three Months Ended March 31, 1987
				(Predecessor)
Cash flows from operating activities				
Net income	$ 18,919	$ 7,390	$ 8,235	$ 17,445
Noncash items included in net income:				
Depreciation and amortization	52,535	43,775	34,844	3,429
Debentures issued in lieu of interest	2,845	5,381	2,502	
Deferred income taxes	1,369	1,601	(5,271)	8,137
Other	260	427	(1,358)	398
Change in accounts payable and accrued expenses	11,002	(22,211)	10,022	(4,610)
Increase in other assets	(901)	(3,647)	(7,786)	(8,000)
Cash provided before change in customer-related balances	86,029	32,716	41,188	16,799
Change in customer-related balances (excluding the effects of the 1989 acquisition of Rose & Company Investment Brokers, Inc.):				
Payable to customers	750,610	635,867	53,472	208,331
Receivable from customers	(134,076)	35,754	101,511	(82,482)
Drafts payable	(514)	6,048	(17,677)	(68,722)
Payable to brokers and dealers	24,211	(46,629)	(11,861)	59,636
Receivable from brokers and dealers	5,454	2,772	2,555	3,386
Short-term investments required to be segregated under Federal or other regulations	(648,611)	(632,844)	(127,944)	(125,578)
Net change in customer-related balances	(2,926)	968	56	(5,429)
Cash provided by operating activities	83,103	33,684	41,244	11,370
Cash flows from investing activities				
Cash payments for businesses acquired, net of cash received	(23,305)		(92,516)	
Purchase of office facilities and equipment	(11,048)	(8,141)	(17,151)	(4,552)
Proceeds from sale of equipment	818	663	8,578	559
Collection on note receivable from Profit Sharing Plan	494	1,729		
Cash used by investing activities	(33,041)	(5,749)	(101,089)	(3,993)
Cash flows from financing activities				
Long-term borrowings			150,000	
Repayment of long-term borrowings	(6,365)	(69,756)	(96,610)	(1,191)
Proceeds from issuance of redeemable preferred stock			6,000	
Preferred stock redeemed			(6,000)	
Payment for surrendered contingent payment rights	(14,505)	(14,451)		
Repurchase of stock appreciation rights	(3,150)			
Dividends paid	(2,287)			
Purchase of treasury stock	(1,829)	(156)		
Net proceeds from sale of common stock	238	298	144,013	
Other			(306)	(2,830)
Cash provided (used) by financing activities	(27,898)	(84,065)	197,097	(4,021)
Increase (decrease) in cash and equivalents	22,164	(56,130)	137,252	3,356
Cash and equivalents at beginning of period	81,262	137,392	140	79,128
Cash and equivalents at end of period	$103,426	$ 81,262	$137,392	$ 82,484

Ethyl Corp.: Consolidated Statement of Cash Flows

CONSOLIDATED STATEMENTS OF CASH FLOWS   Ethyl Corporation & Subsidiaries

(In Thousands of Dollars)

Years ended December 31	1991	1990	1989
Cash and cash equivalents at beginning of year	**$ 38,998**	**$ 79,835**	**$112,084**
Cash flows from operating activities:			
Chemicals and Corporate:			
Income from continuing operations	**206,668**	232,189	219,468
Adjustments to reconcile to cash flows from operating activities:			
Undistributed earnings of Insurance segment	**(99,199)**	(70,208)	(61,519)
Depreciation and amortization	**89,879**	88,522	81,683
Special charges	**11,185**	48,710	—
Gain on sale of subsidiary	**—**	(78,993)	—
Deferred income taxes	**6,469**	5,644	11,692
Change in assets and liabilities, net of effects from acquisitions and sale of subsidiary:			
(Increase) in accounts receivable	**(4,390)**	(8,626)	(11,286)
(Increase) decrease in inventories	**(31,619)**	(37,142)	5,045
Increase (decrease) in accounts payable and accrued expenses	**20,083**	5,012	(20,599)
(Decrease) increase in income taxes payable	**(32,485)**	24,601	(3,010)
Other, net	**(20,206)**	(21,609)	(14,275)
Total Chemicals and Corporate	**146,385**	188,100	207,199
Total Insurance (see Note 18 on page 41)	**181,025**	278,989	328,751
Net cash provided from continuing operating activities	**327,410**	467,089	535,950
Income from discontinued operations	**—**	—	11,864
Net cash provided from total operating activities	**327,410**	467,089	547,814
Cash flows from investing activities:			
Chemicals and Corporate:			
Capital expenditures	**(166,148)**	(151,822)	(119,082)
Acquisitions of businesses (net of $993 cash acquired in 1989)	**(24,035)**	(61,575)	(33,563)
Proceeds from sale of subsidiary	**—**	108,003	—
Other, net	**(17,350)**	(5,614)	3,850
Total Chemicals and Corporate	**(207,533)**	(111,008)	(148,795)
Total Insurance (principally changes in investments, net) (see Note 18 on page 41)	**(760,901)**	(752,057)	(556,919)
Net cash (used in) investing activities of continuing operations	**(968,434)**	(863,065)	(705,714)
(Increase) in net assets of discontinued operations	**—**	—	(6,429)
Net cash (used in) total investing activities	**(968,434)**	(863,065)	(712,143)
Cash flows from financing activities:			
Chemicals and Corporate:			
Additional long-term debt	**138,400**	291,250	42,000
Repayments of long-term debt	**(2,260)**	(108,500)	(152,822)
Regular dividends paid	**(71,008)**	(71,670)	(57,746)
Special dividend paid	**—**	(179,108)	—
Repurchases of capital stock	**(1,838)**	(31,836)	(45,660)
Dividend received from Tredegar Industries, Inc.	**—**	—	100,000
Other, net	**1,253**	233	2,441
Total Chemicals and Corporate	**64,547**	(99,631)	(111,787)
Total Insurance (principally net increase in investment and universal life contract liabilities) (see Note 18 on page 41)	**578,854**	454,770	243,867
Net cash provided from total financing activities	**643,401**	355,139	132,080
Increase (decrease) in cash and cash equivalents:			
Chemicals and Corporate	**3,399**	(22,539)	(47,948)
Insurance (see Note 18 on page 41)	**(1,022)**	(18,298)	15,699
	2,377	(40,837)	(32,249)
Cash and cash equivalents at end of year	**$ 41,375**	**$ 38,998**	**$ 79,835**

In fact, the most helpful cash flow statement for the typical public corporation would not be by major categories of business, as Ethyl does, but by business segments that the parent entity controls. Since most large public entities and almost every major company included in the S&P industrials operates in more than one line of business, investment decisions can be improved if the cash flow analyst has access to that closely held data.

Since entities already compile cash flow statements as part of a full set of financial statements on the individual companies they own and control, the added cost of releasing such information to the public would be small. Of even greater help would be the release of the entity's budgets for all its affiliated companies. Through such information, the analyst could prepare and evaluate a free cash flow prediction in a much more detailed manner, including which affiliates and business segments are truly free cash flow generators, which are cash users, and which are not meeting expectations and which are expected to be, cut the amount of divisional cash flows. Through the release of the budgets, the cash flow analyst can have a clearer understanding of where management is placing its priorities, and the cash effects and divestiture of a company or segment would have on the cash needs on the remaining entity. It might be expected that merger and acquisition activity as well as reorganizations would step up dramatically if, in fact, such information were in the public domain. Investors would force managements of entity's with poor cash-generating divisions to divest such underachievers if the entity as a whole is a high producer of operating and free cash flow.

Example

Zurn Industries operates in four major segments with little correlation among them. Its main segment is the engineering and construction of independent power plants. Their major cash flow contributor is the water control segment, in which they operate a very successful plumbing products business and Californian water-related construction projects. They also operate a negative cash flow business that manufactures and sells golf clubs, and a small operation that manufactures power train drives. The firm does not report cash flows for each of the segments and does not break down cash flows within the water control segment. The cash flow analyst can only rely on data about sales, operating income, and identifiable assets in each of the segments. In cases like this, the analyst can contact the company to obtain further information. For instance, Zurn officials are willing to confirm analysts' estimates that about one-half of the water control revenues relate to the plumbing products, which grow at a high rate of about 15–20 percent per year. Additional information about certain products may be found in the press releases of firms.

Zurn Industries Industry Segment Data

INDUSTRY SEGMENT DATA

(Thousands)	Power Systems	Water Control	Lynx Golf	Others	Corporate	Total
Year Ended March 31, 1994						
Net sales	$462,049	$246,465	$39,284	$37,890		$785,688
Operating (loss) profit	(31,699)	22,095	(14,424)	1,920		(22,108)
Corporate expense						(1,368)
Loss before income taxes						(23,476)
Identifiable assets	122,021	124,042	48,482	27,264	$126,084	447,893
Capital expenditures	1,599	3,923	2,244	1,201	213	9,180
Depreciation and amortization	3,063	3,623	1,631	1,662	708	10,687
Year Ended March 31, 1993						
Net sales	$351,053	$232,393	$39,626	$46,769		$669,841
Operating profit (loss)	10,495	21,549	(3,124)	4,023		32,943
Corporate income						7,885
Income before income taxes						40,828
Identifiable assets	139,592	109,659	54,642	31,113	$155,172	490,178
Capital expenditures	4,373	4,491	2,601	2,386	467	14,318
Depreciation and amortization	3,343	3,498	1,367	1,782	659	10,649
Year Ended March 31, 1992						
Net sales	$270,927	$253,755	$24,789	$47,061		$596,532
Operating profit (loss)	4,628	21,265	(7,271)	(2,702)		15,920
Corporate income						2,102
Income before income taxes						18,022
Identifiable assets	124,161	118,027	41,477	35,054	$122,413	441,132
Capital expenditures	2,715	4,282	744	2,761	195	10,697
Depreciation and amortization	3,412	4,399	1,310	1,737	681	11,539

Example

Utility firms provide to investors and the public not only information about the most recent years but also forecasts for the next five years. This information can be used by the cash flow analyst to predict future financial results and is useful in a firm's valuation. We enclose here the information made public by Minnesota Power.

CPI Corp. begins its cash flow statement with a single-line entry of its operating activities and then immediately goes into financing and investment activities. With net income and depreciation such important parts of CPI's cash flow, it is surprising they have relegated the operating activities to the bottom of the statement.

The 1989 statement of cash flows for CPI is also interesting because it shows net additions to property and equipment of $21,109,188 in 1989 and $19,271,091 in 1988. In the management discussion and analysis section, these expenditures are broken down by lines of business, but the amounts are $25,616,000 and $29,736,000, respectively. Examination of the relevant schedules in Form 10-K, Schedules V and VI, shows that additions were $25,615,968 and $29,736,454 for 1989 and 1988, respectively. However, retirements were $11,159,031 in 1989 and $10,393,852 in 1988. The net additions to PPE in 1989 (i.e., additions minus retirements) come to about $21,325,000 (additions of $25,616,000 minus net book value of assets retired, which had an original cost of $11,159,000 and accumulated depreciation of $6,868,000 from Schedule VI). This is very close to the amount reported in the statement of cash flows indicating that cash proceeds were close to net book value of assets retired. In 1988, the net additions are equal to about $25,502,000 (additions of $29,736,000 minus net book value of $10,394,000 less $6,160,000). On the cash flows from investing activities we find net additions to PPE of only $19,271,091 for 1988. However, under the acquisitions for 1988 we find that PPE of businesses purchased during 1988 was about $6,231,655. Thus, it is likely that CPI included in its capital expenditures (and additions to PPE in Schedule V) the PPE of businesses acquired. This shows that the cash flow analyst should attempt to reconcile amounts in the statement of cash flows with amounts and other information that are available in footnotes, other disclosures in the financial statements, and disclosures in the management discussion and analysis section.

Minnesota Power—Core Electric Utility Operations
Sales, Generation and Capital Expenditures

	Actual		Forecast			
	1991	1992	1993	1994	1995	1996
Electric Sales and Capability						
Electric Sales – Million kWh						
Retail	8,398	8,401	8,382	8,627	8,746	8,962
Resale	728	845	894	876	889	901
Industrial Economy	875	334	307	355	355	355
Electric Generating Capability – MW	1,471	1,471	1,471	1,471	1,471	1,471
Net Participation Purchases – MW	112	112	72	72	40	40
System Peak Demand – MW	1,306	1,299	1,295	1,337	1,357	1,388
Net Firm Capacity Sales – MW	10	10	0	0	0	0
Reserve Margin	20.3%	20.9%	19.2%	15.4%	11.3%	8.9%
Load Factor	82%	82%	83%	83%	83%	84%
Electric Generation Sources						
Steam (Coal)	49%	55%	57%	56%	57%	58%
Hydro	6%	6%	6%	5%	6%	5%
Purchases						
Square Butte (Lignite)	20%	22%	19%	22%	19%	21%
Other	25%	17%	18%	17%	18%	16%
Capital Expenditures – Millions						
Minnesota Power	$38	$44	$46	$46	$45	$46
SWL&P	2	3	1	2	2	2
Rainy River Energy	4	0	0	0	0	0
Total Capital Expenditures	$44	$47	$47	$48	$47	$48

Minnesota Power—Consolidated Financial Forecast (millions of dollars)

	Actual		Forecast			
	1991	1992	1993	1994	1995	1996
Capital Requirements						
Capital Expenditures						
Core Electric Utility	44	47	47	48	47	48
Core Support	2	8	78	46	46	4
Diversification	35	32	29	22	21	17
Total Capital Expenditures	81	87	154	116	114	69
Maturities and Sinking Funds	21	24	21	24	15	17
Total Capital Requirements	102	111	175	140	129	86
Sources of Capital						
Internal Cash Flow						
Depreciation	37	40	45	51	55	57
Deferred Taxes and Deferred ITC	11	(1)	2	7	7	5
Plant and Subsidiary Sales	33	0	0	0	0	0
AFDC	(2)	(2)	(2)	(1)	(1)	(1)
Other	(16)	(2)	20	9	5	11
Total Internal Sources	63	35	65	66	66	72
Percent of Capital Expenditures	78%	40%	42%	57%	58%	104%
External Sources						
Short-Term Debt	(9)	0	0	0	0	0
Long-Term Debt	12	57	59	40	31	0
Preferred Stock	0	0	0	0	0	0
Common Stock	(70)	6	6	6	6	7
Total External Sources	(67)	63	65	46	37	7
Total Sources of Capital	(4)	98	130	112	103	79
Cash For (From) Investments and Other	(106)	(13)	(45)	(28)	(26)	(7)

CPI Corp.: Schedule V, Consolidated Property and Equipment

Fiscal Years Ended February 3, 1990, February 4, 1989 and February 6, 1988

	Balance at Beginning of Year	Additions Charged to Costs and Expenses	Retirements	Balance at End of Year
52 Weeks Ended February 3, 1990:				
Land	$ 1,456,366	$ 6,923	$ 21,912	$ 1,441,377
Building and improvements	30,190,542	8,122,947	3,832,661	34,480,828
Machinery and equipment	80,920,780	11,596,336	4,951,270	87,565,846
Furniture and Fixtures	20,804,091	5,889,762	2,353,188	24,340,665
	$133,371,779	$ 25,615,968	$ 11,159,031	$ 147,828,716
52 Weeks Ended February 4, 1989:				
Land	$ 630,681	$ 840,535	$ 14,850	$ 1,456,366
Building and improvements ...	27,270,896	4,302,969	1,383,323	30,190,542
Machinery and equipment	69,541,673	19,610,391	8,231,284	80,920,780
Furniture and fixtures	16,585,927	4,982,559	764,395	20,804,091
	$114,029,177	$ 29,736,454	$ 10,393,852	$ 133,371,779
52 Weeks Ended February 6, 1988:				
Land	$ 630,681	$ -	$ -	$ 630,681
Building and improvements ...	23,544,778	4,436,182	710,064	27,270,896
Machinery and equipment	63,109,634	10,765,860	4,333,821	69,541,673
Furniture and fixtures	13,753,047	3,289,707	456,827	16,585,927
	$101,038,140	$ 18,491,749	$ 5,500,712	$ 114,029,177

CPI Corp.: Schedule IV, Consolidated Accumulated Depreciation of Property and Equipment

Fiscal Years Ended February 3, 1990 February 4, 1989 and February 6, 1988

	Balance at Beginning of Year	Additions Charged to Costs and Expenses	Retirements	Balance at End of Year
52 Weeks Ended February 3, 1990:				
Building and improvements	$ 13,394,096	$ 3,144,437	$ 2,337,961	$ 14,200,572
Machinery and equipment	32,312,212	11,244,063	3,235,579	40,320,696
Furniture and Fixtures	9,662,873	3,511,588	1,294,771	11,879,690
	$ 55,369,181	$ 17,900,088	$ 6,868,311	$ 66,400,958
52 Weeks Ended February 4, 1989:				
Building and improvements ...	$ 10,995,899	$ 3,179,499	$ 781,302	$ 13,394,096
Machinery and equipment	27,097,655	10,074,016	4,859,459	32,312,212
Furniture and fixtures	7,154,835	3,027,421	519,383	9,662,873
	$ 45,248,389	$ 16,280,936	$ 6,160,144	$ 55,369,181
52 Weeks Ended February 6, 1988:				
Building and improvements ...	$ 8,204,766	$ 3,002,094	$ 210,961	$ 10,995,899
Machinery and equipment	19,959,205	9,029,164	1,890,714	27,097,655
Furniture and fixtures	4,870,228	2,615,326	330,719	7,154,835
	$ 33,034,199	$ 14,646,584	$ 2,432,394	$ 45,248,389

CPI Corp.: Consolidated Statement of Cash Flows

		Fiscal Year		
FISCAL YEARS		1989	1988	1987
ENDED	Cash flows from operating activities	$55,875,733	$50,147,351	$47,530,746
FEBRUARY 3, 1990,	Financing and capital activities:			
FEBRUARY 4, 1989	Net increase (decrease) in debt	(175,344)	474,122	(337,364)
AND	Issuance of common stock to employee			
FEBRUARY 6, 1988	stock plans	1,135,225	1,992,885	871,835
	Investments by minority interests in			
	LBP Partnership	441,440		1,471,432
	Cash dividends	(6,573,188)	(4,138,497)	(2,732,940)
	Purchase of treasury stock	(26,892,827)	(8,097,469)	-
	Cash flows from financing and capital			
	activities	(32,064,694)	(9,768,959)	(727,037)
	Cash flows before investing activities	23,811,039	40,378,392	46,803,709
	Investing activities:			
	Additions to property and equipment, net	(21,109,188)	(19,271,091)	(13,562,147)
	Acquisitions:			
	Property and equipment	(216,060)	(6,231,655)	(1,861,284)
	Intangible assets	(534,634)	(4,729,019)	(1,366,216)
	Long-term investments	2,521,671	(3,148,316)	-
	Restricted stock	(8,581)	(1,030,973)	-
	Cash flows from investing activities	(19,346,792)	(34,411,054)	(16,789,647)
	Net cash and short-term investments			
	generated	4,464,247	5,967,338	30,014,062
	Cash and short-term investments at			
	beginning of period	65,523,321	59,555,983	29,541,921
	Cash and short-term investments at			
	end of period	$69,987,568	$65,523,321	$59,555,983
RECONCILIATION OF	Net earnings from continuing operations	$30,916,066	$31,918,771	$25,770,706
NET EARNINGS TO	Adjustments for items not requiring cash:			
CASH FLOWS FROM	Depreciation and amortization	22,170,876	19,549,090	18,010,576
RESULTS OF	Deferred income taxes	(448,000)	169,000	1,287,000
OPERATIONS	Deferred compensation	3,060,793	1,411,402	1,266,230
	Minority interest in losses of consolidated			
	subsidiaries	(439,364)	(577,020)	(1,143,961)
	Other	(1,160,949)	(323,320)	(247,915)
	Decrease (increase) in current assets:			
	Receivables and inventories	2,666,855	(5,989,902)	1,513,853
	Deferred costs applicable to unsold portraits	(579,637)	(349,505)	(475,959)
	Prepaid expenses and other current assets	(138,064)	(1,184,689)	(1,044,171)
	Increase (decrease) in current liabilities:			
	Accounts payable, accrued expenses and			
	other liabilities	(18,012)	3,969,824	3,065,656
	Income taxes	998,219	880,349	1,431,253
	Deferred income taxes	40,000	2,202,000	(588,000)
	Net cash flows from continuing operations	57,068,783	51,676,000	48,845,268
	Net losses from discontinued operations	(2,245,587)	(1,602,235)	(1,282,600)
	Depreciation and amortization	62,413	399,174	301,919
	Write-off of intangible assets	946,303	-	-
	Decrease (increase) in receivables and			
	inventories	577,354	(523,505)	(303,343)
	Increase (decrease) in accounts payable,			
	accrued expenses and other liabilities	(533,533)	197,917	(30,498)
	Net cash flows from discontinued operations	(1,193,050)	(1,528,649)	(1,314,522)
	Cash flows from operating activities	$55,875,733	$50,147,351	$47,530,746
	Supplemental information:			
	Interest paid	$114,627	$83,039	$80,263
	Taxes paid.	$15,448,019	$17,053,753	$17,526,405

CPI Corp.: Capital Expenditures

C P I C O R P	1989	1988	1987
Capital expenditures:			
Portrait studios	$ 5,391	$ 4,364	$ 4,477
One-hour photofinishing	10,517	13,161	11,771
Other products and services.	2,716	7,224	913
Corporate.	6,730	4,142	888
Discontinued Tender Sender operations. .	262	845	443
	$ 25,616	$ 29,736	$ 18,492

FOREIGN CURRENCY

Changes in the value of a foreign currency do not, by themselves, produce operating or free cash flows as they do not produce cash until converted back to U.S. dollars. This belief is reflected in the statement of cash flows for most entities, where the effects of changes in currency exchange rates are segregated into one line-item, which is shown, typically, right before the change in cash balance.

Most investors believe the value of a foreign investment is enhanced if it is situated in a relatively stable country with a stable currency, but this is a matter of business decision and asset valuation, not cash flow analysis.

Example

Tecumseh Products Co. derives approximately 40 percent of its operating income on just 17 percent of its revenues from its highly successful Brazilian subsidiary. Although Brazil experienced inflation of above 50 percent per year and an unstable government, Tecumseh's Brazilian subsidiary remains the company's jewel.

Although the statement of cash flow does call for a separate line entry for the effect of exchange rate changes on cash, the effects of rate changes on cash are in no way cash flows in U.S. dollars. In fact, many companies prior to *SFAS No. 95* did not obtain cash flow information from their subsidiary but rather prepared a separate statement of changes in financial condition from the subsidiary's balance sheet and income statement.

The new standards call for the financial statement to reflect the reporting currency equivalent of cash receipts and payments that occur in a foreign currency. Because the effect of exchange rate changes on the reporting currency equivalent of cash held in foreign currencies affects the change in an enterprise's cash balance during a period, but is not a cash receipt of payment, the FASB decided that the effect of exchange rate changes on cash should be reported as a separate item on the reconciliation of beginning and ending changes of cash. Under the statement, the company must use the exchange rates in effect at the time of the cash flows to translate the foreign cash flows on the subsidiary's statement of cash flows. A weighted-average exchange rate for the period may be used for translation if the result is substantially the same as if the exchange rates at the dates of the cash flows were used. However, after translating the foreign cash flows from operating, investing, and financing activities using the (weighted-average) exchange rate at the time of the transaction, the foreign cash flows are also translated using the exchange rate at the end of the period. The differences are aggregated and reported, together with the effect of the exchange rate on the beginning cash balance,

PepsiCo.: Industry Segments

Consolidated Statement of Cash Flows

(in millions)
PepsiCo, Inc. and Subsidiaries
Fifty-two weeks ended December 30, 1989, fifty-three weeks ended December 31, 1988 and fifty-two weeks ended December 26, 1987

	1989	1988	1987
Cash Flows from Continuing Operations:			
Income from continuing operations	$ 901.4	$ 762.2	$ 605.1
Adjustments to reconcile income from continuing operations to net cash generated by continuing operations:			
Depreciation and amortization	772.0	629.3	563.0
Deferred income taxes	71.2	20.1	59.0
Other noncash charges and credits–net	128.4	213.4	105.4
Changes in operating working capital:			
Notes and accounts receivable	(149.9)	(50.1)	(95.6)
Inventories	(50.1)	13.8	4.1
Prepaid expenses, taxes and other current assets	6.5	37.8	39.7
Accounts payable	134.9	138.2	(76.9)
Income taxes payable	80.9	55.1	23.3
Other current liabilities	(9.4)	74.7	107.4
Net change in operating working capital	12.9	269.5	2.0
Net Cash Generated by Continuing Operations	1,885.9	1,894.5	1,334.5
Cash Flows from Investing Activities:			
Acquisitions and equity investments	(3,296.6)	(1,415.5)	(371.5)
Purchases of property, plant and equipment	(943.8)	(725.8)	(770.5)
Proceeds from sales of property, plant and equipment	69.7	67.4	98.6
Proceeds from sales of businesses	–	283.2	161.6
Other short-term investments–by original maturity:			
Three months or less–net	667.0	(411.1)	(736.1)
More than three months–purchases	(2,131.1)	(692.6)	(1,311.8)
More than three months–sales	1,476.4	902.0	1,526.2
Other, net	(97.9)	(58.7)	(72.9)
Net Cash Used for Investing Activities	(4,256.3)	(2,051.1)	(1,476.4)
Cash Flows from Financing Activities:			
Proceeds from issuances of long-term debt	71.7	475.3	598.3
Payments of long-term debt	(405.4)	(190.0)	(113.4)
Short-term borrowings–by original maturity:			
Three months or less–net	2,292.2	306.7	114.7
More than three months–proceeds	1,109.5	292.0	547.9
More than three months–payments	(476.2)	(367.4)	(1,157.0)
Proceeds from nonrecourse obligation	–	0.1	299.3
Cash dividends paid	(241.9)	(199.0)	(172.0)
Purchases of treasury stock	–	(71.8)	(18.6)
Other, net	(28.9)	(24.5)	(38.8)
Net Cash Generated by Financing Activities	2,321.0	221.4	60.4
Effect of Exchange Rate Changes on Cash and Cash Equivalents	(17.1)	(1.4)	(8.0)
Net Increase (Decrease) in Cash and Cash Equivalents	(66.5)	63.4	(89.5)
Cash and Cash Equivalents–Beginning of Year	142.7	79.3	168.8
Cash and Cash Equivalents–End of Year	$ 76.2	$ 142.7	$ 79.3

as the effect of exchange rate changes on cash in a single line-item on the statement of cash flows of the parent firm. This item is likely to be small for most firms, even for those with major operations outside the United States.

Example

PepsiCo is a worldwide food company, as shown by the geographic industry segment breakdown. in 1989, PepsiCo had non-U.S. sales of $2.7 billion and non-U.S. assets of over $3 billion. Their foreign currency effect has been minimal, as shown in their statement of cash flows. Therefore, unless the entity keeps large amounts of cash on hand in a currency that depreciates rapidly during a period, the foreign currency effect in the statement of cash flows is bound to be minimal.

PepsiCo.: Consolidated Statement of Cash Flows

Industry Segments:		Net Sales			Operating Profits[a]			Identifiable Assets[b]		
		1989	1988	1987	1989	1988	1987	1989	1988	1987
Soft Drinks:	U.S.	$ 4,623.3	$ 3,667.0	$ 3,112.9	$ 586.9	$ 409.5	$ 363.1			
	Foreign	1,153.4	971.2	862.7	103.2	53.4	46.5			
		5,776.7	4,638.2	3,975.6	690.1	462.9	409.6	$ 6,241.9	$ 4,074.4	$2,779.8
Snack Foods:	U.S.	3,211.3	2,933.3	2,782.8	668.3	587.3	520.0			
	Foreign	1,003.7	581.0	419.2	152.6	49.0	27.6			
		4,215.0	3,514.3	3,202.0	820.9	636.3	547.6	3,366.4	1,641.2	1,632.5
Restaurants:	U.S.	4,684.8	3,950.3	3,499.5	361.8	307.0	281.6			
	Foreign	565.9	430.4	341.0	59.4	44.4	37.8			
		5,250.7	4,380.7	3,840.5	421.2	351.4	319.4	3,095.2	3,105.1	2,782.9
Total:	U.S.	12,519.4	10,550.6	9,395.2	1,617.0	1,303.8	1,164.7			
	Foreign	2,723.0	1,982.6	1,622.9	315.2	146.8	111.9			
		$15,242.4	$12,533.2	$11,018.1	$1,932.2	$1,450.6	$1,276.6	$12,703.5	$ 8,820.7	$7,195.2
Geographic Areas:[a], [b], [c]										
United States		$12,519.4	$10,550.6	$ 9,395.2	$1,617.0	$1,303.8	$1,164.7	$ 9,633.2	$ 7,264.6	$5,699.4
Western Europe		739.0	390.8	308.0	55.5	13.0	6.7	1,754.8	187.7	169.1
Canada and Mexico		899.0	726.3	501.5	126.3	55.0	39.9	460.6	348.0	359.8
Other		1,085.0	865.5	813.4	133.4	78.8	65.3	854.9	1,020.4	966.9
Corporate Assets[c]								12,703.5	8,820.7	7,195.2
								2,423.2	2,314.6	1,827.5
Total		$15,242.4	$12,533.2	$11,018.1	1,932.2	1,450.6	1,276.6	$15,126.7	$11,135.3	$9,022.7
Interest and Other Corporate Expenses, Net					(581.7)	(323.4)	(331.0)			
Income from Continuing Operations Before Income Taxes					$1,350.5	$1,127.2	$ 945.6			

	Capital Spending			Depreciation and Amortization Expense		
	1989	1988	1987	1989	1988	1987
Soft Drinks	$ 267.8	$ 198.4	$ 202.0	$306.3	$195.7	$166.5
Snack Foods	257.9	172.6	195.6	189.3	156.8	154.1
Restaurants	424.6	344.2	370.8	269.9	271.3	237.1
Corporate	9.2	14.9	6.6	6.5	5.5	5.3
	$ 959.5	$ 730.1	$ 775.0	$772.0	$629.3	$563.0

Supplementary Restaurants Data:

	Net Sales			Operating Profits[a]		
Pizza Hut	$2,453.5	$2,014.2	$1,753.2	$208.6	$153.3	$138.0
Taco Bell	1,465.9	1,157.3	1,004.4	112.6	81.6	91.4
KFC	1,331.3	1,209.2	1,082.9	100.0	116.5	90.0
	$5,250.7	$4,380.7	$3,840.5	$421.2	$351.4	$319.4

SUMMARY

This chapter dealt with cash flows from investing, financing, and operating activities, the three most important areas of business. We defined each of these three major activities and illustrated how an analyst may want to interpret these activities and their components. We also provided additional discussion of information that is provided in supplemental disclosure. The next chapter will illustrate how we estimate free cash flow, and why it is preferred to operating income or operating cash flow.

Pfizer, Inc. Statement of Cash Flows

CONSOLIDATED STATEMENT OF CASH FLOWS
Pfizer Inc and Subsidiary Companies

		Year ended December 31	
(millions of dollars)	1993	1992	1991
Operating Activities			
Net income	$ 657.5	$ 810.9	$ 722.1
Adjustments to reconcile net income to net cash provided by operating activities:			
Cumulative effect of accounting changes	—	282.6	—
Depreciation and amortization of intangibles	258.2	263.9	244.1
Divestitures, restructuring and unusual items	752.0	(110.5)	300.0
Deferred taxes	(336.1)	(14.5)	(108.3)
Deferred income amortization	(28.3)	(74.3)	(99.9)
Other	39.3	5.0	24.0
Changes in assets and liabilities, net of effect of businesses acquired and divested:			
Accounts receivable	(160.8)	(193.8)	(101.8)
Inventories	(142.3)	(116.1)	(118.0)
Prepaid and other assets	(44.8)	(246.3)	(158.3)
Accounts payable and accrued liabilities	30.5	69.7	74.3
Income taxes payable	227.9	44.6	61.6
Other deferred items	9.9	85.8	7.8
Net cash provided by operating activities	1,263.0	807.0	847.6
Investing Activities			
Purchases of property, plant and equipment	(634.2)	(674.2)	(593.8)
Purchases of short-term investments	(739.6)	(535.7)	(210.6)
Proceeds from redemptions of short-term investments	846.8	459.8	178.6
Proceeds from sales of businesses	241.2	896.6	195.1
Purchases of long-term investments	(175.9)	(154.6)	(139.3)
Purchases and redemptions of short-term investments by financial subsidiaries	(21.3)	51.0	63.8
Decrease in loans and long-term investments by financial subsidiaries	167.3	283.3	325.5
Other investing activities	118.8	63.7	55.5
Net cash (used in)/provided by investing activities	(196.9)	389.9	(125.2)
Financing Activities			
Proceeds from issuance of long-term debt	6.4	266.0	265.6
(Decrease)/increase in short-term debt	(70.1)	(407.7)	218.4
Employee benefit transactions	42.7	125.1	172.3
Purchases of common stock	(1,019.6)	(665.1)	(463.9)
Cash dividends paid	(536.1)	(486.5)	(437.1)
Other financing activities	9.7	(59.8)	(17.9)
Net cash used in financing activities	(1,567.0)	(1,228.0)	(262.6)
Effect of exchange rate changes on cash and cash equivalents	(26.8)	(29.4)	(12.5)
Net (decrease)/increase in cash and cash equivalents	(527.7)	(60.5)	447.3
Cash and cash equivalents at beginning of year	1,257.1	1,317.6	870.3
Cash and cash equivalents at end of year	$ 729.4	$ 1,257.1	$1,317.6

See Notes to Consolidated Financial Statements which are an integral part of these statements.

Boeing Company Statements of Cash Flow

(Dollars in millions)

Year ended December 31,	1993	1992	1991
Cash flows — operating activities:			
Net earnings	$ 1,244	$ 552	$ 1,567
Adjustments to reconcile net earnings to net cash provided by operating activities:			
Effect of cumulative change in accounting for postretirement benefits other than pensions		1,002	
Depreciation and amortization —			
Plant and equipment	953	870	768
Leased aircraft, other	72	91	58
Deferred income taxes	(536)	(26)	95
Gain/undistributed earnings — affiliates	(1)	(13)	1
Changes in operating assets and liabilities —			
Accounts receivable	(187)	635	(41)
Inventories, net of advances and progress billings	(733)	(138)	458
Accounts payable and other liabilities	606	229	(140)
Advances in excess of related costs	(413)	(28)	(416)
Federal taxes on income	202	206	(453)
Change in prepaid pension expense	(134)	(202)	(403)
Change in accrued retiree health care	144	184	40
Net cash provided by operating activities	1,217	3,362	1,534
Cash flows — investing activities:			
Short-term investments	137	(388)	623
Customer financing additions	(1,560)	(1,156)	(223)
Customer financing reductions	626	16	123
Plant and equipment, net additions	(1,317)	(2,160)	(1,850)
Proceeds from sale of affiliate		50	
Other	8	(19)	(3)
Net cash used by investing activities	(2,106)	(3,657)	(1,330)
Cash flows — financing activities:			
Debt financing	837	482	993
Shareholders' equity —			
Cash dividends paid	(340)	(340)	(343)
Treasury shares acquired		(109)	(127)
Stock options exercised, other	23	35	23
Net cash provided by financing activities	520	68	546
Net increase (decrease) in cash and cash equivalents	(369)	(227)	750
Cash and cash equivalents at beginning of year	2,711	2,938	2,188
Cash and cash equivalents at end of year	$ 2,342	$ 2,711	$ 2,938

See notes to consolidated financial statements.

Hongkong Telecom Statement of Cash Flow

CONSOLIDATED CASH FLOW STATEMENT
For the year ended 31 March 1993

Note		1993 $M	1992 $M
22	**Net cash inflow from operating activities**	**8,285.7**	8,005.9
	Returns on investments and servicing of finance		
	Interest received	**140.4**	143.3
	Interest paid	**(47.8)**	(23.7)
	Dividends received from associated company	**5.0**	0.1
	Dividends paid	**(4,550.4)**	(3,936.9)
	Income from investment	**72.7**	46.8
	Net cash outflow from returns on investments and servicing of finance	**(4,380.1)**	(3,770.4)
	Taxation		
	Profits tax paid	**(1,146.7)**	(571.7)
	Investing activities		
	Purchase of fixed assets	**(3,473.7)**	(2,502.1)
	Proceeds on disposal of fixed assets	**43.0**	19.5
	Decrease (purchase) of investments	**59.0**	(23.4)
	Decrease in long-term deposit	**3.6**	4.1
	Net cash outflow from investing activities	**(3,368.1)**	(2,501.9)
	Net cash (outflow) inflow before financing	**(609.2)**	1,161.9
23	**Financing**		
	Repayment of long-term loans	**(50.1)**	(52.3)
	New short-term loan	**–**	30.0
	Repayment of short-term loans	**(17.4)**	(6.8)
	Proceeds on issue of loan stock to minority shareholders	**–**	8.3
	Net cash outflow from financing	**(67.5)**	(20.8)
	(Decrease) increase in cash and cash equivalents	**(676.7)**	1,141.1
	Cash and cash equivalents at 1 April	**2,203.2**	1,062.1
	Cash and cash equivalents at 31 March	**1,526.5**	2,203.2
	Analysis of the balances of cash and cash equivalents		
	Term deposits	**2,826.4**	2,137.9
	Bank and cash balances	**72.4**	91.6
	Bills of exchange	**(336.6)**	–
	Bank loans and overdrafts repayable within three months	**(1,035.7)**	(26.3)
		1,526.5	2,203.2

Hongkong Telecom Statement of Cash Flow (continued)

22. Reconciliation of operating profit to net cash inflow from operating activities

	1993 $M	1992 $M
Operating profit	**7,255.0**	6,338.3
Depreciation and amortisation	**1,332.1**	1,034.9
Loss on disposal of fixed assets	**37.1**	38.1
Movements in working capital		
Increase in stocks	**(97.6)**	(17.6)
(Increase) decrease in debtors	**(515.9)**	163.3
Increase in creditors	**275.0**	448.9
Net cash inflow from operating activities	**8,285.7**	8,005.9

23. Analysis of changes in financing during the year

	1993 $M		1992 $M	
	Long-term loans (including current portion)	Short-term loans repayable after three months	Long-term loans (including current portion)	Short-term loans repayable after three months
Balance at 1 April	**290.3**	**46.6**	342.6	23.4
Cash (outflow) inflow from financing	**(50.1)**	**(17.4)**	(52.3)	23.2
Balance at 31 March	**240.2**	**29.2**	290.3	46.6

Operating Income, Operating Cash Flow, and Free Cash Flow

INTRODUCTION

This chapter discusses the three principal determinates of worth and value that may be used to analyze and screen a large set of firms, so that a subset of firms can be investigated in depth and possibly included in a portfolio. The three variables are net income, net operating cash flow, and free cash flow. Net profit is a widely used criterion for investment purposes (e.g., in earnings multiples) mostly because earnings are readily available in the financial statements. Net operating cash flow is less frequently used for investment purposes, primarily because prior to *SFAS No. 95*, which required the disclosure of an entire statement of cash flows, net operating cash flow had to be estimated from other financial statements. Finally, free cash flow is used hardly at all for investment purposes because it is fairly complex to estimate, although, intuitively, it seems the most reasonable criterion for investment.[1] Free cash flow is used, however, by credit rating agencies, banks, credit analysts, and corporate treasury departments, among others.

We begin this chapter with a discussion of the limitations of earnings reports in general and of their specific shortcomings for investment purposes. We then review the potential usefulness of net operating cash flows and its pitfalls as an investment criterion. Finally, we introduce the concept of free cash flow and show how it can be estimated and how it can be used for portfolio selection.

---

[1]There are a several simplistic definitions of free cash flows that security analysts and investment firms use. The most common of these is pre-tax profit plus depreciation, minus capital spending. As we show later on, this definition excludes important elements of free cash flows.

EARNINGS AND ITS LIMITATIONS

Security analysts, portfolio managers, and most investment services highlight earnings as one of the most important financial indicators.[2] Most research reports prepared by analysts and published in newspapers include, in addition to stock price and dividend information, the price/earnings ratio of a firm. Financial news services report various earnings numbers:

- The most recent (known) annual earnings per share.
- The running sum of the last four quarterly earnings per share.
- A combination of forecasted and historical earnings.
- Primary earnings per share.
- Fully diluted earnings per share.
- Earnings before extraordinary items.
- Net income.

In short, earnings figures are not uniform across various sources of information.

Example

In a press release to analysts and portfolio managers, Pepsico, the large soft drink manufacturer, wrote the following comments on their third quarterly report for 1991:

As you know we have been very aggressive in disclosing items that we believe are of an unusual nature so that you can make whatever adjustments you deem necessary to understand the quality and underlying trend of our earnings growth. In the third quarter of 1990, there were quite a few such unusual items and, as we recall, some of you found it confusing. Now, to make it even more challenging we are asking you to compare that quarter to the third quarter of 1991, which also has unusual items.

To help in this task, we have added two schedules to the package this quarter. These schedules are designed to make it a little clearer what constitutes an "apples to apples" comparison. One schedule analyzes the impact of unusual items on net income and earnings per share, and the second schedule presents segment operating profits and growth excluding the unusual items. We hope you find them helpful. Of course, if you need any further clarification, we would be happy to assist you.

PepsiCo, Inc., and Subsidiaries: Condensed Consolidated Income Statements

PepsiCo, Inc. and Subsidiaries
Condensed Consolidated Statement of Income
(in millions except per share amounts, unaudited)

	12 Weeks Ended		
	9/7/91	9/8/90 (a)	% Change
Net Sales	$4,881.3	$4,475.7	9
Costs and Expenses, net Cost of sales	2,349.4	2,152.2	9
Selling, administrative and other expenses	1,949.0 (b)	1,714.7 (c)	14
Amortization of goodwill and other intangibles	47.6	45.2	5
Gain on joint venture stock offering	—	(118.2) (c)	—
Interest expense	137.4	158.9	(14)
Interest income	(35.5)	(43.1)	(18)
	4,447.9	3,909.7	14
Income from Continuing Operations Before Income Taxes	433.4 (b)	566.0 (c)	(23)
Provision for Income Taxes (e)	148.0	215.7	(31)
Income from Continuing Operations	285.4 (b)	350.3 (c)	(19)
Discontinued Operation Charge	—	(13.7) (d)	—
Net Income	$ 285.4	$ 336.6	(15)
Per Share:			
Continuing Operations	$ 0.36 (b)	$ 0.44 (c)	(18)
Discontinued Operation	—	(0.02) (d)	—
Net Income per Share	$ 0.36	$ 0.42	(14)
Average shares outstanding	802.2	799.6	

NOTES:
(a) Certain amounts have been reclassified to conform with the 1991 presentation.
(b) Includes an unusual charge of $100.4 million ($62.4 after-tax or $0.08 per share) consisting of a $91.4 million restructuring charge at domestic snack foods and a $9.0 million charge at domestic KFC related to a delayed national roll-out of the new skinless checken product.
(c) Includes an unusual net credit of $70.6 million ($23.8 after-tax or $0.03 per share) consisting of the $118.2 million gain on joint venture stock offering partially offset by $47.6 million in unusual charges (described in the attachments) included in selling, administrative and other expenses.
(d) Represents $14.0 million pre-tax in additional amounts provided for various pending lawsuits and claims relating to a business sold in a prior year.
(e) The effective tax rates were 34.1% in 1991, 38.1% in 1990, and 33.6% in 1990 excluding the unusual tax effects of the gain on joint venture stock offering.

As can be seen, the selling, administrative, and other expenses in 1990 *and* 1991 contain unusual items. In 1990, the unusual items include a $91 million restructuring charge, whereas in 1991 there is a gain of $118 million on a stock offering. Should the analyst include the entire amounts of selling, administrative, and other expenses in income as reported? Should the analyst exclude these items because they are not expected to recur? How about amounts that relate to discontinued operations? The example shows how crucial it is to use the same definition of earnings for all firms in any comparison of firms based on earnings or earnings components. It also shows the danger of using net earnings for comparisons of earnings across time.

To compound the problem, firms are required under generally accepted accounting principles (GAAP) to follow accrual accounting, which introduces many estimates into the financial statements, and which may allow firms to account for identical economic transactions in a differential manner. For example, consider the corner retail store, which keeps its books on a cash basis (i.e., revenues match cash taken in, and pre-tax profits are very close to cash receipts minus cash spent). In contrast, earnings and cash increases are not identical for public companies that use accrual instead of cash accounting. Under accrual accounting, the entity may record revenues before cash is actually collected, and it may record expenses that do not require an outlay of cash, such as recording an accrued liability (e.g., accrued vacation time). Thus, reported income for the public company almost never matches net cash receipts from operations.

When preparing its financial statements, a firm has to make assumptions about future developments, so that it can account for current transactions correctly. For example, accrual accounting requires estimation of the depreciation expense for a period. Most firms estimate the depreciation expense by predicting the useful lives of depreciable assets and the salvage (residual) values of these assets. Clearly, these estimates can be expected to contain errors, which may affect accounting earnings. Indeed, firms update their estimates of useful lives of fixed assets, causing income for the period to increase or decrease, sometimes substantially.

Example

Sometimes firms revise their earnings figures due to new reporting requirements. An extreme case occurred when the SEC changed a reporting requirement for oil and gas firms after they had issued preliminary earnings reports to investors.

Oil Firms Scramble to Restate Earnings in Wake of SEC Ruling in Write-downs

A growing number of oil companies are reporting first-quarter write-downs on their reserves, including some that didn't foresee doing so.

Several large, independent oil companies recently reported results that didn't include substantial write-downs to reflect the sharp drop in oil prices. They had assumed that the Securities and Exchange Commission would approve a staff proposal to postpone such write-downs until year's end.

But on Tuesday, to everyone's surprise the SEC decided to retain rules that require oil companies using full-cost accounting to take quarterly write-downs if the book value of oil and natural gas reserves exceeds current market value. As a result, the companies are scrambling to restate earlier, less-grim earnings reports.

Houston-based Pennzoil Co., for instance, had posted profit of $43.3 million without explaining in its news release that the results were based on what proved to be a poor prediction of the SEC ruling. Just as it was poised to mail out shareholder reports, Pennzoil had to slip a disclaimer into the envelopes saying that "the first quarterly earnings and financial results that appear herein will have to be restated." Pennzoil accountants were busy Friday recalculating the numbers.

On Thursday, Mesa Limited Partnership, based in Amarillo, Texas, restated its results to a $169 million loss, compared with the $31 million profit it posted a few days earlier.[3]

Example

On October 26, 1992, *The Wall Street Journal* reported that Sequoia Systems Inc., which restated its year-end earnings in the prior two weeks, said it would have to restate them again. The most recent restatement related to overstatement of revenues.

---

[3]*The Wall Street Journal*, May 12, 1986.

Example

On October 21, 1992, the *New York Times* reported that Chambers Development Co., a waste management firm, made an accounting change that erased $362 million of earnings from prior years. Essentially, the firm decided to expense the costs of new landfills, instead of capitalizing these costs, which was its previous accounting method.

Example

When Gibson Greetings restated 1993 earnings, reducing it by about 20 percent, its stock price fell 14 percent. The firm discovered that one of its units had overstated inventories. Unfortunately, Gibson Greetings was hurt by two prior items of bad news: its major customer, Phar-Mor Inc., filed for bankruptcy in 1992, and it discovered large interest rate swaps had caused losses.

Example

First Colony Corporation, an insurance firm, reported in a press release on November 1, 1994, that shareholders' equity declined from $20.58 per share at 1993 year-end to $19.24 due to an accounting change required by the FASB. Under *SFAS No. 115*, the firm had to record unrealized losses on its marketable securities in shareholders' equity. This change did not affect income or cash flows, but affected shareholders' equity.

Furthermore, a firm can in many cases choose the accounting method it applies for a specific type of transaction. For example, purchases of inventory may be identical for two firms, but accounting earnings and inventories on the balance sheet may be different because one firm uses LIFO for inventories, whereas the other uses methods such as FIFO or weighted average.

Example

When leaf tobacco prices declined during the second half of 1982, it benefited companies like Philip Morris and R. J. Reynolds which used LIFO, as opposed to companies like American Brands, which used the weighted-average method in accounting for its large leaf tobacco inventories. When prices declined, companies that used LIFO for inventory purposes showed higher accounting income than firms that used other methods.

In contrast, in the computer industry, most firms use the FIFO method for costing inventories. Since prices of computers generally decline, the use of FIFO would tend to inflate cost of goods sold (in comparison to replacement cost), saving these firms some tax payments.

Not only do firms have some latitude in choosing different accounting methods under GAAP, but they also have some latitude in applying accounting standards to their specific situations. Thus, firms may have different approaches to revenue recognition, expense recognition, allocation of costs across periods, and so forth. This flexibility in applying accounting standards may be desirable, because in reality no two businesses are identical. It allows managers to signal the uniqueness of their firms through the selection of accounting methods. However, flexibility makes comparability of earnings across firms, and sometimes even for the same firm across different periods, extremely difficult. Thus, the great focus on earnings in making investment and valuation decisions may be flimsy.

Example—revenue recognition

Are the two methods listed below liberal or conservative accounting practices?

> Sales revenue is generally recorded upon shipment of product in the case of sales contracts and upon installation in the case of sales-type leases. Revenue from service and rental agreements is recorded as earned over the lives of the respective contracts.
>
> Revenue under cost-type contracts is recognized when costs are incurred, and under fixed-price contracts when products or services are accepted and billings can be made. General and administrative expenses are charged to income as incurred. Cost of revenue under long-term contracts is charged based on current estimated total costs. When estimates indicate a loss under a contract, cost of revenue is charged with a provision for such loss.[4]
>
> The Corporation reports profits on long-term contracts on a percentage-of-completion basis determined on the ratio of earned billings to total contract price, after considering accumulated costs and estimated costs to complete each contract. Contracts in progress are valued at cost plus accrued profits less earned billings and progress payments on uncompleted contracts.[5]

Both entities use liberal accounting practices; Unisys recognizes revenues when its products are shipped, and Foster Wheeler records profits on long-term contracts using the percentage-of-completion method. Cash accounting has strong merits when such transactions occur, because cash collected from customers is the same regardless of the particular method that is used for revenue recognition. As a matter of fact, the first element in the debate between accrual accounting and cash accounting revolves around the issue of revenue recognition. The cash flow analyst believes in revenue recognition when collection is made on accounts receivable and cash is deposited in the bank. Under accrual accounting, there is a wide latitude for revenue recognition from progress payments to time of shipment. As seen for the Unisys Corporation, income recognition is subject to much leeway and is certainly different for most industries and entities.

Example—revenue recognition

Warrantech Corp. changed its accounting method for recognizing revenue in the second quarter of 1991, retroactively from the first quarter. This change caused the company to recognize revenues from service contracts on consumer electronics products mostly in the first year of the contract, instead of deferring the recognition of revenues to later years. The firm said that this change reduced its reported net loss for the quarter substantially.

Example—revenue recognition

On May 19, 1994, *The Wall Street Journal* published an article that showed how high-tech firms, which were under pressure to show growth, used revenue recognition methods that were too aggressive. Among the common methods: recognizing sales before the customer signs a firm order, recognizing sales even when a customer does not have the funds to pay for the product, and hiding goods returned by customers.

Example—expense recognition

The deferred asset account, which appears at the bottom of the assets list on the balance sheet, represents expenditures on items that will, hopefully, benefit the firm in future periods, such as advertising expenses, rents paid in advance, and intangible assets such as goodwill. This account should be closely inspected by the cash flow analyst. Changes in deferred assets could be attributed to changes

---

[4]*1988 Annual Report*, Unisys Corporation.
[5]*1989 Annual Report*, Foster Wheeler Corporation.

in policy regarding payment of expenditures for such items as insurance, maintenance, and the costs to redesign and improve existing products, which the firm *hopes* will result in future cash flows. However, the addition to deferred assets usually requires an outlay of cash, whose expense recognition for accounting purposes is deferred for later periods. Advocates of cash flow analysis would differ with the accounting convention of recording an asset of this kind for cash already spent, and will consider it an immediate cash outflow in their analysis. After 1993, firms that adopt the new standard on income taxes, *SFAS No. 109,* are likely to include a deferred tax asset on their balance sheet. This asset is subject to a valuation allowance, which reduces the value of the deferred tax assets that are not likely to be claimed against taxes in the future. As we shall see in Chapter 7, the initial determination and future changes in the valuation allowance are very subjective and may be easily manipulated by management.

Example—expense recognition

Accounting methods for allocation of the cost of purchases between cost of goods sold and ending inventory are another example of expense recognition for accounting purposes, with which cash flow analysts may find a problem. While the purchase (or production) of inventory for cash is a cash outflow, the cost assigned to cost of goods sold may not be a cash outflow and may depend on the particular accounting method chosen for cost allocation. In particular, the inflationary spirals during the 1970s taught security analysts to pay close attention to inventory accounting and its effect on reported profits due to changes in price levels. Investors, for example, realized that if an entity is in a commodity-type industry, subject to swift price movements, LIFO accounting could increase reported profits during disinflationary periods. Furthermore, changes in price levels have a more discriminatory effect on reported earnings than on cash flows. When price levels change quickly, comparisons of earnings across firms are hampered by the amount of inventory held in relation to the company's peers, and the inventory method practiced (LIFO versus FIFO). Free cash flow analysis, by essentially placing all companies on a cash basis and comparing firms according to their cash outlays on purchases or production of inventories, avoids much of the accounting skullduggery.

To complicate matters, most U.S. firms with foreign subsidiaries, that use LIFO for inventory costing in the United States, would *not* use LIFO outside the United States, mostly because LIFO is not allowed for tax purposes in those countries. Indeed, the use of LIFO for tax purposes to shield businesses from inflationary profits is almost singularly a U.S. phenomenon. Most other countries adopted other methods to reduce tax payments on inflationary profits at the time of inventory sale.

During inflationary periods, asset replacement may bear little resemblance to the historical cost represented on the balance sheet and hence earnings are grossly misstated. As an example, consider the LIFO reserve, which has grown substantially for many entities, and which is relegated to an off-balance-sheet asset. Further, strategic liquidations of LIFO inventory layers can increase accounting earnings, albeit at the expense of additional cash outflows for taxes.

Example—write-offs

When Union Carbide Corp., on November 11, 1983, announced it was closing certain facilities resulting in a $140 million charge to net income, the company also pointed out the write-off would have no effect on cash flow. Union Carbide also said that future cash flows would be enhanced as a result of closing down the inefficient facilities. The stock of Carbide reacted very positively to the announcement, as it should have, ignoring the earnings implication of the charge. Write-offs, like that undergone by Union Carbide, are not uncommon and can cause large discrepancies between accounting earnings and cash flows. In fact, write-offs of poor cash flow business units almost always result in increases to a firm's market value.

Setting up reserves has a negative effect on accounting earnings yet has no effect on cash flows.

In the third quarter of 1982, Clark Manufacturing Co. established a reserve of $214.5 million to cover plant shutdown costs at four U.S. and one European location, excess costs during the phasedown period, pension expense, and certain relocation costs. Charges to the reserve amounted to $33.4 million in 1982 and $130.6 million in 1983. In the third quarter of 1983, Clark reversed to income $7.7 million of excess reserves.

Indeed, accounting rule-setters are looking at write-offs, which were abused by some firms by first booking a larger write-off than necessary and then reversing it in the following years to create greater earnings (see related article in The Wall Street Journal, November 2, 1994).

Example

On April 7, 1993, The Wall Street Journal summarized the different accounting methods that IBM used to try and hide its problems.

Among them, booking sales earlier, changing its depreciation methods, leasing contracts, and accounting for the costs of retirement plans.

Example

On June 20, 1994, the *New York Times* reported the problems that IDB had with its auditor. For example, any time the auditor disallowed an item that contributed to income, IDB would replace it with another item that was not booked earlier and that would contribute to income. In one such case, the item was so large that IDB came up with an additional expense to offset the (too high) positive effect of the item on income. The auditor finally decided to resign.

Accountants, bankers, business operators, economists, and security analysts have long debated the role and definition of earnings. It has been recognized by critics of GAAP that because of the multitude of acceptable accounting methods, financial reports across industry lines are usually vastly different, primarily due to peculiarities for the industry. Furthermore, it is difficult for trained security analysts to have a thorough understanding of the accounting methods within the industries of their specialty, and almost impossible outside their specialty, so that they can discern accounting issues of rival industries and comment on matters concerning relative valuation. Unfortunately, without having a thorough knowledge of accounting standards for all industries, it is impossible to conclude how attractive any particular industry is, simply because accounting practices are not uniform. For example, one cannot say with certainty that a particular industry is undervalued because it sells at a discount to the market, as measured by its P/E ratio, if the industry uses very liberal accounting practices relative to the market. Since there is no market accounting practice, one must thoroughly understand the accounting practices and conventions used by all major industries before one is able to identify an attractive industry based on its earnings.

Example

Accounting for research and development (R&D) expenditures is relatively straightforward in the United States; all such expenditures are expensed as incurred, and an asset is not shown for the future benefits of R&D efforts. However, R&D expenditures for computer software projects can be capitalized (i.e., shown as an asset on the balance sheet and amortized over its forecasted useful life) if certain conditions are met. Thus, R&D expenditures for most firms are expensed, but they are capitalized in the computer software industry.[6] The situation is worse when we examine reporting requirements outside the United States, where some countries demand capitalization of R&D costs, others simply allow it in certain cases, while other countries are silent about it altogether.

Many stock analysts attempt to forecast the earnings per share of the firms they follow. A lot of academic evidence shows that analysts usually overestimate earnings per share, although their consensus (median) forecast of earnings per share is reasonably accurate. To understand the difficulty of predicting earnings per share, the analyst should consider not only the prediction of future economic events that affect earnings but also the effects of managerial decisions about investments, financing, and accounting methods. In fact, the most reliable source of earnings estimates is the companies themselves, as most companies will lead analysts to an "acceptable range" of earnings estimates.

Example

To illustrate the complexity of forecasting corporate earnings, we show five schedules from the 1989 United Telecommunications, Inc., Form 10-K. The analyst attempting to forecast expenses using accrual accounting will be confronted with estimating the variables in the expense tables on United Telecommunications, Inc.

The company's consolidated schedule of property, plant, and equipment represents a maze of credits and debits to the balance sheet account as a result of acquisitions, exchanges, purchases, retirements, and other charges or credits. The firm's schedule of accumulated depreciation is also difficult to forecast since it includes retirements of property and property sold and write-offs of fully depreciated assets. Reclassification between other property, plant, and equipment

---

[6]It should be recalled that the 1993 annual report of Quaker Oats (in Chapter 3) included an asset for capitalized software cost. Thus, firms even beyond the software industry may capitalize such costs.

United Telecom: Consolidated Property, Plant, and Equipment

United Telecommunications, Inc.
Form 10–K

SCHEDULE V—CONSOLIDATED PROPERTY, PLANT AND EQUIPMENT
Year Ended December 31, 1989
(Millions of Dollars)

		Additions					
	Balance beginning of year	Business acqui- sitions	Property ex- changes	Addi- tions, at cost	Retire- ments or sales	Other charges (credits)	Balance end of year
LONG DISTANCE COMMUNICATIONS SERVICES							
Digital fiber-optic network	$ 2,814.5	$ 83.1		$ 373.4	$ 18.9	$(39.6)(1)	$ 3,212.5
Data communications equpment	192.8			85.1	24.2	8.4 (2)	262.1
Administrative assets	309.4	145.8		209.1	53.8	(17.4)(3)	593.1
Construction-in-progress	176.3			37.4			213.7
	3,493.0	228.9		705.0	96.9	(48.6)	4,281.4
LOCAL COMMUNICATIONS SERVICES							
Land and buildings	404.4		$6.1	31.7	10.4	0.7	432.5
Other general support assets	321.4		3.6	41.9	30.8	0.9	337.0
Central office assets	2,372.1		31.4	332.8	250.0	(0.7)	2,485.6
Information origination/ termination assets	471.2		5.6	19.3	58.7	(3.2)	434.2
Cable and wire facility assets	3,156.7		76.5	254.4	105.3	(0.3)	3,382.0
Telephone plant under construction	133.8			(28.9)			104.9
Other	41.2		(10.9)	7.4	2.6	2.6	37.7
	6,900.8		112.3	658.6	457.8		7,213.9
COMPLEMENTARY AND OTHER	275.4			25.4	17.9	(23.3)(4)	259.6
	$10,669.2	$228.9	$112.3	$1,389.0	$572.6	$(71.9)	$11,754.9

accounts will also affect the depreciation schedules, as will acquisitions. Since depreciation is often a very large expense item, its estimate is crucial for an accurate earnings forecast.

United Telecom's schedules of valuation and qualifying accounts, and of supplementary income statement information (which includes maintenance and repairs and advertising expenses) are also important when estimating earnings. Many entities will not present a schedule of supplementary information if they deem it to be immaterial. United Telecom's consolidated valuation and qualifying

United Telecom: Consolidated Accumulated Depreciation

United Telecommunications, Inc.
Form 10–K

SCHEDULE VI—CONSOLIDATED PROPERTY, PLANT AND EQUIPMENT
Years Ended December 31, 1990, 1989, and 1988
(Millions of Dollars)

Year ended Dec. 31	Balance beginning of year	Consolidation of US Sprint	Current year provisions Charged to income	Charged to clearing accounts	Retirements, renewals and replacements	Other	Balance end of Year
1990	$3,870.0		$1,022.7 (1)		$432.8 (2)	$ 7.1 (3) $ 11.7 (4)	$4,478.7
1989	$3,339.4		$ 923.7 (1)		$522.0 (2)	$ 26.0 (3) $114.8 (5) $(11.9) (6)	$3,870.0
1988	$2,625.5	$266.2	$ 876.8 (1)	$(1.6)	$410.9 (2)	$ 18.7 (3) $ (5.6) (7) $(29.7) (8)	$3,339.4

	1990	1989	1988
(1) Charged to income as depreciation expense. Reconciliation of depreciation expense to amount disclosed in the Annual Report to Shareholders—Consolidated Statements of Cash Flows:			
Amount charged to income above	$1,022.7	$923.7	$876.8
Amortization of intangibles, plant acquisition adjustment and extraordinary plant retirement credited to amount deferred on balance sheet	60.5	38.2	29.8
Depreciation and amortization expense included in income statement	$1,083.2	$961.9	$906.6
(2) Reconciliation of retirements or sales included in Schedule V—Consolidated Property, Plant and Equipment:			
Amount charged to reserve above	$ 432.8	$522.0	$410.9
Net book value of long distance division retirements and other	75.2	50.6	220.8
Net property, plant and equipment sold or traded			
United TeleSprectrum, Inc.			72.4
United TeleSentinel, Inc.			5.4
Total Schedule V retirements and sales	$508.0	$572.6	$709.5

(3) Net Salvage.

(4) Adjustment primarily represents reclassification of a valuation reserve from plant.

(5) Adjustments resulting from exchange of certain telephone properties in Iowa and Arkansas for similar assets owned by Contel of Kansas and The Kansas State Telephone Company, both Contel Corporation subsidiaries.

(6) Adjustment resulting primarily from the retirement of capital leases prior to full amortization.

(7) Reduction of accumulated depreciation per commission order.

(8) Long-distance communications services' accumulated depreciation reclassified to related property, plant and equipment accounts to record microwave network at estimated net residual value and data communications equipment net balances reclassified for initial contributed assets

United Telecom: Consolidated Valuation

United Telecommunications, Inc.
Form 10–K

SCHEDULE VIII—CONSOLIDATED VALUATION AND QUALIFYING ACCOUNTS
Years Ended December 31, 1990, 1989, and 1988
(Millions of Dollars)

	Balance beginning of year	Consolidation of US Sprint	Charged to income	Charged to other accounts	Other additions (deductions)	Balance end of year
			Additions			
1990						
Allowance for doubtful accounts	$168.8		$361.5	$3.6	$(323.4) (1)	$210.5
1989						
Allowance for doubtful accounts	$202.5		$294.7	$16.7	$(345.1) (1)	$168.8
1988						
Allowance for doubtful accounts	$ 11.9	$305.5	$475.5	$1.6	$(592.0) (1)	$202.5

(1) Accounts charged off, net of collections.

accounts schedule shows a large increase during 1988 in the provision for doubtful accounts, due to the consolidation of U.S. Sprint. The following year, the account is reduced by almost $34 million.

United Telecom's computation of earnings (loss) per share is not difficult to approximate if the earnings applicable to common stock are known, especially given the large number of shares outstanding. Needed, however, are the common stock equivalent shares applicable to options and the employees stock purchase plan.

Since it is very difficult to accurately predict earnings given the vast number of variables needed to formulate the estimate, it is not surprising to find daily earnings surprises during corporate reporting periods. As many academic articles document, there is a strong correlation (relationship) between earnings surprises and stock reaction. That is, negative earnings surprises tend to be quickly followed by drops in the price of the announcing company's stock, and vice versa. We believe that this relationship is true only because there *generally* exists a positive relationship between long-term growth in accounting earnings and cash flows, both cash flow from operations and free cash flow. However, a careful analysis is needed

United Telecom: Consolidated Supplementary Income Statement Information

United Telecommunications, Inc.
Form 10–K

**SCHEDULE X—CONSOLIDATED SUPPLEMENTARY
INCOME STATEMENT INFORMATION
Years Ended December 31, 1990, 1989, and 1988**
(Millions of Dollars)

The following table presents supplementary consolidated income statement information for United:

	1990	1989	1988
Maintenance and repairs (1)	$115.5	$103.6	$ 89.1
Taxes, other than payroll and income taxes			
Property taxes	$115.5	$114.1	$117.3
Gross receipts and other	52.2	64.0	67.6
	$167.7	$178.1	$184.9
Advertising expense	$185.8	$144.8	$127.3

(1) Amount represents maintenance and repairs for long distance communications services. Maintenance and repairs is the primary component of plant operations expense for local communications services companies which totaled $848.1 million, $811.7 million and $737.5 million in 1990, 1989, and 1988, respectively. Complementary and Other businesses had no significant maintenance and repairs expense.

On a consolidated basis, United had no significant depreciation and amortization of intangibles expense or royalty expense during 1990, 1989, and 1988.

to distinguish those cases where the direction of price changes should not follow the direction of the earnings surprise. In particular, when earnings decline due to a noncash accounting adjustment (such as write-offs, restructurings, or other postretirement benefits) but cash flows remain intact or grow, we should expect a positive price reaction to the decline in earnings. Conversely, if cash flows declined but the firm was able to book a larger noncash revenue (such as a gain on early extinguishment of debt), prices should react negatively to the increase in earnings.

Example

Earnings surprises have become so popular that the financial press pays close attention to them. The Wall Street Journal published the following list on July 18, 1990.

United Telecom: Earnings-per-Share Computation

United Telecommunications, Inc.
Form 10–K

EXHIBIT 11

COMPUTATION OF EARNINGS PER COMMON SHARE*
(In Millions Except Per Share Data)

	Year Ended December 31,		
	1990	1989	1988
Earnings applicable to common stock	$306.0	$359.9	$505.6
Add back			
Convertible preferred stock dividends	0.8	1.0	1.2
Interest, net of related income taxes, of 5-percent convertible subordinated debentures	0.1	0.1	0.2
Earnings as adjusted for purposes of computing earnings per share assuming full dilution	$306.9	$361.0	$507.0
Weighted average number of common shares outstanding during the year	211.8	206.2	203.0
Common stock equivalent shares applicable to options and the employees stock purchase plan	2.1	2.9	1.4
Total number of shares for computing earnings per share assuming no dilution	213.9	209.1	204.4
Incremental common shares attributable to			
Additional dilutive effect of common stock options and employees stock purchase plan		0.2	0.8
Conversion of preferred stock			
First series	0.2	0.2	0.2
Second series	1.2	1.6	1.8
Conversion of 5-percent convertible subordinated debentures	0.2	0.2	0.6
Total number of shares as adjusted for purposes of computing earnings per share assuming full dilution	215.5	211.3	207.8
Earnings per common share			
Assuming no dilution	$ 1.43	$ 1.72	$ 2.48
Assuming full dilution	$ 1.42	$ 1.71	$ 2.44

*Common share data reflects the two-for-one stock split effective during 1989.

Quarterly Earnings Surprises

Company Name	Actual EPS	Estimate [# of analysts] 30-Day		Estimate [# of analysts] 120-Day		Percent Diff.
Positive						
Upjohn	$ .62	$.56	[4]	$ .57	[12]	10.71
Tosco	2.62	—		1.38	[3]	89.86
Augat	.27	—		.21	[4]	28.57
Envirosafe Svc	.47	—		.38	[3]	23.68
Adolph Coors	.68	—		.57	[4]	19.30
Fruit of the Loom	.60	—		.52	[4]	15.38
Huffy	.79	—		.70	[4]	12.86
Chemical Banking	1.02	—		.91	[8]	12.09
Intel	.84	—		.76	[24]	10.53
Reynolds Metals	1.75	—		1.59	[9]	10.06
Negative						
FMC Gold	$ .14	$.16	[3]	$ .16	[3]	12.50
Diceon Electron	(.47)	—		(.08)	[3]	—
United Telecom	.18	—		.58	[14]	68.97
Colorado Nat Bkshr	.11	—		.23	[4]	52.17
VF Corp	.37	—		.59	[6]	37.29
Oregon Metallur	.22	—		.30	[4]	26.67
Sundstrand	.57	—		.77	[6]	25.97
Rollins Environ	.12	—		.14	[5]	14.29
Diebold	.58	—		.67	[4]	13.43
Dominion Bkshr	.53	—		.61	[8]	13.11

As can be seen in this list, there were some wide variations with analysts' earnings estimates for earnings that were announced on July 17, 1990. Interestingly, two of the entities that reported large negative surprises, United Telecom and VF Corp. had experienced very different market reactions.

United Telecom stock reacted by dropping 22.9 percent on 12 million shares, almost 17 times its normal trading volume. VF Corp. reacted by rising a quarter point on normal trading volume on a day when the S&P 500 declined slightly.

We believe that the difference in price reactions between the two entities should not be attributed to their earnings but to their free cash flow. United Telecom was generating negative free cash flow, despite positive earnings, mostly because of its large investment in U.S. Sprint. VF Corp. generated positive free cash flow for the quarter, and despite an increase in leverage during the year as a result of a large share buyback, Moody's Investors Service Inc. confirmed its Single-A2 senior debt rating and Prime-1 rating of the company for commercial paper. Moody's said that "despite facing a difficult retail environment, VF continues to generate strong cash flow and should continue to reduce debt levels."

NET OPERATING CASH FLOW

Since firms' earnings may vary widely depending on their accounting methods, accounting estimates, and applications of specific revenue and expense recognition rules to their own situation, one has to rely on some other measure for cross-firm performance comparisons. Ideally, this measure should be free of the effects of as many accounting methods as possible. This leads investors and creditors to forge a measure that is based on cash flows.

Cash flow analysis is an outgrowth of what is known as examining the quality of an entity's earnings. The reason for the growing popularity of cash flow analysis is the expanded use of very liberal accounting practices by firms, and investors' concurrent inability to adequately interpret much of the reported financial statement jargon. For example, the average public investor wonders how an entity selling at a below market price/earnings ratio could ever find itself in a financial predicament.

Example

Integrated Resources was selling at 50 percent below the price/earnings multiple on the Standard & Poor's 500 when it was forced into a bankruptcy filing by its creditors.

Let us review some of the accounting areas that need to be investigated to assess the quality of earnings:

1. The deferred asset account, which appears as the last asset on the balance sheet, should always, to the extent possible, be closely inspected. Changes in deferred assets could be due to prepayment of expenditures for advertising, insurance, and maintenance, or other expenditures such as developmental costs which the company *hopes* will result in future income. But is not an addition to the deferred asset account, which is really an outlay of cash, an expense? Advocates of cash flow analysis would differ with the accounting convention of booking an asset of this kind for cash already spent. Furthermore, the accounting for acquisitions requires the use of the purchase method and the recording of goodwill on the consolidated balance sheet. In some cases, the acquired businesses are sold subsequently, but the related goodwill asset account remains on the consolidated balance sheet.

2. The purchase of inventory, which is an outlay of cash, is not recorded by the accountant as an expense unless the inventory is sold. One should attempt to assess the likelihood that inventory will be sold, and whether the firm has excess inventories. The inflationary spirals during the 1970s conditioned security analysts to pay strict attention to inventory accounting and its effects on reported profits of changes in price levels. When price levels change quickly, depending on the amount of inventory held in relation to the company's peers and the inventory method used (LIFO versus FIFO), earnings comparisons could be very difficult to make. Cash flow analysis, by essentially placing all companies on a cash basis, avoids much of the accounting skullduggery.

3. Asset replacement may bear little resemblance to the historical cost represented on the balance sheet and hence true earnings may be under- or overstated.

4. The accounting method for investments is another area of importance in the determination of earnings quality. The equity method allows the investor company to record its pro-rata share of net profits in the investee if it holds more than 20 percent of the investee's outstanding stock, even if these profits were not received in cash. Under the

new accounting rules, *SFAS No. 115,* unrealized gains and losses on marketable securities would be included in stockholders equity but not in income.

Example

The 1989 statement of cash flows for John Deere Co., which uses the equity method for affiliates in Brazil and Mexico, includes $6.9 million under undistributed earnings of unconsolidated subsidiaries and affiliates. These earnings are included in determining net income, but since they had not been obtained in cash, John Deere subtracts them in its derivation of cash flows from operating activities.

5. Another factor affecting earnings quality is the ratio of profits from operations to interest or dividend income. It has been argued that a high ratio of dividend income to operating profits lowers earnings quality because it is not a result of operations and is therefore unpredictable. It is argued that firms with a high ratio of interest and dividend income to total income from operations should be accorded a lower valuation or free cash flow multiple.

6. Contributing corporate stock or other assets, such as real estate, to the corporate pension fund in lieu of a cash contribution, should be examined by the cash flow analyst or the analyst who is concerned about earnings quality.

7. The analyst should examine when and how revenues are recognized. Is it when the product is shipped, as installment payments are received, or when the contract is signed? Because services are becoming such an important part of revenue growth for many companies (including manufacturing entities), it is important to look at how revenues are recognized for the service portion of the business, including the percentage of service revenues to total revenues.

8. Some accounting rules require the disclosure of a liability in footnotes (such as pensions and other postretirement benefits), but not on the financial statements immediately. Some potential liabilities are not properly disclosed at all (such as the value of stock

options granted to employees, debt of joint ventures and corporate guarantees). The cash flow analyst would wish to make adjustments for noncash items and for items that should be accounted for as additional liabilities in assessing the quality of earnings.

Because of the problems associated with earnings quality, a natural alternative to earnings of a firm is the net operating cash flow, which is subject to fewer accounting manipulations. Operating cash flows are insensitive to the firm's choice of an inventory accounting method because operating cash flows focus on *payments* for inventory purchases (or production), which are the same regardless of the accounting method for inventories. Another example is the choice of a depreciation policy. Whereas the choice of a depreciation method (e.g., straight-line or accelerated depreciation) may affect the earnings of a firm, it does not affect cash from operations at all. Thus, net operating cash flows is a figure that is less affected by the particular accounting methods the firm selects. Furthermore, with the issuance of *SFAS No. 95*, net operating cash flows is more uniformly reported across firms, since the FASB has provided specific definitions for operating, as distinguished from investing or financing, cash flows.[7]

Example

An increasing number of firms discuss not only the change in earnings from one period to another, but also the change in cash flows from operations. For example, Commercial Metals Company, a steel manufacturing firm, discusses in its press release the changes in earnings and operating cash flows:

Commercial Metals Company Reports Earnings of $12 Million

Dallas—October 22, 1991—Commercial Metals Company (NYSE) today reported net earnings of $12.0 million, or $1.12 per share, on sales of $1.2 billion for the year ended August 31, 1991. This compares with earnings of $25.9 million, or $2.27 per share, on sales of $1.1 billion for the same period last year. Cash flow from operations was $38.0 million compared to $48.7 million last year.

---

[7]Nevertheless, firms can still classify transactions in a way that will increase cash from operations rather than investing or financing cash flows, as we showed in the previous chapter.

CMC President and Chief Executive Officer Stanley A. Rabin said, "Following three and a half consecutive years of strong earnings and excellent cash flow from operations, fiscal 1991 results were lower because of the recession."

To understand the limitations of the net operating cash flows for investment purposes, consider the following scenario. Security analysts tell us that a particular security is selling at just three times cash flow and therefore must be a bargain. However, low cash flow multiples being quoted by either corporate officers or security analysts are almost always based on operating cash flow, not free cash flow, a concept we will introduce in more detail below. It is implausible that firms in this era can sell at anything near three times their consistent free cash flow and not be subject to takeover bids, unless the entity is in de facto rapid liquidation. As a matter of fact, companies that sell at less than four times operating cash flow, typically, are net borrowers, as shown in Table 5–1.

Example

Forbes magazine ran the following headline in its January 8, 1990, issue:

At Two Times Cash Flow, Bethlehem Steel Is One of the Cheapest Stocks on the Big Board

Forbes did not specify that Bethlehem Steel's low cash flow multiple was based on its net operating cash flow, but a review of the firm's statement of cash flows indicated that, indeed, net cash from operations was the denominator for the cash flow multiple. However, even a cursory review of Bethlehem Steel's statement of cash flows revealed three pertinent points:

1. A large proportion of its high operating cash flow was consumed by its underfunded pension fund payment (about $170 million out of about $700 million in 1989, and about $515 million out of total operating cash flow of $890 million in 1988).
2. Its operating cash flow was probably near a cyclical peak, given Bethlehem's operating cash flow was just $186 million three years earlier.
3. Bethlehem was operating with the benefit of a very low tax rate due to losses in prior years. This is verified by examining the tax footnote, which reveals a $1.3 billion tax loss carryforward

TABLE 5-1
Firms with Low Multiples of Operating Cash Flows for 1993

Ticker	Name	Market Value (millions)	Operating Cash Flow 1993 (millions)	OCF Multiple	Percent Net Debt Financing	Percent Net Equity Financing	Total Financing/ Market Value
ARONB	Aaron Rents Inc CL B	$ 136.2	$ 55.8	2.4	0.0%	-0.4%	-0.4%
ALK	Alaska Airgroup Inc	184.3	48.5	3.8	2.3	-18.0	-15.7
AEN	Amc Entertainment Inc	195.5	63.7	3.1	-20.7	49.6	28.9
AMOO	Amerco	753.9	202.3	3.7	0.6	19.4	20.1
AWA	America West Airlines CL	383.6	153.4	2.5	-20.2	0.0	-20.2
APS	American President Cos Ltd	617.5	168.6	3.7	-13.7	0.0	-13.7
ASD	Amern Standard Co Inc	526.9	200.8	2.6	-2.9	-2.3	-5.2
AMR	Amr Corp/DE	4,712.0	1,377.0	3.4	-7.2	22.9	15.7
AMTR	Amtran Inc	105.5	33.9	3.1	-23.3	35.5	12.2
ATNI	Atlantic Tele-Network Inc	101.3	31.7	3.2	-5.1	0.0	-5.1
AVL	Aviall Inc	118.8	93.7	1.3	337.4	0.0	337.4
BLY	Bally Entmt Corp	357.8	97.5	3.7	54.8	0.2	54.9
BOR	Borg-Warner Security CP	151.8	52.3	2.9	-26.2	43.9	17.7
BSE	Boston Edison Co	1,061.7	296.5	3.6	15.7	1.0	16.7
BUR	Burlington Inds Inc	754.5	213.9	3.5	2.1	0.0	2.1
CLD	Caldor Corp	381.2	98.7	3.9	-6.3	14.3	8.0
CGF	Carr-Gottstein Foods Co	102.0	35.4	2.9	-81.6	76.1	-5.5
CSNO	Casino America Inc	152.1	44.5	3.4	47.1	-4.4	42.7
CMAG	Casino Magic Corp	175.9	54.1	3.3	42.7	0.0	42.7

TABLE 5-1
(continued)

Ticker	Name	Market Value (millions)	Operating Cash Flow 1993 (millions)	OCF Multiple	Percent Net Debt Financing	Percent Net Equity Financing	Total Financing/ Market Value
CX	Centerior Energy Corp	$1,350.8	$ 516.9	2.6	-1.8%	8.2%	6.4%
CGP	Coastal Corp	3,050.5	809.8	3.8	-16.4	6.7	-9.7
CG	Columbia Gas System	1,314.6	850.4	1.5	-0.1	0.0	-0.1
CDO	Comdisco Inc	926.6	1,873.0	0.5	-30.3	-0.5	-30.9
CQ	Comsat Corp Ser 1	862.1	259.7	3.3	-0.6	0.9	0.3
DIN	Cons G Grupo Dina Spon AD	121.0	59.9	2.0	0.0	107.3	107.2
ACCOB	Coors (Adolph) CL B	632.4	168.5	3.8	0.8	1.2	2.0
JC	Craig (Jenny) Inc	174.2	54.7	3.2	0.0	-9.5	-9.5
CYR	Cray Research	458.8	172.7	2.7	-1.0	-0.5	-1.5
DAI	Daimler-Benz AG Spon ADR	21,141.5	5,699.0	3.7	4.9	0.0	4.9
DARTA	Dart Group Corp CL A	131.7	38.4	3.4	10.4	1.5	11.8
DLCH	Delchamps Inc	124.5	32.9	3.8	-7.0	0.0	-7.0
DLW	Delta Woodside Inds	233.9	62.7	3.7	8.4	0.0	8.4
DTE	Detroit Edison Co	4,074.1	1,140.8	3.6	-10.7	0.9	-9.9
DBRL	Dibrell Brothers Inc	257.7	82.5	3.1	-18.4	0.2	-18.2
EBS	Edison Brothers Stores	327.6	131.0	2.5	22.8	-1.7	21.2
FI	Fina Inc CLA	1,210.6	379.6	3.2	-27.6	0.1	-27.5
FLST	Flagstar Cos Inc	251.6	171.0	1.5	10.0	0.0	10.0
FLM	Fleming Companies Inc	765.6	208.5	3.7	-7.0	1.0	-6.0

TABLE 5–1
(continued)

Ticker	Name	Market Value (millions)	Operating Cash Flow 1993 (millions)	OCF Multiple	Percent Net Debt Financing	Percent Net Equity Financing	Total Financing/ Market Value
F	Ford Motor Co	$27,358.8	$14,007.0	2.0	30.6%	1.4%	32.1%
GM	General Motors Corp	31,747.0	14,655.8	2.2	-23.3	1.9	-21.4
GNV	Geneva Stl Co CL A	182.2	64.4	2.8	25.7	18.2	43.9
GAP	Great Atlantic & Pac Tea Co	807.4	213.6	3.8	10.5	0.0	10.5
GREY	Grey Advertising Inc	215.9	108.0	2.0	13.9	-0.1	13.8
GOU	Gulf Canada Res Ltd ORD	612.1	202.9	3.0	-6.8	0.2	-6.5
HAVAB	Harvard Inds Inc CL B	111.3	51.8	2.1	-32.0	0.0	-32.0
HO	Home Oil Co Ltd	388.5	105.8	3.7	-7.4	2.8	-4.5
HMT	Host Marriott Corp	1,646.9	429.0	3.8	-5.8	0.7	-5.1
HOU	Houston Industries Inc	4,749.4	1,207.7	3.9	-10.9	0.3	-10.6
IMKTA	Ingles Markets Inc CL A	176.8	49.5	3.6	-0.5	0.0	-0.5
ISH	Intl Shipholding Corp	108.9	55.1	2.0	-6.9	-8.7	-15.6
IPT	IP Timberlands LP CL A	1,062.5	373.4	2.8	0.0	0.0	0.0
JCI	Johnson Controls Inc	1,951.1	491.7	4.0	0.3	0.0	0.3
KM	K Mart Corp	5,537.9	1,930.0	2.9	-5.8	0.8	-5.0
KCLC	Kinder-Care Learning Center	251.4	74.4	3.4	-19.3	0.0	-19.3
LHP	Lakehead Pipe Line Ptns LP	113.5	92.5	1.2	21.1	0.0	21.1
MTW	Manitowoc Co	183.2	62.7	2.9	0.0	-16.7	-16.7
MITSY	Mitsui & Co Ltd ADR	11,618.8	4,593.3	2.5	8.6	0.3	9.0

TABLE 5–1
(continued)

Ticker	Name	Market Value (millions)	Operating Cash Flow 1993 (millions)	OCF Multiple	Percent Net Debt Financing	Percent Net Equity Financing	Total Financing/ Market Value
MNT	Montedison Spa ADR	$1,471.5	$ 410.5	3.6	-83.7%	0.0%	-83.7%
NAFC	Nash Finch Co	170.6	83.5	2.0	-1.6	0.0	-1.6
NSH	Nashua Corp	125.9	34.6	3.6	-4.2	-0.1	-4.3
NACC	National Auto Credit Inc	283.2	83.1	3.4	0.0	0.0	0.0
NGE	New York State Elec & Gas	1,467.3	412.2	3.6	-2.8	8.7	5.8
NMK	Niagara Mohawk Power	2,068.4	627.4	3.3	-0.3	3.4	3.0
NAE	Noram Energy Corp	673.6	172.6	3.9	-17.4	0.0	-17.4
NU	Northeast Utilities	2,702.3	920.2	2.9	-4.9	-0.5	-5.4
ORPC	Orion Pictures Corp	121.9	88.3	1.4	-53.1	0.0	-53.1
ORX	Oryx Energy Co	1,088.4	379.0	2.9	4.8	0.0	4.8
OXFD	Oxford Resources Corp CL	150.9	81.5	1.9	66.1	0.1	66.2
PCG	Pacific Gas & Electric	10,532.9	2,792.8	3.8	5.5	-0.9	4.6
PEL	Panhandle Eastern Corp	2,700.7	706.5	3.8	-26.5	8.6	-17.9
PTB	Paragon Trade Brands Inc	169.9	67.6	2.5	0.0	15.8	15.8
PCS	Payless Cashways CL A VTG	363.9	109.0	3.3	-125.9	106.5	-19.4
REC	Recognition Intl Inc	102.9	28.5	3.6	-13.8	31.4	17.6
RP	Rhone-Poulenc SA ADR 1/4	5,381.6	1,873.1	2.9	-12.6	7.3	-5.3
RN	RJR Nabisco Hldgs Corp	6,742.4	1,769.0	3.8	-33.9	17.1	-16.8
RHR	Rohr Inc	187.3	78.7	2.4	-14.4	0.4	-14.0

TABLE 5-1
(continued)

Ticker	Name	Market Value (millions)	Operating Cash Flow 1993 (millions)	OCF Multiple	Percent Net Debt Financing	Percent Net Equity Financing	Total Financing/ Market Value
RLC	Rollins Truck Leasing	$ 561.4	$ 166.5	3.4	5.3%	0.1%	5.4%
R	Ryder System Inc	1,791.5	1,217.9	1.5	-7.2	-3.5	-10.7
SCE	Scecorp	6,940.9	2,002.0	3.5	3.1	-0.2	2.9
SCR.A	Sea Containers Ltd CL A	152.0	127.7	1.2	122.6	-0.8	121.8
SQA.A	Sequa Corp CL A	294.5	121.0	2.4	-32.7	0.0	-32.7
SME	Service Merchandise Co	471.8	236.4	2.0	10.3	0.4	10.7
SHN	Shoney's Inc	427.3	107.8	4.0	-5.5	3.3	-2.3
SHBZ	Showbiz Pizza Time Inc	116.5	44.9	2.6	10.1	-8.4	1.7
SMC	Smith (A O) Corp	415.5	115.4	3.6	-10.7	1.0	-9.7
SWX	Southwest Gas Corp	314.3	89.5	3.5	12.2	-0.1	12.1
STW	Standard Commercial Corp	120.5	47.7	2.5	-7.4	0.0	-7.4
TNH	Terra Nitrogen Co LP	140.9	63.8	2.2	-0.5	0.0	-0.5
TXT	Textron Inc	4,884.2	1,299.4	3.8	-5.8	0.4	-5.4
TDHC	Thermadyne Holdings Corp	146.3	36.6	4.0	-5.0	0.0	-5.0
TNP	TNP Enterprises Inc	162.0	50.7	3.2	-44.7	0.5	-44.2
3TLMXY	Tolmex Sa Spon ADR	1,048.3	313.4	3.3	16.1	0.0	16.1
TOWR	Tower Air Inc	122.3	33.1	3.7	-13.8	35.9	22.1
TPIE	TPI Enterprises Inc	107.0	32.4	3.3	-10.0	16.1	6.0
TTRR	Tracor Inc	103.7	45.5	2.3	90.8	1.5	92.2

TABLE 5–1
(concluded)

Ticker	Name	Market Value (millions)	Operating Cash Flow 1993 (millions)	OCF Multiple	Percent Net Debt Financing	Percent Net Equity Financing	Total Financing/ Market Value
E	Transco Energy Co	$ 772.5	276.2	2.8	-8.3%	-4.8%	-13.0%
UAL	UAL Corp	1,148.1	858.0	1.3	-56.7	51.5	-5.2
UCM	UNICOM Corp	5,247.5	2,249.2	2.3	-1.0	-0.2	-1.2
UIS	UNISYS Corp	1,623.1	1,019.7	1.6	-24.3	0.0	-24.3
UIL	United Illuminating Co	456.1	145.9	3.1	3.7	0.4	4.1
VEN	Venture Stores Inc	197.8	66.3	3.0	5.4	0.6	6.0
VRES	Vicorp Restaurants Inc	152.1	50.9	3.0	-2.2	-3.4	-5.6
VTO	Vitro Sociedad Anonima AD	825.0	283.0	2.9	7.9	0.0	7.9
WOL	Wainoco Oil Corp	102.2	32.8	3.1	-14.6	21.3	6.7
WHX	WHX Corp	292.2	94.2	3.1	30.6	71.2	101.8
YELL	Yellow Corp	488.4	138.8	3.5	-6.8	0.0	-6.8
ZEI	Zeigler Coal Hldg Co	315.5	130.4	2.4	-28.8	0.0	-28.8
	Average				-0.6	6.9	6.3

for tax purposes, and $850 million for alternative minimum tax purposes. The $105.3 million actual tax payment for 1988, as is revealed in the tax footnote, comprises mostly a $99.6 million settlement of audit adjustments and interest related to their federal income tax returns for the years 1971 through 1978.

In fact, Bethlehem Steel's operating cash flow dried up in its first quarter of 1990. During that quarter, operating cash flow fell to $6 million from $119 million in the prior year. This illustrates well why it is preferable to average (or normalize) operating cash flows over four years, as well as analyze its growth rate during both the past four- and eight-year periods.

While Bethlehem Steel was in fact selling at twice its last year's operating cash flow, it was, more importantly, selling at 45 times free cash flow, which is the concept we introduce below. At that time, Bethlehem Steel's free cash flow multiple was twice the market average.

Example

In its December 25, 1989, issue, *Business Week* showed a table that included companies with low cash flow multiples. For example, Universal Health was selling at 2.4 times cash flow and Inland Steel at 2.6 times cash flow. This implies a 42 percent annual return on cash invested for Inland Steel and 38 percent for Universal Health, an obviously exaggerated rate. This, again, is due to the focus on net operating cash flows, a measure that takes into account neither the firm's needs for further investments, nor its retirement of debt.

When corporate officers speak of their firm's cash flow, typically, they are alluding to operating cash flow—but not always. CPI Corporation, in a September 15, 1989, report defined *cash flow* as operating earnings plus depreciation and amortization. However, with the disclosure of the statement of cash flows according to *SFAS No. 95*, many analysts, investors, and creditors have a better-defined measure of operating cash flow. For investment purposes, investors can use the following rule of thumb: do not invest in a firm with negative operating cash flow for even a single year. For example, in stable industries such as consumer non-durable goods, firms should be able to show positive operating cash flow every year and to exhibit growth of operating cash flows that exceeds the rate of inflation over a four- and eight-year period.

Bethlehem Steel: Consolidated Statements of Cash Flows

Consolidated Statements of Cash Flows

(dollars in millions)	Year ended December 31		
	1989	1988	1987
Operating Activities:			
Net Income	$ 245.7	$ 403.0	$ 174.3
Extraordinary gains	—	11.4	70.4
Income before extraordinary gains	245.7	391.6	103.9
Adjustments for items not affecting cash from operating activities:			
Depreciation	325.3	333.6	338.9
Estimated restructuring losses — net (Note C)	105.0	113.0	75.0
Deferred taxes, etc.	12.6	19.7	(3.0)
Working Capital*:			
Receivables	61.6	(89.0)	(99.3)
Inventories	(43.9)	(61.4)	9.8
Accounts payable	29.8	50.3	47.3
Accrued employment costs	(33.6)	81.7	15.0
Accrued taxes	(.1)	(1.7)	5.6
Investment tax credit refund receivable (Note E)	—	130.0	(130.0)
Federal income tax payment (Note E)	—	(99.6)	—
Other — net	4.1	20.5	(1.7)
Cash Provided from Operating Activities	706.5	888.7	361.5
Investing Activities:			
Capital expenditures	(421.3)	(303.9)	(152.7)
Cash proceeds from sales of businesses and assets	38.4	47.2	87.8
Collateral investments	10.1	208.4	(84.2)
Other — net	23.6	18.4	14.3
Cash Used for Investing Activities	(349.2)	(29.9)	(134.8)
Financing Activities:			
Pension financing (funding) — net (Note I)	(172.7)	(514.3)	56.6
Revolving credit payments	—	(240.0)	(120.0)
Long-term debt payments (Note F)	(63.5)	(72.6)	(205.5)
Capital lease payments (Note G)	(34.8)	(155.7)	(52.4)
Restructured facilities payments	(27.5)	(63.2)	(34.9)
Cash dividends paid (Note L)	(37.5)	(45.0)	(11.2)
Common Stock issued (Note L)	1.0	185.4	188.0
Accrued employee investment plan stock	.8	2.0	41.6
Cash Used for Financing Activities	(334.2)	(903.4)	(137.8)
Net Increase (Decrease) in Cash and Cash Equivalents	23.1	(44.6)	88.9
Cash and Cash Equivalents — Beginning of Period	507.4	552.0	463.1
— End of Period	$ 530.5	$ 507.4	$ 552.0
Supplemental Cash Payment Information:			
Interest, net of amount capitalized	$ 65.0	$ 86.0	$ 142.6
Income taxes (Note E)	$ 9.0	$ 105.7	$ 2.6

*Excludes Financing Activities, Investing Activities, Investment tax credit refund receivable and Federal income tax payment.
The accompanying Notes are an integral part of the Consolidated Financial Statements.

Bethlehem Steel: Consolidated Statements of Cash Flows

Bethlehem Steel Corporation

CONSOLIDATED STATEMENTS OF CASH FLOWS
(dollars in millions)

	Three Months Ended March 31	
	1991 (unaudited)	1990 (unaudited)
Operating Activities:		
Net Income (Loss)	$ (39.2)	$ 21.3
Adjustments for items not affecting cash from operating activities:		
Depreciation	58.3	75.8
Other - net (including deferred taxes)	17.3	-
Working capital (excluding financing and investing activities):		
Receivables	(17.7)	(37.3)
Inventories	(41.4)	(2.9)
Accounts payable	(27.7)	(23.9)
Accrued taxes and employment costs	(5.1)	(41.7)
Other - net	(1.3)	14.7
Cash Provided from (Used for) Operating Activities	(56.8)	6.0
Investing Activities:		
Capital expenditures	(102.6)	(100.2)
Cash proceeds from sales of businesses and assets	2.8	3.5
Collateral investments	-	(0.1)
Other - net	(2.0)	3.6
Cash Used for Investing Activities	(101.8)	(93.2)
Financing Activities:		
Pension financing (funding) - net	13.0	(45.5)
Revolving credit borrowings	80.0	-
Long-term debt borrowings	19.8	-
Long-term debt and capital lease payments	(10.8)	(10.2)
Restructured facilities payments	(5.0)	(7.2)
Cash dividends paid	(13.2)	(13.2)
Stock issued	-	0.5
Cash Provided from (Used for) Financing Activities	83.8	(75.6)
Net Decrease in Cash and Cash Equivalents	(74.8)	(162.8)
Cash and Cash Equivalents - Beginning of Period	273.5	530.5
- End of Period	$ 198.7	$ 367.7
Supplemental Cash Payment Information:		
Interest, net of amount capitalized	$ 18.3	$ 17.8
Income taxes	$ 1.8	$ 0.6

However, this rule is probably too strict for more cyclical industries, and one may wish to relax it somewhat, perhaps to exclude only entities that have not produced positive operating cash flow in at least six out of the past eight years.

Example

If the analyst allows for some flexibility in applying the investment rule of no negative operating cash flows, entities such as Boeing and other long-term contractors could be possible investment opportunities. Such firms operate under very long lead times, must operate with large amounts of inventory on hand when beginning projects, and may have negative operating cash flows in the beginning of an operating cycle.

One may then modify the rule, to preclude investment in entities that have two successive years of negative operating cash flows regardless of their industry. However, entities that show negative operating cash flows are probably still riskier, even if there is a sound reason for such a deficit. Such companies are likely to be cyclical in nature. Additionally, if there are operating problems, such firms may find themselves in financial distress.

Example

Morrison Knudsen Corp. showed a negative operating cash flow in 1993, as the firm was building a large inventory of transit railcars for its customers under long-term contracts. Presumably, when the orders were delivered, the firm was to receive cash from its customers and would be able to pay off short-term borrowing that financed their inventories. Thus, over the combined two years, the firm would have shown positive operating cash flow. Unknown to security analysts (as well as to the firm's own board of directors), the firm underbid severely on these contracts in order to obtain them, and the future cash flows in 1994 were insufficient to pay off short-term borrowing. The firm found itself in technical default on its borrowing, and its stock price plummeted.

Negative operating cash flow indicates that management has been unable to employ the assets of the entity properly, or that the entity has encountered economic difficulties in generating cash flows. However, the financial services industry (or firms with a large short-term investment portfolio) is an exception to the negative operating cash flow rule, since the purchase of investments, a use of cash, could cause negative operating cash flows.

CAN NET OPERATING CASH FLOW BE
USED FOR PORTFOLIO SELECTION?

As is well known, many investors consider the P/E ratio their chief investment criterion in making portfolio selections. Fewer investors consider measures that are based on cash flows, primarily net cash flows from operating activities. Can this variable be used to identify investment candidates? This subsection examines the availability of firms with increasing cash flows from operating activities. In Chapter 8, we compare the performance of portfolios that are based on P/E ratios, operating cash flows, and free cash flows.

A casual examination of the data shows that there is no shortage of entities that consistently generate positive operating cash flow each year, and it is simple to construct a diversified portfolio of such entities. For example, limiting ourselves to firms with a market capitalization above $200 million, positive reported net cash flow from operating activities in 1989, and estimated positive net operating cash flow for 1981, we find that 456 out of 606 available firms have shown positive growth rates in operating cash flow during the period 1981–1989. Note that firms with high growth of net income are not necessarily firms with high growth of operating cash flows, or vice versa.

Example

In its 1994 annual report, Jostens, a provider of performance awards, class rings, and yearbooks, showed a net loss of $16.2 million, following a net loss of $12.7 million in 1993. However, for these same two years, Jostens reported positive net operating cash flows of $125 million and $64.4 million, respectively. One item that reduced income substantially in both years was restructuring charges of $69.4 million and $50.6 million in 1994 and 1993, respectively. Out of these charges, $27.3 million and $10.6 million in 1994 and 1993, respectively, were added back to income in the statement of cash flows, indicating that they were noncash charges during these years. The 1994 charge relates to pulling out of a segment in the educational software and hardware placed in schools. The 1993 charges related to the sportswear business, which was subsequently sold, and to restructuring of the photography business. Given that the reduction in development of educational software would save the firm future operating cash flows, one can conclude that Jostens's operating cash flow provided better feedback, that is, gave investors better predictive information than earnings for the year.

Tables 5–2 through 5–5 show large entities (with a market value of greater than $200 million) whose operating cash flow is dramatically different from reported income. Table 5–2 shows entities that had an operating profit for the most recent year, yet were characterized by negative operating cash flow. Table 5–3 shows entities with an operating loss for the most recent year, yet had positive net operating cash flows. Table 5-4 shows entities with average negative operating cash flows during the most recent four fiscal years, but with a positive average operating profit over the same period. Table 5–5 is the mirror image of Table 5–4.

One can also select firms to a portfolio based on their operating cash flow multiples, as opposed to their price/earnings multiples. However, since some nonrecurring cash flows may be included in net operating cash flows, it is more judicious to average the net operating cash flows in the most recent four years, assuming that the nature of the business has not changed. When calculating the average net operating cash flow multiple, adjustments need to be made for material changes affecting the entity, such as changes in financial leverage or changes in the nature of the business as a result of a business combination. For the majority of entities, it is preferable to study the four- and eight-year operating cash flow history. An eight-year period will likely contain at least one industry downturn or other major event (i.e., large acquisition, reorganization). Four- and eight-year periods represent suitable time periods for studying operating cash flows over a typical business cycle; it is important to study how management reacts to or anticipates major turns of the business cycle. This examination offers the cash flow analyst important clues as to how assets and cash flows are managed by the firm.

Typically, corporate managers and directors who have confidence in their entity's products and long-run outlook will continue to make necessary expenditures to ensure that operating cash flows will grow in the future. However, some corporate officers may panic at the first sign of a business downturn and "prune" the entity's balance sheet (primarily receivables, inventories,

TABLE 5–2
Firms with Negative Operating Cash Flow but Positive Income—1993

Ticker	Name	Market Value (millions)	1993 Operating Cash Flow (millions)	1993 Operating Profit (millions)	1994 Annual Return
ANTC	Antec Corp	$ 513.9	$ −2.9	$ 10.1	−26.5%
APOG	Apogee Enterprises Inc	222.6	−10.9	3.3	9.7
AAPL	Apple Computer Inc	4,570.8	−661.8	86.6	35.0
APSI	APS Holding Corp CL A	404.8	−10.2	5.7	41.3
AVID	Avid Technology Inc	276.0	−12.2	3.7	50.3
BBBY	Bed Bath & Beyond Inc	838.3	−1.8	21.9	−13.0
BBY	Best Buy Co Inc	869.7	−126.2	41.7	34.4
BHC	BHC Communications CL A	1,903.5	−55.8	224.3	−10.4
BCL	Biocraft Laboratories Inc	226.1	0.0	6.1	−22.3
BJS	BJ Services Co	317.3	−0.5	14.6	−12.3
CDWC	CDW Computer Centers Inc	460.6	−2.5	12.6	143.8
COMMA	Cellular Commun Inc CL A	478.0	−0.7	11.9	14.4
CTX	Centex Corp	691.0	−56.0	85.2	−45.4
CCN	Chris-Craft Inds	1,016.7	−54.4	149.1	−3.0
RXC	Circa Pharmaceuticals Inc	344.7	−22.2	8.4	90.7
CLF	Cleveland-Cliffs Inc	467.0	−22.8	54.6	2.3
DR	Coastal Healthcare Group Inc	586.6	−18.2	14.1	−31.1
CGEN	Collagen Corp	245.5	−9.1	9.7	−17.4
CPU	CompUSA Inc	355.1	−51.3	12.3	−24.5
CPLY	Copley Pharmaceutical Inc	347.3	−14.5	6.4	−66.5
ESRX	Express Scripts Inc CL A	468.0	−2.6	8.1	56.4
GD	General Dynamics Corp	2,885.6	−148.0	270.0	−3.1
GR	Goodrich (B F) Co	1,096.7	−17.4	15.3	13.2
GC	Grancare Inc	212.2	−9.0	12.2	−3.4
HMY	Heilig-Meyers Co	1,030.3	−74.8	55.0	−35.7
HHC	Horizon Healthcare Corp	540.0	−17.2	16.6	39.1
N	Inco Ltd	3,084.6	−6.4	28.2	8.0
IPSCF	Ipsco Inc	429.7	−24.1	21.6	−8.5
LRCX	Lam Research Corp	1,125.6	−9.5	18.9	14.6
LEN	Lennar Corp	603.4	−68.5	52.5	−31.5
LTV	LTV Corp	1,488.1	−204.0	386.9	2.3
MAG	Magnetek Inc	343.0	−7.4	27.0	−9.2
SUIT	Mens Wearhouse Inc	267.4	−0.2	8.7	−31.0

TABLE 5–2
(continued)

Ticker	Name	Market Value (millions)	1993 Operating Cash Flow (millions)	1993 Operating Profit (millions)	1994 Annual Return
MIKE	Michaels Stores Inc	$ 656.6	$ −28.9	$26.3	−2.8%
MICCF	Millicom Intl Cellular SA	1,143.1	−16.3	32.9	28.2
MK	Monk Austin Inc	231.0	−34.7	28.7	−14.5
MRN	Morrison Knudsen Corp	278.3	−64.3	35.8	−46.1
NMG	Neiman-Marcus Group Inc	541.5	−9.3	58.6	−26.9
TNEL	Nelson (Thomas) Inc	256.6	−0.3	8.7	−0.4
OH	Oakwood Homes	557.1	−75.7	24.5	−9.4
OCR	Omnicare Inc	558.6	−1.0	8.7	37.3
ORLY	Oreily Automotive Inc	227.5	−1.8	8.2	−14.7
OMI	Owens & Minor Inc	429.9	−10.0	18.5	−6.0
PAIR	Pairgain Technologies Inc	319.5	−1.5	7.6	3.6
PGSAY	Petroleum Geo-SVC Spon AD	584.6	−8.9	17.1	12.0
PCTL	Picturetel Corp	435.5	−4.5	7.4	28.0
PRFT	Proffitts Inc	218.7	−39.8	5.7	1.7
PHM	Pulte Corp	621.0	−180.7	77.8	−35.9
QHRI	Quantum Health Resources Inc	291.3	−3.3	16.6	−1.7
RHS	Regency Health Svcs Inc	260.1	−1.3	5.5	−20.5
SFE	Safeguard Scientifics Inc	221.7	−18.9	3.9	43.8
SHLR	Schuler Homes Inc	229.6	−28.3	30.0	−49.1
SCIS	SCI Systems Inc	485.1	−34.2	26.6	2.1
SVGI	Silicon Valley Group Inc	488.9	−27.0	4.5	108.9
RIG	Sonat Offshore Drilling Inc	581.4	−10.7	24.0	12.4
SJI	South Jersey Industries	203.6	−5.8	15.2	−17.6
SP	Spelling Entertnmt Grp Inc	896.4	−48.7	23.7	8.1
WON	Sports & Recreation Inc	364.8	−28.4	11.3	3.0
STA	Starter Corp	237.7	−9.0	28.8	−60.4
SSSS	Stewart & Stevenson Service	1,047.5	−8.0	56.8	−32.2
SHG	Sun Healthcare Group Inc	754.5	−7.9	10.4	51.5
SBL	Symbol Technologies	729.8	−23.4	12.4	70.3
SNTC	Synetic Inc	307.5	−0.3	6.1	77.9
TECD	Tech Data Corp	453.7	−102.7	30.2	−5.6
TRA	Terra Industries Inc	735.5	−1.0	22.8	37.4
TCA	Thermo Cardiosystems	594.8	−1.1	0.4	−11.1

TABLE 5–2
(concluded)

Ticker	Name	Market Value (millions)	1993 Operating Cash Flow (millions)	1993 Operating Profit (millions)	1994 Annual Return
TKN	Thermotrex Corp	$ 288.8	$ –2.4	$ 0.5	–12.2%
TBL	Timberland Co CL A	275.4	–26.7	22.5	–59.0
TOL	Toll Brothers Inc	405.3	–54.9	27.4	–41.6
TRN	Trinity Industries	1,427.1	–45.6	68.3	–25.4
USRX	US Robotics Corp	712.5	–7.4	17.0	24.9
VALM	Valmont Industries	228.0	–2.1	5.3	–13.5
WBB	Webb (Del E) Corp	278.9	–28.8	16.9	11.4
	Average				3.0

TABLE 5–3
Firms with Positive Operating Cash Flow
but Negative Income—1993

Ticker	Name	Market Value (millions)	1993 Operating Cash Flow (millions)	1993 Operating Profit (millions)	1994 Annual Return
COMS	3COM Corp	$3,842.9	$ 127.9	$ –28.7	119.4%
ADLAC	Adelphia Commun CL A	275.1	27.0	–97.4	–54.0
AL	Alcan Aluminium Ltd	5,500.0	444.0	–104.0	23.7
AMH	Amdahl Corp	1,304.9	302.2	–588.7	83.3
AHC	Amerada Hess Corp	4,637.0	819.4	–297.7	2.4
AME	Ametek Inc	609.3	65.3	–7.3	34.2
AMR	Amr Corp/De	4,712.0	1,377.0	–96.0	–20.5
ARA	Aracruz Celulose SA	767.7	26.0	–58.8	44.3
ARTHF	Arethusa (Off-Shore) Ltd	259.2	15.0	–5.0	4.1
AR	Asarco Inc	1,056.2	38.9	–70.7	26.3
BLL	Ball Corp	953.6	185.4	–32.5	6.1
BLY	Bally Entmt Corp	357.8	97.5	–16.0	–27.9
BMG	Battle Mtn Gold Co	789.1	30.1	–4.4	9.1

TABLE 5–3
(continued)

Ticker	Name	Market Value (millions)	1993 Operating Cash Flow (millions)	1993 Operating Profit (millions)	1994 Annual Return
BAX	Baxter International Inc	$ 9,297.3	$ 765.0	$−268.0	20.1%
BEC	Beckman Instruments Inc	843.7	53.3	−33.6	3.3
BS	Bethlehem Steel Corp	1,660.3	203.2	−266.3	−11.7
BCC	Boise Cascade Corp	1,237.8	131.2	−77.1	16.4
BBN	Bolt Beranek & Newman Inc	360.6	13.6	−32.3	24.0
BCU	Borden Chem&Plast LP Com	574.2	38.5	−1.4	150.6
BN	Borden Inc	1,875.4	152.3	−56.9	−26.5
BORL	Borland International	259.7	27.8	−69.9	−58.8
BRG	British Gas PLC ADR	19,471.5	3,251.0	−788.0	1.8
TMBR	Brown (Tom) Inc	216.6	9.7	−2.3	2.2
CTEX	C Tec Corp	367.3	68.8	−5.5	−33.8
CVC	Cablevision Systems CLA	1,284.5	88.7	−246.8	−25.6
CDN	Cadence Design Sys Inc	1,007.5	90.7	−0.6	77.4
CBI	CBI Industries Inc	880.2	106.2	−34.0	−14.1
CCIL	Cellular Communications Int	403.3	0.1	−0.9	196.6
CYCL	Centennial Cellulr CP CL	403.9	1.3	−27.8	−29.9
CX	Centerior Energy Corp	1,350.8	516.9	−875.4	−27.0
CTYA	Century Commun CL A	795.0	106.2	−47.8	−34.8
CEN	Ceridian Corp	1,463.2	44.0	−22.0	41.4
CHA	Champion International Corp	3,670.3	200.8	−134.5	10.0
CMD	Charter Medical Corp	471.2	90.0	−39.6	−16.9
CQB	Chiquita Brands Intl	611.2	30.5	−51.1	20.2
CSN	Cincinnati Bell Inc	1,362.2	198.1	−56.8	−1.1
CMZ	Cincinnati Milacron Inc	707.7	22.2	−45.4	9.0
CIN	Cinergy Corp	3,821.8	341.1	−8.7	−8.3
CITI	Citicasters Inc CL A	314.0	18.4	−66.8	47.8
CCE	Coca-Cola Enterprises	2,721.7	493.0	−15.0	18.4
CDE	Coeur D'Alene Mines Corp	264.8	4.2	−13.3	−23.1
CMCSK	Comcast Corp CL A SPL	3,732.3	345.9	−98.9	−34.2
CMY	Community Psychiatric Cntrs	511.9	16.9	−24.9	−21.4
CNR	Conner Peripherals	537.6	20.2	−445.3	−35.0
CCXLA	Contel Cellular Inc	2,526.9	4.6	−74.9	52.3
CAI.B	Continental Airls Inc CL	216.6	138.4	−1,017.1	−54.9

TABLE 5–3
(continued)

Ticker	Name	Market Value (millions)	1993 Operating Cash Flow (millions)	1993 Operating Profit (millions)	1994 Annual Return
ACCOB	Coors (Adolph) CL B	$ 632.4	$ 168.5	$ −41.9	6.2%
GLW	Corning Inc	7,395.1	589.6	−15.2	9.2
XTO	Cross Timbers Oil Co	228.9	32.2	−4.0	7.4
CYT	Cytec Industries Inc	433.2	82.8	−285.7	194.3
DAI	Daimler-Benz AG Spon ADR	21,141.5	5,699.0	-1,150.0	3.6
DGN	Data General Corp	297.9	74.6	−60.5	6.7
DELL	Dell Computer Corp	1,763.8	113.0	−35.8	81.2
DAL	Delta Air Lines Inc	2,878.3	676.9	−414.7	−7.2
DPGE	Dial Page Inc	291.1	8.7	−8.5	−66.0
DEC	Digital Equipment	4,858.6	46.9	−251.3	−2.9
DTC	Domtar Inc	1,048.4	14.3	−83.7	7.8
DYTC	Dynatech Corp	317.1	35.1	−26.2	41.9
EFU	Eastern Enterprises	543.0	38.5	−32.2	8.4
ELN	Elan Corp Plc ADR	1,094.7	17.3	−72.4	−15.9
ENS	Enserch Corp	945.3	191.8	−14.7	−18.0
EEX	Enserch Exploration	1,025.0	76.4	−3.9	−4.8
ENZ	Enzo Biochem Inc	208.3	0.8	−6.4	−29.9
ETH	Ethan Allen Interiors Inc	342.3	30.2	−2.3	−22.4
FISNY	Fisons PLC Spon ADR	1,598.2	128.0	−33.7	−12.0
FLST	Flagstar Cos Inc	251.6	171.0	−1,648.2	−24.3
FGL	Fmc Gold Company	29.6	33.4	−51.3	−34.8
FMXI	Foamex International Inc	213.5	22.9	−8.9	−41.2
FRAM	Frame Technology Corp/CA	275.5	0.6	−34.0	89.9
FTX	Freeport McMoran Inc	2,498.5	117.3	−83.1	−2.9
GCR	Gaylord Container CP	685.7	15.5	−70.0	100.0
GENZ	Genzyme Corp	983.9	0.3	−6.1	14.5
GP	Georgia-Pacific Corp	6,644.9	389.0	−18.0	6.3
GAMI	Great American Mgmt & Invt	402.3	20.1	−52.6	21.6
GOU	Gulf Canada Res Ltd Ord	612.1	202.9	−23.4	−2.0
HAL	Halliburton Co	4,264.5	243.1	−161.0	7.1
HPH	Harnischfeger Industries Inc	838.5	67.9	−17.7	26.8
HHS	Harte Hanks Commun Inc	345.5	26.4	−45.5	0.0
HL	Hecla Mining Co	468.7	8.6	−11.7	−12.9

TABLE 5–3
(continued)

Ticker	Name	Market Value (millions)	1993 Operating Cash Flow (millions)	1993 Operating Profit (millions)	1994 Annual Return
HSN	Home Shopping Network	$ 849.7	$ 55.0	$ −15.5	−32.8%
HUF	Huffy Corp	218.7	41.4	−3.8	−17.1
ILN	Illinova Corp	1,720.9	397.2	−55.8	2.3
IGL	Imc Global Inc	1,414.8	26.2	−120.0	−3.4
IAD	Inland Steel Industries Inc	1,110.5	112.0	−37.6	6.0
INSL	Insilco Corp	273.7	36.2	−47.5	84.3
INGR	Intergraph Corp	591.5	71.0	−118.5	−23.5
ISLI	Intersolv	231.6	16.2	−29.4	42.2
IBM	Intl Business Machines Corp	48,148.1	8,327.0	−7,987.0	31.9
ICTL	Intl Cabletel Inc	673.4	0.0	−11.1	18.1
IMC	Intl Multifoods Corp	337.5	36.2	−13.4	−1.0
IRF	Intl Rectifier Corp	476.7	18.3	−3.0	73.2
JR	James River Corp of Virginia	1,981.1	440.6	−0.3	8.3
JAPNY	Japan Airlines Ltd ADR	11,785.2	125.5	−367.1	30.2
JOINA	Jones Intercable Inc CL A	318.1	23.7	−25.3	−30.5
JOS	Jostens Inc	943.9	64.4	−7.9	−0.6
KM	Kmart Corp	5,537.9	1,930.0	−328.0	−35.1
KLU	Kaiser Aluminum Corp	596.6	24.2	−123.1	20.8
KMAG	Komag Inc	679.4	40.8	−9.9	47.2
LSO	Lasmo PLC Spon ADR	1,876.3	338.3	−159.6	37.5
LCI	LCI International Inc	625.3	40.2	−2.6	44.6
LINB	LIN Broadcasting	6,257.3	219.6	−60.7	30.9
3LIEL	Lincoln Electric Co	454.3	28.7	−40.5	115.0
LCE	Lone Star Industries	222.7	31.6	−35.3	−71.6
MAI	M/A-Com Inc	265.0	16.2	−22.5	−15.9
MKG	Mallinckrodt Group Inc	2,513.8	136.6	−113.8	−9.6
MAN	Manpower Inc/WI	2,284.0	105.5	−48.9	60.2
MXS	Maxus Energy Corp	726.9	136.6	−37.9	−38.6
MENT	Mentor Graphics Corp	694.6	25.3	−32.1	10.9
MXP	Mesa Inc	344.3	27.9	−102.4	−13.3
MFST	MFS Communications Inc	2,188.4	33.2	−15.8	0.8
MIKL	Michael Foods Inc	226.5	43.5	−16.3	25.9
MNT	Montedison Spa ADR	1,471.5	410.5	−741.7	14.8

TABLE 5–3
(continued)

Ticker	Name	Market Value (millions)	1993 Operating Cash Flow (millions)	1993 Operating Profit (millions)	1994 Annual Return
MCL	Moore Corp Ltd	$ 1,817.1	$ 221.4	$ −77.6	4.8%
NLCS	National Computer Sys Inc	260.1	26.0	−2.5	44.2
NGCO	National Gypsum Co	1,025.7	39.3	−17.8	30.9
NS	National Steel Corp CL B	600.2	59.0	−242.4	22.9
NAV	Navistar Internationl	948.0	35.0	−273.0	−36.0
NWK	Network Equipment Tech Inc	456.6	2.2	−6.3	170.4
CALL	Nextel Communications	1,533.0	29.1	−56.9	−61.4
NSANY	Nissan Motor Co Ltd SP AD	18,526.8	2,153.9	−843.8	25.4
NT	Northern Telecom Ltd	8,725.2	132.0	−878.0	9.6
NOVL	Novell Inc	6,968.3	357.5	−35.2	−17.5
NYN	Nynex Corp	16,559.2	3,655.2	−272.4	−2.5
OLN	Olin Corp	1,064.3	137.0	−92.0	8.8
ORX	Oryx Energy Co	1,088.4	379.0	−93.0	−31.2
OM	Outboard Marine Corp	418.6	39.6	−165.0	−10.5
OI	Owens-Illinois Inc	1,249.5	231.7	−200.8	−11.1
PAGE	Paging Network Inc	1,657.7	79.3	−20.0	11.5
PKD	Parker Drilling Co	254.9	13.7	−10.7	−13.6
PST	Petrie Stores Corp	814.0	4.3	−48.7	−22.5
PNM	Public Service Co of N Mex	522.2	97.3	−61.5	14.9
PBEN	Puritan-Bennett Corp	289.0	23.0	−31.8	34.1
RENL	REN Corp-USA	287.4	2.1	−3.8	68.3
RLM	Reynolds Metals Co	2,976.0	258.7	−322.1	10.2
RN	RJR Nabisco Hldgs Corp	6,742.4	1,769.0	−3.0	−13.7
RDC	Rowan Cos Inc	505.2	18.4	−13.3	−30.6
SK	Safety-Kleen Corp	945.7	136.2	−101.3	−7.0
SFR	Santa Fe Energy Resources	832.5	160.2	−77.1	−13.5
SANYY	Sanyo Electric Co Ltd ADR	10,173.0	581.6	−14.2	49.7
SPP	Scott Paper Co	6,214.1	318.7	−289.1	70.0
SQA.A	Sequa Corp Cl A	294.5	121.0	−55.5	−20.0
SQNT	Sequent Computer Systems Inc	563.4	28.0	−7.5	29.5
SHKIF	SHLSystemhouse Inc	438.6	0.6	−109.9	−29.3
SKFRY	SKF AB ADR	2,048.1	120.7	−77.3	1.5
SII	Smith International Inc	533.4	15.4	−4.0	41.1

TABLE 5–3
(continued)

Ticker	Name	Market Value (millions)	1993 Operating Cash Flow (millions)	1993 Operating Profit (millions)	1994 Annual Return
SNG	Southern New Eng Telecomm	$2,113.7	$ 478.7	$ –43.6	–5.5%
SLCMC	Southland Corp	1,614.3	232.1	–11.3	–33.3
STX	Sterling Chemicals Inc	654.0	50.0	–5.4	228.1
SSW	Sterling Software Inc	759.1	29.7	–33.4	29.5
SW	Stone & Webster Inc	491.3	39.7	–0.4	22.5
8794B	Stone-Consolidated Corp	799.0	61.4	–51.8	10.0
STK	Storage Technology CP CL	875.0	87.5	–117.8	–9.0
SDRC	Structural Dynamics Research	234.3	19.5	–11.7	–68.8
SYMC	Symantec Corp	798.1	1.3	–11.1	–4.1
TDM	Tandem Computers Inc	1,924.9	134.6	–530.1	57.5
TCOMA	Tele-Communications CL A	12,492.0	1,251.0	–7.0	–28.1
TCSFY	Thomson CSF ADR	2,787.5	329.5	–389.3	–4.4
TWX	Time Warner Inc	14,690.1	257.0	–164.0	–19.8
TKR	Timken Co	1,039.5	153.7	–17.7	7.8
E	Transco Energy Co	772.5	276.2	–35.4	21.9
TAM	Tubos de Acero de Mex ADR	207.6	10.8	–16.7	–20.2
TEP	Tucson Electric Power Co	542.4	95.0	–21.8	–17.2
USR	US Shoe Corp	1,152.8	113.9	–15.8	27.1
USS	US Surgical Corp	1,243.3	131.0	–138.7	–15.2
UAL	UALCorp	1,148.1	858.0	–31.0	–12.0
UMC	United Meridian Corp	279.3	42.2	–7.2	6.4
USM	US Cellular Corp	2,533.3	35.3	–25.4	–6.4
MRO	USX-Marathon Group	4,943.3	827.0	–6.0	3.4
X	USX-U S Steel Group	2,303.3	86.0	–169.0	–15.6
VHI	Valhi Inc	890.8	32.8	–64.1	58.1
VCELA	Vanguard Cellular Sys CL	935.9	8.6	–15.3	32.0
VOLVY	Volvo AB SWE ADR	6,839.6	908.0	–415.6	46.4
WBN	Waban Inc	634.4	91.0	–18.7	30.3
WANG	Wang Labs Inc	417.2	31.0	–197.2	–40.4
WS	Weirton Steel Corp	287.0	69.5	–42.9	41.2
WDC	Western Digital Corp	667.1	55.9	–25.1	83.6
WW	Western Waste Industries	221.5	36.2	–10.1	11.1
WX	Westinghouse Electric Corp	5,202.6	561.0	–175.0	–11.9

TABLE 5–3
(concluded)

Ticker	Name	Market Value (millions)	1993 Operating Cash Flow (millions)	1993 Operating Profit (millions)	1994 Annual Return
WPSN	Westpoint Stevens Inc	$ 451.8	$108.3	$–321.6	–23.3%
WONE	Westwood One Inc	351.8	2.0	–8.7	16.4
Z	Woolworth Corp	2,119.7	124.0	–495.0	–37.4
WYMN	Wyman-Gordon Co	208.6	7.2	–17.0	35.1
XRX	Xerox Corp	12,151.8	359.0	–189.0	14.1
ZALE	Zale Corp	406.5	1.6	–285.5	29.7
ZRN	Zurn Industries Inc	$ 212.9	$ 1.8	$ –13.9	–31.0
	Average				10.6%

TABLE 5–4
Firms with Negative Average Operating Cash Flow
but Positive Income—1990–1993

Ticker	Name	Market Value (millions)	Average Operating Cash Flow (millions)	Average Operating Profit (millions)	1994 Annual Return
ANTC	Antec Corp	$ 513.9	$ -0.5	$ 7.0	-26.5%
AVID	Avid Technology Inc	276.0	–6.6	3.0	50.3
BBY	Best Buy Co Inc	869.7	–32.4	18.9	34.4
CAH	Cardinal Health Inc	2,067.3	–3.6	25.4	22.3
CDWC	CDW Computer Centers Inc	460.6	–1.3	0.3	143.8
DR	Coastal Healthcare Group Inc	586.6	–10.5	8.9	–31.1
CPU	CompUSA Inc	355.1	–27.2	4.1	–24.5
CPLY	Copley Pharmaceutical Inc	347.3	–1.8	7.8	–66.5
ESRX	Express Scripts Inc CL A	468.0	–2.8	5.2	56.4
GC	Grancare Inc	212.2	–1.6	2.9	–3.4

TABLE 5–4
(concluded)

Ticker	Name	Market Value (millions)	Average Operating Cash Flow (millions)	Average Operating Profit (millions	1994 Annual Return
HMY	Heilig-Meyers Co	$1,030.3	$–30.2	$ 35.2	–35.7%
HHC	Horizon Healthcare Corp	540.0	–0.4	7.8	39.1
IHS	Integrated Health Svcs Inc	649.5	–2.2	9.2	39.3
KUB	Kubota Corp ADR	9,367.5	–8.9	52.6	34.6
LRCX	Lam Research Corp	1,125.6	–0.8	6.5	14.6
LEN	Lennar Corp	603.4	–32.4	29.1	–31.5
MRNR	Mariner Health Group Inc	299.2	–0.6	1.4	0.0
MWHS	Micro Warehouse Inc	873.4	–2.4	6.5	68.2
MICCF	Millicom Intl Cellular SA	1,143.1	–28.3	7.9	28.2
MK	Monk Austin Inc	231.0	–42.1	26.8	–14.5
TNEL	Nelson (Thomas) Inc	256.6	–1.2	6.3	–0.4
OH	Oakwood Homes	557.1	–58.6	13.2	–9.4
PAIR	Pairgain Technologies Inc	319.5	–2.6	2.8	3.6
PGSAY	Petroleum Geo-SVC Spon AD	584.6	–8.2	9.8	12.0
PRFT	Proffitts Inc	218.7	–7.8	4.4	1.7
QHRI	Quantum Health Resources Inc	291.3	–3.5	8.1	–1.7
RYL	Ryland Group Inc	221.8	–148.3	14.0	–22.0
SFE	Safeguard Scientifics Inc	221.7	–14.5	10.2	43.8
SHLR	Schuler Homes Inc	229.6	–23.1	21.5	–49.1
SVGI	Silicon Valley Group Inc	488.9	–1.9	2.6	108.9
RIG	Sonat Offshore Drilling Inc	581.4	–2.6	12.1	12.4
SP	Spelling Entertnmt Grp Inc	896.4	–15.8	8.0	8.1
WON	Sports & Recreation Inc	364.8	–11.0	6.4	3.0
SHG	Sun Healthcare Group Inc	754.5	–3.8	7.7	51.5
SBL	Symbol Technologies	729.8	–2.8	6.8	70.3
TECD	Tech Data Corp	453.7	–39.5	17.1	–5.6
TKN	Thermotrex Corp	288.8	–0.9	0.3	–12.2
TIF	Tiffany & Co	486.1	–5.0	18.5	23.2
TBL	Timberland Co CL A	275.4	–1.9	12.8	–59.0
TOL	Toll Brothers Inc	405.3	–5.2	14.3	–41.6
WAC	Warnaco Group Inc CL A	662.2	–16.7	18.4	13.6
WBB	Webb (Del E) Corp	278.9	–17.2	13.5	11.4
	Average				11.0%

TABLE 5–5

Firms with Positive Average Operating Cash Flow but Negative Income—1990–1993

Ticker	Name	Market Value (millions)	Average Operating Cash Flow (millions)	Average Operating Profit (millions)	1994 Annual Return
COMS	3 Com Corp	$3,842.9	$ 64.0	$ −3.4	119.4%
ACXT	ACX Technologies Inc	525.4	28.6	−2.3	−0.6
ADLAC	Adelphia Commun CL A	275.1	34.3	−115.8	−54.0
AEM	Agnico Eagle Mines Ltd	415.8	13.1	−25.4	−17.5
AMX	Alumax Inc	1,159.2	15.6	−98.9	32.0
AU	Amax Gold Inc	426.5	32.2	−6.6	−12.7
AMH	Amdahl Corp	1,304.9	126.1	−101.8	83.3
AWA	America West Airlines CL	383.6	79.1	−98.3	−43.3
AMR	Amr Corp/De	4,712.0	912.5	−212.7	−20.5
ARA	Aracruz Celulose SA	767.7	29.2	−62.2	44.3
BLY	Bally Entmt Corp	357.8	129.0	−93.8	−27.9
BMG	Battle Mtn Gold Co	789.1	46.4	−6.1	9.1
BNTN	Benton Oil & Gas Co	245.8	1.4	−1.8	82.5
BS	Bethlehem Steel Corp	1,660.3	202.9	−424.0	−11.7
BSYS	Bisys Group Inc	273.0	10.5	−11.9	28.3
BCC	Boise Cascade Corp	1,237.8	129.7	−58.8	16.4
BBN	Bolt Beranek & Newman Inc	360.6	15.5	−13.5	24.0
BORL	Borland International	259.7	11.5	−50.7	−58.8
BOST	Boston Chicken Inc	692.3	2.6	−2.1	−3.5
BOW	Bowater Inc	1,146.6	118.5	−6.1	18.4
TMBR	Brown (Tom) Inc	216.6	5.4	−3.5	2.2
BUR	Burlington Inds Inc	754.5	75.4	−39.2	−36.3
CTEX	C Tec Corp	367.3	64.2	−9.1	−33.8
CVC	Cablevision Systems CL A	1,284.5	77.6	−249.0	−25.6
CAM	Camco International Inc	460.1	48.9	−4.3	16.5
CRP	Carson Pirie Scott & Co/IL	343.8	15.5	−105.9	34.5
CTYA	Century Commun CL A	795.0	66.7	−58.2	−34.8
CEN	Ceridian Corp	1,463.2	1.5	−14.3	41.4
CDV.A	Chambers Development CL A	263.0	19.2	−23.0	−3.1
CMD	Charter Medical Corp	471.2	132.6	−115.8	−16.9
CNW	Chicago & No Westn Hldgs CP	1,509.6	97.0	−0.2	−22.0
CQB	Chiquita Brands Intl	611.2	43.3	−12.6	20.2

TABLE 5–5
(continued)

Ticker	Name	Market Value (millions)	Average Operating Cash Flow (millions)	Average Operating Profit (millions)	1994 Annual Return
CMZ	Cincinnati Milacron Inc	$ 707.7	$ 14.2	$ –33.6	9.0%
CKL	Clark Equipment Co	885.1	66.7	–7.4	3.6
CMS	Cms Energy Corp	1,995.8	462.3	–213.4	–5.9
CCE	Coca-Cola Enterprises	2,721.7	341.1	–4.7	18.4
CDE	Coeur D'Alene Mines Corp	264.8	0.4	–7.5	–23.1
CG	Columbia Gas System	1,314.6	641.9	–111.8	5.0
CMCSK	Comcast Corp CL A SPL	3,732.3	218.0	–162.7	–34.2
CLT	Cominco Ltd	1,201.8	47.4	–23.5	18.3
CVN	Computervision Corp	271.8	91.0	–277.7	6.9
CNR	Conner Peripherals	537.6	101.5	–25.4	–35.0
CNF	Consolidated Freightways Inc	889.0	172.9	–5.4	–4.9
CCXLA	Contel Cellular Inc	2,526.9	2.8	–92.4	52.3
CAI.B	Continental Airls Inc CL	216.6	109.8	–962.7	–54.9
CNU	Continuum Inc	559.6	8.2	–1.4	58.4
CMOS	Credence Systems Corp	364.4	8.0	–2.2	62.1
XTO	Cross Timbers Oil Co	228.9	16.1	–2.0	7.4
CYT	Cytec Industries Inc	433.2	82.8	–285.7	194.3
DGN	Data General Corp	297.9	84.5	–44.3	6.7
ENRGB	Dekalb Energy Co CL B	211.2	41.1	–27.7	54.5
DAL	Delta Air Lines Inc	2,878.3	488.5	–235.7	–7.2
DPGE	Dial Page Inc	291.1	10.5	–12.0	–66.0
DEC	Digital Equipment	4,858.6	741.9	–776.1	–2.9
ZONE	Discovery Zone Inc	437.0	8.7	–1.1	–43.5
7130B	Dixons Group PLC ADR	1,314.1	69.6	–23.4	–27.0
EUA	Eastern Utilities Assoc	463.5	81.1	–2.4	–16.0
ECO	Echo Bay Mines Ltd	1,098.3	93.2	–20.3	–16.6
ECK	Eckerd Corp	793.7	127.7	–0.5	61.5
ELN	Elan Corp PLC ADR	1,094.7	28.3	–2.0	–15.9
ESV	Energy Service Company Inc	863.0	24.8	–5.9	–8.3
EEX	Enserch Exploration	1,025.0	80.5	–11.9	–4.8
ETH	Ethan Allen Interiors Inc	342.3	25.9	–20.3	–22.4
FJQ	Fedders Corp	219.6	9.6	–19.8	67.6
FD	Federated Dept Stores	2,714.6	391.8	–278.7	–7.2

TABLE 5–5
(continued)

Ticker	Name	Market Value (millions)	Average Operating Cash Flow (millions)	Average Operating Profit (millions)	1994 Annual Return
FLST	Flagstar Cos Inc	$ 2,51.6	$ 200.4	$ –458.8	–24.3%
FMXI	Foamex International Inc	213.5	22.9	–8.9	–41.2
FRAM	Frame Technology Corp/CA	275.5	2.9	–8.7	89.9
FSII	FSI Intl Inc	225.0	2.9	–1.1	125.0
GART	Gartner Group Inc CL A	939.6	9.6	–5.8	126.1
GCR	Gaylord Container CP	685.7	28.3	–101.5	100.0
GIC	General Instrument Corp	3,943.7	68.0	–51.1	6.2
GM	General Motors Corp	31,747.0	9,422.9	–1,783.1	–21.8
GENZ	Genzyme Corp	983.9	3.4	–13.2	14.5
GON	Geon Company	772.2	74.8	–4.5	18.0
GLM	Global Marine Inc	616.3	43.7	–8.5	–12.1
GNR	Global Natural Resources In	224.4	18.3	–7.5	17.2
GAMI	Great American Mgmt & Invt	402.3	17.5	–2.3	21.6
GOU	Gulf Canada Res Ltd Ord	612.1	235.8	–64.5	–2.0
HAL	Halliburton Co	4,264.5	264.4	–15.1	7.1
HHS	Harte Hanks Commun Inc	345.5	25.5	–14.7	0.0
HMSY	Health Mgmt Sys Inc	203.4	8.0	–1.3	66.3
HL	Hecla Mining Co	468.7	12.4	–17.8	–12.9
HTG	Heritage Media Corp CL A	443.6	22.0	–15.8	35.2
HDS	Hills Stores Co	207.4	88.0	–52.2	1.8
HM	Homestake Mining	2,324.7	81.2	–60.6	–21.4
ID	Indresco Inc	286.7	27.1	–14.4	–8.1
INFTA	Infinity Broadcasting CL	1,223.3	22.3	–14.7	4.1
IAD	Inland Steel Industries Inc	1,110.5	76.2	–123.2	6.0
INSL	Insilco Corp	273.7	17.2	–32.4	84.3
IAAI	Insurance Auto Auctions Inc	362.8	4.3	–0.1	–18.0
ISLI	Intersolv	231.6	9.4	–14.7	42.2
IBM	Intl Business Machines Corp	48,148.1	7,199.5	–2,349.0	31.9
ICTL	Intl Cabletel Inc	673.4	2.9	–3.6	18.1
ITL	Itel Corp	1,074.1	264.7	–38.4	23.7
JCOR	Jacor Communications	254.7	2.7	–10.8	–7.8
JAPNY	Japan Airlines Ltd ADR	11,785.2	575.1	–196.0	30.2
JOINA	Jones Intercable Inc CL A	318.1	25.2	–23.6	–30.5

TABLE 5–5

(continued)

Ticker	Name	Market Value (millions)	Average Operating Cash Flow (millions)	Average Operating Profit (millions)	1994 Annual Return
KMET	Kemet Corp	$ 630.2	$ 33.0	$ −0.1	91.1%
KCLC	Kinder-Care Learning Center	251.4	41.1	−26.6	−10.9
KLM	Klm Royal Dutch Air-Ny Re	2,479.3	436.4	−104.1	16.7
KLIC	Kulicke & Soffa Industries	213.8	3.5	−0.2	50.0
LAF	Lafarge Corp	1,207.1	98.2	−7.9	−21.1
LSO	Lasmo PLC–Spon ADR	1,876.3	391.6	−122.0	37.5
LCI	LCI International Inc	625.3	20.7	−22.1	44.6
LINB	Lin Broadcasting	6,257.3	80.7	−124.2	30.9
3LIEL	Lincoln Electric Co	454.3	30.6	−15.2	115.0
LCE	Lone Star Industries	222.7	10.9	−38.3	−71.6
LSI	LSI Logic Corp	3,135.8	96.9	−20.5	154.3
MAI	M/A-Com Inc	265.0	40.1	−6.3	−15.9
MAN	Manpower Inc/WI	2,284.0	66.8	−56.0	60.2
MASX	Mastec Inc	202.5	7.4	−3.7	74.5
MXTR	Maxtor Corp	230.3	36.6	−62.4	0.0
MENT	Mentor Graphics Corp	694.6	24.1	−30.2	10.9
MERQ	Mercury Interactive Corp	203.1	0.6	−1.0	−23.2
MXP	Mesa Inc	344.3	12.1	−119.9	−13.3
MFST	MFS Communications Inc	2,188.4	30.9	−14.4	0.8
MLT	Mitel Corp	488.9	7.1	−20.0	−40.4
MTEL	Mobile Telecommunictns Tech	822.4	10.2	−5.4	−19.6
MNT	Montedison Spa ADR	1,471.5	273.0	−310.2	14.8
NGCO	National Gypsum Co	1,025.7	38.2	−176.1	30.9
NS	National Steel Corp CL B	600.2	83.0	−122.0	22.9
NAV	Navistar Internationl	948.0	99.5	−149.0	−36.0
NWK	Network Equipment Tech Inc	456.6	10.0	−19.5	170.4
CALL	Nextel Communications	1,533.0	13.9	−22.3	−61.4
NSANY	Nissan Motor Co Ltd SP AD	18,526.8	1,856.6	−55.1	25.4
NL	NL Industries	618.9	19.3	−14.6	180.6
NDCO	Noble Drilling Corp	447.4	12.6	−2.8	−32.9
NVA	Nova Corporation	3,355.5	300.2	−25.9	34.7
NMC	Numac Energy Inc	481.1	72.7	−9.7	−4.2
OXY	Occidental Petroleum Corp	6,522.4	852.8	−277.3	19.1

TABLE 5–5 *(continued)*

Ticker	Name	Market Value (millions)	Average Operating Cash Flow (millions)	Average Operating Profit (millions)	1994 Annual Return
ORND	Ornda Healthcorp	$ 735.9	$ 15.6	$ −41.1	−20.6%
OM	Outboard Marine Corp	418.6	74.7	−81.6	−10.5
OCF	Owens Corning Fibrglas	1,508.3	264.8	−65.8	−28.2
OI	Owens-Illinois Inc	1,249.5	244.7	−42.6	−11.1
PAGE	Paging Network Inc	1,657.7	44.6	−9.2	11.5
PKD	Parker Drilling Co	254.9	14.3	−9.7	−13.6
PCS	Payless Cashways CL A Vtg	363.9	100.6	−8.5	−44.8
PGU	Pegasus Gold Inc	385.2	38.0	−6.7	−48.3
PNF	Penn Traffic Co	400.0	49.1	−5.9	4.8
PST	Petrie Stores Corp	814.0	43.4	−3.7	−22.5
PHG	Philips Electr Nv NY Shar	11,478.5	2,487.1	−540.5	43.5
PHYC	Phycor Inc	522.3	1.5	−1.4	39.6
PDQ	Prime Hospitality Corp	277.0	31.0	−103.3	17.6
PNM	Public Service Co of N Mex	522.2	112.1	−35.6	14.9
PBEN	Puritan-Bennett Corp	289.0	18.3	−0.2	34.1
PYRD	Pyramid Technology	247.1	17.9	−5.5	−11.9
QCOM	Qualcomm Inc	1,497.8	5.1	−0.1	−9.4
RYC	Raychem Corp	1,743.1	34.2	−35.9	−4.1
RB	Reading & Bates Corp	447.9	25.0	−15.7	−14.3
RENL	Ren Corp-USA	287.4	3.3	−0.1	68.3
RXR	Revco D.S. Inc	1,288.9	36.7	−87.5	70.7
RDC	Rowan Cos Inc	505.2	13.6	−30.9	−30.6
SAA	Saatchi & Saatchi Plc ADR	293.5	32.9	−261.8	14.9
SFR	Santa Fe Energy Resources	832.5	143.6	−10.8	−13.5
SRL	Sceptre Resources Ltd	324.8	61.5	−38.7	−32.9
SPP	Scott Paper Co	6,214.1	425.3	−10.9	70.0
SFLD	Seafield Capital Corp	229.0	21.6	−1.5	−0.1
SQNT	Sequent Computer Systems Inc	563.4	16.2	−5.7	29.5
SHKIF	SHL Systemhouse Inc	438.6	1.4	−42.6	−29.3
SIER	Sierra On-line Inc	307.3	5.2	−2.0	86.4
SKFRY	SKF AB ADR	2,048.1	190.0	−86.2	1.5
SII	Smith International Inc	533.4	14.6	−1.0	41.1
SDW	Southdown Inc	278.3	19.0	−17.8	−40.8
RSP	Southern Pacific Rail Corp	2,730.0	3.8	−42.7	−8.2

TABLE 5–5 *(concluded)*

Ticker	Name	Market Value (millions)	Average Operating Cash Flow (millions)	Average Operating Profit (millions)	1994 Annual Return
SLCMC	Southland Corp	$ 1,614.3	$ 139.8	$–129.6	–33.3%
STO	Stone Container Corp	1,977.5	138.0	–110.7	80.5
8794B	Stone-Consolidated Corp	799.0	61.4	–51.8	10.0
TDM	Tandem Computers Inc	1,924.9	156.3	–103.6	57.5
TCOMA	Tele-Communications CL A	12,492.0	833.3	–103.8	–28.1
TGT	Tenneco Inc	7,797.6	963.5	–86.3	–16.2
TSO	Tesoro Petroleum Corp	247.1	15.9	–0.4	68.2
TWX	Time Warner Inc	14,690.1	790.8	–101.0	–19.8
E	Transco Energy Co	772.5	196.1	–52.8	21.9
TRY	Triarc Cos Inc CL A	291.6	55.7	–34.6	–53.0
TNV	Trinova Corp	784.7	114.7	–28.4	–4.2
OIL	Triton Energy Corp	1,149.4	15.3	–45.5	12.9
TEP	Tucson Electric Power Co	542.4	67.6	–198.0	–17.2
UAL	UAL Corp	1,148.1	621.8	–171.4	–12.0
UIS	Unisys Corp	1,623.1	1,114.0	–293.1	–31.7
UMC	United Meridian Corp	279.3	33.1	–2.6	6.4
UTR	Unitrode Corp	227.2	13.4	–0.9	28.4
USM	US Cellular Corp	2,533.3	4.8	–14.6	–6.4
U	USAir Group	354.0	75.9	–427.5	–67.0
X	USX-U S Steel Group	2,303.3	108.5	–159.3	–15.6
VLSI	VLSI Technology Inc	576.2	44.8	–4.8	11.6
VOLVY	Volvo AB Swe ADR	6,839.6	575.0	–202.9	46.4
WANG	Wang Labs Inc	417.2	35.5	–390.5	–40.4
WATFZ	Waterford Wedgwood PLC A	620.4	10.6	–18.8	46.9
WS	Weirton Steel Corp	287.0	22.9	–38.4	41.2
WDC	Western Digital Corp	667.1	39.1	–52.0	83.6
WX	Westinghouse Electric Corp	5,202.6	740.3	–159.0	–11.9
WPSN	Westpoint Stevens Inc	451.8	113.1	–537.9	–23.3
WONE	Westwood One Inc	351.8	7.6	–16.9	16.4
WHX	WHX Corp	292.2	92.8	–56.7	–22.6
WGO	Winnebago Industries	239.8	7.6	–6.6	–1.5
WYMN	Wyman-Gordon Co	208.6	28.0	–21.5	35.1
ZALE	Zale Corp	406.5	41.5	–371.4	29.7
	Average				11.3%

payables and fixed assets). Others prudently adjust their level of discretionary spending to match a lower rate of expected growth. Sales of assets during a period of business weakness may be suboptimal because assets would probably be sold at distressed prices just as the U.S. government sold financial institutions to clever purchasers at the bottom of the savings and loan cycle. Thus, the examination of net operating cash flows over an entire business cycle is important for the cash flow analyst.

Although net operating cash flow may be a better indicator of financial health and valuation than operating profits, it still suffers weaknesses. For example, net operating cash flows as reported by firms may include nonrecurring items. Such items as payments or receipts from settlements of legal suits are included in net operating cash flows, as are proceeds from an insurance policy in excess of property book values destroyed by fire. However, such items will probably not recur in the near future and should therefore be excluded from predictions of future cash flows. Since most firms use the indirect method to derive net operating cash flows (see Chapters 3 and 4 for a detailed discussion), the cash flow analyst cannot derive accurately amounts that are not expected to recur in the future.

Another problem associated with operating cash flows is the classification of certain events as either operating cash flows or investing cash flows. For example, some real estate firms classify mortgages as operating cash flows and some as investment cash flows. Cray Research treated its investment in supercomputers that are under operating leases and that are expected to be sold in the future as an operating cash flow in 1987, but as an investing cash flow in 1988. Such classification problems may disappear as firms gain familiarity with *SFAS No. 95.*

Furthermore, net operating cash flow measures only the increase in cash that occurred during the period due to ongoing operations of the firm. However, in most cases, if the firm does not reinvest some of the net cash flow generated by operations, the firm gradually shrinks until it finally liquidates. Most firms have to invest in their productive facilities, their distribution channels, or their administrative facilities every period, just to remain competitive. Thus, net operating cash flow almost always understates the cash that owners of a growth company can consume without affecting the economic viability of their firm. This leads us to the concept of free cash flow.

FREE CASH FLOW

Free cash flow is a very intuitive concept; it focuses on the amount of cash that owners of a business can consume without reducing the value of the business. It recognizes that a business needs to invest in current and long-term assets in order to continue and grow its operations. Thus, free cash flow focuses on the ability of the business to generate cash flows beyond those that are needed to invest in such assets as inventories, plant and equipment, securities of other firms, and the like. *When a firm is able to generate more cash flows from its ongoing operations than are needed to remain in business, the firm has free cash flows.* Such a firm can distribute the free cash flow to its owners through dividends immediately or retain the free cash flow within the firm for further growth and generate even greater free cash flows in the future. Thus, a firm with free cash flows may be a good candidate for investment because these free cash flows will eventually lead to higher security prices.

Example

Hillenbrand Industries states its vision of the firm and comments about the cash that it generates from operations:

How do we put our cash to work? We have five priorities:
- First, we invest in our companies to make sure they remain strong leaders in their markets.
- Second, we invest in add-on product lines that leverage our existing companies.
- Third, we invest in new ventures that enhance our existing companies.
- Fourth, we acquire companies that conform to our strict acquisition criteria.
- Fifth, we buy back Hillenbrand Industries stock.

Unlike operating cash flow, which is now well defined under SFAS No. 95, free cash flow wears many masks and does not have a unique definition. It is known by many names, including raiders' cash flow, surplus cash flow, excess cash flow, distributable cash flow, and disposable cash flow. However, the primary premise behind all these definitions and names is to measure the maximum cash generated during a period that can be distributed to stockholders of the business enterprise without affecting future growth.

The most common definition of *free cash flow*, one which is espoused by Standard & Poor's, is pre-tax income minus capital spending (*The Outlook*, July 20, 1988):

> Analysts believe that capital spending should be deducted because almost every business demands a certain minimal level of nondiscretionary plant and equipment spending. This is especially true of capital-intensive firms in such fields as auto or steel, where cutbacks in capital spending may hurt productivity.

Surplus cash flow as defined by many investors is calculated, typically, by adding to pre-tax income the depreciation expense and subtracting capital spending. Some money management firms believe that 9–10 times surplus cash flow (as defined by Standard & Poor's) is a good gauge of private market value. They arrive at this number by determining the price at which companies were being acquired.

Example

General Dynamics reports data about free cash flows, which it defines as "cash flow from operating and investing activities, excluding investment in marketable securities." This definition is fairly close to that of operating cash flow minus capital expenditures for firms where investing activities other than capital expenditures are minimal.

Example

In its 1991 annual report, RJR Nabisco Holding Corp. provides a condensed statement of free cash flow. The definition that RJR Nabisco uses for free cash flow is operating cash flows minus capital expenditures and dividend payments on preferred stock. This definition does not acknowledge that some of the capital expenditures might have been discretionary, or that some of the other cash expenditures on R&D, on selling, general, and administrative expenses, and even on production or purchase of goods might have been discretionary. Thus, definitions of free cash flows other than those used by RJR Nabisco may be warranted.

RJR Nabisco: Consolidated Statements of Free Cash Flow

Consolidated Condensed Statements of Free Cash Flow*
Years Ended December 31
RJR Nabisco Holdings Corp.
($ millions)

(See Book 2 For Consolidated Financial Statements,
Related Footnotes, and Managements Discussion and Analysis of
Financial Condition and Results of Operations.)

	1991	1990
Income (Loss) from continuing operations	$ 368	$ (462)
Interest expense	2,113	3,000
Amortization of debt issuance costs	104	176
Income tax provision	280	60
Depreciation of property, plant, and equipment	441	450
Amortization (principally intangibles)	683	680
Accretion of other noncurrent liabilities	89	86
Earnings before interest, taxes, depreciation and amortization	**4,078**	**3,990**
Interest paid	(1,397)	(1,424)
Taxes (paid) refunded	(368)	32
(Increase) decrease in working capital, excluding income taxes and interest	(392)	379
Capital expenditures	(459)	(426)
Preferred stock dividends paid	(205)	—
Other, net	167	151
Free cash flow	$1,424	$2,702

* Excludes net divestiture proceeds and financing activities.

It is interesting that neither of the above definitions includes a major cash outflow—principal payments on debt. Unfortunately, there is no simple definition of free cash flow, nor can the analyst simply rearrange a few numbers from the statement of cash flows to come up with an entity's free cash flow. We now show a detailed procedure to estimate free cash flows.

ESTIMATING FREE CASH FLOWS

To estimate free cash flows one can follow two approaches, the direct and indirect approach, just like the derivation of net cash from operations. Under the direct approach the cash flow analyst estimates the components of cash flows of operating activities and then estimates the portion of these components that are discretionary in nature. The cash flow analyst also estimates the discretionary components of the firm's major investments in fixed assets.

Under the indirect approach, the cash flow analyst begins with the change in cash during a period and makes adjustments to that amount for various events that affect free cash flows. Generally, all cash outlays that are not necessary for the firm's continuing operations will be added back to the change in cash, because the firm could have avoided making those payments and still continued its operations. Consequently, free cash flows would have increased had the firm not made those expenditures. Similarly, increases in cash that result from liquidation of fixed assets or from external financing are subtracted from the change in cash, because they do not represent cash flows that were generated by continuing operations of the business, or because they represent the gradual liquidation of the firm.

We begin our estimation procedures by using an example. We present the two approaches to the estimation of free cash flows for this firm.

Example

The Clorox Co. develops, manufactures, and markets household products such as laundry additives, home cleaning products, charcoal briquets, salad dressings, sauces, and water filter systems. It usually has the lead or the strong second brand in each of its product categories. Because of the nature of its products, it is expected to have stable earnings, operating cash flows, and free cash flows.

Clorox reports the following results for the year ending on June 30, 1994:

Clorox Financial Statements

Statements of Consolidated Earnings

The Clorox Company

Years ended June 30	94	93	92
In thousands, except per-share amounts.			
Net Sales	$1,836,949	$1,634,171	$1,547,057
Costs and Expenses			
Cost of products sold	820,434	724,753	678,504
Selling, delivery and administration	359,360	328,088	307,436
Advertising	286,666	242,528	262,586
Research and development	44,558	42,445	42,052
Interest expense	18,424	18,856	24,627
Other expense (income), net	874	2,316	(7,245)
Total costs and expenses	1,530,316	1,358,986	1,307,960
Earnings Before Income Taxes	306,633	275,185	239,097
Income Taxes	126,640	107,267	97,903
Earnings from Continuing Operations	179,993	167,918	141,194
Earnings (losses) from Discontinued Operations	32,064	(867)	(23,429)
Earnings Before Cumulative Effect of Accounting Change	212,057	167,051	117,765
Cumulative Effect of Accounting Change (Note 1)	–	–	(19,061)
Net Earnings	$ 212,057	$ 167,051	$ 98,704
Earnings (losses) per Common Share			
Continuing operations	$ 3.35	$ 3.07	$ 2.60
Discontinued operations	0.59	(0.02)	(0.43)
Earnings before cumulative effect of accounting change	3.94	3.05	2.17
Cumulative effect of accounting change	–	–	(0.35)
Net Earnings	$ 3.94	$ 3.05	$ 1.82
Weighted Average Shares Outstanding	53,800	54,698	54,366

See Notes to Consolidated Financial Statements.

Clorox Financial Statements

Consolidated Balance Sheets
The Clorox Company

Years ended June 30	94	93
In thousands, except share amounts.		
Assets		
Current Assets		
Cash and short-term investments	$ 115,922	$ 71,164
Accounts receivable, less allowance	249,843	226,675
Inventories	105,948	105,890
Deferred income taxes	18,548	19,360
Prepaid expenses	14,014	16,369
Net assets of discontinued operations (Note 2)	–	92,320
Total current assets	504,275	531,778
Property, Plant and Equipment – Net	532,600	538,101
Brands, Trademarks, Patents and Other Intangibles – Net	520,042	463,941
Investments in Affiliates	83,368	68,179
Other Assets	57,284	47,231
Total	$1,697,569	$1,649,230
Liabilities and Stockholders' Equity		
Current Liabilities		
Accounts payable	$ 97,728	$ 84,243
Accrued liabilities	227,197	226,775
Income taxes payable	7,599	20,585
Commercial paper	42,916	39,486
Current maturities of long-term debt	392	481
Total current liabilities	375,832	371,570
Long-term Debt	216,088	204,000
Other Obligations	63,187	50,663
Deferred Income Taxes	133,045	143,703
Stockholders' Equity		
Common stock – authorized, 175,000,000 shares, $1 par value; issued:		
55,422,297 shares	55,422	55,422
Additional paid-in capital	106,554	105,483
Retained earnings	876,832	762,162
Treasury shares, at cost: 1994, 2,050,041 shares; 1993, 572,155 shares	(107,146)	(23,357)
Cumulative translation adjustments	(22,245)	(20,416)
Stockholders' equity	909,417	879,294
Total	$1,697,569	$1,649,230

See Notes to Consolidated Financial Statements.

Clorox Financial Statements

Statements of Consolidated Cash Flows

The Clorox Company

Years ended June 30	94	93	92
In thousands.			
Operations:			
Earnings from continuing operations	$ 179,993	$ 167,918	$ 141,194
Adjustments to reconcile to net cash provided by continuing operations:			
Depreciation and amortization	94,120	83,607	76,507
Deferred income taxes	15,985	32,378	13,330
Other	25,985	9,412	6,849
Effects of changes in:			
Accounts receivable	(18,299)	(36,266)	11,866
Inventories	5,691	(7,892)	183
Prepaid expenses	2,355	(2,850)	4,983
Accounts payable	13,485	(18,071)	(5,399)
Accrued liabilities	(8,134)	2,849	21,772
Income taxes payable	(12,741)	3,498	6,010
Net cash provided by continuing operations	298,440	234,583	277,295
Net cash (used for) provided by discontinued operations	(31,658)	10,877	29,398
Net cash provided by operations	266,782	245,460	306,693
Investing Activities:			
Property, plant and equipment	(56,627)	(77,637)	(124,742)
Net proceeds from sales of businesses	159,293	15,000	709
Businesses purchased	(142,437)	(31,547)	(802)
Disposal of property, plant and equipment	11,264	3,759	1,580
Other	(22,046)	(24,938)	(15,897)
Net cash used for investment	(50,553)	(115,363)	(139,152)
Financing Activities:			
Long-term borrowings	13,000	299	199,532
Long-term debt repayments	(741)	(1,236)	(1,203)
Short-term borrowings (repayments), net	3,430	(42,469)	(333,035)
Cash dividends	(97,095)	(93,509)	(86,408)
Treasury shares acquired	(99,910)	–	–
Employee stock plans	9,845	8,958	8,735
Net cash used for financing	(171,471)	(127,957)	(212,379)
Net increase (decrease) in cash and short-term investments	44,758	2,140	(44,838)
Cash and short-term investments:			
Beginning of year	71,164	69,024	113,862
End of year	$ 115,922	$ 71,164	$ 69,024
Cash Paid for:			
Interest (net of amounts capitalized)	$ 18,267	$ 18,616	$ 18,019
Income taxes	128,210	61,052	73,709
Noncash Transactions:			
Liabilities arising from business purchased	$ 7,200	$ –	$ –

See Notes to Consolidated Financial Statements.

We begin our discussion by using the direct approach to estimate free cash flows.

Estimation procedure I: We first estimate cash that was generated by operations using the simple definition of net income plus depreciation and then subtract from it the capital expenditures of the firm.

Year	6/94	6/93	6/92	6/91	6/90	6/89	6/88	6/87
Net income	212.1	167.1	98.7	52.7	153.6	124.1	132.6	104.9
Add depreciation and amortization	85.6	73.6	80.5	81.4	47.8	41.3	36.6	31.4
Estimated operating cash flow	297.6	240.6	179.3	134.2	201.4	165.5	169.2	136.3
Subtract capital expenditures	56.6	77.6	124.7	109.1	155.9	87.8	153.3	56.0
Free cash flow—I	**241.0**	**163.0**	**54.5**	**25.1**	**45.5**	**77.6**	**15.8**	**80.3**

Year	6/86	6/85	6/84	6/83	6/82	6/81	6/80
Net income	95.6	86.1	79.7	65.5	45.1	38.1	33.2
Add depreciation and amortization	27.0	24.5	22.0	20.5	17.1	12.9	10.5
Estimated operating cash flow	122.6	110.6	101.7	86.1	62.2	51.0	43.7
Subtract capital expenditures	65.2	40.9	37.3	29.6	37.7	32.9	27.0
Free cash flow—I	**57.5**	**69.7**	**64.4**	**56.5**	**24.5**	**18.1**	**16.7**

Note that this simple definition of free cash flows uses a very crude estimate of cash from operations, net income plus depreciation and amortization. This estimate was reasonable as a first approximation when cash from operating activities was not reported and when the data necessary to make other adjustments to income for noncash events or nonoperating cash flows were unavailable. However, now that operating cash flows are routinely disclosed in the statement of cash flows, one can use these figures to estimate free cash flows.

Estimation procedure II:

Year	6/94	6/93	6/92	6/91	6/90	6/89
Reported net operating cash flow	266.8	245.5	306.7	246.7	166.4	158.3
Subtract capital expenditure	56.6	77.6	124.7	109.1	155.9	87.8
Free cash flow—II	**210.2**	**167.8**	**182.0**	**137.6**	**10.6**	**70.4**

This estimation is based on reported operating cash flows, which are available for Clorox since 1989. The above estimation technique uses net cash flow from operations as reported in accordance with *SFAS No. 95*. However, in years prior to 1989, cash from operations is not reported according to *SFAS No. 95* and it has to be estimated using the procedures outlined in Chapter 3. Specifically, we first estimate the individual components of operating cash flows as follows:

Year	6/94	6/93	6/92	6/91	6/90	6/89	6/88	6/87
Total receivables	249.8	226.7	204.6	219.5	151.5	143.4	139.3	121.7
Change in receivables	23.2	22.0	−14.9	68.0	8.1	4.1	17.6	7.8
Net sales	1,836.9	1,634.2	1,717.0	1,646.5	1,484.0	1,356.3	1,259.	1,126.0
Subtract change in receivables	−23.2	−22.0	14.9	−68.0	−8.1	−4.1	−17.6	−7.8
Collection from customers	1,813.8	1,612.1	1,731.9	1,578.5	1,475.9	1,352.2	1,242.4	1,118.2

Year	6/86	6/85	6/84	6/83	6/82	6/81	6/80
Total receivables	113.9	121.6	124.6	100.0	90.1	72.2	57.5
Change in receivables	−7.7	−3.0	24.6	9.9	17.9	14.7	1.9
Net sales	1,089.1	1,054.8	974.6	913.8	867.1	714.0	637.4
Subtract change in receivables	7.7	3.0	−24.6	−9.9	−17.9	−14.7	−1.9
Collection from customers	1,096.7	1,057.8	950.0	903.9	849.2	699.3	635.6

Collections from customers are calculated as sales minus the change in accounts receivable. If one assumes that all sales are on credit, then accounts receivable should have increased during the period by the amount of sales. If they increased by a smaller amount, then some of the accounts receivable were collected during the period. The amount collected can be estimated by subtracting the increase in accounts receivable from annual sales. For example, in 1994, sales amounted to $1,836.9 million and accounts receivable increased by $23.2 million. Thus, collections are estimated as $1,813.8 million (1,836.9 − 23.2, and round-off error). In 1992, however, accounts receivable actually decreased, indicating that not only did the firm collect an amount equal to all 1992 sales but it also collected $14.9 million of the accounts receivable that resulted from 1991 sales. Thus, collections in 1992 are estimated as $1,731.9 million (1,717 + 14.9).

Let us now estimate payments to suppliers, employees, and the like:

Year	6/94	6/93	6/92	6/91	6/90	6/89	6/88	6/87
Total inventories	105.9	105.9	110.5	116.3	128.1	110.6	97.4	77.1
Other current assets	32.6	128.0	34.1	17.1	14.2	127.5	8.3	7.3
Increase in assets	−95.4	89.3	11.1	−8.9	−95.8	132.4	21.4	−13.7
Accounts payable	97.7	84.2	104.2	103.8	79.3	85.8	94.7	68.5
Accrued expenses	227.2	226.8	220.2	214.5	137.1	142.4	126.3	96.3
Increase in liabilities	13.9	−13.4	6.2	101.8	−11.8	7.2	56.2	20.4
Increase in net assets	−109.3	102.7	4.9	−110.6	−84.0	125.2	−34.8	−34.1
Cost of goods sold	758.8	673.2	723.7	722.1	661.8	605.8	549.9	503.6
SG&A expense	690.6	613.1	682.0	629.6	562.1	507.4	473.4	422.1
Add increase in net assets	−109.3	102.7	4.9	−110.6	−84.0	125.2	−34.8	−34.1
Payments to suppliers, employers, etc.	**1,340.0**	**1,389.0**	**1,410.5**	**1,241.1**	**1,139.8**	**1,238.4**	**988.4**	**891.7**

Year	6/86	6/85	6/84	6/83	6/82	6/81	6/80
Total inventories	89.5	90.9	78.6	66.7	72.8	86.0	75.6
Other current assets	8.5	7.6	12.3	16.6	5.6	4.5	3.6
Increase in assets	−0.5	7.6	7.6	4.9	−12.0	11.3	6.8
Accounts payable	68.6	79.3	78.7	76.3	56.3	55.0	40.1
Accrued expenses	75.8	67.6	64.8	53.7	43.2	33.3	31.6
Increase in liabilities	−2.5	3.4	13.5	30.5	11.1	16.6	12.6
Increase in net assets	2.0	4.2	−5.9	−25.6	−23.2	−5.3	−5.8
Cost of goods sold	502.4	500.2	476.4	447.4	466.3	393.1	353.9
SG&A expense	389.9	380.4	340.8	320.1	289.4	241.3	215.9
Add increase in net assets	2.0	4.2	−5.9	−25.6	−23.2	−5.3	−5.8
Payments to suppliers, employers, etc.	**894.4**	**884.8**	**811.3**	**741.9**	**732.5**	**629.1**	**564.0**

Payments to suppliers, employees, and the like, are calculated as cost of goods sold plus selling, general, and administrative expenses. Compustat, Standard & Poor's financial database, which we use here, excludes depreciation and amortization from cost of goods sold, so one can conceive of the sum of these two expenses initially as cash outflows to suppliers and employees. However, one has to add the change in inventories plus the change in prepaid expenses since these represent additional acquisitions of inventory or payments to suppliers and employees due to current operations. We then subtract the change in accounts payable and the change in accrued expenses, because some of the above expenditures may not have been paid during the current period and may actually be paid only in the next period.

To estimate interest payments, we use the interest expense, unless the firm reports interest payables or interest that was capitalized during the period.

Year	6/94	6/93	6/92	6/91	6/90	6/89	6/88	6/87
Interest expense	18.4	18.9	24.7	28.2	3.9	7.2	4.1	5.4
Interest paid	18.4	18.9	24.7	28.2	3.9	7.2	4.1	5.4

Year		6/86	6/85	6/84	6/83	6/82	6/81	6/80
Interest expense		4.8	7.1	9.5	12.7	13.7	5.0	4.3
Interest paid		4.8	7.1	9.5	12.7	13.7	5.0	4.3

A portion of the tax expense may be deferred into the next period with an associated increase in taxes payable, and another portion into later periods, as reflected by the increase in deferred taxes. Thus, normally, the payment for taxes is calculated as the tax expense minus the change in taxes payable and minus the change in deferred taxes.

Year	6/94	6/93	6/92	6/91	6/90	6/89	6/88	6/87
Income taxes payable	7.6	20.6	19.3	19.5	8.3	8.3	12.8	15.7
Deferred taxes	133.0	143.7	117.3	63.2	94.2	89.1	99.5	95.8
Increase in tax liabilities	−23.6	27.7	53.9	−19.8	5.1	−14.9	0.7	13.1
Total income taxes	126.6	107.3	93.1	33.4	90.0	84.1	79.2	81.7
Subtract increase in tax liabilities	23.6	−27.7	−53.9	19.8	−5.1	14.9	−0.7	−13.1
Tax payments	150.3	79.6	39.2	53.2	84.9	99.0	78.5	68.6

Year		6/86	6/85	6/84	6/83	6/82	6/81	6/80
Income taxes payable		14.3	13.1	14.9	14.8	6.5	10.4	11.5
Deferred taxes		84.2	58.2	38.7	30.6	22.6	18.1	13.2
Increase in tax liabilities		27.2	17.8	8.2	16.4	0.6	3.7	5.2
Total income taxes		79.7	69.0	64.4	58.1	35.5	31.2	29.2
Subtract increase in tax liabilities		−27.2	−17.8	−8.2	−16.4	−0.6	−3.7	−5.2
Tax payments		52.5	51.2	56.2	41.8	35.0	27.4	24.0

We can now estimate the net cash from operating activities:

Year	6/94	6/93	6/92	6/91	6/90	6/89	6/88	6/87
Net operating cash flow	305.1	124.7	257.5	255.9	247.3	7.6	171.3	152.6

Year	6/86	6/85	6/84	6/83	6/82	6/81	6/80
Net operating cash flow	145.1	114.8	73.0	107.6	68.1	37.8	43.3

Cash from operations is calculated as collections from customers minus payments to suppliers, employees, interest, and taxes. Note that this procedure does not include in operating cash flows any nonrecurring cash flows. We can now estimate free cash flows by subtracting from reported or estimated net operating cash flows capital expenditures:

Year	6/94	6/93	6/92	6/91	6/90	6/89	6/88	6/87
Net operating cash flow	266.8	245.5	306.7	246.7	166.4	158.3	171.3	152.6
Subtract capital expenditures	56.6	77.6	124.7	109.1	155.9	87.8	153.3	56.0
Free cash flow—III	210.2	167.8	182.0	137.6	10.6	70.4	18.0	96.6

Year	6/86	6/85	6/84	6/83	6/82	6/81	6/80
Net operating cash flow	145.1	114.8	73.0	107.6	68.1	37.8	43.3
Subtract capital expenditures	65.2	40.9	37.3	29.6	37.7	32.9	27.0
Free cash flow—III	79.9	73.9	35.7	78.0	30.4	4.9	16.3

In the above calculations, capital expenditures include all investments in PPE, regardless of whether these capital expenditures were necessary or not. Recall that management has control over the amounts it decides to invest in capital expenditures. Therefore, some of the discretionary capital expenditures may be beyond what is needed to sustain the growth rate of the firm at its current level. Thus, the cash flow analyst should attempt to determine the portion of the capital expenditures that were necessary to sustain growth, and exclude the portion that was not needed to sustain that growth, or the portion that was not necessary at all. The portion which is not needed for future growth represents free cash flow, because it can be paid back to owners without affecting the current growth rate of the firm.

Capital Spending

Of all the discretionary expenditures in a business, capital spending is probably the most scrutinized because of its visibility and its nature. The mere size of capital spending (it is usually the largest use of cash on the statement of cash flows), combined with the fact that cash returns on capital spending occur many periods away, forces investors to investigate whether an entity's capital expenditures are economically justified.

Example

Lukens Inc., a diversified steel manufacturer, has embarked on an ambitious capital spending program, expected to reach $144 million in 1994, as compared to $67 million in 1993. These capital expenditures are designed to (a) significantly increase the company's production of stainless steel, (b) lower costs of carbon steel products, and (c) install a flexible plant capable of producing either carbon steel or stainless steel from the same line.

The total cost of these expenditures constituted about a quarter of Lukens's market value at that point, and the financing required for these projects increased its financial leverage significantly. Additionally, the company was forced to both shut down and curtail production at a time of cyclically high demand and high steel prices.

Forecasting capital spending is difficult because it depends on the economy, on the industry, and the specific conditions of the firm, particularly on its expected rate of growth. Thus, most of the time it is best left up to management estimates. For cyclical entities, capital expenditures can be as volatile as cash flows. For such entities, especially when liquidity deteriorates, capital expenditures reflect the bare minimum that is needed to sustain the business entity. Still, we must devise a way to estimate the component of capital expenditures that is discretionary, and that is not necessary to sustain the growth of the business.

Some security analysts prefer to look at what they consider to be "maintenance" capital spending, that is, capital expenditures that are adequate to keep up the current level of production. This is faulty since it does not take into account the future needs any capital budget should consider. Since capital spending, typically, is the largest investment item, the analysis of capital spending is most important and is the first item to be affected during changes in the economic environment, whether the change is caused by an adverse change in business conditions or by a merger, when only the most important capital spending plans stay on.

One way of estimating the required level of capital expenditures (in the case of a manufacturing concern like Clorox) is to compare the growth rate of cost of goods sold with the growth rate of capital expenditures. Presumably, in order to sustain a specific growth rate of cost of goods sold, capital expenditures should grow by approximately the same rate. If we observe a substantially higher growth rate of capital expenditures than cost of sales during a reasonable period, then it can be assumed that the firm had overinvested in PPE during the period, and this overinvestment represents discretionary capital expenditures that can be considered a free cash flow. To show the estimation for Clorox, we follow these steps:

1. We first estimate the annual average growth rate in capital expenditures and cost of sales over the most recent three years:

Year	6/94	6/93	6/92	6/91	6/90	6/89	6/88	6/87
Capital expenditures (cap exp)	56.6	77.6	124.7	109.1	155.9	87.8	153.3	56.0
Three-year growth rate of cap exp	−19.6	−20.7	12.4	−10.7	40.7	10.5	55.4	14.5
Cost of goods sold (CGS)	758.8	673.2	723.7	722.1	661.8	605.8	549.9	503.6
Three-year growth rate of CGS	1.7	0.6	6.1	9.5	9.5	6.4	3.2	1.9
Excess growth rate cap—CGS	0.0	0.0	6.3	0.0	31.1	4.0	52.2	12.6
Discretionary cap exp	**0.0**	**0.0**	**7.9**	**0.0**	**48.5**	**3.6**	**80.0**	**7.1**

Year	6/86	6/85	6/84	6/83	6/82	6/81	6/80
Capital expenditures (cap exp)	65.2	40.9	37.3	29.6	37.7	32.9	27.0
Three-year growth rate of cap exp	30.1	2.7	4.3	3.1	−1.3	8.8	17.3
Cost of goods sold (CGS)	502.4	500.2	476.4	447.4	466.3	393.1	353.9
Three-year growth rate of CGS	3.9	2.4	6.6	8.1	15.2	−23.4	−17.5
Excess growth rate cap—CGS	26.2	0.4	0.0	0.0	0.0	32.2	34.8
Discretionary cap exp	**17.0**	**0.1**	**0.0**	**0.0**	**0.0**	**10.6**	**9.4**

For example, in 1992, we divide $124.7 by $87.8, to obtain 1.4203. We take the cubic root of 1.4203, which is equal to 1.124, or an average growth rate of 12.4 percent per year.

2. We follow similar calculations to estimate the growth rate in cost of goods sold.
   For example, in 1992, the growth rate of cost of goods sold was 6.1 percent.

3. We subtract the growth rate of cost of goods sold from that of capital expenditures, and substitute zero if the result is negative.
   For example, in 1992, the difference is 6.3 percent (12.4–6.1). In 1984, it is zero because the growth rate of cost of goods sold was 6.6 percent, in excess of the growth rate of capital expenditures of 4.3 percent.

4. We multiply the excess growth rate of capital expenditures by total capital expenditures that year to obtain an estimate of discretionary capital expenditures for the year.
   For example, in 1992, we multiply $124.7 million by the excess growth rate of 6.3 percent to obtain $7.9 million. In 1994, the excess is zero, and no discretionary capital expenditures are designated.[8]

Based on these estimates of the discretionary expenditures on PPE, we obtain the estimated free cash flows by subtracting total capital expenditures from net operating cash flows, and adding back discretionary capital expenditures. This yields:

Year	6/94	6/93	6/92	6/91	6/90	6/89	6/88	6/87
Free cash flow—IV	210.2	167.82	189.8	137.6	59.09	73.99	98.02	103.7

Year		6/86	6/85	6/84	6/83	6/82	6/81	6/80
Free cash flow—IV		96.94	74.07	35.66	77.97	30.36	15.5	25.71

---

[8]The astute reader may ask why should we consider some capital expenditures as discretionary (when the growth rate of capital expenditures exceeds that of cost of sales), but when capital expenditures lag behind sales we do not subtract from operating cash flows an additional amount that is equal to the "required" capital expenditures that were not undertaken. The reason for this seeming inconsistency is that firms can increase productivity due to technological advances and other measures without requiring comparable investments in capital expenditures. Thus, in our calculations we do not penalize firms that became more efficient.

The procedure that we used to estimate discretionary capital expenditures may seem arbitrary at a first glance. We first estimate the growth rate over three years (which requires four years of data) in capital expenditures and cost of sales. The decision to use four years stems from a balancing of two errors; a longer period may yield unfair comparisons because firms change substantially over time. They branch out to other lines of business or decide to dispose of existing lines of business. However, a shorter period than four years is unlikely to include an entire business cycle. Thus, we focus on four years in our analysis.

We compare the rate of growth in capital expenditures with that of cost of goods sold. Ideally, we should have used a physical measure of output to examine the required growth rate of inputs needed to support the growth level of output. However, firms do not provide physical output or input measures, and we have to resort to estimates. We feel that cost of sales is a good measure of growth in output, because it comprises all components of product costs. Given the similarity in price increases between inputs and outputs, the growth rates of cost of sales and capital expenditures should be good proxies for growth rates in physical outputs and inputs.

To assess the extent of a bias that is introduced because of this estimated component of discretionary capital expenditures, we examined the relationship between excess discretionary capital expenditures and market value of firms. First, we found out that, in any given year, fewer than 20 percent of all firms had excess discretionary capital expenditures. Furthermore, fewer than 2 percent of all firms had discretionary capital expenditures that exceed 10 percent of market value of equity. Thus, modifications to our procedure are unlikely to affect the estimate of free cash flows in any significant manner. In Chapter 8, we show that our portfolio results are not sensitive to the exact specification or estimation of discretionary capital expenditures.

Can one identify expenses other than capital expenditures that are discretionary in nature? An immediate candidate is expenditures made in the daily operations of the firm, where management may expend some cash flows in its operations beyond those needed to sustain growth. For example, payments for goods that were acquired or produced, payments for selling, general, and administrative expenses, advertising, and payments for research and development efforts may be in excess of the level that is needed to sustain the current growth rate in sales. Thus, it is important to obtain estimates of discretionary cash outflows for the firm's ongoing operations.

One of the major components of discretionary expenditures is corporate overhead, oftentimes referred to as corporate fat. Unfortunately, few have attempted to quantify the corporate fat portion of overhead. In fact, little has been written about corporate overhead in textbooks on security analysis, investment, and accounting. The current literature has not tied the financial process with the management process, although management consulting firms have long established that corporate overhead is excessive for most firms. For example, whereas corporate overhead represented about 10 percent of total product cost at the beginning of this century, corporate overhead contributes now more than 40 percent to total product costs (e.g., see articles that discuss activity-based costing in the *Journal of Cost Management*).

Corporate restructuring, which became so prevalent during the 1980s, still has a long way to go, according to the measures explained below. Management consultants agree; according to one management consultant: "The Eighties were just the tip of the iceberg, and we're going to see dramatic reductions in the Nineties. Corporate America is still as much as 25 percent overstuffed."[9]

The 1990–1991 recession, as well as the lingering effects of the 1980s debt build-up, caused a frontal attack on corporate cost structure, both in the United States and abroad.

Companies including IBM, Digital Equipment, United Technologies, Colgate-Palmolive, and Hitachi were just some of the more visible companies that took a hard look at their corporate fat and decided it was too high in relation to their rate of growth and their expected rate of growth. The marketplace rewarded these companies as the announcements were made.

Example

The Wall Street Journal published the following news item on September 12, 1991:

---

[9]Ronald Henkoff, "Cost Cutting: How To Do It Right," *Fortune*, April 9, 1990.

AMR, in a Sharp Reversal, Curb Outlays

While the cutbacks ($500 million) represent only about 4 percent of Americans' capital spending, they signal a major strategic shift for the nation's major airline...Now it's going to try to control costs... News of the strategy shift sent the stock of the Ft. Worth, Texas, company higher; AMR was quoted at $59 a share, up $3.125.

On the same date AMR announced its cutbacks, Mr. Robert Stempel, chairman of the General Motors Corporation, said the automotive companies must adopt "lean" production methods. This could mean using about half the traditional factory space, and about one tenth of the inventories. Lean organizations achieved dramatically higher quality and productivity and more efficient and faster product development, with a payoff in lower costs and the ability to bring out different models faster, at lower volumes and with higher quality. (*Financial Times*, September 12, 1991)

The trend in the latter part of the 1990s seems to slash corporate overhead further even in companies that are already very clean. To do this, companies merge and reduce the duplicative overhead functions without affecting revenues. Recent examples include the banking industry, insurance industry, and some utilities.

Currently, security analysts are taught to compare various expenses as a percentage of current sales over five- to- ten-year periods to get an idea if such expenses are out of line. Such analysis is incorrect even if judged compared to its industry, because the company's growth rate and the projected growth rate are what really should determine the appropriate level of many expenses and expense ratios.

Management consultants are well-known for studying an entity's productive and administrative processes to determine how cutbacks could be accomplished while maintaining the same or improved level of production. Continuous process improvement (CPI) techniques in research and development have added to better quality control and better products, which in turn serve to reduce corporate waste.

In order to consider the appropriateness of the level of overhead, it is necessary, first, to examine the unit growth rate of the entity. Unit growth, rather than dollar growth (revenues), should ideally be examined since dollar growth includes the effects of price changes. For example, if prices double with no change in unit growth (in, say, an inflationary spiral), for the entity to double its selling expenses would be unsuitable. The entity's unit growth should also be compared to the unit growth of the industry if possible. This can be done (if price increases for the particular company are not known) by deflating the firm's cost of sales by the deflator for the industry. If discretionary expenditures grow at a rate in excess of the growth rate for sales over a four-year period, especially if its discretionary expenditures growth is greater than that for the industry, one assumes those expenditures are too high.

The amount of the overspending on overhead is directly related to the unit growth rate of the entity, and it should be compared to its expenditures on nondiscretionary items. It is important that we consider the special case of examining high-unit growth industries like technology. When the growth rate of these industries slows down, due to the unavoidable competitive pressures or market saturation, comparing unit growth to expenditures over a long time horizon—even four years—can certainly give the impression that the company has too much corporate fat. This occurs because the long-term growth rate in expenses remains high, while current sales grow at a much lower rate. It is important that these companies quickly reduce their discretionary expenditures to match their new lower long-term unit growth rate.

Although the term *corporate fat* has a negative connotation, every company, like every living being, has and needs some. The question all but the smallest companies ask is, how much corporate fat is justified under the circumstances? Basically, corporate fat represents overspending, which is most often found in selling, general, and administrative (SG&A) expenses; cost of goods sold (COGS), in which both material expense and labor expenses may be included; advertising expenses; and research and development (R&D) expenditures. Thus, we will focus on these items in estimating discretionary cash outflows on the continuing operations of a firm by following three steps:

1. We first calculate the average three-year growth rate of collections from customers and payments to suppliers.

Year	6/94	6/93	6/92	6/91	6/90	6/89
Collections from customers	1,813.8	1,612.1	1,731.9	1,578.5	1,475.9	1,352.2
Three-year growth rate of collections	4.7	3.0	8.6	8.3	9.7	7.2
Payments to suppliers and employers	1,340.0	1,389.0	1,410.5	1,241.1	1,139.8	1,238.4
Three-year growth rate of						

payments	2.6	6.8	4.4	7.9	8.5	11.5
Excess of growth rate of payments over collections	0.0	3.8	0.0	0.0	0.0	4.2
Discretionary payments	**0.0**	**10.6**	**0.0**	**0.0**	**0.0**	**10.5**

Year	6/88	6/87	6/86	6/85	6/84	6/83
Collections from customers	1,242.4	1,118.2	1,096.7	1,057.8	950.0	903.9
Three-year growth rate of collections	5.5	5.6	6.7	7.6	10.8	12.5
Payments to suppliers and employers	988.4	891.7	894.4	884.8	811.3	741.9
Three-year growth rate payments	3.8	3.2	6.4	6.5	8.8	9.6
Excess of growth rate of payments over collections	0.0	0.0	0.0	0.0	0.0	0.0
Discretionary payments	**0.0**	**0.0**	**0.0**	**0.0**	**0.0**	**0.0**

2. We compute the excess of growth rate in payments to suppliers and employees over collections from customers if the excess growth rate is positive, and zero if the growth rate of collections is higher than the growth rate of payments.

3. We multiply the excess growth rate of payments to suppliers over the growth rate in collections by current payments to suppliers. We further multiply this amount by 20 percent to estimate discretionary payments that should be added to free cash flows.

Note that in 1989 the average growth rate of payments to suppliers and employees exceeds the average growth rate of collections from customers by 4.2 percent (11.5 − 7.2). Multiplying this excess by total payments to suppliers and employees of $1,238.4 million and then again by 20 percent yields $10.5 million of discretionary cash flows that were spent on excessive payments to suppliers and employees. The decision to use 20 percent of the excess is based on the observation that most corporate cost reduction programs can cut 20 percent from the excess of discretionary spending without

---

[10]In two closely dated announcements, Tenneco Inc. announced plans to cut a third of its corporate staff to improve performance (10/20/91), and United Technologies Corp. announced reductions of corporate staff by 25 percent (October 1991). The magnitude of these cost reductions is very typical of firms in similar stages of restructuring. It indicates that the level of corporate overhead that can be reduced without affecting growth tends to be around 20 percent-30 percent of the excess of these expenses above the growth rate of the firm.

impairing the progress or development of the firm. Although the correct amount of corporate fat must be determined case-by-case, we have found that when public firms restructure their operations, they are able to trim about 20 percent from what we defined as overspending without affecting future growth.[10] This is the same assumption as that of capital expenditures; not all excess payments to suppliers and employees can be considered discretionary, and to be conservative only 20 percent of these amounts are classified as discretionary cash flows.

Although it seems that our approach is arbitrary, we believe that the data supports our estimation procedure. We checked the distribution of what we termed discretionary payments to suppliers and employees in the entire population of Compustat firms (live ones and those on the Research Compustat database). Only about 15–20 percent of all firms had any discretionary payments to suppliers and employees in any given year. When we compared the magnitude of these discretionary cash flows to total sales of the firm, we found that fewer than 3 percent of the firms in any given year had any discretionary cash flows that exceeded 10 percent of total sales. Thus, errors in our estimates would probably not significantly affect the ranking of firms in terms of their free cash flows. Even if we used other percentages or other approaches to estimate the discretionary components of these expenditures, we would probably have obtained similar results to those obtained in our estimation procedure. In Chapter 8, we show that the performance results of a portfolio chosen according to a low free cash flow multiple does not change much with changes in the method used to estimate discretionary payments to suppliers and employees.

Thus, we add only 20 percent of the excess we conservatively term discretionary cash expenditures to the prior estimate of free cash flows, and get:

Year	6/94	6/93	6/92	6/91	6/90	6/89
Free cash flow—V	210.2	178.5	189.8	137.6	59.1	84.5

Year	6/88	6/87	6/86	6/85	6/84	6/83
Free cash flow—V	98.0	103.7	96.9	74.1	35.7	78.0

Our estimates of free cash flows were focused on a single year. However, firms may have fluctuations in their free cash flows from one year to another, due to shifts in economic and business conditions and business decisions. Thus, it may be more instructive to focus on averages for the most recent years. Based on the above estimates, we obtain the following four-year average free cash flows:

Year	6/94	6/93	6/92	6/91	6/90	6/89
Four-year average free cash flow	179.0	141.2	117.7	94.8	86.3	95.8

Year	6/88	6/87	6/86	6/85	6/84	6/83
Four-year average free cash flow	93.2	77.6	71.2	62.6	56.8	78.0

Note that the average free cash flow of Clorox is consistently positive and generally growing. This is to be expected given the type of products Clorox sells and its market penetration. We can now compare the behavior of Clorox's average free cash flow with its market value for the period 1983–1994.

FIGURE 5–1
Clorox Co.: Average Free Cash Flow and Market Value

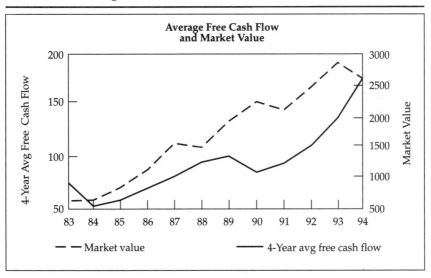

As the graph shows, market value and average free cash flow dovetail each other fairly well. Thus, it may be tempting to select firms for a portfolio based upon their relationship of market value and average free cash flow. We provide results on this investment approach in Chapter 8.

An Alternative Procedure

An alternative procedure is to estimate the free cash flows in an *indirect* way by a process of tracing the changes in cash during the period. This approach is based on the following rationale:
Consider the cash sources–uses identity,

$$OCF + NetDebt + NetEquity = Div + Invest + ChangeCash$$

where OCF is the net cash flow from operating activities, NetDebt and NetEquity are the net cash provided by issuance of debt or equity, respectively, Div represents cash dividends paid by the firm, Invest represents cash investments in capital expenditures and such investments, and ChangeCash is the change in cash balance from the beginning to the end of the period.
Simple algebraic manipulations yield

$$OCF - Invest = ChangeCash + Div - NetDebt - NetEquity$$

On the left hand side of the equation, we have the traditional definition of free cash flows, net operating cash flows—minus net investments during the period, mostly in capital expenditures. By now, we know some of the investments in capital expenditures can be considered discretionary. Let us denote discretionary investments by DiscInv and nondiscretionary investments by NonDiscInv. Similarly, some of the cash outlays, such as payments to employees and suppliers, R&D, and so forth, may be discretionary. Let us denote these discretionary cash outflows by DiscOCF, and the nondiscretionary cash from operations by NonOCF. Thus, the equation can be written as,

$$(NonOCF - DiscOCF) - (NonDiscInv + DiscInv) = ChangeCash + Div - NetDebt - NetEquity$$

Simple manipulations yield

$$\text{NonOCF} - \text{NonDiscInv} = \text{ChangeCash} + \text{Div} - \text{NetDebt} - \text{NetEquity} + \text{DiscInv} + \text{DiscOCF}$$

Note that the left hand side of this equation now contains the free cash flow as we defined it above—the cash generated by ongoing operations of the business during the period, in excess of necessary investments in capital expenditures and other *necessary* payments. Note that this represents free cash flow because net operating cash flow now includes cash receipts from operations in excess of necessary cash outflows for generating these cash receipts during the period, and in excess of investments that are intended to maintain the ability of the firm to generate these cash receipts in the future. Obviously, the excess cash receipts can be distributed to shareholders without affecting the growth of the business.

The right hand side of the equation shows an alternative way of estimating free cash flow from operations. Instead of estimating the cash receipts minus necessary cash flows, one begins with the change in cash during the period and makes adjustments to it as is portrayed on the right hand side of the equation. For example, decreases in cash due to financing events, such as payment of dividends or retirement of debt, are added back to the change in cash. Similarly, decreases in cash due to discretionary capital expenditures, or investing activities beyond those needed to sustain the growth of the firm, are added back to the change in cash. Decreases in cash due to operating expenses beyond those that are needed to sustain the growth of the firm are also added back to the change in cash because they represent discretionary expenditures. Using similar logic, increases in cash due to disinvesting events, such as the sale of PPE, or increases of cash due to financing events, such as the issuance of common stock, are subtracted from the change in cash. This procedure yields another estimate of free cash flow, but it uses an indirect method to estimate the free cash flow. Let us illustrate this approach as it applies to Clorox.

Example

Let us first calculate the change in cash and cash equivalents from the balance sheet:

Year	6/83	6/84	6/85	6/86	6/87	6/88
Change in cash and equivalents	43.2	8.4	60.8	27.3	40.2	13.8

Year	6/89	6/90	6/91	6/92	6/93	6/94
Change in cash and equivalents	−25.9	−108.7	−10.7	−44.8	2.1	44.8

Add to the net change in cash and cash equivalents all financing cash outflows, since they do not represent free cash flows from *operating* activities:

Year	6/83	6/84	6/85	6/86	6/87	6/88
Cash dividends	22.8	27.8	32.7	37.2	42.2	49.6
Stock purchases	0.0	0.0	0.0	0.0	0.0	0.0
Reduction L.T.D.	26.8	30.1	32.2	2.9	20.1	4.4

Year	6/89	6/90	6/91	6/92	6/93	6/94
Cash dividends	60.0	70.9	79.5	86.4	93.5	97.1
Stock purchases	0.0	67.4	4.0	0.0	0.0	99.9
Reduction L.T.D.	3.6	14.2	0.9	1.2	1.2	0.7

Cash dividends will be added back to the net change in cash because they represent cash that can be (and is) returned to stockholders without affecting the growth of the firm's business, that is, its free cash flow. Stock repurchases are very similar to dividends; they represent cash flows that are not needed for the continuing growth of current operations and are used to buy out some shareholders. Finally, the reduction of long-term debt is a disfinancing cash flow—that is, it represents free cash flow that is used to buy out debt-holders instead of stockholders. Thus, it is added back to the change in cash in order to derive the free cash flow which is generated from operating activities.

The next batch of adjustments relates to financing events that increased cash. To correct for their effects on the change in cash, we have to subtract them from the change in cash.

Year	6/83	6/84	6/85	6/86	6/87	6/88
Sale of common and preferred	0.0	53.3	0.0	0.0	0.0	0.0
Increase L.T.D.	0.0	0.0	0.0	0.0	0.0	0.0
Change in current debt	0.6	−0.1	31.8	−16.8	−3.1	66.9
Financing activities—other	40.3	9.5	6.0	0.0	0.0	0.0

Year	6/89	6/90	6/91	6/92	6/93	6/94
Sale of common and preferred	0.0	0.0	0.0	0.0	0.0	9.8
Increase L.T.D.	0.0	0.0	400.5	199. 5	0.3	13.0
Change in current debt	0.8	−79.6	10.4	−333.0	−42.5	3.4
Financing activities—other	0.0	0.0	0.0	0.0	0.0	0.0

The increase in cash during the period that is due to issuance of common stock or preferred stock ($9.8 million in 1994) is a financing cash inflow and does not affect free cash flows from operating activities. Thus, it is subtracted from the change in cash when estimating free cash flows from operating activities. The increases in long-term debt, current debt, and other financing activities represent increases in cash that are caused by financing activities and not by operating activities. Since these events increased cash during the period, they are subtracted from the change in cash when estimating the free cash flow from operating activities.

In a similar manner, we treat other investing activities that reduced cash, and that are added back to the change in cash, because they do not represent free cash flow from operations. Conversely, cash inflows from sale of assets (such as PPE and investments) increase the cash balance during the period, but are not cash flows from operating activities. Thus, we subtract these activities from the change in cash when we estimate free cash flow. In particular, we make the following adjustments:

We first add back the following investing cash outflows:

Year	6/83	6/84	6/85	6/86	6/87	6/88
Increase in investments	14.7	0.0	0.0	15.5	0.0	0.0
Acquisitions	0.0	50.5	0.0	0.0	0.0	43.6
Short-term investments— change	−47.7	−7.9	−56.5	−12.9	−53.3	−10.0

Year	6/89	6/90	6/91	6/92	6/93	6/94
Increase in investments	0.0	0.0	0.0	0.0	0.0	0.0
Acquisitions	11.0	3.8	481.1	0.8	31.5	142.4
Short-term investments— change	0.0	0.0	0.0	0.0	0.0	0.0

We then subtract the following cash inflows from investing activities:

Year	6/83	6/84	6/85	6/86	6/87	6/88
Sale of PPE	2.6	4.0	5.9	2.6	5.5	8.9
Investing activities—other	0.0	0.0	0.0	-0.9	-11.5	-1.8
Sale of investments	0.0	0.0	0.0	0.0	0.0	0.0

Year	6/89	6/90	6/91	6/92	6/93	6/94
Sale of PPE	2.6	3.1	4.4	1.6	3.8	11.3
Investing activities—other	-25.1	113.5	1.6	-6.5	-1.0	137.2
Sale of investments	0.0	0.0	0.0	0.0	0.0	0.0

At this point, we should add back all the discretionary spending for capital expenditures and payments to suppliers and employees. To illustrate another alternative of estimating these discretionary items, we use the following procedure:

1. Discretionary capital expenditures are estimated as before. The only change in the following computations is that the growth rate is estimated as a least-squares growth rate from the four capital expenditures amounts in years t–3 through year t.

Year	6/83	6/84	6/85	6/86	6/87	6/88
Three-year growth rate cap exp	4.2	1.3	4.9	27.9	18.3	46.5
Three-year growth rate COGS	9.1	5.5	2.8	4.0	1.7	2.9
Difference in rates × latest cap exp	0.0	0.0	0.9	15.5	9.3	66.8

Year	6/89	6/90	6/91	6/92	6/93	6/94
Three-year growth rate cap exp	21.0	28.6	-4.4	7.2	-17.8	-21.7
Three-year growth rate COGS	6.7	9.6	9.5	6.4	0.5	0.8
Difference in rates × latest cap exp	12.5	29.6	0.0	1.0	0.0	0.0

2. We now break the discretionary payments to suppliers and employees into several components. The first is the component of R&D expenditures that is discretionary. To estimate it, we use the same procedure as for capital expenditures, i.e., the excess of growth rate in R&D expenditures over the growth rate in cost of goods sold times current R&D expenditures:

Year	6/83	6/84	6/85	6/86	6/87	6/88
Three-year growth rate R&D	13.1	10.7	16.6	17.7	19.1	10.7
Three-year growth rate COGS	9.1	5.5	2.8	4.0	1.7	2.9
Difference in rates × latest R&D	0.7	1.0	3.5	3.7	5.8	2.5

Year	6/89	6/90	6/91	6/92	6/93	6/94
Three-year growth rate R&D	9.5	6.1	12.3	7.7	1.8	−2.3
Three-year growth rate COGS	6.7	9.6	9.5	6.4	0.5	0.8
Difference in rates × latest R&D	1.0	0.0	1.3	0.6	0.6	0.0

3. We proceed to estimate discretionary cash flows in the firm's expenditures on cost of goods sold. The estimation process here is to compare the ratio of cost of goods sold to sales with the long-run ratio (average of the most recent four years). If the ratio exceeds the long-run average ratio, some of these expenditures are considered discretionary, and 20 percent of the excess is multiplied by current sales to determine the amount of excess cost of goods sold, which is considered discretionary cash flows:

Year	6/83	6/84	6/85	6/86	6/87	6/88
COGS percent of sales	49.0	48.9	27.9	46.5	45.2	43.6
Four-year avg COGS percent of sales	53.3	51.7	49.9	48.1	47.1	45.8
Sales	913.8	974.6	873.2	893.7	935.0	1,033.8
Excess COGS	0.0	0.0	0.0	0.0	0.0	0.0
20 percent of difference	0.0	0.0	0.0	0.0	0.0	0.0

Year	6/89	6/90	6/91	6/92	6/93	6/94
COGS percent of sales	45.7	45.9	45.8	43.9	44.3	44.7
Four-year avg COGS percent of sales	45.2	45.1	45.3	45.3	45.0	44.7
Sales	1,199.3	1,309.0	1,468.4	1,547.1	1,634.2	1,836.9
Excess COGS	5.9	11.0	7.8	0.0	0.0	0.0
20 percent of difference	1.2	2.2	1.6	0.0	0.0	0.0

4. We use a very similar process for the selling, general, and administrative expenses, after excluding advertising expenses and R&D expenses, which are usually included in selling, general, and administrative expenses. We also multiply the excess by 25 percent, and not 20 percent as for cost of goods sold, because this item is more subject to managerial discretion:

Year	6/83	6/84	6/85	6/86	6/87	6/88
SGA (Excl. R&D + Adv.) percent of sales	21.3	21.3	18.0	17.9	17.9	18.0
Four-year avg SGA percent of sales	20.5	20.8	20.1	19.6	18.8	17.9
Sales	913.8	974.6	873.2	893.7	935.0	1,033.8
Excess SGA	7.1	5.0	0.0	0.0	0.0	0.4
25 percent of difference	1.8	1.3	0.0	0.0	0.0	0.1

Year	6/89	6/90	6/91	6/92	6/93	6/94
SGA (Excl. R&D + Adv.) percent of sales	18.4	18.3	26.3	19.2	20.1	19.6
Four-year avg SGA percent of sales	18.0	18.2	20.2	20.5	21.0	21.3
Sales	1,199.3	1,309.0	1,468.4	1,547.1	1,634.2	1,836.9
Excess SGA	3.9	2.2	88.5	0.0	0.0	0.0
25 percent of difference	1.0	0.5	22.1	0.0	0.0	0.0

As can be seen, Clorox seems to be a well-managed company, having very little excess selling, general, and administrative expenditures.

5. We now estimate the discretionary component in advertising expenses. The estimation process is very similar to that of the prior two components, except that we consider 50 percent of the excess of advertising expenses to be discretionary.

Year	6/83	6/84	6/85	6/86	6/87	6/88
Advertising expense	108.1	114.3	137.0	139.5	154.8	178.2
Advertising expense percent of sales	11.8	11.7	15.7	15.6	16.6	17.2
Four-year average advertising percent of sales	11.6	11.6	12.7	13.7	14.9	16.3
Excess advertising	2.0	1.1	26.0	17.0	15.6	9.9
50 percent of difference	1.0	0.5	13.0	8.5	7.8	5.0

Year	6/89	6/90	6/91	6/92	6/93	6/94
Advertising expense	200.7	219.1	244.5	270.3	242.5	286.7
Advertising expense percent of sales	16.7	16.7	16.7	17.5	14.8	15.6
Four-year average advertising percent of sales	16.5	16.8	16.8	16.9	16.4	16.1
Excess advertising	2.4	0.0	0.0	8.8	0.0	0.0
50 percent of difference	1.2	0.0	0.0	4.4	0.0	0.0

6. Finally, we estimate the extent to which funding (prepayment) of pension obligations can be considered discretionary. We compute the change in pension prepayment during the year, and assume that 75 percent of it is discretionary, if it is positive. If the change is negative, we disregard it in the estimation of free cash flow.

Year	6/83	6/84	6/85	6/86	6/87	6/88
Pension Prepayment	0.0	0.0	0.0	−3.6	−0.7	1.0
75 percent of difference	0.0	0.0	0.0	0.0	2.1	1.3

Year	6/89	6/90	6/91	6/92	6/93	6/94
Pension Prepayment	7.1	8.1	9.1	8.2	6.4	17.0
75 percent of difference	4.6	0.7	0.8	0.0	0.0	8.0

Let us now summarize all the discretionary items and the resulting net free cash flow:

Year	6/83	6/84	6/85	6/86	6/87	6/88
Discretionary items:						
Capital expenditures value	0.0	0.0	0.9	15.5	9.3	66.8
R&D expense value	0.7	1.0	3.5	3.7	5.8	2.5
Cost of goods sold (20%)	0.0	0.0	0.0	0.0	0.0	0.0
SG&A (25%)	1.8	1.3	0.0	0.0	0.0	0.1
Pension prepayment (75%)	0.0	0.0	0.0	0.0	2.1	1.3
Advertising value	1.0	0.5	13.0	8.5	7.8	5.0
Net free cash flow	115.2	60.8	156.0	138.7	190.0	123.1

Year	6/89	6/90	6/91	6/92	6/93	6/94
Discretionary items:						
Capital expenditures value	12.5	29.6	0.0	1.0	0.0	0.0
R&D expense value	1.0	0.0	1.3	0.6	0.6	0.0
Cost of goods sold (20%)	1.2	2.2	1.6	0.0	0.0	0.0
SG&A (25%)	1.0	0.5	22.1	0.0	0.0	0.0
Pension prepayment (75%)	4.6	0.7	0.8	0.0	0.0	8.0
Advertising value	1.2	0.0	0.0	4.4	0.0	0.0
Net free cash flow	91.9	43.6	163.4	188.0	168.4	218.1

As we did with the direct method of estimating free cash flow, we
can also graph the four-year average free cash flow against market
value and net income (see Figure 5–2). We use slightly different dates
to calculate the market value; December 31 instead of June 30.

Year	6/83	6/84	6/85	6/86	6/87	6/88
Four-year avg FCF	177.2	141.4	135.9	117.7	136.4	151.9
Net income	65.5	79.7	86.1	95.6	104.9	132.6
Market value	803.9	703.4	995.2	1,490.2	1,760.6	1,560.5

Year	6/89	6/90	6/91	6/92	6/93	6/94
Four-year avg FCF	135.9	112.1	105.5	121.7	140.8	184.5
Net income	124.1	153.6	52.7	98.7	167.1	212.1
Market value	2,091.3	2,276.1	2,127.2	2,475.0	2,859.1	3,149.2

Aside from being an efficiently managed firm, the data on Clorox show that efficiently managed firms are more likely to be good free cash flow generators. In Clorox's case, the free cash flow was used, in part, to repurchase stock, which increased the firm's market price.

At this point, we can assess total corporate fat as discretionary capital expenditures plus discretionary R&D expenditures and discretionary COGS, advertising, pension prepayment, and SGA. These items represent corporate fat or additions to free cash flows, because they are not required to sustain the current growth of the firm. As a further illustration, the following table presents the results of an analysis of corporate fat for the largest firms on the New York stock exchange, conducted by Systematic Financial Management Inc. on January 4, 1990:

Company	Corporate Fat (in millions)
IBM	$679
Mobil	670
AT&T	495
General Motors	490
Bellsouth	382
Amoco	347
Philip Morris	269
General Electric	263
G.T.E.	79

Every company has at least some corporate fat, especially if measured in any particular year. That is because in any single year the entity can find itself spending too heavily in such areas as capital spending, research, labor, or cost of sales. But, basically, corporate fat does represent overspending and it can be quantified! The table above shows that our largest companies excessively spent in their last fiscal year to maintain their growth rates. However, with the apparent softening in the economy, these companies have a financial cushion should they desire to cut expenses.

We can examine each of the components of discretionary items, and their proportion to total market value, in Figure 5–3:

The primary reason for the jump in discretionary expenses of Clorox in 1988 was its decision to spend $153 million on capital projects, substantially in excess of prior expenditures that were in

FIGURE 5–2
Clorox Co.: Free Cash Flow Analysis

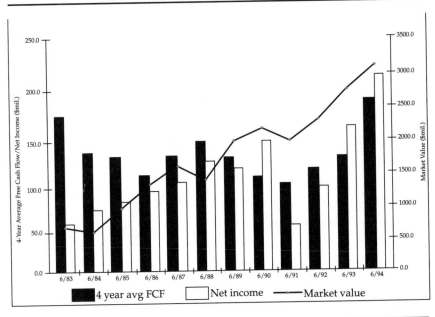

the range of $50 million to $60 million in prior years. Given that free cash flows grew nicely in subsequent years, the investment decision was prudent. Note that Clorox's capital expenditures pattern is lumpy, with large investments in 1988, 1990–1992, and smaller at other years. However, to assess the benefits of a capital expenditures program, one has to look at the long-term benefits of that program. In some cases, one finds that a firm writes down or writes off some of the expenditures made earlier. In Clorox's case, we can see that free cash flows continued to rise, indicating that capital expenditures were justified. However, we also find that the selling, general, and administrative expenses increased beyond their proper level in 1991, possibly because of these capital expenditures.

Note that the estimated free cash flow is reasonably close to those obtained under the direct method of estimating free cash flows. The two are not identical because the methodology of estimating the two was different. Let us now show another example of a firm that generated positive free cash flows from its operations in recent years, but that operates in the service sector of the economy.

FIGURE 5–3

Ratio of Discretionary Expenses of Clorox Co. to its Market Value:

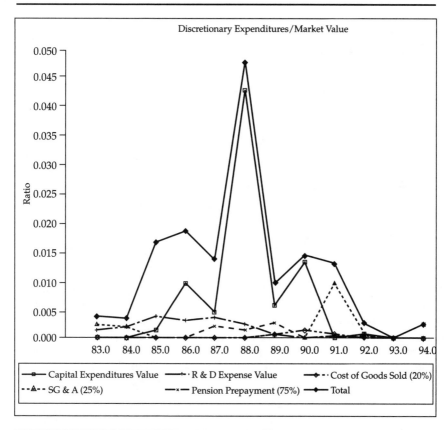

Discretionary Expenditures/Market Value

Legend:
—■— Capital Expenditures Value   —+·· R & D Expense Value   —◆·· Cost of Goods Sold (20%)
--▲-- SG & A (25%)   —×— Pension Prepayment (75%)   —◆— Total

Example

H&R Block is well-known for the tax-related services it provides to customers. However, it also provides computer information (Compuserve) and networking services to corporations and individuals, and also provides and invests in financial products for its customers.

For this example, we use the indirect method to estimate free cash flow. Also, to conserve space, we do not repeat in detail all the computations that were used in the prior example.

H&R Block Financial Statements

CONSOLIDATED STATEMENTS OF EARNINGS

Amounts in thousands, except per share amounts

	YEAR ENDED APRIL 30		
	1994	1993	1992
REVENUES:			
Service revenues	$1,118,566	$ 956,534	$ 865,914
Royalties	96,766	92,529	90,024
Investment income	15,256	15,038	20,089
Other income	8,089	10,162	10,082
	1,238,677	1,074,263	986,109
EXPENSES:			
Employee compensation and benefits	404,367	369,476	359,745
Occupancy and equipment	242,391	203,350	174,863
Marketing and advertising	60,783	47,118	44,869
Supplies, freight and postage	60,182	53,470	62,362
Other	162,698	124,955	97,483
Purchased research and development	25,072	—	—
	955,493	798,369	739,322
Earnings from continuing operations before taxes	283,184	275,894	246,787
Taxes on earnings	119,189	104,877	93,043
Net earnings from continuing operations	163,995	171,017	153,744
Net earnings from discontinued operations (less applicable taxes of $8,706, $9,688 and $8,964)	9,268	9,688	8,509
Net gain on sale of discontinued operations (less applicable taxes of $16,711)	27,265	—	—
Net earnings	$ 200,528	$ 180,705	$ 162,253
Earnings per share from continuing operations	$1.54	$1.59	$1.41
Earnings per share	$1.88	$1.68	$1.49

H&R Block Financial Statements

CONSOLIDATED BALANCE SHEETS

Amounts in thousands, except share data

	APRIL 30	
	1994	1993
ASSETS		
CURRENT ASSETS:		
Cash (including certificates of deposit of $23,519 and $36,074)	**$ 41,343**	$ 43,417
Marketable securities	**473,043**	291,347
Receivables, less allowance for doubtful accounts of $12,744 and $12,000	**165,858**	228,691
Prepaid expenses	**19,551**	26,483
Total current assets	**699,795**	589,938
INVESTMENTS AND OTHER ASSETS:		
Investments in marketable securities	**105,705**	104,762
Excess of cost over fair value of net tangible assets acquired,		
less accumulated amortization of $43,429 and $36,249	**67,679**	125,628
Other	**36,301**	37,120
	209,685	267,510
PROPERTY AND EQUIPMENT, at cost less accumulated		
depreciation and amortization of $192,481 and $172,444	**165,224**	148,386
	$1,074,704	$1,005,834
LIABILITIES AND STOCKHOLDERS' EQUITY		
CURRENT LIABILITIES:		
Notes payable	**$ —**	$ 37,167
Accounts payable, accrued expenses and deposits	**160,592**	132,321
Accrued salaries, wages and payroll taxes	**55,195**	53,495
Accrued taxes on earnings	**120,425**	106,943
Total current liabilities	**336,212**	329,926
OTHER NONCURRENT LIABILITIES	**30,617**	25,420
STOCKHOLDERS' EQUITY:		
Common stock, no par, stated value $.01 per share:		
authorized 200,000,000 shares	**1,089**	1,089
Additional paid-in capital	**90,552**	101,038
Retained earnings	**719,724**	643,757
	811,365	745,884
Less cost of common stock in treasury	**103,490**	95,396
	707,875	650,488
	$1,074,704	$1,005,834

See notes to consolidated financial statements.

20

H&R Block Financial Statements

CONSOLIDATED STATEMENTS OF CASH FLOWS

Amounts in thousands

	YEAR ENDED APRIL 30		
	1994	1993	1992
CASH FLOWS FROM OPERATING ACTIVITIES:			
NET EARNINGS	**$ 200,528**	$ 180,705	$ 162,253
Adjustments to reconcile net earnings to net cash provided:			
Depreciation and amortization	**57,117**	54,698	44,262
Provision for deferred taxes on earnings	**(2,735)**	(2,915)	(2,778)
Gain on sale of subsidiaries	**(27,265)**	—	(328)
Purchased research and development	**25,072**	—	—
Other noncurrent liabilities	**5,197**	4,276	4,392
Changes in assets and liabilities net of effects of purchase and disposition of subsidiaries:			
Receivables	**2,284**	43,171	114,455
Prepaid expenses	**(412)**	(4,619)	2,798
Net assets of discontinued operations	**(17,370)**	—	—
Accounts payable, accrued expenses and deposits	**31,000**	56,593	13,250
Accrued salaries, wages and payroll taxes	**14,659**	(6,672)	(1,913)
Accrued taxes on earnings	**(300)**	19,278	8,226
NET CASH PROVIDED BY OPERATING ACTIVITIES	**287,775**	344,515	344,617
CASH FLOWS FROM INVESTING ACTIVITIES:			
Purchases of marketable securities	**(1,522,609)**	(1,198,102)	(860,260)
Maturities of marketable securities	**1,339,970**	1,179,903	800,569
Purchases of property and equipment, net	**(83,744)**	(71,921)	(55,789)
Excess of cost over fair value of net tangible assets acquired, net of cash acquired	**(46,570)**	(10,981)	(12,224)
Proceeds from sale of subsidiaries	**188,500**	—	14,000
Proceeds from term loan to former subsidiary	**30,000**	—	—
Other, net	**(24,198)**	(13,241)	(4,410)
NET CASH USED IN INVESTING ACTIVITIES	**(118,651)**	(114,342)	(118,114)
CASH FLOWS FROM FINANCING ACTIVITIES:			
Repayments of notes payable	**(2,435,254)**	(1,717,226)	(901,698)
Proceeds from issuance of notes payable	**2,398,087**	1,653,061	779,495
Dividends paid	**(115,451)**	(103,462)	(91,842)
Payments to acquire treasury shares	**(68,899)**	(94,763)	(86,505)
Proceeds from stock options exercised	**50,319**	62,158	55,810
Other, net	**—**	—	(4,984)
NET CASH USED IN FINANCING ACTIVITIES	**(171,198)**	(200,232)	(249,724)
Net increase (decrease) in cash	**(2,074)**	29,941	(23,221)
Cash at beginning of the year	**43,417**	13,476	36,697
Cash at end of the year	**$ 41,343**	$ 43,417	$ 13,476
SUPPLEMENTAL DISCLOSURES OF CASH FLOW INFORMATION:			
Income taxes paid	**$ 131,124**	$ 98,202	$ 84,597
Interest paid	**4,169**	5,933	5,786

See notes to consolidated financial statements.

21

We add the following items which represent increases to free cash flow:

Year	4/83	4/84	4/85	4/86	4/87	4/88
Cash and equivalents—change	-9.2	41.6	23.1	6.6	54.3	8.0
Cash dividends	23.2	25.1	28.6	32.6	36.8	43.0
Increase in investments	12.5	22.9	9.5	24.4	37.2	295.6
Stock purchases	0.0	0.0	21.5	0.0	6.6	76.1
Reduction in long-term debt	0.7	0.4	0.2	0.3	0.9	0.2
Acquisitions	1.8	6.5	2.5	37.6	2.0	4.6
Short-term investments—change	20.7	-17.7	-59.2	25.6	-46.1	7.3

Year	4/89	4/90	4/91	4/92	4/93	4/94
Cash and equivalents—change	-17.3	8.4	-6.5	-23.2	29.9	-2.1
Cash dividends	51.6	64.5	79.0	91.8	103.5	115.5
Increase in investments	547.5	755.7	595.1	860.3	1,198.1	1,522.6
Stock purchases	0.0	38.8	24.2	86.5	94.8	68.9
Reduction in long-term debt	0.1	0.0	0.0	0.0	0.0	0.0
Acquisitions	5.5	14.1	57.0	12.2	11.0	46.6
Short-term investments—change	-54.9	20.6	5.1	-69.3	-30.5	-181.7

We subtract these items that represent decreases of free cash flow:

Year	4/83	4/84	4/85	4/86	4/87	4/88
Sale of PPE	0.0	0.0	0.0	0.0	0.0	0.0
Investing activities—other	-0.6	-0.7	-3.0	-0.5	-2.1	1.4
Sale of common and preferred	1.4	11.5	4.5	19.2	28.7	51.8
Sale of investments	9.6	12.1	46.3	8.5	11.2	290.3
Increase in long-term debt	0.0	0.0	0.0	0.0	0.0	0.0
Changes in current debt	-0.9	51.1	29.2	-33.7	-65.4	32.5
Financing activities—other	0.0	0.0	0.0	0.1	8.2	0.0

Year	4/89	4/90	4/91	4/92	4/93	4/94
Sale of PPE	0.0	0.0	0.0	0.0	0.0	0.0
Investing activities—other	-4.4	-1.7	12.7	9.6	-13.2	194.3
Sale of common and preferred	15.6	37.7	30.6	55.8	62.2	50.3
Sale of investments	511.9	722.5	578.5	800.6	1,179.9	1,340.0
Increase in long-term debt	0.0	0.0	0.0	0.0	0.0	0.0
Changes in current debt	53.2	33.7	-28.6	-122.2	-64.2	-37.2
Financing activities—other	0.0	0.4	-0.2	-5.0	0.0	0.0

We now estimate the discretionary items. However, Standard & Poor's Compustat, which is the popular database we use to retrieve the information, does not provide a breakdown of selling, general, and administrative expenses, or advertising expenses for H&R Block and includes them as part of cost of goods sold. Furthermore, the firm does not have pension assets. Thus, we have fewer discretionary items estimated for H&R Block than for Clorox.

Year	4/83	4/84	4/85	4/86	4/87	4/88
Three-year growth rate capital expenditures	37.0	4.5	17.7	28.1	−7.9	−1.9
Three-year growth rate COGS	15.8	13.7	16.7	22.0	21.5	18.6
Difference in rates × latest cap exp	2.3	0.0	0.3	1.4	0.0	0.0
Three-year growth rate R&D	0.0	0.0	0.0	0.0	0.0	0.0
Diff in rates × latest R&D	0.0	0.0	0.0	0.0	0.0	0.0
COGS percent of sales	83.8	79.2	79.2	80.3	81.8	80.8
Four-year avg COGS percent of sales	80.9	81.3	81.1	80.6	80.1	80.5
Sales	309.5	399.9	475.9	591.3	686.6	778.1
Excess COGS	9.0	0.0	0.0	0.0	11.7	2.4
20 percent of difference	1.8	0.0	0.0	0.0	2.3	0.5

Year	4/89	4/90	4/91	4/92	4/93	4/94
Three-year growth rate capital expenditures	10.8	20.1	11.1	28.7	37.2	29.7
Three-year growth rate COGS	14.2	13.5	13.5	13.7	12.8	0.4
Difference in rates × latest cap exp	0.0	1.8	0.0	8.4	17.6	24.5
Three-year growth rate R&D	0.0	0.0	0.0	0.0	0.0	0.0
Diff in rates × latest R&D	0.0	0.0	0.0	0.0	0.0	0.0
COGS percent of sales	81.2	80.1	78.5	70.0	68.6	72.2
Four-year avg COGS percent of sales	81.0	81.0	80.2	77.4	74.3	72.3
Sales	876.9	1,027.6	1,162.7	986.1	1,074.3	1,238.7
Excess COGS	1.6	0.0	0.0	0.0	0.0	0.0
20 percent of difference	0.3	0.0	0.0	0.0	0.0	0.0

We can now compute the free cash flow:

Year	4/83	4/84	4/85	4/86	4/87	4/88
Discretionary items:						
Capital expenditures						
value	2.3	0.0	0.3	1.4	0.0	0.0
R&D expense value	0.0	0.0	0.0	0.0	0.0	0.0
Cost of goods sold (20%)	1.8	0.0	0.0	0.0	2.3	0.5
SG&A (25%)	0.0	0.0	0.0	0.0	0.0	0.0
Pension prepayment (75%)	0.0	0.0	0.0	0.0	0.0	0.0
Advertising value	0.0	0.0	0.0	0.0	0.0	0.0
Net free cash flow	3.2	40.2	67.8	83.6	205.5	44.9

Year	4/89	4/90	4/91	4/92	4/93	4/94
Discretionary items:						
Capital expenditures						
value	0.0	1.8	0.0	8.4	17.6	24.5
R&D expense value	0.0	0.0	0.0	0.0	0.0	0.0
Cost of goods sold (20%)	0.3	0.0	0.0	0.0	0.0	0.0
SG&A (25%)	0.0	0.0	0.0	0.0	0.0	0.0
Pension prepayment (75%)	0.0	0.0	0.0	0.0	0.0	0.0
Advertising value	0.0	0.0	0.0	0.0	0.0	0.0
Net free cash flow	66.3	70.2	150.8	366.6	320.7	410.2

As before, we concentrate on the four-year average free cash flow and compare it to the market value and net income of the firm. See Figure 5–4.

Year	4/83	4/84	4/85	4/86	4/87	4/88
Four-year average						
free cash flow	73.5	67.5	65.5	48.7	99.3	100.5
Net income	40.8	48.1	55.5	60.1	73.3	87.9
Market value	483.0	482.6	602.2	1,072.4	1,357.8	1,317.7

Year	4/89	4/90	4/91	4/92	4/93	4/94
Four-year average						
free cash flow	100.1	96.7	83.0	163.5	227.1	312.1
Net income	100.2	123.5	140.1	162.3	180.7	200.5
Market value	1,417.6	1,828.7	2,748.7	3,451.1	3,682.5	3,854.3

FIGURE 5–4
H&R Block: Free Cash Flow Analysis

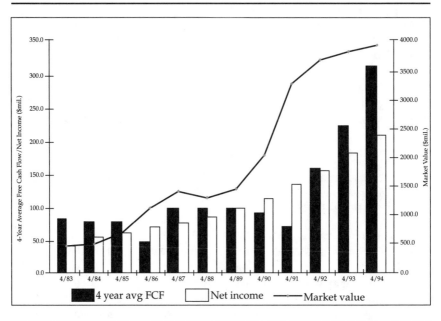

Note the similarity of behavior in the graph between the four-year average free cash flow and the market value of H&R Block. This is a nice example of a growing firm, where both free cash flows and market values increased in recent years. Let us now move to another growth company that for a long time displayed negative free cash flows, but had nevertheless enjoyed an increasing market value, until it stopped being perceived as a growth company.

Example

Toys "R" Us Inc. reports the following results for the year ending on January 28, 1994:

Toys "R" Us: Consolidated Balance Sheets

TOYS"R"US, INC. AND SUBSIDIARIES

CONSOLIDATED BALANCE SHEETS

(In thousands)

	January 29, 1994	January 30, 1993
ASSETS		
Current Assets:		
Cash and cash equivalents	$ 791,893	$ 763,721
Accounts and other receivables	98,534	69,385
Merchandise inventories	1,777,569	1,498,671
Prepaid expenses and other	40,400	52,731
Total Current Assets	2,708,396	2,384,508
Property and Equipment:		
Real estate, net	2,035,673	1,876,835
Other, net	1,148,794	926,715
Total Property and Equipment	3,184,467	2,803,550
Other Assets	256,746	134,794
	$ 6,149,609	$ 5,322,852
LIABILITIES AND STOCKHOLDERS' EQUITY		
Current Liabilities:		
Short-term borrowings	$ 239,862	$ 120,772
Accounts payable	1,156,411	941,375
Accrued expenses and other current liabilities	471,782	361,661
Income taxes payable	206,996	163,841
Total Current Liabilities	2,075,051	1,587,649
Deferred Income Taxes	202,663	175,430
Long-Term Debt	710,365	660,488
Obligations Under Capital Leases	13,248	10,264
Stockholders' Equity:		
Common stock	29,794	29,794
Additional paid-in capital	454,061	465,494
Retained earnings	3,012,806	2,529,853
Foreign currency translation adjustments	(56,021)	14,317
Treasury shares, at cost	(292,358)	(150,437)
	3,148,282	2,889,021
	$ 6,149,609	$ 5,322,852

See notes to consolidated financial statements.

Toys "R" Us: Consolidated Statements of Cash Flows

TOYS"R"US, INC. AND SUBSIDIARIES

CONSOLIDATED STATEMENTS OF CASH FLOWS

(In thousands)			*Year Ended*
	January 29, 1994	*January 30, 1993*	*February 1, 1992*
CASH FLOWS FROM OPERATING ACTIVITIES			
Net earnings	$ 482,953	$ 437,524	$ 339,529
Adjustments to reconcile net earnings to net cash provided by operating activities:			
Depreciation and amortization	133,370	119,034	100,701
Deferred income taxes	36,534	13,998	15,817
Changes in operating assets and liabilities:			
Accounts and other receivables	(29,149)	(5,307)	9,092
Merchandise inventories	(278,898)	(108,066)	(115,436)
Prepaid expenses and other operating assets	(39,448)	(36,249)	(16,176)
Accounts payable, accrued expenses and other liabilities	325,165	112,232	462,152
Income taxes payable	26,588	40,091	7,071
Total adjustments	174,162	135,733	463,221
Net cash provided by operating activities	657,115	573,257	802,750
CASH FLOWS FROM INVESTING ACTIVITIES			
Capital expenditures, net	(555,258)	(421,564)	(548,538)
Other assets	(58,383)	(22,175)	(17,110)
Net cash used in investing activities	(613,641)	(443,739)	(565,648)
CASH FLOWS FROM FINANCING ACTIVITIES			
Short-term borrowings, net	119,090	(170,887)	(94,811)
Long-term borrowings	40,576	318,035	197,802
Long-term debt repayments	(1,335)	(7,926)	(1,590)
Exercise of stock options	29,879	86,323	32,707
Share repurchase program	(183,233)	(27,244)	–
Net cash provided by financing activities	4,977	198,301	134,108
Effect of exchange rate changes on cash and cash equivalents	(20,279)	(8,691)	38,378
CASH AND CASH EQUIVALENTS			
Increase during year	28,172	319,128	409,588
Beginning of year	763,721	444,593	35,005
End of year	$ 791,893	$ 763,721	$ 444,593

SUPPLEMENTAL DISCLOSURES OF CASH FLOW INFORMATION

The Company considers its highly liquid investments purchased as part of its daily cash management activities to be cash equivalents. During the years ended January 29, 1994, January 30, 1993 and February 1, 1992, the Company made income tax payments of $220,229, $151,722 and $155,469 and interest payments (net of amounts capitalized) of $104,281, $83,584 and $46,763, respectively.

See notes to consolidated financial statements.

Toys "R" Us: Consolidated Statements of Stockholders' Equity

TOYS"R"US, INC. AND SUBSIDIARIES

CONSOLIDATED STATEMENTS OF STOCKHOLDERS' EQUITY

(In thousands)	Shares	Amount	In Treasury Amount	Additional paid-in capital	Retained earnings
Balance, February 2, 1991	297,938	$ 29,794	$ (129,340)	$ 353,924	$ 1,752,800
Net earnings for the year	–	–	–	–	339,529
Exercise of stock options (1,640 Treasury shares)	–	–	1,623	15,259	–
Tax benefit from exercise of stock options	–	–	–	15,620	–
Balance, February 1, 1992	297,938	29,794	(127,717)	384,803	2,092,329
Net earnings for the year	–	–	–	–	437,524
Share repurchase program (708 Treasury shares)	–	–	(27,244)	–	–
Exercise of stock options (4,479 Treasury shares)	–	–	4,524	35,301	–
Tax benefit from exercise of stock options	–	–	–	45,390	–
Balance, January 30, 1993	297,938	29,794	(150,437)	465,494	2,529,853
Net earnings for the year	–	–	–	–	482,953
Share repurchase program (4,940 Treasury shares)	–	–	(183,233)	–	–
Exercise of stock options (1,394 Treasury shares)	–	–	41,312	(21,464)	–
Tax benefit from exercise of stock options	–	–	–	10,031	–
Balance, January 29, 1994	297,938	$ 29,794	$ (292,358)	$ 454,061	$ 3,012,806

See notes to consolidated financial statements.

Toys "R" Us: Consolidated Balance Sheets

TOYS"R"US, INC. AND SUBSIDIARIES

CONSOLIDATED STATEMENTS OF EARNINGS

(In thousands except per share information)	January 29, 1994	January 30, 1993	February 1, 1992
Net sales	$ 7,946,067	$ 7,169,290	$ 6,124,209
Costs and expenses:			
Cost of sales	5,494,766	4,968,555	4,286,639
Selling, advertising, general and administrative	1,497,011	1,342,262	1,153,576
Depreciation and amortization	133,370	119,034	100,701
Interest expense	72,283	69,134	57,885
Interest and other income	(24,116)	(18,719)	(13,521)
	7,173,314	6,480,266	5,585,280
Earnings before taxes on income	772,753	689,024	538,929
Taxes on income	289,800	251,500	199,400
Net earnings	$ 482,953	$ 437,524	$ 339,529
Earnings per share	$ 1.63	$ 1.47	$ 1.15

See notes to consolidated financial statements.

For this example, too, we use the indirect method to estimate free cash flow and do not repeat in detail all the computations that we used in the first example.

We add the following items which represent increases to free cash flow:

Year	1/83	1/84	1/85	1/86	1/87	1/88
Change in cash and equivalents	11.1	101.3	−20.6	−79.1	−51.8	−38.4
Cash dividends	0.0	0.0	0.0	0.0	0.0	0.0
Increase in investments	0.0	0.0	0.0	0.0	0.0	0.0
Stock purchases	0.0	0.0	0.0	0.0	0.0	0.0
Reduction of long-term debt	52.3	2.1	2.9	3.8	2.0	1.9
Acquisitions	0.0	0.0	0.0	0.0	0.0	0.0
Short-term investments— change	0.0	0.0	0.0	0.0	0.0	0.0

Year	1/89	1/90	1/91	1/92	1/93	1/94
Change in cash and equivalents	76.9	−82.0	−5.9	409.6	319.1	28.2
Cash dividends	0.0	0.0	0.0	0.0	0.0	0.0
Increase in investments	0.0	0.0	0.0	0.0	0.0	0.0
Stock purchases	36.6	54.2	32.7	0.0	27.2	183.2
Reduction of long-term debt	3.9	1.2	10.9	1.6	7.9	1.3
Acquisitions	0.0	0.0	0.0	0.0	0.0	0.0
Short-term investments— change	0.0	0.0	0.0	0.0	0.0	0.0

We subtract these items that represent decreases of free cash flow:

Year	1/83	1/84	1/85	1/86	1/87	1/88
Sale of PPE	4.4	1.8	2.0	0.0	0.0	0.0
Investing activities—other	−1.8	−4.6	−13.8	0.0	0.0	13.8
Sale of common and preferred	53.5	44.0	8.4	16.1	25.0	15.2
Sale of investments	0.0	0.0	0.0	0.0	0.0	0.0
Increase long-term debt	6.2	15.1	36.1	2.5	0.0	96.6
Changes in current debt	0.3	0.0	20.1	−19.1	−1.1	17.7
Financing activities—other	−9.1	38.3	0.0	11.1	11.0	0.0

Year	1/89	1/90	1/91	1/92	1/93	1/94
Sale of PPE	0.0	0.0	0.0	0.0	0.0	0.0
Investing activities—other	-4.1	-5.1	17.4	-17.1	-22.2	-58.4
Sale of common and preferred	52.4	19.9	30.3	32.7	86.3	29.9
Sale of investments	0.0	0.0	0.0	0.0	0.0	0.0
Increase long-term debt	0.7	0.0	33.2	197.8	318.0	40.6
Changes in current debt	58.5	129.4	181.0	-94.8	-170.9	119.1
Financing activities—other	0.0	0.0	0.0	0.0	0.0	0.0

We now estimate the discretionary items. However, Compustat does not provide a separate breakdown of advertising expenses for Toys "R" Us in recent years and includes it in selling, general, and administrative expenses. Furthermore, the firm does not have pension assets. Thus, we have fewer discretionary items estimated for Toys "R" Us than for Clorox.

Year	1/83	1/84	1/85	1/86	1/87	1/88
Three-year growth rate capital expenditures	56.5	31.7	34.6	50.3	38.2	23.0
Three-year growth rate COGS	29.9	29.6	29.2	23.9	22.9	24.0
Difference in rates × latest capital expenditures	18.1	2.0	9.1	58.6	39.7	0.0
Three-year growth rate R&D	0.0	0.0	0.0	0.0	0.0	0.0
Difference in rates × latest R&D	0.0	0.0	0.0	0.0	0.0	0.0
COGS percent of sales	67.7	66.8	66.9	66.9	68.2	68.8
Four-year average COGS percent of sales	67.4	67.5	67.0	67.1	67.2	67.7
Sales	1,041.7	1,319.6	1,701.7	1,976.1	2,444.9	3,136.6
Excess COGS	2.9	0.0	0.0	0.0	24.7	33.0
20 percent of difference	0.6	0.0	0.0	0.0	4.9	6.6
SGA (excluding R&D + Adv) percent of sales	17.7	17.5	18.6	18.7	17.0	17.1
Four-year average SGA percent of sales	18.7	18.4	18.2	18.1	17.9	17.8
Sales	1,041.7	1,319.6	1,701.7	1,976.1	2,444.9	3,136.6
Excess SGA	0.0	0.0	6.0	11.6	0.0	0.0
25 percent of difference	0.0	0.0	1.5	2.9	0.0	0.0
Advertising expense	22.1	23.1	28.5	38.8	43.2	47.0
Advertising expense percent of sales	2.1	1.8	1.7	2.0	1.8	1.5
Four-year average advertising percent of sales	2.3	2.2	2.0	1.9	1.8	1.7
Excess advertising	0.0	0.0	0.0	1.7	0.0	0.0
50 percent of difference	0.0	0.0	0.0	0.8	0.0	0.0

Year	1/89	1/90	1/91	1/92	1/93	1/94
Three-year growth rate capital expenditures	14.6	11.8	17.6	20.7	4.4	−0.5
Three-year growth rate COGS	28.0	25.9	20.9	15.7	14.3	13.2
Difference in rates × latest capital expenditures	0.0	0.0	0.0	27.5	0.0	0.0
Three-year growth rate R&D	0.0	0.0	0.0	0.0	0.0	0.0
Difference in rates × latest R&D	0.0	0.0	0.0	0.0	0.0	0.0
COGS percent of sales	69.2	69.1	69.3	70.0	69.3	69.2
Four-year average COGS percent of sales	68.3	68.8	69.1	69.4	69.4	69.4
Sales	4,000.2	4,787.8	5,510.0	6,124.2	7,169.3	7,946.1
Excess COGS	35.3	14.6	13.4	36.1	0.0	0.0
20 percent of difference	7.1	2.9	2.7	7.2	0.0	0.0
SGA (excluding R&D + Adv.) percent of sales	17.1	17.0	17.6	18.8	18.7	18.8
Four-year average SGA percent of sales	17.5	17.1	17.2	17.6	18.0	18.5
Sales	4,000.2	4,787.8	5,510.0	6,124.2	7,169.3	7,946.1
Excess SGA	0.0	0.0	20.9	72.7	48.5	27.0
25 percent of difference	0.0	0.0	5.2	18.2	12.1	6.8
Advertising expense	51.0	51.3	55.1	0.0	0.0	0.0
Advertising expense percent of sales	1.3	1.1	1.0	#N/A	#N/A	#N/A
Four-year average advertising percent of sales	1.6	1.4	1.2	#N/A	#N/A	#N/A
Excess advertising	0.0	0.0	0.0	#N/A	#N/A	#N/A
50 percent of difference	0.0	0.0	0.0	0.0	0.0	0.0

We can now compute the free cash flow:

Year	1/83	1/84	1/85	1/86	1/87	1/88
Discretionary items:						
Capital expenditures value	18.1	2.0	9.1	58.6	39.7	0.0
R&D expense value	0.0	0.0	0.0	0.0	0.0	0.0
Cost of goods sold (20%)	0.6	0.0	0.0	0.0	4.9	6.6
SG&A (25%)	0.0	0.0	1.5	2.9	0.0	0.0
Pension prepayment (75%)	0.0	0.0	0.0	0.0	0.0	0.0
Advertising value	0.0	0.0	0.0	0.0	0.0	0.0
Net free cash flow	28.6	10.8	−59.9	−23.4	−40.0	−173.2

Year	1/89	1/90	1/91	1/92	1/93	1/94
Discretionary items:						
Capital expenditures value	0.0	0.0	0.0	27.5	0.0	0.0
R&D expense value	0.0	0.0	0.0	0.0	0.0	0.0
Cost of goods sold (20%)	7.1	2.9	2.7	7.2	0.0	0.0
SG&A (25%)	0.0	0.0	5.2	18.2	12.1	6.8
Pension prepayment (75%)	0.0	0.0	0.0	0.0	0.0	0.0
Advertising value	0.0	0.0	0.0	0.0	0.0	0.0
Net free cash flow	17.0	−167.9	−216.3	345.5	155.1	88.3

As before, we concentrate on the four-year average free cash flow and compare it to the market value and net income of the firm. See Figure 5–5.

Year	1/83	1/84	1/85	1/86	1/87	1/88
Four-year average free cash flow	115.2	88.2	37.4	−11.0	−28.1	−74.1
Net income	64.2	92.3	111.4	119.8	152.2	203.9
Market value	1,418.9	1,733.4	2,494.8	2,862.1	4,513.9	4,109.8

Year	1/89	1/90	1/91	1/92	1/93	1/94
Four-year average free cash flow	−54.9	−91.0	−135.1	−5.4	29.1	93.2
Net income	268.0	321.1	326.0	339.5	437.5	483.0
Market value	4,849.1	7,044.1	7,874.6	9,510.6	11,283.1	8,153.1

Note that the average free cash flow of Toys "R" Us was consistently negative between 1986 and 1992 due to the high expansion rate of the firm. Normally, it is expected that a firm will be able to generate free cash flows from its operations rather than have to finance these negative free cash flows. If a firm shows a consistent pattern of negative free cash flows, it must continuously find sources of funds for its operations; mostly through borrowing or issuance of additional equity. A firm like Toys "R" Us, which experienced a high growth rate in both sales and operating cash flows and which was perceived by the financial

FIGURE 5–5
Toys "R" Us: Free Cash Flow Analysis

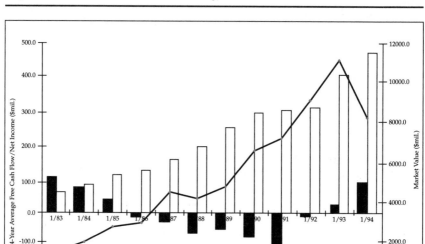

community as a firm with a high future growth rate in operating cash flow, did, in fact, have little trouble raising additional capital for expansion.[11] In the long run, a firm that consistently generates negative free cash flows, if it cannot continually raise new capital, will shrink to the point that it has to liquidate or cease to exist.

A question that needs to be addressed is whether the market ever rewards firms with negative free cash flows. A cursory look into our previous example, Toys "R" Us, indicates that, indeed, the market may reward firms with negative cash flows. Figure 5–5 shows the behavior of stock prices for the firm over the period 1983–1994. It is clear that the stock price showed an

---

[11]This is indeed what Toys "R" Us was able to do in those years. It issued additional debt and additional equity to finance new store openings.

increasing trend over the years 1983–1992, although Toys "R" Us was a negative free cash flow generator over that period. Perhaps one reason for the success of Toys "R" Us stock during that period was that growth stocks did extremely well during that bull market, and Toys "R" Us was the quintessential growth company.

In general, investors may desire to own stocks in a firm that proved to be a net borrower of cash if its operating cash flows grew at a high rate and if there was a high probability that this high growth would continue to be the reason for negative free cash flows. Also, investors in such a firm probably perceive that the expansion of the firm causes negative free cash flows, and that without the expansion the firm can generate positive free cash flows. Note that in 1993 and 1994, when Toys "R" Us started generating positive free cash flows, its market value began decreasing, as investors suspected that the historical high expansion rate of the firm was over. Toys "R" Us began repurchasing its own stock in an attempt to boost its stock price.

Chapter 8 will be devoted to portfolio selection rules and backtesting of a portfolio that are based on investment in firms with low free cash flows multiples.

An alternative criterion for investment is the recovery rate, or the relationship between operating or free cash flows and total assets of the business. This represents a rate of return on assets that are deployed in the business. Such an analysis was conducted by Systematic Financial Management Inc. on September 12, 1989, and is reproduced below. Note that the table is based on operating cash flows as a proportion of total assets, but includes also free cash flows as a percentage of market value of firms. Note also the superior excess returns enjoyed by these firms.

Example

In a recent article published by the *CFO Magazine* in October 1994, National Semiconductor Corp. is described as using a measure that is very similar to the cash recovery rate in assessing the performance of its business units. In particular, managers are judged by the ratio of cash flow generated by the business unit to the cash invested in that business. This ratio has to exceed the cost of capital of the firm.

"Recovery Rate" Leaders

	12 mos. O.C.F./ assets	F.C.F./ market value	O.C.F./ assets (LFY)	4-yr. av. O.C.F./ assets	Market value $ mil.	52-wk. pr. percent change vs. 500
Adobe Systems	0.37	0.89	0.42	1.80	504.2	-6.9
Battle Mtn. Gold	0.29	3.32	0.34	0.69	935.1	-30.0
Buffets Inc.	0.29	3.21	0.33	0.62	149.6	59.2
Compuchem Corp.	0.42	0.65	0.45	0.60	67.7	69.1
Datakey Inc.	0.52	0.65	0.35	0.77	21.8	-21.2
Disney (Walt) Co.	0.31	1.37	0.35	0.51	13416.4	32.4
Georgia Gulf Corp.	0.51	10.70	0.42	0.61	976.6	-6.4
Glaxo Holdings PLC	0.29	4.60	0.33	0.56	16935.1	9.0
King World Production	0.32	4.57	0.79	0.98	727.7	16.9
Micron Technology	0.30	1.01	0.34	0.85	579.4	-37.8
PSE Inc.	0.31	9.63	0.47	0.62	64.1	6.3
Pacificare Health Sys.	0.37	5.55	0.41	0.77	178.6	177.7
Price (T. Rowe) Assoc.	0.33	5.32	0.31	0.50	333.2	13.8
Reuters Holdings PLC	0.30	2.52	0.31	0.48	5516.1	11.9
Sbarro Inc.	0.31	0.86	0.33	0.67	301.5	43.9
Southern Mineral Corp.	0.49	3.11	0.48	0.57	16.1	0.5
Total System Services	0.29	1.03	0.32	0.48	400.8	-6.3
Average	0.38	3.47	0.44	0.71	2419.1	19.5

O.C.F. = Operating Cash Flow
F.C.F. = Free Cash Flow
One of the best measures of corporate performance is the "recovery rate," the relationship between funds provided by operations (O.C.F.) and funds invested in the business (assets). The recovery rate can be considered an index of management's ability to deploy effectively (and earn a good return on) corporate assets. The companies listed above have the highest and most consistent recovery rates, as well as positive free cash flow (F.C.F.).

Note that this ratio is another way of restating free cash flow—operating cash flow divided by cumulative cash outflows required to generate these operating cash flows.

Finally, we provide below a list of the largest free cash flow generators for 1993.

TABLE 5–6
Largest Generator of Free Cash Flow and Operating Cash Flow

		1993 Free Cash Flow
1	Ford Motor Co	7,662.0
2	Philip Morris Cos Inc	5,766.0
3	Intl Business Machines Corp	5,599.3
4	General Electric Co	5,509.6
5	Exxon Corp	4,801.4
6	General Motors Corp-Pre FAS	4,677.9
7	General Electric Co-Pre FAS	3,779.6
8	Royal Dutch/Shell Grp Comb	3,728.9
9	General Motors Corp	3,409.0
10	AT&T Corp	3,387.8
11	Pohang Iron & Steel Co Ltd	3,064.4
12	Nestle SA-Spon ADR	2,771.4
13	Mitsui & Co Ltd-ADR	2,713.3
14	Telefonica de Espana-ADR	2,669.5
15	USG Corp	2,607.0
16	Daimler-Benz AG-Spon ADR	2,562.0
17	Mobil Corp	2,443.8
18	Philip Morris Cos-Pre FASB	2,297.0
19	Merck & Co	2,279.1
20	Royal Dutch Pet-NY Reg	2,237.3
21	Britich Telecom PLC-ADR	2,228.0
22	Total SA-Spon ADR	2,210.6
23	Coca-Cola Co	2,159.0
24	Bristol Myers Squibb	2,124.4
25	DuPont (EI) de Nemours	1,773.6

TABLE 5–6
(*concluded*)

		1993 Operating Cash Flow
1	General Motors Corp	14,655.8
2	Ford Motor Co	14,007.0
3	Royal Dutch/Shell Grp Comb	12,437.0
4	Exxon Corp	11,503.0
5	General Motors Corp-Pre FA	11,406.3
6	General Electric Co	10,187.0
7	Intl Business Machines Corp	8,327.0
8	Royal Dutch Pet-NY Reg	7,462.0
9	Ford motor Co.-Pre FASB	7,389.0
10	AT&T Corp	7,129.0
11	Philip Morris Cos Inc	6,967.0
12	Hitaci Ltd-ADR	6,681.8
13	British Telecom PLC-ADR	6,124.0
14	Daimler-Benz AG-Spon ADR	5,699.0
15	Mobil Corp	5,620.0
16	DuPont (EI) de Nemours	5,380.0
17	General Electric Co-Pre FAS	5,277.0
18	GTE Corp	5,277.0
19	Shell Tran&Trade-NY SH	4,975.0
20	BellSouth Corp	4,786.2
21	Toyota Motor Corp-ADR	4727.3
22	British Petroleum PLC-ADR	4,692.5
23	Mitsui & Co Ltd-ADR	4,593.3
24	BellSouth Telecommunicatio	4,357.0
25	Elf Aquitaine-Spon ADR	4,353.0

STABILITY OF FREE CASH FLOWS

An important element in the analysis of free cash flows is not only the average free cash flow over the most recent four years (and the rate of growth in free cash flows) but also the stability of free cash flows. Firms that are subject to wide fluctuations in free cash flows may be less desirable candidates for investors who are risk-averse. Thus, the cash flow analyst should measure not only the average cash flow but also the variability of free cash flows during the available years. This can be done by eye-balling the free cash flows for the investment candidates, or by a construction of an index, such as the four-year average free cash flow divided by the standard deviation of annual free cash flows. Let us illustrate this index by focusing on the three firms we analyzed in this chapter.

Firm (1)	4-Year Average Free Cash Flow (2)	Standard Deviation of Annual Free Cash Flow (3)	Stability Index (column 2 divided by column 3)
Clorox	$184.5	$53.7	3.43
H&R Block	$312.1	$127.5	2.45
Toys "R" Us	$93.2	$150.3	0.62

As can be seen from this table, Clorox is the most stable firm among the three in terms of its annual free cash flows, whereas Toys "R" Us is the least stable. This seems intuitively reasonable given the lines of business that the three firms are in. Clorox products are the most necessary for daily life, and demand for its products is the most inelastic among the three firms. Thus, it is expected to have the most stable operations in terms of free cash flows. H&R Block provides services that are more dependent on the general economy and are therefore more cyclical. Toys "R" Us is almost completely dependent on economic conditions for sales of its products and its sales are very seasonal. Thus, it should have the least stable operations and cash flows among the three firms.

We can create such an index, or similar other measures to rank all securities we consider for investment. Whereas this index was based on a linear relationship between the average free cash flow and the standard deviation, other measures of the relationship can be used depending on the preferences of the investor.

Chapter Six

Security Valuation Based on Free Cash Flow

INTRODUCTION

In the last chapter, we defined free cash flow and showed several methods of estimating it. In this chapter, we use the definition of free cash flow to determine the value of a firm's securities. Valuation is important because it provides an assessment of a particular security's attractiveness as an investment and to the firm it means to raise capital. The investor is able to compare the security's current market price with its assessed value to determine whether a wide gap exists between the two. If current market prices and the assessed value agree with each other, the investor may decide to continue holding the security. If the assessed value is lower than the current market price, the investor may decide to sell, or take a short position, in the stock. If the assessed value is higher than current market prices, the investor may want to purchase (additional) shares and capitalize on future market increases in prices.

A similar approach can be used by a portfolio manager in making portfolio decisions. The portfolio may be selected on the basis of criteria that point undervalued securities. In addition, the portfolio selection rules may include other restrictions on firms that are included in the portfolio. For example, the portfolio manager may place restrictions regarding minimum size, minimum growth rate in sales or cash flows, stability of cash flows, or maximum leverage. In this chapter, we will present the theoretical foundation for an investment strategy based on free cash flow, relying on a model of security valuation.

THE CONSTANT-GROWTH DIVIDEND MODEL

Most valuation models assume that the price of a security is equal to the present value of dividends that are received on the security throughout its life. The main assumptions in these models relate to the discount rate used to value future dividends in current dollars and the pattern of cash dividends in the future. The valuation models vary in their assumptions about the pattern of future dividends and the methods to estimate those future dividends. Most models assume that the discount rate is constant across periods. This is not a bad assumption because the present value of any stream of future cash flows using a varying discount rate across periods can be converted to the same present value using a constant discount rate across periods.

The first equation in the valuation model can be written as:

$$P_t = \sum_{i=t+1}^{\infty} \frac{E(D_i)}{(1+r)^{i-t}} \tag{1}$$

In this equation, P_t is the market value of the firm at the end of period t, r is the required rate of return on investment in the firm (assumed to be equal across periods), and D_t is the dividend at period t. Note that the equation takes the sum of all future dividends (indicated by the summation sign Σ) from the following period $(t+1)$ through infinity (∞). In each period i, the dividend is discounted to the end of period t by dividing the dividend into one plus the discount rate to the power of $i-t$, which is equal to the number of periods until the dividend is paid. For example, the dividend at period $t+2$ will be discounted to the end of period t by dividing it into $(1+r)$ to the power of 2.

The constant-growth dividend model assumes that dividends grow at a constant rate, g, every period. Thus, assuming that the firm paid a dividend D_t in period t, the dividend in every subsequent period i, will be simply $D_t(1+g)^{i-t}$, the dividend in period t multiplied by the compounded growth rate g for the periods subsequent to period t. Substituting back in equation (1), we get:

$$P_t = \sum_{i=t+1}^{\infty} \frac{D_t(1+g)^{i-t}}{(1+r)^{i-t}} \tag{2}$$

Since D_t is not dependent on the index i and is equal at every period subsequently to period t, we can simplify equation (2) to yield:

$$P_t = D_t \sum_{i=t+1}^{\infty} \frac{(1+g)^{i-t}}{(1+r)^{i-t}} \qquad (3)$$

The last term in equation (3) is a sum of a geometric series, which grows every period by a factor of $(1+g)/(1+r)$. Assuming that $r > g$, the series will converge to $(1+g)/(r-g)$. Thus, equation (3) will become:

$$P_t = D_t \frac{(1+g)}{(r-g)} \qquad (4)$$

Example

To put equation (4) into practical use, let us examine NCH Corp., which at the end of 1993 had a price of about $62 per share. During 1993, NCH paid out a dividend of $2 per share. Assume that NCH had an expected growth rate of 7 percent per year and that the required rate of return on NCH is 10.5 percent per year. Applying the formula in equation (1), we get a market value of about $61 per share. If the market expected a return of 12 percent and the growth rate of dividends is 7 percent, then the value according to equation (1) should have been about $43 per share, substantially below the market price. An investor should at that point sell the stock. However, if the market requires a return of 9 percent on the stock, then the value according to equation (1) should be about $107 per share. An investor should at that point buy the security because it is undervalued in the market.

In practice, it may be less desirable to estimate the growth rate on dividends—firms attempt to avoid any reduction of dividends because a reduction most often affects share prices negatively. Thus, firms maintain dividends at a level that they hope to sustain in the long run and do not hasten to increase dividends. An alternative measurement is to use the growth rate of earnings and an estimate of the dividend payout ratio. The dividend payout ratio is estimated as total dividends divided by total earnings for a period. This ratio is relatively constant across time when it is estimated using a period of at least five years because short-term fluctuations in earnings do not affect the long-term estimation of this ratio.

Suppose that the firm had earnings of E_t in period t, and that the dividend payout ratio equals b. Then, assuming that earnings grow at a rate of g per period, next period's dividend may be estimated by:

$$D_{t+1} = bE_t \,(1+g) \tag{5}$$

Substituting back for the dividend in equation (4) yields:

$$P_t = \frac{b \, E_t \,(1+g)}{(r-g)} \tag{6}$$

To implement equation (6), we need to estimate the payout ratio, b, and the growth rate in earnings, g.

Example

American Brands reported income of \$3.30 per share for 1993. The growth rate of its income over the 10-year period 1984–1993 was about 3.7 percent per year. Its dividend payout ratio, measured over the same 10-year period by dividing total dividends during that period into total income in that period is 46 percent, that is, the firm pays out 46 cents of every dollar of income. Assume that the required rate of return on American Brand's stock is about 5 percent greater than the estimated growth rate. Then, according to equation (6), the price of a share should be about \$31.50 at the end of 1993. The actual price at that time was about \$33.25 per share. Thus, the security seems to have been a little overpriced.

To apply equation (6), we still need to estimate the required rate of return on a firm's security. A well-accepted method for estimating the required rate of return is to use the capital asset pricing model (CAPM), which is very popular in finance theory. Under the CAPM, the expected rate of return on any specific security j is provided by the following equation:

$$E(R_j) = R_f + \beta_j \times E(R_m - R_f) \tag{7}$$

where $E(R_j)$ is the expected return on security j, R_f is the rate of return on a risk-free investment, β_j is the relative risk of a firm, and R_m is the rate of return on the market portfolio.

To understand the relationship established by the CAPM, let us first explain the relative risk measure, β_j. The CAPM posits that the expected return on each security varies systematically with the expected return on all securities in the marketplace, that is, the market portfolio. However, some stocks are defensive—their Beta is lower than 1 and they fluctuate less on average than the market portfolio. Some other stocks are aggressive—their β is greater than 1 and they fluctuate more than the market. With a β of 1, the security is expected to fluctuate identically to the entire market. To illustrate this concept, suppose that β_j is 1.5 and that the expected excess return of the market (market return in excess of the risk-free rate) is about 10 percent. Then, the expected excess return on security j would be 15 percent (1.5 × 10 percent). Similarly, if the expected excess return on the market portfolio is −10 percent, the expected excess return on security j would be –15 percent. Thus, the fluctuations in the market return get magnified for security j because of its aggressive β. However, if security j had a β of 0.8, then the same market fluctuations would translate into 8 percent and −8 percent (0.8 × 10 percent); market fluctuations are attenuated by a defensive β.

Note that the CAPM posits a linear relationship between the expected excess return on security j and the expected excess return on the market portfolio. In practice, this relationship is unlikely to hold precisely for any particular period. However, deviations from this valuation rule are expected to cancel each other over time and over a large subset of securities. Empirical tests of the CAPM generally support the linear relationship between actual return on a security and the actual return on a market index, although this relationship is much stronger at the portfolio level (i.e., measuring the β of a portfolio) than at the individual security level. Also, the literature documents several systematic deviations from the CAPM, such as the effect of the dividend yield, size, and book/market ratio on security returns. Thus, the CAPM is probably not a precise description of the process that generates security returns, but is nonetheless a reasonable approximation for most applications in finance.

In our case, we shall estimate the β of a security by regressing the actual weekly return of that security on the actual return on the index of all NYSE stocks during the 52 weeks before the estimation date. We use the short-term interest rate on new 91-days Treasury bills as the risk-free rate and assume that the excess return on the market portfolio is equal to its long-range historical average excess return of about 8.2 percent. This will provide us with an estimate of the expected return on a security.

Example

American Brands had an estimated β of 1.3 as of 12/31/93, based on a regression of its stock returns on the portfolio of all NYSE stocks during the 52 weeks prior to 12/31/93. On that date, the yield on new 91-day Treasury bills was about 3.08 percent. If the long-term average of excess market return is about 8.2 percent, the required rate of return on American Brands' stock as of 12/31/93, should have been:

$$R_j = 3.08\% + 1.3 \times 8.2\% = 13.74\%$$

The estimated growth rate of dividends per share of American Brands during the most recent 10 years is about 8.66 percent per year. Thus, the price of American Brands on 12/31/93 using the dividend in 1993 of $1.97 per share, is equal to:

$$P = \$1.97 \times 1.0866 / (.1374 - .0866) = \$42.1$$

Note that the actual price of American Brands on 12/31/93 ($31.50) was lower than the price implied by the constant growth-rate dividend model.

The constant growth-rate dividend model assumes that dividends will grow in the future indefinitely. In practice, firms may grow at a high pace initially, but then the rate of growth slows down substantially as the business matures or as competitors enter the market. Therefore, more sophisticated applications of the dividend valuation models assume two or three subperiods in which dividends grow at different rates. However, such applications require assumptions about growth rates in the various subperiods, increasing the likelihood of larger estimation errors.

Let us move now to a valuation model that is similar to a dividend-based valuation model, but that is based on free cash flow.

FREE CASH FLOW–BASED
VALUATION MODEL

We assume again that the market value of a firm is equal to the discounted present value of future dividends, as already described in equation (1). However, to estimate future dividends, we use the identity about sources and uses of cash flows (in excess of cash balance increases or decreases) during a period, which is described as:

$$CFO_t + BOR_t = D_t + CAPEXP_t \tag{8}$$

where CFO is the cash from operating activities after subtraction of cash payments for interest, BOR is net additional borrowing by the firm, and CAPEXP is net cash payments for new capital investments. In this identity, the firm has only two sources of cash flows—the cash that is generated from its ongoing operations and any additional borrowing by the firm. Note that both of these sources can be negative; the firm may actually have more cash outflows than cash inflows from its operations in a particular period, or it may actually be paying down debt at a particular period. However, for simplicity we assume both of these are net cash inflows.

The left-hand-side of equation (8) represents the cash outflows during a period. Again, we assume two main uses of cash—payment of dividends and capital expenditures. In practice, the firm may use its cash inflows to buy back shares, which is another form of dividends, or the firm may acquire other existing businesses instead of acquiring property, plant, and equipment (PPE). Our identity of cash flows assumes a broad definition of cash outflows for capital expenditures and dividends to include the above (and other) examples. Also, the dividends and capital expenditures may be net cash inflows in any specific period if stockholders invest more cash in the firm or if the firm receives greater proceeds for sale of PPE than it spends to acquire new PPE. However, for simplicity, we treat these items in equation (8) as net cash outflows.

Let us define free cash flow, FCF, as cash from operating activities minus capital expenditures, CFO − CAPEXP. Also, let us assume zero future borrowing by the firm. In such cases, the identity about sources and uses of cash flows can be rearranged to yield:

$$D_t = FCF_t \tag{9}$$

As equation (9) shows, the firm can distribute its entire free cash flow as dividends to its stockholders in any given period without reducing its market value, since the firm does not rely on additional borrowing to sustain its current level of growth.

Substitution of equation (9) into equation (1) yields:

$$P_t = \sum_{\tau=1}^{\infty} (1+r)^{-\tau} E(FCF_{t+\tau}) \tag{10}$$

Equation (10) assumes that the price at the end of period t is equal to the sum of all discounted future free cash flows, so, in effect, the free cash flow is simply substituted for dividends in the pricing equation. This makes sense under our stated assumptions about no future borrowing and the 100 percent payment of free cash flow as dividends.

Assume now that the firm is in a steady state; that is, its free cash flows are identical in each future period and are not expected to grow (or to decline) from their current level. Let us denote this level of steady-state free cash flow, AVGFCF, which is estimated as the average free cash flow in the four most recent years. Such a firm would have a market value of:

$$P_t = AVGFCF \sum_{\tau=1}^{\infty} (1+r)^{-\tau} = \frac{1}{r} AVGFCF \tag{11}$$

because the sum of the geometric series (under the summation sign Σ) converges to $1/r$. Note that in equation (11) we do not have any adjustment for growth—the most recent average free cash flow, AVGFCF, is not expected to grow. This introduces a conservative bias in valuing a security if one assumes that the future free cash flows would not decline. To the extent that free cash flows are expected to grow (decline) in the future, the current market value should be higher (lower).

It will become useful later on to work with the free cash flow multiple, which is the relation between market value of a firm and its steady-state free cash flow; it can be written as:

$$\frac{P_t}{\text{AVGFCF}} = \frac{1}{r} \tag{12}$$

Equation (11) will be used to identify firms that are mispriced by the market. When the free cash flow multiple is identical to the inverse of the required rate of return, the security is fairly priced according to this model. However, when the free cash flow multiple is greater than the inverse of the required rate of return, the security is probably overpriced, because the right-hand side of equation (12) can increase with either increases in P_t, or decreases of AVGFCF. Since AVGFCF is assumed to be constant, the actual market price is higher than the indicated price according to equation (12). Using similar logic, the security is underpriced if the free cash flow multiple is below the inverse of the required rate of return because the right-hand side of equation (12) is reduced with reductions in price.

Equation (11) is based on some restrictive assumptions. The firm's recent average free cash flow, AVGFCF, is expected to remain constant across all future periods. This assumption can be justified for firms that have shown a fairly consistent ability to generate free cash flows. Such firms probably operate in stable industries and probably have mature products. Thus, an initial requirement for identifying a subset of firms for which the above free cash flow–based valuation may hold is an ability to consistently generate free cash flows and current forecasts that such cash flows are likely to continue.

The second assumption underlying equation (11) is that the firm would need no future additional borrowing. Let us first emphasize that this requirement does not mean that the firm has no current borrowing. Typically, firms should have some debt in their capital structure to take advantage of the deductibility of interest expense for tax purposes. What the assumption specifies is that these firms should not need to raise money through *additional* amounts of debt. According to the model's specifications, such firms would probably not need additional borrowing because they can generate sufficient cash from operating activities to cover all the cash outflows for replacement of PPE and acquisition of new PPE, required to maintain the current level of growth. Thus, these firms should exhibit a pattern of positive free cash flows in recent periods.

When a firm shows a consistent pattern of positive free cash flows that are expected to continue into the future, the assumptions of equation (11) are expected to hold reasonably well, and we can compare the current market prices through the free cash flow multiple to the inverse of the required rate of return. To the extent that the free cash flow multiple seems to be lower than the inverse of the required rate of return, the security would be underpriced, and model expectations are that the security price would increase in the future.

Example

American Brands' pattern of four-year average free cash flow is described in the table below for the period 1986–1993 (data in millions of dollars):

Year	1986	1987	1988	1989	1990	1991	1992	1993
AVGFCF	308.7	339.1	392.9	588.5	754.2	1,038.4	1,062.5	995.8
Market value	4,668.8	4,899	6,117.7	6,799.6	8,314.8	9,176.3	8,204.4	6,708
Net income	365.3	522.7	580	630.8	596	806.1	883.8	469.8

A graph of the free cash flow, AVGFCF, net income and market value is depicted in Figure 6–1.

As can be seen in the graph, American Brands had a consistent pattern of positive free cash flows that grew during the period 1986–1993. The decline in 1993 stems from price wars in the American tobacco market, which occurred when Philip Morris decided to lower its cigarette prices in an effort to gain market share. Nevertheless, even in 1993, American Brands continued to show positive free cash flow, although not at the same level as in prior years. Note that the market value of American Brands seemed to behave in a similar manner—it generally increased as AVGFCF increased, but it started to decline in 1992, again probably as a reaction to the news of price wars in the domestic tobacco market.

FIGURE 6–1
American Brands Inc.: Free Cash Flow Analysis

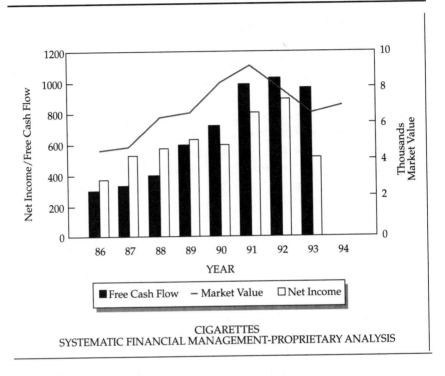

CIGARETTES
SYSTEMATIC FINANCIAL MANAGEMENT-PROPRIETARY ANALYSIS

To determine whether American Brands' stock was underpriced at the end of 1993, note that it had a free cash flow multiple of about 6.7 × ($6,708/$995.8) at the end of 1993. At the same time, its required rate of return (which we estimated in the earlier example using the CAPM) was 13.74 percent at the end of 1993, so the inverse of the required rate of return at the end of 1993 was 7.3 (1/0.1374). Thus, the free cash flow multiple was lower at the end of 1993 than the inverse of the required rate of return, and the stock would seem to be underpriced according to equation (11).

THE IMPORTANCE OF DEBT

The analysis underlying equation (11) emphasizes that a firm should not depend on future borrowing to finance its expansion. This concept is important not only for the analysis in equation

(11) but also for any investor interested in conservatively managed firms. When the capital structure of a firm contains more debt than the firm can service from its cash flows, the firm is financially leveraged, and needed future borrowing may be difficult to obtain at reasonable interest rates. Thus, to maintain financial flexibility, it is useful for a firm to keep a low level of current debt in its capital structure. However, some debt is not specifically included on the balance sheet, but is only reported in footnotes to the financial statements. In the next chapter, we concentrate on the proper measurement of debt, including off-balance-sheet liabilities, and consider what levels of debt increase the risk of a security.

Chapter Seven

Financial Structure and Free Cash Flows

INTRODUCTION

The decade of the 1980s will be remembered for the wave of acquisitions and leverage buyouts that were facilitated by the ease of debt issuance. Many firms issued high-yield debt, "junk bonds" as they became known, which promised investors a high return but offered very little security in terms of the firm's assets. These junk bonds were intended to be paid off by the firm's cash flows or through sales of some business segments that were not focal to the firm. The underlying business rationale for investing in high-yield bonds was that the acquired firms had steady cash flows (or at least adequate operating cash flow to cover debt payments), that the chance of default on these corporate bonds was extremely small, and that the acquisitions that were consummated using the junk bonds were made at attractive prices (high yield) to the acquirers.

With hindsight, it is easy to see that in too many instances none of these three assumptions had been correct. Firms ran into cash flow difficulties and debt payments could not be met from operating cash flows. The actual default rate turned out to be much higher than was initially perceived. Also, the acquisition prices (including the hefty investment banking fees) were just too high in many cases. Still, a very important lesson can be learned from these transactions—the importance of the relationship among free cash flows, corporate debt, and financial structure *for all firms*. In this chapter, we discuss how the financial structure of a firm is related to the concept of free cash flows.

FINANCIAL STRUCTURE OF A FIRM

Most publicly held companies are financed by a mixture of internal and external capital. Internal capital consists of all financial instruments that, in effect, provide holders with an equity position in the firm. Examples include common stocks; convertible instruments such as preferred stocks and bonds that, for all practical purposes, can be considered as already converted into common stock, stock warrants, stock rights, and so on. External capital can be defined as all financial obligations to outsiders who are not likely to become equity holders in the firm. Examples are short-term debt owed to banks, and bonds that do not convert to common stock. Other examples of external capital are obligations of the firm under leases, pension and other postretirement benefits to employees, guarantees made by the firm, and other off-balance-sheet liabilities such as debt related to a joint venture and various derivative securities.[1]

Traditional finance theories show that a firm has an optimal financial structure, which is an optimal balance between internal and external capital.[2] The optimal capital structure is derived from theoretical models that balance costs and benefits for each form of financing. Benefits and costs are associated with external capital. For example, it is well-known that interest payments on debt are tax deductible, whereas dividend payments to preferred and common stockholders are not deductible to the firm and are taxable to shareholders. Thus, a firm has a clear incentive to raise external capital. However, external capital dilutes the control of equity holders because the firm is subject to a greater scrutiny by creditors. Also, if at any period the firm's cash flows are insufficient

---

[1]In some cases, a supplier will provide a customer with free equipment and even inventory in exchange for the customer's promise to purchase future merchandise from the supplier. This promise is another obligation of the customer, although it is an off-balance-sheet liability. Richfood, a high-growth food distribution company, has used this method very effectively.

[2]Miller and Modigliani (*Journal of Business*, 1961) show that it does not matter how a firm finances itself. Ross (*Bell Journal of Economics*, 1977) and Leland and Pyle (*Journal of Finance*, 1977) show that an optimal financial structure exists because of signalling costs. Lewellen (*Journal of Finance*, 1975) and Galai and Masulis (*Journal of Financial Economics*, 1984) show that an optimal financial structure exists because of bankruptcy costs and taxation.

to service its debt, the firm may be forced into bankruptcy or reorganization, and equity holders will be exposed to additional costs (including the issuance of additional equity). Moreover, in bankruptcy or reorganization, the firm may be forced to sell assets it prefers to own.

Other financial theories suggest that entrepreneurs have incentives to issue shares in their firms to the public, in effect raising more internal capital when they consider current stock prices too high. Thus, they issue additional shares of the firm to the public and enjoy the benefits of cash infusion into the firm that is not justified by future cash flows. Conversely, when owners of firms repurchase stock in their firms, they likely consider the firm's price too low compared with future cash flows. Thus, they repurchase the firm's stock, in effect reducing internal capital. Note that this explanation is based on the notion that entrepreneurs have more information about their firms than the public at large, that is, information asymmetries exist between current and future equityholders.[3]

Such information asymmetries, as well as other conflicts of interest, may also exist between stock- and bondholders. For example, stockholders may wish to invest in projects that are too risky for bondholders. These projects may have a negative net present value because of the high risk associated with the project, but they are adopted by owners nevertheless because stockholders are not faced with the risk of losing all capital, as are creditors. On the other hand, they stand to gain immensely if cash flows in the future turn out to meet or exceed expectations.[4]

---

[3]Smith (*Journal of Financial Economics,* 1986) provides a review of the literature. Mikkelson and Partch (*Journal of Financial Economics,* 1986) and Eckbo (*Journal of Financial Economics,* 1986) show the negative effects on stock prices when firms issue debt. Masulis and Korwar (*Journal of Financial Economics,* 1986) and Asquith and Mullins (*Journal of Financial Economics,* 1986) provide evidence of negative reactions to announcements of stock issuances, whereas Dann (*Journal of Financial Economics,* 1981) and Vermaelen (*Journal of Financial Economics,* 1981) provide evidence of positive stock reactions to announcements of stock repurchases. Livnat and Zarowin (*Journal of Accounting and Economics,* 1990) provide evidence that is consistent with the effects of financing events as described in the statement of cash flows on security prices.

[4]However, others argue that bondholders may actually fare better than stockholders in case of bankruptcy or reorganization, so that stockholders actually have an incentive to invest in less risky projects than are optimal for the firm.

One common characteristic of all these theories is that the financial structure of a firm does not usually lie in either of the extreme cases; that is, firms are neither all-equity nor all-debt. Rather, they have a mixture of internal and external capital. Another common characteristic of these theories is that firms are not at their optimal capital structure at all times. Instead, firms continuously make adjustments to their financial structure in an attempt to react to changing economic and market conditions, so that they can reach their new optimal financial structure. Thus, we should observe that firms adjust their capital structure in almost every period, as can, indeed, be verified from any casual examination of financing cash flows of firms.

Can one predict how adjustments to the financial structure of a firm should be related to operating and free cash flows? To answer this question, recall that one of the major disadvantages of external capital is the possibility of bankruptcy and reorganization costs to stockholders. These expected costs relate, of course, to the likelihood of financial difficulties for the firm; the higher the likelihood of financial difficulties, the greater the expected bankruptcy costs, and the more costly external financing becomes. An immediate variable to consider for the likelihood of financial difficulties is the stability of operating and free cash flows. The more stable operating and free cash flows are, the lower the probability of financial difficulties and the lower the probability of bankruptcy. Thus, firms with stable operating and free cash flows are expected to be characterized by higher financial leverage than their counterparts, where financial leverage can be measured by the relative proportion of debt to equity. Such firms are also more likely to be increasing external capital at the expense of internal capital.

Similarly, firms that exhibit volatile operating cash flows and firms that are characterized by negative free cash flows are expected to have lower financial leverage and, on average, are expected to show decreases in debt and increases in equity financing.

Cash flow analysis can provide worthwhile clues of impending financial risk and return. Unfortunately, it has become all too common to identify an entity reporting healthy operating gains that finds itself unprepared to operate during a business downturn because it had been such a heavy user of cash.

Example

Todd Shipyards appeared to be a healthy company when its earnings were considered. But this was not the case when Todd was viewed from a free cash flow perspective.

Todd Shipyards
(amounts in millions)

Year	Net Income	Free Cash Flow	Market Value
1983	$ 30.17	$ 32.4	$141.1
1984	21.87	(12.4)	134.6
1985	18.88	(1.2)	133.6
1986	(2.34)	(35.7)	116.4
1987	(58.29)	(19.0)	86.0
1988	(20.50)	(72.2)	8.4

The contrast between Todd Shipyard's net income and free cash flow is dramatic. Free cash flow turned negative almost four years before the company filed for bankruptcy. Even when Todd had negative free cash flow for three consecutive years, the company still had a very high market capitalization, indicating investors were paying scant attention to the worsening state of Todd's free cash flow.

Investors who relied on the common, but incorrect, definition of *health* that was limited to net income plus depreciation and deferred taxes were left with the impression that Todd was not the poor cash flow entity the table shows. The common definition did not indicate Todd company was a bankruptcy candidate until shortly before it entered Chapter 11.

Also, using the most common, but incorrect, definition of free cash flow (deducting capital spending from net income, depreciation, and deferred taxes) slightly improved the real picture. Even so, during 1985, the company reported an operating cash flow of almost $40 million and a naive definition of free cash flow of $28 million.

Todd Shipyards
(in millions)

Year	FCF	OCF(*)	OCF − Capital Expenditures
1983	$ 32.4	$ 51.52	$ (12.8)
1984	(12.4)	44.55	(.6)
1985	(1.2)	39.55	27.81
1986	(35.7)	8.37	(47.57)
1987	(19.0)	(92.80)	(104.56)
1988	(72.2)	(16.20)	(19.60)

*OCF represents operating cash flow estimated by net income plus depreciation plus deferred taxes.

When low-growth firms have large and stable free cash flows, we expect them to be able to reduce debt, repurchase stock, or increase dividends. The reason is that firms with large free cash flows can divert such free cash flows to the retirement of debt or to the repurchase of equity, without affecting future growth. Recall that the definition of *free cash flows* is that proper investments are made to allow for the normal growth of the firm. Thus, free cash flows represent either growth opportunities beyond expected growth or, if excellent growth opportunities are unavailable, cash that can be used to retire unnecessary debt or unnecessary equity. Thus, firms with good free cash flow profiles are expected to reduce debt on average or to reduce equity. We can use these relationships to identify firms that are good candidates for investment purposes, as described in the next chapter.

We discuss now several specific areas of the financial structure and their relationship to free cash flows.

FINANCIAL LEVERAGE AND DEBT COVERAGE

Financial leverage may be defined as the proportion of total debt to total capitalization of a firm. A firm is considered highly leveraged when the ratio of debt to total capitalization is high. A firm is unleveraged when it has no debt in its capital structure. For most practical applications, debt can be defined as total debt, including lease obligations and any off-balance-sheet liabilities such as unfunded pension and other postretirement benefits. Short-term debt must also be included in total debt since many companies have short-term loans that eventually have to be refinanced with long-term debt. Also, some companies have large balloon payments due within a year. Thus, one should include in total debt of a firm short- as well as long-term debt, and any off-balance sheet liabilities. Total capitalization includes debt plus total stockholders' equity, where the latter is measured either by the market value of equity or by the accounting book value of equity.

Traditional finance thinking views financial leverage as increasing a firm's risk; if operating cash flows at any period are lower than debt payments, the firm has to liquidate some assets or increase its capitalization just to continue operations. Thus, the more leveraged a firm, the riskier it becomes. At the same time, debt has a desirable benefit because interest payments on debt are tax deductible, whereas dividend payments are not. Finance theory suggests that an optimal combination of debt and equity exists for each firm, known as the optimal financial structure. Firms can continuously change their financial structure by issuing debt or equity, so that the optimal level of financial leverage will be attained. Generally, the greater the volatility of operating cash flows and free cash flows, the lower should the financial leverage be. Conversely, the greater the stability of operating or free cash flows, the more leveraged a firm can become.

Example

It is not unusual for financially weak brokerage firms to borrow at the parent level and then send the cash to the broker-dealer where it counts as capital. In the industry this is known as double-leveraging. The Securities and Exchange Commission (SEC) regulates the industry and is in charge of setting capital requirements—how much equity and debt the firm must have invested in the business. The SEC also allows short-term debt to be counted as part of capital.

Since loans are counted as part of capital, Drexel Burnham Lambert, even as it was rapidly heading toward bankruptcy, was able to claim it was exceeding Federal capital requirements. In fact, just before Drexel entered bankruptcy it stated it had almost $300 million more in capital than was required by the SEC. However, much of the capital was in the forms of loans from its parent, Drexel Burnham Lambert

Group, Inc., which was financing itself with short-term loans. Soon afterward, Drexel's house of cards collapsed when the SEC and the New York Stock Exchange refused to allow Drexel's brokerage unit to reduce its capital by repaying loans from its parent.

Example

Japanese and German firms are usually more financially leveraged than their U.S. counterparts. At the end of 1993, Sanyo Electric Co. and Sony Corp. had a debt/equity ratio (short- plus long-term debt to book-value of stockholders equity) of 1.2 and 1.0, respectively. In the same year, Motorola Inc. and Intel Corp. had ratios of 0.3 and 0.1, respectively. Thus, these two U.S. firms relied more heavily on internal capital than the two Japanese firms, which relied more heavily on external capital.

Traditional measures of a firm's ability to pay the interest on its debt include the debt coverage ratio, measured by earnings before taxes and interest divided by interest expense. The greater is this ratio the easier it is for the firm to meet interest payments. However, this ratio measures the short-term ability of a firm to service its debt, *it totally ignores the firm's ability to reduce its financial leverage.* For example, the firm may generate enough operating cash flows to sustain its current level of growth and to cover existing interest payments. But the firm may not have any free cash flows to retire old debt or called for in loan covenants. Consequently, it may be exposed to greater financial risk than a firm that does generate free cash flows. Therefore, we suggest an additional measure of a firm's financial risk: the relationship between total debt and free cash flows.

To assess the ability of a firm to attain its desired financial structure, we focus on the ratio of total debt to the four-year average free cash flows. Thus, we propose an examination of the following ratio for firms that are likely candidates for investment decisions:

$$\frac{\text{Total debt}}{\text{Four-year average free cash flow}}$$

The greater this ratio, the greater the financial risk of the firm, and the lower this ratio, the lower the financial risk of a firm. Ideally, one would like to invest in firms that are able to generate free cash flows consistently but that are also subject to a lower debt burden. Such firms can make appropriate capital investments if they find good investment opportunities because they can either use their free cash flows to do so or they can increase their debt.

Example

During 1987, The Phillips-Van Heusen Corporation acquired G. H. Bass & Co. for $79 million and repurchased $168.6 million of stock through a Dutch tender auction. As reflected on the statement of cash flows, Phillips has been undergoing a series of financial transactions to help spread out the debt payments taken on as a result of the business transactions, initially financed with short-term debt.

As the 1989 statement of cash flows shows, Phillips has not been generating an adequate amount of free cash flow, when taking into account other investing activities, to help pay down its leverage. In 1989, to aid cash flow, Phillips sold businesses for $10.1 million in cash.

According to Phillips' 1989 long-term debt footnote, the company reports the following principal debt payments due over the next five years.

Phillips-Van Heusen Schedule of Principal Payments
1990—$12.9 million
1991—$10.1 million
1992—$14.2 million
1993—$15.9 million
1994—$12.9 million

It seems quite evident by reviewing the past three years' statement of cash flows that Phillips is unlikely to be able to generate sufficient funds to service the principal payments. Subtracting the $8.7 million of operating cash flow from discontinued operations during 1987 and averaging over the three years 1987–1989 yields an average operating cash flow of $10.5 million. Phillips must add to and improve its existing capital base, which has been growing by about 30 percent over the last four years and about 12 percent over the past eight years.

Reviewing Phillips' balance sheet indicates they could draw down some inventory, thus providing cash. But given the large growth rate in revenues during the past four years and eight years of about 13 percent and 7 percent, respectively, it is doubtful inventories could be reduced dramatically.

Example

According to the "Heard on the Street" column, *The Wall Street Journal*, September 23, 1991, Trizec, a Canadian real estate investment firm, saw its debt downgraded due to cash flow difficulties. Apparently, the cash flows that Trizec and its largest subsidiary, Bramalea, generated from operations were insufficient to cover debt payments. Thus, the firm needed to use additional debt to hold on to its properties.

According to finance theory, it is useful to consider not only the ratio of total debt to average free cash flows but also the volatility of free cash flows. The volatility of free cash flows is a measure of an *operating risk* of a firm; the more volatile the free cash flows are, the greater the firm's operating risk. The ratio of total debt to average free cash flow is a measure of *financial risk*; the higher this ratio is, the greater the firm's financial risk. Additionally, measures of stock risk—such as the systematic risk, Beta, or the total variability of stock returns—have been shown to consist of financial and operating risks.

Figure 7–1 portrays the two dimensions of risk. In the figure, we show the risk profile of a hypothetical firm X. We can compare the risk profiles of other firms to this firm. Naturally, most people will prefer firms with lower risks to firms with higher risks. Thus, firms with risk profiles in region C would be superior to firm X because they have both a lower operating risk and a lower financial risk. Firms in region B are inferior to firm X because both dimensions of risk are greater than those of firm X. The selection of a firm in regions A and D depends on the decision maker's tolerance for the two types of risk. Individuals with more tolerance for financial risk than for operating risk may prefer firms in region D over firm X, because they have lower operating risk. The converse would be true for region A.

As mentioned in the previous chapter, the cash flow analyst should always examine the behavior of free cash flows and four-year average free cash flow in the most recent four- and eight-year period to assess how the firm was able to overcome downturns in the economy and how stable are the free cash flows. The analyst should also examine the instances when a firm has negative free cash flows; in most cases, investments in firms with several years of negative free cash flows are justified only if the investor is willing to absorb a higher operating risk.

FIGURE 7–1

Financial Risk and Operating Risk

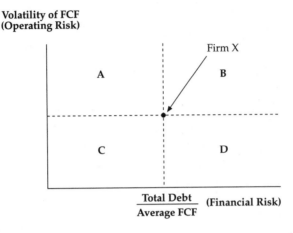

Region A Firms with lower financial risk but greater operating risk
Region B Firms with *both* greater operating *and* financial risk
Region C Firms with *both* lower operating *and* financial risk
Region D Firms with lower operating risk and greater financial risk

DEBT, CAPITAL SPENDING, AND FREE CASH FLOWS

Charles Exley, former chairman of NCR Corporation, now a subsidiary of AT&T, always believed technology companies do not make good LBO candidates because they need growing amounts of research budgets to stay competitive. Similarly, entities that cannot make the necessary cutbacks in capital spending and other discretionary cash outlays also are unsuitable candidates for LBOs because high leverage often impairs potential growth opportunities. When such entities get away from what they should be doing—making better products—and move toward being financially motivated companies, their operating cash flows suffer as they are overtaken by competitors.

We examined Chairman Exley's belief that high rates of R&D and capital spending are important for future growth, with a subsequent positive spillover into the stock price. To test this hypothesis, we investigated the performance of entities—called the leveraged group—that have had positive growth rates in free cash flows; we assumed these entities had the wherewithal to increase their spending on research and new capital. In fact, they even had the creditworthiness to undertake such spending, but for whatever reason had decided not to do so.

We looked at the eight-year period, 1982–1990, a unique period because it encompassed the longest peacetime economic expansion. In order to be included in the "leveraged group," the entity needed a minimum market capitalization of $50 million and a growth rate in either research and development spending or capital spending of less than 3 percent per year over the period. Additionally, the growth rate in total debt had to be greater than 12 percent per year over the eight-year period. We then compared this group with the S&P industrials. See Table 7–1.

The leveraged group had a slightly higher growth rate of free cash flow than that of the S&P. However, the far greater growth rate in debt made that group appear to investors to be a far riskier investment. Indeed, the leveraged group had a total return of slightly more than a third of the S&P. It would take the leveraged group almost 17 years to repay its total debt versus just 6.3 years for the S&P.

The lack of investment has already taken a toll on operating cash flow and book earnings. The entities have been able to continue a positive growth rate in free cash flow through cutbacks in expenditures the marketplace felt were vital to the health of the firm. Of course, an entity can only continue to sacrifice spending on necessary plans and R&D for a finite period, before the effect on operating cash flow is also felt on free cash flow. The managers of the enterprise can only "squeeze the lemon" so hard for so long before it runs dry.

Even for the S&P, leverage has shown a steady rate of growth, indicating that the assumption of debt is not necessarily detrimental to the entity's financial health, nor does the marketplace necessarily shun such enterprises. However, if the rate of growth in financial leverage is greater than the long-term growth of free

TABLE 7-1
When Leverage Comes at the Future's Expense: A Study of the Current Business Expansion

	Eight-Year Growth Rate in R&D	Eight-Year Growth Rate in Capital Spending	Eight-Year Growth Rate Debt	Seven-Year Growth Operating Cash Flow	Five-Year Price Change	Five-Year Earnings per Share Growth	Market Value (million)	Seven-Year Growth Free Cash Flow	Debt/Equity (%)	4/85–4/90 Total Return	Years for Free Cash Flow to Repay Debt
Leveraged group	-1.3	-2.2	22.0	1.3	23.0	7.6	$391.6	7.9	96.5	43.9	16.7
S&P industrials	10.1	8.3	12.6	9.5	92.8	11.6	$398.0	6.8	53.9	124.2	6.3

Positive free-cash-producing entities that have had less than 3 percent annual rate of growth in either capital spending or research, when combined with an annual growth in leverage of greater than 12 percent, have had miserable stock price performance.

Although the free cash flow of this group has grown at a rate slightly in excess of the S&P industrials, the far greater growth in leverage results in a much more risky investment. In fact, it would take the leveraged group almost 17 years to repay its total debt versus 6.3 years for the S&P industrials, with leverage also having a negative effect on operating cash flow and earnings growth.

The moral: Leverage is OK, as witnessed by the returns on the S&P, but not when it comes at the future's expense—even for excess cash generators.

cash flows, especially when it sacrifices necessary expenditures, the market takes good notice.

One might be tempted to believe the leveraged group entities would comprise unknowns. That is untrue. The group included such companies as Avon Products, Borden, Coca-Cola, General Motors, ITT, IBM, Litton, Safeway, Unisys, Westinghouse, and Xerox. Since that period, most of these firms have begun investing larger amounts in capital expenditures and R&D projects, and also reducing their debt levels. For those firms, stock prices have moved up.

IBM, for instance, had a growth rate in its capital spending of negative 2.2 percent per year in the late 1980s, while its growth rate of short-term and long-term debt has increased by 21.8 percent per year! Needless to say, its stock price, having risen at an annual rate of 3.1 percent per year including dividends, has performed dramatically below the S&P. As Table 7–2 illustrates, IBM's capital spending rebounded in 1989, but only back to its 1982 level. It subsequently fell, as IBM's main products encountered stronger competition and decreasing demand. Note that long-term debt increased in the beginning of the 1990s as cash flows from its main products declined. IBM stock has done well in the years 1994 to 1995. However, the growth in the personal computer market accelerated. IBM, aided by large cost-cutting measures, was able to show strong increases in cash flow. Hence, the company's stock price recovered its 1990 level.

In summary, we find that free cash flows and debt are interrelated because firms cannot neglect improving operations and making proper investments without sacrificing future operating and free cash flows. Even if such firms resort to short-run debt because it is less costly initially due to the tax deductibility of interest payments, free cash flows in the future may be hurt by larger interest payments. Thus, firms should probably pay less attention to financial management and more attention to management of operations and future growth. Apparently, the market is able to distinguish among firms along these dimensions, and in the long run penalizes firms that underinvest in future growth and assume too much debt.

Given our analysis in Chapter 6, it is important to identify firms that are less likely to need future borrowing because they can generate sufficient cash from their operations. Thus, we shall select into our portfolios firms that have low financial leverage, as

TABLE 7–2
IBM: Debt and Capital Spending (in millions)

Year	Short-Term Debt	New Long-Term Debt	Long-Term Debt Retired	Capital Expenditures
1993	$12,097	$11,794	$ 8,741	$3,154
1992	16,467	10,045	10,735	4,571
1991	13,716	5,776	4,184	6,497
1990	7,602	4,676	3,683	6,509
1989	5,892	6,471	2,768	6,414
1988	4,862	4,540	3,007	5,390
1987	1,629	408	719	4,304
1986	1,410	1,059	845	4,620
1985	1,293	1,614	928	6,430
1984	834	1,363	768	5,473
1983	532	174	351	4,930
1982	529	480	298	6,685
1981	773	751	181	6,845
1980	591	604	94	6,592
1979	933	1,450	146	5,991
1978	242	74	44	4,046
1977	172	23	42	3,395
1976	116	25	45	2,518

measured by the ratio of total debt to the four-year average free cash flow. However, we have to be careful in our definition of total debt. It should not be restricted only to debt that is classified as such on the balance sheet of a firm; it should also include off-balance-sheet liabilities. In the following sections, we review forms of debt that do not appear on the firm's balance sheet.

LEASES

Accountants distinguish between two major types of leases, capital leases and operating leases. Assets under capital leases are recorded as assets on the balance sheet with offsetting liabilities (usually denoted capital lease obligations) among the long-term liabilities of the firm. Assets under operating leases are not shown on the balance sheet as assets, nor are any liabilities created due to these leases. Information about operating leases is disclosed only through a footnote to the financial statements, not on the balance sheet itself; hence the name *off-balance-sheet liability*. Accounting and disclosure requirements for leases are covered primarily by *SFAS No. 13* (1976), and later pronouncements by the FASB that served to explain *SFAS No. 13* or slightly modify it.

Operating and capital leases are distinguished mainly through tests that are intended to examine whether the benefits and risks of ownership were in fact transferred from the lessor to the lessee. If they were, the lease is classified as a capital lease, and an asset with an offsetting liability is included on the balance sheet. Otherwise, the lease is classified as an operating lease, and the information is reported in a footnote. There are four general tests for the classification of leases as capital or operating leases. If any one of these tests is satisfied, the lease is classified as a capital lease:

1. The legal title to the asset is transferred to the lessee at the end of the lease term.
2. The lease agreement contains an option to purchase the asset from the lessor at the end of the lease term by paying a bargain price (i.e., below-market price).
3. The lease term is for longer than 75 percent of the remaining economic useful life of the leased asset.
4. The present value of payments under the lease term exceeds 90 percent of the asset's fair market value at the inception of the lease agreement.

The accounting standard prevents firms from applying tests (3) and (4) when the leased asset is at the last 25 percent of its remaining economic life.

Test 1 indicates that ownership of the asset is transferred to the lessee at the end of the lease term. Thus, we view the lease agreement as an installment sale, where the lessee agrees to purchase the leased asset through a series of payments, but with an official transfer of legal title at the end of the lease term, instead of at the beginning of the lease term. Similarly, test 2 ensures that a reasonable lessee will exercise the bargain purchase option and, in effect, will purchase the asset. Therefore, as in test 1, we view the lease as an installment sale and show the asset and the liability on the balance sheet immediately. In principle, we treat the lease as a compound transaction where the leased asset is purchased by the lessee, and where the lessor provides the lessee with a loan that is equivalent to the value of the asset. Future lease payments by the lessee pay for both the interest on the loan and for the reduction of the loan's principal.

The leased asset under a capital lease is included among the fixed assets of the firm and is subject to the same depreciation methods as the firm's other fixed assets. The loan is included among the long-term liabilities of the firm, with the current portion included among current liabilities. Note that at the inception of the lease, the asset and the liability are identical and are equal to the present value of the lease payments. However, at any other period, the asset is depreciated using the firm's depreciation methods (with a depreciation period that cannot exceed the lease term), whereas the liability is treated as any other long-term debt; that is, it is carried on the balance sheet using the effective interest rate method. Under that method, the effective interest rate implicit in the lease (at the inception of the lease) is used to discount future payments on the lease. Thus, the liability capitalized lease obligations will usually not represent the market value of these liabilities. The market value of these obligations can be determined by using the market interest rate at the time the calculation is made, whereas the capitalized lease obligations are calculated using the rate in effect at the inception of the lease. The two will deviate from each other because of economic conditions, Federal Reserve Bank policy, and so on.[5]

Test 3 ensures that most of the remaining benefits from the asset (75 percent) will be reaped by the lessee, making the lessee the de facto owner of the asset. Similarly, the lessee in test 4 makes

---

[5]This treatment is not unique to capitalized lease obligations. All long-term debt of the firm is carried at the present value of future payments on the debt, using the interest rate in existence at the time the debt was issued. Thus, the market value of the debt will be different from the accounting value of debt. Starting in 1993, many firms now report in a footnote the estimated fair market value of their obligations in addition to the carrying amount. For example, NCH shows in its 1994 financial statements that its long term debt had a carrying value of $6.79 million, whereas its estimated fair market value on the balance sheet date was only $5.595. The estimated fair market value was derived by discounting the future cash flows, using the company's current borrowing rate for loans of comparable terms and maturities.

payments under the lease that in current values are sufficient to purchase over 90 percent of the asset. Thus, under test 4, we treat the lease as if it represented an outright sale of the asset. Note that tests 3 and 4 are inapplicable at the end of the asset's life because we want to ensure that the lessee will enjoy most of the economic benefits of the leased asset.

The above tests are very restrictive; they guarantee that the lessee becomes the de facto owner of the asset. However, there is really no theoretical reason for classifying any lease agreement as an operating lease. Theoretically, the promise to make any lease payments in the future should be treated as a liability whether or not the leased asset is a de facto purchase. Similarly, the right to obtain benefits from using the leased asset in the future should be construed as an existing asset, whether or not the leased asset is a de facto purchase by the lessee. Thus, conceptually, one should probably record in the financial statements all assets under leases, whether they are capital or operating leases.

Example

Petrie Stores was, for a long time, the largest shareholder of Toys "R" Us. Since Petrie purchased its position in Toys "R" Us at a low cost, disposing of these shares would have resulted in a huge realized gain (over $1 billion), with a substantial tax payment. To avoid it, Petrie Stores agreed to merge into Toys "R" Us, except that Toys "R" Us did not want to own the women's fashion stores Petrie operated. Petrie's management group purchased the clothing chain from Petrie, enabling the merger with Toys "R" Us to go through. However, the agreement stipulated that Toys "R" Us would retain a certain proportion of the Toys "R" Us shares that Petrie holders were supposed to get, until full resolution of all lease agreements that Petrie Stores had with various lessors (a period estimated at five years). This example shows how important lease agreements are; they are an important part of a firm's obligations, even if they do not explicitly appear on the balance sheet.

For our purposes, to estimate total debt of a firm, we need to estimate the present value of future payments under operating leases, because the present value of capitalized lease obligations is already included in the long-term debt of the firm. We therefore add the present value of payments under operating leases to long-term debt of the firm. To do that, we use information that is available in the footnotes to the financial statements.

Example

In its 1994 financial statements, H&R Block Inc. disclosed the following information about its commitments, where data were provided on operating leases:

> Substantially all of the Company's operations are conducted in leased premises. Most of the operating leases are for a one-year period with renewal options of one to three years and provide for fixed monthly rentals. Lease commitments at April 30, 1994, for fiscal 1995, 1996, 1997, 1998 and 1999 aggregated $54,124, $44,341, $29,126, $16,115, and $5,839, respectively, with no significant commitments extending beyond that period of time. The Company's rent expense for the years 1994, 1993, and 1992 aggregated $63,655, $59,016 and $56,406, respectively.

The footnote provides information about actual rent expense for operating leases in 1992, 1993, and 1994, the years for which income statements are presented. Also, the firm reports estimated rent expense under its operating leases for 1995 and for the next four years. According to these estimates, rent expense for 1995 is estimated to be $54,124. Note, however, that this figure is substantially lower than the actual rent expense for 1994, and it is about the same as the actual rent expense incurred in 1992. Is it possible that the firm expects to lease fewer premises? Is the firm expected to shrink its operations or renegotiate its current leases? Note further that after 1995 the forecasted rent expense drops drastically to levels substantially below the actual rent expense in the most recent years. What can cause this phenomenon?

The firm reports in this footnote its actual rent expense for the years 1992–1994. It also reports *current* commitments under leases *in force* for periods beyond fiscal 1994. The firm estimates only payments on those leases that will remain in force beyond the current period. Since most of its leases are for short periods (i.e., for one year), a large portion of leases that are expected to be renewed are not included in the forecasted rent expense for future years, because H&R Block does not have firm commitments to renew those leases. However, H&R Block will very likely incur a greater rent expense in the future, since it is expected to grow. To verify that, we provide in Table 7–3 the actual rent expense in 1990–1994, and the firm's assessments of these expenses as reflected

TABLE 7–3
H&R Block's Expected versus Actual Lease Payments

| Year | Actual | 1989 Forecast | | 1990 Forecast | | 1991 Forecast | |
		Firm[a]	Our[b]	Firm	Our	Firm	Our
1987	38.2						
1988	40.7						
1989	45.5						
1990	52.5	40.3	49.7				
1991	58.3	29.3	54.2	42.8	59.6		
1992	56.4	18.0	59.1	31.1	67.7	46.4	66.0
1993	59.0	9.3	64.6	18.9	76.9	30.9	74.7
1994	63.7	5.5	70.5	10.4	87.4	18.6	84.6
1995				5.7	99.2	10.7	95.7
1996						2.7	108.3
1989 P.V.[c]	218.1	84.1	222.2				
1990 P.V.				89.5	289.2		
1991 P.V.						90.7	317.9
Total debt[d]		211.5		245.5		228.5	
Percent increase in debt[e]		39.8	105.1	36.4	117.8	39.7	139.1

[a]Figures represent future rent payments as reported by the firm in footnotes. The figures from the 1989 footnote are used as the forecast for 1990–1995.

[b]Figures represent our forecast of future rent payments, based on footnote rent expense in the most recent three years. For example, the growth rate in rent expense between 1987 and 1989 is used to predict 1990–1995 rent payments.

[c]The 1989 P.V. is calculated as the net present value of rent payments in the five-year period 1990–1995, using a 10 percent rate.

[d]Consists of short- plus long-term debt.

[e]Represents the percent increase in total debt if the present value of operating lease payments is added to total debt.

in a similar note to the 1989 annual report. As can be seen from the exhibit, rent expense in 1990–1994 actually exceeded rent expense in 1989 and was substantially greater than that forecasted in 1989.

To forecast the level of future rent expenses more accurately, Table 7–3 uses a very simplistic prediction rule. It takes the actual rent expense for the current year and multiplies it by one plus the actual growth rate in actual rent expense over the most recent three

FIGURE 7–2
H&R Block Rent Payments and Revenues

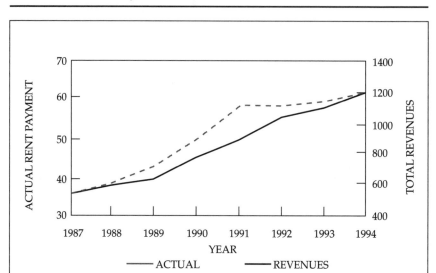

years. For example, to forecast rent expense for 1990, we first estimate the growth rate of the actual rent expense from 1987 to 1989
by finding the square root of the rent expense in 1989 divided by
that of 1987. This yields about 9 percent (square root of 45.5 / 38.2
minus one). We now multiply the actual rent expense in 1989 by
1.09 to obtain the forecasted rent expense in the *Our* column, $49.7.
The estimate for 1991, based on the same data and estimation procedure, is simply $49.7 times 1.09, or $54.2. The estimates for the next
three years follow suit. Notice that these estimates are much
closer to actual rent expense incurred in 1990–1995 than those forecasted by the firm. Thus, to estimate future cash outflows needed
for rent payments, the analyst is better off with forecasts that are
based on current levels of rent payments than on forecasts based
on leases still in force beyond the current year.

Note that actual rent expense increased by almost a constant
rate until 1991, flattened in 1992 and 1993, and increased again
in 1994. Figure 7–2 shows the behavior of rent expense against
revenues of H&R Block. It shows that rent expense had not grown

in 1992 and 1993 at the same rate as revenues, indicating that management was able to keep these costs down for some time. However, these expenses bounced back to their prior level in 1994.

To estimate the effect of capitalizing the operating leases, we discount the forecasted rent expenses in the next five years by using a 10 percent discount rate. These estimates are provided in Table 7–3. Note that the estimated present value of rent payments under these operating leases, *using the forecasted figures by the firm,* yield a liability of about $80 million at the end of 1989. This is compared with total debt of the firm (current and noncurrent) at the end of 1989 of about $212 million. Thus, had we added the off-balance-sheet liability created by operating leases to the total debt of the firm, total debt would have increased by 39.8 percent, as reported at the bottom of Table 7–3. Note that the increase would have been much more pronounced had we used our forecast of future payments for operating leases, 105 percent. Thus, one should examine the off-balance-sheet liability created by operating leases not capitalized or incorporated on the balance sheet. Of course if one were aware of circumstances that would lead to a more accurate forecast (i.e., management discussion, change in real estate market, or change in company growth rate) that should be incorporated.

Let us now show an example of a firm with long-term operating leases.

Example

Club Med, Inc., operates 27 villages (resorts) in the United State, Mexico, and other areas, whereas its parent company, Club Mediterranee, operates another 71 villages in other areas. In its 1994 financial statements, Club Med reports:

> At October 31, 1994, the Company rented villages and/or underlying land pursuant to operating leases (4 villages). The remaining terms of the operating leases range from 10 to 25 years with an average of 17 years. The leases generally provide for the suspension of rental payments in cases of force majeure, such as wars, floods, etc. One lease requires the payment of rentals based upon occupancy levels achieved. Club Mediterranee guarantees the Company's performance with respect to one lease. In addition, the company is committed under noncancellable operating leases with expiration dates through 2000 relating principally to office space.
>
> Minimum rental commitments under noncancellable operating leases, excluding *Sandpiper*, are as follows:

Years Ended on October 31 (thousands of dollars)	Villages	Other
1995	$ 3,101	$4,959
1996	3,723	4,099
1997	3,719	2,197
1998	3,715	1,739
1999	3,387	931
Thereafter	37,841	3
	$55,486	$13,928

Total rent expense consists of the following:

	Years Ended October 31 (thousands of dollars)		
	1994	1993	1992
Operating leases:			
Villages:			
Minimum	$11,365	$ 6,956	$ 7,279
Contingent	259	6,755	6,685
Other	8,740	10,255	10,136
	$20,364	$23,966	$24,100

On November 15, 1993, the Company sold and immediately leased back through the year 2015, the village of *Sandpiper* for $65,700,000. The operating lease requires annual minimal lease payments of $4,162,000.

Future minimal annual rentals and gain amortization on the *Sandpiper* lease are as follows:

Years Ended October 31 (in thousands of dollars)	Minimum Rentals	Gain Amortization
1995	$ 4,225	$ 1,152
1996	4,411	1,152
1997	4,065	1,152
1998	4,808	1,152
1999	5,019	1,152
Thereafter	107,138	17,870
	$130,206	$23,630

On December 5, 1994, the Company sold, and immediately leased
back for a period of 20.5 years, the Mexican villages of *Cancun* and
Ixtapa. The operating lease requires annual minimum lease payments
of $3,200,000, increasing to $4,100,000 by the end of the lease.

To understand Club Med's lease transactions, note that its fiscal
year-end is October 31, 1994. Thus, the sale and leaseback of its
Sandpiper village, which occurred on November 15, 1993,
should be treated as if it took place at the beginning of fiscal
1994. Viewed this way, we find the following actual rent expense
and expected future payments for Club Med:

Year	Minimum	Contingent	Other	Sandpiper	Total
Rent Expense					
1992	7,279	6,685	10,136		24,100
1993	6,956	6,755	10,255		23,966
1994	11,365	259	8,740		20,364
Future Rent Payments					
1995	3,101		4,959	4,225	12,285
1996	3,723		4,099	4,411	12,233
1997	3,719		2,197	4,605	10,521
1998	3,715		1,739	4,808	10,262
1999	3,387		931	5,019	9,337
Thereafter	37,841		3	107,138	144,982

Note that the actual rent expense in 1992–1994 is higher than
the expected rent in 1995–1999. Some of the difference relates to
the contingent rent, which is generally large in 1992 and 1993
but which does not appear in future rent payments. Furthermore,
note that whereas the rent expense on villages is reasonably steady,
the other rent expense declines steeply in 1995–1999, indicating
these are short-term leases.

Let us attempt a de facto capitalization of the operating lease
payments of Club Med. Its leases run on average terms of 17 years,
with a payment of about $3.4 million per year. Using a 10
percent interest rate, these lease payments have a present value
of $27 million. The Sandpiper lease has a remaining term of about

21 years, with lease payments that seem to increase about 4.4 percent per year. Assuming a 10 percent discount rate and an initial payment of $4.2 million, the present value of this lease is about $52 million.[6] We should now add the present value of the other rent payments, which is about $11.3 million, again using a 10 percent discount rate and the future rent payments provided by Club Med. Thus, the present value of all the above lease payments is about $90 million. The firm reports total debt of about $242 million ($162 million of current liabilities, $54 million of long-term debt, and $26 million of other liabilities and minority interest). The de facto capitalization of operating lease payments would have increased total debt by about 37 percent (90/242). Had we used more realistic assumptions about future payments under operating leases, total debt would have increased even more.

The example of Sandpiper also illustrates another dimension of leases, the ability to convert an owned property to immediate cash without showing the liability on the balance sheet. In this case, Club Med sold Sandpiper, but immediately obligated to lease it back for a long period—about 22 years. Proceeds of the sale were about $65.7 million, which the firm can now use to develop other properties. The firm shows the cash (or the other properties) as assets on the balance sheet, so total assets do not decrease due to the transaction, unless the cash is used to pay expenses. At the same time, the liability the firm now assumes— to make annual lease payments of over $4 million per year—is not recorded among Club Med's liabilities. The firm had in this case a gain of about $25 million, which would be incorporated into the income statement over a period of 22 years, the length of the lease, and is shown as a liability on the balance sheet until it is amortized. Over the lease term, Club Med will show annual rental payments of about $5 million, and a gain of about $1 million, or a net expense of about $4 million. This can be compared with a depreciation expense of about $2 million a year, assuming book value of Sandpiper was about $40 million, and the remaining depreciation period was identical to the new lease term. It can easily be seen that the cash flow consequences and

---

[6]This is probably an understatement, since the village was subsequently sold for $65.7 million.

the financial reporting description of the sale and leaseback transaction of Sandpiper are very different.

Table 7–4 provides a list of firms with lease obligation that exceed total debt of the firm.

TABLE 7–4

Additional Liability Due to Operating Leases—1993–94 (amounts in millions)

Ticker	Name	P.V. Operating Lease Obligation (1)	Total Debt (2)	Ratio to Total Debt (1)/(2)	Market Value
ACV	Alberto-Culver Co CL B	$ 77.9	$ 75.8	1.03	$ 810.4
AAL	Alexander & Alexander	262.9	141.0	1.86	1,031.7
AWA	America West Airlines CL	675.2	521.6	1.29	406.1
APS	American President COS LT	450.2	271.7	1.66	600.4
BKS	Barnes & Noble Inc	481.3	190.0	2.53	919.8
BIGB	Big B Inc	67.0	66.8	1.00	211.3
BCF	Burlington Coat Factory	162.9	156.4	1.04	447.7
CLD	Caldor Corp	294.8	291.7	1.01	360.4
CKR	CKE Restaurants Inc	102.5	79.9	1.28	136.8
CML	CML Group	116.4	59.0	1.97	461.1
CA	Computer Associates Intl	170.0	149.6	1.14	10,060.4
CPY	CPI Corp	98.4	60.1	1.64	208.9
DARTA	Dart Group Corp CL A	166.6	121.3	1.37	153.7
DLCH	Delchamps Inc	154.0	51.1	3.01	128.1
DAL	Delta Airlines Inc	3,618.8	3,466.0	1.04	3,137.7
DDC	Detroit Diesel Corp	116.3	62.3	1.87	543.4
EBS	Edison Brothers Stores	421.7	239.1	1.76	316.6
FCA	Fabri-Centers of America	174.1	102.5	1.70	168.5
FDX	Federal Express Corp	1,952.6	1,830.4	1.07	3,846.2
FAF	First Amer Finl CP CA	86.0	85.0	1.01	217.3
FLR	Fluor Corp	90.0	88.3	1.02	3,991.8
GPS	Gap Inc	871.3	82.6	10.55	4,943.3
GME	General Motors Cl E	905.6	695.0	1.30	19,508.9
GMH	General Motors CL H	761.3	494.6	1.54	15,996.0
Grey	Grey Advertising Inc	89.6	78.9	1.14	208.5
HHC	Horizon Healthcare Corp	130.0	109.3	1.19	613.9

TABLE 7–4 (concluded)

Ticker	Name	P.V. Operating Lease Obligation (1)	Total Debt (2)	Ratio to Total Debt (1)/(2)	Market Value
KSS	Kohls Corp	$ 76.0	$ 52.8	1.44	$1,591.9
LECH	Lechters Inc	152.8	85.9	1.78	277.6
LTD	Limited Inc	2,056.4	665.7	3.09	7,869.0
LOTS	Lotus Development Corp	103.0	78.5	1.31	1,915.1
MGA	Magna International CL A	72.7	63.5	1.15	2,279.1
MES	Melville Corp	1,694.2	571.0	2.97	3,684.3
MESA	Mesa Airlines Inc	199.7	100.2	1.99	202.9
MIKE	Michaels Stores Inc	126.7	110.8	1.14	705.8
MCL	Moore Corp Ltd	133.2	100.9	1.32	1,929.1
MLG	Musicland Stores Corp	415.9	135.0	3.08	325.3
NIN	Nine West Group Inc	72.4	51.1	1.42	1,003.4
OMC	Omnicom Group	330.4	326.4	1.01	2,055.1
ORCL	Oracle Systems Corp	193.3	89.7	2.15	14,072.9
PST	Petrie Stores Corp	298.9	145.0	2.06	269.4
PGSAY	Petroleum Geo-SVC Spon	70.6	66.8	1.06	589.4
PIR	Pier 1 Imports Inc/DE	287.1	147.9	1.94	353.5
PZS	Pittston Co-Services Group	172.4	88.8	1.94	1,135.9
RGIS	Regis Corp/MN	97.5	64.5	1.51	211.5
RTRSY	Reuters Holding PLC ADR	260.0	218.7	1.19	12,558.4
RDK	Ruddick Corp	116.9	115.2	1.01	443.2
SPLS	Staples Inc	226.3	125.0	1.81	1,745.2
TLB	Talbots Inc	123.3	58.0	2.13	1,151.9
TJX	TJX Companies Inc	457.0	219.6	2.08	896.1
USR	US Shoe Corp	486.7	190.6	2.55	1,204.9
UAL	UAL Corp	4,834.9	4,050.0	1.19	1,281.7
U	USAir Group	2,834.7	2,531.9	1.12	376.6
VEN	Venture Stores Inc	108.3	103.2	1.05	208.6
WBN	Waban Inc	387.7	189.1	2.05	626.1
WPO	Washington Post CL B	55.3	51.8	1.07	2,915.3
WIN	Winn-Dixie Stores Inc	729.2	98.3	7.42	4,195.2
Z	Woolworth Corp	1,566.4	901.0	1.74	2,334.9
WOA	Worldcorp Inc.	179.3	136.1	1.32	133.3
	Median	176.7	113.0	1.43	758.1

UNFUNDED PENSION AND OTHER POSTRETIREMENT OBLIGATIONS

Most entities in the United States have plans that promise employees various postretirement benefits, most notably pension, life insurance, and health care benefits. It is important to study and understand the entity's postretirement liabilities in any cash flow and credit analysis. We shall describe in this section some of those postretirement benefits, their accounting rules, and their effects on debt.

Firms use two general types of pension plans—defined benefit and defined contribution plans. *Defined benefit plans* promise the employees specific monetary payments to be made to them (or to their remaining spouses) upon retirement. The firm has the responsibility to have funds available to pay for those future benefits. *Defined contribution plans* specify the contribution the employer has to make currently to the plan. Employees are paid from funds available in the plan when they retire, based on number of years of service and salary. Under defined benefit plans, the employer bears the risk of a shortfall in funds if the employee reaches retirement and the plan's assets are insufficient to make the required payments. In that case, the employer must make supplemental payments so that retirees will receive their promised benefits. Under defined contribution plans, the employer discharges most responsibilities as soon as the necessary contributions are forwarded to the plan; any risk of shortfall in funds is born by the employees. Many firms have attempted in the last two decades to terminate their defined benefits plans and to offer instead defined contributions plans, which would effectively eliminate their risk, once the required contributions are made.

Typically, firms will set up a separate entity, the pension fund, which is administered jointly by employees and the firm's management (called the investment or employee benefits committee). Employer contributions to the fund (called funding) increase the assets of the pension fund. Fund assets are also invested (mostly in equities and governmental or corporate bonds), and the return on these investments increases fund assets. Fund assets decrease when payments are made to current retirees and, to a much smaller extent, due to expenses in managing the fund. Pension plans are subject to the provisions of the Employee Retirement Security Act of 1974, known as ERISA.

Defined contribution plans pose few accounting problems. When employees earn the right to the contribution by the employer, the employer accrues the obligation as a current liability. Funding (payment) of the contribution to the designated fund discharges the employer's obligation. The employer is not legally concerned with the value of the assets in the fund or with making additional payments to existing and future retirees. Fund managers are hired to maximize the long-term returns on the plan assets. An example for a defined contribution plan is one in which the employer transfers a specified percentage of the employee's current compensation to a fund chosen by the employee. Typically, these contributions are not taxable by the employee until drawn from the fund.

Defined benefit plans, on the other hand, pose great difficulties from an accounting point of view. Here, the employer retains the responsibility for the specified future benefits until the employee or the employee's survivors are no longer eligible for those benefits. Thus, the employer is liable for these benefits until all future payments are made. The major accounting issues are how to estimate the value of this liability and how it should be recorded in the financial statements. The major concern for the cash flow analyst is the effect of the liability on cash flows and the long-term solvency of the firm.

Initially, firms reported no liability for pension obligations and included in the income statement an expense that was equal to the actual payment to existing retirees during the accounting period. This practice was stopped by *APB Opinion No. 8*, which required firms to estimate their liability to employees and disclose in a footnote to the financial statements some information about the liability. The next example will help you better understand the nature of the liability, and the associated accounting disclosure.

Example

This is a hypothetical example, although many firms have most features employed in this example.

The pension plan is a defined benefit plan. It promises that employees who reach retirement age (65 years) will get, for each year of service, annual compensation that is equal to 2 percent of their average annual salary during the five-year period prior to retirement. Thus, an employee who worked for the firm 30 years is entitled to 60 percent of the average annual salary prior to retirement. These benefits will continue until the employee dies, at which point only 50 percent of these benefits will be paid to the surviving spouse. The plan has other restrictions. For example, employees who leave the firm before they have spent at least five years with the firm are not eligible to any pension benefits. Employees who remain at the employment of the firm for more than five years, but for less than 10 years, will get only 50 percent of their pension benefits when they reach retirement age, even if they are no longer employed by the firm. After 10 years, employees are eligible for 100 percent of the earned pension benefits when they reach retirement age, even if they are no longer employed by the firm.

Several factors affect the estimation of the firm's liability under this plan. First, the firm has to consider the current age of employees, so that it will know how many years are left before pension benefits begin. Second, the firm has to estimate the life expectancy of the employees and their spouses, so it can assess how long benefits will have to be paid. Third, the firm should estimate the turnover rate of employees, because it is *not* necessary to accrue pension obligations for employees who will not remain with the firm for at least five years, and only 50 percent of the benefits for employees who remain with the firm between five and ten years. The firm should then estimate the average annual salary of the employee upon which pension benefits will be based.[7] Finally, these future payments should be discounted to estimate the present value of the pension obligation. The estimated liability is called actuarial present value of pension benefits, because actuarial assumptions are made in estimating future payments under the plan.

Typically, when firms initiate pension plans or when firms make amendments to existing pension plans (e.g., increasing the rate of compensation from 1.5 percent to 2 percent for each year of service), the benefits are applied retroactively to employees who were eligible for these benefits when the plan was adopted or

---

[7]In some pension plans, payments received from Social Security reduce payments to employees. In such cases, it is important also to determine the future level of payments from the Social Security system.

amended. Thus, in addition to the continuous accumulation of pension benefits for current services by employees, firms may be liable to pay pension benefits to employees for past and prior services. These lump-sum additions to the pension liability may be spread over future periods by amortizing the liability for prior services over the remaining time until employees retire.

As already explained, the firm makes contributions to the pension fund, and fund assets are invested further to yield greater assets in the future.[8] Thus, at any point in time, the pension plan will have a liability for future pension benefits and assets from which this liability can be paid in the future. We describe the fund as *underfunded* when liabilities exceed assets and as *overfunded* when assets exceed the liabilities.

The funding status of the plan may change every year. The firm may increase contributions to the plan, or investments may yield a rate of return beyond that which was initially expected. Also, there may be actuarial gains and losses that are caused by changes in the actuarial assumptions that underlie the estimated liability. For example, when the turnover rate of employees surpasses expectations, the pension liability decreases because fewer employees will reach the point at which benefits vest, which is the point when benefits will have to be paid even if the employee leaves the firm before retirement.[9] Another example is when employees die earlier than the actuarial projection. This reduces future benefits as well as current liabilities, thus producing an actuarial gain. Such gains and losses are not incorporated into income at the year they occur, but are amortized over future years, if they are material.

APB Opinion No. 8 (1968) required firms to estimate the pension liability using an acceptable actuarial method and to include in the pension expense an amortization of prior service costs. It also

---

[8]Sometimes the contribution to the pension fund will not be in cash but will be in the form of real-estate properties, or even the firm's own common stock. In an effort to reduce its liability in its underfunded pension plans, General Motors contributed its own common stock to the pension fund.

[9]For the pension liability one cannot necessarily use the rule of thumb according to which increases in liabilities are economically bad for the firm and decreases are necessarily beneficial to the firm. For example, an increase in the turnover rate will decrease the pension liability, but it also means the firm loses skilled, trained employees. Thus, the economic loss from the higher turnover ratio may actually exceed the economic benefits from reduced pension payments in the future.

required firms to disclose in a footnote to the financial statements the unfunded vested benefit obligation and the pension expense for the period. Unfunded vested benefits are equal to the actuarial present value of pension obligations that will be paid whether or not employees remain with the firm, minus fund assets that are available for payments to employees. In addition, the SEC required firms to disclose the unfunded prior service cost.

In 1976, the FASB changed the accounting and disclosure requirements as they relate to the pension fund. First, fund assets were required to be disclosed using the fair market value of those assets, and not at their accounting carrying cost. This usually tended to increase the value of fund assets because equity and real estate investments, typically, were understated when historical-cost values were used. Second, the FASB required additional disclosure about pension plans in a footnote to the financial statements. Firms had to supply information about the actuarial present value of their vested and nonvested pension benefits; about the fair market value of pension plan assets, about the average discount rate used in the estimation of the liability, and about the projected rate of return on pension plan investments. Still, no liabilities or assets were incorporated into the financial statements by these pronouncements.

In 1985, the FASB issued *SFAS No. 87*, which imposed new accounting and disclosure requirements on firms. *SFAS No. 87* required for the first time the recording of a pension liability on the balance sheet under certain conditions (described below). It also broadened the disclosure in the footnotes to the financial statements. The standard became effective in 1987, although some firms chose to adopt it earlier. Let us examine some of these major changes.

Probably the largest effect of this standard is the requirement to use the "projected benefit obligations" instead of the "accumulated benefit obligations" in some tests employed by the standard and in disclosure of the liability. The difference between projected and accumulated benefits relates to the forecast of future salary increases. Recall that a pension plan usually sets a formula for pension benefits based on the average salary at some point close to retirement. Naturally, the longer the service is with the firm, the more likely the employee is to have a higher salary due to promotions and salary increases as a result of inflation. Thus, in estimating the actuarial present value of *projected* benefit obligations, the actuary takes into account expected future salary increases. However, to estimate the actuarial present value of *accumulated* pension benefits, the actuary uses current salary levels. The difference between the two measures is substantial; for the average firm it increases the actuarial present value of the liability by about 20 percent to 40 percent.

The second major change in *SFAS No. 87* is the requirement to accrue a liability *on the balance sheet* that is equal to the excess of the actuarial present value of accumulated pension benefits over plan assets. Thus, if a firm's actuarial present value of accumulated pension benefit is larger than the value of plan assets to satisfy this liability, the difference is shown as a liability on the balance sheet. This requirement becomes effective for firms with large shortfalls in their pension plans and is known as the *minimum liability* requirement.

The third major change in *SFAS No. 87* is the treatment of the transition amount. At the initial adoption of *SFAS No. 87*, the difference between the actuarial present value of *projected* pension benefits and the plan assets is denoted the transition amount. This difference is amortized over the average remaining service of employees or 15 years. Note that if the plan is overfunded at the adoption of *SFAS No. 87*, the transition amount is an asset that is incorporated into the balance sheet (through the amortization) over a period of time. If the plan is underfunded at the adoption of *SFAS No. 87*, a liability will be incorporated into the balance sheet over the amortization period. Note that the transition asset/liability is a one-time event, and subsequent additional net assets or liabilities will not be recorded on the balance sheet, unless a minimum liability occurs.

SFAS No. 87 also required firms to disclose information in a footnote to the financial statements, some of which is just a carryover of prior FASB pronouncements, but most of which is new and broadened information. The required information is generally of three types: (*a*) information about pension plan assets and liabilities, whether incorporated on the balance sheet or not, (*b*) information that provides additional details about the pension expense for the period, and (*c*) information about the pension plan, funding policy, and assumptions used in estimating the liability. Later we will provide a description of these information items.

The standard requires firms to disclose information about the actuarial present value of accumulated pension benefits and of projected pension benefits. Since the old disclosure requirements are still in effect, the pension liability is broken down into vested and nonvested benefits. The footnote also discloses the fair market value of pension plan assets, so the analyst can determine if the pension plan is overfunded or underfunded. The standard also requires firms to reconcile the funding status, or the amount of over- or underfunding with the pension plan assets/liabilities that were not yet recognized and incorporated on the balance sheet. For example, the transition amount is likely to appear for most firms in the late 80s and the 90s, since it is amortized over a period of about 15 years for the majority of firms. The firm is likely to disclose those unamortized actuarial gains/losses that are not yet incorporated on the balance sheet. The firm is also likely to include such items as prior period pension costs that are not yet incorporated into the balance sheet.

Example

Monsanto, a chemical firm, also produces NutraSweet, chemicals for agricultural uses, and various drugs through its Searle group. In its 1993 annual report, the firm includes the following information (in millions of dollars):

	1993	1992
Plan assets at fair value	$3,827	$3,751
Actuarial present value of plan benefits:		
Vested	3,266	2,848
Nonvested	120	123
Accumulated benefit obligation	3,386	2,971
Effect of projected future salary increases	373	426
Projected benefit obligation	$3,759	$3,397
Excess of plan assets over projected benefit obligation	68	354
Less:		
Unrecognized initial net gain	161	221
Unrecognized prior service cost	(261)	(216)
Unrecognized subsequent net gain	305	538
Accrued net pension liability	$ 137	$ 189

The accrued net pension liability was included in:

Postretirement liabilities	$ 185	$ 232
Less: Other assets	(48)	(43)
Accrued net pension liability	**$ 137**	**$ 189**

First, let us note that the plan was overfunded in 1993 and in 1992; plan assets exceeded the projected benefit obligations by $68 million and $354 million in 1993 and 1992, respectively. Further note that the projected benefit obligation exceeded the accumulated benefit obligation by about $373 million in 1993, or about 11 percent of the accumulated pension benefit obligations. Thus, the incorporation of future salary increases into the estimation of the liability has affected the pension liability materially.

Second, we should note that although Monsanto had an overfunded plan in 1993 and 1992, it recorded on the balance sheet a net liability of $137 and $189 million, respectively. The reason for recording a liability—although Monsanto had more assets than obligations in its pension plans—was explained at the bottom of the schedule. Monsanto had an unrecognized initial net gain (i.e., a transition asset) of $161 million which had not yet been incorporated into the balance sheet. It would be incorporated slowly in the future through an amortization. Similarly, the firm had subsequent net gains of $305 million, which were yet to be incorporated into the balance sheet. These gains were mostly from the success of their investments, as we shall see later. However, the accounting standards do not allow a firm to recognize these net gains (or losses) immediately in the period they occur. Instead, they are spread over a long period. Finally, there are prior service costs that arise when plans are adopted or amended to include benefits retroactively, which increased the benefit obligation by $261 million in 1993, but had not yet been shown on the balance sheet. It would be incorporated into the balance sheet slowly through an amortization of this liability. Thus, the net effects of these three items would be: net assets of $ 68 million should be reduced by the assets that are not yet recognized, $161 million and $305 million, but would increase by $261 million of liabilities that do not have to be recognized yet, to yield a net liability of $137 (68 − 161 − 305 + 261).

The cash flow analyst would note that Monsanto actually should show fewer liabilities on its balance sheet than it shows. Its liabilities should actually be reduced by $137 million, and its assets should increase by $68 million, or an increase in net assets (assets minus liabilities) of $205 million (68 + 137). Furthermore, Monsanto would not need to contribute cash into its retirement plans, and cash outflows for the firm would be unnecessary. Indeed, Monsanto stated: "Because the company's pension plans are well-funded, contributions to these plans were neither required nor made in 1993, 1992, and 1991."

Example

Aluminum Co. of America, Alcoa, is the largest manufacturer of aluminum and aluminum products in the United States. In its December 1993 financial statements, it disclosed the following information about its pension assets and liabilities (in millions):

	Assets Exceed Accumulated Benefit Obligations		Accumulated Benefits Obligations Exceed Assets	
	1993	1992	1993	1992
Plan assets, primarily stocks and bonds at market	$3,688.4	$1,702.1	$ 90.6	$1,662.1
Present value of obligation:				
Vested	3,154.8	1,450.0	197.1	1,697.7
Non-vested	310.9	147.8	17.3	161.2
Accumulated benefit obligation	3,465.7	1,597.8	214.4	1,858.9
Effect of assumed salary increases	328.1	60.3	20.0	236.7
Projected benefit obligation	3,793.8	1,658.1	234.4	2,095.6
Plan assets greater (less than) projected benefit obligation	(105.4)	44.0	(143.8)	(433.5)
Unrecognized:				
Transition (assets) obligations	7.7	(40.3)	10.8	67.2
Prior service cost	138.6	27.0	53.8	45.6
Actuarial (gains) losses, net	(113.3)	56.0	(4.1)	200.8
Minimum liability adjustment			(43.4)	(78.5)
Prepaid (accrued) pension cost	$ (72.4)	$ 77.7	$(126.7)	$ (200.4)

In this disclosure, Alcoa reports separately the assets and liabilities of its various pension plans along two dimensions—those plans in which assets exceed accumulated benefits and those in which the reverse occurs. The analyst should note, however, that both of these types were underfunded in 1993, as indicated by the entry plan assets greater (less than) projected benefit obligations. The total underfunding of Alcoa at the end of 1993 is $249.2 million (105.4 + 143.8) if measured by comparing the plan assets to the projected benefit obligations. The total amount of liabilities incorporated on the balance sheet is $199.1 million (72.4 + 126.7). Thus, the analyst should assume that the total debt of Alcoa should be increased by $50.1 million (249.2 − 199.1), which is the net pension liability that is yet to be recorded on the balance sheet.

As in the previous example, note that the effect of projecting future salary increases is to increase the accumulated benefit obligation by a total of $348.1 million (328.1 + 20.0), or 9.5 percent. Unlike Monsanto in the prior example, Alcoa had a net transition liability, which is incorporated on the balance sheet after the proper amortization. All other items are the same as we saw for Monsanto, except for the entry minimum liability adjustment. This item represents the minimum liability on pension plans that had accumulated benefits that exceed their assets. Note that in 1993, the accumulated benefit obligations of $214.4 million exceeded plan assets of $90.6 million by $123.8 million. Thus, Alcoa needed to include on the balance sheet a minimum liability of this amount. It actually shows an accrued liability of $126.7 on the balance sheet.

The standard requires firms to disclose information about the major components of the pension expense for the accounting period. The first component is the normal service cost for the period. This represents the additional pension benefits that employees earned during the period simply because they spent one additional year of service with the firm. Recall that the pension plan has a formula that provides pension benefits according to the number of service years with the firm. Thus, this additional year entitles employees to greater pension benefits, and the actuarial present value of those additional benefits is the normal service cost.

The second component of the pension expense is the interest expense. This component represents the fact that the balance of the pension liability as of the beginning of the year has come one year closer to maturity. As is true of debt, when a loan is one year closer to maturity its present value increases, and the increase in the present value of the loan from the beginning of the year to its end represents interest expense. Similarly, since the actuarial present value of the pension liability that existed at the beginning of the year is larger at the end of the year, the increase in the present value is considered interest expense and is shown as the second component of the pension expense for the year.

The third component of the pension expense is actually a pension revenue in most cases—the rate of return on pension plan assets. As a mirror image of the interest expense on the pension plan liability at the beginning of the year, the return on plan assets represents the interest revenue on assets that existed at the beginning of the year. Recall that in most cases the pension plan will have assets in the fund at the beginning of the period. These assets were intended to offset the liability that existed at the beginning of the period. Just as we recognize the increase in the present value of the liability over the year as interest expense, we should recognize as revenue the increase in plan assets due to profitable investments during that same year.

The final component of the pension expense in the footnote to the financial statements is the amortization and deferral of various amounts. Among the amounts that need to be amortized and included in the pension expense are items such as actuarial gains and losses, which are incorporated into the balance sheet over a period of time.[10] Other items that will be amortized are prior service costs due to adoption and amendments of pension plans, and the transition amount. As a matter of fact, most of the firms that had a large overfunding at the time they adopted *SFAS No. 87*, which meant that they also had a large transition asset, reduced pension expense that year because of the amortization of the transition asset. Also, if the pension fund had an actual return on assets that exceeded or fell short of the assumed long-term rate of return, the excess (or shortfall) is deferred and is amortized slowly if it exceeds a minimum amount. Finally,

---

[10]*SFAS No. 87* allowed firms to amortize actuarial gains and losses only if they exceed a certain minimum amount. This is the "corridor" approach adopted by this standard.

firms may from time to time decide to provide current retirees with benefits increases. These would also be added to the pension expense. Let us review examples of disclosure of the components of pension expense.

Example

In its note to the 1993 financial statements, Monsanto reports the following information about the components of pension cost (income) (in millions):

	1993	1992	1991
Service cost for benefits earned during the period	$ 75	$ 65	$ 63
Interest cost on benefit obligation	285	272	259
Assumed return on plan assets*	(342)	(291)	(269)
Amortization of unrecognized net gain	(26)	(41)	(33)
Total	$ (8)	$ 5	$ 20

*Actual returns on plan assets were $550 million, $230 million, and $689 million in 1993, 1992, and 1991, respectively.

Note that Monsanto not only did not show an expense on its defined benefit pension plans but actually showed income on these plans. The reason is that the firm showed a high return on its assets, $342 million, whereas the increase in the value of the pension obligation as of the beginning of the year was only $285 million. Thus, the firm had an excess income of $57 million (342 − 285) to offset pension costs for the year of $75 million. In addition, the firm had an amortization and deferral amount that also *decreased* the expense by $26 million, with a net result of income on pension plans of $8 million. A large portion of the $26 million that were amortized during the year was due to the amortization of unrecognized net gains and the transition amount. Indeed, if we go back to the data provided above on Monsanto's pension assets and liabilities, we can see that the transition amount consisted of $161 million at the end of 1993, and the unrecognized gains amounted to $305 million on that date. Note further that Monsanto had an actual return that exceeded the assumed long-term return in 1993 and 1991 by large amounts, but was lower by a small amount in 1992. Thus, over these three years, the unrecognized (unamortized) gains were substantial.

Example

In a footnote to its 1993 financial statements, Alcoa reported the following information about its components of pension expense (in millions
of dollars):

	1993	1992	1991
Benefits earned	$102.4	$ 92.2	$ 82.6
Interest accrued on projected benefit obligation	253.9	250.7	240.9
Net amortization	59.8	29.7	21.2
	416.1	372.6	544.7
Less: Expected return on plan assets*	268.1	259.2	249.0
Pension costs	$148.0	$113.4	$ 95.7

*The actual returns were higher than the expected returns by $324.2 in 1993, $82.4 in
1992, and $253.9 in 1991 were deferred as actuarial gains.

Note that unlike Monsanto above, Alcoa reported an expense from
its pension plan in 1993. Further note that, although the return on
plan assets in all years shown exceeded the interest cost component,
the net amortization and deferral figure *increased* the expense by $59.8
million in 1993. This figure represents (primarily) amortization of
prior service costs because, as we saw before, the transition amount
was a small net liability.

The last type of information disclosed in the footnote on pensions
is about assumptions made to estimate the pension liability, a
description of the pension plans and pension formulas, and the
funding policy of the firm. For example, the firm will usually
disclose the discount rates, the rate of return on plan assets, and
the rate at which salaries are expected to grow in the future. Interestingly enough, most firms assume that the rate of return on plan
assets and the rate used to discount the pension liability are higher
than the rate at which salaries are expected to grow. Thus, employees in these firms are estimated to have an erosion of their real
earnings power.

The firm usually describes its pension plans in general terms:
who is eligible for participation in the plan, the major elements of
the plan formula, and any other plans that are not standard U.S.
plans. Thus, information is separately provided about foreign
pension plans and about multiemployer plans within the United

States (multiemployer plans are common to all employees of a particular union, regardless of the specific employer. All employers are responsible together for pension liabilities and assets). The firm will also describe its funding policy (i.e., what contributions to the fund are expected to be made every year, or at least normally).

Example

Monsanto discloses the following information about its pension plans:

> Most Monsanto employees are covered by noncontributory pension plans...Pension benefits are based on the employee's years of service and/or compensation level. Pension plans are funded in accordance with Monsanto's long-range projections of the plans' financial conditions. These projections take into account benefits earned and expected to be earned in the future, anticipated future returns on pension plan assets, and income tax and other regulations.

> Pension costs are determined by using the preceding year-end rate assumptions. Assumptions used as of Dec. 31 for the principal plans were:

	1993	1992	1991
Discount rate	7.25%	8.5%	8.5%
Assumed long-term rate of return on plan assets	9.50	9.5	9.5
Annual rates of salary increase (for plans that base benefits on final compensation level)	4.25	6.0	6.5

It should be noted that Monsanto expects the rate of return on plan assets to be 9.5 percent, although the discount rate is assumed to be only 7.25 percent. To compensate for the decline in the discount rate, however, the company that year also reduced the salary assumption. It is common to find significant changes in the discount rate, to go hand in hand with changes in either or both the investment and salary assumption. Furthermore, note that employees should expect salary increases of only 4.25 percent. Note further that the assumed discount rate was reduced in 1993 to reflect lower interest rates during that year. This change increased the pension benefit obligation substantially, as can be seen by comparing the accumulated (and projected) benefit obligation in 1992 and 1993. The firm reports that the change in the interest rate assumption caused an increase of $277 million in the projected benefit obligation. Thus, changes in assumed rates can have a major effect on the funding status of a pension plan.

Let us now check whether the interest expense and rate of return components of the pension expense are consistent with the assumed discount rate and the rate of return on plan assets. Recall that the projected benefit obligation as of 12/31/92 was reported by Monsanto as $3,397 million, and plan assets as of that date were $3,751 million. Multiplying the projected benefit obligation at the beginning of 1993 by the discount rate of 8.5 percent yields $289 million, which is very close to the reported interest cost component for 1993 of $285 million. Similarly, the expected rate of return on plan assets can be estimated as $339 million (9.5 percent of 3,751), which is close to the reported return on plan assets of $342 million in 1993.

Example

Alcoa reports the following information in the footnotes to its 1993 financial statements:

> Alcoa maintains pension plans covering most US employees and certain other employees. Pension benefits generally depend upon length of service, job grade and renumeration. Substantially all benefits are paid through pension trusts that are sufficiently funded to ensure that all plans can pay benefits to retirees as they become due.

It further provides the following information:

	1993	1992	1991
Settlement discount rate	6.75%	6.75%	7.25%
Long-term rate for compensation increases	5.5	5.5	5.5
Long-term rate of return on plan assets	9.0	9.0	9.0

Note that just like Monsanto, Alcoa also lowered its discount rate in 1992 and 1993. However, it did not change its assumptions about either salary increases or the rate of return on plan assets.

Alcoa further states that it "also sponsors a number of defined contribution pension plans. Expenses were $34.5 in 1993, $23.9 in 1992 and $22.1 in 1991." This shows the simplicity of accounting and disclosure for defined contribution pension plans.

Note that the pension plan assumptions disclosed by the firm relate only to a "closed" group of employees—its current active and current retirees. Long-term assumptions regarding growth in the workforce, while not covered under existing accounting regulations, are routinely covered by the company's actuarial valuations. Unfortunately, these assumptions are not normally disclosed to investors outside the company.

What are the implications of the pension plan liabilities and assets to total debt and free cash flows? The easy answer is that a firm may have an underfunded pension plan, and the liability that is recorded on the balance sheet (if one is recorded at all) may be smaller than the projected benefit obligation. In such cases, the cash flow analyst should add to total debt the difference between the present value of projected benefit obligations and the pension liability that is incorporated on the balance sheet. This additional liability is an off-balance-sheet liability, just like operating leases.

Example

American Brands, a manufacturer of tobacco and alcohol products, as well as plumbing fixtures and golf products, disclosed pension information in its 1993 reports about its U.S. and non-U.S. plans. Selecting the proper information from this footnote, we construct the following table (in millions):

	Overfunded U.S. Plans	Underfunded U.S. Plans	Non-U.S. Plans	Total
Projected benefit obligation	$903.2	$810.0	$857.8	$2,571.0
Fair value of assets	883.0	848.0	1,021.8	2,752.8
Excess (deficiency) of plan assets	(20.2)	38.0	164.0	181.8
Prepaid pension cost (liability)	62.5	73.1	182.1	317.7
Overstated net plan assets	82.7	35.1	18.1	135.9

Note that American Brands show total plan assets of $2,752.8 million, which exceeds the pension obligation of $2,571 million by $181.8 million. However, the firm has already incorporated on its balance sheet assets in the amount of $317.7. Thus, the financial analyst should regard the firm as having a book value that is lower by $135.9 million (317.7 − 181.8) than that reported on the balance sheet.

Example

In its 1994 annual report, Sysco discloses that on July 2, 1994, its projected benefit obligation reached $129.5 million, while its plan assets amounted to $110.3 million. The firm had an underfunding of

$19.2 million, but included on its balance sheet an accrued pension liability of only $18.2 million. Thus, the cash flow analyst needs to add $1 million to Sysco's debt for this off-balance-sheet liability. Sysco's long-term debt on that date amounted to $538.7 million, so the addition of the pension liability would not have been material for this particular firm. However, for some firms such an addition to total debt can have a material effect on the financial statements.

In some cases, the pension plan is overfunded to such a degree that the plan has more assets than what is already incorporated on the balance sheet. In those cases, the cash flow analyst could increase net assets of the firm and net equity by the difference between these two amounts. The difference represents additional assets that will save future cash inflows into the plan by the firm.

Example

National Service Industries Inc. operates in seven industries, but derives most of its revenues and cash flows from three core businesses—lighting equipment, textile rental, and specialty chemicals.

In its 1990 financial statements, National Service Industries reported a projected benefit obligation of $49.325 million as of 6/30/1990 and plan assets of $73.780 million on that date for its overfunded plans, so that net assets for these plans were $24.455 million. The firm reported that it had incorporated on the balance sheet an asset in the amount of $7.652 as of 8/31/90.[11] Thus, net assets should increase due to this plan by the difference, or $16.803 million (24.455 − 7.652).

For its underfunded plans, the actuarial present value of projected benefit obligations amounted to $15.464 million, whereas plan assets on that date were only $10.765 million. Thus, these plans were underfunded by $4.699 million. The firm reported that the pension liability on the balance sheet for these plans was only $3.806 million, so that the total debt of the firm should *increase* by $0.893 million (4.699 − 3.806). For convenience, one can probably net the increase in net assets with the increase in total debt.

The cash flow analyst should also attempt to evaluate the cash flow that the firm will fund into its pension plan, and compare that amount with the pension expense. Any discrepancies should be

---

[11]According to *SFAS No. 87*, the actuarial estimates and the balance sheet date should be no more than three months apart. Earlier, firms could have made the actuarial estimation on any day during the year.

added to free cash flows if the expense is greater than the cash outflow, or subtracted from free cash flows if the cash outflow is greater. In most cases, however, the firm provides only very general information about its funding policy, which does not permit the cash flow analyst an adequate assessment of the contributions to the pension plan. Such information is described in the company's "Annual Valuation," which is not normally given to shareholders or investors. Thus, the cash flow analyst can in most cases assume that the pension expense is equal to the cash outflow to the plan, and the only adjustment will be to total debt of the firm.

Table 7–5 shows the effects of the additional liability due to pension obligation for a sample of firms with large underfunded pension plans.

Table 7–6 provides another example in which we adjust total debt to include both additional debt due to operating leases and to pensions. To show the importance of these items, we selected an extreme example, Delta Airlines Inc., which has a significant liability due to operating leases of equipment, including aircraft.

As can be seen in Table 7–6, using 10 percent to discount payments under capital leases yields the capitalized amount $144.1 million, which is remarkably close to the capitalized obligation reported by Delta. When we capitalize the payments under operating leases net of sublease revenues, we obtain an additional liability of $5.87 billion, which increases total debt of $1.4207 billion by about 413.2 percent!

When we examine the footnote on pensions, we find that Delta has an underfunding of about $382.6 million, whereas the liability that has been incorporated on the balance sheet as of the end of 1990 is only $21.7 million. Thus, additional liability due to pensions in the amount of $360.9 million should be included in total debt. This increases reported total debt by about 25.4 percent. Together with operating leases and before considering the effects of other postretirement benefits, total debt increases by 438.6 percent! This shows the importance of considering off-balance-sheet liabilities.

PENSION PLAN SURPLUS OR DEFICIENCY

The growth in corporate unfunded pension liabilities made firms, unions and union members, employees, Congress, security

TABLE 7–5
Additional Liability Due to Pensions—1993–94 (amounts in millions)

		Additional Pension Liability (1)	Total Debt (2)	Ratio to Total Debt (1)/(2)	Market Value
AMT	Acme-Cleveland Corp	1.3	3.5	0.38	102.9
ACXT	ACX Technologies Inc	31.6	71.0	0.44	542.1
ADCT	ADC Telecommunications Inc	1.0	0.8	1.19	1,875.3
ATLI	Advanced Technology Lab Inc	4.5	3.7	1.24	196.6
AFL	Aflac Inc	60.7	122.1	0.50	4,108.3
AKST	AK Steel Holding Corp	167.5	402.4	0.42	658.0
ALS	Allegheny Ludlum Corp	64.4	135.1	0.48	1,413.0
ATK	Alliant Techsystems Inc	32.5	56.9	0.57	375.9
AFIL	American Filtrona Corp	0.5	1.3	0.36	104.6
AZO	Autozone Inc	4.5	4.3	1.06	3,534.1
AVP	Avon Products	73.1	194.1	0.38	4,132.3
BA	Boeing Co	843.0	2,630.0	0.32	17,592.7
BMY	Bristol Myers Squibb	332.0	765.0	0.43	32,938.7
CCC	Calgon Carbon Corp	6.5	9.0	0.72	439.3
CASC	Cascade Corp	1.4	4.2	0.34	165.1
ECP	Central Newspapers CLA	1.2	2.7	0.45	685.6
CEN	Ceridian Corp	83.7	19.4	4.31	1,524.8
KOF	Coca-Cola Femsa De C V A	1.9	2.7	0.71	855.0
CG	Columbia Gas System	31.0	6.1	5.09	1,384.2
CTB	Cooper Tire & Rubber	24.8	44.1	0.56	2,404.3
ACCOB	Coors (Adolph) CL B	108.9	225.0	0.48	613.2
CORD	Cordis Corp	7.1	11.6	0.61	1,178.1
CRD.A	Crawford & Co CL A	45.4	10.9	4.18	550.9
ESY	E-Systems Inc	187.5	33.1	5.66	1,527.2
ECL	Ecolab Inc	51.2	143.7	0.36	1,537.9
ELF	Elf Aquitaine Spon ADR	4,317.0	12,179.0	0.35	19,381.2
EBF	Ennis Business Forms	4.4	0.5	8.74	213.7
FICI	Fair Isaac & Company Inc	1.8	2.7	0.64	276.5
FLK	Fluke Corp	10.1	14.9	0.68	281.2
AJG	Gallagher (Arthur J.) & Co	12.6	25.7	0.49	522.9
GD	General Dynamics Corp	63.0	196.0	0.32	2,937.2
GPC	Genuine Parts Co	27.2	12.4	2.20	4,859.1

TABLE 7–5 *(concluded)*
Additional Liability Due to Pensions—1993–94 (amounts in millions)

		Additional Pension Liability (1)	Total Debt (2)	Ratio to Total Debt (1)/(2)	Market Value
GRB	Gerber Scientific Inc	12.8	7.9	1.62	335.5
GDMK	Goodmark Foods	1.9	5.5	0.34	119.7
GRO	Grow Group Inc	3.3	3.2	1.05	235.6
HDI	Harley-Davidson Inc	30.3	21.4	1.42	1,802.5
HRL	Hormel Foods Corp	22.0	10.7	2.06	2,120.0
ID	Indresco Inc	10.8	16.7	0.65	286.7
MNI	McClatchy Newspapers CL A	0.8	0.1	13.73	709.7
MKRL	MK Rail Corp	0.6	0.9	0.60	154.3
MRC	Moorco International Inc	2.8	7.4	0.37	148.3
3MBEN	Moore (Benjamin) & Co	4.1	11.8	0.35	679.5
MRN	Morrison Knudsen Corp	14.4	47.0	0.31	192.3
MII	Morton Intl Inc	87.1	267.3	0.33	4,178.2
GOSHA	Oshkosh B'Gosh Inc CL A	4.9	1.3	3.78	199.6
PZM	Pittston Co-Minerals Group	32.2	0.3	104.22	156.1
PCP	Precision Castparts Corp	12.8	15.7	0.82	501.8
ROK	Rockwell Intl Corp	600.5	991.2	0.61	8,478.6
3RVTL	Roseville Telephone Co	15.4	40.0	0.39	443.7
SHW	Sherwin-Williams Co	59.8	21.4	2.79	2,852.3
SMF	Smart & Final Inc	4.3	2.5	1.75	300.7
TSA	Sports Authority Inc	0.2	0.1	2.76	400.3
SREG	Standard Register Co	14.9	24.0	0.62	494.5
STH	Stanhome Inc	11.4	0.8	13.68	536.3
TER	Teradyne Inc	16.3	17.2	0.95	1,511.2
TKIOY	Tokio Marine & Fire Ins AD	180.5	518.1	0.35	18,046.0
TSS	Total System Services Inc	1.1	1.7	0.67	1,058.3
X	USX-US Steel Group	1,148.0	1,551.0	0.74	2,455.0
VH	Value Health Inc	11.4	7.2	1.59	1,600.4
VOD	Vodafone Group Plc ADR	10.1	24.1	0.42	10,150.3
WNT	Washington Natl Corp	3.0	2.4	1.25	221.8
WDHD	Woodhead Industries Inc	0.4	0.2	2.60	127.5
WYL	Wyle Electronics	6.1	10.1	0.60	298.9
	Median	12.8	11.8	0.64	658.0

TABLE 7–6
Delta Airlines 1990 (millions of dollars)

	Capital Leases	Operating Leases	Subleases	Net Operating Leases
1988		$ 435.3		
1989		536.2		
1990		545.5		
1991	$ 24.4	533.9	$ 6.0	$ 527.9
1992	24.7	533.1	6.0	527.1
1993	19.7	523.4	5.9	517.5
1994	20.6	515.5	5.5	510.0
1995	18.3	512.9	5.2	507.7
Thereafter	108.6	6,984.8	72.1	6,912.7
Total	216.3	9,603.6	100.7	9,502.9
Interest—capital leases	69.6			
Present value of capital leases	146.8			
Present value assuming 10 percent	144.1			5,870.0
Total debt	$1,420.7			
Increase in total debt (%)—leases				413.2
Projected benefit obligation	3,904.1			
Plan assets (FMV)	3,521.5			
Net pension obligation	382.6			
Accrued pension costs (liability)	21.7			
Additional pension liability	360.9			
Increase in total debt (%)—pensions				25.4
Increase in total debt (%), total				438.6

analysts, and investment bankers aware of the potential risk in these long-term liabilities. Prior to the 1970s, a detailed analysis of an entity's pension plan was usually not undertaken until after a merger. With the enormous growth in the pension liability and its effects on cash flows, that situation changed dramatically. Now, due to the potentially large impact of contributions to the pension plan on cash flows, the pension liability is examined very closely by potential buyers, investors, analysts, and creditors.

Several entities with positive operating and free cash flows have chosen to file for bankruptcy protection in order to avoid large pension payments.

Example

LTV Corporation, a large steelmaker, bought Republic Steel for $712 million in stock and assumed about $800 million in debt. What it ignored was Republic's large unfunded pension liability, which at the time of LTV's bankruptcy petition had been paying close to $250 million a year on its $2 billion unfunded liability. The management of LTV transferred the entire pension obligation to the U.S. government's Pension Benefit Guarantee Corporation (PBGC), the government's sponsored and administered program that insures the private pension system. Because the PBGC became liable for the LTV pension payments of about $250 million annually, LTV could use those funds to modernize. LTV was further able to improve its free cash flow by renegotiating onerous union agreements and contracts for iron ore and coal. It was further relieved from paying the $16 per person annual insurance premium the PBGC charged for ongoing pension plans. While the PBGC continued to foot the pension obligation, LTV recorded in 1988 an operating cash flow of $410 million on $1.4 billion in revenues.[12] At the same time, the financial position of the PBGC deteriorated considerably, and, in essence, there was no guaranty that the PBGC could have undertaken payments for another large pension plan that defaulted on its obligations. Eventually, to free itself from bankruptcy status, LTV negotiated a solution for its pension obligation.

For firms with overfunded pension plans, plans in which pension assets exceed pension obligations, there is a temptation to terminate the pension plan, settle existing obligations, and use the excess assets in the firm. This, of course, may be viewed as hidden free cash flows, which get recognized with a formal action of the firm.

Example

In 1989, Alexander and Alexander Inc. purchased annuity contracts for $37.4 million to settle the accumulated benefit obligations to certain retirees and recorded a pre-tax gain of $15.7 million. Alexander and Alexander recognized the gain as a reduction of its 1989 pension expense.

---

[12]See Sarah Smith, "The Joys of Bankruptcy," *Corporate Finance Magazine*, April 1990, for a thorough review of the LTV case.

However, note that not all the net pension assets can be taken over by the firm. During the LBO era of the 1980s, the pension plan, once perceived to be a cost center for the firm, began to be considered a profit center because the investments of the pension plan yielded higher returns than were expected. A careful examination of the surplus of assets in the pension fund revealed, however, that only a small portion could have been utilized by the firm immediately.

Example

When speculation spread that USX was a candidate for a hostile takeover, many security analysts and financial reporters pointed to the seemingly large surplus of pension assets in the fund. Presumably, the acquired firm could have used cash from the pension plan to pay down debt used to acquire USX. The same argument was raised by security analysts in 1989 when investor Harold Simmons acquired a large stake in Lockheed Corp.

However, the large surplus that seemed to exist when security analysts simply subtracted pension liabilities from the fair market value of pension assets at year-end were drastically reduced in reality. What analysts ignored were:

1. Taxes on the gains in the pension assets, including a 15 percent excise tax.
2. The rates on Guaranteed Insurance Contracts (GICs) were lower than the discount rates assumed by the pension plan at that time. Thus, to satisfy the pension obligations, more assets would have had to be invested in low yielding GIC's.
3. For Lockheed, the U.S. government would be entitled to most of the surplus, since the Pentagon funded the plan.

It is vital that investors have a thorough understanding of the magnitude of the pension plan's liabilities that are assumed as a result of a business combination. Often, due to the haste with which many deals are put together, the acquiring company is not fully aware of the extent of the liabilities it is assuming. Other entities are more than happy to sell divisions because of the large extent of their pension fund liabilities and the future negative impact on cash flows of funding those liabilities. The wording in a purchase agreement concerning the meaning of a particular liability can be so vague that not all parties can later agree on what was meant when the initial agreement was signed.

Example

Banner Industries charged Pepsi-Cola that Pepsi dumped a large liability in its lap when Banner purchased its trucking subsidiary.

If the acquiring entity continues the plan of the acquired entity, it assumes a liability for that portion of the plan's vested liability that is not funded (the unfunded vested liability) up to 30 percent of the acquiring entity's net worth. The vested liability is the actuarial present value of benefits that must be paid even if current employees leave the company. In addition, the acquiring company may assume other liabilities. Nonvested benefits or benefits that will become vested only if the employee remains employed by the company may be assumed, and such liabilities may be substantial. If the acquired entity was publicly held, information about vested and nonvested benefits is included in the pension footnote to the annual report. More typically, the acquiring entity elects to terminate the acquired entity's plan, preferring to meld the new employees into its own plan, with appropriate credits given for length of service.

Liabilities under a multiemployer pension plan must be evaluated by the analyst because of the penalties associated by withdrawal. Severe withdrawal penalties could be imposed on the acquirer if it decided to terminate a pension plan. The extent of outstanding claims must also be reviewed, including other postretirement benefits such as life insurance or catastrophic claims. It is therefore important to learn of the annual (cash) pension expense from the company if it is not well specified. However, as we argued above, very few firms reveal the annual contribution to the pension plan.

LIABILITIES FOR POSTRETIREMENT BENEFITS OTHER THAN PENSIONS

In November 1984 the FASB issued *SFAS No. 81*, which required firms to disclose information about postretirement health care and life insurance benefits. Under that standard, firms were to disclose the cost of health care and/or life insurance benefits to retirees, their dependents, or survivors. If such costs to retirees could not be separated from costs to current employees, total costs were required to be disclosed, as well as the number of active employees and the number of retirees covered by the plan. A general description of the plan, covered employees, and benefits was also required.

Example

Brush Wellman Inc. is a leading international supplier of high-performance engineered materials. It is a fully integrated source of beryllium, beryllium alloys, and beryllia ceramic. It also supplies specialty metal systems and precious metal products.

In a note to its 1990 financial statements, Brush Wellman states:

> In addition to providing pension benefits, the Company provides health care and life insurance benefits for certain retired employees. The costs for these benefits are charged to expense as paid or accrued, and amounted to $803,000 in 1990; $1,044,000 in 1989; and $906,000 in 1988.
>
> In connection with operations discontinued in 1985, the Company retained certain obligations for these employees' postretirement medical benefits. At December 31, 1990 and 1989, $4,600,000 and $5,200,000 respectively, relating to such medical benefits were included in Other Long-Term Liabilities.

To get an idea about the magnitude of these benefits, total expenses of Brush Wellman in 1990, excluding taxes and interest, were about $270 million. Thus, the expenses on the two items to current retirees seem small (only $0.8 million in 1990). However, note that the firm also discloses the magnitude of its obligation for medical benefits to employees in discontinued operations, which amounted to about $4.6 million in 1990. Again, to put it in its proper perspective, total liabilities of Brush Wellman as of 12/31/90 were about $123 million, with long-term liabilities of about $60 million. Thus, the postretirement medical liability to those employees seems significant in relation to both total debt and certainly for long-term debt. Had the firm also accounted for future postretirement benefits to its *current* employees, total liabilities would have been increased significantly. Indeed, when the firm adopted *SFAS No. 106* in the beginning of 1991, the transition obligation amounted to about $25 million, which increased total liabilities and long-term liabilities significantly.

In December 1990, the FASB issued *SFAS No. 106,* which deals with accounting for postretirement benefits other than pensions. Under *SFAS No. 106,* firms have to accrue postretirement benefits expected to be paid to *active* employees, their beneficiaries, or their covered dependents for services that the active employees provide today. Thus, instead of showing in the financial statements an expense for *current payments to retirees,* firms have to also include an expense that is equal to the actuarial present value of additional benefits that *current active employees* earned during the period. In addition, footnote information provides data about the liability associated with these benefits, as well as any assets that were set aside to discharge the liability.

The requirements of *SFAS No. 106* are similar to those of *SFAS No. 87* for pension benefits, but with proper modifications. Similar to *SFAS No. 87,* a transition amount is created and is either included immediately in income as the effect of an accounting change, or it can be spread over 20 years (or the average remaining service period of active plan participants). Since most firms had not provided any funds to offset this liability, most firms have to set a transition liability, which either reduces net income in the period of adoption substantially or affects future income over a long period. Similarly, total debt of the firm is usually materially affected if the transition liability (with future adjustments due to additional services and reductions due to contributions) is added to the firm's existing liabilities.

Example

In a press release issued in September 1991, General Electric announced it had decided to adopt *SFAS No. 106* in the third quarter of 1991. GE wrote that "the new accounting will be applied by the Company on a catch up basis rather than prospectively and will result in a one-time, after-tax charge to net earnings of approximately $1.8 billion, less than 10 percent of GE's equity."

To place the expected decline of GE's 1991 earnings in perspective, note that total earnings of GE for 1990 were $4.303 billion and 1991's first quarter earnings were initially reported as $999 million.

Indeed, in its 1990 financial statements, GE provided the following data about postretirement benefits:

GE and its affiliates sponsor a number of plans providing retiree health and life insurance benefits. GE's aggregate cost for the principal plans, which cover substantially all employees in the United States, was $249 million in 1990, $283 million in 1989 and $302 million in 1988.

Generally, employees who retire after qualifying for optional early retirement under the GE plan are eligible to participate in retiree health and life insurance plans. Health benefits for eligible retirees under age 65 and eligible dependents are included in costs as covered expenses are actually incurred except for certain accruals provided in connection with business acquisitions and dispositions. For eligible retirees and spouses over age 65, the present value of future health benefits is funded or accrued and is included in costs in the year the retiree becomes eligible for benefits. The present value of future life insurance benefits for eligible retirees is funded and is included in costs in the year of retirement.

Most retirees outside the United States are covered by government programs, and GE's cost is not significant.

In December 1990, The Financial Accounting Standards Board issued *SFAS No. 106* , Employers' Accounting for Postretirement Benefits Other Than Pensions" establishing accounting principles for retiree health and life insurance plans. At January 1, 1991, GE had obligations for postretirement benefits other than pensions estimated at $4.2 billion while related assets in trust and cost accruals totaled $1.5 billion. *SFAS No. 106* must be adopted by 1993 either by amortizing this net transition obligation (about $2.7 billion) over 20 years or by charging it immediately to operations; earlier adoption is encouraged.

As can be seen from GE's 1990 footnote, postretirement payments for health and life insurance benefits were about $249 million in 1990. The transition amount at the end of 1990 was estimated as $2.7 billion, before applicable taxes. Thus, adopting SFAS No. 106 at the beginning of 1991 would have increased total liabilities by $2.7 billion, or about 2 percent (total liabilities of GE amounted to about $131 billion at the beginning of 1991). They also reduced stockholders equity, which amounted to about $22 billion at the beginning of 1991, by the net of tax effect of the accounting change or $1.8 billion. Thus, the change had a substantial impact on GE's financial statements.

It should be noted that within a month of GE's announcement of this large expense to its 1991 financial statements, Westinghouse Electric also announced a $1.68 billion pre-tax charge to earnings due to problems at its credit unit. Westinghouse announced plans to cut 3.4 percent of its workforce in an effort to reduce future cash outflows. Westinghouse's stock price declined over 10 percent after the announcement, whereas GE's stock price was largely unaffected by its announcement of the charge against earnings because of the adoption of *SFAS No. 106*. The difference in the market reaction can probably be attributed to expectations about future cash flows. GE's postretirement liability was known by the market, and the adoption of *SFAS No. 106* had no cash flow effect. Westinghouse's announcement may have taken the market by surprise, because the problems at its credit subsidiary may have been greater than expected by market participants.

To understand the provisions of *SFAS No. 106*, let us assume initially that it relates only to health care benefits that are paid after retirement. Suppose that the plan promises health care benefits to all employees who attain age 55 while in service, and only if they have at least 10 years of service with the firm. Suppose we wish to determine the obligation for an employee who is 45 years old, who had been with the firm for 13 years already, and who is expected to remain employed by the firm until retirement at the age of 65. The employee is expected to live until the age of 75, and health care benefits are assumed to be $1,500 during the first year after retirement and to increase by 8 percent each year. For simplicity, assume that the employee is single, and that all benefits are paid at the end of the year. The firm assumes a discount rate of 9 percent for the postretirement benefits. Table 7–7 contains the calculation of the future claims, the present value of these claims at four different ages, and the amount of the expected benefit obligation and the accumulated benefit obligation up to that age.

The first step in estimating the obligation is to determine the expected payments after retirement age (i.e., at ages 66 through 75.) We then discount the obligation to the present, when the employee is at age 45 (or 50, 55, and 56, in the other columns). The discounting is done by using the assumed rate of 9 percent. At the current age, 45, the present value of these future postretirement costs is $2,357. This is the actuarial present value of *expected* benefit obligations. It is the actuarial present value because we had to make actuarial assumptions about life

TABLE 7–7
Estimation of Expected and Accumulated Benefit Obligation

Future Age	Cost	Present Value at Age 45	50	55	56
66	$1,500	246	378	581	634
67	1,620	243	374	576	628
68	1,750	241	371	571	622
69	1,890	239	368	565	616
70	2,041	237	364	560	611
71	2,204	234	361	555	605
72	2,380	232	357	550	600
73	2,571	230	354	545	594
74	2,776	228	351	540	589
75	2,999	226	348	535	583
Total benefits	$21,730	$2,357	$3,626	$5,579	$6,081
Actuarial present value– expected benefits		$2,357	$3,626	$5,579	$6,081
Years from hiring date		13	18	23	24
Years until full eligibility		10	5	0	0
Ratio of accumulated services		13/23	18/23	23/23	23/23
Actuarial present value– accumulated benefits		$1,332	$2,838	$5,579	$6,081

expectancy, length of service, marital status, and the like. However, note that at present the employee is not yet fully eligible for the postretirement benefits. The employee will only become fully eligible at the age of 55, and then only if still at the employment of the firm. Thus, the employee has not yet attained the date of *full eligibility*.

SFAS No. 106 attributes postretirement benefits to years of service in an equal manner. Thus, at the age of 45 with 13 years of service, the employee has 10 more years to attain the full eligibility age of 55. *SFAS No. 106* requires the recognition of the portion of the obligation that accumulated by the employee to date using the number of years of service to date divided by the total expected number of years until the employee become fully eligible. At the age of 45 this yields 13/(13 + 10), and at the age of 50 the ratio increases to 18/23. Thus, the actuarial present value of the *accumulated* benefit obligations at the age of 45 is 13/23 of the *expected* benefit obligations, or $1,332. Similarly, at the age of 50, the accumulated benefit obligation is valued at 18/23 of the expected benefit obligation, or $2,838. However, at the age of 55, the employee becomes fully eligible, and the accumulated and expected benefit obligations are identical, $5,579. From then on, the actuarial present value of the two benefit obligations is identical.

Note that from the age of 55 to the age of 56 the actuarial present value of the accumulated benefit obligation increased by $502 (6,081 − 5,579). This increase represents the interest cost component of the expense, and is equal to 9 percent of the accumulated benefit at the age of 55, $5,579. This seems intuitively reasonable, because at the age of 55 the employee is fully eligible and an additional year of service does not add any new postretirement benefits. The only change is that the obligation's maturity is one year shorter at the age of 56 than at the age of 55, which represents the interest expense component, as we saw for pension benefits. However, before age 55, the increase in the liability comprises both an interest expense and a service cost component, because some of the postretirement benefits are attributed to that year's services.

SFAS No. 106 requires firms to estimate the actuarial present value of the accumulated postretirement benefits at the date of adoption of the new accounting rule, and subtract from it any assets that were set aside for satisfying this liability. This difference is denoted the transition amount and it can be treated in one of two approaches. The first approach is to include the offset to the transition amount in income immediately, as the effect of a change in an accounting principle, which means placing it after extraordinary items and just before net income on the income statement. The second approach is the delayed recognition approach; here the transition amount is amortized into income over 20 years, or the average remaining service years of active employees.

The FASB required the adoption of the standard for fiscal years beginning after December 15, 1992, for public U.S. firms. Thus, firms had to adopt the standard in their 1993 financial statements at the latest. Unlike pension plans, postretirement plans are largely unfunded and, typically, highly underfunded, so the transition amount is usually a liability for most firms, with an offsetting expense in the financial statements. Whether a firm chooses to recognize the expense immediately or delay its recognition depends on the firm's earnings status and its expectations about future earnings. If earnings for the year are very high or very low, the firm may choose to incorporate the transitional charge into income immediately. If earnings in the future are expected to be high, the firm may delay the incorporation of the expense into earnings of future years. Also, firms had some flexibility in adopting the standard earlier (before 1993) or later in their financial statements. Successful firms generally adopted the standard earlier (just like GE) to signal that they are in a better position.

Note that regardless of the date and method of adoption, there is no effect on cash flows. The only cash flow effects are the payments by the firm to current retirees and contributions to a fund that will make future payments to retirees. These cash outflows are unlikely to change because of the adoption of the standard. Indeed, in its press release announcing the adoption of *SFAS No. 106* in its 1991 financial statements, General Electric wrote: "There will be no cash flow impact from the charge to earnings, and the Company has been informed by both Moody's and Standard & Poor that the adjustment will have no impact on GE's triple-A debt ratings." Thus, credit rating agencies behave as if they were aware of this liability even prior to its incorporation into a footnote or the balance sheet itself. Since it has no cash flow effects (the expense is handled on a pay-as-you-go basis), it is only an accounting change and is likely to have very little effect on stock prices.

Other disclosure requirements of *SFAS No. 106* parallel those of *SFAS No. 87* for pensions. For example, a firm is required to disclose the amount of the net periodic postretirement cost, showing separately the service cost component, the interest cost component, the actual return on plan assets for the period, amortization of the transition amount, and other amortization and deferrals. A firm is also required to provide information about assets and liabilities: the fair value of plan assets, the actuarial present value of the accumulated benefit obligation (identifying separately the portion attributable to retirees, other fully eligible employees, and other active plan participants), unrecognized prior service cost, unrecognized net gain or loss, unrecognized transition amount, and the amount included on the balance sheet (whether an asset or a liability).

A firm is also required to disclose information about the terms of the plans, the participants, the assumed rates (including health care cost trend rate), the effects of a one-percentage-point increase in the assumed health care cost trend rates, and the type of assets held to discharge postretirement obligations. Because of its similarity to pension benefits, we will not expand the discussion of these items here.

Some firms began to take steps to prepare for the adoption of *SFAS No. 106* even before the standard was issued. For these firms, the effects on income or on the balance sheet due to the formal adoption of *SFAS No. 106* are likely to be small.

Example

In a footnote to its 1990 financial statements, Vulcan Materials Inc. includes the following paragraphs:

> In addition to pension benefits, the Company provides certain health care benefits and life insurance for some retired employees. Substantially all of the Company's salaried employees and, where applicable, hourly employees may become eligible for those benefits if they reach at least age 55 and meet certain service requirements while working for the Company. Generally, company-provided health care benefits terminate when covered individuals become eligible for Medicare benefits or reach age 65, whichever first occurs.
>
> Effective January 1, 1989, the Company changed to accrual method of accounting for the aforementioned postretirement benefits based on actuarially determined costs to be accrued over the period from the date of hire to the full eligibility of employees who are expected to qualify for benefits. In the first quarter of 1989, the Company recorded the full amount of its estimated accumulated postretirement benefit obligation, which represents the present value of the estimated future benefits payable to current retirees and a pro rata portion of estimated benefits payable to active employees after retirement period. The pretax charge to 1989 earnings was $15,331,000 with a net earnings effect of $9,562,000 ($.23 per share). The latter amounts were reflected as cumulative effects of the accounting change in the consolidated statement of earnings.
>
> The cost of providing postretirement benefits under the new accrual method amounted to $2,985,000 in 1990 and $2,549,000 in 1989. In prior years the Company recognized the cost of providing

the postretirement benefits by expensing the contributions when made. The amount included in expense for 1988 under the previous method approximated $629,000. If the 1990 and the 1989 costs had been determined under the previous method, the amounts recognized would have been $1,157,000 and $1,064,000, respectively.

In December 1990 the Financial Accounting Standards Board issued *Statement No. 106*, "Employer's Accounting for Postretirement Benefits Other Than Pensions," which requires the use of an accrual method. The method adopted earlier by the Company, as described above, is substantially in compliance with the new standard. The Company expects to modify its methodology in 1991 to fully comply with *SFAS No. 106*. No significant effect on earnings is expected as a result of this modification.

The Company funds the postretirement benefits plan each year through contributions to a trust fund for health care benefits and through payments of premiums to providers of life insurance. All assets of the plan relate to life insurance and are composed of reserves held by the insurer.

As indicated by Vulcan Materials, the firm has already adopted *SFAS No. 106* in substance, and it expects no significant effects from the complete adherence to the standard in 1991. Probably, the only major change for the firm will be the additional disclosure that is required by the new standard, as discussed above. Note that in terms of the annual expense, the expense for postretirement benefits more than doubled under the new standard than under the old method of "pay as you go." This is likely to be accentuated for firms that have not yet attempted to switch to accrual of the liability.

Example

American Brands adopted *SFAS No. 106* using the catch-up adjustment method. This required the firm to accrue a transition liability of $310 million on 1/1/93, of which $41.3 million was recorded earlier. The income statement effect (net of $119 million of deferred taxes) was a charge of $191 million on income before this charge of $668.2 million. Since the standard was adopted as of the beginning of 1993, there was also an increase in the annual expense for postretirement benefits from the pay-as-you-go method to complete accrual. The pre-tax expense in 1993 increased by $19.6 million. Note that this additional expense, as well as the transition liability, are noncash amounts. The firm reported that the total 1993 postretirement expense amounted to $36.4 million, of which $28.9 million represented service cost and $7.5 million represented interest cost. Thus, the cash outflow to current retirees in 1993 amounted to $16.8 million (36.4 − 19.6), which is the total expense for the year minus the noncash accrual. In 1992 and 1991, the cash expenses were $14.3 million and $11.2 million, respectively.

In reporting the funding status of the plans, American Brands disclosed the following (in millions of dollars):

	1993	1992
Accumulated benefit obligation		
Retirees	$265.7	$231.0
Fully eligible active plan participants	42.2	40.7
Other active plan participants	98.7	79.6
	406.6	351.3
Unrecognized net loss from experience differences	(34.9)	
Accrued postretirement costs	$371.7	$351.3

As can be seen, the firm does not have any assets in its postretirement plans. This is reasonable because there is no tax advantage to any funding of these liabilities, which are not tax deductible. Thus, the entire amount is shown on the balance sheet as a liability. Indeed, the firm reports on the balance sheet a liability of $520.3 million for postretirement and other liabilities and long-term debt of $2,492.4 million. Thus, postretirement benefits add a significant amount to total debt of the firm.

Note further that the firm reports an actuarial loss of $34.9 million, which occurred in 1993 between 1/1/93, the adoption date, and 12/31/93, the balance sheet date. This loss would be incorporated into income in the future through amortization if it exceeds a certain minimum threshold. To gain an understanding of this actuarial loss, we find that the firm reported the discount rate at the beginning of the year as 8.5 percent, and as 7.4 percent at year-end. This was the most important factor in increasing the actuarial present value of the liability.

The firm reports some other assumptions, such as a health care cost trend rate of 13.25 percent in 1993, declining to 6 percent by 2,007 and level afterwards. It also reports that an increase of 1 percent in this rate would have increased the accumulated benefit obligation on 12/31/93 by 9 percent. Thus, we can see the sensitivity of the obligation to the assumed health care cost trend rate.

What are the implications for the cash flow analyst? As stated above, the direct effects of the standard on cash flows are likely to be minimal. However, firms may take certain steps to decrease future cash payments to its retirees. For example, American Airlines wanted its workforce to pay a monthly fee to prepay future health benefits. Ralston Purina introduced an ESOP instead of its retiree medical plan. Other firms discontinued such benefits to new employees or asked their employees to share in the costs of these postretirement benefits, and others introduced HMOs (health maintenance organizations) to reduce future medical costs. Thus, the direct cash flow effects are likely to be insignificant, although the indirect effects are likely to be more beneficial to future cash flows than would otherwise have been the case. Indeed, the lower rate of increase in health care costs during the mid-1990s has saved firms cash and reduced the required liability for retirees' health care benefits.

The cash flow analyst should, however, remove the effect of the amortization of the transition amount, or the catch-up adjustment due to the new standard, from earnings because it represents a noncash expense just like depreciation. The cash flow analyst should also add the difference between the net obligation (excess benefits over assets) and the amount incorporated in the balance sheet to total debt. Just as for pensions, this amount represents an additional off-balance-sheet liability that should be incorporated as total debt.

Example

In the above example for American Brands, the cash flow analyst would disregard the charge to income of $191 million, net of taxes, and should add to total debt $34.9 million, which is an additional off-balance-sheet liability (the unrecognized net loss due to actuarial changes). This amount was not incorporated on the balance sheet by 12/31/93.

Example

The adoption of *SFAS No. 106* by firms had generally occurred in 1993, the last year the FASB permitted for adoption. Thus, the financial analyst may have seen a sharp decline in earnings of many firms, due just to the effects of this accounting change. However, the decline in net income had usually not been accompanied by a decline in cash flows, which were reasonably robust during the expansion stage of the business cycle. A notable exception was the adoption of the *SFAS No. 106* by General Motors Co. in 1992, which resulted in an extremely large decrease in earnings, along with an 80 percent decrease in shareholders equity. A possible motivation for this early adoption by GM was the change of management that occurred during 1992. The new management team realized that this standard would have to be adopted no later than 1993. Since the management change occurred in late 1992, the new management would not have been held accountable for 1992 results, which would be attributed to the old management. Furthermore, 1992 was not a profitable year for GM, and it is psychologically better to incur additional charges to income in years of losses (to begin a new slate). Thus, GM adopted the standard as of the beginning of 1992, punishing earnings substantially not only for the beginning of the year liability, but also for the 1992 additional noncash charge to earnings for accrued postretirement benefits. Naturally, results in 1993 stood to improve when compared with 1992 results. In the professional literature, this is called a big-bath phenomenon.

CONTINGENT LIABILITIES

Another potential off-balance-sheet liability can be found in contingent liabilities. If large enough, contingent liabilities can severely impair the entity or even induce bankruptcy. These are obligations that occurred before the fiscal year-end, but whose effect on the financial statements is not clearly determinable on that date. The FASB postulated in *SFAS No. 5* three degrees of uncertainty: probable, reasonably possible, and remote. The firm must set a liability for an expected obligation if it is probable that a liability has been incurred *and* the amount of the liability can be reasonably estimated. For example, when a firm distributes coupons that can be redeemed with purchases of future merchandise, a contingent liability exists and must be accrued. In such a case, it is almost certain that a large proportion of the coupons will be presented in the next accounting period. Furthermore, the firm can reasonably forecast what percentage of the coupons will be presented by the due date. Thus, a liability is accrued on the balance sheet with an offsetting charge against income.

SFAS No. 5 specifies that if a contingent liability is probable but the amount cannot be reasonably estimated, or if the likelihood that a loss occurred is only reasonably possible, a footnote disclosure is necessary. Thus, most legal proceedings against a firm are disclosed in a footnote on contingencies because the firm either deems their chances of success to be less than probable or because the firm cannot reasonably estimate the extent of the liability.

The cash flow analyst should examine the footnote on contingencies closely to determine if any events occurred that may affect cash flows in the future, although they had not been given accounting recognition in the financial statements.

Example

In footnotes to its 1991 financial statements, Kennametal reports the following:

> In 1991, a trial court awarded $7.1 million in damages, plus attorneys' fees in an amount not yet determined, to GTE Products Corporation (GTE) in a patent infringement suit filed against the company in the Federal District Court for the Western District of Virginia. The suit involved an infringement of a GTE patent on certain styles of carbide cutter bits used in the road planning industry. Kennametal is currently appealing the decision.
>
> In connection with this litigation, the company recorded a pretax charge to earnings in fiscal 1991 totalling $6.4 million, or $0.36 per share after tax. While the outcome of the appeal cannot be predicted at this time, management believes that the ultimate resolution of the litigation will not have a material adverse effect on the financial position of the company.

Note that in the above litigation, a loss contingency is probable, and the amount is measurable reasonably well, due to the court's award. Thus, Kennametal recorded a liability on its financial statements, although it still plans to pursue the decision in court. However, Kennametal also reports other pending litigation in its 1991 financial statements:

> In the ordinary course of business, there have been various legal proceedings brought against the company, including certain product liability cases. Since 1984, the company, along with varying numbers of other parties, has been named as a codefendant in numerous complaints which allege that former or existing employees of competitors and customers suffered personal injury as a result of exposure to certain metallurgical substances or other materials during their employment. The involvement of many of the defendants, including the company, is based on assertions that these defendants sold metallurgical materials or other products to the plaintiffs' former or existing employers.
>
> Damages are sought jointly and severally from all defendants, with certain of the complaints seeking both compensatory and

punitive damages and others seeking compensatory damages only. The company is vigorously defending these cases and, to date, a significant number of these cases have been either dismissed or settled for a nominal amount. All such dismissed or settled cases have been resolved without a finding of liability of the company. It is management's opinion, based on its evaluation and discussions with outside counsel, that the company has viable defenses to the remaining complaints and that, in any event, this litigation will not have a material adverse effect on the financial position of the company.

The second footnote discloses information about litigation concerning product liability. In this case, the firm had not set up a liability, and was merely reporting the fact in a footnote to the financial statements. These liabilities may have a material effect on future cash flows if any of the product liability suits is successful in court. This is very well known in the tobacco industry, where investors pay close attention to court cases regarding product liability.

Example

Scimed Life Systems Inc. disclosed on 9/25/91 that it expected three lawsuits against it due to patent infringement. In reaction to this announcement, the stock price of Scimed dropped 30 percent, although second quarter earnings were up about 70 percent due to a large increase in sales. The lawsuits against the firm were for the segments with the greatest growth, and theoretically all the products of the firm were subject to a risk of litigation. On March 7, 1994, Scimed announced the verdict on the last of these suits, which amounted to approximately $60 million to $66 million. At that time, Scimed had over $100 million in cash and cash equivalents, so the firm could have easily paid for the damages in the court verdict. Interestingly, the stock price of Scimed went up after the announcement, indicating that the market expectations were probably much bleaker about the verdict. After the announcement, the volume of trading in the stock rose substantially, as can be seen in Figure 7–3.

On November 8, 1994, Boston Scientific Corp. announced a merger agreement with Scimed Life Systems to be effected through stock exchange of Boston Scientific for Scimed stock. This announcement drove the price of Scimed stock, as well as trading volume, considerably, as can be seen in Figure 7–4.

FIGURE 7–3
Scimed Price and Volume after Court Decision

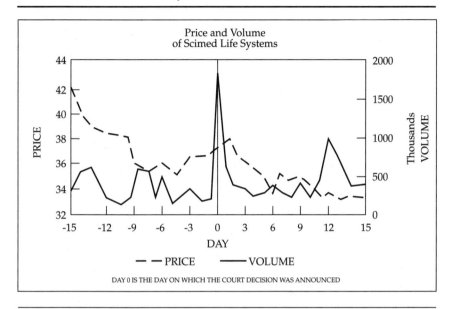

Price and Volume
of Scimed Life Systems

DAY 0 IS THE DAY ON WHICH THE COURT DECISION WAS ANNOUNCED

CONVERTIBLE BONDS

Convertible bonds have the characteristics of a straight-debt bond, plus an additional option to purchase a specified number of shares at a fixed price. Thus, the holder of a convertible bond enjoys a fixed interest payment until the bond reaches maturity (or is converted to equity) and, at the same time, enjoys the option of partaking in the capital appreciation of the stock. If the stock of the firm increases in value to a point above the fixed price implicit in the convertible bond, then the bondholder is likely to exercise its option and convert the bond to common stock. In such cases, the convertible bonds should be viewed as equity rather than debt of the firm. However, when the firm's stock sells below the exercise price implicit in the conversion option, the holder is unlikely to convert the bond to common stock, and the bond should be considered as part of total debt.

FIGURE 7–4
Scimed Price and Volume after Merger Announcement

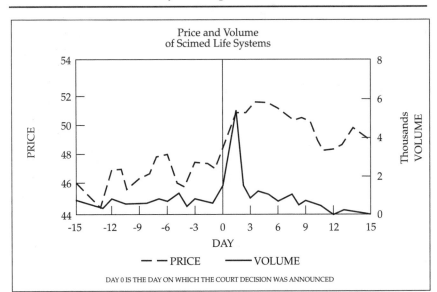

Price and Volume
of Scimed Life Systems

DAY 0 IS THE DAY ON WHICH THE COURT DECISION WAS ANNOUNCED

Example

Hercules has convertible bonds outstanding with a maturity date of 06/30/1999. These bonds pay 6.5 percent interest rate, and as of 8/30/91, every $1,000 bond could have been converted to 28.571 shares of common stock with a common stock price of $40.375, whereas the price of the bond on the same date was $1,140. Assuming the bond was converted to common stock, a bondholder can receive 28.571 common shares which could be sold in the marketplace for $1,154 (28.571 × $40.375). Thus, it pays for a bondholder to convert the bonds into common stock, and the bonds should be considered common stock.

Example

NBI has convertible bonds with coupon rate of 8.25 percent which will mature on 11/15/2007. The bonds were traded at a price of $1,375 for each $1,000 par value on 8/30/91. At that date, each bond could be converted in to 22.727 common shares, which had a market price of $0.141 per share on 8/30/91. Thus, if a bondholder would have converted the bond into common stocks and sold the proceed immediately, the proceeds from the sale of the common stocks would have been \$3.20 (22.727 × \$0.141). Thus, a bondholder is unlikely to convert the bond into common stock at that time, and the convertible bond should be considered debt and not common stock.

DEFERRED TAXES

Most firms include among the long-term liabilities on the balance sheet a liability for future tax payments, or deferred taxes. This liability has attracted the attention of investors, creditors, managers, and accountants for a long time. At issue is the difference between the tax expense reported in the financial statements and the actual tax payment to the tax authorities. The two are different because of different treatment of items for tax and for financial reporting purposes. Some differences are permanent (i.e., they are not expected to reverse in the future), whereas others are temporary differences that are expected to reverse.

A firm may depreciate an asset using a straight-line depreciation method for financial reporting purposes and accelerated depreciation schedule for tax purposes. The firm enjoys lower tax payments in the beginning of the asset's life, but greater tax payments towards the latter part of the asset's life. Since the entire amount to be depreciated (the asset's original cost) is the same, regardless of the depreciation method, the difference between the depreciation for tax and financial reporting purposes is nothing but a temporary difference. Cash flow, of course, would be enhanced in earlier years and impaired in later years. Any lower tax payments at the beginning of the asset's life are expected to be offset by greater tax payments toward the end of the asset's life. On the other hand, interest received on municipal bonds is tax deductible and would never be included in taxable income, but financial reports must incorporate such interest as income. Thus, interest on a municipal bond is an example of a permanent difference.

The accounting profession requires firms to record a liability for temporary differences based on the assumption that the situation will be reversed in the future and larger tax payments will be made in the future. Thus, the firm creates a liability on its books for these future tax payments based on expected tax rates in the future. Such a tax liability is not required for permanent differences, presumably because these will not be reversed in the future.

Opponents of the deferred tax liability argue that, in reality, most firms have a large buildup of deferred taxes that are unlikely to ever be paid to the government. They argue that as long as the firm keeps on growing, and as long as additional temporary differences are created, deferred taxes will continue to grow. This is empirically verified by observing the steady growth of the deferred tax liability on most firms' financial statements over the last two decades. Furthermore, opponents of the deferred tax liability argue that this liability is never discounted to the present, unlike other long-term liabilities of the firm. Indeed, this issue has not been satisfactorily resolved by the FASB, which issued *SFAS No. 96* to deal with accounting for income taxes. Also, the FASB deferred the effective date of the new standard with the issuance of *SFAS No. 100*, deferred it again with *SFAS No. 103*, and finally set new accounting rules with *SFAS No. 109*.

SFAS No. 109 changed the accounting for income taxes in several material ways. First, it established the "liability" approach for deferred tax liabilities. Second, it defined and expanded the disclosure rules for temporary and permanent differences between tax and financial reporting. Finally, it allowed firms to include deferred tax assets on the balance sheet if it is "more likely than not" that the firm can utilize these deferred tax assets in the future. Let us explain each of these issues, and illustrate them by several examples.

In the past (before *SFAS No. 96*, which most firms did not adopt, or before *SFAS No. 109*), firms used to set a deferred tax liability as the difference between the tax expense on a temporary item and the actual current tax liability on that item. For example, if a financial reporting expense was shown at $5,000, whereas on the tax return the same expense was shown as $6,000, a temporary difference of $1,000 would have been created. Suppose further that the firm was subject to a 46 percent tax rate. The firm would create a deferred tax liability for $460 (46 percent of $1,000), which is equal to the expected tax payment on the item when the expense is smaller on the tax return than on the financial statements. One can also derive $460 by comparing the financial statements appost tax credit on the item of $2,300 (46 percent of $5,000) and the actual tax credit of $2,760 (46 percent of $6,000). Note that both computations give the same result if one uses the same rate of 46 percent. Prior to *SFAS No. 109* (or its predecessor, *SFAS No. 96*), firms used the second method to set up their deferred tax liability.

Suppose now that two years later, but before the item reverses, the government decides to reduce the tax rate to 40 percent. Using the first approach, the expected tax liability in the future is now $400 (40 percent of $1,000) instead of $460 as computed earlier. Thus, the "liability" approach, which is adopted by *SFAS No. 109* (and *SFAS No. 96*), would reduce the deferred tax liability on the balance sheet by $60 ($460 – $400), and would incorporate in income a $60 gain due to lower taxes. Under the approaches prior to *SFAS No. 109* (and *SFAS No. 96*), such a decrease in the liability would not have been made, since at the time of the initial expense of the item, the difference in the tax and financial statement expense that was incorporated into the income statement was exactly $460. Note that if tax rates are expected to increase, the reverse effect would occur; an increase in the deferred tax liability and a loss on the income statement due to tax increases.

Prior to *SFAS No. 109*, firms found it very difficult to record a deferred tax asset. Deferred tax assets occur when a firm has greater expense for financial reporting purposes than for tax purposes. For example, the accrual of postretirement benefits is a financial reporting expense under *SFAS No. 106*, but it is not a taxable expense until cash is actually paid to retirees. Firms did not set up deferred tax assets unless they were reasonably certain that the tax benefits from the assets would indeed be obtained in the future. Under the current tax rules, one can carry tax losses backward three years to offset prior taxable income, and forward up to 15 years. However, to utilize tax carryforwards, the firm must have future taxable income. Prior to *SFAS No. 109*, firms rarely created deferred tax assets because the uncertainty about utilization of these assets in the future was significant. *SFAS No. 109* allowed firms to set up a deferred tax asset if "it is more likely than not" that the tax asset would be utilized in the future. It also required firms to show the entire amount of deferred tax assets, but then reduce the tax assets by a "valuation allowance," which is similar to an allowance for uncollectible receivables. This allowance reduces the deferred tax asset to the amount that is likely to be utilized in the future.

SFAS No. 109 requires firms to continue with prior disclosure about income taxes and mandates some additional disclosure. Accordingly, firms usually report separately in a footnote their current and deferred tax expense for the period, as well as their federal state and local taxes and, if applicable, their domestic and foreign taxes. Firms are also required to reconcile the statutory tax rate with their effective tax rate, in effect providing information about permanent differences between financial reporting and taxable income. Firms are also required to disclose the major components of deferred tax assets and liabilities, in effect providing information about temporary differences. Let us examine several such disclosures.

Example

Stride Rite Corp., a shoe manufacturer and merchandiser, reports in its 1994 financial statements the following information on deferred tax assets and liabilities:

	1994
Deferred tax assets:	
Inventory valuation reserves	$ 7,447
Distribution center relocation cost accrual	3,844
Accounts receivable allowances	4,004
Compensation accruals	2,272
Other accounting reserves and accruals	15,679
	33,246
Deferred tax liabilities:	
Undistributed earnings of foreign affiliates	1,730
Depreciation and amortization	4,825
Other items	1,577
	8,132
Net deferred tax assets	$25,114

Deferred tax assets are set up for inventories that were probably reduced to market (below cost) for financial reporting purposes, but not for tax purposes, until they are sold, resulting in an accounting expense that is larger than the tax expense. Similarly, the relocation costs of the new distribution center represent an accounting expense (accrual of future losses and expenses), but not a current cash outflow, which would be a taxable expense. The firm also records an accounting expense on its receivables that are not expected to be collected, whereas for tax purposes such allowance is not taxable. Finally, expenses for various compensation arrangements such as sick and vacation pay, which are accrued for financial reporting purposes, but which are not taxable until actually paid to employees, also result in deferred tax assets.

Deferred tax liabilities result from tax depreciation that is greater than financial reporting depreciation, mainly because accelerated depreciation schedules are available for tax purposes. Stride Rite, unlike most firms, also includes a deferred tax liability for undistributed earnings of foreign affiliates. These earnings are included in accounting income but are not taxable in the United States until such earnings are repatriated (e.g., through dividend payments). Most firms indicate that they expect such earnings to be permanently reinvested abroad and thus do not create a liability on the foreign income (because it represents a permanent difference). Stride Rite expects to repatriate these earnings, which then become a temporary item, on which a deferred tax liability is required.

Note that Stride Rite had not set up a valuation allowance on its deferred tax assets because "the Company expects to fully realize the benefits of such tax assets." A valuation allowance would have increased the tax expense of the firm and reduce income.

Stride Rite also reports the following information about permanent differences:

	1994
Statutory federal tax rate	35.0%
State income taxes, net of federal income tax benefit	8.7
Tax benefit from manufacturing operations in Puerto Rico	(1.1)
Tax benefit related to company-owned life insurance program	(4.3)
Other	0.9
Effective income tax rate	39.2%

Note that the effective tax rate of Stride Rite is 39.2 percent, mostly due to state income taxes of 8.7 percent in addition to the federal rate of 35 percent. Further note that Stride Rite set up manufacturing facilities in Puerto Rico, enjoying permanent tax benefits in the United States, when Congress wanted to encourage firms to manufacture goods in Puerto Rico. Indeed, most pharmaceutical firms have operations in Puerto Rico for this reason. Another permanent difference is the tax benefits on their in-house life insurance program.

Example

Digital Equipment Corp. (DEC) suffered net losses during the period 1990–1994, with a net loss of $2,156 million in 1994. Its pretax loss in 1994 was $2,020 million, and it provided a provision for income taxes of $85 million on the loss, although most firms in this situation show tax benefits. In the notes to the financial statements, DEC reported no current tax expense in the United States and a reduction of deferred taxes of $14 million. However, on its foreign operations DEC reports tax expense of $99 million, with $93 million of deferred taxes. In addition, DEC reports the following information about deferred tax assets and liabilities:

	Assets	*Liabilities*
Inventory-related transactions	$ 101,933	$ 8,437
Depreciation	61,335	44,693
Deferred warranty revenue	80,506	
Postretirement/postemployment benefits	400,037	18,323
Restructuring	446,505	
Tax loss carryforwards	1,424,927	
Tax credit carryforwards	149,013	
Intangible assets	106,368	
Other	168,392	98,465
Gross deferred tax balances	2,939,016	169,918
Valuation allowance	2,677,673	
Net deferred tax balances	$ 261,343	$169,918

Note that DEC reports gross deferred tax assets of $2,939 million, but it provided a valuation allowance of $2,678 million, so the net deferred tax assets included on the balance sheet is only $261 million. Thus, DEC assumes that it is more likely that it would *not* be able to utilize the tax benefits of the deferred tax assets. Given DEC's losses in the prior years, this seems reasonable. However, as DEC became profitable again, it may reduce the valuation allowance in the future, thereby increasing profits.

Since the cash flow effects of deferred taxes are extremely difficult to ascertain, we recommend that the cash flow analyst should *not* include deferred taxes among long-term liabilities of the firm when considering total debt of the firm.

TAX-BASED TRANSACTIONS

When the cash flow analyst examines a firm as an investment candidate, tax considerations usually play a major role. In some cases, transactions are carried out in a specific manner to ensure a favorable tax treatment. In these cases, the firm may have carried out a completely different transaction, or used a completely different approach, had there been no taxes to be paid. However, the firm chose the particular transaction to minimize tax payments on the corporate or the individual-stockholder level. In many cases, the cash flow analyst can predict the nature of the transaction ahead of time, and may utilize this knowledge for profitable investments. Let us provide several examples.

Example

Petrie Stores was a large shareholder of Toys "R" Us stock, with a very low cost basis in the stock. If it had sold its shares of Toys "R" Us at the then current market price, Petrie Stores would have recognized a capital gain of over a billion dollars, with a tax payment of over $400 million. To save these taxes, the cash flow analyst could have predicted a merger between Petrie and Toys R Us, in which shareholders of Petrie receive share of Toys R Us. Such a tax-free merger had indeed taken place at the beginning of 1995, and stockholders of Petrie became stockholders of Toys R Us, with much greater liquidity.

Example

Seagram has been a major stockholder of DuPont for over ten years, in which the stock price of DuPont increased substantially, resulting in potentially large capital gains taxes to Seagram upon sale of its position in DuPont. To reduce this tax liability Seagram chose to obtain a special dividend from DuPont, which is subject to a corporate dividend exclusion of 70 percent. For instance, when a corporation receives a dividend of $100,000 it does not have to pay taxes on 70 percent of the dividend, and it has to pay ordinary income taxes on $30,000 of the received dividends. DuPont had repurchased its own stock held by Seagram, and had issued warrants to Seagram, which entitled Seagram to purchase back the same amount of stock at an unrealistically-high value. Although Seagram is extremely unlikely to ever exercise the warrants, the IRS rules deem the repurchase of stock as a dividend, because Seagram's ownership interest in DuPont was not reduced, given its warrants. Seagram preferred to pay the ordinary income tax rate on the 30 percent of the entire dividend, instead of capital gains tax rate only on the capital gain. The choice is a function of the magnitude of the capital gain and the difference between the capital gain tax rate and the ordinary income tax rate. Subsequent to the publicity about the Seagram transaction, legislators introduced legislation that would prevent such transactions in the future.

Example

A similar transaction to Seagram's and DuPont occurred for Franklin Electric and Goulds Pumps, who were equal owners of a joint venture in Oil Dynamics Inc. (ODI). In November 1994, Goulds Pumps received a cash dividend for its share, which it probably treated using the dividend exclusion . Franklin Electric received a stock dividend, and ended up controlling most of ODI's stock.

Example—The Morris Trust

When a firm A owns shares in another firm B, it can effect a tax-free distribution to its shareholders using a "Morris Trust" transaction, similar to that of Petrie Stores and Toys R Us. The corporation A first transfers all its assets, except for the shares in Corporation B and a five-year-old small business to a new corporation which is spun off to shareholders. This spin-off is tax-free to shareholders of A, until they sell the shares in the new corporation. In the second step, the remaining corporation A (which now consists of shares in Corporation B and a small five-year-old business) merges with Corporation B, and stockholders of Corporation A receive shares in Corporation B in a tax-free merger, until they sell the shares of B.

To comply with the tax rules, the spin-off must ensure that both firm A and the new corporation that is spun off would be viable business entities with a five-year history. Also, Corporation A must distribute at least 80 percent of the new corporation's shares. There should also be a good business reason for the separation of the two businesses. Currently, the IRS has stopped issuing favorable tax rulings on such "Morris Trust" transactions, leaving firms with a tax uncertainty.

Example

Cooper Industries operated in four business segments, including one which is more volatile because it is dependent on oil and gas-related activities. Cooper wanted to spin this volatile segment back to shareholders, but decided to do it as a split-off. In this transaction, Cooper offered shareholders stock in the spun-off division, Cooper Cameron. However, Cooper asked its shareholders to tender a specified number of Cooper shares for each ten shares of the new entity Cooper Cameron. Thus, Cooper effects not only a spin-off, but also a stock repurchase, which is usually considered to be a favorable signal for market prices of the repurchasing firm. To be considered a tax-free transaction, Cooper must convey at least 80 percent of Cooper Cameron to shareholders. Furthermore, Cooper may record a loss (or a gain) if the book value of Cooper Cameron is higher (lower) than the market value of Cooper's shares tendered back to Cooper. A similar transaction has been considered by Eli Lilly with respect to its public subsidiary Guidant.

As can be seen from the above examples, the cash flow analyst can scenerio forcast types of transactions that a firm may enter into if it holds a minority position in another firm. The analyst can also assess the cash flow consequences of such transactions, once they are announced to the public.

SUMMARY

In this chapter, we examined the relationship between capital structure of the firm and the firm's ability to generate consistent operating and free cash flows. We showed that firms with stable and large free cash flows are likely to be better-off, because they can use these free cash flows to consistently reduce debt, repurchase stock, or take advantage of investment opportunities depending on the economic environment. Firms with volatile cash flows that issue too much debt are exposed to a greater financial risk.

We also proposed a ratio to measure the ability of a firm to retire debt without affecting its growth opportunities—the ratio of total debt to average free cash flows. The higher this ratio, the less likely is a firm to be able to repay its debt without impairing its future growth. The lower this ratio, the more likely the firm will be able to retire its debt, withstand adverse business conditions, maintain or increase dividends, and repurchase common stock.

However, to apply this ratio properly, the cash flow analyst should consider what constitutes total debt of the firm. We show that certain liabilities are not included on the balance sheet, such as operating leases, pensions, other postretirement benefits, contingencies, and the like. In contradistinction, some liabilities that are included on the balance sheet should be excluded from total debt because they represent equity, such as convertible bonds that are likely to be converted, or when there is too much uncertainty about the substance and timing of the liability, such as for deferred taxes.

The examination of total debt is important for portfolio selection, because we wish to identify firms that are unlikely to need additional borrowing in the future, as suggested in Chapter 6. Such firms should also be characterized by stable, consistent free cash flows. The next three chapters show how the cash flow analyst can use the relationship between financial structure and free cash flows for portfolio selection.

Chapter Eight

Free Cash Flow and Portfolio Selection

INTRODUCTION

In the previous chapters, we discussed the differences between earnings, operating cash flows, and free cash flows. We illustrated the derivations of these three measures, reviewed their effects on the financial structure of the firm, and discussed their potential usefulness for portfolio selection. The purpose of this chapter is to compare the performance of U.S. portfolios that are based on these three measures, or to be more precise, on price multiples of earnings, net operating cash flows, and free cash flows.

In this chapter, we describe investment strategies based, not only on price multiples, but also on investment considerations such as size and debt restrictions. We provide results of back-testing these investment strategies and show the superiority of free cash flow for investment purposes. In addition, we show the performance of live portfolios that were selected using an investment strategy based on free cash flows. This chapter is the first of three that ratify the intuitive appeal and economic sense of using a free cash flow–based investment strategy.

BACK-TESTS OF A P/E STRATEGY

Basu (*Journal of Finance*, 1977) has shown that an investment strategy based on P/E ratios can outperform the market index. In particular, Basu showed that portfolios having a "long" position in securities with low P/E ratios and a "short" position in securities with high P/E ratios consistently obtained excess returns for many years. These excess returns would have been earned after adjusting for transaction costs and various measures of risk. Other researchers claimed that Basu's results were due to the fact that firms with extreme high or low P/E ratios tended to be small capitalization stocks. Indeed, Keim (*Journal of Financial Economics*, 1981) and Reiganum (*Journal of Financial Economics*, 1981) showed that portfolios of small capitalization firms yielded better returns than the market as a whole. As a reaction to this research, mutual funds that specialized in small market-capitalization firms became more attractive to investors. However, with the dramatic stock market fall of October 1987, it became evident that these small firms are subject to another dimension of risk: the low level of liquidity that prevents investors from quickly or easily liquidating a position in these securities.

Basu (*Journal of Financial Economics*, 1983) has also shown that the P/E effect is independent of the small-capitalization effect, and that it exists for large market-capitalization firms as well as for small firms. Thus, it seems an investment strategy based on buying firms with low P/E ratios and short selling firms with high P/E ratios may provide excess returns to investors. The rationale behind such an investment strategy is that the P/E ratio may be perceived as the number of years it would take for the investment in a firm (the price) to be paid back through the earnings of the firm. The longer it takes to recapture the original investment, the worse-off is the investor. However, one should note that the P/E ratio serves as an indication of a payback period only if one assumes that earnings are equivalent to free cash flows, and only if earnings are expected to remain at the same level. Indeed, some high P/E ratios are justified if cash flows of the firm are expected to grow at higher rates in the future than the historical or even current growth rates. Also, the market price presumably adjusts for differential effects on earnings of various accounting methods (Beaver and Dukes, *The Accounting Review*, 1973). In recent years, money managers who based their investment decisions solely on P/E ratios seemed to have had inferior returns to the S&P (Standard and Poor's) 500 index.

In this section, we describe the results of back-testing, an investment strategy based on P/E ratios. To make sure we did not introduce any survivorship bias into the back-tests, we included in the sample all firms available for investment, regardless of whether they survived to the date of the study. Specifically, firms were selected for the study from the universe of stocks covered by Standard & Poor's Compustat Annual and Quarterly Industrial File, as well as the Compustat Research File. To ensure that the P/E ratio would include the most recent information at the time of the portfolio formation date, we used information from the most recent four quarters prior to the portfolio formation date. The portfolio selection date was always December 31, and securities included in the portfolio were held for the entire calendar year following the portfolio formation date. The portfolio was assumed to be sold at the end of that year and a new portfolio constructed at that time. All securities in a portfolio were equally weighted at inception.

For each of the firms in the Compustat universe, we retrieved the market value on the portfolio formation date and the sum of the four most recently announced quarterly earnings before the formation date. Because a firm's fiscal year-end may not coincide with the calendar year, we used as the most recently announced quarterly earnings the quarters ending in August, September, or October prior to the portfolio formation date. This procedure was intended to ensure that earnings for the most recent four quarters were indeed known to market participants by the portfolio formation date. Thus, we reduced the information bias that may be introduced in back-testing. Specifically, one may be using information that was not yet available at the time portfolios were assumed to be formed. For example, if we allowed all firms to be used for the P/E portfolios, we may have sorted firms according to P/E ratios that are based on earnings that were not yet known on the portfolio formation date, because the firm's fiscal year-end occurred subsequent to the portfolio formation date. However, this procedure may be slightly biased for firms that have August as their fiscal quarter-end and that managed to disclose earnings for the quarter ending in November prior to the portfolio formation date. We prefered to use some stale financial statement data in back-tests rather than risk introducing information bias (i.e., using information that is available to the researcher ex-post, but which was not available to the market on the portfolio formation date).

We further restricted our analysis to firms with market capitalization of at least $100 million as of the portfolio selection date because we wanted our portfolios to include only firms with reasonable levels of liquidity in their stock trading. We also restricted ourselves only to "long" portfolios. Unlike Basu and the prior research, we did not assume the possibility of shorting a security for an entire year. In practice, it may be impossible or sometimes very costly to short a stock for long periods of time because the security may be unavailable for borrowing. Thus, we chose to concentrate only on the long side of P/E-based portfolios, which meant we wanted to include in the portfolio securities with low P/E ratios.

A practical problem with P/E ratios is that a nontrivial proportion of the population of firms report negative earnings. For such firms, the P/E ratio is meaningless, and we omitted them from our analysis. We focused on earnings before extraordinary items to reduce the influence of nonrecurring items. Note also that by using the ratio of market value to total earnings, we abstracted from the arbitrary accounting method used to calculate earnings per share. As is well known, the number of shares used to calculate earnings per share is not simply the number of outstanding shares at the portfolio formation date, on which the price per share is based.

To select firms into the portfolio, we sorted, according to their P/E ratios, all firms in the Compustat universe, excluding firms in financial services (SIC codes 6000–6999).[1] To make reasonable comparisons among the P/E, OCF, and FCF strategies, we restrict the populations to be the same.[2] To eliminate firms with negative earnings, we assigned to these firms a very high positive P/E ratio. We then selected into the portfolio those firms that fell into the bottom decile of P/E ratios among all firms remaining in the universe.[2]

---

[1]We exclude firms in the financial sector because the estimation of free cash flow for such firms is more difficult given their estimates of loan reserves or expected claim losses.

[2]It should be recalled that the universe now excluded firms with market capitalization below $100 million and financial services firms.

To assess the performance of a portfolio, we needed a benchmark against which the portfolio performance was measured. The most widely used measure of performance in the domestic financial services is the performance of the S&P 500 index, which is a value-weighted index of 500 selected firms. Because our firms were of different size groups, and because we assumed an equal weighting of our securities in the portfolio, we needed another measure of performance. The academic literature has shown that a good proxy for risk and most other dimensions of security returns is the size of a security, measured by the market value of equity. Thus, we also used size-adjusted returns to assess the performance of our portfolio. The procedure using size-adjusted returns began by classifying all securities in the universe into 10 portfolios according to their size (market capitalization) on the portfolio formation date. For each of these 10 portfolios we computed the equally weighted return in the following calendar year. The size-adjusted return of a security was the return on that security minus the return on the portfolio of firms in the same size decile.

We repeated the process of portfolio selection for all years 1980 through 1994. To illustrate the portfolio selection, we ranked all firms on December 31, 1980, according to their P/E ratios. We selected only the firms at the bottom 10 percent of P/Es and held the portfolio from January 1, 1981, until December 31, 1981. We then repeated the process on December 31, 1981, and held securities during all of 1982, and so forth.

Table 8–1
P/E Portfolio Results

Year (1)	N* (2)	Median P/E (3)	Median Market Cap† (4)	P/E Portfolio Annual Return (5)	P/E Portfolio Size-Adjusted Return‡ (6)	S&P 500 Return (7)	P/E Portfolio minus S&P 500 (8)
80	31	3.7	269	–0.8	–34.2	32.4	–33.2
81	61	4	303	–4.4	–3.6	–4.9	0.5
82	61	4.1	323	23.1	0.4	21.6	1.5
83	93	4.2	390	35.5	10	22.4	13.1
84	175	6.7	545	8.2	11.8	6.1	2.1
85	133	6.1	475	37.5	8	31.6	5.9

Table 8–1
(concluded)

Year (1)	N* (2)	Median P/E (3)	Median Market Cap† (4)	P/E Portfolio Annual Return (5)	P/E Portfolio Size-Adjusted Return‡ (6)	S&P 500 Return (7)	P/E Portfolio minus S&P 500 (8)
86	152	7.2	732	21.1	5.1	18.2	2.9
87	132	7.8	523	–3.1	–5.5	5.2	–8.3
88	121	6.2	633	29.7	7.6	16.5	13.2
89	173	6.6	717	25.1	1.9	31.4	–6.3
90	144	6.6	435	–18.5	–6.2	–3.2	–15.3
91	97	5.1	323	46.2	8.6	30.5	15.7
92	125	8.4	488	9.6	1	7.7	1.9
93	155	9.8	528	26.4	9.4	10	16.4
94	208	10.5	421	–1.2	2.4	1.3	–2.5
Mean	124		474	15.6	1.1	15.1	0.5
t-statistic				3.4	0.4	4.7	0.2

Note: The P/E portfolio is created on 12/31 of year t – 1. Securities included in the portfolio are for firms that are not in the financial services industry and that had market values of equity in excess of $100 million on the portfolio formation date. The portfolio includes the 10 percent of the remaining firms with the lowest positive P/E ratios on the portfolio formation date. Returns are for the equally weighted portfolio during year t.

* N = the number of firms in the P/E portfolio.

† Market Cap = the median market value of equity on the portfolio formation date.

‡ Size-adjusted returns are the returns on a security minus the equally weighted return on a portfolio of securities which fall into the same market-cap decile on the portfolio formation date.

The mean is the average return across all years. The t-statistic is estimated as the mean return divided by the standard error of the return across the 15 years 1980–1994.

The results of this investment strategy are shown in Table 8–1. As can be seen in the table, the mean size-adjusted return on this portfolio was 1.1 percent per year, which the t-statistic shows to be statistically indistinguishable from zero. The exhibit also shows that the average annual return on the low P/E portfolio was 15.6 percent, which is barely greater than the average annual return on the S&P 500 index of 15.1 percent. As a matter of fact, the table reports the differences in returns between the P/E portfolio and the S&P 500 index and tests whether the mean difference is equal to zero. As can be seen from the t-statistic for that column, the P/E portfolio does *not* provide returns that are statistically different than the S&P 500 index. Thus, prior results about the superiority of the P/E strategy may be different from our results because of any one or a combination of the following reasons:

1. Prior studies used a hedge portfolio, investing not only in long positions but also in short positions. We use only long positions, which realistically were more easily implementable.

2. We excluded stocks whose market capitalization was below $100 million. These stocks have provided the excess return to the P/E strategy in prior studies. A strategy that systematically invests in securities of firms with capitalization below $100 million can be very difficult to implement, except for the small investor. We also tested the same P/E strategy but with a restriction that the market value of the firm should be greater than $1 million on the portfolio formation date. This test yielded mean annual return of 21.9 percent, and a size-adjusted return of 2.8 percent per year. However, the size-adjusted return was statistically indistinguishable from zero (t-statistic of 1.0).

3. We excluded firms in the financial services. Such firms may have provided the excess returns in prior studies.

4. We used the period 1980–1994. Prior studies in this area used earlier periods in which the P/E effect may have held. It is plausible that the P/E effect dissipated in the 1980s, after the publication (and possible implementation) of those studies that documented the P/E effect and after removal of the technological barriers of implementing this strategy. For example, access of individual investors to databases that have P/E ratios from home computers has become widely available. In recent studies, Fama and French (*Journal of Finance*, 1992, and *Journal of Financial Economics*, 1993) showed that the P/E ratio cannot be used to explain the cross-sectional distribution of returns in recent periods.

Figure 8–1 illustrates the annual returns on the P/E portfolio and the S&P 500 index for the period 1980–1994. It reinforces the

Figure 8–1
Low Decile P/E Portifolio Annual Returns

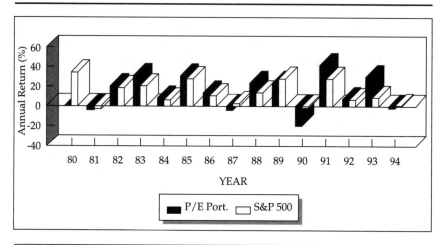

FIGURE 8–2
Low Decile P/E Portifolio Cumulative Returns

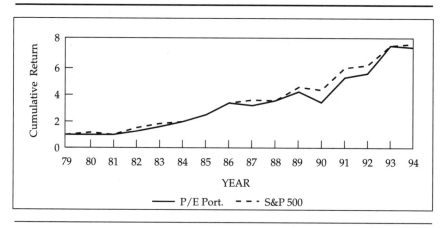

impression that we gained earlier from Table 8–1 (i.e., we cannot
see any dominance of the P/E portfolio over the S&P 500 index).
In some years one performs better, whereas in other years the
reverse is true. Figure 8–2 shows the cumulative return on a $1
investment in the P/E portfolios at the end of 1979 through the

end of 1994, and the performance of an investment in the S&P 500 index over the same period. It is easy to see that the S&P 500 dominated the P/E portfolios for most of that period.

In conclusion, the strategy of investing in securities that have the lowest P/E ratios (the bottom 10 percent) did not earn abnormal returns during the period 1980–1994. The returns on the P/E portfolios have not been greater than the S&P 500 index, nor did they outperform the portfolio of stocks with the same size.

THE IMPORTANCE OF LOW DEBT

As we pointed out in Chapter 6, it is important to identify firms that have low financial leverage because these firms, which are conservatively managed, are unlikely to utilize extensive borrowing in the future. Furthermore, a firm with lower financial leverage is less risky because the firm can borrow in difficult economic times more easily than a firm with high financial leverage. Such firms are also in a better position to take advantage of appropriate business opportunities. Thus, it seems reasonable to examine whether we can improve the performance of the portfolio if we restrict it to firms with low financial leverage.

In order to apply a strategy of low P/E ratio and low financial leverage, we follow the same selection criteria as before (i.e., the market value has to be above $100 million on the portfolio formation date, and we exclude all the financial services firms). We also require firms to have a debt to equity (D/E) ratio below 40 percent, where the debt is measured as book value of short-term and long-term debt plus the present value of operating leases and the off-balance-sheet pension liability, if the latter exists. To allow a reasonable number of firms to pass the above selection criteria, we select all firms with a positive P/E ratio in the bottom two deciles, as compared to the bottom decile above. The results of this investment strategy are available in Table 8–2, and are portrayed as before in Figures 8–3 and 8–4.

As can be seen in Table 8–2, introducing a low debt/equity ratio does improve the performance of the P/E portfolio from an average annual return of 15.6 to 17 percent (see Table 8–1, column

Table 8–2
Low Debt/Low P/E Portfiolio Results

Year (1)	N (2)	Median P/E (3)	Median Market Cap (4)	P/E Portfolio Annual Return (5)	P/E Portfolio Size Adjusted Return (6)	S&P 500 Return (7)	P/E Portfolio Minus S&P 500 (5)–(7)
80	27	5.1	269	18.7	–14.7	32.4	–13.7
81	35	4.9	280	12.5	12.9	–4.9	17.4
82	42	5.6	379	22.4	–0.2	21.6	0.8
83	52	5.6	353	33.7	8.2	22.4	11.3
84	99	9.7	493	4.0	8.2	6.1	–2.1
85	66	8.0	308	29.1	0.6	31.6	–2.5
86	73	9.0	448	19.2	4.9	18.2	1.0
87	86	11.0	238	–3.1	–4.0	5.2	–8.3
88	59	8.5	307	28.0	5.1	16.5	11.5
89	93	8.8	353	23.7	1.8	31.4	–7.7
90	95	8.6	315	–9.0	4.4	–3.2	–5.8
91	72	7.3	311	34.1	–4.6	30.5	3.6
92	110	11.4	275	16.2	7.0	7.7	8.5
93	116	12.8	351	20.9	4.0	10.0	10.9
94	148	12.6	252	4.4	8.7	1.3	3.1
Mean	78		329	17.0	2.8	15.1	1.9
t-statistic				5.2	1.7	4.7	0.8

(5). Similarly, the size-adjusted mean return is now 2.8 percent per year, as compared to 1.1 percent in Table 8–1. However, the annual returns on the portfolio do not show any superior performance against the S&P 500 index. The differential return has a mean of 1.9 percent, which is statistically indistinguishable from zero (t-statistic of 0.8). Similarly, the mean size-adjusted return, although positive, is statistically indistinguishable from zero, as is evident by the low t-statistic of 1.7 at the bottom of column 6 in Table 8–2.

Figures 8–3 and 8–4 seem to support the results in Table 8–2. One cannot say conclusively that the annual return on the P/E portfolio with low financial leverage has superior returns than

Figure 8–3
Low Debt/Low P/E Portfolio Annual Returns

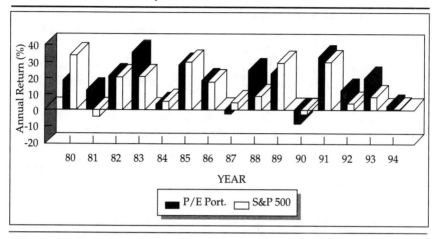

Figure 8–4
Low Debt/Low P/E Portfolio Cumulatiave Returns

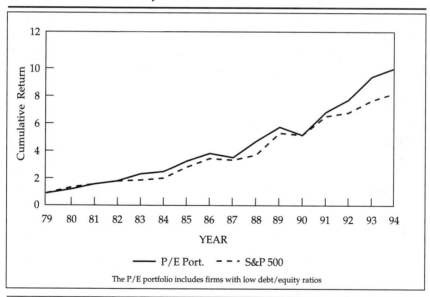

The P/E portfolio includes firms with low debt/equity ratios

the S&P 500 index. However, the cumulative return of the P/E portfolio in Figure 8–4 has done better than the S&P 500 index, but mostly due to the years 1992 and 1993.

We should note, however, that the S&P 500 index is a high quality portfolio, especially compared to the average publicly listed company or a large index portfolio such as the Russell 3,000 index. Thus, it is much more difficult to outperform the S&P 500 index than other, more broad indexes.

Note that the number of firms in the P/E portfolio with low D/E ratios actually declined to an average of 78 firms in Table 8–2 from 124 in Table 8–1. This is expected given the additional low debt requirement. Recall that to offset the decline in the number of firms due to the low D/E ratio, we allowed the P/E multiple to be at the bottom 20 percent of firms and not 10 percent, as in Table 8–1. This is evident by the slightly higher median P/E in Table 8–2 than that of Table 8–1.

BACK-TESTS OF NET OPERATING CASH FLOW MULTIPLES

The investment strategy based on P/E ratios assumed that investors wish to invest in firms with low P/E ratios because these firms have shorter investment recapture periods. As explained above, this is true if earnings and free cash flows are very close to each other and if such free cash flows are constant or continue to grow at the same rate in the future. As an alternative to P/E ratios, one can use the net operating cash flow multiple. The net operating cash flow multiple can be defined as the market value of equity divided by the net operating cash flow. This multiple uses as the denominator the net cash flow generated by operations, or if one wishes to abstract from an extreme observation in a particular year (i.e. normalize the data), the average cash flow generated from operations over the most recent four years.

The net operating cash flow multiple can be more useful than the P/E ratio for of several reasons. The P/E ratio is affected by accounting methods that underlie the earnings computation in general, and the earnings per share computations in particular. Net operating cash flows, on the other hand, are free from many of the assumptions that underlie earnings and are less influenced by managerial selection of accounting methods. Net operating cash flow (as defined by *SFAS No. 95*) is, therefore, a better measure than earnings of cash flow returned on the investment in the business.

Moreover, by averaging net operating cash flows over the most recent four years, we obtain a more useful measure of expected net cash flows in the future.

Example

Tandy Corp. reports on its 1991 statement of cash flows a sale of customer receivables that contributed about $350 million to net operating cash flows, which totaled about $617 million in 1991. (Net operating cash flows were $58 million in 1990, and $353 million in 1989). The sale increased operating cash flows, thereby producing an artificially low net operating cash flow multiple for 1991. Thus, an averaging of cash flows over four years may abstract from temporary increases in operating cash flows. Note that Tandy sold its receivables again in 1995.

To examine the performance of the net operating cash flow multiple for investment in securities, we again form portfolios of stocks with low net operating cash flow and debt multiples. We first retrieve or estimate (using balance sheet changes) the average net operating cash flow for all firms during the period 1980–1994. We then define the net operating cash flow multiple as the market value of equity on the portfolio formation date divided by the four-year average net operating cash flow for the year *before* the portfolio formation date. For example, we used the average net operating cash flows during the four years 1977–1980, together with the market value of equity on December 31, 1981, to form the OCF (operating cash flow) portfolio held during 1982.

Note that unlike the previous section, we rely on annual estimates of operating cash flows, and not on the most recently announced four quarters, as we did for earnings. The reason is that earnings were disclosed on a quarterly basis throughout the testing period, whereas operating cash flow has been required by *SFAS No. 95* only from 1987 and onward. Note also that to reduce the information bias, we use average OCF from the year before the year of the portfolio formation date. For example, for a firm with a December fiscal year-end, we use the 1985 operating cash flow data, together with the market value on December 31, 1986, to form our OCF portfolio for 1987. The 1985 data would be published before April 1986, so market participants would have had access to these data for at least eight months before the portfolio formation date. For firms with a fiscal year-end that falls

Table 8-3
OCF Portfolio Results

Year (1)	N (2)	Median OCF Multiple (3)	Median Market Cap (4)	OCF Portfolio Annual Return (5)	OCF Portfolio Size-Adjusted Return (6)	S&P 500 Return (7)	OCF Portfolio minus S&P 500 (5)–(7)
80	23	3.1	395	19.5	−13.4	32.4	−12.9
81	23	3.6	353	2.5	3.1	−4.9	7.4
82	28	3.2	591	27.1	5.2	21.6	5.5
83	34	3.2	384	49.0	23.8	22.4	26.6
84	46	4.3	531	−6.5	−2.6	6.1	−12.6
85	41	3.9	448	13.7	−15.6	31.6	−17.9
86	51	3.9	609	2.0	−12.6	18.2	−16.2
87	47	4.2	292	12.7	12.0	5.2	7.5
88	33	3.9	656	27.2	5.6	16.5	10.7
89	48	4.3	529	33.8	11.5	31.4	2.4
90	49	4.5	403	−19.6	−6.4	−3.2	−16.4
91	31	3.8	639	19.5	−18.6	30.5	−11.0
92	45	4.1	373	9.7	0.7	7.7	2.0
93	62	4.9	341	22.5	5.8	10.0	12.5
94	82	6.1	336	12.9	16.9	1.3	11.6
Mean	43	4.1	459	15.1	1.0	15.1	−0.1
t-statistic				3.6	0.3	4.7	−0.0

between June and August, the information would have been available even longer. Thus, we are more conservative in our selection approach in order to reduce the information bias (i.e., that we would have used on the portfolio formation date information that had not yet been available to the market on that date).

As before, we restrict our selection to firms with a market value in excess of $100 million, and firms with a positive average net operating cash flow. Furthermore, these firms had to have an OCF multiple at the bottom 20 percent of all firms and a leverage ratio of debt to equity below 40 percent. The performance of each of the portfolios is measured by the average return on the portfolio and is compared to the performance of the S&P 500 index and to similar-size stocks. The results for the OCF portfolios are reported in Table 8–3.

As can be seen in Table 8–3, the mean annual return on the OCF portfolio is 15.1 percent, which is identical to the average annual return on the S&P 500 index during the period 1980–1994. Furthermore, the average annual size-adjusted return is 1.0 percent, with a t-statistic of 0.3, which indicates that the size-adjusted return is statistically indistinguishable from zero. Similarly, the difference between the OCF portfolio and the S&P 500 index is statistically indistinguishable from zero (with a t-statistic of 0.0). Thus, the OCF portfolio does not appear to provide any superior returns to the S&P 500 index or to similar size firms. Figures 8–5 and 8–6 show the annual returns and the cumulative returns for the period 1980–1994. They also indicate the superiority of the S&P 500 index over the OCF portfolio.

PERFORMANCE OF A FREE CASH FLOW PORTFOLIO

The investment strategy we recommend is based on low free cash flow multiples. Recall that free cash flows represent the amount of cash that stockholders can receive without hampering the future growth of the firm at its current rate of growth. Thus, a multiple based on free cash flows measures more accurately the investment recapture period. The free cash flow multiple has an additional advantage; it is less affected than earnings by the selection of accounting methods and managerial decisions about dividends. At the same time, it incorporates into the cash generated by operations the capital expenditures, in effect, making sure that the firm's capital assets would grow and sustain the firm's current growth levels.

Recall that in Chapter 6 we developed a free cash flow–based valuation model that assumed free cash flows will remain constant at their most-recent four-year average level and that the firm has low debt levels and is unlikely to need additional future borrowing. Under these assumptions, we showed that the free cash flow multiple (i.e., the market value of the firm divided by the four-year average free cash flow) is equal to the inverse of the required rate of return on the security (the discount rate). Thus, to select firms into the portfolio, we need to iden-

Figure 8–5
OCF Portfolio Annual Returns

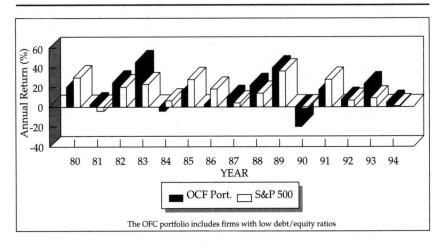

The OFC portfolio includes firms with low debt/equity ratios

Figure 8–6
OCF Portfolio Cumulative Returns

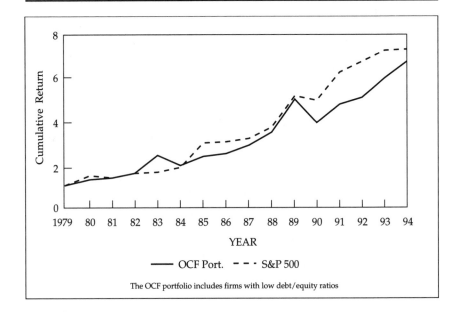

The OCF portfolio includes firms with low debt/equity ratios

tify firms with low free cash flow multiples because these firms are likely to be temporarily underpriced by the market. Since the average free cash flow and the required rate of return are fixed, any stock that sells below the inverse of its required rate of return is likely to do so because its current market value is below its fundamental value. Thus, we concentrate on the quintile of firms with the lowest free cash flow multiples for our free cash flow (FCF) portfolio.

The model in Chapter 6 assumed that free cash flows are constant. If we assume that free cash flows grow over time, we can construct another model by using a simple extension of the dividend discount model. Instead of dividends, we use free cash flow as the variable of interest. This makes sense because management has discretion over the amount of cash that it decides to distribute. However, management has almost no discretion over free cash flows as we define it. Similarly, when a firm pays no dividend, the dividend discount model will show a value of zero for the stock unless an arbitrary amount is substituted for the dividend (such as earnings times an assumed payout ratio). For our simple model, there is no need to worry about the dividend policy of the firm.

Let us define the variables that we use in the analysis:

V_t = The value of the firm at the end of period t. We assume that period 0 is the current period.

FCF_t = The free cash flow generated during period t. For simplicity, we assume that the free cash flow is generated at the end of period t.

k = The required rate of return on the security of the firm (cost of capital). The required rate of return is assumed constant across periods.

r = The growth rate of free cash flows from period to period. This rate is assumed constant across periods (i.e., free cash flows grow by a rate of r every period).

M = The free cash flow multiple (i.e., V_t/FCF_t).

The current market value of the firm is equal to the present value of the free cash flow in the next period and the market value at the end of the next period. Formally:

$$V_0 = \frac{FCF_1}{1 + k} + \frac{V_1}{(1 + k)} \tag{1}$$

Substituting for V_1 in the above equation the present value of the free cash flow in period two, FCF_2, plus the value at the end of period 2, V_2, we get:

$$V_0 = \frac{FCF_1}{1 + k} + \frac{FCF_2}{(1 + k)^2} + \frac{V_2}{(1 + k)^2} \tag{2}$$

Similar substitutions for all future values of the firm yields:

$$V_0 = \frac{FCF_1}{1 + k} + \frac{FCF_2}{(1 + k)^2} + \frac{FCF_3}{(1 + k)^3} + \ldots \tag{3}$$

Assuming that the free cash flows grow at a constant rate, r, we get the following series:

$$V_0 = \frac{FCF_0 (1 + r)}{(1 + k)} + \frac{FCF_0 (1 + r)^2}{(1 + k)^2} + \frac{FCF_0 (1 + r)^3}{(1 + k)^3} + \ldots \tag{4}$$

Using the formula for a sum of a geometric series, and assuming that k is larger than r, we get:

$$V_0 = FCF_0 \sum_{}^{\infty} [\frac{(1 + r)}{(1 + k)}]^t = FCF_0 \frac{(1 + r)}{(1 + k)} \frac{1}{1 - \frac{(1 + r)}{(1 + k)}} \tag{5}$$

After some simplifications, this yields:

$$V_0 = FCF_0 \frac{(1 + r)}{(k - r)} \tag{6}$$

Thus, we get the following free cash flow multiple:

$$M = \frac{V_0}{FCF_0} = \frac{(1 + r)}{(k - r)} \tag{6}$$

Note that when the growth rate of the free cash flow is assumed to be zero (i.e., when $r = 0$), then equation (7) reverts back to the free cash flow multiple being equal to the inverse of the required rate of return ($1/k$). To see the sensitivity of the valuation to the assumed growth rates, we can find the theoretical multiple for combinations of the growth rate in free cash flows, r, and the difference between the required rate of return and the growth rate, $k - r$. Table 8–4 illustrates the theoretical multiple for several such combinations.

As can be seen in Table 8–4, the free cash flow multiple is very sensitive to the difference between the required rate of return and the assumed growth rate of free cash flows. For example, when the required rate of return, k, exceeds the growth rate of free cash flows, r, by more than 6 percent, it is unlikely that the free cash flow multiple will exceed 20. For a security with a cost of capital of 15 percent, and a growth rate of free cash flows of 9 percent, the theoretical free cash flow multiple from the table should be 18 ($r = 0.09$, and $k - r = 0.06$). The table also shows that the free cash flow multiple is not very sensitive to the growth rate in free cash flow. Thus, as long as the required rate of return is larger than the growth rate by more than 5 percent, indicating that the real discount rate is in excess of 5 percent, we should expect the free cash flow multiple to be lower than 20.

To implement the free cash flow–based investment strategy, we use similar requirements to those we used earlier for the P/E and OCF strategies. In particular, we require that firms have a market capitalization of at least $100 million on the portfolio formation date and that portfolio firms would not belong to the financial services sector. In addition, we require firms to have a low financial leverage (i.e., a debt to equity ratio [D/E] less than 40 percent). Finally, we require the free cash flow multiple to be in the bottom 20 percent of all firms, and we assign an arbitrary large positive multiple to any firm having a negative free cash flow.

TABLE 8–4

Free Cash Flow Multiples for Several Combinations of r and k − r

	The Required Rate of Return in Excess of the Growth Rate (k − r)									
Growth of FCF (r)	*0.01*	*0.02*	*0.03*	*0.04*	*0.05*	*0.06*	*0.07*	*0.08*	*0.09*	*0.1*
0.01	101	51	34	25	20	17	14	13	11	10
0.02	102	51	34	26	20	17	15	13	11	10
0.03	103	52	34	26	21	17	15	13	11	10
0.04	104	52	35	26	21	17	15	13	12	10
0.05	105	53	35	26	21	18	15	13	12	11
0.06	106	53	35	27	21	18	15	13	12	11
0.07	107	54	36	27	21	18	15	13	12	11
0.08	108	54	36	27	22	18	15	14	12	11
0.09	109	55	36	27	22	18	16	14	12	11
0.1	110	55	37	28	22	18	16	14	12	11
0.11	111	56	37	28	22	19	16	14	12	11
0.12	112	56	37	28	22	19	16	14	12	11
0.13	113	57	38	28	23	19	16	14	13	11
0.14	114	57	38	29	23	19	16	14	13	11
0.15	115	58	38	29	23	19	16	14	13	12

Just as we did for the OCF-based strategy, we use the market value of equity on the portfolio formation date (December 31) and the four-year average free cash flow for the prior year in order to reduce information bias. Thus, for the first year in our sample, 1980, we used the market value on December 31, 1979, and the average free cash flow over the years 1975–1978. We assume that the equally weighted portfolio is held for all of 1980. A new portfolio is selected on December 31, 1980, and the process continues until 1994. The results of this strategy are reported in Table 8–5 and Figures 8–7 and 8–8.

The free cash flow portfolios earn an average annual return of 19.2 percent, which is 4.1 percent above the S&P 500 index. Furthermore, the size-adjusted returns on the portfolio have a mean of 5.3 percent per year, statistically and economically better

Table 8–5
Free Cash Flow–Based Portfolio Results

Year (1)	N (2)	Median FCF Multiple (3)	Median Market Cap (4)	FCF Portfolio Annual Return (5)	FCF Portfolio Size-Adjusted Return (6)	S&P 500 Return (7)	FCF Portfolio minus S&P 500 (8)
80	78	7	395	26.5	–6.6	32.4	–5.9
81	67	8.2	363	7.1	7.5	–4.9	12
82	53	8.3	355	36.7	13.8	21.6	15.1
83	52	7.1	311	29.1	3.5	22.4	6.7
84	105	9.4	300	–1.3	4.3	6.1	–7.4
85	100	7.6	331	30.8	2.1	31.6	–0.8
86	99	9.1	370	10.6	–2.4	18.2	–7.6
87	67	8	292	6.2	5.5	5.2	1
88	40	5.9	316	33.7	10.9	16.5	17.2
89	78	8.8	326	27.3	5.7	31.4	–4.1
90	71	8.3	286	–13.9	0.1	–3.2	–10.7
91	60	7.3	329	41.7	3.1	30.5	11.2
92	92	9.2	309	16.9	7.4	7.7	9.2
93	99	9.9	292	31.7	15.1	10	21.7
94	139	11.4	302	4.6	8.8	1.3	3.3
Mean	80	8.4	325	19.2	5.3	15.1	4.1
t-statistic				4.8	3.6	4.7	1.6

than zero (t-statistic of 3.6). Thus, the FCF portfolio outperforms not only the S&P 500 index, but also portfolios with similar size securities.

As can be seen in Figures 8–7 and 8–8, the free cash flow portfolios outperform the S&P 500 in most years, and the cumulative returns of the FCF portfolios exceed the S&P 500 Index handsomely over the entire period 1980–1994. Figure 8–9 compares the FCF strategy with the OCF strategy, the P/E strategy and the S&P 500. It clearly indicates the superiority of a FCF-based strategy over all the other strategies, including an earnings-based strategy.

Figure 8–7
FCF Portfolio Annual Returns

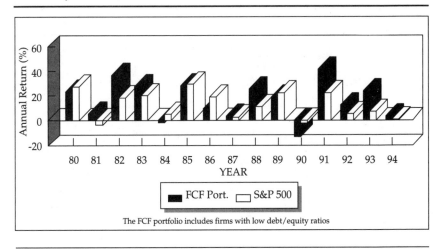

The FCF portfolio includes firms with low debt/equity ratios

FIGURE 8–8
FCF Portfolio Cumulative Returns

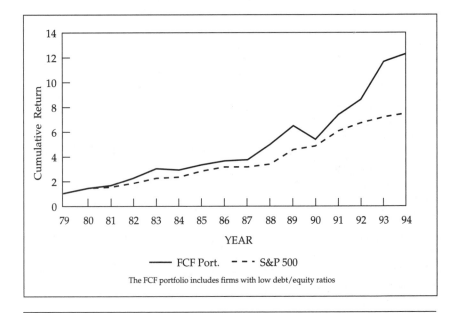

The FCF portfolio includes firms with low debt/equity ratios

FIGURE 8–9
Cumulative Returns of All Portfolios

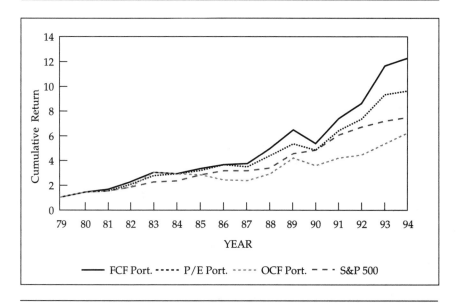

The superiority of cash flow–based multiples over earnings-based multiples in selecting undervalued stocks for a *value* portfolio is documented by Lakonishok, Shleifer, and Vishny (*Journal of Finance*, 1994). Their study, shows that the value style of investment outperforms the *growth* or *glamour* style of investment. Value investors attempt to identify securities that are temporarily undervalued by the market, although their intrinsic (or fundamental) value is higher. Glamour investors attempt to identify securities that are undervalued because the market has not captured their superior growth opportunities (due, for example, to a unique market share or product). Lakonishok et al. not only document the superior performance of value stocks over glamour stocks, but also provide evidence that this superior performance is slightly better with value stocks that are selected according to low cash flow multiples. The authors use a simplified measure of cash flow that is similar to net operating cash flow. Our results about the superiority of free cash flow portfolios is consistent with their evidence.

COMPARING LIVE PORTFOLIOS
TO BACK-TESTS

In the previous sections of this chapter, we evaluated our investment strategy by back-testing. However, what seems to be working well in back-testing may not work when implemented on a live portfolio. To convince academicians and practitioners that a particular strategy can be beneficial to an investor, it is important to provide results on live portfolios as well as the results of back-tests. Superior performance of a live portfolio is stronger evidence of investment strategy success because many biases can be inadvertently introduced by the researcher in back-testing a strategy. For example, the researcher may not be controlling properly for survivorship bias, timing of information disclosure, missing data, restated data, and so on. Also, back-tests of a strategy may be affected by the selection bias of firms into a database. For example, firms may be included in a database only if they pass some initial data requirements, including survival for a period of two or more years. A back-test using data from that database may already be biased for more successful firms, even if the database includes firms that were delisted subsequently. Thus, the superior performance of a live portfolio should be more credible than the performance of portfolios in back-tests of a strategy. Nevertheless, back-tests of an investment strategy are useful in proving that the portfolio was indeed selected according to a specified strategy. In buying or selling securities of a live portfolio, the portfolio manager may actually use decision rules that are not explicitly stipulated in the strategy. Back-testing ensures that such extraneous decision rules do not become part of the investment strategy. Furthermore, back-testing usefully measures portfolio performance sensitivity across a range of selection criteria. For example, we compared the results of a low P/E strategy, with those of a strategy featuring low P/E combined with a low debt level to ascertain whether the low D/E requirement enhanced performance significantly. The usefulness of such comparative exercises should be apparent.

Real-life portfolio strategies are inherently different from assumed strategies in back-tests. In reality, portfolio managers make decisions in a manner that cannot be captured entirely by any investment strategy. For example, our investment strategy indicated forming the portfolio once a year and holding the securities in a portfolio for an entire year. Our investment strategy also assumed that we invested an equal amount in each security in the portfolio. In reality, portfolio managers may hold different proportions of the portfolio in each of the individual securities. They also examine the performance of securities in the portfolio throughout the year, purchasing additional securities or selling securities according to market conditions. Another difference between back-tests and a live portfolio relates to the effects that trades have on market prices. When a large block of securities is traded, the effect on the market price may be such that the transaction cannot be implemented at the price that is assumed in the back-test of the model. In practice, money managers may execute trades in a particular security over an extended period of time. Also, if a strategy assumes that stocks are quickly turned over (bought and sold frequently), transaction costs may actually hamper the investment performance considerably. Thus, it is impossible to design a back-test of an investment strategy that will replicate real-life decisions by a professional money manager. We therefore provide additional evidence about the performance of live portfolios that are selected according to the concept of free cash flows.

LIVE PORTFOLIO RESULTS

Systematic Financial Management, L.P., (Systematic), has managed portfolios that are based on the free cash flow concept stipulated throughout this book. (Kenneth Hackel is president of Systematic and Joshua Livnat is a consultant for the firm.) To be included in Systematic's core portfolio, a firm must have a market capitalization of at least $200 million. It has to have a low free cash flow multiple (i.e., market value divided by the four-year average free cash flow of between 5 and 15). The firm usually has total debt that is less than 40 percent of net worth and a low debt multiple (i.e., total debt divided by the average free cash flows is less than 5). Finally, the firm exhibits strong growth rates in operating and free cash flows over the most recent four years and eight years and shows consistent free cash flows over a long horizon that will include at least one business cycle. Systematic also diversifies the

Table 8–6
Systematic Financial Management, Inc., Portfolio Results

Year	Live Systematic Annual Return	S&P 500 Return	Live Systematic minus S&P 500	Cumulative Returns S&P 500	Cumulative Returns Live Systematic
85				1.00	1.00
86	14.1	18.2	−4.1	1.18	1.14
87	4.5	5.2	−0.7	1.24	1.19
88	29.0	16.5	12.5	1.45	1.54
89	26.3	31.4	−5.1	1.90	1.94
90	2.0	−3.2	5.2	1.84	1.98
91	27.3	30.5	−3.2	2.40	2.52
92	11.8	7.7	4.1	2.59	2.82
93	14.9	10.0	4.9	2.85	3.24
94	−1.3	1.3	−2.6	2.89	3.20
Mean	14.3	13.1	1.2		
t-statistic	5.2	4.4	0.9		

portfolio firms across economic sectors. The portfolio includes about 35 stocks out of the universe of over 5,000 stocks having financial information available to calculate the relevant variables.

Table 8–6 reports the results of a composite of Systematic's fully discretionary portfolios since the beginning of 1986. As can be seen in the exhibit, Systematic's live portfolio managed to outperform the S&P 500 index during the period 1986–1994 by about 1.2 percent per year. The live returns are after transaction costs, so they show that free cash flow–based investment strategy can outperform the market. Further analysis of the quarterly returns (not shown here) indicates that, not only did Systematic's live portfolios have a larger return than the S&P 500, but they also had a lower standard deviation of return (with 14.2 percent for the live portfolio, compared to 15.0 percent for the S&P 500). Thus, Systematic's superior performance is likely not due to the additional dimensions of risk. Furthermore, an analysis of Systematic's returns during quarters when the S&P 500 increased or decreased shows that during 1986–1994, Systematic's portfolios

FIGURE 8–10
Cumulative Return—Systematic Live Portfolios

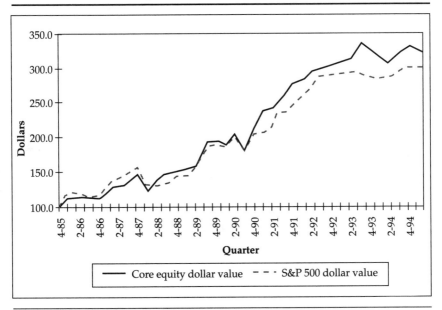

captured about 90 percent of the increases in the market, but declined only about 58 percent of the market's decline. Thus, the superior performance of Systematic's portfolio comes mostly from periods in which the market declines. This is to be expected given the conservative investment approach inherent in the portfolio construction—selection of firms with consistent free cash flows, low financial leverage and low free cash flow multiples.

Figure 8–10 portrays the cumulative returns of Systematic's core portfolios against the S&P 500 Index from 1986 onward. As can be seen from the graph, Systematic's live portfolio returns, which are net of transaction costs, exceeded the returns on the S&P 500 index during the same period. Figure 8–11 portrays the behavior of Systematic's core portfolios during up and during down markets, to illustrate the superior performance of Systematic's portfolios during market declines.

An affiliate of Systematic, Cash Flow Investors (CFI), has managed separate portfolios from Systematic's, but with the same investment strategy. Instead of investing in just 35 firms as does

FIGURE 8–11

Relative Performance of Equity Composite in Bull and Bear Markets
(Gross performance results for the nine years ended December 31, 1994)

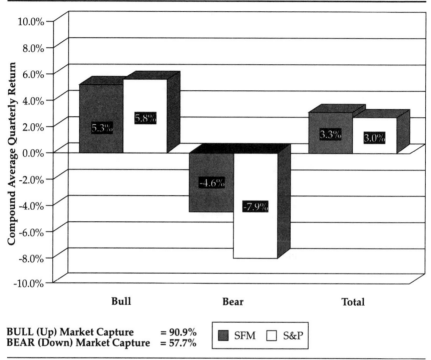

BULL (Up) Market Capture   = 90.9%   ■ SFM   □ S&P
BEAR (Down) Market Capture = 57.7%

Systematic, CFI invests equal amounts in about 150 firms according to the following characteristics. Firms must have a market value of at least $200 million, have free cash flow multiples below 20 and above 5, have low financial leverage (total debt/free cash flow below 10), and positive growth rates in free cash flows. A small proportion of the portfolio firms may not pass all of the above criteria, but may have shown a superior growth in either operating or free cash flows over the most recent four years. The CFI portfolios are more similar to a market index than the regular Systematic portfolio—they include substantially more stocks and are more diversified. Thus, the comparison with an index like the S&P 500 is more reasonable for these portfolios.

Table 8–7 provides annual returns and cumulative returns on the live CFI portfolios and the S&P 500 index during 1988–1994.

As the table shows, the CFI portfolios outperformed the S&P 500 index by 1.5 percent per year during 1988–1994. Also, as can be seen in the table and Figure 8–12, the cumulative returns of the CFI portfolios over the period exceeded that of the S&P 500 index. Additional analysis of the quarterly returns (not shown in the exhibit) indicated that the CFI portfolio captured about 100 percent of the increases in the S&P 500 index, but declined only about 60 percent of the market decline. Thus, the CFI portfolio added the conservative dimension of firms with low free cash flow multiples and low levels of debt.

The live performance results of Systematic and CFI indicate it is possible to implement the investment strategy advocated in this book. One can identify firms with low free cash flow multiples and low levels of debt for investment purposes. In fact, one can create both a small but diversified portfolio of such firms and an index-like portfolio of such firms that can outperform the S&P 500 index. Such strategies can yield superior returns even after transaction costs and trading liquidity considerations.

SUMMARY

The results presented in this chapter unambiguously show that to identify securities for a long position, do not use low P/E ratios or low net operating cash flow multiples. These measures may have been useful in identifying firms for long positions in the early 1980s. At the end of the 1980s and the beginning of the 1990s, however, these investment strategies have not outperformed the general market.

In contrast, an investment strategy based on the selection of firms with low free cash flow multiples and low debt ratios, as well as a consistent ability to generate operating and free cash flows, yielded returns that outperform the market. This result is validated by the performance of live portfolios as well as by the back-tests of the model. Thus, this evidence establishes the importance of free cash flows for portfolio selection. In the next two chapters, we shall show two more applications of the free cash flow strategy, for small-capitalization stocks and for international investments.

FIGURE 8–12
Cumulative Return—CFI and S&P 500

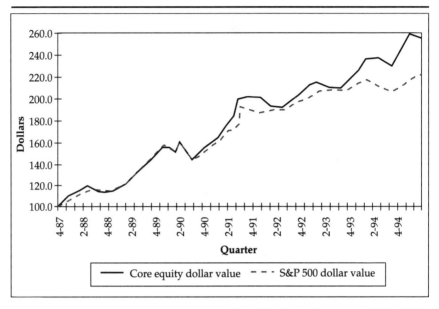

Table 8–7
CFI Portfolio Returns: Annual and Cumulative

Year	Live CFI Annual Return	S&P 500 Return	Live CFI Minus S&P 500	Cumulative Returns S&P 500	Cumulative Returns Live CFI
87				1.00	1.00
88	15.4	16.0	–0.6	1.16	1.15
89	29.6	31.4	–1.9	1.52	1.50
90	1.3	–3.2	4.5	1.48	1.51
91	33.2	30.5	2.6	1.93	2.02
92	6.9	7.7	–0.8	2.07	2.16
93	12.5	10.0	2.5	2.28	2.43
94	5.7	1.3	4.4	2.31	2.56
Mean	14.9	13.4	1.5		
T-statistic	5.1	4.2	2.5		

Chapter Nine

Investment in Small-Capitalization Stocks

INTRODUCTION

In the previous chapter, we showed the superiority of an investment approach based on identifying firms with consistent free cash flows, low levels of debt, and low free cash flow multiples. This portfolio strategy outperformed portfolios based on low P/Es, low multiples of operating cash flows, the S&P 500 index, and portfolios with firms of similar sizes. In this chapter, we show that the same strategy can be applied to investments in small- and mid-capitalization stocks, which were shown to outperform their large counterparts over a long period of time. The investment strategy we advocate enjoys the benefits of the free cash flow–based strategy, as well as the superior returns of small-capitalization stocks. We show that this strategy selects securities into a "long" portfolio that outperforms the market index, returns of similar size securities, returns of firms with similar book/market ratios, and returns of similar risk (beta) securities.

THE SMALL-CAPITALIZATION ANOMALY

The finance literature at the beginning of the 1980s documented the existence of higher abnormal returns to securities of small-capitalization stocks than their large-capitalization counterparts. For example, the studies by R. Banz (*Journal of Financial Economics*,1981), D. Keim (*Journal of Financial Economics*, 1983), and M. Reinganum (*Journal of Financial Economics*, 1981) documented a negative association between returns and a firm's size where size is the market value of equity. Indeed, the financial markets immediately capitalized on this research by offering investment portfolios consisting of small-capitaliaztion securities. Although the performance of small-capitalization companies has not always been better than that of large firms (a notable example is the market crash of October 1987), recent studies (e.g., see Fama and French, *Journal of Finance*, 1992) continued to document the importance of size in determining security returns.

To gain a good perspective on the differential returns of small- and large-capitalization firms, we constructed portfolios based on size alone and compared the performance of the top decile and bottom decile. To construct these portfolios, we sort all firms with a market value of at least $1 million into 10 groups (portfolios) according to their market value of equity on the portfolio formation date, December 31. We then assume that we hold the portfolio during the entire calendar year after the portfolio formation date. For each of the 10 groups (size portfolios), we calculate the value-weighted return for the year after the portfolio formation date. The portfolios are held during the 15 years 1980–1994.

Table 9–1 contains data about the value-weighted returns, as well as information about the median market value (in millions of dollars) and the percentage of firms that went bankrupt within three years after the portfolio formation date, for firms in the largest and smallest decile.

As the table shows, the average annual return on the largest-size decile was 14.5 percent, whereas the average annual return on the smallest-size decile was 30.7 percent. A casual observation of the data also shows that the return on the smallest-size decile is much more variable than the return on the largest-size decile. This is confirmed by the lower t-statistic of the smallest-size decile (2.9), as compared with the largest-size decile (4.5). Note further that the median firm in the largest-size decile has a market value of over $2.2 billion on the portfolio formation date, whereas the median firm in the smallest-size decile has a market value of only $3 million. Interestingly, both the largest-size and the smallest-size portfolios dominated the average returns on the market as a whole of 12.8 percent. The market is defined as all firms with a market value of $1 million or higher on the portfolio formation date.

Table 9–1
Large-Capitalization Firms versus Small-Capitalization Firms: Portfolio Returns

Year	Largest Firms Median Market Value ($ millions)	Largest Firms Percent Bankrupt in the Next Three Years	Largest Firms Value-Weighted Annual Return	All Firms Value-Weighted Annual Return	Smallest Firms Median Market Value ($ millions)	Smallest Firms Percent Bankrupt in the Next Three Years	Smallest Firms Value-Weighted Annual Return
80	1,069	0.0%	32.2%	6.8	$2	3.9%	74.1%
81	1,333	0.0	-6.8	-4.6	3	4.2	2.9
82	1,181	0.0	17.2	18.7	2	2.5	38.3
83	1,387	2.1	22.2	23.8	2	3.9	77.6
84	1,494	1.0	4.0	1.8	3	6.1	-10.1
85	1,577	1.2	32.2	31.8	2	6.1	15.6
86	2,001	1.5	23.2	20.3	3	5.0	8.4
87	2,249	0.0	8.1	5.5	3	5.6	-7.0
88	2,153	0.0	17.4	18.1	2	3.7	17.8
89	2,407	2.0	27.2	25.7	3	7.7	8.9
90	3,070	0.0	-5.5	-7.2	3	9.6	-25.0
91	2,755	0.0	27.5	29.8	2	21.6	125.3
92	3,411	0.0	3.2	5.2	3	14.3	59.4
93	3,576	0.0	13.8	14.9	4	9.1	72.7
94	3,681	0.0	2.0	0.8	6	0.0	1.3
Average	$2,223	0.5%	14.5%	12.8	$3	6.9%	30.7%
t-Statistic			4.5	4.1			2.9

FIGURE 9–1
Cumulative Returns for Large-Capitalization versus Small-Capitalization Portfolio

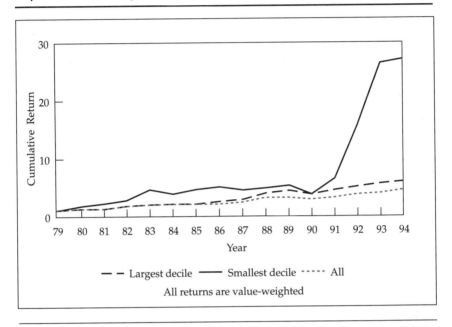

Figure 9–1 presents the cumulative returns of the smallest-size portfolio, the largest-size portfolio, and the market as a whole for the period 1980–1994. The figure clearly indicates the superiority of the smallest-size portfolio over both the largest-size portfolio and the market portfolio. Of course, we should also note that superiority of the smallest-size portfolio is due to the very high returns during the three years 1991–1993. However, the smallest size portfolio seems to dominate the other portfolios throughout the testing period, although it was hurt substantially in 1990.

Investors usually require higher returns if the underlying securities have greater risks (assuming that their growth prospects are captured in prices properly). To gain some insights into the possible additional risk of small-capitalization stocks, we provided the percentage of all portfolio firms that went bankrupt within three years after the portfolio formation date. The largest firms had a bankruptcy rate of about 0.5 percent, whereas the smallest-size portfolio had a bankruptcy rate of 6.9 percent during the testing period 1980–1994. Thus, smaller firms face a greater bankruptcy risk than large firms, which may partially explain the greater returns on small firms' securities.

A question that immediately comes to mind is whether a strategy of investing in the smallest-size stocks is indeed feasible. Note that the median market value of firms in the smallest-size portfolio is about $3 million. With such a low market value of equity, trading liquidity in the stock is very low, and the stock is probably both infrequently and thinly traded (with a large spread between the bid and asking price). Thus, a professional investor with a reasonable-size portfolio cannot invest in these stocks because of liquidity concerns. Furthermore, returns on these stocks may be limited to a very low level of trading, sometimes at a volume of just several thousands shares a month. Consequently, except for small investors with very long time horizons, the smallest-size securities cannot be used by professional investors to obtain abnormal returns.

To illustrate this point, we focus on all firms with a market value of equity below $100 million on the portfolio formation date. We use the same portfolio selection rules as before; firms had to have a minimum market value of $1 million on the portfolio formation date and were held for the entire calendar year immediately after the portfolio formation date. Table 9–2 presents the value-weighted annual returns on this portfolio.

As can be seen in Table 9–2, the number of firms with market capitalization below $100 million on the portfolio formation date is quite large—over 3,500 firms from about 6,000 firms with market capitalization above $1 million in the database. The median market value of this portfolio is $18 million, substantially greater than the median value of the smallest-size decile ($3 million), but still not sufficiently liquid for most investment professionals. The value-weighted annual return on this portfolio is 13.5 percent per year, slightly greater than the annual return on the market portfolio of 12.8 percent, but not significantly better. Note further that the portfolio of firms with market capitalization below $100 million yielded negative returns in 5 of the 15 years presented in Table 9–2, compared with only 2 years for the market as a whole. Thus, the return on this portfolio is much more volatile than that of the market. Note also that the percentage of firms that

Table 9–2
Small-Capitalization Firms Portfolio Results

Year	Number of Firms	Median Market Value ($ million)	Percent Bankrupt in the Next Three Years	Value Weighted Annual Return	Value Weighted Annual Return
	Firms with Market Value between $1 Million and $100 Million				*All Firms*
80	2,879	$16	2.3%	38.9%	6.8%
81	2,906	18	2.5	-0.7	-4.6
82	3,443	14	1.7	26.2	18.7
83	3,334	15	1.9	34.4	23.8
84	3,496	18	4.3	-12.7	1.8
85	3,598	16	3.9	27.4	31.8
86	3,463	18	4.4	2.9	20.3
87	3,752	19	4.7	-13.6	5.5
88	4,059	17	3.5	18.6	18.1
89	3,855	18	5.7	11.5	25.7
90	3,699	18	6.5	-25.8	-7.2
91	3,800	15	11.4	48.8	29.8
92	3,573	18	8.1	23.3	5.2
93	3,679	23	7.2	29.4	14.9
94	3,853	29	0.0	-6.5	0.8
Average	3,559	$18	4.5%	13.5%	12.8%
T-Statistic			6.3	2.5	4.1

went bankrupt within three years of the portfolio formation date is a significant 4.5 percent, but still lower than the 6.9 percent for the smallest-size decile. This indicates that the firm-specific risk of these firms is not as great as those of the smallest firms.

Table 9–3 shows similar statistics for two similar portfolios—a portfolio of firms with market capitalization between $100 million and $2,000 million on the portfolio formation date, and a portfolio of firms with market capitalization above $2,000 million. The portfolio of firms with market capitalization between $100 million and $2,000 million, what we call SMID (small- and mid-capitalization stocks), has over 1,700 firms on average with a median market value of about $290 million. This magnitude is large enough for most professional investors. Note that this portfolio had an average annual return of 16.3 percent, as compared with the average annual return on the market portfolio of 12.8 percent. Note further that the bankruptcy risk of these firms is much lower than those in Table 9–2; only about 1 percent of these firms went bankrupt within three years after the portfolio formation date, compared with 4.5 percent for the firms in Table 9–2.

Table 9– 3 also contains information about the portfolio of large firms—those with a market capitalization in excess of $2 billion on the portfolio formation date. The number of firms in this portfolio is about 300 per year, and this group constitutes between 5 and 10 percent of all firms in the market. However, the median firm for the large-capitalization group has a market capitalization of about $4 billion, so these firms are very important in driving the value-weighted overall market return. Note that the portfolio of large firms had an average annual return of 14.3 percent, above the market portfolio's annual return of 12.8 percent. These firms did not experience bankruptcy within the following three years after the portfolio formation period, presumably because their sheer size gave them leverage in negotiations with lenders, which smaller firms do not enjoy.

Figure 9–2 presents the cumulative returns of the three portfolios in Tables 9–2 and 9–3, as well the market return for the period 1980–1994. As can be seen in the graph, the portfolio of firms with market value below $100 million outperformed the other portfolios in the beginning of the 1980s, but then lagged behind the other portfolios. This portfolio also suffered the worst returns in 1987 and 1990, the two years with adverse market conditions (the stock market crash of October 1987 and the Gulf War in 1990). The SMID portfolio dominated the portfolio of large firms for most of the period 1980-1994, and, in particular, enjoyed a better recovery than the portfolio of large firms in the years 1991-1993. The market portfolio (marked "ALL" in the graph) underperformed both the portfolio of large firms and the SMID portfolio.

Based on the foregoing evidence, it seems that a careful investment strategy in small- and medium-capitalization stocks may yield better returns for an investor over the long run. The investor

Table 9-3
Small- and Medium-Capitalization Firms versus Large-Capitalization Firms: Portfolio Results

Year	Market Value between $100 Million and $2,000 Million				Market Value above $2,000 Million			
	Number of Firms	Median Market Value ($ millions)	Percent Bankrupt in the Next Three Years	Value-Weighted Annual Return	Number of Firms	Median Market Value ($ millions)	Percent Bankrupt in the Next Three Years	Value-Weighted Annual Return
80	1,213	$288	0.9%	30.0%	89	3,877	0.0%	33.9%
81	1,340	289	1.0	1.1	130	3,361	0.0	-9.9
82	1,310	290	0.7	22.5	117	3,531	0.0	14.0
83	1,406	296	1.5	24.4	161	3,396	0.0	22.2
84	1,667	283	1.7	-0.7	189	3,650	0.0	4.9
85	1,523	295	0.9	32.7	198	3,593	0.0	31.5
86	1,644	302	1.1	16.0	269	3,651	0.0	23.7
87	1,696	284	1.2	-0.6	315	3,890	0.0	9.1
88	1,603	297	1.0	20.4	320	4,058	0.0	17.2
89	1,748	302	1.4	22.8	349	4,188	0.0	27.4
90	1,772	295	1.0	-12.1	425	4,509	0.0	-5.3
91	1,630	293	1.5	41.1	381	4,609	0.0	26.2
92	2,063	282	1.6	12.8	486	4,508	0.0	3.0
93	2,407	287	0.0	18.2	520	4,455	0.0	13.6
94	2,844	291	0.0	-3.8	595	4,635	0.0	2.3
Average	1,724	$292	1.0%	16.3%	303	3,994	0.0%	14.3%
t-Statistic				4.4				4.3

FIGURE 9-2
Cumulative Returns for Various-Size Portfolios

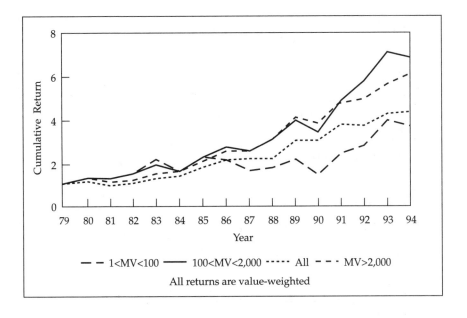

can benefit from the superior returns that small- and medium-size firms yield, although there are greater risks involved in investments in smaller firms. The two major risks involved in small-firm investments are due to lower diversification and to greater financial risk. Smaller firms are generally much less diversified than their larger counterparts. For example, large firms are usually involved in several business segments. Even if a large firm operates in only one major business segment, it usually enjoys a wide selection of products and is less dependent on any particular product for its success. Smaller firms are much more dependent on a single product, and their cash flows and market prices often fluctuate widely, depending on the success of that product and on where the economy and industry stand in the business cycle.

FIGURE 9–3
Russ Berrie and Co.

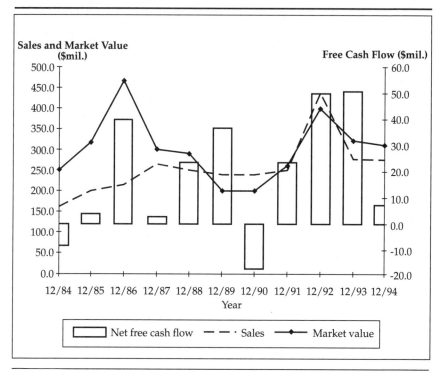

Example

Russ Berrie and Co. is a manufacturer and merchandiser of gift items
and items for impulse shopping. The firm enjoyed a large increase in
revenues and cash flows around 1992, mainly due to the popularity
of its Trolls (1991–1993). When the popularity of its Trolls declined
(1994), the firm's cash flows and prices declined, as can be seen in
Figure 9–3.

The other dimension of risk inherent in small-capitalization
firms is their financial risk. Small firms with high levels of debt
may find it impossible to raise new money for expansion, or just
to cover shortages when business conditions worsen. Banks are
much more eager to lend additional amounts of money to large
firms than to smaller firms. First, banks see the chance of bankruptcy

of a larger entity to be lower than that of a smaller entity. Larger firms can exercise greater political pressure on government officials, labor unions, customers, creditors, and suppliers when facing financial failure. For example, Chrysler Corp. managed to obtain government loan guarantees, so that the firm could continue in business. Similarly, employees of TWA purchased the company when it encountered financial difficulties in the 1980s and early 1990s. Small firms, which lack the wherewithal of large businesses, may be unable to obtain additional levels of debt when necessary and can more easily become bankrupt than large firms.

The portfolio selection process advocated in the previous chapter seems to be ideal for the selection of smaller firms with more stable free cash flows, lower levels of debt, and low prices as reflected in their free cash flow multiples. Such small firms are likely to be more diversified than other small firms, as is evident by their ability to consistently generate free cash flows. Furthermore, because of their low levels of financial leverage, they are likely to be less susceptible to bankruptcy than their small counterparts with higher levels of debt. Thus, a portfolio strategy that combines the benefits of small-capitalization investing with those of free cash flow investing may provide very attractive returns to shareholders. We describe such a strategy below.

SMALL-CAP INVESTING COMBINED WITH FREE CASH FLOW INVESTING[1]

Introduction

The purpose of this strategy is to select into the portfolio small-capitalization firms that have, among other logical criteria, low free cash flow multiples. The investment strategy takes a long position in securities of small firms that have shown an ability to consistently generate free cash flows, that have low financial leverage, and that are selling at low free cash flow multiples. Although these

---

[1]Adapted, with permission, from *Financial Analysts Journal*, Sptember/October 1994. Copyright 1994, Association for Investment Management and Research, Charlottesville, VA. All rights reserved.

firms are small, they are unlikely to be in their embryonic or initial growth stages; instead, typically, these companies operate in a stable business environment and are likely mispriced by the market because of lower earnings or lower earnings growth. Thus, instead of looking at the strong free cash flows of these firms, investors overreact to negative earnings or to negative earnings prospects.

The recommended investment strategy is intuitively appealing because it combines the benefits of growth and value investing. On the one hand, prior studies indicate that small firms are likely to grow at a faster rate than large firms. On the other, small firms are likely to be exposed to greater risks; they are less diversified (which implies a greater operating risk) and have a greater financial risk than large firms. Thus, the selection of small firms with low operating and financial risks seems to reduce the inherent risk of small firm investments.

The results of this strategy indicate that it is possible to construct a portfolio of small firms that outperforms the market portfolio, as well as portfolios of other firms with similar size, book/market ratio, or systematic risk.

Data and Portfolio Formation Rules

Data. The data for estimation of free cash flows are taken from the 1991 Compustat Annual Industrial (PST and Full Coverage) and Research Files. To reduce the survival bias, the initial population consists of all industrial firms, whether their securities are actively traded as of the time the study is conducted or not. The returns data are obtained from the 1991 CRSP data files for NYSE, AMEX, and NASDQ firms. Thus, to be included in our portfolio, firms must have available data on both Compustat and CRSP files.

Portfolio Formation. The portfolio formation date is assumed to be the last day of December every year. On that day, we examine the average free cash flow for the prior year and estimate other variables from the financial statements for the prior year. For example, in December 1989, we use data from the 1988 financial statements. Thus, for a firm that reports on a calendar basis, and assuming a lag of about three months between the balance sheet date and the disclosure date, the financial statements are available for about nine months before the portfolio formation date. Since firms with fiscal year-end before May 31 are classified by Compustat as reporting data for the prior calendar year, we minimize the risk that we use information that had been unavailable on the portfolio formation date (hindsight bias). Note that this conservative procedure actually introduces a bias against finding any abnormal returns.

On the portfolio formation date, we examine all securities (in the PST Annual Industrial, Full Coverage, and Research Files) and select those that pass our selection criteria. We then assume that we invest equal amounts in each of the securities selected for the portfolio, that we buy these securities on the portfolio formation date (December 31), and that we hold the securities until the end of the following year. For example, we use the 1988 financial statement data to construct the portfolio in December of 1989 and then examine the return on the portfolio during the period January 1 through December 31 of 1990.

Selection Criteria. We impose the following selection criteria for the portfolio:

1. To ensure that the stock of a selected firm will be adequately traded (i.e., reasonable liquidity), we require that the firm will have a market value of at least $50 million as of the portfolio formation date. We also require a maximum market value of equity of $2 billion in order to limit the portfolio to small- and mid-size firms. We will provide results later that illustrate the sensitivity of portfolio performance to these rules.

2. The four-year average (and the most recent) operating and free cash flows of the firm are positive. This criterion is intended to identify firms that can finance current growth rates from internally generated cash flows.

3. The growth rate of net operating cash flow and free cash flow in the most recent four years must be above 5 percent. This criterion is intended to ensure that selected firms would be consistent cash flow generators and have positive real rates of return.

4. The ratio of total debt (short- and long-term debt) to the four-year average free cash flow should be less than 10. The rationale for this criterion is that such firms have favorable debt capacity and are relatively unleveraged. These firms are unlikely to borrow in the future, given their ability to generate free cash flows internally, and in any event have strong financial flexibility. The upper bound of 10 is determined a priori, given past data about this ratio; the median in years prior to the portfolio formation date is substantially higher than 10.

5. The free cash flow multiple should be between 5 and 20. This multiple is estimated by the ratio of market value of equity as of the portfolio formation date to the four-year average free cash flow in the prior year. Recall that the free cash flow multiple is equal to the inverse of the required rate of return according to the no-growth model of valuation based on free cash flows. Thus, for securities with multiples below the inverse of the required market rate of return, capital appreciation is likely. Given the period of estimation, we set the a priori required rates of return in the range of 5–20 percent. The requirement of an upper bound of 20 stems from our observation that the median free cash flow multiple on the S&P industrials during years prior to the portfolio formation date fluctuated around 25. Therefore, by using information that was available on the portfolio formation date, the selection of 20 as an upper bound yields firms with lower cash flow multiples than the median.

As a result of applying all these screening or filtering rules, the final portfolio in any specific year is rather small. We obtain in our sample a minimum of 77 firms in 1990 and a maximum of 167 in 1984.

Returns. The portfolio strategy assumes that we invest equal amounts in each stock and that the average return for a portfolio is estimated over the following 12 months. For each year, we calculate raw returns, size-adjusted returns, beta-adjusted returns, book/market-adjusted returns, and market-adjusted returns. The size-adjusted return is estimated as the cumulative raw return on a security during the portfolio holding period minus the equally weighted average cumulative return on a portfolio of stocks that belong to the same decile of market capitalization as of the portfolio formation date. The book/market-adjusted return is estimated in two stages—(a) firms are classified into decile according to size (market value of equity on the portfolio formation date); (b) within each size decile, firms are classified into book/market (as of the prior year) decile. Thus, firms are classified into 100 portfolios arranged according to combinations of size and book/market ratio. The book/market-adjusted return reflects the return on a security minus the equally weighted return on all securities with the same combination of size and book/market ratios. For simplicity, in the remainder of this section, we shall refer to book/market-adjusted returns, although these returns adjust for *both* size and book/market ratios. Beta-adjusted return is cumulative raw return during the portfolio holding period minus the equally weighted average cumulative return on a portfolio of securities that fall into the same decile of beta on the portfolio formation date. Beta is estimated on the portfolio formation date by regressing the security's return on the equally weighted market return from CRSP using all available daily returns during the year, which ends on the portfolio formation date. Market-adjusted returns are raw returns minus the return on the value-weighted CRSP index.

Results

Table 9–4 reports the portfolio mean and median returns for the period 1978–1991. The exhibit also includes size-adjusted returns, book/market adjusted returns, beta-adjusted returns, market-adjusted returns, and the return on the CRSP value-weighted index. As can be seen in the exhibit, the portfolio returns averaged 21.6 percent per year during the period 1978–1991, whereas the CRSP value-weighted index produced an average annual return of 16.6 percent during that same period. Furthermore, in 10 of 14 years, the portfolio return exceeded the value-weighted index. Note that the median and the average returns on the portfolio are reasonably

Table 9-4 Small-Capitalization Portfolio Returns

Year*	N	Portfolio Mean†	Portfolio Median†	Size Adjusted††	Book to Market Adjusted††	Beta Adjusted††	Market Adjusted††	Value-Weighted Index
78	140	0.204	0.132	0.067	0.046	-0.023	0.120	0.084
79	120	0.320	0.196	-0.041	-0.085	-0.083	0.084	0.236
80	110	0.241	0.126	-0.086	-0.099	-0.107	-0.087	0.328
81	99	0.109	0.088	0.069	0.040	0.044	0.153	-0.044
82	139	0.389	0.349	0.143	0.107	0.108	0.186	0.202
83	134	0.360	0.326	0.071	0.043	-0.025	0.136	0.225
84	167	0.067	0.032	0.092	0.093	0.124	0.018	0.049
85	166	0.321	0.280	0.014	0.036	0.061	0.010	0.311
86	89	0.195	0.147	0.072	0.076	0.098	0.025	0.170
87	99	0.015	0.010	0.042	0.033	0.074	-0.012	0.027
88	92	0.295	0.238	0.081	0.050	0.083	0.129	0.166
89	101	0.208	0.182	0.008	-0.009	0.064	-0.106	0.314
90	77	-0.102	-0.142	0.061	0.077	0.099	-0.052	-0.049
91	104	0.405	0.334	-0.010	-0.009	-0.108	0.097	0.308
Average§	117	0.216	0.164	0.042	0.029	0.029	0.050	0.166
t-Statistic§		5.4	4.4	2.6	1.8	1.3	2.0	4.7

* Returns for year † are cumulated over calendar year t (using daily data), since the portfolio formation date is December 31 of year t − 1. On that date, securities are selected into the portfolio based on free cash flow and other information derived from year t − 2's financial statements

† Portfolio mean (median) is found by the average (median) annual return on the individual securities in the portfolio.

†† Adjusted returns are found by subtracting from each security's annual return the mean annual return on all securities that belong to the same decile, as of the portfolio formation date. The table reports the mean adjusted return over all securities in the portfolio for any given year. Size is determined by the market value of equity. Book/market ratio is book value of equity divided by market value of equity. Beta is estimated from all available daily returns during the year of the portfolio formation date. The market model is used with the equally weighted CRSP index proxying for the market return. Market-adjusted returns are average return on the portfolio minus the return on the value weighted CRSP index.

§ Mean returns are calculated as the average annual return on the portfolio during the period 1978–1991 (using 14 observations). The t-statistic is calculated as the mean return divided by its standard error over the same 14 observations.

460

close to each other, indicating that the portfolio superiority is not caused by extreme observations. Also, the free cash flow portfolio performed better than the market in the "down" year 1981 (but not in 1990), indicating that the selected securities do not have a greater risk in adverse market conditions.

A further examination of Table 9–4 reveals that the adjusted returns on the portfolio are significant from an economic point of view, with annual abnormal returns of 2.9 percent on the average for beta-adjusted returns, 4.2 percent for size-adjusted returns, 5.0 percent for market-adjusted returns and 2.9 percent for book/market-adjusted returns. Furthermore, most of the annual abnormal returns are positive, indicating the superiority of the free cash flow portfolios over the various control portfolios. The table also provides t-statistics to test whether the mean annual abnormal return is equal to zero. Thus, we divide the average annual adjusted return by its standard error across the 14 years to obtain the t-statistic.[2] All the t-statistics are significant at the 10 percent level or less, except for the beta-adjusted returns. However, according to Fama and French (*Journal of Finance*, 1992), it is more important to control for size and book/market ratios than for beta.

Table 9–5 reports some statistics about the free cash flow portfolios. The median market value of the portfolio is about $194 million during the period, consistent with our selection criteria. The mean free cash flow multiple is very stable between 12.5 and 14.2, and the mean debt multiple is between 2.8 and 3.5. The average dividend yield on the portfolio is 4.0 percent, in excess of the market average during the same period of 2.1 percent. This is a further indication of the stability of operations for the portfolio firms. The mean E/P ratio varies along the years, with a mean of 9.6 percent for the entire period. The unexpected earnings variable (first difference in earnings divided by price at the beginning of the period) is negative on the average for the entire period, and is negative for 8 of the 14 years in the period 1978–1991. Thus, the average firm in our free cash flow portfolios experiences a "negative earnings surprise" before the portfolio formation date, although free cash flows of the firm actually grew during the most

---

[2] This method is used by E. F. Fama and James MacBeth, "Risk, Return, and Equilibrium: Empirical Tests," *Journal of Political Economy* 81 (1973), pp. 607-36.

Table 9–5 Financial Characteristics of Portfolio Firms

					Mean			
Year	N	Median Market Value*	FCF Multiple**	Debt Multiple†	Dividend Yield††	E/P Ratio§	UE/P"	Beta#
78	140	173.9	12.5	2.9	0.042	0.137	0.007	1.092
79	120	161.3	13.1	2.9	0.047	0.146	0.004	0.950
80	110	171.7	12.7	2.9	0.043	0.140	0.013	0.973
81	99	188.0	12.6	3.1	0.050	0.129	−0.044	0.929
82	139	175.7	12.8	3.2	0.046	0.127	−0.018	0.898
83	134	181.7	12.7	3.2	0.045	0.089	−0.026	0.905
84	167	194.1	13.3	3.4	0.035	0.067	0.003	0.843
85	166	211.3	13.1	2.9	0.036	0.089	0.003	0.924
86	89	208.7	14.2	3.1	0.034	0.055	−0.024	0.910
87	99	229.4	13.6	3.1	0.028	0.047	−0.026	1.017
88	92	186.7	13.4	2.9	0.029	0.078	−0.008	0.951
89	101	198.2	13.4	2.8	0.031	0.079	0.009	0.962
90	77	180.5	13.6	3.4	0.052	0.078	−0.006	1.057
91	104	251.5	12.6	2.8	0.042	0.082	−0.035	1.137
Average	117	193.8	13.1	3.1	0.040	0.096	−0.011	0.968
T-Statistic	29.6		101.0	55.6	19.2	10.8	−2.2	44.5

* Market value of equity is calculated as of the portfolio formation date, December 31, of year t − 1 for year t in the table.

** FCF multiple is market value of equity on the portfolio formation date (year t − 1), divided by four-year average free cash flow as of year t − 2.

† Debt multiple represents total debt, divided by four-year average free cash flow.

†† Dividend yield is dividend divided by price, as of the portfolio formation date.

§ Earnings-to-price ratio is earnings per share at t − 2, divided by price at the end of t − 1, all adjusted for stock splits and stock dividends.

" Unexpected-earnings-to-price ratio is earnings per share at year t − 2 minus earnings per share at t − 3, divided by price per share at the end of t − 1, all adjusted for stock splits and stock dividends.

\# Beta is estimated from all available daily returns during year t − 1. Security returns are regressed on the value-weighted CRSP index return.

FIGURE 9–4
FCF Portfolio Cumulative Returns

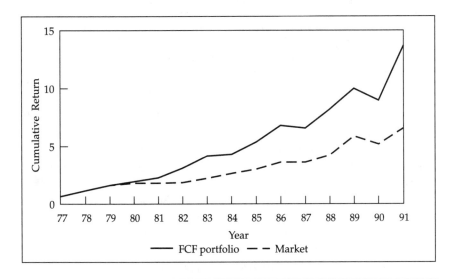

recent four years. This bad earnings news may be a partial explanation for the abnormal returns on our portfolios, if investors in
the short term are fixated on earnings to the exclusion of free
cash flows. Finally, the average beta of the portfolio is 0.968, with
four years that exhibit betas only slightly larger than 1.0.

Figure 9–4 portrays the cumulative returns on the portfolios
constructed according to the free cash flow strategy, and the value-
weighted market return from CRSP. As can be seen, the free cash
flow portfolios clearly outperform the market return.

Sensitivity Analysis

The abnormal returns documented above may be derived by the
restrictions on market capitalization in the portfolio selection. In
particular, we restricted firms to a market capitalization between

$50 million and $2 billion. To test the sensitivity of our results to the specific market capitalization of portfolio firms, we alter the bounds on market value as follows:

1. Market value between $50 million and $500 million.
2. Market value between $50 million and $1,000 million.
3. Market value between $100 million and $1,000 million.

The portfolio average annual returns are available in Table 9–6. A comparison of the results in Table 9–4 above with those in Table 9–6 indicates that average portfolio returns are almost completely insensitive to the exact specification of bounds on market value. Also, in all cases, the portfolios outperform the CRSP value-weighted market index. Thus, we feel confident that it is the combination of restrictions on size and free cash flow multiples that drives the results, and not the exact bounds placed on market value.

To see if the firms selected into our portfolio are concentrated in any particular industry, Table 9-7 provides the distribution of firms in three-digit SIC industries. As can be seen, we find no particular industry clustering in the free cash flow portfolios.

Summary and Conclusions

This section examined the performance of an investment strategy that identifies small- and mid-capitalization firms with a consistent pattern of operating and free cash flows, low financial leverage, and low free cash flow multiples. It shows that portfolios based on this investment strategy are able to generate superior returns. These portfolios performed better than the CRSP value-weighted market index, similar size portfolios, similar beta portfolios, and similar book/market portfolios. Thus, the superior results of the free cash flow portfolios are likely not due to additional dimensions of risk.

RESULTS OF A LIVE PORTFOLIO

Systematic Financial Management, Inc., has managed small- and mid-capitalization portfolios of stocks that were selected based on the general criteria used in the prior section. The portfolio

Table 9–6
Average Portfolio Returns for 1978–1991: Various Bounds on Firm Market Value

N	Portfolio Mean	Portfolio Median	Size Adjusted	Book to Market Adjusted	Beta Adjusted	Market Adjusted	Value-Weighted Index
Market Value: $50 Million to $500 Million							
89	0.210	0.154	0.038	0.024	0.023	0.044	0.166
	5.102	3.795	2.071	1.267	1.068	1.524	4.685
Market Value: $50 Million to $1,000 Million							
105	0.213	0.164	0.041	0.027	0.026	0.047	0.166
	5.390	4.327	2.391	1.515	1.160	1.801	4.685
Market Value: $100 Million to $1,000 Million							
73	0.213	0.166	0.040	0.033	0.027	0.047	0.166
	5.863	4.724	2.149	1.729	1.003	1.980	4.685

Notes:

1. Mean values are shown in the top rows; t-statistics are shown in bottom rows. Variable definitions are in notes to Tables 9–4 and 9–5.

2. N is average number of firms in the portfolio during 1978–1991.

Table 9–7
Three-Digit SIC Code Distribution of Portfolio Firms

							Year							
SIC	78	79	80	81	82	83	84	85	86	87	88	89	90	91
100	•	•	•	•	•	•	•	1	1	1	2	1	1	•
800	•	•	•	•	•	•	•	•	•	•	•	•	1	2
1000	1	•	•	1	5	1	2	•	•	1	1	2	1	3
1200	1	•	•	•	•	•	1	1	1	2	•	1	1	1
1300	2	2	•	•	•	3	3	2	2	1	1	2	2	2
1400	•	•	1	2	1	•	•	•	1	•	2	1	1	2
1500	1	1	1	•	1	•	1	1	1	2	•	1	•	•
1600	5	5	2	2	•	•	•	1	1	•	•	•	1	•
1700	•	•	•	•	•	•	•	1	•	•	•	•`	•	•
2000	8	9	9	8	13	9	11	15	4	5	3	3	2	1
2100	•	•	2	•	•	1	1	•	•	•	•	•	•	•
2200	2	2	4	6	5	6	7	2	2	3	3	1	2	1
2300	4	•	1	2	1	1	2	4	•	4	2	3	•	1
2400	0	1	2	3	3	1	1	•	1	•	1	•	2	1
2500	2	1	1	•	2	1	•	3	1	1	2	•	2	4
2600	5	3	3	5	4	4	3	2	4	5	4	2	4	6
2700	6	7	9	6	7	8	6	4	3	2	1	3	5	2
2800	8	10	7	7	9	16	16	19	7	6	6	7	3	6
2900	•	•	•	•	1	2	•	1	1	2	2	2	1	1
3000	2	•	•	3	6	1	6	1	4	3	4	1	1	2
3100	2	3	•	2	•	1	1	•	•	1	1	1	1	•
3200	2	3	7	5	4	1	1	3	1	3	3	2	3	•
3300	3	6	3	4	9	5	4	1	3	2	3	3	5	7
3400	6	5	4	2	7	11	14	14	4	4	4	4	1	7
3500	17	11	13	4	9	15	23	23	10	11	9	12	5	12
3600	12	11	4	6	5	6	9	13	4	5	6	9	5	6
3700	17	11	13	4	8	4	10	9	10	11	7	9	2	3
3800	7	5	1	1	1	4	9	13	6	4	2	3	3	2
3900	1	2	2	2	3	3	4	3	•	2	1	2	2	3
4000	1	•	1	2	1	3	2	2	1	•	•	•	•	•
4200	1	1	2	•	1	•	•	2	•	•	•	•	•	•
4400	•	•	•	•	•	•	•	•	•	•	•	•	1	•
4500	1	2	2	1	2	2	•	1	1	1	•	1	•	•
4600	•	•	•	•	•	1	•	•	•	1	1	•	•	•

Table 9–7 *(concluded)*

SIC	78	79	80	81	82	83	84	85	86	87	88	89	90	91
											Year			
4700	•	•	•	•	•	1	•	1	•	•	•	•	•	1
4800	8	5	7	4	4	3	3	4	2	4	2	2	2	1
4900	3	1	1	•	•	2	3	3	1	1	•	1	•	•
5000	4	1	2	1	2	3	3	1	2	3	2	2	1	1
5100	1	3	2	4	5	4	4	3	•	3	•	•	1	1
5200	1	•	•	•	•	•	1	•	•	•	•	•	•	•
5300	2	3	1	2	1	1	2	2	1	•	1	•	•	2
5400	1	3	2	•	2	•	1	1	•	2	1	•	•	•
5600	4	2	1	3	2	•	2	•	•	•	2	•	2	2
5700	1	•	•	•	•	1	•	1	•	•	•	•	•	•
5800	•	•	•	•	2	2	3	•	1	•	•	•	1	1
5900	2	2	•	2	2	2	1	3	•	1	1	•	•	•
6000	•	•	•	•	•	•	•	•	•	•	1	•	•	•
6200	•	•	•	1	1	•	•	•	•	•	2	2	2	4
6300	1	1	•	•	•	•	•	•	•	•	•	•	2	2
6400	2	3	4	2	3	1	1	2	0	2	3	1	•	1
6500	•	•	•	•	•	•	•	1	1	•	1	•	•	2
6700	1	1	1	1	3	6	3	3	7	4	3	7	3	4
7000	•	•	1	•	1	•	•	•	•	•	•	•	•	•
7200	•	•	•	•	•	•	•	•	•	•	•	1	•	1
7300	2	5	4	5	8	5	9	8	3	1	4	7	2	6
7800	•	•	2	1	3	•	•	1	1	•	1	1	2	3
7900	•	•	2	2	2	2	•	2	2	•	2	2	1	2
8200	•	•	•	•	•	•	•	1	1	2	•	1	•	1
8700	1	2	2	•	1	5	4	1	2	•	•	2	2	1

generally consists of about 45 stocks, which are held in roughly equal proportions. To be included in the portfolio, firms had to have a market capitalization of between $100 million and $2,000 million and low free cash flow and debt multiples. The market value to four-year average free cash flow of a firm should have been less than 15 on the inclusion date of the security in the portfolio, and its ratio of total debt (including off-balance-sheet

Table 9–8
Systematic Financial Management, Inc.,
SMID Capitalization Composite

Quarter/Year	SMID Cap Composite	Russell 2000
4-92		
1-93	7.4%	4.3%
2-93	2.0	2.2
3-93	8.1	8.7
4-93	4.6	2.6
1993	23.7	18.9
1-94	1.7	–2.7
2-94	–1.8	–3.9
3-94	5.6	6.9
4-94	–4.2	–1.9
1994	1.1	–1.8
1-95	4.6	4.6
YTD	4.6%	4.6%

Annualized Performance Summary, March 31, 1995

	SMID Cap Composite	Russell 2000
One year	4.0%	5.5%
Two years	10.4%	8.2%
Since inception	12.7%	9.3%
Up capture	109.9%	
Down capture	52.1%	

liabilities) to four-year average free cash flow less than 5. Furthermore, free cash flows should have grown in the most recent four-year period.

Systematic's small- and mid-capitalization (SMID) portfolio began on January 1, 1993. The returns on this portfolio are reported in Table 9–8, which also compares the portfolio's performance to the Russell 2000, a widely-used index of small and mid-cap securities. As can be seen from the table, Systematic's SMID portfolio earned average annual return of 12.7 percent since inception, while the Russell 2000 index earned an average annual return of 9.3 percent during the same period. More interestingly, and consistent with the results for the regular Systematic portfolios described in the previous chapter, the SMID portfolio captures all the market increases (109.9 percent) during the portfolio period, but declines only about half (down capture of 52.1 percent) of the market declines. This explains the superiority of the free cash flow portfolio over the market portfolio and is consistent with the nature of firms that are selected into the portfolio.

Figure 9–5 portrays the cumulative returns on Systematic's SMID portfolio and the Russell 2000 index. It shows clearly the superiority of the SMID portfolio over that of the Russell 2000 index.

FIGURE 9-5
SMID Portfolio Results versus Russell 2000 Index

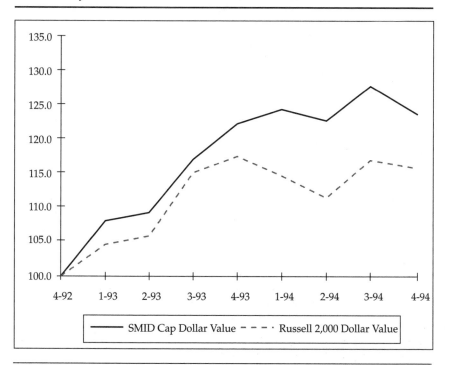

SUMMARY

In this chapter, we showed how an investor can combine two known anomalies—the superior returns on small- and mid-capitalization stocks with the superior returns on a low free cash flow strategy—to obtain returns that outperform market indices, portfolios of similar-size firms, portfolios with the same beta risk, and portfolios of firms with similar size and book/market ratios. These results were obtained in back-tests of the strategy for a long period, as well as live portfolios for a shorter period. The strategy is successful because it identifies small firms with stable operating and free cash flows, low levels of debt, and low free cash flow multiples. Such small firms are usually more diversified, stable, and liquid than their counterparts, which explains why they perform better than their peers in declining markets.

In the next chapter, we show you how to utilize the same portfolio strategy to select international (foreign) firms.

Chapter Ten

International Investments Based on Free Cash Flow

INTRODUCTION

This chapter shows how we can implement the same free cash flow strategy that we saw in the previous two chapters to investments in foreign equities. This strategy is particularly appealing for foreign firms because it reduces the need to rely on earnings information from financial statements, which vary across countries just due to differential accounting methods. The chapter illustrates how one can use information from foreign financial statements to estimate free cash flows of firms. As before, the investment strategy selects firms that are consistent free cash flow generators, have low financial leverage, and have low free cash flow multiples.

The results of this investment strategy yield returns in excess of an international market index, which consists of all firms in the Global/Vantage database. These results are not due to additional risk because abnormal returns are obtained even after adjusting for size and book/market ratios. It is shown that the selected portfolio firms perform significantly better than firms with similar sizes and book/market ratios.

BENEFITS AND COSTS OF FOREIGN INVESTMENTS

Benefits of Foreign Investments

With the recent improvements in communication links across countries and continents, the ever-increasing globalization of businesses and capital markets, and the growth opportunities available abroad, investors can no longer afford to forgo foreign

investments.[1] There are two major benefits from foreign investments: additional dimensions of diversification from foreign investments will lead to lower total portfolio risk and additional growth
opportunities that arise when every one's universe is expanded.

The theory of portfolio diversification suggests that investments
in foreign markets offer additional opportunities for diversification beyond the local market. To assess the magnitude of this
diversification, we examine the matrix of correlations among the
returns of various countries reprinted here with permission of
Morningstar American Depository Receipts (Morningstar, Inc., 225
West Wacker Drive, Chicago, Illinois 60606; phone 312-696-
6100). As can be seen in the World Market Correlations Chart
published in May 19, 1995 (Figure 10–1), the long-term correlation between the S&P 500 index in the United States and the Canadian index is 0.56, which is high but probably lower than most
investors expect, given the strong relationships among these
two economies. The correlation is much lower for the United States
and Japan, 0.27 for the five-year correlation, which suggests that
international diversification can be substantial. A good analysis
of international correlations is available in Odier and Solnik (*Financial Analysts Journal*, March–April 1993).

Foreign markets may offer not only additional diversification
but also additional growth opportunities if in those markets one
can find companies that are underpriced relative to domestic
concerns. It is generally believed that investments in firms traded
on emerging stock markets can yield tremendous returns simply
due to the growth potential of such firms. For example, the
economies of many countries in the Far East expanded rapidly
during the 1980s and 1990s due to direct foreign investments and
more open economies. Local firms enjoyed expanding local
markets, as well as the possibilities of joint ventures with foreign firms. Consequently, the market values of these local firms
mushroomed, and investors in these firms fared very well. The
stock index of an emerging market often yields returns in excess

---

[1]Indeed, on January 5, 1993, *The Wall Street Journal* began publishing a world
Dow-Jones index, which includes returns on equity securities from about 10
countries. This index is maintained using several currencies and reports data for
three continents and many industries.

FIGURE 10–1
World Market Correlations, April 30, 1995

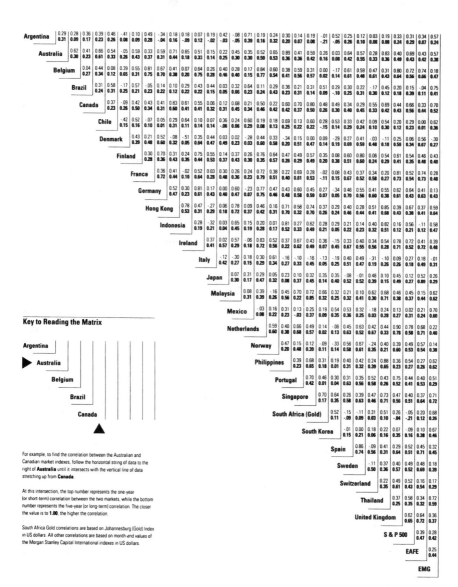

Key to Reading the Matrix

Argentina

▶ Australia

Belgium

Brazil

Canada

▲

For example, to find the correlation between the Australian and Canadian market indexes, follow the horizontal string of data to the right of **Australia** until it intersects with the vertical line of data stretching up from **Canada**.

At this intersection, the top number represents the one-year (or short-term) correlation between the two markets, while the bottom number represents the five-year (or long-term) correlation. The closer the value is to **1.00**, the higher the correlation.

South Africa Gold correlations are based on Johannesburg (Gold) Index in US dollars. All other correlations are based on month-end values of the Morgan Stanley Capital International indexes in US dollars.

of 50 percent in a given year. Furthermore, foreign economies are likely to mitigate current negative trends in the domestic market because not all markets are affected by the same economic events. At times, the local economy may be in a recession because of a restrictive monetary or fiscal policy or because of a political crisis, while economies in other counties may be expanding steadily. Investment in foreign securities at such times may offer additional rewards to investors.[2]

However, investments in foreign equity securities usually carry additional dimensions of risk as well: (1) foreign investments are subject to currency exchange risks, (2) foreign firms are subject to their own local accounting and disclosure rules, which, for the most part, are less stringent than those prevailing in the United States, (3) greater political risk, and (4) foreign markets may react differently to economic and noneconomic events than does the local market just because of differing social/psychological/cultural settings. Let us address each of these dimensions.

Foreign Exchange Risk

Foreign investments are affected, not only by the stock return in the local market, but also by the conversion of that return to the currency of the investor.

Example

An extreme effect on performance has been felt according to Reuter (January 3, 1995) by Wright EquiFund Mexico, an open-ended pure-Mexico mutual fund. Its assets declined 31.7 percent between December 19, 1994, and December 28, 1994, due to the Mexican peso devaluation. However, it should be emphasized that this is an extreme example, and most currency fluctuations tend to reverse themselves over long time horizons.

This foreign currency exchange risk may work also for the benefit of the U.S. investor if the local currency appreciates against the U.S. dollar. In such cases, the U.S. investor obtains not only

---

[2]See, for example, Becker, Finnerty and Gupta (*Journal of Finance*, 1990), Bergstrom (*Journal of Portfolio Management*, 1975), Hunter and Coggin (*Journal of Portfolio Management*, 1990), Lessard (*Journal of Finance*, 1974), Maldonado and Saunders (*Financial Management*, 1981), and Solnik (*Journal of Quantitative Finance*, 1974).

the local return, but also the gain in value of the foreign currency relative to the U.S. dollar. Also a decline in the value of a local currency can make exports more competitive.

Example

Stock in TECUMSEH Corp., rallied after Brazil devalued its currency and felt competitive pressure due to an artificially high value placed on the currency earlier, increased exports of its Brazialian output.

Example

During the first quarter of 1995, Japan's Nikkei index declined by about 17 percent, but Japanese ADRs (American depository receipts—American claims against Japanese securities, where the claims are denominated and traded in U.S. dollars) actually rose during that period, mostly because of the declining dollar against the Japanese yen.

The U.S. investor may decide either to absorb the foreign exchange risk inherent in the investment or to hedge it. Most investors in foreign equities choose to absorb the foreign exchange risk. Hedging of a foreign investment is costly and may in most cases as far from perfect hedge. The investor can hedge by entering a forward exchange contract for a specific currency for a specific duration. However, since the duration of the foreign investment may exceed or be shorter than that of the forward contract, he or she may have to assume additional hedging, or fold a position early. Furthermore, hedges of some currencies are not widely available or are very costly because there is no organized foreign exchange market in that currency. An investor may also benefit from not hedging because foreign exchange rates are unpredictable. Thus, a long-term foreign investment may in most cases be little affected by short-term fluctuations in foreign exchange rates.

Accounting and Disclosure Rules

A major obstacle to foreign investment is the different accounting rules in foreign countries. For example, it is well known that the price/earnings ratio of Japanese stocks is about two to three times greater than their American counterparts. This gap occurs not only because of Japanese overpricing, risk, or growth, but also because of Japanese conservatism in reported earnings, which are also used for tax purposes. Similarly, even casual observation of accounting reports and methods across countries shows how much international diversity exists currently, in spite of efforts at harmonization of accounting methods. Thus, some of the most frequently used tools for valuation and relative ranking of firms may no longer be valid when branching to other countries.[3]

Example

Although an increased number of companies, in the interest of fair disclosure, are adopting international accounting standards, a company can opt out of inconvienent clauses if mentioned in the annual report.

Example

Property, plant, and equipment (PPE) is carried on the books of a U.S. firm at its historical acquisition cost minus accumulated depreciation. During the high inflation period in the 1970s the SEC and the FASB experimented with supplementary disclosure about current values of PPE and inventory in (unaudited) footnotes to the financial statements.

In the United Kingdom, Australia, and New Zealand, firms often revalue their PPE, and carry it on the balance sheet at revalued costs. A footnote would generally break down the carrying value to the original cost, the additional value due to the revaluation, and the date of the revaluation. Firms have the option of choosing when they want to revalue their PPE. Such revaluation can occur before a firm raises new capital or when current prices of its properties are very different from their carrying values on the balance sheet. Typically, when the firm revalues its PPE, the additional value increases (debits) assets of the firm, and the offsetting credit causes an increase of stockholders equity. However, some countries allow certain firms (such as real estate firms) to include the value appreciation of PPE in current income. In most countries that allow revaluations, subsequent annual depreciation expense increase because they now include the revaluation as well.

In the Netherlands, firms may account for PPE on the balance sheet using current values. Due to the high inflation after the first world war, Dutch accounting has accepted (and even recommended) current values of PPE. Current values may be obtained by annual appraisals of PPE, or by the replacement costs of these properties.

---

[3]See, for example, Choi and Levitch, *The Capital Market Effects of International Accounting Diversity*, (Homewood, IL: Dow Jones–Irwin, 1990), Gray (*Journal of Accounting Research*, 1980), Lee and Livnat (working paper, New York University, 1991), Meek (*The Accounting Review*, 1983), Meek (*Journal of International Financial Management and Accounting*, 1991), Nobes and Parker (*Comparative International Accounting*, Oxford, UK, 1981), Pope and Rees (working paper, University of Strathclyde, Glasgow, 1992), and Weetman and Gray (*Accounting and Business Research*, 1991).

In Latin America, many countries subject to high inflation recommend the constant-currency valuation of PPE. Firms in these countries increase the carrying value of the property by the inflation rate during the period, and then subtract depreciation expense from the adjusted value. In contrast to current values of the PPE, all that is needed for constant-currency valuation is the knowledge of the (general) inflation rate during the period. Note that the carrying value would not be adjusted to reflect changes in the specific values of the PPE. They would only adjust for the effects of the general inflation in the economy.

Example

In the United States, when a firm acquires another firm for a price that exceeds the fair market value of the acquired firm's assets, the acquiring firm incorporates an additional asset on its consolidated balance sheet, usually called goodwill. In future years, this goodwill is amortized and earnings are lower due to the goodwill amortization charges.

In the U.K. and other countries, purchased goodwill is deducted directly from stockholders equity in the year of acquisition. Thus, earnings of the firm in future years are not affected by goodwill amortization. This discrepancy in goodwill amortization has been mentioned in the financial press as one of the reasons for higher prices paid by British acquirers than their U.S. competitors in acquisition contests.

Example

Japanese and German accounting standards do not require a firm to disclose segment information, as is required in the United States. When Daimler Benz wanted to have its stock traded in the United States as an ADR, it had to begin disclosure of segment data. According to newspaper accounts at the time, this disclosure was the largest stumbling block in its decision to have its securities traded in the United States.

In a study described by *The Wall Street Journal* (February 23, 1995), Shelley Taylor & Associates, a London consulting firm, surveyed money managers about disclosure practices of 170 publicly listed firms in 10 countries. Only 58 percent of these firms provided segment data, and only 65 percent provided any geographical data about operations. Money managers expressed concern about the lack of disclosure in this important area.

Not only are there differences in accounting methods across countries, but the enforcement mechanisms are much different across countries. In the United States, if a firm deviates from Generally

Accepted Accounting Principles (GAAP) and the deviation is material, the auditor has to issue a qualified audit opinion. This is not
true for many other countries, where auditors have a less-power-
ful position in their confrontations with audited firms. Furthermore, in the United States, firms comply well with the SEC
requirements for disclosure of annual data within 90 days of the
balance sheet date, and quarterly reports within 45 days. In many
foreign countries, a sizable portion of publicly listed firms do not
comply with the local disclosure rules, and their annual or
interim reports are issued after the mandatory date.

Another dimension on which U.S. and foreign countries differ
is on the frequency of disclosure within the year. In the United
States, publicly listed firms (with a minimum market value) are
required to issue quarterly reports to shareholders, as well as
immediate announcements about specific important events (Form
8-K). Due to the frequency of litigation in the United States,
firms usually comply with these disclosure requirements. In
other countries, firms do not have to report every quarter and
may have only one interim report at midyear. Furthermore, in
many foreign countries (but especially in new and emerging
markets), material information about the firm is not immediately disclosed to the market, and in some cases, insiders are
known to trade on that information before it is disclosed to
the public.

Thus, foreign markets may be characterized by accounting information prepared according to different accounting standards. The
mandatory information in these accounting reports may be less
comprehensive than that required in the United States, and the
reports may not be as timely as U.S. reports. Additional information about the firm may be less forthcoming outside the United
States than it is here.

Differences in Market and Social Settings

The U.S. capital markets are for the most part large and reasonably efficient. Although it is possible to find securities that trade
in illiquid fashion and with a low trading volume, many securities in the market are traded continuously. In emerging markets,
however, liquidity may be a major concern for investors. The

volume of trading of smaller stocks in emerging market may be so low that an individual investor may be able to affect security prices materially with small amounts of money.

A large proportion of the stocks in the United States are held by institutional investors, who are presumed to be knowledgeable and disciplined about their investment decisions. In many of the emerging markets, the stock market is dominated by individual investors with little or no knowledge about investments, who may use it as an instrument of legal betting. In such markets, security prices may reflect noneconomic dimensions of attractiveness that are based more on speculation than reality.

Some established foreign markets have a tradition of favoring creditors at the expense of shareholders. For example, the stock market in Germany is relatively small (in terms of the number of publicly listed firms) and is heavily controlled by institutional investors. Firms in Germany and Japan, traditionally, have relied more on borrowing than on public issuance of capital. Thus, the stock market in Germany is much less developed than the U.S. stock market, although the economy in Germany is well developed.

Finally, local customs and culture play an important part in the behavior of investors. For example, news about illness or wounding of the U.S. president have sent the market skidding in the United States, but news of a coup d'etat in Thailand has not prevented the Thai stock market from resuming its normal daily trading and price increases. In some countries, announcements by public officials are taken very seriously, while in others they are discounted completely; statements made by the chairman of the U.S. Federal Reserve Bank may have a material effect on the stock market, whereas similar statements made in other countries would have no effect on security prices (if the central bankers have a low credibility). Similarly, as became known subsequently, Japanese brokerage firms used to compensate large investors for trading losses, until the crash in the Japanese stock market, when these losses became too big for the four large Japanese brokerage firms to sustain.

Thus, foreign investments offer the local investor a prudent way to diversify investments and to obtain future growth that may be impossible in the local market. However, foreign investments carry additional dimensions of risk: in particular, the risk of foreign exchange rate loss, a less favorable information and disclosure environment about foreign firms, and thin markets with differing sensitivities than those of the local market. The investor may decide to ignore the risk inherent in foreign exchange rates by investments in many countries, but he or she should attempt to minimize the risks of the information environment and the low trading liquidity. We suggest a portfolio strategy based on free cash flows that reduces the latter two types of risk.

ESTIMATING FREE CASH FLOWS OF FOREIGN FIRMS

In the case of foreign firms, we follow the direct method of estimating free cash flow (see Chapter 5); that is, we estimate the components of operating cash flows and subtract capital expenditures from it, but add back unnecessary discretionary capital expenditures and discretionary payments. However, we have to make an additional modification because of the presence of reserves in foreign firms' financial statements.

Foreign firms in some countries use a noncash charge against income with an offsetting amount to untaxed reserves. The estimation of cash flows from operating activities has to take into account this charge and, even more important, the change in the untaxed reserves that occurs when actual cash payments are made with an offsetting reduction in untaxed reserves. Thus, a direct method of estimating cash flows from recurring operating activities seems to be warranted because it abstracts from dealing with many of the foreign firms' reserves.

We estimate cash collected from customers as sales minus the change in accounts receivable. Operating cash outlays are estimated as operating expenses (cost of goods sold and selling, general and administrative expenses)[4], minus those noncash expenses (depreciation and amortization), plus changes in inventories and prepaid expenses, minus changes in trade accounts

---

[4]In some countries, the information about operating expenses is available only in the aggregate, without a breakdown into cost of goods sold, selling, general and administrative expenses, and the like.

payable and accrued expenses. In certain countries, firms reduce their earnings by appropriation of a certain amount to untaxed reserves. This is a noncash expense that is similar to depreciation or to bad debt expense with an offsetting increase in a reserve account (in the liabilities section of the balance sheet) or a provision account. When the firm falls into bad times, the firm makes cash payments to cover its expenses, but instead of charging these payments against income, it reduces the reserve account. Thus, to obtain an estimate of cash outlays for such firms, we add to operating expenses the appropriation to untaxed reserves. We then subtract the change in the balance sheet reserves, as well as changes in balance sheet provisions for pension and other provisions.[5]

To illustrate the potential impact of these items, let us examine the 1993 financial statements of Daimler-Benz.

Example

Daimler-Benz Corp. filed Form 20-F with the SEC in 1993. This form is filed when a foreign firm presents its financial statements according to its local GAAP (generally accepted accounting principles) and is intended to provide a reconciliation of income and equity to U.S. GAAP. Thus, we have an opportunity to assess the magnitude of accounting differences between the two. In Note 2 to the financial statements contained in the Form 20-F, Daimler-Benz describes and reconciles the differences between U.S. and German GAAP. This note is incorporated here.

As seen on page 488 in 1993, Daimler-Benz reported income of DM602 million ($346 million using the exchange rate on December 31, 1993), according to its German GAAP, after adjusting for minority shareholders' share of the losses. However, its net income according to U.S. GAAP amounted to a loss of DM1,839 million ($1,057 million). Thus, the magnitude of the adjustment is considerable. Conversely (see page 489) in 1993, majority shareholders' equity amounted to DM17,584 million according to German GAAP, but to DM26,281 million according to U.S. GAAP. Thus, it seems that Daimler Benz's 1993 income was overstated when compared to U.S. GAAP, whereas its stockholders equity was understated. This can occur when

---

[5]See Todd and Sherman, *Handbook of International Accounting* (New York: John Wiley and Sons, 1991), on this issue.

Daimler-Benz

DAIMLER-BENZ AG

Consolidated Statements of Income
(in millions, except per share amounts)

		Year Ended December 31,			
	Note	1993 (Note 1)	1993	1992	1991
Revenues		$ 56,187	DM 97,737	DM 98,549	DM 95,010
Increase in inventories and other capitalized in-house output..............	4	1,010	1,757	2,330	3,556
Total output............................		57,197	99,494	100,879	98,566
Other operating income...................	5	4,237	7,370	4,506	3,545
Cost of materials........................	7	(29,362)	(51,076)	(49,084)	(49,456)
Personnel expenses	8	(19,425)	(33,790)	(32,003)	(29,372)
Amortization of intangible assets, depreciation of fixed assets and of leased equipment		(4,633)	(8,059)	(7,085)	(5,977)
Other operating expenses	6	(8,785)	(15,281)	(15,254)	(13,824)
Income from affiliated, associated and related companies	10	59	103	118	56
Interest income, net	11	262	456	577	623
Write-downs of financial assets and of securities.............................	13	(173)	(300)	(121)	(134)
Results from ordinary business activities.....		(623)	(1,083)	2,533	4,027
Extraordinary results......................	14	1,496	2,603		(544)
Income taxes	15	(296)	(515)	(586)	(1,039)
Other taxes		(223)	(390)	(496)	(502)
Net income..............................		354	615	1,451	1,942
Earnings per share.......................	1	$ 7.43	DM 12.92	DM 30.46	DM 40.21
Allocation of net income:					
Net income..............................		354	615	1,451	1,942
Profit carried forward from previous year				2	8
Transfer to retained earnings		(122)	(212)	(816)	(1,275)
Income applicable to minority stockholders ...		(195)	(339)	(184)	(99)
Loss applicable to minority stockholders		187	326	151	29
Unappropriated profit		224	390	604	605

See accompanying Notes to Consolidated Financial Statements.

Daimler-Benz

DAIMLER-BENZ AG

Consolidated Balance Sheets
(in millions)

	Note	1993 (Note 1)	1993	1992
			At December 31,	
ASSETS				
Non-current assets				
Intangible assets....................................	16	$ 301	DM 523	DM 611
Property, plant and equipment........................	17	10,877	18,921	19,254
Financial assets	18	2,317	4,031	3,991
Leased equipment..................................	19	6,829	11,879	9,777
		20,324	35,354	33,633
Current assets				
Inventories...	20	13,948	24,262	23,138
Advance payments received		(4,207)	(7,317)	(5,549)
		9,741	16,945	17,589
Receivables from leasing and sales financing	21	5,042	8,771	6,166
Other receivables	22	8,824	15,349	14,771
Other assets.......................................	22	2,354	4,095	3,503
Securities...	23	3,961	6,889	6,089
Cash		1,698	2,954	2,968
		31,620	55,003	51,086
Prepaid expenses and deferred taxes	15	327	569	1,465
Total assets		52,271	90,926	86,184
STOCKHOLDERS' EQUITY AND LIABILITIES				
Stockholders' equity	25			
Capital stock		1,339	2,330	2,330
Additional paid-in capital...........................		1,217	2,117	2,117
Retained earnings..................................		7,328	12,747	13,440
Minority interest...................................		323	561	1,228
Unappropriated profit of Daimler-Benz AG (DBAG)		224	390	604
		10,431	18,145	19,719
Provisions				
Provisions for pensions and similar obligations	9	7,335	12,759	12,217
Other provisions	26	13,295	23,128	22,478
		20,630	35,887	34,695
Liabilities	27			
Liabilities from leasing and sales financing..............		7,853	13,660	10,971
Accounts payable trade		3,943	6,859	6,517
Other liabilities		9,081	15,796	13,725
		20,877	36,315	31,213
Deferred income		333	579	557
Total stockholders' equity and liabilities		52,271	90,926	86,184

See accompanying Notes to Consolidated Financial Statements.

Daimler-Benz

DAIMLER-BENZ AG

Consolidated Statements of Cash Flows
(in millions)

	Year Ended December 31,			
	1993 (Note 1)	1993	1992	1991
Cash flows from operating activities:				
Net income..	$ 354	DM 615	DM 1,451	DM 1,942
Adjustments to reconcile net income to net cash provided by operating activities:				
Extraordinary results..	(1,496)	(2,603)		
Depreciation and amortization of non-current assets (including amounts related to leased equipment of DM 2,536 ($1,458), DM 2,178 and DM 1,764 in 1993, 1992 and 1991, respectively)....	4,804	8,357	7,168	6,092
Increase in provisions, net..................................	1,428	2,483	1,296	1,482
Gain on sale of AEG KABEL.................................				(490)
Gain on disposal of non-current assets........................	(120)	(208)	(69)	(177)
Gain on sale of securities	(954)	(1,659)		
Change in assets and liabilities, net of change in companies included in consolidation				
Inventories, net	1,766	3,072	(976)	(2,241)
Receivables...	94	163	(2,014)	(2,263)
Accounts payable and other operating liabilities	(413)	(718)	(1,835)	1,282
Other	236	411	307	117
Cash provided by operating activities	5,699	9,913	5,328	5,744
Cash flows from investing activities:				
Purchase of non-current assets	(3,053)	(5,310)	(6,710)	(7,399)
Increase in leased equipment................................	(3,089)	(5,373)	(5,206)	(4,191)
Proceeds from disposal of non-current assets (including net change in leased equipment of DM 1,396 ($803), DM 1,343 and DM 853 in 1993, 1992 and 1991, respectively)........................	1,548	2,693	1,995	1,841
Payments for acquisition of investments in businesses.............	(567)	(986)	(807)	(1,937)
Proceeds from disposals of investments in businesses.............	330	573	669	42
Net change in short-term investments	584	1,016	1,644	1,344
Increase in leasing and sales financing receivables, net	(1,497)	(2,605)	(1,911)	(1,085)
Cash provided by (used for) change in companies in consolidation	25	43	2,018	(32)
Other	(330)	(574)	785	89
Cash used for investing activities	(6,049)	(10,523)	(7,523)	(11,328)
Cash flow from financing activities:				
Change in commercial paper borrowings, net......................	(272)	(473)	1,655	(311)
Additions to financial liabilities (including amounts for leasing and sales financing, net of DM 2,689 ($1,546), DM 2,858 and DM 1,465 in 1993, 1992 and 1991, respectively)................	1,719	2,990	3,532	5,515
Repayment of financial liabilities	(693)	(1,205)	(1,495)	(842)
Dividends paid	(364)	(633)	(640)	(607)
Other			20	7
Cash provided by financing activities	390	679	3,072	3,762
Effect of foreign exchange rate changes on cash	(48)	(83)	81	46
Net increase (decrease) in cash	(8)	(14)	958	(1,776)
Cash at beginning of year	1,706	2,968	2,010	3,786
Cash at year-end	1,698	2,954	2,968	2,010

See Note 24 for additional cash flow information.

See accompanying Notes to Consolidated Financial Statements.

Daimler-Benz

DAIMLER-BENZ AG

Notes to Consolidated Financial Statements — (Continued)
(in millions of DM)

2. Significant Differences Between German and United States Generally Accepted Accounting Principles

The Daimler-Benz consolidated financial statements comply with German GAAP, which differs in certain significant respects from U.S. GAAP. The significant differences that affect the consolidated net income and stockholders' equity of Daimler-Benz are set out below.

a. *Appropriated Retained Earnings — Provisions, Reserves and Valuation Differences*

According to German GAAP, accruals or provisions may be recorded for uncertain liabilities and loss contingencies. The amount of such accruals or provisions represents the anticipated expense to the Group. Accruals for potential losses on open production orders take into consideration all internal costs, including indirect selling and administrative expenses. Application of German GAAP may also lead to higher accrual balances and reserves for possible asset risks than are allowed under U.S. GAAP. To the extent that provisions, reserves and valuations under German GAAP are more conservative than the corresponding U.S. GAAP amounts, such differences can be viewed in a manner similar to appropriated retained earnings. Under U.S. GAAP, in accordance with Statement of Financial Accounting Standards ("SFAS") No. 5 "Accounting for Contingencies," an accrual for a loss contingency is recorded by a charge to income if it is both probable that an asset has been impaired or a liability has been incurred and the minimum amount of loss can be reasonably estimated. Unspecified liability reserves for future losses, costs or risks do not meet the conditions for accrual under SFAS No. 5.

The adjustments to stockholders' equity of DM 5,770 and DM 9,931 would have reduced other provisions at December 31, 1993 and 1992 by DM 4,883 and DM 8,105, respectively. The remainder of the adjustments would have increased property, plant and equipment, inventories and other receivables under U.S. GAAP.

b. *Long-term Contracts*

Daimler-Benz generally accounts for revenues and costs on long-term contracts using the completed-contract method with recognition of performance milestones where practicable. Under U.S. GAAP, revenues and costs on long-term contracts are recognized using the percentage-of-completion method of accounting.

c. *Goodwill and Business Acquisitions*

In accordance with German GAAP, goodwill may be charged directly to stockholders' equity or capitalized and amortized over its useful life, generally ranging between 5 years and 15 years. Prior to 1988, net assets acquired as part of a business combination were valued at historical cost. Net assets acquired after 1987 have been recorded at their estimated fair value. Under U.S. GAAP, the difference between the purchase price and fair value of net assets acquired as part of a business combination is capitalized as goodwill and amortized through the income statement over its estimated useful life, which may not exceed 40 years. For the purpose of the reconciliation to U.S. GAAP, goodwill is being amortized through the income statement over estimated useful lives ranging between 15 and 40 years.

Daimler-Benz

DAIMLER-BENZ AG

Notes to Consolidated Financial Statements — (Continued)
(in millions of DM)

d. Business Dispositions

German GAAP requires the accounting for the disposition of a business based upon the date of a signed contract. Under U.S. GAAP, a gain on the sale of a business is reflected in the period in which a closing occurs with the exchange of consideration. The gain on the sale of AEG KABEL which was recognized in 1991 for German GAAP purposes is recognized in 1992 under U.S. GAAP. In addition, applying the differing accounting principles between German and U.S. GAAP results in differing book values of the underlying businesses. As a result, the German and U.S. GAAP accounting gain or loss on a business disposition may be different.

e. Pensions

Daimler-Benz provides for pension costs and similar obligations including postretirement benefits based on actuarial studies using the entry age method as defined in the German tax code. U.S. GAAP, as defined by SFAS No. 87, "Employers' Accounting for Pensions" is more prescriptive particularly as to the use of actuarial assumptions and requires that a different actuarial method (the projected unit credit method) be used. In addition, the Group adopted SFAS No. 106 "Employers' Accounting for Postretirement Benefits Other Than Pensions" as of January 1, 1992. The application of this standard, to provide fully for the transitional liability, is included in the net income reconciliation as a cumulative effect adjustment net of income taxes.

f. Foreign Currency Translation

The Group's foreign currency accounting policies are disclosed in Note 1. Under U.S. GAAP, in accordance with SFAS No. 52, "Foreign Currency Translation", assets and liabilities denominated in a foreign currency are recorded at period end rates with any resulting unrealized gain or loss recognized in the income statement. The balance sheets of foreign companies are translated at period end exchange rates, and income statements are translated using an average rate during the period. The assets and liabilities of foreign companies operating in highly inflationary countries are remeasured into the functional currency (DM) by translating monetary items at current rates and non-monetary items at historical rates, with all resulting translation gains and losses being recognized in income.

g. Financial Instruments

The Group enters into contracts using financial instruments to cover certain foreign currency risks related to future transactions. In accordance with the German Commercial Code a reserve is set up for unrealized losses relating to such financial instruments whereas unrealized gains are not recognized until realized. Under U.S. GAAP, there are prescriptive rules that govern the application of hedge accounting. Financial instruments that do not qualify for hedge accounting are marked to market with any resulting unrealized gains or losses recognized in the income statement.

h. Deutsche Aerospace Airbus GmbH ("Deutsche Aerospace Airbus")

As discussed in Note 3, under German GAAP Deutsche Aerospace Airbus was not consolidated as part of the Group for periods prior to 1992. Under U.S. GAAP, Deutsche Aerospace Airbus would have been consolidated to reflect Daimler-Benz' 80% ownership interest during 1991. The adjustments to net income included in the reconciliation to U.S. GAAP represent the U.S. GAAP earnings of Deutsche Aerospace Airbus.

Daimler-Benz

i. *Other*

Other differences in accounting principles include adjustments for LIFO inventory, treasury stock and the minority stockholders' interest in U.S. GAAP adjustments.

j. *Deferred Taxes*

Under German GAAP deferred tax assets are generally recognized for the elimination of intercompany profits. Other deferred taxes are calculated on the liability method but are recognized only to the extent that consolidated deferred tax liabilities exceed consolidated deferred tax assets. Under U.S. GAAP as prescribed by SFAS No. 109 "Accounting for Income Taxes" deferred taxes are provided for all temporary differences using the liability method based on enacted tax rates.

The deferred tax adjustment included in the following reconciliation to U.S. GAAP also includes the income tax effects of the above U.S. GAAP adjustments, where appropriate.

In addition, the 1991 extraordinary charges under German GAAP would have reduced operating income under U.S. GAAP.

Daimler-Benz

DAIMLER-BENZ AG

Notes to Consolidated Financial Statements — (Continued)
(in millions)

Reconciliation to U.S. GAAP

The following is a summary of the significant adjustments to net income for the years 1993, 1992 and 1991 and to stockholders' equity at December 31, 1993 and 1992, which would be required if U.S. GAAP had been applied instead of German GAAP. The translation of 1993 amounts from marks into dollars is unaudited and has been made solely for the convenience of the reader at the December 31, 1993 Noon Buying Rate of DM 1.7395 = $ 1.

	Note	1993	1993	1992	1991
Net income as reported in the consolidated income statements under German GAAP....		$ 354	DM 615	DM 1,451	DM 1,942
Less: Income and losses applicable to minority stockholders		(8)	(13)	(33)	(70)
Adjusted net income under German GAAP		346	602	1,418	1,872
Add: Changes in appropriated retained earnings – provisions, reserves and valuation differences	(a)	(2,450)	(4,262)	774	64
		(2,104)	(3,660)	2,192	1,936
Other adjustments required to conform with U.S. GAAP:					
Long-term contracts	(b)	45	78	(57)	(32)
Goodwill and business acquisitions	(c)	(165)	(287)[1]	(76)	(270)
Business dispositions	(d)			337	(490)
Pensions and other postretirement benefits	(e)	(359)	(624)[2]	96	(66)
Foreign currency translation	(f)	(23)	(40)	(94)	155
Financial instruments	(g)	(129)	(225)	(438)	86
Earnings of Deutsche Aerospace Airbus ...	(h)				636
Other	(i)	168	292	88	57
Deferred taxes.......................	(j)	1,510	2,627[3]	(646)	(126)
Net income in accordance with U.S. GAAP before cumulative effect of a change in accounting principle....................		(1,057)	(1,839)	1,402	1,886
Cumulative effect of change in accounting for postretirement benefits other than pensions as of January 1, 1992, net of tax of DM 33	(e)			(52)	
Net income in accordance with U.S. GAAP		(1,057)	(1,839)	1,350	1,886
Earnings per share in accordance with U.S. GAAP		$(22.69)	DM (39.47)	DM 29.00[4]	DM 40.52
Earnings per American Depositary Share in accordance with U.S. GAAP[5]		$ (2.27)	DM (3.95)	DM 2.90[4]	DM 4.05

[1] Includes write-downs of goodwill related to the businesses of AEG and Dornier.
[2] Includes reversal of DM 237 gain recognized for German GAAP. See Note 31.
[3] Includes significant tax benefits relating to net operating losses recognized under U.S. GAAP. See Note 15.
[4] Includes the negative effect of the change in accounting for postretirement benefits other than pensions of DM 1.12 per share (DM 0.11 per American Depositary Share).
[5] Earnings per American Depositary Share are calculated on the basis of ten American Depositary Shares for every Ordinary Share.

Daimler-Benz

DAIMLER-BENZ AG

Notes to Consolidated Financial Statements — (Continued)
(in millions)

	Note	1993	1993	1992
Stockholders' equity as reported in the consolidated balance sheets under German GAAP		$10,431	DM 18,145	DM 19,719
Less: Minority interest		(322)	(561)	(1,228)
Adjusted stockholders' equity under German GAAP........		10,109	17,584	18,491
Add: Appropriated retained earnings — provisions, reserves and valuation differences	(a)	3,317	5,770	9,931
		13,426	23,354	28,422
Other adjustments required to conform with U.S. GAAP:				
Long-term contracts	(b)	119	207	131
Goodwill and business acquisitions...................	(c)	1,313	2,284	1,871
Pensions and other postretirement benefits	(e)	(1,047)	(1,821)	(1,212)
Foreign currency translation	(f)	49	85	(342)
Financial instruments	(g)	219	381	580
Other	(i)	(402)	(698)	(1,708)
Deferred taxes....................................	(j)	1,431	2,489[1]	(138)
Stockholders' equity in accordance with U.S. GAAP ...		15,108	26,281	27,604

[1] Includes significant deferred tax assets relating to net operating losses recognized under U.S. GAAP. See Note 15.

New U.S. Accounting Standards — not yet adopted

SFAS No. 112 — "Employers' Accounting for Postemployment Benefits" establishes an accounting standard for employers who provide benefits to former or inactive employees after employment but before retirement. The Statement was issued in November 1992 and is effective in 1994.

SFAS No. 114 — "Accounting by Creditors for Impairment of a Loan" addresses the accounting by creditors for the impairment of certain loans. The Statement was issued in May 1993 and is required to be adopted in 1995.

SFAS No. 115 — "Accounting for Certain Investments in Debt and Equity Securities" prescribes accounting for investments in equity securities that have readily determinable fair values and all investments in debt securities. The Statement was issued in May 1993 and is effective in 1994.

Daimler-Benz has not yet addressed the impact of each of the above Statements on its financial position or results of operations.

Daimler-Benz

---

14. Extraordinary Results

	1993	1992	1991
Extraordinary income	2,603		490
Extraordinary expense			(1,034)
	2,603		(544)

In 1993 extraordinary income of DM 2,603 results from the Group's change of its methods of application of valuation measures as well as accounting policies. The extraordinary credit resulted from adjustments to provisions of DM 1,935, receivables of DM 445 and inventory of DM 223.

In 1991 the extraordinary income results from the gain on the sale of AEG KABEL and its subsidiaries. Extraordinary expenses in 1991 are in connection with the withdrawal from the office and communication technology business of AEG.

Under U.S. GAAP, the 1991 extraordinary expenses would be reductions in operating profit.

Daimler-Benz

---

26. Other Provisions

	At December 31,	
	1993	1992
Estimated future losses on open contracts	5,280	5,393
Employee benefits and social costs	1,734	2,333
Accrued warranty and contract costs	5,753	5,139
Provisions for taxes	1,668	1,655
Restructuring programs	3,397	1,384
All other	5,296	6,574
	23,128	22,478

Provisions for taxes include DM 833 and DM 764 at December 31, 1993 and 1992, respectively, which pertain to Daimler-Benz AG open tax years awaiting final assessment.

some U.S. GAAP expenses bypass the income statement and are charged against stockholders equity directly. Alternatively, the German GAAP–based income statement may contain credits (income or adjustments of previously recognized expenses) that the U.S.-based GAAP may not recognize.

In the case of Daimler-Benz, the 1993 income statement shows losses from ordinary business activities of DM1,083 million, which are transposed to net income of DM615 by an extraordinary credit of DM2,603 million (see page 482). In Note 14 (on page 490), we find that this credit is the result of adjustments (reductions) made to other provisions, receivables, and inventories. This is a noncash credit, as can be seen in the statement of cash flows, where this item is subtracted from income to derive net operating cash flow. We should also note that no extraordinary items appear in 1992 income, and a DM544 million charge appears in 1991, when income (in both years) is positive and high. Thus, it seems that the firm makes adjustments to income based on the level of its income for the particular year.

Note further that income according to German, as well as U.S., GAAP is positive and high in 1991 and 1992 (see page 488). In these two years, after adjustment of German GAAP income to U.S. GAAP income in Note 2, the changes in appropriated retained earnings, provisions, reserves, and valuation differences are positive; that is, they are added to German GAAP income because the firm was more conservative in these two years than U.S. GAAP would allow. The situation reverses in 1993, when the firm is substantially less conservative than U.S. GAAP, and additional charges have to be recorded in income according to US GAAP. Thus, the transfer in and out of provisions and reserves seems to be timed to smooth out income; in good years these provisions and reserves increase because of additional (noncash) charges, and in bad years they decrease (or not increase as much as they should) so that income would be greater.

This example shows clearly the importance of using the information about charges, provisions, and other adjustments to reserves that appear on the income statement, together with changes in those balance sheet items, to derive the estimated cash payments to suppliers and employees.

Exhibit 10–1 contains a worksheet to estimate free cash flow for Daimler-Benz in 1993. We first estimate collections from customers as sales minus the changes in receivables, plus the change in advance payments received from customers. To estimate payments to suppliers and employees, we include operating expenses from the income statement, which are cost of materials, personnel expenses, and other operating expenses. As explained above, Daimler-Benz reduced the operating expenses with an extraordinary credit of DM2,063, which is used to offset some of the above operating expenses. We now add the changes in inventories and prepaid expenses, and subtract the increases in payables, other liabilities, and provisions, since these increases reflect expenses that were not paid in cash.

To estimate tax payments, we use the tax expenses in the income statement and add to it the increase in other assets, which include (among other things) tax refunds and deferred taxes. Finally, we estimate other cash flows by using the income statement items for other income, net interest income, and other operating income. Ideally, we should subtract from these amounts the items that are nonoperating in nature, such as gains on sale of PPE. However, absent enough breakdown in footnotes, we use the entire amount.

At the bottom of the worksheet, we estimate discretionary capital expenditures and discretionary expenses in the usual manner. First, we estimate the growth rate in capital expenditures, sales, and expenses over the three years 1991–1993. We use three instead of four years, because the statement of cash flows was changed in 1993, and earlier numbers cannot be comparable. We now compare the growth rate in capital expenditures to that of sales. Since the growth rate in sales is greater (1.4 percent compared with -4.0 percent), discretionary capital expenditures are estimated as zero. The discretionary expenses are equal to the difference between the growth rate in expenses (2.3 percent) and that of sales (1.4 percent) times current expenses of DM97,544 times 20 percent.

Free cash flow consists of operating cash flow minus capital expenditures plus discretionary expenses, and is equal to DM(2,557).

DATA AND PORTFOLIO FORMATION RULES

Data

The data for this study are taken from the Global/Vantage database, which is produced by a joint venture of Compustat and Extel. The database contains financial information about U.S. and foreign firms, as well as monthly security prices of these firms. The database begins in January 1982, although available data for our variables are more prevalent in recent years. To reduce a potential selection bias, the initial population consists of all industrial firms

EXHIBIT 10–1
Daimler Benz 1993

(Millions of DM)	1993	1993	1992
Sales	97,737		
Minus changes in leasing receivables	–2,605	8,771	6,166
Minus changes in other receivables	–578	15,349	14,771
Plus chages in advance payments received	1,768	7,317	5,549
Collections from customers	**96,322**		
Cost of materials	–51,076		
Personnel expenses	–33,790		
Other operating expenses	–15,281		
Extraordinary results	2,603		
Increase in inventories	–1,757		
Decrease in prepaid expenses	896	569	1,465
Increase in payables	342	6,859	6,517
Increase in other liabilities	2,071	15,796	13,725
Increase in provisions	1,192	35,887	34,695
Payments to suppliers and employees	**–94,800**		
Income taxes	–515		
Other taxes	–390		
Minus changes in other assets	–592	4,095	3,503
Payments for taxes	**–1,497**		
Other income	103		
Interest income	456		
Other operating income	7,370		
Other cash inflows	**7,929**		
Net operating cash flow	**7,954**		

whether their securities were actively traded on April 1993 (the last month of data available when this study was conducted) or not.

Our estimates of net cash flow from operations require the change in balance sheet accounts and therefore can only be estimated from 1983 onward. Our free cash flow estimates require averages over four (or at least two) years; hence, the first year of average free cash flow data is 1984.

EXHIBIT 10–1
(continued)

(Millions of DM)	1993	1993	1992
Capital expenditures:			
Purchase of noncurrent assets	**–5,310**	–6,710	–7,399
Increase in leased assets	**–5,373**	–5,206	–4,191
Total capital expenditures:	**–10,683**	**–11,916**	**–11,590**
Discretionary capital expenditures:			
Three-year growth rate in capital expenditures		–4.0%	
Sales	97,737	98,549	95,010
Three-year growth rate in sales		1.4%	
Max (0, differences in rates)		0.0%	
Discretionary capital expenditures:	**0**		
Discretionray expenses:			
Costs of materials	51,076	49,084	49,456
Personnel expenses	33,790	32,003	29,372
Other operating expenses	15,281	15,254	13,824
Extraordinary results	–2,603	0	544
Total expenses	97,544	96,341	93,196
Three-year growth rate in expenses		2.3%	
Max (0, differences in rates)		0.9%	
Discretionary expenses	**172**		
Free cash flow	**–2,557**		

Portfolio Formation

The portfolio formation date is assumed to be the last day of December every year. On that day, we examine the average free cash flow for the prior year and estimate other variables from the financial statements for the prior year. For example, in December 1989, we use data from the 1988 financial statements. Thus, if a firm reports on a calendar basis, and assuming a lag of six months between the balance sheet date and the disclosure date, the financial statements are available for about six months before the portfolio formation date. For a typical Japanese firm with a March 31 fiscal year-end, the data are available about three months prior to the portfolio formation date. Since firms with fiscal year-end after May 31 are classified by the database as reporting data for the prior calendar year, we feel that the risk of using information that had not been available at the portfolio formation date is minimized.

On the portfolio formation date, we examine all securities and select those that pass our selection criteria. We then assume purchases of these securities on the portfolio formation date (December 31) and hold them until the end of the following year. For example, we use the 1988 financial statements to construct the portfolio in December 1989 and then examine the return on the portfolio during the period January through December 1990.[6]

Portfolio Selection

We impose the following selection criteria for the portfolio:

1. Average free cash flow of the firm in the most recently available year is positive.
2. The growth rate of net operating cash flow in the most recent four years (or at least two years if data are unavailable) must be positive.
3. The ratio of total debt (short- and long-term debt) to the four-year average free cash flow should be less than 10.[7] This number is selected a priori because evidence prior to the portfolio selection date indicates that about 75 percent of all firms have higher debt multiples. It also yields a sample of firms that have low traditional measures of financial leverage, as we shall see below.
4. Average free cash flow should have grown during the most recent four years (or at least two years if data are unavailable).

---

[6]Note that in some cases we may use data from financial statements that are already available to market participants for over 12 months. This is done purposely to reduce the risk of using information that was unavailable on the portfolio formation date. This conservative approach is likely to introduce a bias against findings of superiority for the portfolios based on free cash flows.

[7]As we show in Chapter 7, it is better to estimate total debt by inclusion of off-balance-sheet liabilities. However, the information about these liabilities of foreign firms is very limited and varies considerably from one country to another.

5. The free cash flow multiple should be between 5 and 25 for the portfolios selected in 1990–1992, and between 5 and 30 for the portfolios selected in 1987–1989 (to increase the number of firms selected into our portfolio). The lower bound (of 5) is used as an efficient way of deleting outliers. Our experience indicates that data (from financial statements and prices) for firms with free cash flow multiples below five are likely to be erroneous. The upper bound eliminates overpriced securities. The free cash flow multiple is estimated by the ratio of market value of equity, as of the portfolio formation date, to the four-year average free cash flow in the prior year. Note that foreign firms may have more than just one publicly traded issue. For such firms, market value is the sum of the market values for each of the firm's issues.

6. To ensure an adequate liquidity in the stock of a firm, we require the firm to have a market value in excess of $200 million (U.S.) as of the portfolio formation date. Note that all the prior selection criteria were denominated in the native currency of the firm. This is the only criterion where we translate the market value into U.S. dollars; it allows meaningful comparisons among firms from different countries.

The portfolio strategy assumes we hold the stock for a whole year, so that returns for a portfolio are estimated over the 12 months following the portfolio formation date. For firms with more than one publicly traded issue we include all issues in the portfolio. The security returns represent the local market return, and do *not* include any losses/gains due to changes in foreign exchange rates. Thus, they represent the returns to a U.S. investor who chose to fully hedge the portfolio for currency fluctuations. This seems to be a better measure of a successful portfolio strategy because it abstracts from gains and losses that may be induced simply by changes in exchange rates between the U.S. dollar and other currencies.

We report the returns for the portfolio of foreign firms with low free cash flow multiples and the returns on two benchmark portfolios for comparison. The first benchmark is the value-weighted return on all the foreign firms included in the Global/Vantage database. This index is very highly correlated with the MSCI index for EAFA and Canada, which consists of securities in 13 European countries, Canada, and 5 Pacific countries (including Japan, Australia, New Zealand, and Hong-Kong).[8]

The second benchmark is the return on portfolios with the same combination of size and book/market ratio as the free cash flow portfolio. The reason for the second benchmark is that firms in the free cash flow portfolios are chosen to be larger than the median firm in the database. As is well documented, smaller firms have larger average returns than larger firms, possibly due to additional risk. Similarly, Fama and French (*Journal of Finance*, 1992) show that firms with large book/market ratios have larger average returns than firms with low book/market ratios. As Fama and French show, the size and book/market ratio of firms are better at explaining the cross-sectional variation of returns than such variables as beta and the P/E ratio. Thus, we assign all foreign firms in the Global/Vantage database to one of five size groups, and to one of five book/market ratio groups. We then calculate the equal-weighted return on all firms in each of the 25 combinations of size and book/market ratio. To assess the performance of the free cash flow portfolio, we match the return on each security in the portfolio with the average return on the portfolio of firms that have the same size and book/market combination.[9]

RESULTS

Table 10–1 presents the means of some variables of interest for the portfolios based on free cash flows during the years 1987–1993. Note that the portfolios have a small number of securities, ranging from 45 securities in 1987 to 74 in 1992. In 1993, the portfolio included only 20 securities because the database had not been fully updated at the time of this study. The table also

---

[8]We use the value-weighted return on all firms in the Global/Vantage database because the database includes some countries that are not followed by the MSCI index. For example, South African firms are included in the Global/Vantage database but not in the MSCI index for EAFA and Canada.

[9]Initial examination shows that the returns on foreign securities exhibit similar sensitivity to size and book/market ratios as U.S. firms. The authors are currently conducting research on this subject.

TABLE 10-1

Means of Variables for the Free Cash Flow Portfolios

Variable	1987	1988	1989	1990	1991	1992	1993
Number of firms	45	61	74	66	68	74	20
Market value ($U.S.)	1,909	1,823	1,806	1,873	1,918	2,223	4,132
FCF/Market value	0.071	0.061	0.067	0.072	0.080	0.072	0.072
OCF/Market value	0.122	0.110	0.113	0.122	0.137	0.133	0.136
Debt/Market equity	0.147	0.170	0.156	0.145	0.168	0.186	0.218
Debt/Book equity	0.327	0.354	0.337	0.388	0.205	0.494	0.511
Book equity/Market	0.427	0.446	0.438	0.453	0.556	0.459	0.559
Size decile	7.6	7.7	7.7	7.1	7.5	7.6	8.4
FCF decile	9.4	9.4	9.3	9.4	9.2	9.2	8.8
OCF decile	8.3	8.0	8.1	8.6	8.0	8.0	7.1
Debt/market decile	4.9	4.9	5.2	5.0	4.8	4.9	4.3
Debt/Book equity decile	3.5	3.8	3.8	3.7	3.3	4.0	4.8
Book/market decile	5.8	5.4	5.7	6.1	5.6	5.1	4.4
Number of two-digit SIC codes	20	22	26	23	30	26	14

Notes:

1. Mean market value is in millions of U.S. dollars at the beginning of the year.
2. FCF/Market value (OCF) represents the four-year average free (operating) cash flow in year t-2, divided by total market value at the end of calendar year t−1.
3. Debt/Market equity represents total debt at the end of year t−2 divided by market value of equity at the end of calendar year t−1.
4. Debt/Book equity represents total debt at the end of year t−2 divided by book value of equity at year t−2.
5. Book equity/market represents total book value of equity at year t−2 divided by market value of equity at the end of calendar year t−1.
6. All firms in the Global/Vantage database were ranked in ascending order of a variable and assigned into deciles (where 1 is the lowest and 10 the highest). The average decile rank for the firms in the free cash flow portfolios is reported in the table. The deciles are for the six variables in the table (e.g., size is market value in $U.S. dollars, FCF is the ratio of average free cash flow to market value).
7. The table reports the number of distinct 2-digit SIC industries in which the portfolio firms operate.

shows that the mean size (market value of equity) of our firms is over U.S. $1,800 million in each of the years, which is not surprising given the stringent selection criteria we used. Furthermore, the average size decile to which the portfolio firms fall is between 7 and 8, indicating that our portfolio firms are among the top 30 percent of all firms in terms of size. Given the strong effects of size on returns, it is clear that an adjustment for size is needed in return comparisons.

Table 10–1 also reports that the mean free cash flow to market value of the portfolio is about 7 percent, or a free cash flow multiple of about 14. This ratio is generally at the top 10 percent of all firms in the database, as indicated by the mean decile to which the portfolio firms fall. A similar picture emerges with respect to operating cash flows, where the multiple is about 8–9 and the portfolio firms fall into the top 20 percent of all firms.

The portfolio firms were also selected to have a low debt/average free cash flow ratio. Table 10–1 reports some statistics about the debt/equity ratios of the portfolio firms. Generally, portfolio firms fall into the bottom 50 percent in terms of their financial leverage, as measured by both debt/equity ratios. The table also reports that the portfolio firms fall into the median decile in terms of book/market ratio (i.e., they do not exhibit any special book/market risk). Also, the table clearly indicates the wide distribution of firms across two-digit SIC industries.

Table 10–2 provides information on the returns of the free cash flow portfolios, the market portfolio and the portfolios of firms with the same combination of size and book-to-market ratio (B/M). The table presents the average percentage returns in each of the months January 1987 through April 1993, the cumulative returns for the same period, and the two adjusted returns— returns adjusted for the entire market and adjustment for other firms with the same combination of size and B/M ratio. It should be recalled that the portfolio composition changes only once a year, so that the returns reported for all months in the same calendar year contain the same portfolio of securities.

As can be seen at the bottom of Table 10–2, the portfolio based on free cash flow has an average monthly return of 1.26 percent, which is statistically different from zero with a t-statistic of 2.31 (about 1 percent significance level). Similarly, the average return

TABLE 10–2
Monthly Returns, Cumulative Returns, and Adjusted Returns

Month	Percentage Return			Cumulative Return			Adjusted Return	
	Portfolio	Market	Size and B/M	Portfolio	Market	Size and B/M	Market	Size and B/M
Jan. 87	3.31	1.96	4.15	3.31	1.96	4.15	1.34	−0.85
Feb. 87	5.79	3.63	4.73	9.29	5.67	9.08	2.15	1.06
Mar. 87	2.03	1.81	3.69	11.50	7.58	13.11	0.22	−1.66
Apr. 87	4.64	3.84	2.39	16.68	11.71	15.81	0.81	2.25
May. 87	7.42	4.38	1.92	25.34	16.60	18.04	3.04	5.49
Jun. 87	4.99	1.68	2.84	31.60	18.55	21.39	3.32	2.15
Jul. 87	9.41	3.93	7.40	43.98	23.21	30.37	5.48	2.01
Aug. 87	0.37	1.89	1.18	44.51	25.54	31.91	−1.52	−0.81
Sep. 87	0.75	2.06	1.32	45.60	28.12	33.65	−1.30	−0.56
Oct. 87	−22.98	−17.53	−23.62	12.14	5.66	2.08	−5.45	0.64
Nov. 87	−7.10	−5.95	−7.03	4.18	−0.63	−5.10	−1.15	−0.07
Dec. 87	6.51	−1.41	3.09	10.96	−2.03	−2.17	7.92	3.42
Jan. 88	1.00	4.97	1.95	12.07	2.84	−0.26	−3.97	−0.95
Feb. 88	2.84	6.24	5.53	15.25	9.25	5.26	−3.40	−2.69
Mar. 88	3.94	3.10	3.19	19.80	12.64	8.62	0.85	0.75
Apr. 88	2.11	3.26	3.13	22.33	16.31	12.02	−1.15	−1.02
May. 88	0.39	−0.48	1.78	22.80	15.75	14.02	0.87	−1.39
Jun. 88	7.03	4.34	5.19	31.43	20.78	19.93	2.68	1.84
Jul. 88	1.41	2.17	1.70	33.29	23.40	21.97	−0.75	−0.28

TABLE 10–2 (*continued*)

Month	Percentage Return			Cumulative Return			Adjusted Return	
	Portfolio	Market	Size and B/M	Portfolio	Market	Size and B/M	Market	Size and B/M
Aug. 88	-3.16	-3.53	-3.11	29.08	19.05	18.18	0.36	-0.05
Sep. 88	2.91	2.25	3.44	32.84	21.72	22.24	0.67	-0.52
Oct. 88	3.84	0.20	3.20	37.94	21.96	26.14	3.64	0.64
Nov. 88	-0.80	1.63	-1.31	36.84	23.95	24.48	-2.42	0.52
Dec. 88	3.03	2.36	2.25	40.98	26.88	27.29	0.66	0.78
Jan. 89	8.97	6.43	8.02	53.63	35.05	37.49	2.54	0.96
Feb. 89	-0.87	-0.75	-0.37	52.30	34.03	36.98	-0.11	-0.49
Mar. 89	3.59	2.76	3.67	57.76	37.73	42.00	0.82	-0.08
Apr. 89	1.72	2.49	3.23	60.48	41.16	46.59	-0.77	-1.51
May. 89	-1.49	1.67	1.60	58.09	43.52	48.93	-3.16	-3.09
Jun. 89	0.94	-0.60	1.98	59.58	42.66	51.88	1.54	-1.04
Jul. 89	4.97	6.52	4.48	67.51	51.96	58.69	-1.55	0.49
Aug. 89	1.94	0.25	3.21	70.76	52.34	63.78	1.69	-1.27
Sep. 89	0.69	1.35	0.00	71.94	54.40	63.78	-0.66	0.69
Oct. 89	-4.77	-3.10	-5.63	63.74	49.62	54.56	-1.67	0.86
Nov. 89	2.38	3.90	1.71	67.63	55.45	57.20	-1.52	0.67
Dec. 89	2.56	2.77	3.65	71.93	59.76	62.95	-0.21	-1.09
Jan. 90	-0.52	5.70	-0.74	71.04	68.86	61.75	-6.22	0.22
Feb. 90	-3.33	-2.87	-1.89	65.35	64.02	58.69	-0.46	-1.44

TABLE 10-2 *(continued)*

Month	Percentage Return			Cumulative Return			Adjusted Return	
	Portfolio	Market	Size and B/M	Portfolio	Market	Size and B/M	Market	Size amd B/M
Mar. 90	3.65	−0.30	1.36	71.39	63.52	60.85	3.95	2.30
Apr. 90	−1.93	−7.65	−2.48	68.08	51.02	56.86	5.72	0.54
May. 90	5.20	7.23	6.48	76.82	61.93	67.03	−2.02	−1.28
Jun. 90	1.21	−8.00	0.69	78.96	48.97	68.18	9.21	0.52
Jul. 90	−1.46	8.23	0.48	76.35	61.23	68.98	−9.69	−1.93
Aug. 90	−8.68	−11.63	−10.71	61.04	42.47	50.89	2.95	2.02
Sep. 90	−9.71	−12.30	−11.51	45.40	24.95	33.52	2.59	1.80
Oct. 90	4.04	6.16	2.00	51.28	32.65	36.19	−2.12	2.04
Nov. 90	−0.73	−6.15	−2.23	50.18	24.49	33.16	5.43	1.50
Dec. 90	1.33	2.19	0.62	52.18	27.22	33.99	−0.86	0.71
Jan. 91	−1.06	−0.71	−1.33	50.57	26.31	32.21	−0.35	0.27
Feb. 91	12.63	13.65	13.17	69.58	43.55	49.63	−1.02	−0.54
Mar. 91	3.46	1.97	3.72	75.45	46.39	55.18	1.49	−0.25
Apr. 91	1.62	−0.20	0.39	78.30	46.09	55.79	1.82	1.23
May. 91	0.96	1.49	0.95	80.00	48.26	57.26	−0.53	0.01
Jun. 91	−0.27	−3.67	−1.89	79.52	42.83	54.29	3.40	1.62
Jul. 91	3.86	2.66	1.77	86.45	46.63	57.01	1.20	2.10
Aug. 91	−0.11	−2.60	−0.98	86.25	42.82	55.48	2.49	0.86
Sep. 91	0.47	1.95	−0.71	87.11	45.61	54.38	−1.49	1.18

TABLE 10–2 *(continued)*

Month	Percentage Return			Cumulative Return			Adjusted Return	
	Portfolio	Market	Size and B/M	Portfolio	Market	Size and B/M	Market	Size amd B/M
Oct. 91	0.30	0.76	-0.77	87.67	46.72	53.20	-0.46	1.06
Nov. 91	-3.58	-5.89	-4.46	80.96	38.08	46.37	2.31	0.88
Dec. 91	1.01	0.25	-1.12	82.79	38.42	44.73	0.76	2.13
Jan. 92	6.18	2.77	5.08	94.08	42.25	52.08	3.41	1.10
Feb. 92	-0.07	4.33	1.25	93.94	48.41	53.98	-4.41	-1.32
Mar. 92	0.09	8.61	-2.04	94.12	61.18	50.84	-8.51	2.13
Apr. 92	4.40	-0.14	2.49	102.66	60.96	54.58	4.54	1.92
May. 92	3.19	4.94	2.64	109.14	68.91	58.67	-1.75	0.55
Jun. 92	-4.26	-3.43	-4.87	100.22	63.11	50.93	-0.83	0.61
Jul. 92	-6.27	-4.74	-5.56	87.66	55.37	42.54	-1.53	-0.71
Aug. 92	-3.16	-0.97	-3.17	81.74	53.86	38.02	-2.18	0.01
Sep. 92	0.22	-1.19	-0.20	82.14	52.03	37.75	1.41	0.41
Oct. 92	3.30	5.37	1.40	88.15	60.20	39.68	-2.07	1.90
Nov. 92	2.32	4.31	3.11	92.51	67.10	44.03	-1.99	-0.80
Dec. 92	4.33	2.66	2.71	100.84	71.54	47.93	1.67	1.62
Jan. 93	4.68	0.08	1.62	110.24	71.69	50.33	4.60	3.06
Feb. 93	3.99	2.52	2.95	118.63	76.02	54.77	1.46	1.04
Mar. 93	5.59	2.47	3.95	130.86	80.38	60.88	3.12	1.64
Apr. 93	2.84	1.37	2.68	137.42	82.85	65.19	1.47	0.16

TABLE 10–2 (concluded)

Month	Percentage Return			Cumulative Return			Adjusted Return	
	Portfolio	Market	Size and B/M	Portfolio	Market	Size and B/M	Market	Size and B/M
Average	1.26	0.92	0.78				0.35	0.48
Standard error	0.55	0.55	0.54				0.37	0.16
t-Statistic	2.31	1.66	1.44				0.95	2.93

Notes:

1. *Portfolio* indicates the returns on the free cash flow portfolio. *Market* indicates returns on the value-weighted index of all firms in the Global/Vantage database. *Size and B/M* indicates the return on the portfolio with the same combination of size and book/market as the security in the free cash flow portfolio.

2. Percentage returns are equally weighted average returns over all securities in the free cash flow and the size and B/M portfolio, and value-weighted for the Market portfolio. Cumulative returns are the multiplication of one plus the return during the entire cumulation period minus one.

3. Adjusted market returns are the return on the free cash flow portfolio minus the Market return. Adjusted size and B/M return is the return on the free cash flow portfolio minus the return on the portfolio with the same size and B/M.

4. Average returns, standard errors, and t-statistics are calculated over the 76 monthly observations Jan. '87 to Apr. '93.

on the portfolio of all firms in the database (market) is 0.92 percent per month, with an associated t-statistic of 1.66 (about 5 percent significance level). Finally, the return on firms with the same combination of size and B/M as the free cash flow firms is the lowest, 0.78 percent per month, with an associated t-statistic of 1.44 (about 7 percent significance level).

The table, as well as Figure 10–1, show the cumulative returns of the free cash flow portfolio, the portfolio of all securities in the database, and similar combinations of size and B/M portfolios. As can be clearly seen, the portfolio based on free cash flow yields the highest cumulative return (137 percent over the 76 months), with the other two benchmarks trailing behind (83 percent and 65 percent, respectively). Thus, the portfolio based on free cash flows clearly dominates the other two benchmark portfolios throughout the study period.

Table 10–2, as well as Figure 10–2, also presents results for the market-adjusted and the size-B/M adjusted returns. The former is achieved by subtracting from the return on the free cash flow portfolio the return on the market portfolio, where the market portfolio is the portfolio of all securities in the database. The second adjusted return is simply the return on each security in the portfolio minus the return on the portfolio with the same combination of size and B/M. As the table reports, the average monthly market-adjusted return is 0.35 percent, which is not statistically significant. However, securities chosen for the free cash flow portfolio are much larger than the median security in the market (usually at the top 30 percent of all securities), so the returns on these securities should be compared to similar size and B/M securities. When this is done, the average monthly adjusted return is 0.48 percent, with a t-statistic of 2.93 (significance level of less than 1 percent). Thus, the free cash flow portfolio clearly indicates superior returns. Furthermore, as Figure 10–3 illustrates, the cumulative market-adjusted returns are never negative during the study period, and the cumulative size-B/M–adjusted returns are negative only for two months at the beginning of the study period.

Note that in Figure 10–3, the graphs show cumulative excess returns, not raw returns. The line marked market shows the return on the portfolio based on FCF minus the return on the market portfolio. Similarly, the line marked *size&B/M* indicates returns on

FIGURE 10–2
Cumulative Returns

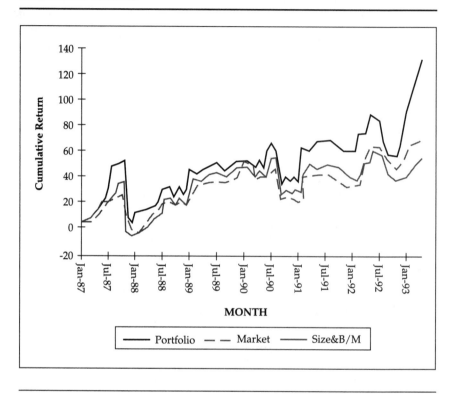

the portfolios in excess of returns on similar size and book/market securities. Thus, as long as the cumulative return is above 1, the FCF-based portfolio outperforms its benchmarks.

Finally, one should note that the returns in Table 10–2 do not provide any evidence of a "January" effect. The adjusted returns for January are not larger than other months and do not support any abnormal performance in January. Thus, the assumption of portfolio formulation on December 31 of each year is not what drives the superior returns of the free cash flow portfolios.

FIGURE 10–3
Cumulative Adjusted Returns

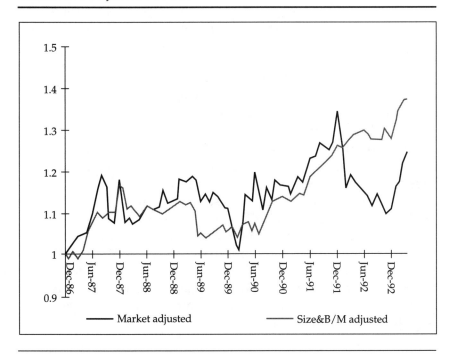

SUMMARY AND CONCLUSIONS

This chapter advocates an approach to foreign investments that is based on free cash flows. Free cash flow is superior to earnings or even net operating cash flow for foreign investments because it mitigates spurious effects caused by the selection of different accounting methods across different countries. The study also shows how to estimate free cash flow for foreign firms.

The chapter shows that returns based on a portfolio of foreign stocks selected according to the free cash flow strategy outperforms an index of all foreign firms on the Global/Vantage database as well as portfolios of firms with the same combination of size and book/market ratios. This is consistent with the intuition for selecting these firms into a portfolio—these firms are stable cash flow generators, have low levels of debt, and are larger than the median foreign firm.

The evidence in the last three chapters points out unequivocally the merits of investments that are based on free cash flow. Firms with low financial leverage can outperform the market, whether restricted to small- and mid-capitalization firms, international firms, or even for entire population of stocks.

In this book, we showed a systematic method to estimate free cash flows, a method that does not simply use operating cash flows minus capital expenditures. Instead, our method acknowledges the existence of capital expenditures and other payments that are discretionary and that can be saved without affecting future growth. We show extensive examples of applying this method to estimate free cash flow, as well as numerous examples to illustrate the analysis of cash flow activities.

Unlike many other methods of security analysis, free cash flow analysis makes a lot of intuitive sense and is reasonably easy to apply in practice in screening a large set of firms, in analysis of industries, and in analysis of individual firms. With investors' growing emphasis on cash flow analysis, the market should be moving toward a better pricing of securtities on the basis of cash flows instead of on the basis of earnings. This book certainly prepares the reader for this imminent change.

Index